To Connie

Colleen Sen

THE
CHICAGO
Food Encyclopedia

THE
CHICAGO
Food Encyclopedia

EDITED BY

Carol Mighton Haddix, Bruce Kraig, and Colleen Taylor Sen

FOREWORD BY

Russell Lewis

UNIVERSITY OF ILLINOIS PRESS
Urbana, Chicago, and Springfield

Library of Congress Cataloging-in-Publication Data
Names: Haddix, Carol Mighton, 1946- editor. | Kraig,
    Bruce, editor. | Sen, Colleen Taylor, editor.
Title: The Chicago food encyclopedia / edited by Carol
    Mighton Haddix, Bruce Kraig, and Colleen Taylor
    Sen; foreword by Russell Lewis.
Description: Urbana: The University of Illinois Press,
    [2017] | Series: Heartland foodways | Includes
    bibliographical references and index.
Identifiers: LCCN 2017006116 (print) | LCCN
    2017007883 (ebook) | ISBN 9780252087240 (pbk. :
    alk. paper) | ISBN 9780252099779 (ebook)
Subjects: LCSH: Food—Illinois—Chicago—History—
    Encyclopedias. | Food industry and trade—Illinois—
    Chicago—History—Encyclopedias. | Chicago (Ill.)—
    History—Encyclopedias.
Classification: LCC TX360.U63 C4534 2017 (print) | LCC
    TX360.U63 (ebook) | DDC 664.00973/11—dc23
LC record available at https://lccn.loc.gov/2017006116

Contents

Color illustrations follow page 162

Foreword

Students of Chicago history are all too easily tempted to turn to a narrative of urban inevitability that posits that the city's evolution over the past two centuries was destined. Most typically, this view reflects a geographical determinism, arguing that Chicago's uniquely favorable location for transportation and industrialization gave it a head start over other cities. According to this understanding, location is at the root of the city's rise as the crossroads of America. Chicago's culinary history is especially vulnerable to this approach. Named after a local food source (wild onion), positioned adjacent to some of the nation's most fertile and productive agricultural lands, and home to a distinctive cuisine that Chicagoans enthusiastically embrace as an essential element in constructing an identity, Chicago's historic status as the nation's food capital does indeed seem destined.

But there is another way to interpret Chicago's culinary traditions and its history, and happily this volume has embraced this perspective wholeheartedly. According to this explanation, Chicago was shaped by a number of national, regional, and local factors during the nineteenth and twentieth centuries. Two of the most significant were national transformations from craft to industrialized work and from rural to urban living. Those Chicagoans who stood at the intersection of these momentous trends and influences envisioned different city futures, making decisions and taking action in the context of the prospects offered by a nation undergoing fundamental change. Food was not only essential to sustain the city, it also presented a unique opportunity for urban growth. The procurement of agricultural products, the processing of them into food, and their distribution became major enterprises in Chicago.

This national transformation found fertile ground in Chicago and was critical to the city's growth and expansion. Indeed, between 1830 and 1890, Chicago was the fastest growing city on the globe. For a better sense of this remarkable and unprecedented growth, a few comparisons are helpful. During the same 60-year period, the population of London almost doubled, increasing by 1.8 times; Paris more than doubled, growing 2.3 times; and Berlin more than quadrupled, increasing 4.1 times. On this side of the Atlantic, New York City's population grew 4.1 times. Chicago during the same period grew from 29,963 citizens to 1,099,850, an increase of almost 37 times. And during the decade from 1890 to 1900, Chicago increased its land area to 182.9 square miles, making it physically the largest city in the world. Chicago was indeed the shock city of the nineteenth century.

How did all of this happen? Through a combination of a geographic location that was unusually well suited for industrialization, westward expansion of American settlements, civic vision, imagination, shrewd business acumen, and sheer luck, Chicago became a national crossroads where people, ideas, and products moved east and west, north and south. Initially through an interconnected system of waterways, and by the 1850s via a national railroad network, Chicago became the national center for the processing and shipping of agricultural products and implements, a leading port for grain, the world leader in lumber production and shipping, and the center for the processing and shipping of meat. With the completion of the Illinois & Michigan canal in 1848 and the construction of the first railroad the same year, Chicago had the unique advantage of two intertwined layers of transportation—water and rail—that allowed the city and its businesses to tap into regional raw materials (especially agricultural products), process them, and distribute them nationally.

In Chicago, industrialization went hand-in-hand with rapid urbanization—the processes fueled each other—and the result was a new kind of city. This remarkable fusion of two powerful nineteenth-century juggernauts played out in Chicago on a massive scale. Population growth and the physical growth of the city expanded boundaries, and new housing and infrastructure provided the resources for new industries to develop and to grow. Likewise, industrial development brought immigrant and migrants to Chicago for work and demanded new land for production facilities and new infrastructure to transport raw materials and finished products. These immigrants and migrants brought ethnic and regional traditions with them to a nation and a city that was rapidly changing. They adapted these traditions to American habits and practices, as well as to new opportunities they discovered in Chicago, creating a swirling, ever-changing urban cultural stew that reshaped work, leisure, and foodways.

Together, industrialization and urbanization also fostered two important characteristics that supercharged nineteenth-century Chicago: innovation and new markets. Although we celebrate invention and innovation in America as creative expressions that are worthy ends in themselves, the person who develops new markets for an innovation is likely to be more successful. Chicago was fertile ground for new ideas, and the city's position as a national crossroads allowed businessmen to think more imaginatively and expansively about creating new markets.

Chicago's food history is replete with examples of entrepreneurs developing new methods, technology, recipes, products, and markets, and these risk takers had a profound impact on the city's relationship with food. Once Gustavus Swift had perfected a system of rail stations to replenish the ice in refrigerated railroad cars, enabling him to ship meat to the eastern seaboard, he turned his attention to developing markets to consume his new cuts of beef. His success hinged on his understanding of the link between fostering novel food-related technology and creating new markets. Likewise, immigrant and migrant entrepreneurs brought innovation to ethnic and regional cuisines and especially to street food, building thriving local business and, in some cases, national food empires. Chicagoans were more successful than their urban counterparts in their innovative approach to the procurement, processing, and distribution of food and to creating new markets, and this became the foundation of the city's national and international food business and its enduring reputation as the nation's food city.

The Chicago Food Encyclopedia offers an original interpretation of the transformation of food in an urban setting and makes a significant contribution to culinary history scholarship. Nothing to date rivals this volume in terms of its scope and comprehensiveness. By combining sound urban history scholarship with fresh and compelling culinary history research, this encyclopedia charts new territory for understanding Chicago's ongoing relationship with food and why the city has become a major food destination today. It introduces the novice to Chicago's long association with the cornucopia of food produced or consumed in the city over two centuries, yet it also provides seasoned scholars in-depth interdisciplinary analyses of urban food as a business and how it evolved as an essential part of daily life in a city. It certainly will become an essential reference work for students of Chicago history and a trusted guide for all Chicagoans who love their city and its amazing food offerings.

RUSSELL LEWIS
Executive Vice President and Chief Historian,
Chicago History Museum

Preface

······································

Located at the center of America's agricultural heartland and bordering the nation's great waterways, Chicago is one of the world's great food cities. Chicago has not only been home to some of the world's top restaurants but has an enormous diversity of ethnic neighborhoods and cuisines, with few counterparts in other cities. It is not surprising that many of the city's nicknames relate to food: Carl Sandburg's "hog butcher for the world" and "stacker of wheat," "the big onion" (an homage to the original Native American name for the place on which the city stands), and, more positively, City in a Garden (a translation of its Latin motto *Urbs in Horto*), and Paris on the Prairie (from Daniel Burnham's 1909 plan for the city).

As editors, our goal was twofold: to create a reference work that describes the full tapestry of the city's rich gastronomical scene; and to provide historical and cultural perspective. It is meant to be a resource for citizens and a handbook for the tens of millions of visitors who come to the city—to browse through, savor the illustrations, wonder at the stories of amazing people and interesting events, and even try some classic recipes. *The Chicago Food Encyclopedia* will also serve as a resource for students, historians, and scholars researching the city's culinary history.

The book is divided in two parts. The first is a brief general history of Chicago's food from before the city's founding to the present day. We believe that the narrative is necessary to tie the entries into a coherent whole. Readers can dip into individual entries and learn about a specific person, place, event, or food, but the story of Chicago's food puts them into a historical and cultural context. For instance, the connections between Chicago's role in America's food production systems and what people in the city actually eat is told piecemeal in entries but set into a historical fabric by the narrative. However, the first part is not a comprehensive account of Chicago food. That would be redundant with entry subjects and

would require another book or even as massive a project as the *Encyclopedia of Chicago*.

The second part consists of 375 well-researched entries in alphabetical order written by more than 70 writers, educators, scholars, and industry experts. Our initial step was to draw up a list of headwords of potential topics and potential contributors. This list was based on our long experience in planning, writing, and contributing to other reference works such as *The Oxford Encyclopedia of American Food* and *Street Food around the World*. It also was grounded in our decades-long work researching, writing, and editing articles, columns, and books about Chicago food. We drew up a list of contributors from the ranks of journalists, scholars, bloggers, and authors, including many of the leading names in the Chicago food scene. They in turn suggested new or related topics. Even during the writing of the actual entries, we discovered topics we had overlooked and commissioned new entries.

Our first task was to determine geographical scope. Looking at the Chicago region's physical and economic extension outward to ever more distant suburbs and into a midwestern megalopolis, we realized that covering all of what is now the Greater Chicago region would be too massive for a single volume. Historical overviews of each area, suburb, and beyond, would take multiple volumes. Therefore, we decided to confine the book's contents to the current city limits, more or less. Since we posit a model of the city's neighborhoods, most of which are ethnically composed, moving outward from their original locations, the collar suburbs such as Berwyn (Bohemians) and Skokie/Buffalo Grove (Jews) are implicitly covered by discussions of the Chicago communities. Some businesses that relocated to suburbs, such as Kraft Foods to Glenview (and back to the center city in 2016), do not warrant a full discussion of that suburb in this scheme. Perhaps another volume will cover the subject. Only the Period Kitchen, Dining Room, Pantry, and Recipes Resources discusses near-suburban historical societies and museums as ways of looking at Chicago food history.

Chicago is a city of neighborhoods. Looking at historical city maps along with historical statistics gives perspectives on any moment or periods in time. James T. Farrell's great pentalogy of the Irish American O'Neill-O'Flaherty families set around Washington Park illuminates how neighborhoods are ephemeral and ethnic boundaries are constantly changing. That is why we chose not to take a strictly geographical approach in the selection of entries. Nor is this book a historical geography or ethnography that studies each neighborhood in detail. Rather, in its entries for the food of ethnic groups we see changes over time. An example is the Mexican entry where we see that the formerly Bohemian-Polish Pilsen became Mexican in character. We also were selective in what ethnic groups we included. There are more than 150 ethnicities in the city, and their numbers continue to grow. For example, the past few years alone have seen the settlement of refugees from Bhutan, and Somalia, and the Rohingas from Burma (Myanmar). Because their numbers are still small and they have not yet made a mark on public dining, they are not included in this work. Other ethnic groups, such as Germans, Swedes, and Irish, have been largely assimilated; nonetheless, these communities are covered in some detail because of their historical contributions to Chicago's food culture. When one community's cuisine has close similarities with another, we have included them in a single entry—for example, countries that were once part of Yugoslavia.

Elements of the Encyclopedia

Entries range in length from 100 to 1,500 words. The shortest entries focus on a specific dish, restaurant, person, or event. The longer entries are overviews of a broader topic, often with historical background, such as important ethnic groups, business and industries, organizations, and historical periods. Eating establishments are such an important category that we have broken them down into fifteen separate entries, the largest being fine-dining restaurants. Similarly, the category of wine has six separate entries.

The Chicago Food Encyclopedia has some special features that are not found in similar volumes. One is an entry on Literature. Chicago is not just a physical entity; it is a group of ideas that Chicagoans have about themselves and their hometown (as in the famous television skit, "da Bears" spoken with a ripe Chicago accent). Literature is one way to glimpse those ideas. Anyone reading about the heroine of Theodore Dreiser's *Sister Carrie* dining in a downtown restaurant gets an instant picture of life around 1900. The same can be said for the ill-starred Studs Lonigan, Augie March, and many more. A discussion of cookery books published in and about Chicago going back to Isaac A. Poole's 1857 *The Cake Baker, A Book of Practical Receipts for Making Cake* shows how ideas and culinary fashions changed over time. The unique Period Kitchen, Dining Room, Pantry, and Recipes Resources is of special importance. Going to the places listed gives a physical quality to the city's and near suburbs' life through time periods.

The other main elements of the book are an introduction placing Chicago food in a historical context, a timeline of Chicago food history, illustrations, short biographies of the contributors, sidebars, a topical list of entries, and an index. We spent a great deal of time searching for and obtaining illustrations, especially those of historical interest that readers may not have seen before, such as archival pictures of ethnic groups. The numerous sidebars include recipes of iconic Chicago dishes, literary excerpts and quotations, and bits of interesting but peripheral information related to the main entries.

For readers who want more information, a bibliography with more general and some important topical works about Chicago and its food appears at the end of the book. Cross references are provided when useful and necessary.

Like any work of this scope, it may contain omissions and errors. The editors take full responsibility and welcome readers' input for future editions.

We hope *The Chicago Food Encyclopedia* will inspire those in other cities to write similar works. Our goal with this book is to help readers understand how foods and beverages have shaped—and continue to shape—this great city.

Acknowledgments

There are many people to thank for their help with *The Chicago Food Encyclopedia* during the last three years. First, to all contributors, thanks for your expertise and diligence. Thanks also go to Les Dames d'Escoffier Chicago and The Julia Child Foundation for their generous grants in support of the project. Our gratitude also goes to Professor Perry Duis and Russell Lewis, who reviewed the proposal and encouraged us to move forward.

Elizabeth Carlson, alias Miss Ellie, gets special thanks not only for her groundbreaking research but for her great help in finding and gathering illustrations.

Thanks to all who reviewed our topics list, especially Peter Engler and Professor Lynn Weiner. Special thanks also go to the eminent historian of America's food, Andrew Franklin Smith, for sharing tips on how to do this project and whose own work in New York spurred us on.

To the staff at University of Illinois Press, we thank you for your enthusiastic collaboration and support for this ambitious project. Special thanks goes to former director, Dr. Willis Regier of the Press, whose enthusiasm for the project ensured that it would go forward.

THE
CHICAGO
Food Encyclopedia

Introduction

Chicago was, in historian Donald L. Miller's phrase, the "City of the Century." The nineteenth century was an age when America changed itself from a rural small-scale manufacturing economy into the world's greatest agricultural and industrial power. American economic power rose on triple pillars. The first was comprised of iron, steel, steam engines, ships and railroads, machine tools, and farm machinery, the hard visible signs of the first industrial age. An immense inflow of immigrants was another pillar, and, perhaps most important of all, massive food production was a third. Much of the machinery and human labor went toward making America the world's foremost food supplier. Chicago was both the product and a main engine of this national transformation.

The city was founded as a commercial enterprise, a trade and manufacturing center. Many of the founders came from New England and New York. They were people of their times, entrepreneurs of many stripes determined to exploit the riches of the American interior and thereby make their fortunes. Wealth was to be made not in gold and silver, not in furs or luxury goods, but in foodstuffs. The men who became the city's first elected commissioners came here because they knew that the Erie Canal would link the small town of Chicago to New York City's markets. They soon planned more canals and later railroad lines to create a network running from the east to the Mississippi River and New Orleans. These new transportation systems made Chicago America's commodity center. But people do not live by industrial food production alone.

The story of Chicago's food consists of several strands, one of which is commodity production, the processing and manufacturing of food for national distribution. The other is what Chicagoans actually ate—public and private dining. Much of that came from the people who settled in the city. While basic American fare was the foundation—meat, bread, dairy, and potatoes—immigrants from across the globe brought their own food traditions. Eventually, these ethnic food preparations burst their community boundaries to form whole new dishes. Chicago's iconic dishes such as hot dogs, deep-dish pizza, and Italian beef are examples not only of eclectic cuisine but of Chicago's food identity. The story became more complex in the late twentieth century when the city became an international food center once again, not with commodities but with cuisine created by world-class chefs.

Chicago's food story starts with unprepossessing origins. Earliest Chicago was not blessed with great natural resources. A river flowed out of flat prairie land into one of the world's great freshwater seas, Lake Michigan. Fed by two small streams not much more than a few yards wide, the river was nothing grand. The floodplain was a sodden marsh for much of the year with a few areas of higher ground and some mud islets emerging in the sluggish stream. At the river's mouth sandbars and mud flats blocked direct access to the Great Lake. In the spring, the place was alive with black flies, and in summer, mosquito swarms feasted on any warm-blooded creature that they found. William H. Keating, a professor of mineralogy sent to the area on a military expedition in 1823, found the climate to be awful: cold and wet in winter, hot and humid in summer with capricious weather patterns. He might just as well have coined the phrase known to all modern Chicagoans, "if you don't like the weather, wait a minute." Keating said that the village called Chicago could never feed its few hundred people, "a miserable race of men," because of the climate and bad soils. But the place had promise, great promise, as envisioned by the city's founders.

The greater Chicago region was rich in wild and cultivated food. Native Americans harvested the plentiful fish in the lakes and rivers and game in the wooded areas. There were wild midwestern foods to be gathered, such as sunflower seeds, black walnuts, pawpaws, persimmons, and the wild onion (either leek or ramp or garlic) that gave Chicago its name. They also raised corn, beans, and

Wild onions for which Chicago is named. *Wikimedia Commons.*

squash in small fields near the rivers. The early American and métis (people of mixed French-Canadian and Indian ancestry) settlers lived on these foods, while listening to predatory wolves howling not far from their homes along Lake Street as late as the 1830s. Food was brought into the small town from the nearby fields and woods, setting a kind of pull-and-push economic pattern. That is, Chicago was and remains a raw food catchment area to which raw materials were brought and then sent out to national and international markets in either original form—wheat for instance—or as processed products. Meat was the most famous example.

Keating, despite his reservations, recognized the site's potential importance and growth as the link between the Great Lakes and the Mississippi River. Chicago was one of the few places that offered both a harbor—the Chicago River as it merged into the lake—and a passageway westward into the great agricultural wealth of the Midwest and the Mississippi River basin beyond. Natural passes by land and by water also led eastward across Indiana and Ohio to New York. As the eminent historical geographer William Cronin, in his book *Nature's Metropolis*, said geography is not destiny, but a fortuitous location, plus human ingenuity, planning, determination, and hard work were the engines of Chicago's extraordinary growth. The city was a natural landscape conquered and reordered. Even Keating admitted, albeit sourly, that was possible and necessary.

J. S. Wright's map of 1834 shows the city laid out on a grid, one that could be expanded in three directions almost without limit. The survey was done by James Thompson, who was hired by a commission set up by the city fathers to finance and build the Illinois and Michigan Canal. The grid created spacious blocks that led to a real estate boom that rapidly built the city's specialized spaces: housing and small shops that became neighborhoods, public buildings and squares, large shopping areas such as State Street, warehouses and factories, and eventually the great public parks along the lakefront. In early Chicago, all were packed in and near the Loop. Later the grid expanded outward to form new neighborhoods, and the city grew to accommodate the population that expanded so quickly between 1837 and 1930.

The proposed canal was critical. In a great era of canal building, it was modeled on the Erie Canal (finished in 1825) that cut across New York State to carry the abundant foods of the Midwest (through Chicago) to New York City. In return, easterners sent prized items such as the fresh Atlantic oysters that could be had in Chicago's newly built hotels as early as 1837. By the 1848 completion of the Illinois and Michigan Canal, barges filled with coal, iron, food, and produce moved both east and west to fuel the city's emerging industries and to make it America's commercial food center.

Chicago's settlers and builders set the stage for a good portion of the city's food history. Chicago was a cultural stew, built by immigrants from other parts of the nation and, later, from around the world. As mentioned earlier, prominent among first settlers were métis, including the Beaubien, Ouilmette, and Robinson families. Alexander

1,000 YEARS AGO
Miami and Potawatomi give
Chicago its name.

1803
Canadian John Kinzie takes
command of the trading post
and builds Fort Dearborn.

1700s   1800s

1780s
Afro-French Jean Baptiste
Point du Sable builds a
trading post.

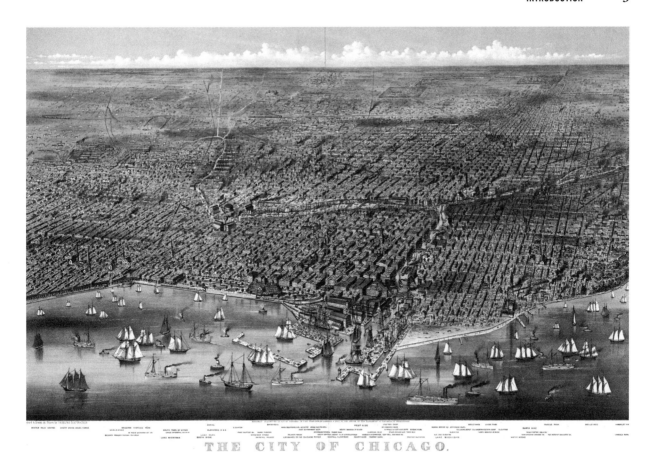

THE CITY OF CHICAGO.

Currier and Ives print of Chicago's Harbor, 1874. *Library of Congress.*

Robinson, the colorful Scottish-Potawatomi leader, remained in Chicago. The family integrated into the emerging Chicago society, and descendants still live in the area. The majority of immigrants came from the northeastern states, bringing their food preferences with them. Yankee-style oysters, fish, beef, root vegetables, and plenty of sugary desserts were on the menu. Great numbers of new European and some Asian immigrants brought new foodways.

Immigrants were drawn into the city by the promise of employment, no matter how poorly paid the jobs were. They settled into the city's blocks, building homes or renting homes built by the businesses that employed them. Spaces became defined ethnic neighborhoods, cultural ecologies, with their own languages, including dialects of English. As in today's neighborhoods, they were physically defined by street and landmark boundaries (parish churches, for instance) and food shops' and restaurants' signage. Food preferences, even the smells of cooking, are important parts of these localized cultures. A famous example is the Maxwell and Halsted Street area from

810s

1820s

1827
John Kinzie and Archibald Caldwell build the first real tavern at Wolf Point with homemade hard liquor featured.

Pioneer settler John Kinzie's house purchased from Jean Baptiste Point du Sable, ca. 1804. www.idaillinois.org. *Courtesy of the Plainfield Historical Society.*

around 1880 to the 1930s, with its Yiddish store signs and kosher foods. Irish immigrants, who dug the Illinois and Michigan Canal, stayed on in places such as Bridgeport at the head of the canal. Their food preferences were largely the same as Anglo-Americans. When the Germans, the first major "foreign" ethnic group, arrived after 1848, their preferences for breads, beer, potatoes, sausages, and meats cooked into hearty dishes fit right into Chicago's food profile. The foods of the Scandinavians, Jews, Czechs, Poles, and other East Europeans, followed by Mexicans, Central Americans, Puerto Ricans, and others, all became important to Chicago life.

The city founders who built the food catchment and processing industries planned to make Chicago a major center from the beginning. In the 1820s, the city's first butcher and constable, Archibald Clybourn, brought cattle and pigs to the city from as far away as Sangamon County and the Wabash River. His slaughtering operation on the river's north branch not only supplied the small town, but also the East Coast. Grocers and millers set up shop. In 1839, Chicago had four mills for a population of 4,100. In the early 1830s, Clybourn and fellow entrepreneurs,

especially George W. Dole and his partner Oliver Newberry, began to process and manufacture meat and flour for distribution across the nation. In 1848, merchants set up what would be the ancestor of the Chicago Board of Trade to deal in contracts for commodities. Fully developed as the market for commodity futures after the Civil War, Chicago became the center of the nation's food business.

Business boomed once engineers cleared the large sandbar blocking direct entrance to the Chicago River, and the Illinois and Michigan Canal opened the way to the Mississippi and New Orleans. Major economic depressions and recessions every few years slowed economic activity, but never for long. Even the Great Fire that burned down the whole central city hardly stopped the city's vital economy. Visitors were amazed at how quickly the city was rebuilt, beginning only days after the fire ended. Radiating out from the city center, the landscape came to be filled with bleak warehouses, factories, and venues to feed workers. By the 1880s, about 25,000 ships docked at Chicago ports each year. Sail- and steamboats moved back and forth to ports along the Great Lakes; some commodities were hauled along canals. The Chicago Sanitary

1831
George W. Dole, later called the "Father of the Provisions, Shipping and Elevator Business," opens Chicago's second grocery store at Dearborn and Water Streets.

1835
Lake House Hotel on Kinzie Street is the first eating place to use menu cards, napkins, and toothpicks and to serve oysters.

1838
Steamer "Great Western" carries the first shipment of wheat from Chicago, 75 bushels.

1847
Cyrus McCormick moves to Chicago to manufacture his mechanical grain reaper.

1848
The Illinois and Michigan Canal opens; corn exports to the east rise eightfold.

1830s   **1840s**

1832
Dole begins slaughtering and packing beef at his store, processing 150 head per day.

1836
First Irish immigrants come to Chicago.

1844
The Exchange Coffee House on Clark Street is the first eating house not connected to a hotel or tavern.

1848
Capt. Robert C. Bristol builds the first large steam-powered grain elevator.

The Chicago Board of Trade is founded, establishing market rules; it eventually controls the national commodities futures market.

and Ship Canal, completed in 1900 after a decade of labor, permanently reversed the flow of the Chicago River, sending the city's sewage westward to the Illinois River. Larger and longer barges could move bulky freight such as coal into the city. This was the age of coal-fired everything, from factories to building heating systems and electrical generation plants. Soot covered the city, including its food.

Railways Create New Chicago Markets

Technologies revolutionized the food industry and the new city, with canals and railroads as the most visible signs of change. Before 1848, lumbering "prairie schooner" wagons traveled along rough roads to the lakeside settlement. Cattle plodded along the same routes, in an early version of the Texas and Kansas cattle drives that Chicagoans later helped organize. This changed dramatically beginning in 1848.

Visionary entrepreneurs and civic-minded elected officials (often the same people) created a Chicago railroad system. William B. Ogden, the city's first mayor, worked fervently to open the Galena & Chicago Union railroad. He persuaded farmers to the west of the city to give land and put up money for construction; the railroad's first run, from near Galena to what is today's Oak Park, carried a load of grain. The Illinois Central Railroad, running from Cairo, Illinois, to Chicago, opened the market for southern and central Illinois wheat and fruit growers. Within 12 years, 11 railway lines covering 4,000 square miles led into the growing city, and by 1903, the number grew to 27 rail routes. Chicago's wheat imports by rail grew nine times and corn four times from 1852 to 1856. To accommodate the traffic, grain silos serviced by railcars sprang up. Captain Robert C. Bristol built the city's first large steam-powered grain elevator. A decade later, more than four million bushels of grain passed through the city. By the 1880s, Chicago was the world's largest wheat shipper. Carl Sandberg's epithets, "Player with Railroads" and "Stacker of Wheat," well described this American breadbasket.

Some of the wheat, barley, rye, oats, and corn that poured into the city became baked goods. The city had

commercial bakeries from the start. Large-scale commercial baking began as early as 1858 and developed into regional and national businesses. The same held for meat. Businessmen and city leaders decided to rationalize the booming meat industry by building a centralized stockyard with rail lines to serve it. By 1865, The Union Stock Yards became the symbol of the gritty industrial city that city fathers called the greatest pork-packing city in the

MURDER IN A FAMOUS RESTAURANT

During Thanksgiving festivities on November 25, 1875, "one of the best known restaurateurs in town, Charley Whyland, the head of the firm managing the St. Elmo's Restaurant, attached to Kuhn's Hotel" had been murdered by a vile ruffian, gambler, and drunk named Henry Davis, reported the *Chicago Daily Tribune*.

Davis, who was drunk, accosted Whyland in the restaurant, brandishing a six-shooter. After calling his victim names too vile for newspapers to print, Davis shot Whyland in the face. He then ran through the restaurant, pursued by restaurant personnel, throwing sauce bottles at them and threatening them with his weapon. After a chase out into the street, Davis returned to the restaurant kitchen where he was confronted by the butcher wielding his cleaver. Just then a policeman arrived and talked the murderer into handing over his weapon.

The *Tribune* suggested that Davis was aggrieved because his lady friend of dubious repute, a Mrs. Salsbury, had been insulted by Whyland (she denied the story). At the trial, Davis claimed that he had been subject to bouts of insanity and was drunk. After a hung jury, Davis pleaded guilty to manslaughter and received 21 years in Joliet prison. The newspapers and many reformers called for gun control, especially in the many saloons and gambling dens in the city.

—BRUCE KRAIG

1850s	1854		1861–1865	1868
Large numbers of German immigrants settle in the city, bringing sausages, bread, beer, and confections.	Eighty-three million bushels of grain are shipped via rail and canal.		The Civil War creates an economic boom for Chicago; one-third of all rail lines lead to Chicago to supply food for troops.	Philip Henrici opens the first Viennese coffee house on Dearborn Avenue. The first known cookbook published in Chicago is Poole's *The Cake Baker*.

850s   **1860s**

	1853	1858	1865	1868
	The earliest existing hotel menu is from the St. Nicholas; the menu is entirely in French.	Chester E. Morse's place at the "C & R.I. RR Station," is probably the first named railway lunch counter.	The Union Stock Yards are established.	Philip Armour founds Armour & Company.

world, the new "Porkopolis," or in Sandberg's words, "Hog butcher for the world." New communities followed the industry. A new packing town grew, beginning in 1868, when Benjamin P. Hutchinson bought land next to the yards for his operations. It was called Back of the Yards. Irish, Lithuanians, Poles, and other groups lived side by side, not always peacefully.

Further technical and business innovation made Chicago's food industries the most advanced in the nation. In 1847, Cyrus McCormick moved his reaping machine business to Chicago. Merged with two other manufacturers in 1902, the new company controlled 80 percent of the agricultural machinery market. A host of other inventions followed. Today, Chicago remains a center for food technology and mechanical innovation in food processing. Swift and Armour developed the ancestor of the assembly line at their slaughterhouses. With their resulting higher production rates, the packers needed better ways to get product to distant markets. Ice cut from lakes and rivers cooled factories and refrigerated cars. Those cars, pioneered by George H. Hammond and Gustavus Swift in the late 1860s and 1870s, allowed Chicago beef to reach New York still cold and at lower prices than local farmers could offer.

City Farms, City Gardens

Chicago's founders called it Urbs in Horto, city in a garden, soon after 1837. In her memoir of a childhood in 1860s and '70s Chicago, Louise de Koven Bowen recalled that when her maternal mill-owner grandfather built the family mansion on a tree-filled lot at the corner of Adams Street and Wabash Avenue, their old neighbors living on Lake Street were sad to see them move so far away. Country folks, she called her family, who used to picnic at Gage Farm on Michigan Avenue and 16th Street. It took a whole day to get there and back. Bowen fondly remembered Alice the family cow, who was kept in a field on Adams Street and milked daily. Growing up in Lakeview in the 1880s, Caroline B. King, who later became one of America's leading food writers and teachers, wrote fondly about the large garden her

family kept and the adjacent small farms that supplied eggs, butter, milk, and vegetables. Lakeview was a major celery-growing region up to the early twentieth century, while Bridgeport and West Ridge were famous for cabbages. Who could forget Mrs. O'Leary (who lived on DeKoven Street) and her infamous cow in the apocryphal story of the Chicago Fire. As the city expanded, houses and paved roads covered the old farms; and only a few gardens were in the park system.

Chicago's growth amazed not just its own residents but visitors, especially after the Great Fire. First came draining the city of its polluted water from frequent floods. An extensive network of drainpipes were laid down, a number of them still in use in 2015. Historian Perry Duis observes in *Challenging Chicago* that Chicago authorities knew that foul water carried diseases, even if they did not understand germ theory. The process of sewage disposal was fixed with one of the great engineering feats in American history, the Sanitary and Ship Canal. Begun piecemeal in the 1870s and finished in 1900, the project reversed the flow of the Chicago River. Instead of waste going into Lake Michigan it went to the Des Plaines River and eventually the Illinois and Mississippi Rivers, much to the chagrin of communities along them.

Visitors could hardly believe the "can do" nature of the city that was filled with the most modern buildings of the era. They marveled at the world's best transit systems focusing on six railroad terminals, all of them busy. The Loop, a light rail system begun in 1858, ran around the center city. The elevated version came into existence in 1892, and Chicago's landscape was changed by the now-familiar "El." An estimated three-quarters of a million people traveled into the city using the El and trolleys. By century's end, Chicago carried the densest concentration of people and businesses in the United States. Because the throngs of workers and visitors had to be fed, many visitors commented on the city's food scene. What may have been America's first-named lunch counter, Chester E. Morse's place, was booming at the Chicago and Rock Island Railroad station by 1858. Many more fast-service eateries followed.

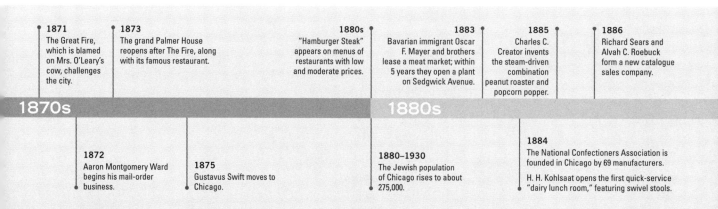

1871
The Great Fire, which is blamed on Mrs. O'Leary's cow, challenges the city.

1873
The grand Palmer House reopens after The Fire, along with its famous restaurant.

1880s
"Hamburger Steak" appears on menus of restaurants with low and moderate prices.

1883
Bavarian immigrant Oscar F. Mayer and brothers lease a meat market; within 5 years they open a plant on Sedgwick Avenue.

1885
Charles C. Creator invents the steam-driven combination peanut roaster and popcorn popper.

1886
Richard Sears and Alvah C. Roebuck form a new catalogue sales company.

1870s

1880s

1872
Aaron Montgomery Ward begins his mail-order business.

1875
Gustavus Swift moves to Chicago.

1880–1930
The Jewish population of Chicago rises to about 275,000.

1884
The National Confectioners Association is founded in Chicago by 69 manufacturers.

H. H. Kohlsaat opens the first quick-service "dairy lunch room," featuring swivel stools.

In housing, income, and food, class distinctions divided Chicagoans, as they still do. Anyone with money employed housekeepers, cooks, and handymen. Caroline B. King's family employed Anna, a wonderful German cook and baker, and her future husband Emil. The wealthy Frances Macbeth Glessner hired Irish cooks, one of whom quit in disgust when the family purchased one of the new-fangled electric stoves shown at the Columbian Exposition of 1893. Studies done at the end of the century show that upper-middle-class people ate greater varieties of fresh food than working-class families. Yet, working families managed to eat more calories than middle-class people. Small shop and restaurant owners and street vendors in neighborhoods could make a living in this small-scale economy.

Chicago has always been a place to dine out. Ten taverns served the city in 1837; there were more taverns than churches. Mark Beaubien operated the most famous of them, the Sauganash (meaning "English speaker" in a Native American language) Tavern. Travelers often slept on the floor of the primitive building after a night of drinking and fiddling by the cheerful proprietor. Tavern cookery consisted of boiling, roasting, and frying local foods. Good as the ingredients might have been, as James Parton claimed 30 years later, cooks prepared their foods badly, mainly by boiling. At the same time, fine dining could be found at Chicago's first grand hotel, the Lake House (later renamed the Sherman House). R. B. Macy, visiting from Wisconsin, described it as "the most magnificent hotel in the universe," its dining room having the city's first printed menus and napkins. The Lake House and the grand hotels that followed in the nineteenth century served dishes made in the French style of the day, with German touches and using American game animals. As in a Briggs House menu of 1859, oysters were the de rigueur appetizer, followed by fish dishes, boiled meats, and then roasted meats, all accompanied by ornamental dishes such as quail pie. Wild game followed—the likes of roast bear loin, roast squirrel, and ever-present prairie chickens (now almost extinct on the American prairies). Dessert and a range of imported German and French wines and brandies helped get the feast down.

One of Chicago's first hotels and taverns was operated by the celebrated Mark Beaubien. www.idaillinois.org. *Courtesy of the Plainfield Historical Society.*

Visitors and the well-off locals often dined in Chicago hotels in the city's commercial center. Their menus reflected national dining styles, as did Chicago's great restaurants: Wright's at Crosby's Opera House, Kinsley's, Rector's, Burcky and Milan, and Henrici's among the best known. They were the equal of any in the country, though the dishes were not as ornamental as in the hotels. As the center of the meat industry, Chicago had renowned steak houses. Some, Billy Boyle's Chop House a prime example, were considered more upscale than others. The first free-standing restaurant, the Exchange Coffee House, in 1844 served somewhat simpler versions of grand dishes. Its menu listed pigs feet, tripe, tongue, pies, tarts, custard, Indian and graham breads, prairie and tame chickens, game, birds, "welsh rare-bits," and oysters fried, stewed, or in soup. On the second floor, ladies could partake of ice cream and other dainties. Many other middle-price-range places followed; one of them, the well-known New York Restaurant, sold 25-cent meals and bragged that it never reused leftovers. As early as the 1880s, budget-priced "hamburger steak" appeared on menus. These kinds of restaurants, such as the twentieth century's Toffenetti's chain (opened in 1914), eventually become dining spots for families and shoppers.

1891
William Wrigley sets up his chewing gum business in Chicago.

1900–1910
Fifteen thousand Greek immigrants arrive in Chicago.

Roughly 170,000 Poles arrive in Chicago.

1903
Joseph L. Kraft and brothers establish a wholesale cheese business in the Water Street market.

1906
Upton Sinclair publishes *The Jungle.*

890s

1900s

1893
The World's Columbian Exposition introduces new food and cooking products.

1901
The Quaker Oats Company is founded; it acquires the Aunt Jemima brand in 1926.

1904
Brach's Candy begins.

1908
The African American Frinch family begins Frinches Pantry on Evanston Avenue (now Broadway), the first integrated restaurant in Chicago.

ROYKO'S TAKE ON ETHNIC CHICAGO

"The neighborhood-towns were part of larger ethnic states. To the north of the Loop was Germany. To the northwest was Poland. To the west were Italy and Israel. To the southwest were Bohemia and Lithuania. And to the south was Ireland. . . . You could always tell, even with your eyes closed, which state you were in by the odors of the food stores and the open kitchen windows, the sound of the foreign or familiar language, and by whether a stranger hit you in the head with a rock."

—MIKE ROYKO IN *BOSS*

While the rich feasted, the working masses ate faster and cheaper. To serve its dense downtown crowds of working people and shoppers, Chicago developed innovative restaurants. Snacks, including fruit and prepared foods, had always been the province of street vendors. Bananas brought in from the new train service to New Orleans and oranges from California became main snack foods. In the 1880s, food wagons appeared on the scene. The ancestors of today's food trucks, wagons serviced factories, schools, and the nighttime entertainment crowds. New fast-service restaurants that catered to Loop workers were invented in the 1880s and 1890s. Simple counters with stools or chairs with one arm for holding food popped up across the city. Five- and ten-cent meal places were located in working-class parts of town and at the edge of the downtown business district. William Weeghman, onetime owner of the Chicago Cubs and builder of Wrigley Field, made his fortune with one-arm lunchrooms. H. H. Kohlsaat's dairy restaurants catered to young working women. A Loop restaurant owner dubbed his places "cafeterias" and the name stuck. Drugstores installed lunch counters and larger chains,

Thompson's, B/G Foods and Pixley & Ehlers the largest, dominated the new cafeteria market. So numerous were the quick-service places along Madison and Clark Streets that the area became known as "Toothpick Alley." These quick-service places, urban in origin, broke out of their environments to become national chains, including the Chicago area–based McDonald's.

Although eating out has always been important in Chicago's culinary life, most people ate home-cooked meals. When they ate out it was at locally based, often ethnic, eateries. They still do. Unlike other cities, Chicago did not have a permanent central market where consumers could buy directly from food wholesalers and farmers. In 1848, the city built a market hall on State Street near Madison, but it failed within a decade because people kept moving further and further from the old Lake Street center. Shoppers got their food from small grocers, butchers, bakers, and dairy shops. The earliest Chicago newspapers carried advertising, such as from J. B. Doggett, who "would respectfully call the attention of the citizens of Chicago to his large stock of Family Groceries which were purchased for the retail trade in the city. The stock is of the highest quality and the prices will suit . . . free delivery." Then as now, grocers listed prices as inducements. Hundreds, later thousands, of small shops in every neighborhood covered the city's food shopping needs. Grocers picked up food at the wholesale market on Water Street or had it delivered by wagon. Butchers got their meat from the stockyards, but milk often came from city dairies that kept cows in their own yards. Scandals about bad milk brought about the first food regulations and, in 1916, laws requiring pasteurization.

One star on Chicago's four-star flag stands for the 1893 World's Columbian Exposition or World's Fair. A landmark event in American history, it was also one for food history. A stunning array of official exhibits within the fairgrounds and unofficial ones on the Midway attracted roughly half of America's population within a nine-month period. Visitors packed Chicago restaurants, highlighting the city as a culinary center. International pavilions all had restaurants that introduced their cuisines to Americans, while

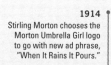

1914
Stirling Morton chooses the Morton Umbrella Girl logo to go with new ad phrase, "When It Rains It Pours."

1916–1918
The "Great Migration" of African Americans to the north and Chicago begins.

1920
Prohibition goes into effect.
H. Teller Archibald opens his Fannie May candy store.

1927
Kraft Cheese introduces Velveeta Cheese.

1910s   1920s

1915
The *Chicago Defender* publishes its first recipe column in March.

1919
The U.S. Constitution is amended for the eighteenth time to prohibit the manufacture, transport, and sale of alcohol.

1922
Ivar Coulson invents the malted milkshake at a Walgreens drugstore.

1929
Mars, Inc., builds a new plant on Oak Park Avenue in Chicago.

Lunch Wagon, South Side, 1941. *Library of Congress.*

Neighborhood grocery stores received supplies from wholesalers and packers such as Gabel, 1920. *Courtesy of the Chicago History Museum, ICHi-85009; M. J. Schmidt.*

on the Midway all kinds of delectable dishes appeared, including sausages from the precursor of the Vienna Beef Company and Oscar Mayer. The famous cooking teacher Sarah Tyson Rorer lectured on cookery at the Illinois Corn Exhibit model kitchen, located in the Women's Building, and Ellen Swallow Richards taught women about healthful diets. Jane Addams and other reformers were greatly influenced by Richards's ideas about efficiency, economy, and good nutrition for both middle-class and poor people. Commercial companies at the Exposition—such as Heinz, Swift, Armour, and others—introduced packaged foods that would become the future of America's industrialized food systems. Although one of the worst depressions in American history followed, the grand exhibition showed the triumph of technology and the primacy of the city in American life, all centered on Chicago.

The first two decades of the twentieth century, culminating in World War I, marked major changes in Chicago and American food. Restaurant menus became simpler, home cooks relied more on processed foods, the city enforced more food regulations, and Prohibition began in earnest. Because of production problems on the East Coast and

changing tastes, oysters ceased to be the number one appetizer on most restaurant menus. The numerous cafeterias, lunch counters, and affordably priced restaurants served dishes as simple as melted cheese sandwiches, soups, baked ham, chopped beef steaks, chicken a la king, baked potatoes, and canned vegetables. Home cooks made similar dishes as taught in numerous newspaper and magazine articles. Economy and speed became common cooking themes, especially during World War I. Food will win the war, the federal government said, and farmers responded with huge production increases. Home cooks also economized in every way by using cheaper ingredients, substitutes, and growing large amounts of vegetables in home gardens. Armour's Veribest Brand canned food division and other Chicago companies printed pamphlets showing how to economize, especially by using their brands.

Electric household devices, including vacuum cleaners, irons, and toasters, arrived on the market, and gas stoves began to replace old coal-fired stoves. Cooking became easier and more sanitary. Food hygiene became more important with the passage of the Pure Food and Drug Act in 1906 among others. Though sensationalized by Upton

A typical butcher shop of the era with carcasses hung in front. *Courtesy of the Chicago History Museum, ICHi-85014.*

Sinclair's still powerful novel, *The Jungle*, rotted and adulterated food had long plagued Chicagoans. The federal law and city ordinances, such as those on milk purity and even dealing with street vendors (one medical authority in 1915 claimed that syphilis was passed on by hot dog vendors), made Chicago a national leader in food purity.

In the years following World War I, Chicago remained one of America's fastest growing major cities and a mecca for immigrants. The city's expandable grid allowed new building developments to the north, west, and south largely as ethnic neighborhoods. By 1920, its population reached 2.7 million people, around a third foreign-born and a quarter second-generation immigrants, mainly of European origin. The largest immigrant populations were the Poles, Germans, Russian and East European Jews, followed by Italians, Swedes, Irish, and Czechs.

All these groups brought their own culinary traditions. From the 1920s on, some of their dishes crossed ethnic and neighborhood boundaries to become iconic Chicago dishes. Italians, most from the southern part of the country, created Italian beef, which was probably first served at weddings in the Taylor Street neighborhood known as "Little Italy. The first pizzeria in Chicago was likely Granato's on Taylor Street, opened in 1924. Deep-dish pizza was invented (probably based on or related to the thick pizza bread made in Italian bakeries) in 1943 at Riccardo's restaurant by two restaurateurs who wanted to turn pizza into a full meal. Jews went into the meat, sausage, and delicatessen business. Their all-beef products became the hot dog of choice in Chicago and "kosher-style" delis dotted the city, including several in the downtown business districts. Greeks came to dominate the wholesale fruit and vegetable business, as well as confections and ice cream. Many of the nation's Greek diners, soda shops, and candy makers were trained in Chicago from the 1920s to the 1950s. African Americans settled on the South Side and, post 1950s, on the West Side. Restaurants serving such traditional southern dishes as fried chicken and barbecue became popular, the latter becoming a nationally recognized Chicago style. Mexicans arrived just before World War I and formed small communities graced by grocery stores, tortillerias, bakeries, and storefront eateries. Treated as exotic, Mexican cuisine would not expand into other parts of the city until the 1960s.

The Age of Speakeasies

In January 1919, the Volstead Act (to carry out the 18th Amendment to the Constitution) made the manufacture, sale, and transport of alcohol illegal in Illinois. The law

1950s
This decade brings the second great African American migration to Chicago.

1953
Sunbeam improves the electric frying pan design (invented in 1911) with a heat controller in handle.

1955
Ray Kroc opens the first McDonald's franchise in Des Plaines.

1960
Chicago-based Kraft Foods Company introduces its first bottled barbecue sauce.

LATE 1950s
Nancy's Pizza develops the stuffed pizza.

1962
The first Crate and Barrel store opens in Old Town.

The Treasure Island supermarket chain opens.

1963
Chef Louis Szathmary opens The Bakery, bringing a modern continental menu.

1964
The Civil Rights Act is signed after protests and sit-ins; "soul food" becomes the new term in Chicago for southern cooking.

1965
The Immigration and Nationality Act expands immigration of Mexican, Chinese, and Southeast Asians to Chicago, changing culinary tastes.

1966
Tootsie Roll opens a plant in the Ford City Industrial Park.

1968
McDonald's introduces the Big Mac.

1968
Peter Lo inaugurates Mandarin-Szechuan-Hunan cooker in Chicago at the Chinese Tea House.

1950s

1960s

ushered in one of the most colorful and notorious eras in the city's history. Although Chicago had its share of gangsters before Prohibition (including "Big Jim" Colosimo, owner of the famous Colosimo restaurant), the new order offered opportunities for profit. Gangsters ran illegal breweries and stills, smuggled alcohol from Canada and Cuba, and owned and supplied Chicago speakeasies—some 20,000, by estimates. They ranged from small neighborhood joints to lavish downtown nightclubs. Unlike pre-Prohibition bars that served only men, they welcomed women; drinking became fashionable among "flappers." Cocktails were in vogue, mainly to mask the flavor of bootlegged liquor. A few of the city's most celebrated speakeasies turned legal with the end of Prohibition in 1933 and still flourish, including Schaller's Pub, The Green Mill Cocktail Lounge, the Green Door Tavern, and Twin Anchors. But many famous old restaurants closed because they could not legally sell most kinds of alcoholic beverages.

The day after Prohibition ended, two of Chicago's most famous restaurants opened their doors: The Cape Cod Room in the Drake Hotel and The Berghoff (begun in 1898 as a saloon, it reopened with its own signature beer). Some speakeasy owners opened legitimate nightclubs and supper clubs, and in the late 1930s and 1940s, Rush Street became the place for nightlife. In the early 1930s, Chicago boasted over 40 nightspots, among them Chez Paree, the New College Inn, the Venetian Room, The Limehouse, the Canton Tea Room, the Marine Dining Room in the Edgewater Beach Hotel, and El Harem, known for its "perfumed' Turkish atmosphere. On the South Side, the Great Terrace and other African American nightclubs flourished.

Chicagoans always have had a sweet tooth. It was the Candy Capital of the World, at its peak in the mid-1950s when more than 100 candy companies were in operation here. Chicagoans flocked to the ice-cream parlors and soda fountains that sprang up throughout the city and suburbs. Many are in business today, including Gertie's Ice Cream, Margie's Candies, Oberweis Dairy, and Homer's Gourmet Ice Cream. The malted milkshake was invented by Ivar Coulson in 1922 at a Walgreens Drug Store. Chicago also

Chinese-owned nightclubs like the Limehouse on Howard Street featured big bands and Cantonese Food. *Courtesy of the Rogers Park / West Ridge Historical Society.*

was home to the soda fountain industry, with leaders like Sam Schy, whose American Soda Fountain sold and repaired fountain equipment nationwide. Fizzy chocolate soda was probably created by a Chicagoan, Frederick Sanders Schmidt.

By 1933, underemployment and unemployed reached 50 percent and hunger was rampant. More people emigrated from the United States than came to it, including several hundred thousand Mexicans who were forcibly repatriated. Government agencies, churches, and other private organizations set up soup kitchens, also called "breadlines," that served meals to the poor. The fare was spartan: soups and stews made of whatever could be bought locally and cheaply, plus bread and coffee. One of the most famous soup kitchens was opened in 1931 by Al Capone who, facing federal indictment, wanted some favorable publicity. Over a two-year period, it served breakfast, lunch, and dinner to some 120,000 people. Food writers, such as Mary Meade in the *Chicago Tribune*, offered housewives creative ways of using ingredients such as rice, beans, and cheese instead of meat.

1970
Cuisinart introduces the food processor at the National Housewares Show in Chicago.

Jewel Foods offers the first generic food brand.

1976
The American Egg Board is formed and creates "The Incredible Edible Egg" campaign.

1979
Chicago opens the first farmers markets since the nineteenth century.

The Greater Chicago Food Depository opens on the Southwest Side.

1984
Consolidated Foods Co. changes its name to Sara Lee Corp. after its frozen cheesecakes.

1970s   **1980s**

1971
Rich Melman opens R. J. Grunt's; the seeds of a culinary empire are sown.

1973
Le Français opens, owned by Jean and Doris Banchet.

The era of Chicago as "Meatpacker to the World" ends; the Union Stock Yards close.

1978
Arnie Morton opens Morton's The Steakhouse on State St.

1980
The first Taste of Chicago is held on Michigan Avenue; later, it moves to Grant Park.

1987
Charlie Trotter opens his soon-to-be top-rated restaurant on Armitage Avenue; Rick and Deann Bayless open a high-quality Mexican place, Frontera Grill.

For a gyros sandwich, lamb or beef is formed into a cone around a skewer and roasted vertically. *Photograph by Mary Valentin.*

truth. A Chicago diner could choose among Russian, Bohemian, Greek, Filipino, Japanese, French, English, Louisiana Creole, Italian, Mexican, Middle Eastern, Roumanian, and Chinese restaurants. Some iconic Chicago dishes surfaced at this time, including Chicken Vesuvio, which appeared on the menu of the Vesuvio Restaurant in the 1930s. During the 1930s, popular self-service cafeterias and lunch counters sold such classic sandwiches as BLTs, ham and cheese, and tuna or chicken salad for 15 to 25 cents. New products came on the market, including Kraft's Velveeta (first introduced in 1931) and its Macaroni and Cheese.

In 1933–34, Chicago's second world's fair held on the lakefront, "A Century of Progress," painted an optimistic picture of America's scientific achievements and industrial development, especially in food. Model homes showcased modern appliances, such as electric refrigerators, ranges, and dishwashers. Kraft Foods displayed its new "emulsifying machine," the Miracle Whip, which gave its name to the company's new salad dressing that became wildly popular. Fairgoers could enjoy meals from a wide choice of cuisines at kosher hot dog stands, doughnut shops, French cafes, a Jewish deli, beer gardens sponsored by the leading breweries, and even elegant sit-down restaurants featuring live music and dancing.

World War II and the 1950s

During World War II, sugar, meat, butter, whiskey, canned goods, and other items were rationed, and Americans were encouraged to grow fruits and vegetables in their "victory gardens," transforming cityscapes into patches of green garden amid bungalows and factories. In Chicago, more than 250,000 home gardens were planted. The Chicago Horticultural Society and the Chicago Park District supported the creation of 15,000 victory gardens on vacant sites that in 1943 alone produced 55,000 pounds of food.

The end of World War II saw dramatic changes in Americans' lifestyles and eating habits. There was a massive move to peripheral parts of the city and the suburbs. What had been farms and vacant lots along what is now the Far West and Northwest sides were filled with rows

Despite this, many people did have jobs and ate out. The same pattern of neighborhood and downtown destination restaurants held. Chicago had a thriving cosmopolitan restaurant scene that journalist John Drury chronicled in his *Dining in Chicago*, published in 1931. A Chicago booster, Drury claimed that the "moules marinieres" served in Chicago restaurants were as equal to those in any restaurant in France, and that Chicagoans could do a tour of the world in food in Chicago—a claim not very far from the

1990s   **2000s**

1998
Abby Mandel founds Green City Market, a sustainable farmers market.

2001
Doug Sohn opens his hot dog emporium, Hot Doug's.

2005
Chef Grant Achatz opens Alinea on North Halsted St.

2006
Chicago bans the sale of foie gras; this is rescinded in 2008.

The first Chicago Gourmet food festival is held in Millennium Park.

2007
The U.S. Census reports that 21.7 percent of Chicago's population is foreign-born.

of small homes. By the end of the 1950s, 40 percent of Americans lived in suburbs, a movement driven by the baby boom. Starting in the late 1930s, supermarkets began replacing small neighborhood stores by offering lower prices, nationally branded packaged food, and more convenient service. After 1945, they expanded rapidly over the rest of the century, often driving out old neighborhood food shops and changing the visible face of communities. Jewel Foods became a market leader in 1950s by remodeling the old Loblaw Groceries chain and opening supermarkets in new suburban shopping centers.

By the late 1930s and early '40s, electric stoves and refrigerators with freezers, many manufactured in Chicago, became common in home kitchens. Convenience was the new mantra, and companies began to sell frozen and prepackaged food. Frozen orange juice, instant cocoa, cake and cookie mixes, brown-and-serve rolls, prestuffed turkeys—all made their appearance in the 1950s. Many of the new items were manufactured by Chicago companies—for example, Swift (Butterball turkeys), Quaker Oats, Kraft Foods, and Sara Lee. Cookbooks, food company brochures, and popular women's magazines gave their readers recipes for meatloaf, casseroles—tuna and green bean casseroles were especially popular—made with canned soups and vegetables. Emblematic dishes of the era include three-bean salad, jello molds, bacon wrap-arounds, dips and chips, canapés, and tidbits in "blankets." Some instant foods originated in the field rations developed during the war, including cake mixes, dehydrated soups, powdered eggs, and canned meats. Chicago companies were at the forefront of changes in food technology, and the industry trade group was located in the city.

Home entertaining became fashionable. Cocktails were in vogue—Manhattans and martinis were the most popular—and cocktail lounges multiplied. Wine was enjoyed only by a few epicures or on special occasions, such as Christmas or Yom Kippur. Several establishments began selling wine in the 1940s and '50s, including Sam's, Schaefer's, and Binny's.

In the 1950s and '60s, fast-food chains, epitomized by McDonald's, began to revolutionize the restaurant industry.

Robert's kosher fish market on the North Side. *Photograph by Ashish Sen.*

Oak Park native Ray Kroc opened the first McDonald's franchise in Des Plaines, Illinois, in 1955, and by 1958, the company sold its 100 millionth hamburger. The franchise model was adapted to other types of food, notably pizza. By 1953, more than 100 pizza parlors did business in the Chicago area. Pizza had been a local urban dish, became regional as people moved to the suburbs, and then grew into a national craze, driven by new manufacturing technologies and corporate marketing.

Shifting Populations and the Family Dinner

The latter half of the twentieth century marked more dramatic changes in Chicago's food scene. Along with the rest of the country in the 1960s, the Midwest's largest city was set to experience a half-century of shifting politics, growing awareness of civil rights and women's liberation, expanding and waning war efforts, student protests, recessions and prosperity, and evolving food habits. The food scene ranged from fast-food and supermarket

2013
Dominick's stores are closed by Safeway Brands.

2016
The number of restaurants in the Chicago metro market reaches about 19,000.

010s

2020s

2015
The James Beard Foundation Awards ceremony is held for the first time in Chicago.

expansions to gourmet and exotic food imports, from the first celebrity chefs and award-winning restaurants to farmers markets and the "locally grown" movements. New immigrants brought new flavors. It was a time of increasing sophistication about food and cooking—and of the growing importance of Chicago as an American food destination.

For the first time, the city of Chicago began losing population, almost 2 percent in 1960, according to census figures. From there, the trend continued downward, with losses of about 4 to 11 percent per year. The suburban lifestyle lured folks away from the city: better schools, safer streets, and bigger kitchens and lawns. At the same time, women continued to leave their kitchens to join the workforce. Thirty percent of U.S. women worked in 1960, increasing to almost 60 percent in 2012.

It's little wonder that new convenience foods kept appearing on store shelves. Frozen and packaged and "ready to cook" foods helped busy households put meals on the table. As such convenience products mushroomed, so did area supermarkets, helped by Chicago's status as the middle-of-the-country transportation hub. Chicago was built with the help of an expanding railway system in the 1800s, but by the early 1960s, trucks had taken over many food transportation duties. New expressways eased the transition, and trucks supplied the city's growing number of produce markets, supermarkets, and restaurants. The introduction of the microwave oven brought cooks a new tool for getting fast meals on the table, though it took many years to become accepted as something more than a beverage warmer. By 1988, more than 900 new microwave food products had appeared on supermarket shelves.

But it was not all convenience cooking in home kitchens. After all, the '60s brought Julia Child, TV's *The French Chef*, who encouraged Americans to try their hand at what most thought of as "fancy French fare." Her now-classic book, *Mastering the Art of French Cooking* was published in 1961, and "gourmet was groovy," as Beverly Bundy wrote in *The Century in Food*. In Chicago, the Pope family continued their popular cooking school, focusing on international dishes. Chef John Snowden opened a new cooking school, Dumas Pere L'Ecole de Cuisine Française, on the North Side, where he taught thousands of students who were hungry for the ins and outs of classic French food.

Home cooks were ready to tackle French food and other fancy dishes. Socializing meant inviting friends over for a dinner or cocktail party. Quiche became one of the most popular dishes of the entertaining set in the 1970s. Fondue was soon to follow. Backyard grilling became a weekend event, especially after the introduction of the soon-to-be-iconic, bucket-shaped Weber Grill, locally made in Palatine. Backyard barbecuing was a special feature of African American neighborhoods that became widely popular among all Chicagoans. Noting the trend, Chicago-based Kraft Foods Company introduced its first bottled barbecue sauce in 1960, kicking off a competitive segment of the grocery aisle that continues to this day.

More cooking classes for home cooks appeared, offering a growing audience techniques and guidance for parties and everyday meals. One of them, Cook's Mart, on North LaSalle Street, brought in nationally known culinary experts Diana Kennedy and Marcella Hazan among many others. The shop was well-stocked with culinary tools and gadgets, many from local firms such as EKCO, Chicago Metallic Bakeware, and Chicago Cutlery Co. Geared for those who loved to entertain, the first Crate and Barrel store opened in Old Town in 1962. The warehouse-like store offered inexpensive china and cooking tools that could be placed in those newfangled dishwashers in many Chicago homes. Television cooking shows such as Chicago-produced *Frugal Gourmet* encouraged a new generation to try cooking—and to buy cooking gear.

Rising food costs, beginning in the early 1970s, and the stock market crash of 1987 had home cooks turning more to inexpensive ingredients. Cookbooks and the media offered recipes for such foods as ground beef, dried beans, and rice. "Comfort food" became a well-used phrase and included old-time favorites such as macaroni and cheese, long-cooked stews, and pot roasts. Many of Chicago's classic street foods—hot dogs, Italian beef, and pizza—fit into this economical niche; some cooks turned to making them at home. Manufacturers helped put comfort foods in the supermarket aisles and freezers. In 1984, Chicago's Consolidated Foods Company changed its name to the Sara Lee Corporation, named after its popular frozen cheesecake products. The National Live Stock and Meat Board, representing beef producers and located on Michigan Avenue, continued to promote meat well into the 1990s, launching the famous "Beef, It's What's for Dinner" advertising campaign with actor Robert Mitchum. After the September 11, 2001, terrorist attacks on the World Trade Center, the term "comfort foods" reappeared in the Chicago media and on restaurant menus, with recipes for classic dishes to prepare while "cocooning" at home.

A Changing Supermarket Scene

Provisioning was easier as the second half of the twentieth century advanced. A number of Chicago-area multidepartment supermarkets competed for the family food dollar as they replaced the old specialized butcher, baker, and greengrocer shops. In the new millennium, more specialized stores entered the Chicago market. Trader Joe's emphasized well-priced wines and creative frozen appetizers, entrees, and desserts. Whole Foods Market filled the natural foods niche. Formerly suburban stores such as Target reentered the city along with warehouse markets—Costco with its low-cost bulk items, for example. Wal-Mart also arrived, first in the suburbs. A new player, Mariano's, bought up many of the vacant Dominick's stores. Owned by Milwaukee-based Roundy's, it offered full supermarket services and a strong ethnic foods selection. Specialty foods were a mark of the new population. The Whole Foods and Trader Joe's chains were among the new stores, but there were local ones as well. In 1963, a small Greek-owned supermarket, Treasure Island, opened. It stocked imported products, wine, and unusual meats and produce for shoppers now willing to cook "foreign" food and drink French wines. Debbie Sharpe opened a small market in Bucktown, the Goddess and Grocer, offering a deli and products along the lines of pastas, sauces, dressings, wine, and beer. Sharpe, also a caterer to rock bands, such as Madonna and The Rolling Stones, grew the business into multiple locations. Later, in 2001, Fox & Obel offered packaged gourmet fare and an in-house bakery, cafe, and prepared foods kitchen. But profits dwindled and it closed in 2013. Plum Market, a specialty supermarket, opened in 2013 in Old Town, featuring locally made products and prepared foods.

Beginning in the '60s and '70s, more health-focused food stores came to Chicago. While some markets, Kramer's on Wabash the best known, had been around since the 1940s, the newer trend began with the back-to-nature creed of the hippies, who embraced whole grains and organic produce. One of the first markets to feature such foods was The Bread Shop, opened by Kay Stepkin in the late 1960s on North Halsted Street. The interest in healthier eating led to a surge of farmers markets, sponsored by the city of Chicago and neighboring towns, and in 1998, the opening of the Green City Market, with Abby Mandel as founder. It featured only farmers who subscribed to sustainably grown or raised foods. In the new century, every supermarket—large and small—expanded its own organic food selections.

Food manufacturers noted consumers' new interest in diets and began producing all manner of "light" and allegedly healthy convenience products. In 1989, for example, Conagra introduced one of the first lines of frozen diet foods, Healthy Choice meals. Kraft created light mayonnaise and salad dressings. Meanwhile, The American Egg Board, based in Park Ridge, attempted to persuade Americans that eggs were not unhealthy, cholesterol-raising items as was thought in the 1990s. Science has proved them right, and free-range and cage-free eggs are a whole new product range.

Kosher Sushi shows merging culinary traditions. *Photograph by Colleen Sen.*

The New Immigrants

Always a city of "newcomers," Chicago saw a new influx of immigrants, thanks to The Immigration and Nationality Act of 1965, signed into law by President Lyndon Johnson. It allowed, for the first time, larger numbers of immigrants from Asia and eased some restrictions for others, such as Mexicans, South Asians, and Middle Easterners. From the late 1960s through the 1990s, waves of immigrants arrived in Chicago, bringing new flavors to the neighborhoods. They also included people from Ecuador, Colombia, Ethiopia, West Africa, and the Balkans. Like immigrant groups before them, each settled into neighborhoods, turning them into small versions of their homelands with

A PIE FROM THE EARLY DAYS

Herma Naomi Clark, born in 1871, wrote a column for the *Chicago Tribune* from 1932 to 1956 called "When Chicago Was Young." Her papers, deposited in the Chicago History Museum, include letters from prominent Chicagoans. One letter described a Patterson family cookbook, begun in 1843, that included this recipe for squash pie. It is one of the earliest written recipes from Chicago. Note: No directions for baking were given!

—BRUCE KRAIG

Squash Pie

1 pint boiled squash
2 cups sugar
1/2 t. nutmeg
1 T ginger
1 t. cinnamon
1 T melted butter
2 cups milk
1 T molasses
1 t. salt
3 eggs
Pie crust
1 cup butter
1 cup lard
enough flour with ice water
Do not knead!

Chicagoans to the vibrant cooking of Southeast Asia, with its fresh herbs, chilies, and pungent curries. Thai immigrants came to the area, too, and their cooking became one of the most popular ethnic cuisines in Chicago.

Because the new Immigration Act gave preference to those in certain professions or who had family ties, new waves of Filipino immigrants also arrived in Chicago, largely health-care professionals. They opened restaurants featuring *pancit*, their stir-fried noodles, meat, and vegetable dish, and *adobo*, a vinegar-soy braise of pork or chicken. The city's Korean population also jumped in the 1960s, concentrating in Lincoln Park and Lakeview and then spreading out to northwest areas, especially Albany Park, which became one of the most diverse neighborhoods in Chicago.

New Mexican immigrants joined family members already living in the Pilsen and Little Village neighborhoods. They opened restaurants, such as the popular Nuevo Leon on Eighteenth Street in the 1960s. As more people from various regions of Mexico moved to the Chicago region—786,000 in 2000—their eateries and food stores spilled out of Pilsen into other neighborhoods. Puerto Ricans also arrived and settled around Humboldt Park and along Division Street, where small restaurants served up a made-in-Chicago creation, the jibarito sandwich made with plantains. Devon Avenue became home to Indian and Pakistani food stores and restaurants. Some Japanese newcomers created restaurants that began a sushi craze in Chicago. By the early 1970s, Chicago had a half dozen sushi bars and, by the 2000s, hundreds across the city.

The construction of the University of Illinois at Chicago campus in the 1960s provided a singular example of changing cultural ecology. To make way for the growing campus, a group of older immigrants, the Italians and Italian Americans who lived in the Taylor Street area, or "Little Italy," were forced out of their homes and moved to the suburbs. Only a small strip of Italian restaurants and shops and a museum remain today on Taylor. North of Little Italy, Greektown also was affected by campus expansion, but most restaurants survived along Halsted Street. A 1968 newcomer, The Parthenon (closed in 2016), was known for its dramatic flaming saganaki appetizer. The campus development also forced the Maxwell Street Market from its longtime home to a stretch of Canal Street for several years before it moved again to Des Plaines Avenue near Roosevelt Road. The market evolved through those years into a mainly Mexican affair, with stands selling tamales, tacos, and churros amid the flea-market clothing and electronics. By the 2007 community survey for the U.S. Census, 21.7 percent of the population was foreign-born. About 56 percent came from Latin America, 23 percent from Europe, 18 percent from Asia, and 2.6 from other parts of the world. Today,

food stores and restaurants each known by signage and language. As Dominic Pacyga in Melvin Holli and Peter d'A Jones's *Ethnic Chicago, A Multicultural Portrait* demonstrates, neighborhood geography was the same, but cultures were not.

The new Chinese immigrants came from diverse regions—northern China, Hunan, and Szechwan the most representative. Some opened restaurants that featured regional cuisines unfamiliar to Chicagoans, including Peter Lo's and House of Hunan. Their popular Mongolian hot pot dishes highlighted a marriage of disparate styles: Mandarin-Szechuan (Sichuan). An influx of refugees from the Vietnam War, including Laotians and Cambodians, settled in the Argyle Street area of Chicago, joining newer Chinese immigrants there. This new "Chinatown" helped introduce

Chicago has the fifth highest foreign-born population in the United States. As John Drury wrote in 1933, one can visit world cuisines by traveling through Chicago's neighborhoods.

Beginning in the 1950s, increased numbers of African Americans moving from the South settled in Chicago's West Side, joining the well-established black communities on the South Side.

Mostly hailing from Mississippi and Arkansas, the new Chicagoans brought regional variations of standard dishes, though many were categorized as soul food restaurants. West Side Food stores now sold specifically Mississippi foods such as spicy pork sausages. Over time, however, eating habits in the black community changed. As years went on, many of the soul food restaurants were forced to close: Army & Lou's, Queen of the Sea, Izola's, Gladys' Luncheonette. Some southern-style restaurants and many rib and chicken shacks remain as reminders of a unique Chicago cuisine.

Many residents in less-advantaged neighborhoods had to deal with "food deserts," areas with a lack of full-service supermarkets, in addition to low incomes. The passage of the Food Stamp Act of 1964 helped. Those in the economically challenged neighborhoods, mainly on the South and West Sides of the city, now had a helping hand from the federal government. The program later became known as Supplemental Nutrition Assistance Program (SNAP). But the challenge of getting supermarket chains to open in these areas remained. In September 2016, Whole Foods opened a store in Englewood on the south side of Chicago. However, hunger was a constant threat for families. In 1979, The Greater Chicago Food Depository opened on the Southwest Side. The nonprofit distributed donated groceries to food pantries across the city and became a training center for the disadvantaged.

A small dent in the food-access problem came after the passage of The Farmer-to-Consumer Direct Marketing Act of 1976, which made it easier for farmers to sell directly to consumers. The city and suburbs began opening farmers markets in the neighborhoods. Though prices at the markets could not compete with the bulk prices of the large supermarkets, they did provide fresher, locally grown produce. Many city markets and independent markets accept the Link cards of the SNAP program. As of 2015, more than 150 farmers markets existed in the Chicago area.

The Dining Revolution

The most dramatic changes in how Chicagoans ate could be found through their restaurants. From its steak-and-potatoes beginnings, the city soon expanded its menu with

A sign advertising stuffed pizza. *Image licensed by Ingram Image. Courtesy of Philip V. Wojciak.*

fast food, fancy French food, regional American food, fusion food, farm-to-table food, and molecular gastronomy—and all permutations between. Chicagoans' growing sophistication about food and a crop of new, young chefs created one of the fine-dining capitals of the world by the early 2000s.

First, the growth of fast-food chains certainly changed Chicago's eating-out habits. Inexpensive burgers now competed with the city's popular hot dog stands and the suburban drive-in restaurants of the 1950s. Fast food captured Chicago's hearts and stomachs. Though not a fast food, pizza in Chicago continued and expanded in popularity. Independent operators popped up with thin-crust, stuffed, and tavern-style, square-cut pies. Then came Gino's East in 1966, and Giordano's, Lou Malnati's, Connies, and Nancy's. It seemed every neighborhood had its own pizza parlor. As the 1990s and 2000s arrived, Italian-style thin crust pizzas cooked in wood-burning ovens became the newest trend, and diners could find them in all sorts of restaurants beyond pizza joints.

In 1971, the era of Chicago as "Meatpacker to the World" came to an end. The cattle market at the Union Stock Yards was closed, and the nearby Stock Yard Inn served its last steak in 1976. Meat processing had shifted west, closer to where livestock was raised. But that did not deter Chicagoans' taste for a prime steak, and the city continued its reputation as the steakhouse capital of the country with favorites such as Gene & Georgetti's and Eli's the Place for Steak, and newcomers Morton's The Steakhouse and Gibson's.

Fine dining in the 1960s meant French or Continental food. As with the old downtown upscale restaurants, these were destination places that catered to a more affluent population. In 1963, The Bakery opened in a storefront on North Lincoln Avenue. Chef Louis Szathmary offered fine continental cuisine, with dishes like beef Wellington with Cumberland sauce. The most influential of French chefs was Jean Banchet, who opened Le Français in Wheeling in 1973 with his wife, Doris. They turned the restaurant into what some called a "temple of gastronomy." Jovan also was a French restaurant, but it was owned by a Yugoslavian, Jovan Trboyevic, one of the most influential restaurateurs in the city. He later opened Le Perroquet on Walton Street, which became the first place in Chicago to emphasize the imported "nouvelle cuisine" of France.

During the 1970s, while French and continental places did well, a new American cuisine began to appear. In Chicago, Richard Melman and Jerry Orzoff opened a casual restaurant in 1971 called R. J. Grunts, where they created an eclectic menu and one of the country's new, hipper iterations of salad bars (and smorgasbords). As the 1980s progressed and living was high, diners enjoyed more dining out than ever before. Practitioners of what was called "new-American" cuisine included Gordon Sinclair, with his 1976 Gordon restaurant, and chef Michael Foley, with Printer's Row restaurant. In 1984, the Levy Brothers opened a high-end Italian place called Spiaggia on the Magnificent Mile and launched the career of chef Tony Mantuano. It set the bar for Italian food in Chicago that has not been matched since.

Top ingredients became the focus for another pioneer chef, Charlie Trotter. In 1987, he created an elegant, fine-dining establishment that bore his name. It became the top restaurant in Chicago, and one of the country's most celebrated. The same year that Trotter began his restaurant, Rick and Deann Bayless opened a casual, art-filled

Mexican cafe on North Clark and called it Frontera Grill. It would become as influential for its modern but authentic take on Mexican food as Trotter's was for top fine dining.

In the 1990s and 2000s, restaurants boomed in the city, pausing briefly during the 2008 recession. As the economy struggled to bounce back, a number of less-expensive restaurants appeared (some from chefs looking to diversify their properties or downscale, and some from chains), leading the food website Eater to call it the "fast casualization of Chicago."

In 2005, Grant Achatz opened a restaurant that would reach fame around the world for its daring, creative fare that utilized what would be called "molecular gastronomy." Alinea was like no other restaurant in town. With partner Nick Kokonas, he soon earned kudos for one of the best restaurants in the world. Chicago's fine-dining mode continues with restaurants such as Acadia and Grace.

Chefs embraced local ingredients and seasonal cooking, often handcrafted in casual bistros. "Farm to table" became buzzwords, along with "artisan." Charcuterie, nose-to-tail meats, and in-house butchering were trendy, not very different in ingredients from nineteenth century cookery. Wine lists offered bottles from around the world, new lounges sold "craft cocktails," made by "mixologists," and brewpubs touted local craft beers. By 2015, restaurants in the Chicago market numbered 20,039, according to research firm NPD Group. Food in Chicago today comes more varied, lighter, and fresher than ever. The selection of imported products has widened, with choices from places unimaginable just 20 years ago. At the same time, many ingredients grow or are raised closer to home.

Much of the food scene today reboots what existed earlier in Chicago's history. For example, in 1910, more than 200 milk bottlers existed in Chicago, but they disappeared with the growth of large dairy operations far from Chicago. Yet, in 2015, a new dairy plant opened in the Fulton Market neighborhood, where it produces artisan milk, cream, and yogurt made from grass-fed cows. The plant, named the 1871 Dairy, recalls the year Mrs. O'Leary's cow became famous for its rumored role in the Great Chicago Fire, and it signals how the city's food has evolved and revolved—like the history of the city itself.

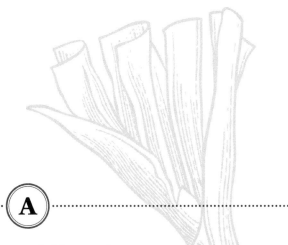

A

Achatz, Grant

Chef/restaurateur Grant Achatz (b. 1974) learned the kitchen trade in his family's restaurants in Michigan. After graduating from the Culinary Institute of America, Achatz worked at Charlie Trotter's legendary restaurant and then Thomas Keller's French Laundry in Napa Valley, rising to become sous chef. In 2004, he moved back to Chicago to become executive chef at Trio, where he earned a legion of enthusiastic customers, including Nick Kokonas, who later became a partner with Achatz at Alinea, which opened in 2005. Though Achatz resisted being called a practitioner of molecular gastronomy, he pushed the boundaries of cooking, using sci-fi technology such as the Smoking Gun (a handheld device used to smoke food instantly) and the Anti-Griddle (a very cold cooking surface). In 2006, *Gourmet* named Alinea the best restaurant in America. In 2011–16, Alinea earned Michelin's top 3-star rating.

In 2011, Achatz opened Next, a restaurant in Fulton Market with a revolutionary ticketing system and a constantly changing menu reflecting different historic periods and geographic locations. In the same year, he opened Aviary, a remarkably innovative cocktail lounge and, downstairs, The Office, a modern-day speakeasy. In mid-2016, Achatz and Kokonas opened a more casual restaurant, Roister. With Kokonas, Achatz wrote *Life, on the Line*, a book about his career and successful battle with tongue cancer.

Contributor: David Hammond

See also: Alinea; Chefs; Molecular Gastronomy; Restaurants and Fine Dining; Restaurateurs and Restaurant Groups

BIBLIOGRAPHY

Achatz, Grant, and Nick Kokonas. *Life, on the Line: A Chef's Story of Chasing Greatness, Facing Death, and Redefining the Way We Eat.* New York: Gotham, 2011.

Sifton, Sam. "At Alinea, Three Stars Come with a Mischievous Taste of Autumn." *New York Times*, November 17, 2010.

Addams, Jane

Laura Jane Addams (1860–1935), cofounder of Hull House, feminist and pacifist, was born in Cedarville, Illinois, one of nine children. Her father, a Quaker, was a wealthy member of the Illinois state senate for 16 years (1854–70) and a friend of Abraham Lincoln (letters from the president began, "My dear Double-D'ed Addams"). Her education took her from the Rockford (Illinois) Female Seminary (later Rockford College) to the Women's Medical College of Pennsylvania in Philadelphia and then to Johns Hopkins University in Baltimore.

But it was during a second tour of Europe that her devotion to public service, and in particular a dedication to the needs of the poor, crystallized. Her model for Hull House was Toynbee Hall, a settlement house in East London. She and a school friend, Ellen Gates Starr launched their Chicago settlement in 1889 in a tired mansion on Halsted Street built by Charles Hull. In 1905, a craftsman-style dining hall was built next to Hull House, and nutritious food was distributed to the neighborhood immigrants—mainly Italians in the immediate vicinity, but also Jews, Greeks, Irish, and some Germans. Concerned that the poor immigrants did not have proper diets for healthy living, Addams and her colleagues created kitchens and a coffeehouse in 1893. Their dishes were based on the latest scientific nutritional standards that were being developed by Ellen Swallow Richards in Boston and shown at the World's Columbian Exposition. Neighborhood homemakers were supposed to learn from them. Workers in nearby factories received coffee, soups, and stews every day for 5 cents, children and young working women got lunches cheaply, and anyone could purchase food to take home. Oyster, cream of tomato, cream of potato, or cream of celery soup cost 10 cents a pint, 15 cents a quart. Chicken, mutton, and beef broth could be had for a nickel a pint. The experiment failed because the food was bland and Italian women preferred their own vegetable dishes, sauces, and pasta. But the idea of healthful cooking was a landmark in creating new organizations such as the Chicago-based American Dietetics Association and the home economists groups. Later, Addams was involved in peace movements before and during World War I, devoted herself to women's suffrage, and supported the founding of the National Association for the Advancement of Colored People and the American Civil Liberties Union. Her Nobel Peace Prize, in 1931, was the first awarded to an American woman.

Contributor: Alan Solomon

See also: Hull House; Settlement Houses

BIBLIOGRAPHY

Addams, Jane. *Twenty Years at Hull-House.* New York: Signet Classics, 1961.

Pacyga, Dominic A. *Chicago: A Biography.* Chicago: The University of Chicago Press, 2009.

Advertising

Chicago long has been America's second most prominent advertising center, after New York. Where New York had the more glamorous accounts, such as cars, liquor brands, and travel, Chicago advertising was associated with the more common, everyday products of the heartland—industrial and agricultural brands, specifically the

The 1920 test kitchen of advertising firm J. Walter Thompson showing new kitchen appliances and testing of products in their portfolio. Courtesy of J. Walter Thompson Iconographic Collection, John W. Hartman Center for Sales Advertising and Marketing History, David M. Rubenstein Rare Book and Manuscript Library, Duke University.

household products known in the business as "packaged goods."

The dominant advertising media in Chicago in the late nineteenth and early twentieth century included newspapers, what is now called *outdoor* (everything from billboards around ballfields to posters pasted on walls of downtown buildings), and mail order, particularly the giant catalog operations of Sears, Roebuck & Co., Montgomery Ward, and Spiegel.

Food was a relatively minor category in newspaper advertising in the postwar period until the advent of grocery store chains with their weekly sale ads. It was not a significant product in the catalog world either, though appliances were sold that way. (One of the more interesting and popular mail-order products to come out of Chicago in the pre-WWI era was the Vegetarian Society Mill, used by vegetarians nationwide to grind nuts and other proteins into meat substitutes.) Outdoor was the most common medium at this time for food products, and old photographs of every part of town capture ephemeral advertisements for Chicago products, from Cracker Jack and Wrigley chewing gum to the many local breweries.

It would take a new medium to make Chicago a major advertising center and to create Chicago's most influential advertising agencies: radio. Between 1927 and 1931, the Lord & Thomas (later Foote, Cone & Belding) agency invented the Monday through Friday domestic dramas that would come to be known as soap operas (so called because their primary sponsors were Procter & Gamble detergent brands). Lord & Thomas not only wrote the advertisements but also produced the entire program with minimal to no input from the networks. The company also pioneered comedy, police, and variety shows.

Though prepackaged foods were still in relative infancy at that point, food brands such as the cereals made by Kellogg's and General Mills were among the biggest spenders on radio. The Lone Ranger, produced at WGN in Chicago, was sponsored by Cheerios and other General Mills brands over its tenure. The National Barn Dance, a hugely popular country music program, was produced at WLS and sponsored by a food-related medicine, Alka-Seltzer. And Chicago-based Kraft created and sponsored the most popular variety program, the Kraft Music Hall, hosted by Bing Crosby. How messages were integrated into the program varied greatly. Kraft, for instance, took care to keep its messages separate from the program's stars, always having them delivered by an announcer, but other brands worked themselves (clumsily by modern standards) directly into the program content.

Packaged food brands took off with the postwar boom and the rise of another new medium, television. That fostered the growth of what was called the Chicago School of

Billboard advertisement for Chicago's Williamson Company, 1923. Library of Congress.

Advertising, mainly associated with Leo Burnett, founder of the agency bearing his name. Burnett eschewed cleverness for its own sake, something he felt the ad men of New York were too often guilty of, making people remember the ad rather than the product. At the same time he had little taste for the kind of repetitive, hard sell associated with St. Louis–based Ted Bates, creator of animated stomachs curing heartburn. Burnett felt that every worthwhile product had an "inherent drama," which could be brought to life in a folksy, approachable manner acceptable to easygoing midwesterners.

That nearly always meant using a "critter," an animated spokesman for the product. Some of Burnett's critters, often designed by the ubiquitous Paul Coker (who also drew Hallmark cards, Mad magazine parodies, and character designs for Rankin Bass animated Christmas specials in the era), remain iconic 60 years on. Charlie the Tuna, who wished he were tasty enough for Star-Kist; Snap, Crackle, and Pop, who personified the noise made by a bowl of Rice Krispies in milk; the Green Giant, which proved such a perfect image for the Minnesota Canning Co. that it changed its name to his. Tony the Tiger, the Pillsbury Dough Boy, the Keebler Elves, and not least, the Marlboro Man, all flowed out of Burnett at this time. Critters were taken with enormous seriousness—a common story inside the agency was of the meeting where someone shouted angrily, "Snap would NEVER say that to Pop!"

Another type of food business that became a major advertising category in the 1960s and 1970s was the fast-food chain (or "quick-service restaurant" in industry parlance). By far the most successful and influential was Oak Brook–based McDonald's. The hamburger chain's early advertising was fairly crude, with a low-rent critter in the form of "spokesclown" Ronald McDonald.

Chicago-based Needham, Harper & Steers (later DDB Needham) introduced the theme "You deserve a break today," aimed at assuaging the guilt of moms for taking the family for burgers instead of a home-cooked meal. Under Needham's creative chief, Keith Reinhard, McDonald's shifted from a focus on food to a wide range of image-building advertisements in the 1970s, stressing McDonald's as a friendly occasion for family bonding. The kids got a full set of critters (Hamburglar, Mayor McCheese, and so forth), while adults were assured of McDonald's wholesomeness and even winking sophistication with ads like the Stan Freberg-esque musical production number of a restaurant crew getting ready for work ("There is nothing so clean/As my burger machine"). In 1981, however, Burnett won the account away from DDB Needham by arguing that moms didn't even need to justify a McDonald's "break" to themselves anymore (they also cut their commission on McDonald's huge advertising budget).

The focus on TV advertising, however, meant that as the mass-media market fragmented and online media appeared, traditional ad agencies were slow to react. Food is no longer one of the top categories for TV advertising, as clients have shifted dollars into point of sale (in-store) advertising, online marketing, event sponsorship, direct mail, and other media targeted to specific slices of their customer base. Meanwhile, the decline of grocery advertising in newspapers has significantly impacted the staffing, and even existence, of food sections and coverage in daily newspapers.

These more targeted areas are obviously lucrative for those working in them and effective for their clients. But the days of the Chicago School of Advertising, using mass media to successfully communicate a high-level brand image capable of lasting half a century or more in the public consciousness, seem to have passed.

Contributor: Michael Gebert

See also: Media

BIBLIOGRAPHY

Cummings, Bart. *The Benevolent Dictators: Interviews with Advertising Greats.* Lincolnwood, Ill.: NTC Business Books, 1987 (1984).

"Lord & Thomas." *Advertising Age,* September 15, 2003. http://adage.com/article/adage-encyclopedia/lord-thomas/98753/.

African Americans

Jean Baptiste DuSable, who referred to himself as a "free Negro," established the area's first permanent residence on the river's north bank in the 1780s. Historian Lerone

COFFEEHOUSE CONFRONTATION

··

One of the first attempts by African Americans to desegregate restaurants came in 1942 at Jack Spratt Coffee House on East 47th Street and Kimbark in the Kenwood neighborhood. A group of white and black students at the University of Chicago, led by James Farmer, staged a sit-in at the modest cafe, refusing to leave until the black students were served. The coffeehouse staff called the police, who did not remove the students, saying no laws had been broken. The students were served, and, later, Jack Spratt dropped its policies toward blacks. The early sit-in tactic of the Chicago students became one of the tools of the civil rights nonviolence movement in the 1960s South.

—CAROL MIGHTON HADDIX

Bennett described the fur trader as Chicago's first "meat-packer," as well as the city's first "builder" and wholesaler. Today, a small bust at the northeastern edge of Pioneer Court honors DuSable on the land where he lived and maintained a house, two barns, a mill, a bakehouse, a poultry house, a dairy, and a smokehouse for pork. Du Sable sold his land in 1800 and moved to Missouri, but his pioneering legacy remains.

By the 1850s, Chicago's African American population was firmly established, though it was only 1–2 percent of the total population. It included free blacks and fugitive slaves who had made use of the Underground Railroad to travel north to freedom. (Chicago was called by antebellum critics "a sinkhole of abolition.") Chicago was an island of freedom in a state that had notoriously discriminatory Black Laws (1819–65) that deprived African Americans of basic civil liberties. One such group of men and women met in private homes for prayer, followed by covered-dish shared dinners. This group made up the beginnings of Quinn Chapel A.M.E. (African Methodist Episcopal) Church, Chicago's oldest black church congregation, on the corner of 24th Street and South Wabash Avenue. At Quinn, the tradition of fellowship suppers continues today as congregation members prepare meals using recipes reflecting their southern heritage, such as greens, fried fish, chicken, cornbread, soft yeast rolls, sweet potato pie, and pound cake.

By 1860, city directories included occupations for some of the 1,500 Negroes who resided in Chicago at that time. They included one butcher, one hotel keeper, sixteen hairdressers, and five barbers. In 1867, black businessman J. O. Grant and his wife are recorded as opening an all-night lunchroom called The Break of Day.

The Pullman Palace Car Company, founded by George Pullman in 1867, designed and manufactured sleeping cars for the rapidly developing railroad industry. With the Civil War recently ended, Pullman sought out formerly enslaved blacks for service jobs, such as Pullman porters, waiters, and chefs. By the 1920s, the Pullman Company is credited with employing more African Americans than any other company in America. Four decades after the company formed, Pullman chef Rufus Estes published a cookbook, "Good Things to Eat, as Suggested by Rufus." Estes, who had been born into slavery in Murray County, Tennessee, in 1857, included directions for dishes he had grown up watching his mother prepare, such as fried chicken, broiled pig's feet, corn fritters, ginger cookies, and tapioca pudding. Other recipes, such as lamb curry, chicken timbales, beef marrow quenelles, and eclairs, were based on the chef's extensive national and international travel.

In the booming postwar era, caterer Charles H. Smiley was a notable success. After moving to Chicago in 1885, Smiley became a wealthy man and "one of the city's foremost caterers." When Booker T. Washington visited Chicago to meet with distinguished black businessmen, Washington referred to Smiley as having "character, good powers of observation, ambition and brains." He is considered to have been one of the leading culinary forces, changing the face of African American catering during the early decades of the twentieth century by offering a full range of services, including food, pastries, and floral arrangements. His clientele included both prominent African Americans and whites in Chicago.

More "country" Southern food traditions arrived with the first wave of the Great Migration in 1915. During the early decades of the twentieth century, railroads offered southern blacks easier transportation access to northern and western destinations. Between 1915 and the Civil Rights Movement in the 1970s, six million black people changed their address from the segregated and "separate but equal" Jim Crow South to move to the urban north. Chicago and New York City were the top two destinations. Many of the newcomers were attracted to Chicago by articles in the *Chicago Daily Defender* describing jobs in the meatpacking industry and other opportunities in the city. The *Defender*, founded in 1905, was the most popular and influential black newspaper read in the South. A 1923 *Defender* directory of Chicago African American–owned businesses listed 120 grocery stores, 100 restaurants, 13 bakeries, 28 ice-cream and candy shops, and 18 stores specializing in soft drinks. Many of these businesses were located in the modern Bronzeville neighborhood.

Older African Americans in Chicago, the "Old Settlers," were often aghast at the new immigrants' food shops and restaurants. Instead of "respectable" dining places such as the Elite in Bronzeville, the newcomers patronized fried chicken and fish shacks and barbecue joints, and they were accused by the *Defender* of eating watermelon in public. Such restaurants and foods were the basis of a cuisine later called "soul food."

In 1919, a year of infamous race riots in the city, Judge H. Parker migrated from Montgomery County, Tennessee, with his family's sausage recipes and began selling products from a horse-drawn wagon. By 1921, he had acquired several trucks and a small plant for his Parker House Sausage Company. Highly successful with its smoked sausages and hot links, the family-run company remains at 4605 S. State St.

The magazines *Ebony* (launched in 1945) and *Jet* (1951), founded by black media pioneer John H. Johnson, often showcased African American food and dining, along with content highlighting politicians, entertainers, and issues in the black community. *Ebony*'s first food editor, Freda DeKnight, played a transforming role in the perception of African American cooks. Before DeKnight, most magazine ads and films promoted the stereotype of childlike, smiling black men and broad-breasted women "cooking for white people." DeKnight's "Date with a Dish" columns have been described as "offering food preparation as "a gateway toward expanded social and cultural literacy." Her cookbook, *A Date with a Dish* (Hermitage Press, 1948), is considered the first national African American cookbook. Following De Knight's death, *Ebony* later published much of the original book as *The Ebony Cookbook* in 1962. During later years, home economists Charla L. Draper and Charlotte Lyons served as food editors. Lyons, food editor from 1985 to 2010, edited *The New Ebony Cookbook* in 1999.

Memorable cookbooks from Chicago-based black authors include *Mama's Tea Cakes* (1998), *The New Soul Food Cookbook* (2005), and *Smothered Southern Food* (2006) by Wilbert Jones, *Cooking with Kocoa* (2001) by Kocoa Scott-Winbush, *Real Men Cook: More than 100 Easy Recipes Celebrating Tradition and Family* (2005) by Kofi Moyo and Yvette Moyo, and *Real Women Cook: Building Healthy Communities with Recipes that Stir the Soul* (2012) by Yvette Moyo with Sharon Mogan.

Small restaurants featured southern-style dishes to welcome newcomers during the early days of the Great Migration. Many of the noted early black-owned restaurants,

Shopowner sets out produce in a South Side grocery store, ca. 1941. Library of Congress.

bars, and cocktail lounges were located on a long stretch on or near the commercial district of 47th Street. Busy with activity from early morning to the wee hours of the next morning, these thriving businesses featured national celebrities as performers and guests. They once included Lee's Fried Chicken and Lee's Barbecue (536 E. 47th St.), Arie's Soul Food (114 E. 47th St.), the original Regal Theater on 47th Street, The Parkway Ballroom, Mack's Chili, Sunset Cafe/Grand Terrace (315 E. 35th St.), Morris Restaurant, and Gerri's Palm Tavern (446 E. 47th St.).

As black soldiers returned to civilian life after World War II, many moved north to Chicago with their families. This second wave of the Great Migration (1945–70) brought almost 750,000 African Americans to Chicago. The city's old racial boundaries were broken as people moved from the old Black Belt to the southern boundaries and westward into Lawndale, Garfield Park, and all the way to Austin. Restaurants and food stores catering to this new population sprang up. The Moo and Oink grocery store chain with locations on Stony Island Avenue and West Madison Street is a well-known example. New restaurants reflected the new Chicagoans' tastes with southern recipes including smothered or fried chicken, chitterlings, cabbage, black-eyed peas, Brunswick stew, brains, barbecue, biscuits, catfish, deviled eggs, grits, greens, gumbo, banana pudding, caramel cake, chess pie, peach cobbler, and pound cake. All served the iconic Soul Food dish, macaroni and cheese. Such dishes were referred to as "down-home" cooking, until the term "soul food" began to be used during the 1960s. Army and Lou's (1945–2010),

Gladys' Luncheonette (1946–2001), Izola's (1950–2011), and Soul Queen (1970–2009) were among the best known on the South Side. On the West Side, Edna's, now revived as Ruby's, and a host of barbecue, fried fish, and chicken restaurants along West Madison Street and Chicago Avenue are examples of soul food restaurants that arose from population changes.

Classic black restaurants remaining include Harold's Chicken Shacks, a chain owned and franchised by Harold Pierce for more than 50 years, and Lem's Bar-B-Que House owned by the Lemons family for half a century. Popular and well-known African American–owned restaurants and food businesses that celebrated more than a decade of business are Captain's Hard Time Dining Original Soul Vegetarian, B. J.'s Market & Bakery, Brown Sugar, Karyn's Raw Bistro, and Sweet Maple Cafe.

Black-owned food companies operating in Chicago for more than a decade include Grandma Maude's, founded in 1994 by Paul Fregia, offering southern-style food and seasoning mixes, and Comfort Cake, founded by Amy Hilliard in 2001, featuring pound cakes and other desserts.

Contributor: Donna Pierce

See also: Pullman Porters; Soul Food

BIBLIOGRAPHY

Grossman, James. *Land of Hope: Chicago, Southerners, and the Great Migration*. Chicago: University of Chicago Press, 1991.

Miller, Adrian. *Soul Food: the Surprising Story of an American Cuisine One Plate at a Time*. Chapel Hill: University of North Carolina Press, 2013.

Reed, Christopher Robert. *The Rise of Chicago's Black Metropolis, 1920–1929*. Urbana: University of Illinois Press, 2012.

Spear, Allen H. *Black Chicago: The Making of a Negro Ghetto (1890–1920)*. Chicago: University of Chicago Press, 1967.

Africans

Immigrants from Africa did not settle in Chicago in large numbers until relatively recently. Initially, they were refugees, especially from the Biafran war in Nigeria (1967–70) and from the repressive Derg regime in Ethiopia and the ensuing civil war beginning in the late 1970s. Since then, other migrants have followed, bringing with them varied food traditions from different regions of Africa.

Ethiopians (including Eritreans, since Eritrea had not yet seceded from Ethiopia) were the first to open restaurants. Mama Desta's Red Sea Restaurant on Broadway in Lakeview was the pioneer, opening in 1984. Ethiopian restaurants in Washington, D.C., which hosted a far larger Ethiopian population than Chicago, had demonstrated that they could successfully appeal to adventurous American tastes and did not have to rely on an Ethiopian clientele. Mama Desta's, located in an increasingly trendy neighborhood with no African population to speak of, followed suit. The food was appreciably different from any other kind of food in Chicago. The meal was served on a spongy pancake called *injera* made with fermented *teff*, a grain exclusive to Ethiopia, over which different stews were placed: *wats*, stews with a spicy red sauce with a *berbere* base; or *alitchas*, a milder yellow stew; along with various vegetable preparations. The wide range of vegetable dishes made Ethiopian restaurants attractive destinations for vegetarians. Additional loaves of *injera* were served alongside the platter, and diners were expected to break off a piece and eat their food with their fingers.

Other Ethiopians emulated Mother Desta's success, opening similar restaurants, first near Wrigley Field and later in Edgewater, Rogers Park, and Evanston. After Eritrea declared its independence in 1993, several restaurants openly identified themselves as serving Eritrean food, although these restaurants, unlike their predecessors, catered primarily to Africans, especially the growing number of Eritrean cab drivers. Nevertheless, the food they served was largely identical to that served in Ethiopian restaurants. At the same time, a few Somali restaurants opened in Edgewater, also largely serving cab drivers. Somali food is somewhat reminiscent of Ethiopian and Eritrean food, although with more pasta, a legacy of Italian colonization, and with halal meat.

Unlike Ethiopian restaurants, West African restaurants have always catered primarily to Africans. African entrepreneurs served from food trucks to cab drivers in the Loop. The largest West African population in Chicago was Nigerian. In 1991, one of these Nigerian entrepreneurs opened Vee Vee's Restaurant on Broadway in Edgewater. The food at Vee Vee's and other West African restaurants typically consists of a starchy staple—rice, *foo foo* (pounded yam), or *gari* (pounded cassava)—accompanied by a "soup," a meat or fish stew that can be very spicy, especially "pepper soup." Other Nigerian as well as Ghanaian restaurants, all serving similar kinds of food, opened in Edgewater and Uptown. Certain dishes are specific to Nigerian cuisine, notably *egusi* soup, made with crushed melon seeds; while others are more typically Ghanaian, particularly in their copious use of dried fish. Groundnut stew, a peanut-based dish, is more typical of Ghanaian cuisine, but can also be found in many Nigerian restaurants.

A smaller French-speaking West African community had opened a number of now-closed restaurants, including La Pirogue, a Togolese restaurant on 18th Street; Le Maquis, an Ivoirian restaurant on Howard; and Le

Conakry, also on Howard, from Guinea. Though the food they offered was quite distinctive, their clientele was not only tiny but widely dispersed throughout the Chicago area, and they were not successful in reaching a broader audience. Senegalese restaurants have been more successful. Le Village in Uptown lasted several years, and Senegalese restaurants still operate on the South Side (Yassa) and Rogers Park (Badou). These establishments have managed, at least to a limited extent, to attract a wider clientele.

A few grocery stores in Chicago carry ingredients for African food. The largest number are along or near Broadway on the North Side and in the Uptown and Edgewater neighborhoods, but there is also an African grocery on 79th Street on the South Side and on Madison Avenue on the West Side. Some of the foods they carry are geared exclusively to an African clientele, such as teff as well as *attieke*, grated fermented *manioc* from Cote d'Ivoire. However, many staple foods, such as yams (not sweet potatoes), cassava, and palm oil are common to West Africa, the Caribbean, and South America.

On the other hand, North African restaurants are exclusively geared to American patrons. Moroccan restaurants are far and away the most common. L'Olive on Sheridan Road near the Irving Park El station was among the first, but various Moroccan restaurants (for example, Marrakesh and Shokran) have come and gone on the North Side. Typical dishes include couscous, fine-grained semolina accompanied by grilled or stewed meats, vegetables in broth, chickpeas, and *harissa*, a fiery paste made from red peppers; *tagines*, stews individually baked in conical clay dishes, often featuring meat (lamb or chicken) with preserved lemon, prunes, olives, or dried apricots; and *bastilla*, made from filo dough stuffed with shredded chicken and flavored with cinnamon. For several years, Icosium Café, an Algerian restaurant, which featured exotic crepes, was located on Clark Street in Andersonville.

Contributor: Robert Launay

BIBLIOGRAPHY

Cavanagh, Amy. "Best African Food in Chicago." *TimeOut*, December 13, 2013.
Pang, Kevin. "Yassa in Bronzeville." *Chicago Tribune*, March 9, 2015.

Agriculture, Urban

Incorporated in 1837 with the motto Urbs in Horto (City in a Garden), Chicago's location as a shipping terminus of the rich, developing farmland of the Midwest meant

PROMOTING SUSTAINABLE URBAN FARMING

Advocates for Urban Agriculture (auachicago.org) is a group formed to promote sustainable urban agriculture in the Chicago area. From home- and community-based growing to market gardens and small farms, the group promotes local food economies through newsletters, blogs, and meetings. Since 2010, the group has offered an online mapping project to show locations of urban farms and gardens (at cuamp.org).

—CAROL MIGHTON HADDIX

that agriculture would play a central role in the city's development. Both agricultural products and technological innovations would eventually bring renown to the city.

From Chicago's earliest days, civic leaders were vegetable gardeners and fruit growers, and they gained prestige by fostering technical knowledge and the exchange of best practices for farming at all scales. Farms, dairies, and orchards flourished within the grid laid down when Chicago was platted in 1830.

By the late 1830s, Chicago was already sending out produce, grains, and livestock to various parts of the Midwest. Neighborhoods or outlying towns that were annexed into the city in the late 1800s became identified with their products: Bridgeport for cabbages (1850s), Roseland (1840s) for flowers and vegetables, and Lakeview for its celery (1880s). Such products were sent on horse-drawn wagons into many open-air markets, an important part of provisioning of the city.

Chicago nurserymen cultivated and shipped the best varieties. Some of the world's largest seed catalog companies were in the Loop in the 1890s, shipping seeds produced locally. Chicago also was prominent for greenhouse technology; large glasshouses, such as those operated by Luxembourger immigrants in West Ridge at the turn of the century, would become essential components of urban truck farming. Agricultural and livestock journals published in Chicago, as well as trade associations, were central to developing standards of quality in labeling and packaging. As rail networks expanded, Chicago became a hub for the processing, brokering, and shipping of local and regional products.

Innovation and technology in several areas, including specialized production, preservation (meatpacking),

VERTICAL FARMING AT THE PLANT

Eerie magenta grow-lights hover over small arugula greens in water in one room at The Plant. Nearby, tanks of swimming tilapia provide the plants with fertilizer in a closed-loop system (in which waste from one farming activity fuels others). Conventionally grown fruits and vegetables nestle in real dirt, just outside the door. Housed in and around a still mostly empty former meat-processing plant in the Back of the Yards, The Plant was founded in 2010 by entrepreneur John Edel, who is building the self-sufficient food production operation in the middle of the city. The 93,000-square-foot facility so far includes a variety of small commercial food operations—a baker, a mushroom grower, and, eventually, a brewer.

With a grant from the state of Illinois, Edel is working on an anaerobic food digester that will consume 30 tons of food waste daily from The Plant and surrounding businesses and produce enough energy to meet all of The Plant's power needs.

—CAROL MIGHTON HADDIX

consolidation of wholesale activities, and refrigerated transport contributed to a developing industrial model of agriculture that became dominant in the nineteenth and twentieth centuries. The growth of a commodity economy is apparent in the stockyards (founded 1865) and the Chicago Board of Trade (founded 1864). Following the Chicago Fire of 1871, which was popularly if erroneously linked in popular history to a dairy cow in a barn near the Loop, more stringent building codes, rapidly increasing population and land values, and denser patterns of housing contributed to a definitive reorganization of spaces separating the rural and the urban. For more than a hundred years forward, the city would be reorganized as the locus of industrial production. Food production seen as an inextricable part of living within an urban context would be increasingly marginalized to the point of near invisibility.

Farms receded as the city grew; patterns of land use and transportation affected notions of local sources of food. Small market gardens continued to thrive within pockets of Chicago and nearby suburbs. Truck farms from rural areas in Illinois and surrounding states also had local channels to Chicago consumers through outdoor markets, wagons (later trucks) making neighborhood rounds, and deliveries to small groceries. Roadside

stands at farms were common in the 1920s. Milk, dairy products, butter, and eggs were delivered into the 1940s and 1950s directly to homes and small groceries. Poultry farms persisted in metro Chicago into the late 1970s; the *pollos vivos* vendors of today can be seen as remnants of this tradition.

Immigrants maintained habits of gardening, and Chicago developed a strong tradition of community gardens. One of the earliest shared gardens was organized at Hull House; plots were raffled off to recent arrivals living near the settlement house, and went quickly. Later waves of immigrants with agrarian traditions arrived to overcrowded tenements with little land available for cultivation. Wherever they could, they found ways to grow food and maintain their own culture by growing foodstuffs not offered by mainstream purveyors. For every immigrant group there are rich stories of farming, such as that of Mexican railroad workers living in boxcar camps in South Side neighborhoods, permitted during the Great Depression to use railroad land for growing corn and other crops. This immigrant gardening tradition continues today in herb and vegetable gardens cultivated by Asian immigrants in Uptown and Rogers Park.

Community gardens producing food for home consumption and extra income were important during periods of economic depression, financial crisis, and public food shortages. There was a turn to gardening during the Great Depression to alleviate hunger and later in the 1970s with rise of the environmental movement, but especially during the two World Wars. City and federal government programs, accompanied by heavy promotions in the media, actively promoted these efforts, providing technical and organizational assistance. During World War II, Chicago led the nation in urban food production—55,000 pounds of food were produced from 172,000 Victory Gardens in 1943.

From the 1970s to the 1990s, nutrition, food security, and sustainable living became major themes in rethinking Chicago's relationship to agriculture. Urban gardening continued to be seen as a source of self-sufficiency, but also reflected progressive ideals. Community gardens were organized in 1993 as the Brownfields initiative—named for conversion of vacant lots. These and other local economic development efforts were organized by and for various groups, including African Americans, youth, formerly incarcerated persons, and the homeless. Rising land costs, zoning issues, and toxic soil were challenges, experienced differently around the city. In gentrifying areas, there was controversy over garden sites, as at Belden/Halsted (Lincoln Park) and sites in Humboldt Park.

Children's Garden Club, Pottawottomi Park, 1945. Courtesy of the Rogers Park / West Ridge Historical Society.

A focus on organic, sustainable, and artisanal products heralds a renewed interest in local production. Growing one's own food or buying local products now are fashionable urban pastimes. Celebrity chefs encourage local and seasonal cooking, farmers' markets are increasingly popular, and "heritage" crops are being revived. A more direct relationship between food producers and consumers, similar to what existed earlier in Chicago's history, is emerging with new farmers' markets and the popular restaurant concept of "farm to table." Contributing are social enterprises, restaurants with rooftop gardens, specialty producers such as mushroom growers and beekeepers, and small farmers from surrounding rural areas (including the Thurman family from the historic African American farming village of Pembroke, Illinois). In 2011, the Chicago Zoning Ordinance was amended, with community gardens allowed up to 25,000 square feet (eight city lots) and larger urban farms by permit, regulating commercial production and other agricultural activities.

This resurgence of urban agriculture is a trend fed from many directions: food fads, a network of nonprofit organizations, progressive African American and Latino activism, churches, restaurants championing local foods, and upscale groceries trying to "do well by doing good." As at the beginning of the story of urban agriculture in Chicago, specialization, technological innovation, and opening of new markets are critical, as new models like vertical farming and urban aquaponics look for commercial viability. Meanwhile, throughout Chicago, community gardening traditions continue with more than 50 in the city and 45 organizations working in local food sustainability.

Contributors: Ann Barnds and Richard S. Tan

See also: Chicago Botanic Garden; Chicago High School for Agricultural Sciences; Community Gardens; Community Supported Agriculture; Wholesale and Distribution

BIBLIOGRAPHY

Advocates for Urban Agriculture. https://auachicago.org/resources/chicago-urban-agriculture-directory/.

Hoyt, Homer. *100 years of Land Values in Chicago*. Chicago: University of Chicago Press, 1933.

Maloney, Cathy Jean. *Chicago Gardens: The Early History*. Chicago: University of Chicago Press, 2008.

Albert Pick Company

The Albert Pick Company revolutionized the concept of wholesaling restaurant, hotel, and bar supplies on a national scale. In a yearly catalog similar to Sears, it offered every item, other than food, necessary to run such operations. Czech-born Albert Pick founded the company with his brother Charles on 5th Avenue in Chicago in 1857. They later relocated their business to Randolph Street and eventually Wells Street. The enterprise grew into one of the nation's largest restaurant supply houses by the early 1900s and played a major role into the 1950s.

The firm purchased and relabeled a wide array of products under its own brand name, everything from frying pans to linen tablecloths. It also produced a line of products such as silverware made in its Bridgeport, Connecticut, factory and bar fixtures/furnishings produced in Cincinnati and New York City. Pick also designed cafeterias, hotels, and restaurants from the ground up, focusing on kitchen design and interiors. It expanded into the hotel business during the Great Depression and had 16 properties by 1937. Pick purchased five Holiday Inns in 1955 and ventured into motels. American Airlines bought out Pick in 1979, retiring the famous brand name.

Contributor: Stefan Osdene

BIBLIOGRAPHY

Jakle, John A., Keith A. Sculle, and Jefferson S. Rogers. *The Motel In America*. Baltimore: Johns Hopkins, 2002, 125.

Pick, Albert. *At Your Service: Supplies for Hotels, Restaurants, Clubs, and Taverns*. Chicago: Albert Pick, 1936.

Alinea

The name of this fine-dining restaurant in Chicago's Lincoln Park neighborhood is a nod to the *pilcrow* (¶)—a typographical paragraph mark—or, in Latin, *a lineā* (meaning "off the line"). The brainchild of chef Grant

Achatz and partner Nick Kokonas, Alinea is known internationally for its molecular, modernist approach to American cuisine. It was one of the first U.S. restaurants to use science to manipulate ingredients. The multicourse tasting menu from Achatz and chef de cuisine, Mike Bagale, features avant-garde creations served on unusual dishware, wires, or even as art drawn right on the table. The ever-changing, amazing selections have included an edible balloon of dehydrated apple and helium, a "camp fire" of parsnip logs, and a course called "hot potato, cold potato."

Opened May 5, 2005, on Halsted Street, Alinea holds a 3-star rating from the *Michelin Guide*. Additionally, Alinea received the AAA's highest recognition, the Five Diamond Award, from 2007 to 2014. On the San Pellegrino World's 50 Best Restaurants List, it ranked ninth in 2014. Achatz and Kokonas published the eponymous hardcover book, *Alinea*, in 2008, a photo-heavy tome offering a behind-the-scenes look into the Alinea kitchen, coupled with 100-plus recipes. In 2016, the owners introduced a new concept in which diners move from place to place for different courses.

Contributor: Jennifer Olvera

See also: Achatz, Grant; Chefs; Restaurants and Fine Dining

BIBLIOGRAPHY

Alinea restaurant. http://website.alinearestaurant.com/site/recognition/.

"Alinea." The World's 50 Best Restaurants. http://www.theworlds50best.com/list/1–50-winners/alinea.

http://en.wikipedia.org/wiki/The_New_York_Times.

Allen Brothers

Founded in 1893 in the city's historic Union Stock Yards, this South Side institution is famed as a wholesale purveyor of meat to some of the nation's top restaurants, hotels, casinos, and country clubs. It also is an online retailer to consumers. The company, family-run (lastly by Robert A. Hatoff and his son Todd) until its 2013 sale to Connecticut-based The Chefs' Warehouse Inc., is noted for its USDA prime beef. It also offers "humanely raised" heritage-breed veal, lamb, pork, seafood, ready-to-eat side dishes, and prepared desserts. Company headquarters are located at 3737 S. Halsted St.

Contributor: Bill Daley

BIBLIOGRAPHY

Allen Brothers. http://www.allenbrothers.com.

Shropshire, Corilyn. "Robert A. 'Bobby' Hatoff: 1943–2012; Businessman Always Sealt in Relationships, Family Firm Sells High-end Meats to Local Restaurants." *Chicago Tribune*, October 14, 2012.

Allgauer, Gustav

Allgauer (1904–72) arrived in Chicago from his native Germany at age 25, with, as he often stated, "$3.65 in [my] pocket." He worked as a busboy, cook, waiter, and bartender throughout the city. In 1936, he left his bartending job at the Bismarck Hotel. Although he was broke, he was able to borrow money from a bank to purchase the Black Forest restaurant on North Clark Street. The refurbished restaurant, serving mostly German foods, became successful.

In 1947, Gene Nüfer's historic 1857 restaurant and tavern, Nufer's Sea Grill, an old stagecoach stop and Chicago's second oldest restaurant was put up for sale. Allgauer bought it the next year with $5,000 borrowed from his attorney. He renamed it Allgauer's Nufer Restaurant. A later name change made it Allgauer's-On-Ridge because of its location on North Ridge Avenue. Under Allgauer's ownership, the restaurant became known for its eclectic menu: tender beef, fresh seafood including garlic-laced shrimp Neufer, and game entrees, such as broiled bear steak and rack of venison.

During 1951, Allgauer bought three other restaurants in quick succession: the Fireside in Lincolnwood, renamed Allgauer's Fireside; the Old Heidelberg and Rathskeller in downtown Chicago, renamed Allgauer's Heidelberg; and one of the oldest restaurant in Chicago, the 1836 Ridge Inn, south of Allgauer's-On-Ridge. He immediately demolished the decrepit Ridge Inn and then revamped the remaining restaurant's menus to feature his now-famous steak and seafood specialties, but he included a smattering of German dishes at the Heidelberg.

Tragedy struck Allgauer in 1958. His popular Fireside restaurant was destroyed by two masked, armed men who invaded the premises, held seven employees hostage, and then doused the entire establishment with gasoline. The fire made national news, bringing it to the attention of Robert F. Kennedy, counsel for the Senate Rackets Committee. In testimony before that Committee, Allgauer denied knowing who had torched his business but admitted paying "special group dues" to Local 450 of the Hotel and Restaurant Employees and Bartenders International Union, which was allegedly "under the thumb of Claude Maddox, an old-time Capone hoodlum."

Contributors: Ellen F. Steinberg and Jack H. Prost

See also: Beer Gardens; Germans; Restaurants and Fine Dining

BIBLIOGRAPHY

Daley, Bill. "Villa Moderne Memories." *Chicago Tribune*, January 28, 2014. http://www.chicagotribune.com/features/life/ct-villa-moderne-remembered-20140128–4,0,7436660.column.

Rannells, Elizabeth. "Have You Heard? Gentlemen in the Kitchen." *Chicago Daily Tribune*, April 15, 1951, F1.

Alliance for the Great Lakes

Residents of states that border the Great Lakes are understandably proud and protective of the natural treasure at their shores, particularly as concerns about water use become issues worldwide. Based in Chicago since 1970, the mission for the Alliance for the Great Lakes has been to conserve and restore the world's largest freshwater resource for generations of people and wildlife. In the summer of 1967, there was a massive die-off of alewives—an estimated one billion pounds. Chicago's North Side had no access to clean drinking water because the dead fish clogged the pumps in the lake, and the whole city was under an order to boil water because it was so polluted with decaying fish. The cause was arguably blue-green algae near Gary. Other killing blooms in Lake Erie, likely exacerbated by a warming climate, suggest possible outbreaks within the Lake Michigan environmental community. In addition to programs that conserve water and coastlines, the Alliance outlined options to fight the invasive Asian carp that threaten native fish populations and the $7 billion fishing industry.

Contributor: Janine MacLachlan
See also: Asian Carp; Zebra Mussels

BIBLIOGRAPHY

Alliance for the Great Lakes. http://www.greatlakes.org/.

American Dairy Association

In 1940, U.S. dairy farmers formed the American Dairy Association (ADA). Designed to promote U.S.-made dairy products, the ADA is best known for its "REAL Seal," an icon used to designate and encourage sales of U.S.-made dairy products at that time. In 1970, the ADA merged with the National Dairy Council to form the United Dairy Industry Association. Based in Rosemont, it is now known as Dairy Management, Inc., or the National Dairy Council. It runs one of several commodity checkoff programs in the United States, funded through industry fees assessed on each hundred-weight unit of milk. Fees are pooled to promote the generic promotion and research of American-made dairy products.

Contributor: Tia M. Rains
See also: Dairy Industry

BIBLIOGRAPHY

Dairy Management, Inc. http://www.dairy.org/about-dmi/.
USDA Agricultural Marketing Service. http://www.ams.usda.gov/.

American Egg Board

In 1976, the American Egg Board was established as a national checkoff program. The program collected an assessment fee on all egg production from companies with more than 75,000 hens. The goal was to increase the public demand for eggs through marketing and advertising. The Board consists of 18 representatives and 18 alternates from all areas of the country, all of whom are appointed by the U.S. Department of Agriculture. The AEB staff, based in suburban Park Ridge, executes the programming under the Board's direction to promote The Incredible Edible Egg. In 1984, the Egg Nutrition Center was formed under the auspices of the Egg Board with the sole purpose of understanding and promoting the nutrition and health benefits of eggs.

Contributor: Tia M. Rains

BIBLIOGRAPHY

American Egg Board. http://www.aeb.org/.

Ann Sather Restaurants

After 21 years of working in a meatpacking plant, Ann Sather used her life savings to buy the 76-seat Swedish Diner on Belmont Avenue for $4,000 in 1945. She ran the renamed Ann Sather restaurant until her retirement in 1981, selling the business to Thomas Tunney, who later became a city alderman representing the 44th Ward.

"I always strived for a friendly atmosphere. It's like entertaining. I'd never serve anything I wouldn't eat in my own home," she told the *Chicago Tribune* in 1996. Ann Sather was the daughter of a Norwegian immigrant and grew up in North Dakota. She died in 1997 at the age of 90.

Tunney was 24 and a graduate of the Cornell University School of Hotel and Restaurant Management in New York when he purchased the restaurant. But first, he worked alongside Ann Sather for a year learning the ropes. Tunney relocated the Belmont Avenue restaurant to larger quarters and opened various satellites in other areas of Chicago, including Hyde Park and Andersonville (both now closed). Three locations remain: 909 W. Belmont St.; 3145 N. Broadway St.; and 1147 W. Granville Ave.

Ann Sather restaurants perhaps are best known for cinnamon rolls, a Swedish-accented menu, and a tradition of support of community and grassroots organizations.

Contributor: Bill Daley

ANN SATHER'S CINNAMON ROLLS

Prep: 30 minutes
Rise: 1 hour, 45 minutes
Cook: 12 minutes

This popular recipe has appeared in many places, including the restaurant's website, the *Chicago Tribune*, and *Better Homes and Gardens New Cookbook*.

Makes: 12 rolls

1 envelope (1/4 ounce) active dry yeast
1 teaspoon sugar
1/4 cup warm water (110 degrees)
1 cup milk, scalded, cooled
1 stick (1/2 cup) butter, half melted, half at room
    temperature
1/3 cup granulated sugar
1 1/2 teaspoons salt
2 1/2 to 3 cups all-purpose flour
1/2 cup brown sugar
1 tablespoon ground cinnamon
Glaze, optional, recipe follows

1. Stir the yeast and 1 teaspoon of the sugar into the warm water in a large bowl; let stand 5 minutes. Mix in milk, the melted butter, 1/3 cup sugar, and salt. Add 1 cup of the flour; beat with a spoon or an electric mixer until smooth.

2. Gradually stir in 1 1/2 cups of the flour until smooth. If the dough is still moist, stir in 1 tablespoon flour at a time to make a soft dough. Cover with a dry cloth; let rise in a warm place until doubled in bulk, about 1 hour.

3. Divide the raised dough in half. Roll out (with a lightly floured rolling pin) on a lightly oiled board. Stretch 1 piece of the dough to make a 12-by-8-inch rectangle. Spread 2 tablespoons of the soft butter over the top of the dough. Sprinkle with brown sugar and cinnamon. Beginning on the long side, roll up tightly, jelly-roll fashion. Repeat with remaining dough.

4. Cut the dough into 2-inch slices. Place on greased and floured baking sheets. Let the dough rise (in a warm place) until doubled in bulk, about 45 minutes. Bake in the oven until golden brown, 12 to 15 minutes. Remove from oven; place the cinnamon rolls on a wire rack. Top rolls with a glaze immediately, if desired. Serve warm or at room temperature.

For the glaze: Combine 1 cup confectioners' sugar, 1/4 teaspoon vanilla extract, and 1 tablespoon milk in a small bowl. Mix until smooth. Stir in additional milk, 1 teaspoon at a time, until icing is loose enough to drizzle.

BIBLIOGRAPHY

Armour, Terrence E. "2nd Generation Ann Sather." *Chicago Tribune*, November 15, 1987.
Heise, Kenan. "Ann Sather, 90: Founder of Namesake Restaurant." *Chicago Tribune*, April 24, 1997.

Armour & Company

One of America's leading food producers from the late nineteenth century onward, the company was founded by Philip Danforth Armour (1832–1901). Born on a farm in Stockbridge, New York, to a family of eight children, Armour left home at age 19 for the California gold fields where he made a large sum of money selling supplies to miners. Experienced in wholesaling, the young Armour moved to Milwaukee where he began a provisioning company and eventually partnered with the city's leading meatpacker, John Plankinton. Meanwhile in 1860, his brother George teamed with pioneer Chicago butcher and grocer George Dole to build a grain storage business.

Eventually, Armour brought two other brothers to Chicago, moved the company to the city, and formed a provisioning, grain storage, and meatpacking business in 1863 called Armour & Company. The company was a success from the start, becoming the city's leading grain elevator

View of the Armour & Co. packing plant in the Union Stock Yards area, 1910. In "Notable Men of Chicago and Their City," 1910. ttps://archive.org/details/notablemenofchi00chic.

business and holding more than 6 million bushels a year by 1881.

As soon as the Union Stock Yards were established in 1865, Armour began a slaughtering and packing operation. One of Chicago's big three packers (Swift and Morris, the others), Armour became a national company by the 1880s. The main plant was built in levels where animals were killed at the top floor and disassembled in stages until, at the bottom level, rendering and sausages were done. Such efficiency was matched by shipping meat in the 1,200 refrigerated cars that the company owned at the end of the century.

Armour produced a wide range of products, using every bit of the slaughtered animals. Sold nationally and internationally, margarine, lard, glue, gelatin, and soaps were among its many products. One of the earliest makers of canned meats, Armour supplied the British army fighting in the Sudan and American troops in the Spanish American war. The company's retail lines, called Veribest, included canned vegetables, soups, margarine, evaporated milk, juices, and even fresh eggs. Soaps were always part of Armour's line, and in 1948, it developed an antibacterial product labeled Dial, which remains a major label.

Armour's labor relations were notorious in the age of rampant Robber Baron businesses. His 7,000 Chicago workers were poorly paid, receiving well under the living wage for families. They struck several times, but the strikes were brutally broken: Armour was the model for unsympathetic figures in Upton Sinclair's expose of the meat industry, *The Jungle*. Things became better for workers under his son, J. Ogden Armour, thanks to intervention by Jane Addams and later unionization. Nonetheless, Philip D. Armour was a philanthropist, funding orphanages and endowing a technical institute to help young people without financial means to gain educations.

The Armour Institute was the foundation for the modern-day Illinois Institute of Technology.

The Armour family sold their major interest in the early 1920s, but the company continued as a major force in American food production into the late 1950s. Then acquisitions by other firms and spinoffs left the Armour brands in the hands of the John Morrell Group, owned by Smithfield Farms (now merged with China's Shuanghui International Holdings Limited) and Pinnacle Foods, which markets the Armour Star brands.

Contributor: Bruce Kraig

See also: Union Stock Yards

BIBLIOGRAPHY

Lau, Karen Y. "Armour, Philip Danforth." Ken Albala and Allen Gary, eds. *The Business of Food*. Westport, Conn.: Greenwood, 2007.

Leech, Harper. *Armour and His Times*. New York: D. Appleton-Century Co., 1938.

Arun's

Arun Sampanthavivat and business partner Sunny Leon opened the fine-dining destination Arun's in 1985. A native of Southern Thailand, Sampanthavivat grew up on a rubber plantation. He went on to secure degrees in Thai literature and foreign languages from Bangkok's Chulalongkorn University, a master's degree in international relations from Sophia International University in Tokyo, and a master's degree in political science from the University of Chicago.

During his studies in Chicago, Sampanthavivat decided to open a Thai restaurant with a group of investors. Those plans didn't materialize, so he opened one on his own in a small rented space on Irving Park Road. His only prior cooking experience was gained from family members and cooking for friends.

He moved the restaurant to Kedzie Avenue in Albany Park in 1998, and it features intimate, semiprivate alcoves and a gallerylike, Thai art- and artifact-adorned setting, helping to place it as one of Chicago's most elevated dining experiences. The prix-fixe menu changes, based on the chef's whim and seasonality. It is customized to individual diners' preferences and diets and features top-notch Thai ingredients—such as chilies, galangal, tamarind, and basil—traditional techniques, and exciting flavors. Since 2002, Arun's has been awarded AAA's highest Five-Diamond rating. Sampanthavivat was awarded Best Chef: Great Lakes in 2000 by the James Beard Foundation.

Sampanthavivat also helped develop Taste of Thai Town on Pulaski Road. Opened in 2015, it is a converted police station that houses a casual restaurant and community center.

Contributor: Jennifer Olvera

See also: Restaurants and Fine Dining; Southeast Asians.

BIBLIOGRAPHY

http://www.wbez.org/can-arun-sampanthavivat-create-chicago-neighborhood-scratch-108701.

Ruby, Jeff. "Arun's in Albany Park: The Accidental Masterpiece." *Chicago Magazine*. http://www.chicagomag.com/Chicago-Magazine/January-2012/Aruns-in-Albany-Park-The-Accidental-Masterpiece/.

Asian Carp

In the United States, this refers to a group of large, bony freshwater fish that have invaded the Mississippi River Basin in great numbers, crowding out native species. Filter feeding fish, which eat plankton, they were imported by Southern fish farmers to clean their ponds in the 1970s, escaped into the wild, and began reproducing. One species, the silver carp, is known for leaping from the waters when disturbed and occasionally injuring boaters. In 2014, the U.S. Army Corps of Engineers operated three underwater electric barriers to help prevent their spread into the Great Lakes.

In 2010, a group of Chicago chefs experimented with preparing the carp as food. While most chefs agreed the flavor of the fish was good, it was difficult to butcher, given the fish's extremely bony skeletal structure, and most decided it was not worth the effort. Still, the fish can occasionally be found in Chinatown markets and served in restaurants. They are considered a viable food source in Asia and in Israel, where they are processed into gefilte fish. In 2012 a downstate fish processor considered a plan to exploit those markets, but later changed course, deciding it would be more profitable to process them into fishmeal, oil, and bone meal.

Contributor: Mike Sula

See also: Alliance for the Great Lakes

BIBLIOGRAPHY

"Asian carp threat to the Great Lakes," National Wildlife Federation. http://www.nwf.org.

Sula, Mike. "The Culinary Solution." *Chicago Reader*, March 25, 2010. http://www.chicagoreader.com/chicago/asian-carp-cooking-chicago-chefs/Content?oid=1571974.

Atomic Cake

Since the 1950s, this legendary Chicago cake has been an essential part of birthdays and other celebrations, especially in Chicago's southwest suburbs. While there are variations, a standard version consists of three layers of cake—yellow, banana, chocolate—and three layers of filling—fresh strawberries, banana chocolate pudding, and vanilla pastry cream—the whole slathered with whipped cream. One explanation for its name is that the cake was so spectacular that it reminded people of the atomic bomb. Some old-timers still order an "atomic bomb cake."

Contributor: Colleen Sen

BIBLIOGRAPHY

Zeldes, Leah. "Chicago Ushers in the Atomic Age—and Its Cake." http://www.diningchicago.com/blog/2010/12/03/chicago-ushers-in-the-atomic-age-and-its-cake/.

Automatic Canteen Company of America

A leading manufacturer of automated vending machines, the company was founded in July 1929 by Nathaniel Leverone after he had acquired the Chicago Automatic Canteen Corporation, the American Legion's vending operations in Chicago. The firm began operations with 100 5-cent candy machines, and expanded to about 230,000 machines nationwide by 1940. The company added cigarettes as a vending offering following World War II and hit a peak of $200 million in sales by the mid-1960s, with a strong presence in factory lunchrooms. The company merged with International Telephone and Telegraph in 1968 in a deal, the *Chicago Tribune* reported, worth $242.5 million. It was later sold to the Trans World Corporation in 1973, when operations management moved away from Chicago. Currently operating under the name Canteen Corporation, it is part of British-based Compass Group North America—a major caterer and vending machine company that serves 8 million meals daily.

Contributor: John Carruthers

See also: Equipment, Commercial

BIBLIOGRAPHY

"Automatic Canteen Co. of America." *Encyclopedia of Chicago*. http://www.encyclopedia.chicagohistory.org/pages/2558.html.

Azteca Foods Inc.

The nationally known manufacturer of refrigerated tortillas got its start in 1970 when Arthur Velasquez and nine business partners, all Mexican Americans, each invested $8,000 to create the Azteca Corn Products Corp., in Chicago's Pilsen neighborhood.

At the time, tortilla operations were primarily local, with nonrefrigerated products sold in nearby groceries. Azteca changed everything, developing a product that could be shipped and sold in supermarkets with minimal preservatives.

In 1984, the company was purchased by the Pillsbury Co. Five years later, Pillsbury, taken over by London-based conglomerate Grand Metropolitan PLC, sold the company back to Velasquez (with a partner), who renamed it Azteca Foods Inc. It remains a family-owned company, led by CEO Velasquez, who grew up across the street from Hull House, Jane Addams's pioneering settlement, and his daughter, Renee Togher, the company's president.

Azteca's refrigerated product line includes multiple versions of the basic tortilla (including one with no preservatives), bake-and-fill salad shells, and tortilla chips; the company also markets flour tortillas and flavored wraps under its Baja brand. Its 100,000-square-foot manufacturing facility in the Garfield Ridge neighborhood on the city's Southwest Side employs more than 150 people.

Contributor: Alan Solomon

See also: Mexicans; Tortillas and Tortillerias

BIBLIOGRAPHY

Palmer, Ann Therese. "Ready to Lead the Family's Business." *Chicago Tribune*, December 29, 2008.

"Talking Management," video interview with Arthur Velasquez. *Crain's Chicago Business*, November 14, 2008. http://topics.chicagobusiness.com/v/53416134/arthur-velasquez-azteca-foods.htm.

B

Baby Ruth

This chocolate-covered candy bar made of peanuts, caramel, and nougat was listed by *Time* magazine in 2014 as "One of the 13 Most Influential Candy Bars of All Time."

The Curtiss Candy Co. of Chicago developed Baby Ruth in 1920 and marketed it for seven decades. The candy bar was a reformulated version of owner Otto Schnering's unsuccessful Kandy Kake recipe, also using milk chocolate, peanuts, and nougat. It competed with another local product, Oh Henry!, a bar made by Williamson Candy. Baby Ruth achieved success through its name, a lower price point than Oh Henry!, and unique and extensive marketing strategies.

There is much debate as to the name. Because Curtiss was located on the same street as Wrigley Field (where the Chicago Cubs played), many people assumed that the bar was named after the popular slugger Babe Ruth. The company claimed it was named after President Grover Cleveland's deceased daughter. But that story was suspected as an effort to avoid paying royalties to the "Babe." In 1931, Babe Ruth sued over the name when he tried to market his own candy bar, "Ruth." He lost the suit because the name had already been trademarked by Curtiss.

Schnering heavily marketed the candy bar, using slogans, circuses, hot-air balloons, and airplanes.

In 1923, the company dropped thousands of Baby Ruth bars attached to mini parachutes from an airplane over Pittsburgh. For four decades after Ruth called his famous home-run shot in the 1932 World Series at Wrigley Field, an illuminated sign advertising Baby Ruth stood atop a rooftop across the street, though not at the ball's landing place.

In 1995, the Ruth estate licensed his image to be used for marketing the candy bar. In 2006 the candy bar was designated as official candy bar of Major League Baseball. It was listed in the 2007 Chicago Cubs program as a proud sponsor of the Chicago Cubs.

Curtiss was bought in 1964 by Standard Brands; in 1981 by Nabisco; and, in 1990, Curtiss sold to Nestle, Switzerland, who now markets Baby Ruth.

Contributor: Geraldine Rounds

See also: Candy

BIBLIOGRAPHY

Broekel, Ray. *The Great Candy Bar Book*. Boston: Houghton, Mifflin, 1982.

Goddard, Lewis. *Chicago's Sweet Candy History*. Mount Pleasant, S.C.: Arcadia Publishing, 2012.

Badonsky, George

A well-known, outspoken restaurateur, Bodonsky was behind successful restaurants such as Le Bastille, Tango, George's, and for a time, Maxim's de Paris, which he bought in 1984. After a stint as a record producer, he opened The Brewery on Broadway in the late 1960s. Then came Tango in the Belmont Hotel, a hip, seafood restaurant filled with modern art by Andy Warhol and Peter Max, and a menu of fish flown in from the East Coast. In the 1970s, he opened La Bastille, an authentic French bistro where he initiated popular Bastille Day and Beaujolais Nouveau festivals on Superior Street. At George's on Kinzie Street, he combined a love of food and music by bringing in well-known jazz and other artists in a cabaret-jazz club venue. A fire closed the restaurant in 1984; he rebuilt it, but had to sell shortly afterward. He also resurrected the closed Maxim's de Paris on Astor Street, a venture that lured chef Jean Joho from France, but which closed after two years. He died at 78 in 2015 at his Stevensville, Michigan, home.

Contributor: Carol Mighton Haddix

BIBLIOGRAPHY

O'Donnell, Maureen. "George Badonsky, 78; Restaurateur 'Was Ahead of His Time.'" *Chicago Sun Times*, January 12, 2015.

The Bakery Restaurant

In 1963 with his wife and partner, Sadako Tanino, the Hungarian-born chef Louis Szathmary opened The Bakery on the Near North Side of Chicago. In the first year, more than two hundred articles were written about the Bakery. Many restaurant critics across the nation gave rave reviews. Of those who did not, Szathmary observed, "They don't know shiitake from shinola." Guests came from around the world, and Szathmary hosted almost every celebrity who visited Chicago.

When Szathmary opened The Bakery, the standard for fine dining in Chicago was typically a meal of shrimp cocktail, iceberg lettuce with Thousand Island dressing, prime rib of beef, asparagus with hollandaise sauce, and baked Alaska. Szathmary, however, served such "exotic" fare as grated celery root salad, *paprikás csirke* (also called chicken *paprikash*) drizzled with sour cream, and his signature dish, beef Wellington made with rich foie gras rather than the usual duxelles. Szathmary called his cuisine Continental with American undertones and soon had diners waiting weeks for reservations.

It mattered little to the public that the 117-seat restaurant was in an old and rickety building in a then-seedy neighborhood and that Szathmary had filled his three dining rooms with secondhand silverware and furniture he described as "early restaurant and late Salvation Army." All diners saw were the cheery red-and-white candy-striped awning outside, the clean white tablecloths, the spotless wooden floors, and Szathmary's family greeting them and seating them. After accomplishing a more than 25-year successful run, Szathmary closed the restaurant in 1989 and retired.

Contributor: Scott Warner
See also: Restaurants and Fine Dining; Szathmary, Louis

BIBLIOGRAPHY

Rice, William. "Louis Szathmary, Noted Chef, Ex-Restaurant Owner." *Chicago Tribune*, October 5, 1996.
Warner, Scott. "Louis Szathmary." T*he Oxford Encyclopedia of Food and Drink in America*. Oxford: Oxford University Press, 2004.

Baking and Bakeries

In the early 1800s, women did most of their own baking at home; hearth fires took skill and constant stoking, and the results were usually rustic and simple. The growth of Chicago meant the housewife could contemplate purchasing bread and sweet baked items from neighborhood bakeries. Ingredients for baking became more accessible and allowed for a variety of baked goods.

The Chicago River and Lake Michigan provided Chicago's milling power. With the invention of the John Deere plow in 1837 and Cyrus McCormick's reaper in 1847, midwestern grain production boomed; grain elevators, flour mills, and warehouses opened in Chicago, and soon shipments of grains moved eastbound for trade by way of the Great Lakes. From 1858 to 1871, The Chicago Board of Trade recorded sales for bushels of rye, corn, oats, barley, and wheat. Also recorded were millions of barrels of wheat flour milled throughout the city.

By 1880, with a city population of about 500,000, there were 280, mostly small, bakeries recorded. But the mid-1800s also yielded enormous bakeries. Mechanical Bakery, founded in 1858, employed hundreds of workers baking crackers, cookies, and pies. But Dake Bakery, founded in 1861, took over as the largest cracker manufacturer in the city. After the 1871 Chicago Fire brought ruin to Mechanical and rebuilding for Dake, David F. Bremner saw an opportunity. Bremner set up shop and began making crackers, using the worn Mechanical Bakery ovens. He initialed the crackers with a DFB so his customers would remember his product. Bremner's crackers are still sold today, though the firm's headquarters was moved to Denver. Paul Schulze Sr., an immigrant from Germany, established the Schulze Baking Co. in 1896. It became a major commercial bread bakery and created the Butternut Bread brand.

ARTISAN BREADMAKERS

Breadmakers of the Old World found their way to the new young city of Chicago and found a ready market. Their simple, hearty loaves of rye, whole grain, or pumpernickel kept the working classes of Chicago coming back to their small bakeries. But with the advent of commercial bakeries, the white-bread boom, and fully stocked supermarkets, demand for their style of breads faded.

In the 1960s, the natural foods movement reintroduced Chicagoans to hearty, fermentation-started loaves of bread at places such as The Bread Shop on North Halsted. And then a second wave of artisan breads appeared in small bakeries in the late 1990s and early 2000s, encouraged by the consumer's desire for more authentic, simple foods. The older ethnic bakeries had resurgences. Italian bakers such as Ferrara Bakery on Taylor St., and D'Amato Bakery on Grand joined the Polish Racine Bakery and Anne's Ukrainian, among others, to spark interest in high-quality, locally made breads.

In the city and suburbs, such bakeries included Ambrosia Euro-American Patisserie in Barrington, Bittersweet Bakery on Belmont, Red Hen Bakery on Milwaukee Ave. (and later on West Diversey), Flourish Bakery on Bryn Mawr, and LaBriola in Lombard. Among newer entries are Baker Miller Bakehouse on North Western Avenue, Bon Bom Bakery in Pilsen, Floriole on Armitage, Hendrickx Belgian Bread Crafter on East Walton Street, Hewn Bakery in Evanston, Hoosier Mama Pie Co. on West Chicago Avenue and Evanston, La Boulangerie on North Milwaukee, La Farine in Avondale, La Fournette on North Wells Street, Little Goat Bread on West Randolph Street, Publican Quality Breads on West Lake, and Upper Crust Bakery on West Grand.

—CAROL MIGHTON HADDIX

Mass production of cookies and biscuits was in full swing by 1898. Hardtack (for the army and navy) and crackers were produced by professional bakers and shipped in barrels and boxes via Chicago's rail system. The National Biscuit Company (Nabisco) was formed when the American Biscuit and Manufacturing Company (which took over 40 midwestern bakeries) combined with New York Biscuit Company (consisting of 7 eastern bakeries) and the United States Baking Company. Nabisco moved its headquarters to New York in 1906. By that year, the company was earning $40 million annually, but still employed 1,300 men and women locally.

One unusual bakery, The Women's Baking Company, was founded in 1892 in a response to food safety concerns. It advertised that "every family must have bread . . . it is a woman's work to supply it . . . we will supply more wholesome bread, pies, cakes . . . for less money than the housewife can make at home." Unfortunately, the bakery folded in 1894.

Chicago attracted professional bakers and confectioners from their European homelands. The rapid demand for "bakers" and factory helpers grew, and so did an organized group of laborers, the Bakery and Confectionery Workers International Union, which claimed 28,000 members by 1920. The Retail Bakers of America was founded in 1918. It partnered sellers and buyers for profitable bakeries and offered training for the industry. The organization also helped formulate industry standards and industry research. In 1887, *The Baker's Helper*, a national industry journal was established in Chicago. It later morphed into the *National Baker* and other industry journals.

The industrialization of food during the 1920s and 1930s brought about sliced, packaged white bread and box cake mixes. As World War II ended, women returned from the factories and spent more time at home again. Baking rebounded again, with time-saving products and more available exotic ingredients such as cocoa, coconut, and pineapple. Gas stoves and electric refrigerators also helped women bake more quickly, consistently, and successfully.

Further industrialization in the 1940s led to more baking changes. Chicago's Edward Weidenmiller Foundry created embossing and stamp-cutter machinery for cookies and crackers. Nabisco, for example, used the new sugar wafer plates for their products. This allowed for thousands of new designs and shapes, such as animal crackers and Oreo's. Charles W. Lubin bought three Community Bake Shops in Chicago in 1935. He created a rich cheesecake and named it, and his business, after his daughter, Sara Lee. In the 1950s, Lubin invented a pound cake that could be frozen, distributed, and baked in a single foil pan.

Levinson's Bakery. Photograph by Ashish Sen.

Eventually, grocery stores began to include in-house bakeries. Heineman's, starting as a small Chicago retail bakery, became a self-service bakery department within Jewel and Dominick's supermarkets by 1959. Other supermarkets started their own baking operations. Consumers now could purchase their freshly baked bread in the same store while shopping for groceries.

Beginning in the late 1960s, hippies and other young people began demanding more natural, healthful breads. The Bread Shop on North Halsted was one of the first made-in-house natural bakeries in Chicago. Other shops and health food stores also started carrying sprouted-wheat breads, multigrain breads and 100 percent whole wheat breads. The trend grew, so that today, such breads are found in many supermarkets, including Whole Foods and Trader Joe's.

Starting in the 1990s, warehouse-style supermarkets with discount prices gave the consumer unprecedented exposure to a quantity of baked goods. Store bakeries grew in size, and "quality" and "freshly made" were interpreted by the grocery seller rather than the consumer. And, while consumers selected their baked goods from freezers and grocery store bakeries, many small, corner bakeries were disappearing. And yet a few stalwarts continued baking, including Roeser's in Humboldt Park, which celebrated its 105th anniversary in 2016, Dinkel's Bakery on Lincoln Avenue since 1922, and Weber's Bakery on the South Side since 1930.

In recent years, Chicagoans have seen small bakeries and pastry shops open throughout the city. Their focus is on artisan, handmade baked goods, prepared with minimal or no preservatives and often local ingredients (see sidebar). The French Pastry School opened in 1995 on Grand Avenue and then moved to West Jackson Boulevard, giving Chicago a leg up in the pastry arts. It is now part of the City Colleges of Chicago. Many of its graduates have opened their own pastry shops in town. Other bakeries devote themselves to doughnuts and cupcakes throughout the city and suburbs. It appears that the local/corner bakery may be making a comeback.

Contributor: Jenny Lewis

See also: Bremner, David Francis; Doughnuts; Dressel's Bakery; Fingerhut Bakery; Keebler Company; Lutz's Café and Bakery; Sara Lee Corporation; Turano Baking Company; Twinkies

BIBLIOGRAPHY

Achilles, Rolf. "Baking Tools." *Made in Illinois: A Story of Illinois Manufacturing*. Chicago: Illinois Manufacturers' Association, 1993.

Andreas, Alfred Theodore. "Bakers." *History of Chicago, Volume I.* Chicago: A. T. Andrea, 1884.

Baldwin Ice Cream

In 1921, seven African American postal workers decided to link their resources to start an ice-cream business: Seven Links Ice Cream Company. They opened an ice-cream parlor, 5314 S. State St., in the Grand Boulevard community, an ideal location to draw customers from DuSable High School and the historic Regal Theatre.

In the 1930s, the company was reorganized as the Service Links Ice Cream Co. In the next decade, Kit Baldwin, one of the founders, bought out the remaining partners, and in 1946, he renamed the firm the Baldwin Ice Cream Company and opened more parlors. The ice cream was popular, and in 1955, Baldwin starting selling the ice cream through major grocery stores in Chicago's African American communities.

After Baldwin's death in 1961, the company changed hands a few times, and in 1967, it was purchased by Joseph Robichaux, an executive of the Wanzer Milk Company, who applied his expertise in the dairy industry to the company. Robichaux died suddenly in 1971, and his wife Joelyn took the helm.

As an African American woman business owner, Robichaux was an anomaly and faced many challenges in growing the business. In 1983, she obtained concession rights for five Baldwin stores at O'Hare airport and maintained one ice-cream parlor in the Chatham neighborhood. In 1989, several chain stores began selling Baldwin brand ice cream throughout the Midwest.

In 1992, Baldwin Ice Cream was purchased by entrepreneur Eric G. Johnson. Today, the more than 90-year-old brand is one of the products of the Baldwin Richardson Foods Company.

According to Dairy Foods magazine, Baldwin Ice Cream is the "only sizable and continuously black-owned ice-cream business in the United States."

Contributor: Charla L. Draper

See also: African Americans

BIBLIOGRAPHY

Chavez, Donna M. "A Scoop of Sweet Success: The Man behind the Revitalized Baldwin Ice Cream." *The Chicago Tribune*, May 8, 1994.

DeMille, Darcy. "Baldwin Ice Cream Founder Was Inspired by Booker T." *Chicago Defender*, July 5, 1958.

Balkan Immigrants

The region called the Balkans comprises Albania, Bosnia-Herzegovina, Bulgaria, Croatia, Kosovo, Macedonia, Montenegro, Serbia, Slovenia, and sometimes Romania and Greece (see entries.) All but Albanians, Kosovans, Romanians, and Greeks speak closely related Slavic languages. Until the early 1990s, these countries (except for Bulgaria and Albania) were part of the Socialist Federal Republic of Yugoslavia.

For centuries much of the region was under the rule of the Ottoman Empire, while Slovenia and parts of Croatia were part of the Austro-Hungarian empire. The region's food incorporates elements of Turkish, German, Central European, even Italian cuisine. The main religions are Islam, Eastern Orthodoxy, and Roman Catholicism.

Immigrants from the Balkans came to Chicago in several waves. In the late nineteenth and early twentieth century, thousands of immigrants, mainly unskilled men, found work in the stockyards, steel, and construction industries. Political refugees fled during and after World War II, while the collapse of socialism in 1989 brought thousands more, especially Bulgarians. The war in Bosnia-Herzegovina from 1992 to 1995 led to a large influx of Bosnian refugees to Chicago.

According to the 2010 U.S. Census, 28,500 first-generation Serbians lived in Chicago, plus 35,000 Croatians, and 15,000 who called themselves Yugoslavians. No official census figures exist for Bosnians and Herzegovinians, but Chicago is believed to have one of the largest populations in the United States, estimated as high as 50,000. A small, but growing, community of Bulgarians live mainly in the northwest suburbs.

A number of restaurants, butcher shops, and coffee shops serve this growing community. Most of the businesses are located in the north and northwest parts of the city and suburbs. Stores include Serbian-owned Beograd Meat Market; Lalich Delicatessen; Sandy's Bakery and Deli; and City Fresh Market. Eating establishments include Restaurant Sarajevo; Caffé & Restaurant Yugoslavia; Beograd Café; Serbian Village Restaurant; and Coffee Slasticarna Drina. Restaurant Mehanata in Des Plaines has an extensive menu featuring Bulgarian dishes such as *kavarma*, a pork and vegetable stew, and *lukanka*, a semidried flattened sausage.

Although there are regional variations, the different nationalities share many common dishes, among them: *Burek*, a baked or fried pastry made of a thin flaky dough filled with cheese, minced meat, vegetables or fruits; *ćevapi* and its diminutive *ćevapčići*, ground pork, beef, or lamb formed into long sausage-shaped tubes and grilled. They may be served with white bread or rolls and a paprika spread, or alone with sour cream, ketchup, roasted peppers, mayonnaise, onions, and other condiments; *raznjici*, a shish kabob made with large chunks of pork tenderloin; *kaymak*, a creamy dairy product made from the milk of cows, sheep, or goats that is eaten as an appetizer, a condiment, or with bread; *lepinja*, a thick, round bread similar to pita; *suvi vrat*, semidried smoked pork shoulder; *ajvar*, a condiment made of roasted red peppers and eggplant; *plejskavica*, a large patty made of mixed ground meats (beef, pork, lamb) served hot on a plate with side dishes or on bread with grilled onions, like a hamburger; *shopska* salad, chopped tomatoes, cucumbers, peppers, onions, and feta cheese; *sarma*, cabbage stuffed with ground meat and rice and a tomato-based sauce; and black, viscous Turkish-style coffee served in a small pot.

Contributor: Colleen Sen

BIBLIOGRAPHY

Day, Jennifer. "Balkan Comforts: You Might Not Know the Dishes' Names but You'll Recognize the Flavors." *Chicago Tribune*, December 8, 2011.

Pridmore, Jay. "Yugoslavian Fare Simple, but Watch It." *Chicago Tribune*, August 29, 1986.

Ballpark Food

If "Take Me out to the Ball Game" had been written in 2015, Jack Norworth would have had a hard time working Asian barbecue pork sandwiches and mahi mahi fish tacos into the seventh-inning-stretch anthem. Back in 1908, when Norworth penned the iconic song, peanuts, popcorn, Cracker Jack, and hot dogs (and beer) were the extent of ballpark fare. It is likely Norworth spotted a mention of Cracker Jack—a caramel-coated popcorn and peanut snack started

by Chicago brothers Frederick and Louis Rueckheim—on a subway ad for a game in New York.

Baseball had been around as an organized sport since 1846, but it wasn't until 1887 that Harry M. Stevens opened the first concession stand at a minor league ballpark in Columbus, Ohio. Stevens, a book salesman who developed scorecards so fans could track the players, also is credited with peanuts' strong association with baseball. In 1895, the Cavagnaros peanut company wanted to place an ad in one of Stevens's scorecards and paid with peanuts, which Stevens then sold to the stadium. The first link between hot dogs and baseball is less clear. It could be in 1880s when a St. Louis bar owner, who also was part-owner of the St. Louis Browns, may have sold the sausages outside the ballpark, or when Harry Stevens's son Frank pedaled a cart of hot dogs (though his father thought ham and cheese sandwiches would be more popular) outside Madison Square Garden.

A 1947 Chicago Cubs program lists Oscar Mayer red hots for 15 cents, Borden's ice cream and Coca-Cola for 10 cents, and cheese sandwiches and Pabst beer for 25 cents. In the previous season 1,342,970 customers consumed 1,368,876 hot dogs, accounting for close to half the club's food sales. Through the 1970s, ballpark fare did not venture too far afield, but in the 1980s, that started to change. In 1982, Chicago-based Levy Restaurants was persuaded to cater the corporate skyboxes at Comiskey Park, home to the White Sox, taking orders the day before games and trucking food from its restaurants to the park. The first dessert cart also appeared at Comiskey Park, offering guests individual portions of a variety of sweets. In 1985,

Members of the Chicago White Sox eat hot dogs between halves of a doubleheader, 1931. Library of Congress.

Levy Restaurants also started serving the skyboxes at Wrigley Field. When the 1990s saw a dozen new professional ballparks open, they included wood-fired ovens and large kitchens for on-site food preparation. Concessions and skybox menus became another way teams distinguished themselves.

In 2015, fans at Wrigley Field noshed on the city's signature Vienna Beef hot dogs, but also grazed on the Joe Maddon Italian Hoagie, named after the Cubs' manager and loaded with salami, ham, cheese, and cherry-pepper relish. Across town at Guaranteed Rate Field, Sox fans ordered the likes of maple-glazed bacon-on-a-stick, beef barbacoa tacos, Chinese steamed dumplings, and a hot Cuban ham-and-pork sandwich that pays homage to the late Sox great Minnie Minoso.

Contributor: Deborah Pankey

See also: Cracker Jack; Hot Dogs

BIBLIOGRAPHY

Jacobstein, Bennett. T*he Joy of Ballpark Food: From Hot Dogs to Haute Cuisine.* San Jose, Calif.: Ballpark Food Publications, 2015.

National Hot Dog and Sausage Council. http://www.hot-dog.org/.

Banchet, Jean and Doris

Dinner at Le Français, when Jean Banchet was in the kitchen, and Doris, his wife and business partner, was in charge of the dining room, was more than a meal. It was an event. People came to the small suburb of Wheeling from all over the country just to eat there. When famed French chef Paul Bocuse, a close friend and ally, celebrated his 60th birthday, Jean Banchet hosted the party.

Banchet, often described as dashing and charming, was born in Roanne, France, in 1941, one of triplets. Starting as an apprentice as a teenager, he trained in several famous kitchens in France, including La Pyramide. Restaurateur Arnie Morton brought Banchet to the United States to head up the kitchen at the swank Playboy Club in Lake Geneva. In 1973, Banchet opened his signature restaurant Le Français, choosing a location in the northern suburbs that, he would later say, was all he could afford. Named the best restaurant in the United States by *Bon Appetit* in 1980, the restaurant introduced classic French dining to the Midwest. When the original restaurant was destroyed by fire two years later, the Banchets replaced it with a building reminiscent of a French country inn. The Banchets' home was on the property, maximizing the time Jean could spend in the kitchen and Doris rule the front of the house.

As charismatic as he was talented, Banchet was a perfectionist who demanded nothing less from everyone who

Chef Jean Banchet, chef/owner of Le Français. Courtesy of Doris Banchet.

worked for him. If a dish went awry, you tossed it and started over. And if you wanted to keep your job, you made sure it didn't happen again. Jean Banchet died in 2013. He is memorialized in the Jean Banchet Awards for Culinary Excellence for culinary originality and talent in the Chicago area.

Contributor: Barbara Revsine

See also: Chefs; French; Le Français; Restaurateurs and Restaurant Groups

BIBLIOGRAPHY

Gordinier, Jeff. "Jean Banchet, Chef Who Translated French Cuisine, Dies at 72." *New York Times*, November 25, 2013.

Vettel, Phil. "Le Français Chef Set High Standard for Fine Dining in Chicago." *Chicago Tribune*, November 25, 2013.

The Bannos Family

Jimmy Bannos Sr., chef/owner of the popular Cajun/Creole restaurant Heaven on Seven, began his career working at his family restaurant the Garland Coffee shop, a deli on the seventh floor of the Garland Building at 111 N. Wabash. Both of his Greek grandfathers had run restaurants (Bannos Diner at 134th and Canal, and J&P

in Cicero). After discovering Cajun food via the cookbooks of New Orleans chef Paul Prudhomme, he worked with Prudhomme in New Orleans. On his return, Bannos added New Orleans–inspired items to the Garland's menu. The items proved so successful that in 1986 he changed the name of the restaurant to Heaven on Seven and served only New Orleans dishes, including oyster and catfish po' boys, hoppin' john, etouffeé, gumbo, and jambalaya. He opened a second branch at 600 N. Michigan, and a third in Naperville, both in partnership with Bob Vick.

His son Jimmy Bannos Jr. studied at Johnson & Wales University and worked for Emeril Lagasse and Mario Batali before returning to Chicago. In 2013, in collaboration with his father, Scott Harris, and Tony Mantuano, he opened The Purple Pig, 500 N. Michigan Ave., featuring housemade charcuterie, cheese, Mediterranean fare, and an extensive wine list. In 2013, Bannos Jr. won a James Beard award as "Rising Star Chef of the Year."

Contributor: Colleen Sen
See also: Chefs; Restaurateurs and Restaurant Groups

BIBLIOGRAPHY

Kogan, Rick. "Jimmy Bannos Jr. Pushes Restaurant Legacy in New Directions." *Chicago Tribune*, January 5, 2015.

Barbecue

Chicago's reputation for barbecue is built on ribs as surely as the city was built on the wreckage of the Great Chicago Fire. Although plenty of chicken and beef barbecue can be found in town, there was a reason Carl Sandburg called the city "hog butcher for the world."

Barbecue and the blues both came to the South Side from the Mississippi Delta as hundreds of thousands of African American farm workers displaced by mechanization moved north during the First Great Migration, from 1910 to 1930. Then, because Chicago was a major wargoods manufacturer, from 1940 to 1960, there was a Second Great Migration, and the South Side became known as the "Capital of Negro America."

Southerners made barbecue by fire-roasting their meats low and slow over dirt pits. Health regulations eventually forbade restaurants from cooking in holes in the ground, so aboveground brick and concrete-block pits, such as the Texas "pulley pit," became the standard. It is a large rectangle, perhaps 4 feet high, 10 feet long, and 4 feet wide, with a cooking grate below the top and a flat metal lid that was lifted by a rope through a pulley hanging from the ceiling. To prevent another Great Chicago Fire, and to prevent smoke from filling the room, a unique variation called the "aquarium pit" evolved in Chicago. A large box of thick, tempered glass rises from the bricks and connects to the chimney making it look like a giant aquarium. They are still used in a dozen or so restaurants, mostly on the South Side and, although a few can be found elsewhere, they remain emblematic of Chicago barbecue.

Chicago's reputation for ribs was given a boost in 1974 when, in an episode of the Korean War sitcom, M.A.S.H., Dr. Hawkeye Pierce got so fed up with the food that he called a restaurant named Adam's Ribs in Chicago and placed an order to be delivered to his mobile hospital in South Korea as medical supplies. In real life there was no Adam's Ribs, although years later a restaurant renamed itself to take advantage of the fame of the story.

Then, in 1982, the *Chicago Sun-Times* Pulitzer Prize–winning columnist Mike Royko bragged that he made the best ribs anywhere and launched the annual Royko Ribfest in Grant Park. One of the nation's first large barbecue competitions, the event became an overnight sensation with more than 400 contestants. Almost from the outset, vegetarians began pestering Royko for permission to enter nonmeat "ribs." The crotchety columnist wrote that he had nothing personal against vegetarians, "In fact, I occasionally eat vegetables—a tiny onion in a martini or a stalk of celery in a Bloody Mary." The contest grew to almost 1,000 entrants, but Royko tired of the hassle and wriggled out of the job in 1987. Without him, it petered out and shut down in 1990.

The winner of the inaugural Royko Ribfest was an African American from Mississippi, Charlie Robinson, who parlayed his instant fame into the restaurant Robinson's No. 1 Ribs in the near western suburb of Oak Park and a line of sauces and spices. In 1985, brothers Dave and Larry Raymond came in second in the Royko Ribfest. Their sauce was so good that Dave bottled it and started selling it wholesale from the trunk of his car. In 2001, the brand was bought by the large food processor, Ken's Foods. Now Sweet Baby Ray's is by far the most popular barbecue sauce in the nation with about 40 percent of the market, although it is no longer made in Chicago.

Today there are five distinct styles of Chicago ribs: Delta style, "boilbecue," smokeless roast, digital, and fusion barbecue.

1) Delta style. A dozen or so pitmasters, mostly South Side African Americans, still cook in aquarium pits over wood. Ribs, rib tips, hot links, pulled pork, and chicken are their signature dishes, often served on top of slices of white bread, smushed into a cardboard boat, doused with a sweet-tart tomato-based sauce, and topped with

fries. Many sell carryout only, pretty much like their antecedents did back home under the big shade tree in the Mississippi Delta. Among the remaining Delta-style are Lem's, founded in 1954, and Leon's, founded in 1940.

2) Boilbecue. Meanwhile, Eastern Europeans, many of whom came to rebuild the city after the Great Chicago Fire in 1871, simmered their ribs with cabbage, potatoes, onions, and caraway seeds as they did back home, making a rich stew. But they liked the sweet red sauces of the South, so they pulled the ribs out of the pot, slathered them in sauce, and tossed them on the grill. Boilbecue can be found in scores of restaurants and carryouts around town. Although the boiling makes the meat very tender, alas, much of the meat's flavor comes out in the water.

3) Smokeless roast. Restaurants such as Twin Anchors Restaurant & Tavern, founded in 1932 and a favorite of Frank Sinatra, pop their ribs in the oven to roast, then sauce them, and finish them on the grill. The Gale Street Inn, opened in 1963, also became famous for sweet fall-off-the-bone ribs that are first steamed, then roasted, and then broiled.

4) Digital. Since the year 2000, a dozen or so first-rate restaurants on the North Side and in suburbs have opened, several gaining national renown, among them Smoque and Chicago q. They use gas-fired pits supplemented with logs for flavor, and are fitted with digital thermostats and timers. Many of the old timers have upgraded to the digital smokers, among them Russell's, in Elmwood Park, founded in 1930, and Carson's, a chain launched in 1977 with three locations.

5) Fusion barbecue. Most barbecue tends to stick to the classic Southern canon of ribs, pulled pork, beef brisket, burnt ends, and chicken. But contemporary chefs, many influenced by Asian cuisines, have taken barbecue to exotic new places with creative spices, tomato-free sauces, unusual buns, and unexpected side dishes. Such fusion can be found at places such as bellyQ and Lillie's Q.

Because grilling also is a form of barbecue (from a technical, culinary, historical, and lexicography standpoint), Chicago's worldwide-famed steakhouses are related to the city's equally famed barbecue restaurants.

Contributor: Craig Goldwyn

See also: African Americans

BIBLIOGRAPHY

Amazing Ribs. http://amazingribs.com/index.html.

Robinson, Charlie. *The Charlie Robinson Story from the Son of a Mississippi Delta Sharecropper to the Top of the Chicago Barbecue Charts.* New York: W. P. Norton, 2012.

Wiviot, Gary. *Low & Slow: Master the Art of Barbecue in 5 Easy Lessons.* Philadelphia: The Running Press, 2012.

Bars, Taverns, Saloons, and Pubs

Chicago has a rich history of drinking culture that begins in its earliest days of European settlement. As soon as Chicago became a fur-trading hub in the early 1800s, visitors would travel through and need hotels, which had restaurants and also taverns as part of their hospitality. The first tavern was opened by Archibald Caldwell in 1828 or 1829 at Wolf Point, where the Chicago River's north and south branches meet. Other taverns followed: for example, the Eagle Tavern was turned into The Sauganash Hotel (and Tavern) by its jolly proprietor, Mark Beaubien.

By the mid-1800s, the city was full of drinking establishments, and the term "saloon" came to be used for them. A saloon could be either a tavern, which was attached to an inn, or a grocer dealing with liquor sales. These establishments originally had sample rooms where people could purchase liquor wholesale and sample the goods.

The number of saloons grew dramatically in the late 1800s, due to an increase in population as well as social factors. In 1877, 1,017 saloon licenses were issued in the city; by 1895, there were 6,522. They were frequented predominantly by the working and merchant classes, as the higher classes socialized in private clubs, homes, or bars in elegant hotels. Saloon drinking was mostly a male affair, though some saloons had a side door for women. In working-class neighborhoods, women sometimes joined their husbands for a beer or two, since this was often the only day off in a week. In many places, women did not stand at the bar and might not even enter into the front room, which was a male space, with mustache towels on the bar and spittoons by the brass foot rails full of the disgusting sludge of chewing tobacco.

Bars became social centers of neighborhoods, often divided by ethnic group: Lithuanians went to Lithuanian bars and the Germans went to *biergartens*. (The word *pub*, derived from *public house*, generally was used for Irish establishments.) Customers could find out about job openings or housing possibilities, read the newspapers, and cash paychecks. The saloon came to be knit into the fabric of local politics: Everyone knew and respected the barkeeper, and they often progressed to become alderman or have other political assignments. The most famous was the colorful saloon-keeper Mathias "Paddy" Bauler (1890–1977), a 43rd Ward alderman and political boss known for his statement, "Chicago ain't ready for a reform mayor."

In the late 1800s and early 1900s, bars sold mostly beer and whiskey, and sometimes French brandy. Whiskey was drunk straight and then perhaps with a chaser of water, milk, or buttermilk. Other products included cigars, cigarettes, headache powders, and chocolate bon-bons. These were named "wife pacifiers," because men grabbed them on the way out to appease wives for not being home. Other products sold were laxatives, cola (originally to help with headaches and fatigue), and beef tea, which was considered a hangover cure as well as a quick way to get nutrients.

Bars started to compete with each other with the "free lunch." Buy a drink and your lunch was free. This would consist of pickled vegetables, hard boiled eggs, and sandwiches made with cheap meats. One writer said that the free lunches "would kill a horse." Other activities at saloons included games, such as billiards or handball, and gambling and prostitution.

Up to the turn of the century, bars were the primary public spaces for the working class in Chicago. In many neighborhoods, people were packed into tenement housing and worked backbreaking jobs, and the saloon was a place to "medicate" and escape from toils of work and family life. The neighborhood saloon was the most significant institution outside of the family and church parish and often a place for union meetings and political organizing. By the time of Prohibition, the saloon was intrinsically tied to politics, and politics was tied to the illegal activities in these spheres. In the beginning of Prohibition, saloon business was mostly business as usual, except clientele might enter through a side door.

Even before Prohibition, reformers spoke out against saloons. Jane Addams called for more public parks to allow people to congregate. With the rise of the movie theater and the movement to the suburbs, the old urban saloon culture began to fade even before Prohibition. After Prohibition, the word "saloon" almost disappeared because of its unsavory reputation, even in official licenses issued by the state of Illinois. "Bar" and "cocktail lounge" became the trendy vocabulary.

Neighborhood bars for decades functioned with the rhythms of the workers nearby. People drank at the bar before work, during lunch, and after work. Factories operated 24/7. The 1950s saw the rise of the cocktail lounge. Bars evolved with changing social needs. The 1970s saw the rise of the "singles club."

With the deindustrialization of Chicago from the 1970s into the 1990s, entire neighborhood economies disintegrated. When factories closed, all the bars around them closed, too. In the 1990s, Mayor Richard M. Daley revoked hundreds of liquor licenses, saying, "A bad liquor establishment can tear the fabric of a neighborhood and send it into decline."

Contributor: Amanda Scotese
See also: Prohibition; Speakeasies

BIBLIOGRAPHY

Duis, Perry Duis. *The Saloon: Public Drinking in Chicago and Boston, 1880–1920*. Urbana: University of Illinois Press, 1999.

Moser, Whet. "The Decline of the Chicago Neighborhood Tavern: A Daley and Demographic Legacy." *Chicago Magazine*, February 13, 2012. http://www.chicagomag.com/Chicago-Magazine/The-312/February-2012/The-Decline-of-the-Chicago-Neighborhood-Tavern-A-Daley-and-Demographic-Legacy/.

Smith, Henry Justin. *Chicago's Greatest Century, 1833–1933*. Chicago: Consolidated Publishers, 1933. http://archive.org/stream/chicagosgreatcen00smit/chicagosgreatcen00smit_djvu.txt.

Bayless, Rick and Deann

Rick Bayless refers to himself as a "gringo from Oklahoma," yet he has become one of America's leading emissaries of Mexican cuisine. With his wife and partner, Deann, Bayless has been on a culinary odyssey as an award-winning chef, restaurateur, author, TV personality, salsa manufacturer, and teacher. Bayless was born in Oklahoma City in 1953 into the fourth generation of a family of restaurateurs and grocery store owners. Although without Mexican roots, Bayless has said he felt a spiritual connection to Mexico from childhood. He pursued an undergraduate degree in Spanish language and literature and Latin American culture at the University of Oklahoma and a master's degree in linguistics at the University of Michigan. Here he met Deann Groen (born 1949), who had graduated earlier with advanced degrees in English Language and Literature. He had nearly completed his PhD in anthropological linguistics when he decided to leave academia and devote himself full time to teaching cooking classes, running a catering business, and hosting *Cooking Mexican*, his first PBS show in 1979, the same year he married Deann.

Rick and Deann Bayless. Photograph by Chris Cassidy.

In the early 1980s, the Baylesses began a five-year, 35,000-mile grassroots exploration of Mexico's diverse regional cuisine, taking copious notes. In 1987 they published *Authentic Mexican: Regional Cooking from the Heart of Mexico*, which is still considered a classic today. Immediately after the book's publication, The Baylesses opened Frontera Grill, a casual 70-seat restaurant on Clark Street.

Working closely with local farmers and purveyors, Bayless showcased the vibrant flavors of authentic Mexican cuisine, such as complexly spiced moles, light citrus marinades, grilled quail, smoky chilies, and cilantro-enhanced dishes. Frontera Grill was an immediate success. In 1989, the Baylesses opened Topolobampo, a 75-seat fine-dining restaurant, adjacent to Frontera. In 2010 they opened Xoco, a smaller eatery offering Mexican street food: in 2016, they opened both Leña Brava and Cerveceria Cruz Blanca, a brewery. They also operate several quick-service restaurants.

Over his career, Bayless has won most of the food industry's top awards, including the James Beard Award as Outstanding Chef in the United States (1995) and Humanitarian of the Year (1998). Frontera Grill won the James Beard Award for Outstanding Restaurant in the United States (2007). Bayless also won Bravo's "Top Chef Masters" competition in 2009.

Saying they wanted to give back to the community, the Baylesses launched Frontera Farmer Foundation to provide grants for small family-owned farms in the Midwest. The couple started their own company, Frontera Foods, which produces sauces and salsas from regional recipes. In September 2016, the Baylesses sold Frontera Foods to ConAgra for a reported $108.9 million.

Rick Bayless's celebrity chef status took a quantum leap in the early 2000s, when he began his PBS series *Mexico—One Plate at a Time*, with Deann as producer. To date, the couple has produced eight cookbooks. The Baylesses say they intend to further their crusade to make authentic Mexican cuisine accessible to the home cook and to help Americans appreciate Mexican food for the world-class cuisine it is.

Contributor: Scott Warner

See also: Chefs; Frontera Grill, Mexicans; Restaurateurs and Restaurant Groups

BIBLIOGRAPHY

Bayless, Rick. *The Oxford Companion to American Food and Drink*. Oxford: Oxford University Press, 2007.

Daley, Bill. "Deann Groen Bayless, Restaurateur." *Chicago Tribune*, November 3, 2013.

Beatrice Foods

Founded in Nebraska in 1894, the Beatrice Creamery Co. purchased dairy products from farmers and then graded, packaged, and distributed them. The founders, George Everett Haskell and William W. Bosworth, introduced cream separators for farmers to use to speed up production.

Beatrice moved to Chicago in 1913 and the firm thrived. By the 1930s, 30 million gallons of milk and 10 million gallons of ice cream were produced annually. The firm acquired creameries through the years, and was recognized for its "Meadow Gold" brand by World War II. Government rationing of dairy products may have momentarily slowed the company's progress during the war, but ultimately it grew and became known as Beatrice Foods by 1946.

From the 1950s until the 1970s, the company expanded further with the acquisition of Tropicana, Good & Plenty, Shedd's, La Choy, and Peter Pan, to name a few food companies. By 1970, 8,000 Chicagoans called Beatrice their employer. The original dairy distributor was a major player in a variety of food distribution companies. A policy of decentralized management had local managers overseeing the acquired companies and proved to be an enormous success. Beatrice also began to acquire nonfood companies such as Avis Rent-a-Car, Culligan, and Playtex, a profitable move to diversification.

But the model of "let the companies manage themselves" did not prove profitable enough for investors during the 1980s. The demise of Beatrice, according to some, was the acquisition of Esmark in 1984 for $2.7 billion. Outside consultants were called-in and "The sales and marketing functions, including advertising . . . were taken out of the capable hands of plant managers and brokers and assigned to a centralized sales staff," wrote Neil Gazel.

In 1986, the investment firm of Kohlberg Kravis Roberts & Company agreed to buy out Beatrice for $8.7 billion—the largest buyout in history up to that time. By 1991, ConAgra acquired what remained of Beatrice Foods, including Hunt's tomato products, Wesson Oil, and Orville Redenbacher's popcorn. After further brand spinoffs, Beatrice's food manufacturing is limited to snack products and salad dressings.

Contributor: Jenny Lewis

BIBLIOGRAPHY

Cole, Robert J. "Beatrice Is Seeking Esmark." *New York Times*, May 21, 1984. nytimes.com/1984/05/22/business/beatrice-is-seeking-esmark.html.

Gazel, Neil R. *Beatrice: From Buildup through Breakup*. Urbana: University of Illinois Press, 1990.

Chicago City Hall features beehives on its green roof. Courtesy of the Chicago Honey Co-op.

Beekeeping

The practice of providing hives for bees to produce honey for personal household use came to Chicago with European immigrants. Extra honey may have been sold or bartered with friends and neighbors, but it was considered a hobby, not a business, until the mid–twentieth century.

One of these hobby beekeepers who documented her work was Mrs. Frances Glessner, socialite and renowned hostess on Prairie Avenue. Her hives reportedly harvested more than 1,000 pounds of honey a year, which was not only for her renowned table, but used liberally as gifts. Glessner House records include a 1908 note from the future secretary of the treasury in President Taft's cabinet who thanked her for her annual jar of honey, a "chief treasure of our house."

In the late 1970s and early 1980s, horticulturalist and landscaper Michael Thompson installed hives on the roof of Chef Louis Szathmary's The Bakery restaurant on Lincoln Avenue and produced honey there in a quantity enough to sell about 100 pounds a year to Macy's in New York. This convinced Thompson that there was enough business to sustain a change in career paths, and he began building hives and teaching urban beekeeping at the Learning Exchange. Late in the 1970s, Thompson entered Chicago honey in the Illinois State Fair competition and won the "Twenty Pounds Light Honey" category.

The 2000s brought a renewed interest in farm-to-table food products, and interest in bees, honey, and urban beekeeping grew at an astonishing rate. In 2000 Thompson began to jar and sell products at farmers markets and partnered with another beekeeper, Tim Brown, to form the Chicago Honey Co-Op, which sells honey, candles, and other products online, at farmers markets, and in a few boutique retail stores.

In 2005, Brenda Palms Barber founded Sweet Beginnings, a nonprofit group that provides job training to men and women recently released from prison. They care for hives and make, package, and sell products made from the honey. In addition to maintaining more than 100 hives around the city, Sweet Beginnings, in partnership with Chicago's Department of Family Support Services and the North Lawndale Employment Network, installed an apiary at O'Hare Airport. The project has grown to 75 hives, making O'Hare the first and largest on-site airport apiary in the world.

Chicago's unique quality and quantity of honey is exceptional because bees have access to so much flora in the inner city. Built on what was originally farmland, much of the city has sweet clover, many parks and parkways feature linden trees blooming at just the right time for honey production, and residents and the city maintain flower gardens and boxes everywhere, including in the street medians.

Today's harvests also include about 30 urban hives on the grounds of the old stockyards under the modern wind turbine installed by Testa Produce, as well as hives on the roof of City Hall and other downtown city-owned buildings. Thompson estimates that the Co-op harvests more than 2,000 pounds, and other beekeepers are harvesting and selling about 5,000 pounds per year.

Contributor: Judith Dunbar Hines
See also: Agriculture, Urban

BIBLIOGRAPHY

Chicago Honey Co-Op. http://www.chicagohoneycoop.com.
Cook-Dupage Beekeepers Association. http://cookdupagebee keepers.com/.
Sweet Beginnings. http://www.sweetbeginningsllc.com/.

Beer, Breweries, and Brewpubs

Chicago's love of beer is older than the city itself. Before Chicago was even established in 1833, the would-be city was already home to a handful of taverns at Wolf Point, the intersection of the three branches of the Chicago River. Among them was Wolf Point Tavern, which sold a rustic house-brewed ale for six cents per pint to supplement

BEER FESTS

Chicago beer enthusiasts staged small-scale gatherings, such as dinners paired with imported European beers, as early as the 1970s. But beer festivals didn't sink roots in the city for years to come. Among the city's first major beer fests was the Real Ale Festival, started in 1996 by prominent beer enthusiasts Steve Hamburg and Ray Daniels. Staged annually until 2003, the festival was dedicated to "real ale" (or cask beer), and grew from 32 beers at Goose Island's Clybourn Avenue brewpub in its first year to 220 during its last year at the Finkl steel plant in west Lincoln Park.

The same year Real Ale Festival ended, one of the city's signature beer festivals emerged. The Illinois Craft Brewers Guild launched the Festival of Wood and Barrel-Aged Beers (FOBAB for short) to pay homage to a beer style widely credited with being popularized in Chicago by Goose Island Brewing: beer aged in wood barrels. The barrels had formerly been used for bourbon, but also included second-use wine, rye whiskey, and other barrels. FOBAB would come to be one of the nation's great beer festivals, selling out nearly as soon as tickets went on sale.

A year later, Three Floyds Brewing Co. began what would become another signature annual event: Dark Lord Day. At first hatched as a means to release Three Floyds' Dark Lord coffee-vanilla imperial stout, Dark Lord Day quickly became a national attraction, with beer fans descending upon Floyds's Munster, Indiana, brewery to share rare bottles of beer that attendees brought from home. Dark Lord Day grew into an increasingly complex event, eventually featuring ticketed admission and a day of heavy metal music, food, and beer from multiple breweries.

When craft beer saw a spike in popularity in 2010, beer festivals gained further traction. Beer Hoptacular, which would be staged at venues across the city, debuted that year. Chicago Craft Beer Week also began in 2010, and created another of the city's signature beer events as its opening event: Beer Under Glass, which features mostly local brewers pouring beer under the glass of Garfield Park Conservatory.

During the following years, the city and suburbs became home to dozens of festivals, both big (dozens of breweries pouring at Soldier Field and Union Station) and small.

—JOSH NOEL

---

the small amount of drinkable beer that arrived from the Eastern United States.

The city's first proper brewery soon followed. German immigrants William Haas and Konrad Sulzer, who arrived in Chicago from Watertown, New York, in 1833, launched the Haas & Sulzer Brewery, and it was a fast success among the city's fewer than 1,000 residents. Sulzer (who would one day have a large, regional Chicago Public Library named for him near Lincoln Square) sold his stake to William Ogden, the city's future mayor. The brewery thrived and expanded before ownership was sold to William Lill and Michael Diversey, which led to the brewery being renamed Lill & Diversey. They had a four-story brewery at the southeast corner of Chicago Avenue and Pine Street (later renamed Michigan Avenue) that withstood large Chicago fires in 1860 and 1864. It became the largest brewery west of the East Coast. Its flagship beer was Lill's Cream Ale.

Beer became an economic engine for the fast-growing city. Growth brought ample union jobs and a rash of smaller breweries trying to cash in on the beer craze. Some of those breweries shut down quickly, while others grew and profited. Among the latter was the Conrad Seipp Brewery (which would eventually become the city's

largest) and the John A. Huck Brewery. Initially a city of ales, Chicago increasingly embraced lagers, thanks mostly to the surge of German immigrants who opened bars and breweries (and also populated them). As those German immigrants increasingly dominated the beer landscape, lager—the popular style back home—came to dominate.

Largely a draft product in its earliest Chicago days, beer was increasingly bottled during the 1850s. Intense demand caused a ripple effect that helped spawn Milwaukee and St. Louis as the nation's beer-making capitals; because Chicago brewers were unable to make enough beer for its swelling population, its neighbors to the north and south filled the gaps by exporting beer on newly built railroads.

As beer production grew in Chicago, so did the presence of saloons. By 1855, there were 675 of them, a mere 50 of which were owned by native-born Americans; German and Irish immigrants owned most of the rest. The infusion of immigrant-owned bars intensified an anti-immigrant movement and led Mayor Levi Boone of the anti-immigrant Know-Nothing Party to enforce an ordinance requiring bars to close on Sundays (one of the most popular drinking days for many working-class immigrants). Boone also sought to raise the cost of a liquor license from $50 per year to $300, which also was seen as targeting the immigrant population. The result was a riot on April 21, 1855, known as the "Lager Beer Riot," which led to 1 death and 60 arrests.

But the riot did nothing to quell the city's fervor for beer, as bars and breweries continued to open. The brewing industry was particularly fluid, with openings, closings, and consolidations occurring at a rapid clip. By 1869, Chicago brewing had grown into a $2 million industry, with almost as many barrels of beer made per year (246,212) as there were people (298,977). The Great Chicago Fire of 1871 devastated the brewing industry. It was the third major fire for Lill & Diversey, which sustained $500,000 of damage; the Huck brewery was destroyed. However, the disaster opened an even greater avenue for Milwaukee brewers, especially Schlitz, to take advantage of Chicago's need for imported beer.

As the city and its breweries rebuilt in the late nineteenth century—led by the Conrad Seipp Brewing Company, which began exporting outside the city—the number of Chicago taverns reached record numbers. Schlitz increasingly opened "tied houses" (bars bearing its logo and serving its beer), which included close to 60 such bars in the 1890s and early 1900s. In 1882, Chicago also became a beer education center, as Dr. John Ewald Siebel opened such a program bearing his name. It expanded during the 1890s and in 1910 became the Siebel Institute of Technology.

Prohibition began asserting itself in Chicago in 1915, when Mayor William Thompson signed a decree mandating that all city bars be closed on Sundays. The (near) deathblow was dealt with the proclamation of national Prohibition in 1919, which reduced Chicago's 43 breweries to 16. However, with the assistance of organized crime, beer production kept humming, albeit with limited numbers and with the help of the black market.

With the end of Prohibition, local breweries again began to thrive, including Atlas, Berghoff, and Schoenhofen breweries. Meanwhile, Milwaukee again flooded Chicago with beer, further cementing itself as a beer-making capital. By September 1933, 23 breweries operated in the city and, despite great initial demand after Prohibition, overproduction caused prices to tumble. A predatory market emerged in which breweries used free kegs, signage, and glassware to get their product into bars. It was a practice that would endure in Chicago for decades.

A nation of homogeneous and consolidating tastes took a toll on Chicago's brewing industry in the decades that followed. St. Louis and Milwaukee continued to assert their dominance, while Chicago breweries closed and consolidated amid dying local brand loyalty. Those that held on—such as Meister Brau, which was the city's

Beer drinkers in a saloon, 1905. Courtesy of the Chicago History Museum, DN-0003265; Chicago Daily News, Inc.

preeminent local beer—lost market share year-by-year while the big breweries invested increasingly heavily (and to great success) in marketing and advertising. Miller ultimately bought the Meister Brau brand and its idea of "light" beer to solidify its place as one of the nation's major brewers.

The slow death of the Chicago brewing industry was complete in 1978 with the closing of the Peter Hand Brewery on Division Street west of Halsted. Chicago, then second-largest city in the nation, was left to be a battleground for macro brewers to assert supremacy. Budweiser was the early leader, but Schlitz took the lead in the early 1970s; for a time, it seemed so bulletproof that it opened a distribution facility in Chicago. Old Style soon replaced Schlitz as the city's go-to beer, but the Wisconsin-made beer began to lose prominence after the early 1980s with rise of beer imports from Canada, Jamaica, Mexico, and Europe, and the rise of "lite" beer.

While macro beer took hold of the Chicago market, dissension and a longing for diversity began bubbling at the edges. It started with the founding in 1977 of the Chicago Beer Society, which remained dedicated to the best in (mostly) imported beer from Europe served in the proper glass at the proper temperature. It remained a small, but devoted group; 10 years after its founding, it still had fewer than 100 members (though by the mid-1990s, it rocketed upward of 630).

The brewing scene began stirring back to life during the 1980s with the founding of Pavichevich Brewing (and its signature brand, Baderbrau pilsner), Golden

Prairie Brewing Company, and Chicago Brewing Company, among others. None would last.

A smattering of suburban breweries popped up during the 1990s—Two Brothers, Flossmoor Station, and Three Floyds—but the surge began in earnest in 2009 with the opening of Metropolitan Brewing in the Ravenswood neighborhood. In a boom that would mirror national growth, breweries began opening across the city and suburbs at a rapid clip, including Half Acre, Pipeworks, and Revolution, all of which would attract sizable followings for each new product release.

Dozens more production breweries and brewpubs followed, including a second brewery for Lagunitas Brewing, which had been founded in Northern California in 1993 and established itself as one of the nation's most successful brands. By 2015, the Chicago area was home to more than 70 breweries and brewpubs, and the city had launched a website to guide people to craft beer locales: choosechicago.com/craftbeer.

First emerging in the United States on the West Coast in the late 1970s, brewpubs—restaurants where beer is brewed and consumed on-site—didn't reach Chicago until the late 1980s. The city's first, Sieben's River North Brewery, named for a defunct Chicago brewery started by a German immigrant in the 1800s, opened in 1987 at 432 W. Ontario St. The Tap and Growler, at 901 W. Jackson Blvd., followed in 1987. The following May, a retired vice president of Container Corporation launched the city's third brewpub at 1800 N. Clybourn Ave., which he named for a small island in the north branch of the Chicago River—Goose Island. The novelty of such brewpubs briefly captivated the city, though all met struggle. Sieben's closed in 1990 and the space was taken over by the Berghoff Restaurant, which opened a brewpub of its own that would also close after three years. Tap and Growler lasted until 1992. Goose Island would come close to closing when a major construction project next door dramatically deflated business, but it survived, thrived, and eventually opened a production brewery that it would sell to Anheuser-Busch for $38.8 million.

Further brewpubs would sporadically open and close, including Weeghman Park Brewery, a block from Wrigley Field, which declared bankruptcy and become the second Goose Island location in 1999. National brewpub chains soon landed, including three Rock Bottom locations and a Gordon Biersch in suburban Bolingbrook. Brewpubs would find accommodating homes scattered throughout the suburbs, including Mickey Finn's in Libertyville and Flossmoor Station in Flossmoor.

In 2001, Piece Pizza opened in the gentrifying Wicker Park neighborhood, serving New Haven–style pizza. A small brewery in the back produced dozens of award-winning beers. Brewpub openings largely were dormant for the next 10 years, but, mirroring the national rise in craft brewing, a new wave of brewpubs began opening in Chicago: Haymarket Pub and Brewery, Atlas Brewing, Revolution Brewing, Horse Thief Hollow, and DryHop. In 2014, the owner of DryHop, Greg Shuff, announced he would be opening a second brewpub—Corridor Brewing, which would have a different food and beer focus from DryHop—and that he would be opening a chain of brewpubs in the city.

Contributor: Josh Noel

See also: Beer Gardens, Germans

BIBLIOGRAPHY

Agnew, Michael. *A Perfect Pint's Beer Guide to the Heartland.* Urbana: University of Illinois Press, 2014.

Johnson, Julie. "Brew It Yourself: Getting into Homemade Beer." *Chicago Reader,* January 1, 1994.

Neu, Denese. *Chicago by the Pint: A Craft Beer History of the Windy City.* Mt. Pleasant, N.C.: The History Press, 2011.

Skilnik, Bob. *Beer: A History of Brewing in Chicago.* Fort Lee, N.J.: Barricade Books, 2006.

Beer Gardens

German immigrants introduced beer gardens to the United States, as well as the light-colored, bottom-fermented lagers served in them. Chicago, home to many Germans and German Americans, beginning in the mid–nineteenth century, supported numerous outdoor beer gardens, which were affiliated with local brewers. The gardens, some as small as a few tables, others as large as ballrooms, were typically situated above or next to cellars where brewers' beers were aging. These venues helped build brand loyalty because prices were low. People of every ethnicity were welcome.

The first lager beer garden in Chicago was opened in 1847 by a German immigrant brewer from the Rhineland, John Anton Huck (1819–78) and his partner, John Schneider. Huck's Brewery on the Near North Side produced malt liquor and lager beer. The company operated its popular *biergarten* until it and the brewery were destroyed during the Great Chicago Fire of 1871.

As more Germans arrived in Chicago following the unrest in their homeland in 1848, the numbers of brewers and *biergartens* swelled. As early as 1869, the number of "lager beer saloons," which also included *biergartens* and *bierstubes*, was reputed to be "not far short of a thousand." By 1900, Chicago's 60 brewers operated many of the estimated 1,700 beer gardens and taverns throughout the city.

During good weather, families socialized, ate, sang, and enjoyed music in Chicago beer gardens. These settings, planted with trees to provide respite from summer heat, were extensions of their community and home lives. Formal entertainment and traditional German foods, such as soft pretzels with mustard, liverwurst, knockwurst, and bratwursts, were secondary to the *gemütlichkeit* to be found at the gardens. The mostly middle-class men, who often brought their wives and children, frequented these establishments primarily on weekends, including Sundays.

The "Chicago Lager Beer Riot" of 1855 was precipitated when the ultraconservative, xenophobic Know-Nothings pressured fellow party member Mayor Levi Boone to raise the taxes on liquor sales by 600 percent and to enforce laws prohibiting Sunday alcohol and beer sales. The beer lovers won their bloody battle to keep the *biergartens* open on Sundays, although owners were occasionally brought to court for breaking those laws as late as 1859.

Over time, some Chicago *biergartens* became increasingly elaborate, offering professional music, variety shows, dancing, and full German menus in landscaped, parklike, year-round settings. One of the most famous Chicago beer gardens was the Frank Lloyd Wright–designed Midway Gardens in Hyde Park. This indoor/outdoor garden complex was constructed in 1914, but, because of speculator Ed Waller's financial problems, it was sold to the Edelweiss Brewery Company in 1916, then renamed Edelweiss Gardens. The gardens originally catered to an upscale clientele, but after the Edelweiss Company assumed ownership, revamping the complex to appeal to a broader range of patrons, it began to deteriorate. The building, which had been sold again to an automobile tire and supply company, was totally demolished in 1929, a victim of three ownership changes, World War I, and Prohibition.

The Sieben Brewery on the Near North Side operated one of the last brewery-related beer gardens in Chicago until 1967. Michael Sieben (1859–1925), a German immigrant from Ebersheim near Mainz, had established his brewery business in 1865. It narrowly avoided destruction during the Great Chicago Fire, was relocated to North Larrabee Street in 1876, and as of 1903 featured both a *bierstube* and garden. Customers could sing along with a specially written song to King Gambrinus, the patron saint of brewers, while munching on mustard-dipped pretzels, eating hot dogs or liver sausage sandwiches, and drinking beer.

During Prohibition, the brewery was unwittingly leased to associates of Al Capone who were supposed to produce nonalcoholic "near beer" under the name "The George Frank Brewery." In 1933, the Sieben family resumed operation, reopening the *bierstube* and garden.

By 1967, changing demographics and competition from mass-produced beer companies made it unprofitable to continue. A fire destroyed the bottling house in 1968; the brewery buildings were bulldozed a year later.

Contributors: Ellen F. Steinberg and Jack H. Prost

See also: Germans

BIBLIOGRAPHY

Skilnik, Bob. "Building Chicago Was Thirsty Work." *Chicago Tribune*, July 16, 1997.

"The Sunday Gardens at Cottage Grove: Application to Restrain Them." *Chicago Press and Tribune*, July 14, 1859.

"Sunday Resorts: Where and How People Spend the Sabbath." *Chicago Tribune*, July 18, 1869.

The Berghoff

Known for its classic German dishes and namesake beer, this historic Loop eatery stands among a handful of American restaurants that are not only more than a century old, but also family-owned and -operated from day one.

In 1878, Indiana brewery owner Herman Berghoff (1852–1934) opened the Berghoff Café (really a saloon) to serve his own beer. The entrepreneurial Berghoff, who had immigrated to the United States from Germany, sold his beer for 5 cents a glass and 10 cents a stein, along with a free corned beef sandwich. In 1913, the building housing the Café at West Adams and State Streets was razed, and Berghoff moved his business to a 45,000-square-foot facility one door down at 17 W. Adams, where it stands today.

Sons Lewis and Clement turned the place into a full-fledged restaurant. They expanded the menu and created the oak-paneled west dining room with its stained-glass windows, murals, and chandeliers—giving customers a sense of old-world Europe.

During Prohibition, Berghoff survived by serving legal near beer and his own line of soda pops. The restaurant

GLORIA STEINEM DRANK HERE

Until 1969, The Berghoff bar was an all-male stronghold where no female dared set foot on its brass rail. Then, one November day that year, several women who belonged to the National Organization for Women (NOW) walked in, bellied up to the bar with the good old boys—and made history. Not long afterward, New York feminist Gloria Steinem came in for a much publicized drink. The bar has been desegregated ever since.

—SCOTT WARNER

BERGHOFF RESTAURANT CREAMED SPINACH

Creamed spinach is one of the most requested recipes from The Berghoff. Photograph by Carol Mighton Haddix.

Prep: 10 minutes
Cook: 20 minutes
Makes: 8 servings

This popular dish's ingredients were a secret until the restaurant closed temporarily in 2006. This version is adapted from *The Berghoff Family Cookbook.*

2 cups half-and-half
1 cup milk
1 1/2 teaspoons chicken base
1/2 teaspoon hot red pepper sauce
1/2 teaspoon ground nutmeg, plus more for garnish
1/8 teaspoon celery salt
1/2 stick (1/4 cup) unsalted butter
3 cloves garlic, minced
1/4 cup flour
3 packages (10 ounces each) frozen chopped spinach, thawed, squeezed dry
Salt, pepper to taste
Cooked crumbled bacon, optional

1. Place half-and-half, milk, chicken base, red pepper sauce, nutmeg, and celery salt in a medium saucepan; heat over medium-high just until simmering. Remove from heat; keep warm.

2. Heat butter in a separate medium saucepan over medium heat. Add garlic; cook, stirring, 1 minute. Whisk in flour; cook, stirring often, 2 to 3 minutes. Slowly whisk warm milk mixture into butter mixture a little at a time. Cook over medium heat, stirring, until thick, about 5 minutes. Stir in spinach; simmer 5 minutes. Season with salt and pepper to taste. Garnish with bacon and additional nutmeg, if desired.

began serving wiener schnitzel, sauerbraten, German pot roast, apple strudel, potato pancakes, and other classics. The Berghoff butchered its own meat and made its own bread and pastries.

At Prohibition's end in 1933, Herman managed to obtain retail liquor licenses Number 1 (for the bar) and Number 2 (for the restaurant), which are on permanent display. Herman worked at the restaurant regularly until his sudden death in 1934.

When Herman's namesake grandson turned 70 years old in 2005, he announced he wanted to retire and closed the restaurant in February 2006. Crowds lined up for what appeared to be a last meal. Meanwhile, the founder's great-granddaughter Carlyn Berghoff, a successful caterer and graduate of the Culinary Institute of America, found that her catering facility lease was up for renewal. At her father's invitation, she moved her business into the Berghoff space and began a new company called Berghoff Catering & Restaurant Group. Carlyn reopened the restaurant spaces, keeping many of the classics on the menu and giving new life to the family business. As the Berghoff's fourth-generation owner, Carlyn preserved the Berghoff legacy by writing two books, coauthored with Nancy Ross Ryan: *The Berghoff Family Cookbook* and *The Berghoff Cafe Cookbook.* In 2016, Carlyn retired and her brother, Peter Berghoff, who

Herman Berghoff with the city's first liquor license after Prohibition. Courtesy of The Berghoff Restaurant.

had run The Berghoff Café in O'Hare International Airport, took over operation of the restaurant.

Contributor: Scott Warner
See also: Beer and Breweries; Germans, Prohibition; Restaurateurs and Restaurant Groups

BIBLIOGRAPHY
Berghoff, Carlyn, Jan Berghoff, and Nancy Ross Ryan. *The Berghoff Family Cookbook*. Kansas City, Mo.: Andrews McMeel Publishing, 2007.

Berolzheimer, Ruth

Theresa Ruth Berolzheimer (1886–1965) served as the director and editor of the Chicago-based Culinary Arts Institute (CAI), a cookbook-focused imprint of Consolidated Book Publishers. Berolzheimer's family relocated to Chicago Heights from Missouri around the turn of the century where she founded the town's first Hebrew school at the age of 17. After graduating from the University of Illinois with a degree in chemical engineering—the second woman in the school's history to do so—she began a career in social work with stints at Milwaukee's Abraham Lincoln House, where she worked on the fifth edition of founder Lizzie Black Kander's *Settlement Cookbook*, and in New York City, where she served as managing editor of *Good Eating Magazine*.

She returned to Chicago in 1938 to take the reins at the CAI, whose origins go back to the 1860s with a New York–based fashion magazine called the *Delineator* that published recipes for homemakers. With an enormous catalog of recipes, the CAI published hundreds of titles between 1937 and 1989, and operated a test kitchen at several locations in Chicago with a staff of women overseen by Berolzheimer. Despite this, Berolzheimer apparently wasn't much of a cook, according to her nephew, who said her talents were in publishing.

Her name appeared on every title published during her tenure, including the CAI's most notable *The American Woman's Cookbook*, an 800-plus page compendium that sold a million copies by 1943. Berolzheimer also oversaw publication of titles as diverse as *The Encyclopedic Cookbook*, *The Dairy Cookbook*, *Body-Building Dishes for Children*, *500 Sandwiches*, and *250 Ways to Prepare Meat*. She retired to southern California in 1949.

Contributor: Mike Sula
See also: Cookbooks

BIBLIOGRAPHY
Daniels, Frank, "A Cookbook Lover's Guide to the Culinary Arts Institute." 2000. http://friktech.com/cai/cai.htm.

Sula, Mike, "The Cookbook Queen." *Chicago Reader*, September 11, 2008. http://www.chicagoreader.com/chicago/the-cookbook-queen/Content?oid=1106100.

Beverage Testing Institute

Founded in 1981, Beverage Testing Institute's (BTI) mission is to provide the public and commercial firms unbiased information about wine, beer, and spirits. The institute originally tested only wines to provide reviews for wineries and for the public. Craig Goldwyn, a wine writer, began the review service to help consumers make more informed buying decisions. It since has expanded testing to include all alcoholic beverages. When Goldwyn departed the institute, Jerold O'Kennard took the helm as director.

Today, the institute offers buying guides in publications across the world and on its website, www.tastings.com. Tasting panels include staff members and guest experts such as restaurateurs, sommeliers, retailers, and writers who taste the products blind. BTI organizes annual world competitions in wine, beer, and spirits and produces an annual World Value Wine Challenge. Scores are based on an 80- to 100-point scale. Medals are awarded for the best beverages in their categories. Scores also are published in an e-newsletter called "e-Tastings." Through the years, BTI has become one of the most respected testing services in the beverage industry and a reliable guide for consumers everywhere.

Contributor: Carol Mighton Haddix

BIBLIOGRAPHY
Gray, Joe. "Chicago-based Tasting Panel Rates the Top Bargains in Wine." *Chicago Tribune*, January 10, 2006.
Nachel, Marty. "Beverage Testing Institute." Real Beer, 1997. www.realbeer.com.

Big Baby

The Big Baby is a double cheeseburger that originated and is still found mainly in the working-class neighborhoods of the Southwest Side around Midway Airport. Though the burger isn't radically different from some other inexpensive double cheeseburgers, the preparation as well as the name have been widely copied locally.

The Big Baby was introduced in the late 1960s at Nicky's, a small local chain of hot dog and hamburger shops started by Nicky Vaginas on West 63rd Street in Summit. The classic Big Baby consists of two griddle-cooked thin beef patties (often one-sixth pound) with a single slice of processed American cheese in between on a toasted sesame seed bun. Condiments are limited to ketchup, mustard, and several dill pickle slices beneath the patties and a tangle of sliced, sautéed onions on top. It's not uncommon to find lettuce, tomatoes, and even mayonnaise as options, but such additions were not found on the original and are shunned by the purists.

A handful of Nicky's founded by Mr. Vaginas, some still run by his associates, are found around Midway, but most Big Babies are served by newer establishments (sometimes named Nicky's) scattered throughout the Southwest Side and spreading through the Chicago region.

Contributor: Peter Engler

BIBLIOGRAPHY

"The Burger That Ate Chicago." *Time Out Chicago*, July 29, 2005. http://www.timeout.com/chicago/food-drink/the-burger-that-ate-chicago.

Billy Goat Tavern

The tavern and grill was founded by Greek immigrant William "Billy Goat" Sianis, and now is run by his nephew Sam Sianis. The most famous of several locations is located on the lower level of 430 N. Michigan Ave.

The Billy Goat began when the elder Sianis bought the Lincoln Tavern at 1855 W. Madison St.—across the street from the Chicago Stadium—in 1933 with a bounced personal check for $205 (later repaid with the first weekend's receipts). Sianis changed the name of his tavern in 1934, when he rescued and adopted an injured baby goat that had fallen from a truck onto the road in front of the bar.

Sianis scored an early public relations success when he posted a "No Republicans served here" sign in the window while Chicago was hosting the 1944 Republican National Convention. The bar was swarmed with delegates demanding to be served, and Sianis reported receipts of $2,600 for a single day.

The Michigan Avenue location opened in March 1964. Owing to its proximity to the major Chicago newspapers and bureaus, it soon became known as a late-night hangout for journalists, columnists, and printers. Notable local journalists with their bylines posted on the tavern's wall include Mike Royko (who often wrote about the Billy Goat), Roger Ebert, and Dave Condon. Other locations have since opened in Chicago and one in Washington, D.C.

The Billy Goat gained national fame through a series of *Saturday Night Live* television sketches written by Bill Murray and Don Novello, both Billy Goat regulars who admitted basing the sketch on Sianis's tavern. John Belushi starred in the sketches, in which a series of customers attempt to order and find out that the restaurant serves only cheeseburgers. Catchphrases from the sketch involving attempted orders for Coca-Cola ("No Coke, Pepsi!") and French fries ("No fries, chips!) are still in use at the original location. The sketch's biggest contribution to the Billy Goat's reputation is the pronunciation and repetition of its signature menu item: "Cheeseborger! Cheeseborger!"

The Billy Goat also is known for a "curse" placed on the Chicago Cubs by Sianis, following game four of the 1945 World Series against the Detroit Tigers. Sianis and his goat (wearing a sign saying "We Got Detroit's Goat") were ejected from Wrigley Field over complaints from Cubs owner P. K. Wrigley about the animal's smell. Following the series, won in seven games by Detroit, Sianis sent a telegram to Wrigley reading "Who stinks now?"

The team and tavern have undertaken efforts to lift the curse after an epic collapse in the 1969 pennant race. The Cubs invited a goat into the stadium and onto the field, including it in opening day ceremonies in the 1984 and 1989 seasons, years in which the Cubs won division titles. The curse apparently was lifted when the Cubs won the World Series in November 2016. But oddly enough, the only Billy Goat location ever to fail was located at 3516 N. Clark St., a stone's throw from Wrigley Field.

Contributor: John Carruthers
See also: Greeks

BIBLIOGRAPHY

http://www.billygoattavern.com/legend/our-history/.
Kogan, Rick. *A Chicago Tavern: A Goat, a Curse, and the American Dream*. Chicago: Lake Claremont Press, 2006.

Binny's Beverage Depot

When Harold Binstein died in August 1995, he left behind a 13-store retail chain of liquor stores called Gold Standard Enterprises Inc., headquartered in Skokie. Binstein had started Gold Standard in 1952 with a small store near Wrigley Field. His son Michael took over the chain after his father's death. He expanded the family business by opening new stores and acquiring others, including those owned by Sam's Wine & Spirits, Chalet Wine & Cheese, Zimmerman's Liquors, and Armanetti's Fine Wines & Liquors. By mid-2016, the chain had 35 stores in Illinois, most of them in the Chicago area but one as far south as Champaign, all under the Binny's Beverage Depot banner.

Contributor: Colleen Sen
See also: Wine and Wineries

BIBLIOGRAPHY

White, Monée Fields. "Binny's Growth Cocktail." *Crain's Detroit Business*, October 30, 2009.

Blackbird Restaurant

Consistently on the top lists of Chicago's best restaurants, and earning a 4-star review from the *Chicago Tribune* and a Michelin star each year since 2011, Blackbird has earned a national reputation. Opened in 1997 by Rick Diarmit, Donnie Madia, Eduard Seitan, and chef Paul Kahan (they later formed the One Off Hospitality Group Ltd.), the restaurant at 619 W. Randolph St. is known for casual elegance in food, service, and decor. Architect Thomas Schlesser earned the James Beard Foundation's award for Best Restaurant Design in 2002 for Blackbird's spare room in white, gray, and red oak. Kahan and his kitchen staff produce seasonal, local dishes with creative flair. Their fixed-price lunch is one of the city's best fine-dining bargains. According to *Chicagoist*, Blackbird is "for foodies who want to experience culinary mastery, but can't afford to empty a month's pay into one evening."

Contributor: Carol Mighton Haddix

See also: Kahan, Paul; Restaurants and Fine Dining

BIBLIOGRAPHY

Ram, Chandra. "The Blackbird Project." *Plate* magazine online. 2015. http://www.blackbird/plateonline.com.

Blackhawk Restaurant

The Blackhawk restaurant sated the appetites of food and music lovers from the moment Otto Roth opened the doors at 139 N. Wabash Ave. on December 27, 1920, until his son Don Roth closed them 64 years later. Father and son were savvy innovators, tapping into diners' desires and setting trends before the word "trendsetter" became part of America's vernacular.

By 1926, Otto Roth had become one of the first restaurateurs to mix dinner and dancing. He put in a dance floor and settled Carlton Coon, Joe Sanders, and their Kansas City Nighthawks on the bandstand. Shows were broadcast live over WGN radio and were so popular—other entertainers included Louis Prima, Glenn Miller, Perry Como, and a 4-year-old Mel Torme—that Western Union put a ticker tape on the bandstand to field requests from across the country.

When Otto Roth died in 1944, Don Roth nurtured the restaurant for another 40 years, transitioning in 1952 from the dinner-and-dancing concept to a restaurant where "the food's the show." "We were a hearty restaurant," said Roth, "But we knew that we had to replace the big bands with something revolutionary if we were to survive." Food carts of prime rib rolled through the dining room, a 15-shrimp

cocktail and Boston scrod were on the menu. The star? A spinning salad bowl. The tableside theatrics featured a salad bowl set on ice and surrounded by 21 ingredients, including a secret dressing.

Roth opened several other restaurants (on Pearson Street and on Wabash Avenue north of the Chicago River) plus Don Roth's Blackhawk in Wheeling. The original Blackhawk restaurant closed in 1984. Much of its memorabilia became part of the Wheeling location, which ran 30 years before closing in 2009. Don Roth, one of the creators of Taste of Chicago, also was involved in national and local restaurant organizations, often serving in leadership roles. He died on November 21, 2003.

The restaurant, a legend to several generations, was named for the U.S. Army's Blackhawk infantry division, which in turn was named for the chief of the Fox and Sauk tribes in Illinois. The restaurant proved just as resilient. A stink bomb was tossed into the restaurant on opening night, which cleared the restaurant until "a lake breeze supplied a new atmosphere," according to news reports, sending guests back into The Blackhawk to continue celebrating. And when a statewide horse-meat scandal erupted, civic authorities closed the restaurant. Roth challenged the charges in court, where a jury found the restaurant innocent. Upon reopening, business went up.

Contributor: Judy Hevrdejs

BIBLIOGRAPHY

Black, Lisa. "Don Roth's Blackhawk Takes One Last Spin Around: Wheeling Landmark Closes after 30 Years with Memories for All." *Chicago Tribune*, January 1, 2010.

Leonard, Will. "Blackhawk's 40th Anniversary Stirs Fond Memories." *Chicago Sunday Tribune*, October 23, 1960.

Blogs (See: Media, New)

Blommer's Chocolate Company

The oldest and largest cocoa bean processor in North America, Blommer's produces chocolate coatings, compound and specialty products, carob coatings and drops, chocolate liquor, cocoa powder, and cocoa butter. In addition to supplying the wholesale market with chocolate products, Blommer also has a retail outlet store at its Kinzie Street location.

Blommer's is a fourth-generation family company, founded in 1939 by Henry Blommer Sr. with brothers Al and Bernard. The Blommer brothers made their first delivery of liquid chocolate from their new plant on Kinzie

Street. They laid a foundation for their business by offering chocolate pricing based on the New York Cocoa Exchange quotes.

After Henry's death in 1992, the family averted a takeover from Cargill Corporation through a buyback program. In 1997, Blommer's produced 275 million pounds of chocolate and processed 5 percent of the world's cocoa beans. By 2008, it was processing 50 percent of all U.S. cocoa bean imports. Blommer's joined six other companies to develop the World Cocoa Foundation in 2000, and in 2007, expanded its sustainable initiatives program to West Africa. It now has four factories around the United States and Canada.

Blommer's has long been noted for the chocolate aroma emanating from its factory: It is a feature of downtown Chicago life. In a 2006 segment of National Public Radio's "This American Life," a reporter described the smell emanating from Blommer's as the "smell of magic."

Contributor: Geraldine Rounds

See also: Candy

BIBLIOGRAPHY

Amer, Robin. "Blommer, Where the Bridges Smell like Chocolate." www.wbez.org. April 11, 2012.

Rosenthal, Phil. "Inside Blommer Chocolate: Family and Cocoa at 75." *Chicago Tribune*, May 18, 2014.

Boka Restaurant Group

Kevin Boehm and Rob Katz met, formed their company, and opened their first restaurant in 2003 in Lincoln Park. They called it Boka, using their last names for inspiration, and served an eclectic menu of modern American dishes. From there, the duo created a series of chef-driven restaurants, all with unique differences and cuisines that steadily earned 3-star reviews and awards for rising-star chefs, best restaurants, and best restaurateurs. Chef/partners include some of the top names in fine dining: Mark Hellyar at Momotaro, Stephanie Izard at Girl & the Goat, Chris Pandel at Balena, Giuseppe Tentori at G. T. Fish & Oyster, Paul Virant at Perennial Virant, and Lee Wolen at Boka. The group runs a dozen popular restaurants, including a bar, a diner, a coffee shop, and the latest, Swift and Sons steakhouse. It also created the Boka Catering Group in 2012.

Contributor: Carol Mighton Haddix

See also: Izard, Stephanie; Restaurateurs and Restaurant Groups

BIBLIOGRAPHY

Vettel, Phil. "The Boka Restaurateurs behind Star Chefs." *Chicago Tribune*, February 19, 2014.

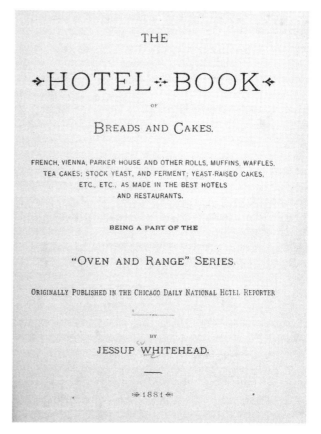

THE

✦ HOTEL ✦ BOOK ✦

OF

BREADS AND CAKES.

FRENCH, VIENNA, PARKER HOUSE AND OTHER ROLLS, MUFFINS, WAFFLES, TEA CAKES; STOCK YEAST, AND FERMENT; YEAST-RAISED CAKES, ETC., ETC., AS MADE IN THE BEST HOTELS AND RESTAURANTS.

BEING A PART OF THE

"OVEN AND RANGE" SERIES.

ORIGINALLY PUBLISHED IN THE CHICAGO DAILY NATIONAL HOTEL REPORTER

BY

JESSUP WHITEHEAD.

✦ 1881 ✦

One of Jessup Whitehead's many publications, 1881. Archive.org.

Books and Publishers

Food and drink books about Chicago, written by Chicagoans or published in Chicago, would fill a sizable bookcase. Cookbooks of every kind were produced in the city, from nineteenth-century recipe collections and household-tips manuals to publications from newspapers throughout the years. Ethnic books, written in native languages and intended to celebrate immigrant cultures, reflected Chicago's diverse communities. So did the ubiquitous community cookbooks that date to the Civil War Sanitary Fairs. The range was, and still is, wide.

Cookbooks published before about 1900 were usually addressed to upper- and upper-middle-class women who had servants to do the cooking. Because the burgeoning economy produced a number or such household managers, cookbooks sold well. By World War I, servants had largely disappeared from all but the wealthiest households, and cookbooks became more democratized with simpler recipes for families who did their own cooking. That is when compilations taken from newspaper columns appeared and continue to be published to this day. Other

COOKBOOK STORES

Chicago's first store exclusively devoted to cookbooks and books about food was Season to Taste, opened in 1988 by Barry Bluestein and Kevin Morissey at 911 W. School St. In addition to serving as a center for food and cooking information, it hosted receptions and readings by authors. Faced with competition from discount book stores, Season to Taste closed in October 1992.

In 2015, Esther Dairiam, inspired by Paris' Librarie Gourmande, opened Read It and Eat at 2142 N. Halsted St. In addition to general and specialty cookbooks, the store stocks food biographies and memoirs, books on diet and nutrition, and food histories. It also has a working kitchen for classes.

Chicagoan Laura Maye founded an online, used cookbook store in 2013 called Edible Type Books. With more than 1500 titles available, it offers modern and vintage choices such as a rare copy of a limited edition 1976 Italian-English cookbook ($450).

—COLLEEN SEN

kinds of books about food include guides to the city and special events. They are snapshots of what public and some private dining were like at the time of publication.

Major publishing houses in Chicago (the first was started by Roger Fergus in 1839) seldom addressed cooking. There were popular nationally distributed cookbooks, and, occasionally, an individual would publish a book. Such is the case of the earliest known Chicago-produced cookbook: Isaac A. Poole's 58-page *The Cake Baker, A Book of Practical Receipts for Making Cake* (1857), based on recipes from Cooper's bakery in New York City.

In 1858, S. C. Griggs & Co. published a new edition of the nationally popular *The American Housewife*, but with a new title, *An Experienced Lady. The Kitchen Directory and American Housewife: Containing Valuable and Original Receipts in All the Various Branches of Cookery.* Like others in this era, the book contained recipes for home remedies and household cleaning.

Cookbooks used as fund-raisers were abundant; many were nonprofit community cookbooks composed of recipes from club or church members. Naomi Donnelley, whose husband founded the R. R. Donnelley (Lakeside Press) printing company, wrote cooking manuals to support the fledgling business. In 1878, she wrote two books, *The Lakeside Cook Book: A Complete Manual of Practical, Economical, Palatable and Healthful Cookery* and *The Lakeside Cook Book No. 2; A Manual of Recipes for Cooking, Pickling, and Preserving.*

Newspapers began the tradition of compiling recipes from their food columns in book form in the late 1800s. One of the first was something of a community cookbook: *The Chicago Daily Tribune: The Home Guide; or, a Book by 500 Ladies, Embracing about 1,000 Recipes and Hints, Pertaining to Cookery, the Household, the Sick Room, the Toilet, etc.* (1877). Jessup Whitehead's *The Chicago Herald cooking school: A Professional Cook's Book for Household Use* (1883), consisted of a series of menus and recipes for everyday meals and entertaining, with minute instructions for making every dish named. The information came from his "Oven and Range" columns. Whitehead was a prolific author of professional manuals between 1870 and 1910. *The Chicago Record Cook Book* (1896) was another popular volume. Later newspaper-based recipe books included Jane Eddington's *The Tribune Cookbook* (1925) and Mary Martensen's *Mrs. Mary Martensen's Recipes Reprinted from the Chicago American* (1932).

The World's Columbian Exposition of 1893 brought forth fair-related books, including Carrie V. Schuman's compilation, *Favorite Dishes, A Columbian Autograph Souvenir Cookery Book* (1893) and Juliet Corson's edited volume, *The "Home Queen" World's Fair Souvenir Cookbook: Two Thousand Valuable Recipes on Cookery and Household Economy, Menus, Table Etiquette, Toilet, etc. / Contributed by over Two Hundred World's Fair Lady Managers, Wives of Governors and Other Ladies of Position and Influence.* Sarah Tyson Rorer's *Recipes Used in Illinois Corn Exhibit Model Kitchen, Women's Building, Columbian Exposition, Chicago, 1893* was specific to one major exhibit, as was Mary J. B. Lincoln's discussion of scientific cooking, *Extracts from Cookery, or Art and Science versus Drudgery and Luck. In The Congress of Women, Held in the Women's Building, World's Columbian Exposition, Chicago, U. S. A., 1893.* Adele Hollingsworth's *The Columbia Cookbook* was a repurposed book previously published in Philadelphia though with some recipes (uncredited) from prominent Chicago restaurateurs.

Chicago's world's fairs also produced many guides to the city's attractions. The 1893 World's Columbian Exposition brought forth *Chicago by Day and Night, A Pleasure Seeker's Guide to the Paris of America* (1892), with a section on dining out, ranging from top restaurants to moderately priced cafeterias. Railroads promoted Chicago tourism with such books as 1912's *Chicago for the Tourist* by the Illinois Central Railroad. It particularly recommended the city's fabulous "Chop Suey" restaurants. One of the best guides was written for the Century of Progress world's fair: Newspaperman John Drury's *Dining in Chicago* (1931) is a treasure trove for anyone interested in food history.

With its huge immigrant population in the late 1800s, the city produced a number of ethnic cookbooks. François Tanty's *La Cuisine Française, French Cooking for Every Home Adapted to American Requirements* (1893) was for middle-class and elite homes. Scandinavian and German cookbooks reflected those populations in the city still using their native languages. One popular book among immigrant groups, Mrs. F. L Gillett's *White House Cookbook*, was translated into German by Hugo Ziemann as *Das Weisse Haus Kochbuch* (1893). An early Asian book was published by Rand McNally, the Chicago map and guidebook firm: *The Chinese-Japanese Cookbook* by Sara Bosse and Onoto Watanna (Winnifred Eaton, 1914). Descendants of immigrants were fully American by the second and third generations, so community cookbooks were written in English. One of them, the *Lawndale Chapter Book of Recipes* (1931), by Emily Kerner (sister of Governor Otto Kerner), came from the West Side Bohemian community.

A notable source for cookbooks, Consolidated Book Publishers, produced a series of Culinary Arts Institute (CAI) books from 1938 to the late 1980s. The publisher's *The American Woman's Cookbook* (1939), edited by Ruth Berolzheimer, sold a million copies within its first five years. CAI published so many cookbooks that most used bookshops in America today have one or more of them on their shelves.

After World War II, women returning from factory jobs found more time to cook. Book publishers, mainly in New York City, slowly increased their cookbook acquisitions. As dining out and entertaining at home became popular, so, too, did books on food. Perhaps the most iconic Chicago cookbook was the *Antoinette Pope School Cookbook* (1948) by Antoinette and François Pope, owners of The Antoinette Pope School of Fancy Cookery.

While important, the Pope book had considerable competition. Meta Given, for example, after teaching home economics at the University of Chicago, wrote the popular *Modern Family Cookbook* (1942), followed by her two-volume Meta Given's *Modern Encyclopedia of Cooking* (1947). Ruth Ellen Church, who also wrote under the pen name Mary Meade, edited the *Chicago Tribune*'s food columns from 1936–74. Her books included Mary Meade's *Magic Recipes for the Electric Blender* (1952), *The Indispensable Guide for the Modern Cook*

(1955), and *Entertaining With Wine* (1978). Later *Tribune* cookbooks would include *The Chicago Tribune Good Eating Cookbook* and many more.

Alma Lach, the food editor of the *Chicago Sun-Times* from 1957 to 1965, wrote *A Child's First Cookbook* in 1950. She went on to host an early television cooking show and to earn the Grand Diplome at Le Cordon Bleu in Paris. Her best-known book *Hows and Whys of French Cooking* was published in 1974 by the University of Chicago Press. The press's list includes mostly scholarly food books, but it has published some cookbooks, such as Lach's and, most recently, *The Big Jones Cookbook: Recipes for Savoring the Heritage of Regional Southern Cooking*, by Chicago chef Paul Fehribach.

Several of the Chicago area's resident cookbook writers have been especially prolific, a category that includes Elaine Gonzalez, Barbara Grunes, Sue Spitler, and more. Also prolific are the many community cookbooks from churches and groups in the city and suburbs. The two volumes done by the Ravinia Festival Women's Board, *Noteworthy* and *Noteworthy Two*, are probably the best known. Others include *One Magnificent Cookbook* and *Soupcon I: Seasonal Samplings* from the Junior League of Chicago.

Many of Chicago's new crop of cookbook writers are working with Evanston-based Agate Publishing and its imprint, Surrey Books, headed by Doug Seibold, a publisher with an interest in both food and culture. Surrey Books was founded in 1982 by Susan Schwartz and published many cookbooks with a focus on diet and health. Agate bought Surrey in 2006 and made it Agate's food and dining imprint. One best-selling Surrey title is *Gluten-Free Baking Classics* by Annalise Roberts (2006). Another top seller was *Indian Slow Cooker* (2010), by Anupy Singla.

Since the mid-1970s, Publications International in Lincolnwood has churned out cookbooks on many topics and books for food companies and products such as Campbell Soup Co., M&Ms, Crock-Pot, and Coca-Cola. Chicago Review Press and its Academy Chicago Imprint bring out occasional books such as *The Jane Austen Cookbook* and *The Supper Club Book*.

As Chicago chefs have become celebrities, many of them have taken up the pen to write books about their restaurants and recipes. One of the first celebrity chefs was Louis Szathmary of The Bakery restaurant. He wrote many books, including *The Bakery Restaurant Cookbook* (1980). Later chef/authors include such well-known Chicago names as Rick Bayless, *Authentic Mexican: Regional Cooking From the Heart of Mexico*, 1987; and Charlie Trotter, *The Charlie Trotter Cookbook*, 1994. Other more recent chef/authors include Grant Achatz, Stephanie Izard, Doug Sohn, Ina Pinkney, Graham Elliot, and Mindy Segal.

Reflecting Chicago's prominence as a national and international food center, many books about the food scene have appeared, including *Chicago Chef's Table*, by Amelia Levin; *The Chicago Homegrown Cookbook*, by Heather Lalley; *Chicago Cooks: 25 Years of Chicago Culinary History and Great Recipes from Les Dames d'Escoffier*, edited by Carol Mighton Haddix; and *The Food Lover's' Guide to Chicago*, by Jennifer Olvera.

Contributors: Carol Mighton Haddix, Bruce Kraig, Barbara Revsine, Ellen Stein

BIBLIOGRAPHY

Kirch, Claire. "Agate Grows through Diversification." *Publishers Weekly*, July 22, 2011.

Brach's Confections

In 1904, Emil J. Brach, son of German immigrants, opened a retail candy store with his two sons in Chicago called the Palace of Sweets. That store became the foundation for Brach's nationally sold candies. Brach's first products were caramels, but now it is the number-one candy-corn maker in the United States. Over the years, its successes also included penny candy, barrel displays, glass candy counters, and, eventually, the "pick a mix" concept.

In 1923, Brach moved his operation to a five-story factory near the street that would become Cicero Avenue. In the 1930s, Brach's became recognized worldwide for high-quality candy. After Brach's death in 1947, control went to his sons, who expanded the Chicago plant and started outsourcing. Over 500 chocolate and hard candy varieties were offered by Brach's by the 1950s.

In the 1980s, internal and external elements, such as the rising cost of sugar, cut into the company's profits. The company president, Ned Mitchell, threatened to close the plant. The city of Chicago, not wanting to lose thousands of jobs, gave Brach's a $10,000,000 loan to rebuild the factory and tie it to a city energy production facility.

In 1966, Brach's was sold to American Home Products. Through the following years, it was bought and sold several more times, eventually ending up as a division of Ferrara Candy Company in 2012. The Chicago factory closed in 2003, and production moved to Mexico, Tennessee, and Minnesota.

Contributor: Geraldine Rounds

See also: Candy

BIBLIOGRAPHY

"Exploring America's Gritty History. Brach's Candy Factory." American Urbex. http://www.americanurbex.com/wordpress/?p=779.

Brach's Original Candy Store, ca. 1910. Courtesy of the Chicago Public Library, Special Collections and Preservation Division.

Bremner, David Francis

In 1848, Canadian-born David Francis Bremner (1839–1922) moved to Chicago with his parents. He served with distinction in the Civil War, after which he opened several bakeries, first in Cairo, Illinois, and then in Chicago. But the Great Chicago Fire of 1871 destroyed Bremner's business, so he rented space in the still-standing Mechanical Bakery building. Within 48 hours of the conflagration, he was supplying bread to Chicagoans. Another fire in 1872 destroyed that structure, so Bremner simply reopened at another site.

Bremner Bakery quickly became known for butter wafers, gingersnaps, oyster crackers, "Eureka" digestive health bread made with milk, and soda biscuits. In order to ensure a fresh, safe milk source for his bread, Bremner purchased a dairy. Each loaf of bread sported an attached tin tag impressed with "DFB," and every cracker was embossed with Bremner's name, guaranteeing the public it was buying genuine products. Company lore is that "DFB" stood for "damn fine bread."

CANDY CRUMBS

For the 2007 Batman film, *Dark Knight*, Brach's vacant administration building on the West Side of Chicago was made to look like "Gotham General Hospital," and then dramatically blown up. There are still remnants and debris left from this scene.

—GERALDINE ROUNDS

Bremner became president of the Chicago-based conglomerate of 40 midwestern bakeries, the American Biscuit & Manufacturing Company. In 1898, American Biscuit merged with two smaller conglomerates to form Chicago-based National Biscuit Company, known as Nabisco. The company was created by Chicago lawyer Adolphus Green with Bremner as a member of its board of directors. When Bremner retired in 1906, the new company moved its headquarters to New York City.

In 1905, Bremner's sons opened the Bremner Brothers Biscuit Company. Incorporated in 1907, it became known for Elfin biscuits, butter, sesame, and cracked wheat wafers, as well as for distinctive tin containers. Facilities were moved to Denver in 1984; the company was sold to Canada-based Dare Foods, Inc., in 1999.

Contributors: Ellen F. Steinberg and Jack H. Prost

See also: Baking and Bakeries

BIBLIOGRAPHY

Andreas, Alfred Theodore. *A History of Chicago*, Vol. 3. Chicago: AT Andreas, 1886, 326–27.

"Extra Dividend on I. C." *Chicago Daily Tribune*, July 20, 1905, 11.

Breweries (See: Beer, Breweries, and Brewpubs)

British

A triple-thick mutton chop at St. Hubert's Old English Grill was once emblematic of British fare in Chicago. Now, the options are more diverse, but equally hearty, as the city's new "gastropubs" take on a pronounced U.K. "flavour."

The British were some of the first people to settle near the southern shores of Lake Michigan, taking part in the lucrative fur trade. One of them, John Kinzie, an ambitious British subject from the Detroit area, controlled the Chicago-area fur trade in the early 1800s and became known as the "father of Chicago." Like all the early settlers, the Kinzie family ate wild game, corn, locally found greens, and distilled spirits. Frontier fare was hardly traditional British.

By 1850, about 12 percent of Chicago's immigrants were English, about 1,881 people. Illinois was third in the nation in English-born residents. By 1890, the number mushroomed to about 27,000 people. The "greatest wave" of Scottish newcomers arrived in the years after World War I and through the 1920s. But the Scots were clearly in Chicago before then. The Illinois Saint Andrew Society, the oldest charitable institution in the state, was established by Scottish immigrants on December 1, 1845. The society celebrates Scottish culture and food with the annual "Feast of the Haggis." (Its 170th anniversary was in 2015.) A decade-by-decade look at immigration from U.S. Census records has 4 percent of Chicago's immigrant population in 1850 as Scottish, about 627 people. The number rose to 1,638 in 1860. The Welsh began arriving in the Midwest in 1840 but numbered only about 1,800 immigrants in Chicago by the turn of the twentieth century. They settled in scattered locations, discouraging a strong ethnic community from forming. By 2000, census data numbers for total United Kingdom immigrants for Metro Chicago show about 16,000.

One of the first well-known English restaurants, with its signature mutton chop, was St. Hubert's Old English Grill, located at 316 Federal St. next to the Union League Club. St. Hubert's was described by Duncan Hines as "a bit of Old England with carved oak beams, stained glass windows and red-coated waiters bearing aloft, most likely, platters of mutton chops two inches thick! Amazing, those chops!" Writers also would mention the chops and recall, fondly, being ushered to a comfortable chair by the fire while their order was being prepared. The grill occupied two stories; the first was for men only, so Clarence Darrow, the famed attorney, had to hold his wedding breakfast upstairs. There are three different stories of St. Hubert's origin: One credits William Abson with launching St. Hubert's and his own eponymous Abson's English Chophouse, "a celebrated place in the '90s, with the same fine food"; another claims that a sea captain named Thomas McKenzie opened St. Hubert's after getting into a disagreement with the Union League club; and a third story places the restaurant in the Great Northern Hotel at least as far back as 1909, before being shuttered by fire in 1911.

These days, British foods may best be epitomized by Spencer's Jolly Posh Foods, which in 2010 began selling bangers, rashers, and black puddings wholesale and at farmers markets. Owner Nicholas Spencer also opened a "contemporary British" restaurant on Southport Avenue, aimed at "Anglophiles and ex-pats," but he closed it in 2016 to concentrate on his wholesale food business.

Other notable U.K. outposts include nine Chicago locations for London's Pret a Manger restaurant chain, the first of which opened in September 2010 at 211 W. Adams St.; the Duke of Perth, 2913 N. Clark St., which opened in 1989 and boasts the largest collection of single malt whiskies in Chicago; The Red Lion Pub, which reopened at 2446 N. Lincoln Ave. in 2014 after being shuttered for six years; Blokes & Birds Public House & Karaoke Lounge, a gastropub at 3343 N. Clark St.; and Pleasant House Pub, at 2119 S. Halsted St., which makes British-style pot pies and desserts.

Contributor: Bill Daley

BIBLIOGRAPHY

"Grill Manager to Retire after 50 Years on Job." *Chicago Tribune*, May 16, 1943.

http://blokesandbirdschicago.com/.

Loring, Kay. "Café Is for Making History: Dining Guide Recalls 1931." *Chicago Tribune*, December 4, 1966.

"Saint Hubert's Heads." The Chicago Architecture Blog. www.chicago architecture.org, December 12, 2012.

Butchers (See: Meat and Poultry)

Butterfinger

Chicago's accessibility to ingredients helped it grow to a sweet-confection capital. One entrepreneur took advantage: Otto Schnering founded the Curtiss Candy company in 1916, using his mother's maiden name for the firm, and began preparing candy in small batches. Later, with a purchase of $100 worth of candy-making equipment, Schnering entered the new and popular chocolate candy bar market, competing with the likes of Mars and Hershey, who sold bars for 10 cents. Schnering knew he would have to attract attention, so he created a bar made of peanuts and chocolate and sold it for just 5 cents. The company sponsored a public event to name the new candy bar and came up with a winner, based on a sportscaster term for a player who dropped a baseball, "butterfinger." Curtiss was bought by RJR Nabisco in 1981, and then Nestle purchased some of the old Curtiss brands, including Butterfinger, in 1989.

Contributor: Jenny Lewis

See also: Candy; Curtiss Candy Company; Baby Ruth

BIBLIOGRAPHY

Kimmerle, Beth. *Candy: The Sweet History*. Portland, Ore.: Collectors, 2003.

Cafeterias and Lunchrooms

While upscale, white-tablecloth restaurants attracted both visitors and locals beginning around 1835, downtown workers and shoppers gave rise to the city's "cheap eats" destinations, a trend that began in 1880 with H. H. Kohlsaat's "dairy lunch room." From there, casual, quick-serve eateries began offering inexpensive midday lunches to the burgeoning number of workers in the Loop, many of them young women: 10,000 stenographers in 1900.

However, it wasn't until the 1890s that a subcategory of these quick-serve establishments appeared—the cafeteria—thanks to entrepreneur John Kruger. At the time, smorgasbord restaurants were popular for lunch in and near the Loop, adopted from Chicago's large Scandinavian population. After a visit to Cuba, he changed the name of his to *cafeteria*, the Spanish word for *coffee shop*. Accordingly, it served quick lunches at low prices.

Before long, chains, such as Charles "Lucky" Weeghman's, John Raklios's, and John R. Thompson's, founded in 1891, tried their hands at the increasingly popular "one-arm lunchroom" craze. Like the places of its ilk that followed, they featured one-arm, wooden chairs intended for quick, solitary eating. This made them a popular midday choice among time-crunched business types. Typically, menu items were simple and comfort-food–driven. At John R. -Thompson's, that translated into frankfurters, cold corned beef sandwiches, and Herkimer County cheese on house-made "Milwaukee Rye Bread." Other chains, including "greasy spoon" Pixley & Ehlers and B/G Foods, jumped on the bandwagon. The epicenter for these eateries was "Toothpick Alley"—otherwise

Interior of Thompson's Cafeteria/One-Arm, ca. 1920. Courtesy of the Chicago History Museum, ICHi-85001; Hornby & Freiberg.

known as Madison and Clark Streets. A hotbed was established; the popularity of lunchrooms and cafeterias spread nationwide.

The Chicago tradition lives on at still-notable locales, such as Valois Cafeteria on the South Side and Manny's Coffee Shop & Deli in the South Loop. Valois got its start in 1921, thanks to William Valois, former chef of the Chicago Beach Hotel. The casual, counter-serve spot is renowned to this day for its snaking lines—not to mention its self-explanatory motto, "See Your Food." Meanwhile, Manny's origins can be traced to post–World War II. It has stood at its current address on Jefferson Street since 1964, serving legendary pastrami and corned beef sandwiches, matzo ball soup, and potato pancakes. In 2002, a second Manny's location opened at Chicago Midway International Airport. More modern interpretations exist in Chicago as well, among them Foodlife, a Water Tower Place venue with 14 different, counter-serve kitchens that dispense everything from barbecue to Asian fare, tacos, and Chicago-style hot dogs.

Contributor: Jennifer Olvera

BIBLIOGRAPHY

Levenstein, Harvey. *Revolution at the Table, The Transformation of the American Die*t. New York: Oxford University Press, 1988.

Zuber, Amy. "Samuel & William Childs." *Nation's Restaurant News*, February 1996.

Candy

The tantalizing fragrance emanating from the Blommer Chocolate factory teases the senses with the promise of sweetness—a promise that the city has been keeping for almost 150 years. The Windy City once was known as the Candy Capital of the World. Some say it still is. However, though Chicago remains a haven of sweetness, many of the candies that were "born" here have been carried away by mergers, acquisitions, or moves to overseas production facilities.

Candy began to evolve from rare luxury to plentiful treat in the mid-to-late 1800s in the United States. Annual consumption of sweets grew from approximately 2.2 pounds per person in 1880 to 13.1 pounds by 1919. Chicago became a candy-making center because manufacturers had easy access to ingredients and shipping. Abundant milk, cream, and butter came from Wisconsin; corn syrup and cornstarch from midwestern farms; and sugar from Michigan's sugar beets. Everything else needed came aboard the increasing network of trains that made Chicago the country's transportation hub. Once several companies succeeded, others soon followed, as happens in business, and no city came close

to matching Chicago's candy output. At the height of its candy-centricity, Chicagoland was home to more than 100 candy companies that employed about 25,000 Chicagoans.

Candy production in Chicago predates the Civil War, though it did not really take off until the conflict ended. During the war, Charles F. Gunther sold candy for a Chicago firm, but then went to Europe to learn more. He returned to Chicago in 1868, knowing how to produce a treat unfamiliar to Americans: caramels. His caramels attracted a wealthy clientele and made Gunther a success. Gunther was far from alone, even at that early date. When the National Confectionery Association was founded in Chicago in 1884, it represented 69 companies. The association (which has since moved to Washington, D.C.) published *Manufacturing Confectioner* magazine and worked to advance candy-making standards.

In 1891, William Wrigley Jr. founded the Wrigley Company and began working to change the popular notion that chewing gum was only for women. In 1893, he introduced the flavors that would soon identify the company: Spearmint and Juicy Fruit. By 1907, Wrigley's gum was known nationwide. The Wrigley Building on Michigan Avenue, completed in 1921, became a Chicago landmark.

It was during the Columbian Exposition of 1893 that the Rueckheim brothers were inspired to add peanuts to their candy-coated popcorn. They trademarked the name *Cracker Jack* in 1896, and it went on to be another American icon. E. J. Brach's and Sons began producing confections in Chicago in 1904. By 1911, the company was producing 25 tons of candy a week, and by 1918, 1,000 tons a week. The company grew to dominate the bulk candy market, with 3,500 employees by the 1980s; it was also a leading employer on Chicago's West Side. In 1994, a corporate merger carried it out of the area.

Postcard of Charles F. Gunther's famous Loop candy store, 1887. Courtesy of the Chicago History Museum, i21804.

ARTISAN CHOCOLATIERS

In the past, Chicago had many chocolate makers, some of whom became large manufacturers. Today, there is a new crop of modern artisans, homegrown chocolatiers who create candies worth a bite.

Katrina Markoff, founder and owner of Vosges Ltd., started making truffles in her kitchen in 1998 and selling them at specialty food stores. The following year, she opened her first Vosges Haut-Chocolate store in Bucktown, which was followed by eight more and a 43,000-square-foot manufacturing facility at 2950 N. Oakley. Vosges is known for its offbeat combinations, such as chocolate with wasabi, bacon, or beef jerky. In 2012, Markoff launched Wild Ophelia, a premium brand for the mass market.

Belgian Chocolatier Piron in Evanston was started by Master Chocolatiers Robert and Fred Piron in 1983. Their signature chocolates, all handmade in the store, include ganache, chocolate buttercreams, Cognac, Grand Marnier, and crème caramels.

Heather Johnston, a pediatrician turned chocolatier, opened Veruca Chocolates (named after a character in *Willy Wonka and the Chocolate Factory*) in October 2012 in a storefront at 2409 N. Western Ave. Her signature chocolates are bonbons, caramels, and "gelt for adults," originally developed for Hanukkah. The shop has kosher certification.

Cocoa & Co. on North Wells Street stocks an impressive supply of chocolates. But several Chicago-area stores selling imported high-end chocolates have closed in the past decade, including Chocolates by Bernard Callebaut; Leonidas; BonBon; Canady le Chocolatier, Ltd.; and Chocolate Box.

Artisan chocolate was the subject of tastings, demonstrations, and lectures at the Chicago Artisan Chocolate Festival April 16–17, 2016, at the Stephen M. Bailey Auditorium in Chicago.

—COLLEEN SEN

Curtiss Candy Company was founded in 1916. By 119, it employed 400 men and women. Baby Ruth and Butterfinger were its best-known contributions to the candy scene. By the 1960s, Curtiss was ranked as one of the top-10 candy companies in the country. However, in 1964, the company was sold and, while its most popular brands are still produced by the current owner, it is no longer in the Chicago area.

In 1926, Le Noble and Company combined two Chicago staples, caramel and chocolate, creating Milk Duds. (They were called "duds" because creator Sean Le Noble was disappointed that he couldn't make them perfectly spherical.) In 1928, another Chicago candy maker, Milton J. Holloway, took over production of Milk Duds, which would be his company's flagship product for another 60 years. However, Milk Duds would outlive the M. J. Holloway company. Holloway was purchased by Beatrice Foods in 1960, but when Beatrice began to fall apart, the history of Milk Duds became intertwined with that of another early Chicago candy company: Leaf.

Leaf Brands was a collection of confectionary companies founded in the 1920s by Sol S. Leaf. Leaf Brands was bought in 1983 by Huhtamäki, a Finnish company. Two years later, Huhtamäki bought the confectionery companies Beatrice Foods was selling, including M. J. Holloway, and rolled them all into Leaf Brands, though moving them all out of Chicago. Huhtamäki would go on to buy Hollywood Candies (Payday and Zero candy bars) as well as Heath and other companies. By the early 1990s, Leaf Brands was the fourth largest candy producer in North America. Then, in 1993, Huhtamäki sold Leaf Brands (including Milk Duds) to Hershey in Pennsylvania.

In 1929, Frank Mars moved his company and 200 employees from Minnesota to Chicago, bringing his successful Milky Way bar with him. The next year, the Snickers bar was introduced, and 3 Musketeers followed two years later. The company continued to grow and diversify, but M&M/Mars still produces most of its best-known candy bars at their Chicago location.

M&Ms were first produced in 1940 by a new company called M&M, founded by Forrest Mars, Frank's son, and Bruce Murrie, the son of the president of the Hershey Co. The name came from the first letters of their last names. These small, round, color-coated chocolate candies were packaged in paper tubes at first. The original colors were red, yellow, green, orange, brown, and violet, which have changed over the years; later peanuts were added. Company tradition has it that the idea came to Forrest Mars during a visit to Spain when he saw soldiers eating a similar product. An alternative origin may be Smarties, small, colorful sugar-coated candies introduced in England by Rowntrees of York in 1937. Forrest Mars bought out Murrie in 1949 and changed the name of the company to Food Manufacturers, Inc. It later merged with Mars, Inc.

The high number of confectioners made Chicago a great town for those who supplied needed ingredients, from milk processors to sugar refiners to flavoring producers to package makers. Henry, Aloysius, and Bernard Blommer started Blommer's Chocolate in 1939 as part of this rush to get close to the action. Blommer processed the chocolate that the candy-makers needed.

Tootsie Roll moved to Chicago from New Jersey in the 1960s. Today, its 1,500 employees turn out the famous chewy candy and its many siblings, enjoying the city's transportation infrastructure.

Just outside the city, in Oakbrook Terrace, The Ferrara Candy Company is best known for Lemonheads. Founded in 1908, it is the number one manufacturer of nonchocolate candy in the United States. And then there are the area's big multiproduct companies that include candies as part of a larger package. For example, Kraft Food is responsible for prodigious numbers of caramels and marshmallows.

The story of confections, once made here and still made here, also include Frango Mints, Dove Bars, DoubleMint, Slo Pokes, Whoppers, Andes Mints, AffyTapple, Primrose, DeMets, Charleston Chew, World's Finest Chocolate, Fannie May, Charms, Junior Mints, Oh Henry!, and so many more. Nor has the age of start-ups ended, as local entrepreneurs such as Vosges, Veruca, and Belgian chocolatier Piron have started producing artisanal chocolates.

The city may no longer be the center of the world for confection production, but the sweet stuff is still abundant. Independent chocolate shops all across the city offer handmade delights. Some of them (such as Margie's Candies, founded in 1921) are as much a part of the city's candy history as the bigger players.

Contributor: Cynthia Clampitt
See also: Baby Ruth; Blommers Chocolate; Brach's; Butterfinger; Curtiss Candy; Dove Bars; Fannie May; Ferrara Pan; Frango Mints; Gunther, Charles; Margie's Candies; Mars, Inc.

BIBLIOGRAPHY

Cavanaugh, Amy. "Explore Our Candied Past in Sweet Home Chicago." *Chicagoist*, January 19, 2013.

Goddard, Leslie. *Chicago's Sweet Candy History*. Charleston, S.C.: Arcadia Books, 2012.

http://chicagoist.com/2013/01/19/explore_our_candied_past_in _sweet_h.php.

Lydersen, Kari, "Chicago Is Sweet Home to Fewer Candy Factories." *Washington Post*, February 7, 2006.

Canonne, Sébastien

Together with Chef Jacquy Pfeiffer, Canonne founded the French Pastry School in 1995, which became part of Kennedy-King College, part of the City Colleges of Chicago, in 1999.

Born in 1968, Canonne grew up in Normandy and apprenticed under the iconic pastry chef Gaston Lenôtre in Paris. After several years he moved on to several world-class establishments, like the Beau Rivage Palace in Geneva, Switzerland, and the Palais de L'Elysée, where he made pastries for French President François Mitterand.

In 1992, Canonne moved to Chicago to work for the Ritz-Carlton Hotel. After several years here, and with Chicago as his home base, Canonne turned to teaching and consulting in prominent properties worldwide, such as the Ritz-Carlton and Four Seasons Hotels and Resorts companies.

Canonne took his passion for teaching to another level when he and Chef Pfeiffer cofounded The French Pastry School. Since then he has earned numerous honors, including the Taittinger Champagne Pastry Chef of the Year in America, 1995, and the prestigious title of M.O.F. (Meilleur Ouvrier de France, or Best Craftsman of France), 2004.

Contributor: Scott Warner
See also: Baking and Bakeries; Cooking Classes
Source: Information supplied by The French Pastry School, Chicago.

Cantu, Homaro

One of Chicago's "molecular gastronomy" chefs, Cantu (1976–2015) helped bring the city nationwide fame as a home for cutting-edge cuisine. His Moto restaurant, opened in 2005 in the Fulton Street Market area, was one of the first to feature such creations as edible menus and Kentucky Fried ice cream. Moto earned a Michelin star in 2012, and maintained it in following years. Cantu converted the basement of Moto into an indoor farm. Later he opened iNG, a more casual but still experimental, restaurant next to Moto. It closed in 2013.

He filed many patent applications for his food and equipment innovations and created Cantu Designs to develop foods for aerospace, commercial, and humanitarian uses.

He wrote *The Miracle Berry Diet Cookbook* in 2012, after discovering the sweetening properties of the so-called miracle berry (a native of West Africa) in his experiments for his restaurants, where he turned sour ingredients into sweet ones. His 2014 coffee shop, Berrista, made use of the berry in doughnuts and pastries.

Cantu was the cohost of the television series *Future Food* for Planet Green, and in 2011, gave a Ted Talk on postmodern cuisine. He appeared on *Iron Chef America* and *The Ellen Degeneres Show*. He was board president of the Trotter Project, a nonprofit group named for the late Charlie Trotter that offers career guidance for young people with an interest in cooking.

Growing up in Washington and Oregon, his family at one time was homeless. But he ended up attending the Western Culinary Institute (later Le Cordon Bleu) in Portland and working for many restaurants, before moving to Chicago to work with Charlie Trotter.

Contributor: Carol Mighton Haddix

See also: Molecular Gastronomy

BIBLIOGRAPHY

Wells, Pete. "Homaro Cantu, Science-Minded Chicago Chef, Dies at 38." *New York Times*, April 15, 2015.

Cape Cod Room

Tucked into a comfortable niche on the first floor of The Drake Hotel, the Cape Cod Room was one of Chicago's best known and longest-running restaurants. It opened on December 6, 1933, the day after the official end of Prohibition. Periodic updates kept the restaurant current without diminishing its vintage charm. Its most famous artifact, the wooden bar where Marilyn Monroe and Joe Dimaggio carved their initials, just like it was when the couple dined at the restaurant more than a half-century ago.

Certain of the Cape Cod's dishes also had a long tenure. Items such as Dover sole meuniere and Maine lobster with mashed potatoes were perennial best sellers, but the Bookbinder's soup is arguably the restaurant's best known dish. The original recipe came from Bookbinder's Original Restaurant in Philadelphia, where it was made with snapping turtle. The Cape Cod's version was made with red snapper. The Drake closed the restaurant for good in 2016, during the hotel's remodeling.

Contributor: Barbara Revsine

See also: Restaurants and Fine Dining, Seafood Restaurants

BIBLIOGRAPHY

Nunn, Emily. "First Bite: Cape Cod Room." *Chicago Tribune*, April 24, 2008.

Caribbeans

Chicago's Caribbean population is dominated by the Puerto Rican community, which numbered just more than 100,000 in the 2011–13 American Community Survey. It is the city's second-largest Hispanic community after Mexicans. In addition to Puerto Ricans, almost 9,000 people of Cuban origin and almost 3,000 people of Dominican origin call Chicago home. Additionally, about 11,000 Chicagoans identified themselves as non-Hispanic people of West Indian origin, the largest groups being from Jamaica (almost half) and Haiti.

The cuisines best represented in Chicago are those of the largest groups listed above, most traditionally found on the North and Near Northwest Sides of the city.

Rogers Park and Chicago's Far North Side neighborhoods, along the border with Skokie and Evanston, have been a point of congregation for Chicago's Caribbean population since the mid–twentieth century. There, residents and visitors alike have become familiar with Jamaica's eponymous jerk chicken, available at restaurants and take-out stands around the neighborhood. The chicken is prepared with a dryrub of spices, dominated by hot peppers but balanced with other savory and sweet flavors. This jerk spice also is used to marinate other meats. Plates of spicy grilled chicken are often served with plantain, rice, and beans, accompaniments familiar to consumers of other Caribbean fare. Jamaican cuisine now has followed Jamaicans throughout the Chicago area and is easily found beyond the North Side.

Chicago's Puerto Rican community began to arrive about the same time as the Jamaican community in the mid–twentieth century. It dwarfs the other Caribbean communities, partly because of the comparably few legal barriers to entry. As the community grew, it began to consolidate on Chicago's Near Northwest Side. Today, the heart of the Puerto Rican community is around Humboldt Park and along Division Street. The annual Puerto Rican parade is a highlight of the neighborhood, as are its colorful murals that offer a rich glimpse into life on the island. Also lined along the street are many restaurants that exemplify the Caribbean flavors of Puerto Rico.

The food relates to other Caribbean cuisines, with a focus on plantain, yucca, rice, and beans. In addition to featuring panfried, grilled, and baked sweet plantains, the Puerto Rican community has made a significant mark on the development of their national cuisine by pioneering the *jibarito*, a sandwich that substitutes large fried strips of green plantain for bread and is filled with meat, garlic mayonnaise, lettuce, tomato, and cheese. Another popular dish brought from the island is *mofongo*. Typically, it is made of mashed, fried green plantain, filled with meat, vegetables, and/or seafood, or often covered in a broth or a meat stew in place of a filling. Though traditionally featuring plantain, the dish also can be made of mashed yucca or a blend of yucca and plantain.

In addition to mashing green plantains, cooks thickly slice discs of the fruit and fry them to make *tostones*, a traditional side dish. Softening and then flavoring green plantains is another tradition across the Caribbean and is reflected in dishes such as *mangú* from the Dominican

Republic and *fufu de platano* in Cuba. The process continues a tradition brought from West Africa during the era of the slave trade.

Prior to the import of plantain, yucca, a native tuber, was a dominant starch. Growing underground, it was resilient in the face of hurricanes and thus a dependable food that could be fried, boiled, and mashed into dough. Another highly visible African import are pigeon peas, a prominent ingredient in *arroz con gandules* (rice with pigeon peas), an orange rice that is omnipresent along Division Street, though customarily served in Puerto Rico only around the holidays.

Contributor: Andres Torres

See also: Jibarito

BIBLIOGRAPHY

Cohn, D'Vera, Eileen Patten, and Mark Hugo Lopez. "Puerto Rican Population Declines on Island, Grows on U.S. Mainland." Pew Research Center's Hispanic Trends Project. Washington, D.C., August 2014.

Keating, Ann Durkin, ed. *Chicago Neighborhoods and Suburbs: A Historical Guide.* Chicago: The University of Chicago Press, 2004.

Ready, Timothy, and Allert Brown-Gort. *The State of Latino Chicago.* Notre Dame, Ind.: Institute for Latino Studies University of Notre Dame, 2005.

Carl Buddig and Company

Family-owned and family-operated Carl Buddig and Company has deep roots in the Chicago area. In 1943, South Side butcher, Carl John Buddig (1895–1957), founded the wholesale meat business still bearing his name. His first clients were small northern Illinois groceries and meat markets. Today, Carl Buddig and Company is one of the largest meatpacking and distribution corporations headquartered in Illinois.

A LITTLE CURED MEAT WITH YOUR MORNING PAPER?

On April 1, 1959, Carl Buddig and Company famously brought the aroma of its smoked beef to *Chicago Tribune* readers. The company created a scented, full-page advertisement in that day's paper by mixing color inks with a concentrate composed of cassia, oil of clove, and maple syrup. These three ingredients were the same as those used in Buddig's meat-curing process.

—BRUCE KRAIG

Known for lean delicatessen-style meats and poultry, Buddig sells under its own brand name as well as private labels throughout North America and Puerto Rico. Their vacuum-packed product lines include Buddig Original smoked meats and poultry, Buddig Premium and Deli Cuts, as well as Fix Quix grilled poultry strips, all of which are gluten-free with no added monosodium glutamate (MSG).

In 1970, the company acquired a 1,000-acre cattle farm near Fall River, in south-central Wisconsin, planning to operate it under the newly formed subsidiary, Buddig Farms, Incorporated. Eleven years later, the parent company purchased the Old Wisconsin Sausage Company in Sheboygan, Wisconsin, which continues to produce, sell, and distribute beef sticks, summer sausage, wieners, and bratwurst under that name. In 2013, the company leased the Munster, Indiana, facilities formerly occupied by Dawn Foods in preparation for relocating its South Holland, Illinois, warehouse distribution center.

Contributors: Ellen F. Steinberg and Jack H. Prost

See also: Union Stock Yards

BIBLIOGRAPHY

"Buddig Relocates Distribution Center to Munster, In." November 26, 2013. http://www.economicdevelopmenthq.com/blog/buddig-distribution-center-munster-in.

"Reaching Our Full Potential." http://www.oldwisconsin.com/about-us/history.

Carlos' Restaurant

For 30 years, Carlos' was one of the Chicago area's most celebrated fine-dining restaurants, opened in 1981 at 429 Temple Avenue, Highland Park, by Carlos Nieto and his wife Debbie. The restaurant was distinguished by its superb service, formal atmosphere, extensive wine list, and modern French dishes, such as escargots in a Roquefort Pernod cream sauce and a chervil-and-black-truffle–crusted ahi tuna with roasted kabocha squash and a truffle-thyme reduction. Roland Liccioni and Gabriel Viti are among the well-known chefs who worked at Carlos'.

Nieto came from Mexico City in 1968 and worked as a busboy at Escargot and then as a waiter at Le Français. The Nietos opened a second restaurant, Cafe Central, also in Highland Park in 1995, and the Happ Inn in Northfield in 2009. On New Year's Eve 2011, they closed Carlos', renovated it, and four years later opened a new casual dining restaurant called Nietos at the same location.

Contributor: Colleen Sen

See also: Chefs; Restaurants and Fine Dining; Restaurateurs and Restaurant Groups

BIBLIOGRAPHY

Pollack, Penny. "5 Questions for Carlos Nieto." *Chicago Magazine*, January 10, 2012.

Catering

Born out of union halls, church halls, private social clubs, civic institutions, and restaurants, early catering mostly occurred in hotel meeting rooms or ballrooms. Before World War II, using catering firms was a status symbol for the rich, though most had their own house staff to execute all manner of entertaining. For more modest events, restaurants would cater prepared foods, or a local parish or synagogue would host special occasions with community and family assistance. The catering industry's fortunes rose and fell with political and economic changes.

Chicago's Herbert M. Kinsley enjoyed much success at his lavishly decorated establishment in The Opera House on Washington Street, which he purchased in 1865. It was the largest single hall of its kind in the country, accommodating 1,500 guests,

Kinsley's business was known for elegance, quality, and style. He catered to the whims and tastes of businessmen in the daytime, catered gala events in the evening, and supplied private parties in the suburbs, in railcars, and on steamboats. Kinsley served the first meal in George Pullman's new dining car in 1867. While most of the foods first served on trains were cold sandwiches, cakes, and ice cream, full menus soon became available, and by 1892, the railway cars were serving 4.4 million meals a year. Kinsley's extensive menus and wine lists often were written in French and English and offered as many as twenty different preparations of veal, mutton, beef, and poultry. In 1892, Daniel Burnham tapped Kinsley to plot restaurant logistics for the Chicago World's Fair, where he also catered a decadent inaugural dinner for the fair, hosted by the vice president, former President Hayes, and countless U.S. government dignitaries. Kinsley met an untimely death in 1894.

Evidence shows that Kinsley worked for a time with Harriet Brainard Moody. Although she had never cooked before, Moody built a thriving catering business in 1890. Despite being a divorcee, she remained a fixture among society women, friendly with Mrs. Potter Palmer, and a member of several clubs, including the Fortnightly. She called her business The Home Delicacies Association, 705 N. Michigan Ave., and served Chicago's elite, plus Pullman Cars, Marshall Field tearooms, and other Chicago restaurants. Eventually, Moody opened another branch of The Home Delicacies Association in London, supplying Selfridge's department store.

Joseph H. Biggs worked for a time with Moody and then opened his own catering firm at 50 E. Huron St. His business was geared to society events and galas, including the widely covered and elegantly appointed wedding of George Pullman's daughter in his Prairie Avenue home in April 1896. When Florence Pullman married Frank O. Lowden, no expense was spared, and the guest list was a who's who of society and business elite—Palmer, McCormick, Fields, Armour, McClurg, Glessner, Dawes, and Sprague, to name a few.

By the early 1900s, several catering companies were of note. Burton White, 153 and 155 La Salle St., advertised "proper service at proper prices for any occasion. Choicest china, silver and linens." Hull House Coffee House, 240 W. Polk St., took orders and sent out dinners. In 1910, John B. Gaper Catering Company, originally at 161 E. Chicago Ave., also had a retail store on Randolph Street across from the public library. The Gaper Catering Co. enjoyed long success well into this millennium. In 1930, Le Cerf opened for business at 120 E. Oak St. Le Cerf was run by Mary Dunning, who allowed patrons to sample catering options at a tea or luncheon.

Chicago's multicultural population, urban growth, and worldly recognition created more demand for catering. Throughout the decades, despite the often hard economic climates, there always were occasions to celebrate and ask, "Could you recommend a good caterer?"

Closer to date, Jewell Catering has served every U.S. president for the last 45 years, as well as dignitaries and notables throughout the world. George L. Jewell was schooled in his native England and apprenticed at some of the finest hotels in Europe before settling in Chicago and opening George Jewell Catering Services in 1967. It remains in business today.

In 1983, Sue Ling Gin was served a half-frozen breakfast muffin on a Midway Airlines flight. Gin decided to open an airline catering business of her own, the Flying Food Group, Inc. It has produced meals for 80 airlines worldwide, built kitchens in nine U.S. airports, and employed thousands. Gin died in 2014, but the firm remains one of Chicago's largest minority-owned companies.

Michael Roman became known as the "catering guru," after running his family's The Mixing Bowl catering firm and then teaching and motivating other caterers around the city and country. He died in 2013.

Many restaurant companies also added catering services, including Phil Stefani Signature Events and Smoque BBQ. Carlyn Berghoff of the famous restaurant family ran Berghoff Catering & Restaurant Group. Other popular catering firms today, among many, are Entertaining Company, Blue Plate, and Limelight.

Contributors: Rita Gutenkanst and Margarite Lytle

See also: Flying Food Group; Gin, Sue Ling; Kinsley, Herbert M.; Moody, Harriet

BIBLIOGRAPHY

"Miss Pullman Weds." *Chicago Times Herald*, April 30, 1896.

Mulligan, Terrance. "The Delights of Pullman Dining USA 1866–1968." Pullman Car Services Supplement Edition, 2007.

Whitaker, Jan. "Anatomy of a Restaurateur: H.M. Kinsley" and "Anatomy of a Restaurateur: Harriet Moody." *Restaurant-ing through History*. http://restaurant-ingthroughhistory.com.

Central Americans

About 35,000 Chicagoans identify as Hispanic or Latino from Central America (Guatemala, Honduras, El Salvador, Belize, Nicaragua, Costa Rica, or Panama), according to the U.S. Census Bureau's 2011–13 American Community Survey, just less than 5 percent of the city's total Hispanic population. Two-thirds of Chicago's Central Americans were born abroad.

More than half of Chicago's Central Americans are Guatemalan, with Hondurans (about 17 percent) and Salvadorans (about 15 percent) making up the next largest populations. Consequently, Guatemalan cuisine dominates Chicago's Central American culinary offerings but is often served alongside Salvadoran and Mexican dishes. These pairings attest to cultural similarities across the Yucatan peninsula that date back to the Mayans but also reflect the dominance of Mexican culture in Chicago's Hispanic community.

Despite strong economic and political contrasts between Central American nations, their geographic similarities, proximities, and a shared history (from Mayan times, but particularly as Spanish colonies, with the exception of Belize, which was a British colony) help explain culinary consistencies across the region. Central American cuisine reveals a blend of Spanish, Caribbean, and Indian flavors.

Corn, beans, and chilies feature prominently across the region. Rice, potatoes, plantains, and yucca interchange as starch staples, while roasted vegetables, chilies, and seeds—from pumpkin to sesame—thicken and enrich traditional stews, many of which reference Mayan or other Amerindian traditions. For example, Guatemalan restaurants often describe *pepián*, a thick chicken stew spiced with roasted chilies and nuts, as of Mayan origin. And it isn't difficult to imagine the pre-Columbian roots of other Guatemalan chili-based stews, such as *pulique* (a chicken or beef stew) and *hilachas* (a shredded beef and potato stew).

Tamales are a recognizable Central American crossover, but unlike Mexican tamales dominant in Chicago, most Guatemalan and Salvadoran tamales are wrapped in plantain leaves and tend to be a bit larger. Guatemalan *chuchitos* more closely resemble Mexican tamales. Similarly, *pupusas*, traditional Salvadoran grilled corn patties usually stuffed with beans, cheese, pork, and/or loroco, an edible flower, might remind some diners of Mexican *gorditas*.

Chicago's Central Americans are quite diffuse, so restaurants, bakeries, and grocery stores that serve them are distributed across Chicago's North Side. From Brianna's Restaurant in Lincoln Square, which serves Guatemalan, Salvadoran, and Mexican dishes, and then west and south through Albany Park to Humboldt Park, there is a scattering of principally Guatemalan restaurants, many of which double as *pupuserías*. Las Delicias restaurant in Albany Park has long been a popular destination for *pupusas* and Guatemalan food. Several other small *pupuserías* dot the Chicago's Northwest Side. In Andersonville, Isabella's Bakery offers not only freshly Guatemalan bread and desserts but also sells imported Central American food products. One of Guatemala's most recent culinary imports is *Pollo Campero*, a popular fried chicken fast-food chain in Central America.

Other Central American foods are found mostly on pan-Latin menus, with some exceptions, such as at Costa Rican restaurant Irazu in Bucktown or the Honduran Super Pollo in Belmont Cragin (which also serves Mexican and Salvadoran dishes). For a different perspective on Central American cuisine, Belizean food reveals much stronger Caribbean flavors, similar to that of other British colonies, such as Jamaica or Trinidad and Tobago. In Marquette Park on Chicago's South Side, Garifuna Flava celebrates the cuisine of the Garifuna people, often associated with Belize but who live across Central America, descendants of Africans and Caribbean natives.

Contributor: Andres Torres

BIBLIOGRAPHY

Jones, Sandra. "Levy Brings Pollo Campero to Chicago." *Crain's Chicago Business*, July 27, 2005.

Sula, Mike. "A Caribbean Rarity." *Chicago Reader*, August 6, 2009.

A Century of Progress, Chicago World's Fair

From May 27 to November 12, 1933, and May 26 to October 31, 1934, Chicago's A Century of Progress Exposition sprawled across 427 acres along Lake Michigan from 12th Street (now Roosevelt Road) south to 39th Street (now Pershing Road) and on Northerly Island. Like its predecessor, the World's Columbian Exposition of 1893, Chicago's second world's fair punctuated a period of great societal turmoil, and its organizers had similar aims: to showcase American goods and culture, educate the public, promote

American technology and commerce, and, above all, push consumerism.

Although planned well before Black Tuesday in 1929 that commenced the Great Depression, A Century of Progress ultimately became a light in the darkness of that grim period. Oil tycoon Rufus C. Dawes, chairman of the exposition board, steered the fair toward its highlight on scientific and industrial development. Prominent Chicago doctors and scientists had urged the theme—"Science Finds, Industry Applies, Man Conforms"—in hopes of educating the public, restoring trust in science eroded by the chemical weapons of the Great War, and allying science and industrial interests. That included the science of food. In the Hall of Science, fair visitors could see a 10-foot-tall, talking, moving, transparent mechanical man who discussed healthful foods and demonstrated chewing and digesting them. Chemistry exhibits included a model of a molecule of table salt, with spheres representing the positive ion of sodium and the negative ion of chlorine and lights depicting electrons and nuclei. Biology displays covered vitamins, courtesy of North Chicago's Abbott Laboratories, and yeast and fermentation.

Pavilions from more than 20 corporations pushed visitors to open their wallets and modernize their homes and lives. Model homes, such as George Keck's House of Tomorrow, showcased sleek, futuristic kitchens with unheard of time-saving gadgets. In her booklet, "A Century of Progress in Cooking," home economist Grace Viall Gray gushed over "magic electric servants" that would aid the modern housewife:

> "In the General Electric Kitchen a faithful electric refrigerator guards the family's food and her household budget . . . eliminates frequent trips to the market in all sorts of weather. An electric dishwasher *washes and dries all her dishes* in but a few minutes. The electric range keeps her kitchen cool and clean . . . permits her to cook an entire meal while she is shopping."

Displays in the Foods and Agricultural Building showcased innovations in the food industry with dioramas, moving models, and mechanical processes. A collection of cookbooks, menus, and manuscripts tracked developments in cuisine from the first cookbook on. The dairy industry's display charted milk production from the first cows brought to Plymouth colony on up to modern milking methods, represented by a robotic Holstein that blinked her eyes and switched her tail while giving milk via a hygienic McCormick-Deering milker. Farming exhibits also included a poultry show and egg-laying contest.

In a glossy tile and glass kitchen, Chicago's Kraft Foods demonstrated its new, patented "emulsifying machine," the "Miracle Whip" invented by Charles Chapman. Oil, vinegar, eggs, and more than 20 spices were continuously piped into the appliance to become thoroughly whipped and blended into Kraft's new salad dressing. Kraft touted the blend of mayonnaise and less expensive boiled salad dressing as a way to make "fresh foods such as fruit, vegetables and salads better tasting, more appealing and less expensive to Depression-weary consumers." Within 22 weeks of its introduction at the fair, the fame of Miracle Whip, the product named for the mixer, had spread to the point that it outsold all other brands of salad dressing and mayonnaise.

Another mixing innovation wowed fairgoers at the Coca-Cola exhibit, where the first automatic fountain dispenser created well-blended Cokes with the pull of a handle. The machine, invented by Chicago's Dole Valve Co., rendered the hand-stirred drinks of the past obsolete. Coke also ran an exhibition bottling line in the Food and Agriculture building.

Wilson & Co.'s exhibit sliced and packed its Certified Sliced Bacon continuously for 12 hours a day, turning out 400 "always delicious, always uniform" slices each minute. The Wilson building also offered terrace and roof-garden restaurants, a lobby snack bar, and soda fountains, joining ten more Wilson food stands throughout the fairgrounds. Chicago meatpacker Armour & Co. hosted exhibits and a restaurant at the fair. In 1934, its rival Swift & Co. told its story on the "Swift Bridge of Service" stretching across the lagoon to Northerly Island, enticing visitors past its promotional exhibits with an open-air amphitheater featuring free concerts by the Chicago Symphony Orchestra, pet shows, diving exhibitions, and more, plus a pair of restaurants.

Wonder Bread sponsored a modern bakery with a restaurant, and the Continental Baking Co. and National Biscuit Co. also were represented. After the repeal of Prohibition in 1933, the fair's second year brought in a brewery exhibit, telling the story of beer from grain to beverage, with a German rathskeller for sampling, and Schlitz and Miller High Life opened fairground taverns.

For its display, Chicago-based Quaker Oats Co. nodded toward an innovation of the past. Aunt Jemima pancake mix, the first ready-mixed, self-rising pancake flour, had launched at the 1893 World's Columbian Exposition, where actress Nancy Green, in character as the product's namesake cook, sang songs, told stories, and demonstrated the mix, serving thousands of pancakes to fairgoers. Quaker, which still owns the brand, acquired Aunt Jemima in 1926. For the Century of Progress Exposition, the company brought back Aunt Jemima in the person of Anna Robinson, who promoted the product until her death in 1951.

Canning-jar manufacturer Ball Brothers Co. of Muncie, Indiana, sponsored the International Canning Contest, with $10,000 in cash prizes, and displayed the entries, hundreds of jars of food from every state and many countries.

International and ethnic pavilions showed traditional folkways and foods, such as the Belgian Village with its cafes and reproductions of medieval homes, an old church, town hall, fish market, and dog-drawn milk carts. In an authentic tea garden at the Japanese pavilion, women in kimonos performed the ancient Japanese tea ceremony, while at the Czechoslovakian pavilion, a cafe served Bohemian and Slovak dishes. Italy contributed an exhibition of wines as well as food. Chinese, Swiss, German, Austrian, Dutch, Tunisian, Middle Eastern, French, Spanish, Mexican, English, Irish, Welsh, early American, Southwestern, Southern . . . fairgoers had a varied choice of cuisines.

Other dining at the fair ranged from kosher hot dog stands, milk bars, and sandwich shops to sit-down restaurants with live music and dancing, such as Hiram Walker's Canadian Club, situated on another of the bridges between Northerly Island and the mainland. Thompson's Restaurants, a Chicago-based chain of "one-arm" lunchrooms, ran two eateries on the lakefront along the Avenue of Flags; Walgreens operated four stores with soda fountains; and many of the exhibit areas, from the Hall of Religion to the Midget Village, featured restaurants.

The fair cost more than $100 million to produce. Although conceived as a single-summer event, organizers extended the exposition to a second year, partly due to its popularity, partly to raise funds to pay off its debts, and partly for its value in selling American capitalism. President Franklin D. Roosevelt (who contributed favorite recipes for Italian rice and kedgeree to Gray's cookbook) was among those urging the reopening, which he saw as stimulating the U.S. economy. Even before the second year, the exposition had had such an impact that in its honor the city added a third star to the municipal flag.

By the fair's end, nearly 49 million visitors had ponied up the 50-cent daily admission fee (25 cents for children) to get a taste of A Century of Progress.

Contributor: Leah A. Zeldes

See also: Cafeterias and Lunchrooms; Kraft Foods; Restaurants and Fine Dining; Swift & Co.; Wilson & Company.

BIBLIOGRAPHY

Ganz, Cheryl R. *The 1933 Chicago World's Fair: A Century of Progress*. Urbana: University of Illinois Press, 2008.

Gray, Grace Viall, *A Century of Progress in Cooking*. Chicago: Gray Institute of Home Economics, 1934.

Rydell, Robert W. *World of Fairs: The Century of Progress Expositions*. Chicago: University of Chicago Press, 1993.

Check, Please!

Airing first on WTTW (Chicago's PBS member station) in 2001, the now successful *Check, Please!* has expanded to several other U.S. regional markets. In each market, the format is the same: three citizen-reviewers and a host sit around a dinner table and offer heartfelt critiques of both a restaurant of their choosing and a restaurant chosen by each of the other reviewers.

The program concept was developed by Chicagoans David Manilow and Joel Cohen, both of whom continue to be closely involved with production and brand management. Chicago hosts have included Amanda Puck, Alpana Singh, and Catherine De Orio.

Contributor: David Hammond

See also: Media, Television

BIBLIOGRAPHY

Check, Please! http://en.wikipedia.org/wiki/Check,_Please!

Cheese

From the mid–nineteenth to the early twentieth century, Illinois was covered with small dairy farms, many of which produced butter and cheese. In its early days, Chicagoans got their milk from a family member's or neighbor's cow, and milk production remained small scale until the mid-1880s. But as Chicago grew and refrigerated railroad and truck cars made transportation feasible, farmers switched to the production of fluid milk for the city market. As a result, cheese production virtually disappeared except for local farmhouse products. In 1903, Canadian James L. Kraft moved to Chicago and began packaging cheese under the Kraft name. He and his brothers developed a method of processing cheese to increase its shelf life. Today, Kraft's worldwide headquarters are in downtown Chicago, and the company is closing its one processing plant in the state.

In 1978, Rene and Pasquale Caputo founded Wisconsin Corp., which manufactures Italian-style Parmesan, Romano, mozzarella, and other cheeses at its 200,000-square-foot facility in suburban Melrose Park. An adjacent Caputo Cheese market carries more than 10,000 cheeses from around the world and stores them in its aging room. A few restaurants and markets have started making their own cheeses, including Eataly. A pioneer wholesaler was Sofia Solomon, who started providing imported cheeses to top restaurants through her company Tekla in 1992. The American Cheese Company, founded in 1988 by Giles Schnierle, represents about 60 small artisan producers in 28 states and supplies restaurants with some 300 cheeses.

Today more imported and domestic cheeses are available than ever before in Chicago, at farmers markets, ethnic markets, supermarkets such as Whole Foods, and specialty stores such as Pastoral Artisan Cheese, Bread & Wine, Provenance Food and Wine, and Say Cheese.

Contributor: Colleen Sen
See also: Dairy Industry; Kraft Foods; Kraft, James L.

BIBLIOGRAPHY

Daley, Bill. "Sofia Solomon, Cheese Advocate." *Chicago Tribune*, May 19, 2013.
"The Five Best Cheese Shops in Chicago." *Chicagoist*, September 4, 2013. http://chicagoist.com/2013/09/04/the_best_cheese_shops_in_chicago.php.

Chefs

At first, there were just cooks. In Chicago taverns, inns, and restaurants, those who prepared food for customers toiled in obscurity. Like elsewhere in the United States, local cooks were mostly unrecognized and underappreciated. But as restaurants became more important in the years after World War II, the word *chef* gradually emerged. It signified professional training and greater skill with ingredients.

Through the '50s and '60s, Chicago's restaurants improved and fine dining became more available to more people. Chefs often became restaurateurs. One of the most colorful was Louis Szathmary, who opened The Bakery restaurant on North Lincoln Avenue in 1963. With his quintessential chef looks—white mustache and beard, a rotund middle, and a tall, white toque—he brought Continental (with a Hungarian inflection) cuisine to Chicago. Next to follow, Jean Banchet earned a national reputation with his Le Français restaurant in Wheeling, a far distance from downtown Chicago, but that didn't deter diners who appreciated Banchet's classic take on fine French fare.

Szathmary and Banchet were forerunners of today's celebrity chef. Since their contributions, countless other chefs have worked to make Chicago the culinary destination it is today.

A group of French chefs followed Banchet's lead, all preparing French classic or nouvelle cuisine dishes with skill: Bernard Cretier, Didier Durant, Fernand Gutierrez, Jean Joho, Roland Liccioni, Jean Claude Poilevey, Gabino Sotelino, Dominique Tougne, and others.

By the 1980s, the interest in food and dining out, and the rise of the "foodies," brought in the age of the star chef. Among the more well-known were Rick Bayless and the late Charlie Trotter, who each opened restaurants, Frontera Grill and Charlie Trotter's, respectively, in 1987. Each chef ran a popular restaurant, wrote cookbooks, starred in television series, and started food companies. They attracted national—and even international—audiences.

At the same time, some of the popular French restaurants gave way to other cuisines as Italian, Japanese, Chinese, and Thai chefs opened restaurants: Yoshi Katsumura, Jackie Shen, and a young Arun Sampanthavivat, who in 1965 started what would become the elegant, highly rated Thai restaurant, Arun's, on North Kedzie Avenue. Tony Mantuano helped the Italian restaurant, Spiaggia, earn 4-star ratings from local critics for its top-notch, high-end menu.

But chefs preparing upscale American cuisine also earned their share of the press. Michael Foley at Printers Row was one of the first to embrace local, midwestern ingredients. Others included John Terczak at Gordon; Rick Tramonto at Trio and Tru; Shawn McClain at Spring, Green Zebra; Michael Taus at Zealous; Michael Kornick at mk; Bruce Sherman at North Pond; Paul Virant of Vie; Paul Kahan of Blackbird; and more recently, Curtis Duffy of Grace.

Women slowly made inroads as chefs in the 1980s and 1990s, after years of cooking on the line with little recognition. Carolyn Buster was an early groundbreaker at The Cottage in Calumet City. She was followed by such chefs as Monique Hooker, Sarah Stegner, Carrie Nahabedian, Suzy Crofton, Susan Goss, and pastry chefs such as Gale Gand, En-Ming Hsu, and Mindy Segal. More recently, Stephanie Izard and Iliana Regan have created a great number of fans with their Girl & the Goat and Elizabeth restaurants, respectively.

With the molecular cuisine movement sweeping the country in the 2000s, several chefs rose to national spotlight with their modernist food: the late Homaro Cantu, Graham Elliot, and, especially, Grant Achatz, whose Alinea has been rated one of the top restaurants in the world. The era of great Chicago chefs continues.

Contributor: Carol Mighton Haddix
See also: Individual chefs' entries; Restaurants and Fine Dining; Restaurateurs and Restaurant Groups

BIBLIOGRAPHY

"Chicago's Best Chefs." *Chicago Magazine*. June 5, 2007.
Haddix, Carol Mighton. *Chicago Cooks: 25 Years of Food History with Menus, Recipes and Tips from Les Dames d'Escoffier Chicago.* Chicago: Agate Publishing, 2006.

Chef's Hall of Fame

In 2005, the ACF Chicago Chefs Association created the Chefs Hall of Fame to honor Chicago's top food industry leaders, an idea first proposed in 1978 by Chefs John Castro and John Kaufman. The first inductee was Charlie Trotter. Subsequent awardees, honored at annual dinners, include Jean Banchet, Louis Szathmary, Graham Elliot, Rick Bayless, Art Smith, Carrie Nahabedian, Paul

Kahan, and Stephanie Izard. Categories for top Pastry Chef and Industry Leader were later created. The Association, whose mission is to "promote and celebrate Chicago as a culinary mecca," also runs The Chicago Culinary Museum, a collection of culinary artifacts and cookbooks that is looking for a permanent home.

Contributor: Colleen Sen

See also: Restaurant Awards and Honors

BIBLIOGRAPHY

Lalley, Heather. "Chicago Culinary Museum Honors Rick Bayless." *Chicago Tribune*, August 27, 2008.

The Chicago Culinary Museum. http://www.thechicagoculinary museum.org/.

Chicago Botanic Garden

The Regenstein Garden, located on an island within the sprawling 365-acre Chicago Botanic Garden (CBG), holds 400 types of edible plants, including apples, grapes, chilies, berries, and greenhouse-grown plants such as herbs. Located at 1000 Lake Cook Road in Glencoe, the garden offers educational resources for Chicago-area home gardeners, including website information on plants, and workshops, tastings, festivals, exhibits, classes, and demonstrations. Classes include such topics as "The History of Tea," "Mushrooms," "Wellness Gardens," "Edible Container Gardening," and "Homescale Aquaponics."

From May to October, the Garden Chef Series brings area chefs to the Regenstein's outdoor demonstration kitchen area to share recipe techniques using fresh produce. Recipes are posted on the CBG's website. Occasional farm dinners are held in the Regenstein Garden, featuring the produce grown there.

CBG recently joined in the local urban agriculture trend with The Windy City Harvest program for youth. Participants learn job skills and provide fresh produce to underserved communities in the area. In 2014, they produced about 92,000 pounds of produce.

A partnership between the Garden and Kraft Foods Group Foundation in 2010 had Windy City Harvest participants help the Kraft Food Garden in Northfield. By 2013, they harvested a record 14,294 pounds of fresh fruits and vegetables, much of which went to low-income and homeless people. And in 2013, CBG launched the McCormick Place Rooftop Farm. About 20,000 square feet of roof became a productive urban farm as part of a three-year agreement with McCormick Place, and SAVOR . . . Chicago (the McCormick Place food-service operator).

Contributor: Carol Mighton Haddix

See also: Agriculture, Urban

BIBLIOGRAPHY

Sabin, Katje. "The Garden in Winter: Behind the Scenes at the Regenstein Fruit and Vegetable Garden." LTH Forum. http://www .lthforum.com/2014/01/regenstein/.

"Urban agriculture." Chicago Botanic Garden. http://www.chicago botanic.org/urbanagriculture.

Chicago Exchanges

The Chicago of the early 1800s was becoming a shipping and processing hub for the increasing agricultural wealth of the Midwest. Chicago merchants bought and sold commodities, especially grain, thus setting prices and, from the 1830s, some degree of quality control. It was a risky business, with disputes rising among brokers. In 1848, a group of merchants assembled to create an organization to mitigate risk. Called the Board of Trade, it was granted the right to control grain grinding, and in 1859 the state granted it powers to formulate rules for trade and to mediate business disputes.

During the Civil War, when massive supplies were needed by the Union armies, a system rose where contracts for commodities were given and payments made upon delivery. That arrangement became the futures market by the 1870s. The Chicago Board of Trade (CBOT) became the place where U.S. merchants, farmers, and grain traders came to haggle over price and formalize sales and delivery terms for crops still in the field or in storage. While CBOT focused its agriculture expertise largely on corn and wheat, it also served as the foundation for the Chicago Butter and Egg Board, which was formed in 1898 to trade, as its name implied, butter and egg contracts. In 1919, the Chicago Butter & Egg Board was reorganized as the Chicago Mercantile Exchange (CME or the Merc or Chicago Merc). The CME traded butter and eggs, but it also traded onions, pork bellies, live cattle, and hogs. Attempts to introduce shrimp and turkey futures, however, never took off.

The exchanges thrived for decades, each within the trading niches they had carved for themselves. As they are today, they were essential to balance commodity price swings caused by natural disasters, crop failures, and political or economic shifts, all which, if left unchecked, could affect the entire supply chain. Stability and predictability have been associated with exchanges since their start.

In 2007, after nearly a century apart, the CBOT and CME were reunited when CME purchased the CBOT for $8 billion in stock. Today, futures and options contracts on more than 50 products, from pork bellies to Eurodollars and stock market indices, are traded at the combined CME Group. It is the world's leading derivatives marketplace.

Trading exchanges have embraced more than just ownership changes during their existence. The advent of

BOARD OF TRADE PIT

The Chicago Board of Trade (CBOT), founded in 1848, is the oldest grain futures market in the United States. It was a capitalist innovation that made Chicago not only into a stacker of wheat but a center of speculation and trading for food commodities and futures. The CBOT was famous for its "pit," a place where hundreds of frenetic traders yelled out and used hand signals to place buy and sell orders. The scene was made famous by Frank Norris's 1903 novel *The Pit* and revisited during a scene in the 1986 film *Ferris Bueller's Day Off*. Modern technology took its toll on the old trading system; in July 2015 the pit was closed, replaced by silent electronic trading.

—ERIK GELLMAN

electronic trading has shuttered every futures trading floor in the world, including most of those in Chicago in 2015, putting an end to the 150-year reign of the open outcry trading pit. The pits once were chaotic places, filled with yelling and disorderly conduct. But trading now is a 24/7 activity in which monitoring of world trends and price swings is commonplace and done anywhere via computer or mobile device. The competitive battle to secure a buy or sell comes down to the technological advantage that a firm has. A nanosecond edge can be a huge advantage.

The trading pit became an element of American folk culture: the famous trading pit hand signals, often referred to as a fascinating "lost language." Traders recall how, for instance, Goldman Sachs was referenced by a quick point to a gold watch, or Bear Stearns by forming a hand into a claw. In the very basic of pit signals, palms in toward the body indicate the action of buying, and palms out indicate selling. Price is indicated at an arm's length away from the body, and quantity is displayed close to the face. Numerical quantities of 1–5 are displayed with vertical fingers and 6–9 are displayed with horizontal fingers. Quantities of 1 to 9 are indicated at chin level, while increments of 10 are indicated at the forehead. It has all disappeared but remains as a piece of Chicago's business history.

Because of fluctuations in supply and demand, agricultural commodity prices remain highly unstable. Adding to the instability is the vast number of countries vying for a share of the world's market. But the exchanges will remain an integral part of the food production system as it continues to develop into a complex, globalized business.

Contributor: Sarah Muirhead

BIBLIOGRAPHY

"CBOT Trading Pit Hand Signals." Trading Pit History. http://trading pithistory.com/.

Chicago Board of Trade. http://cmegroup.com/company.cbot.html.

Gregory, Owen K. "Commodities Markets." *The Encyclopedia of Chicago*. http://www.encyclopedia.chicagohistory.org/pages/317.html.

Chicago Gourmet (See: Festivals)

Chicago High School for Agricultural Sciences

A college preparatory public high school in the Chicago Public School system, The Chicago High School for Agricultural Sciences is a 72-acre campus at 3857 W. 111th St. Founded in 1984–85 to prepare students from urban backgrounds for careers in the agriculture industry, it is unique in the Midwest and a model for school districts across the nation.

It enrolls 720 students from across the city annually, 60 to 65 percent of whom are from minority groups. The rigorous curriculum is modeled on the Future Farmers of America agricultural education program. The high school is the largest chapter of FFA in the state and fifth largest in the nation.

The curriculum emphasizes mathematics, sciences, and agricultural sciences. As juniors and seniors, students can choose to follow one of several areas of concentration called Pathways. These include Animal Science, Agricultural Mechanics—a hands-on program of agricultural construction and building maintenance—Food Science, Horticulture/Landscape Design, and Agricultural Finance—including macro and micro economics and accounting. Career advising and practical workshops are regularly organized, and an extensive program of internships and summer programs is offered by colleges, universities, and businesses in the Chicago area. Eighty-five percent of graduating students go on to higher education, forty-five percent to the nation's top agricultural universities.

CHSAS students get practical farming experience on the school's 40-acre farm. A farm stand on site sells fresh produce on weekdays from July to the winter holidays, including squash, tomatoes, corn, collard greens, peppers, okra, zucchini, eggplant, cabbage, watermelon, and cantaloupe. The farm is the last working farmland in the city of Chicago.

Contributor: Bruce Kraig

See also: Agriculture, Urban

BIBLIOGRAPHY

Chicago High School for Agricultural Sciences. http://www.chicago agr.org/index.jsp.

Chicken Vesuvio

The basic preparation for the dish now commonly called Chicken Vesuvio is so simple it seems likely to have been served elsewhere before it appeared on a 1930s Chicago menu (apparently for the first time) at the Vesuvio Restaurant (15 E. Wacker Dr.). This Italian American dish includes chicken on the bone with potato wedges. Ingredients are sautéed in garlic, oregano, olive oil, and wine; the chicken skin is usually baked crisp, and peas are sometimes added.

Chicken Vesuvio still is served at many Chicago restaurants, including Harry Caray's and Gene & Georgetti's. The precise origins of this dish are often debated, with a counterargument to the alleged Chicago origins of Chicken Vesuvio offered by Dr. Anthony Buccini, Chicago-based linguist and food historian: "At risk of being attacked for a lack of appreciation of Chicago's place in culinary history, I fail to grasp the basis of the claim that 'Vesuvio' style chicken was in any meaningful sense invented in Chicago. There are a number of variants that can be legitimately called 'Chicken Vesuvio,' and the kinds of variation allowed place the dish squarely amidst a continuum of southern Italian roasted chicken preparations."

Contributor: David Hammond

BIBLIOGRAPHY

LTH Forum. "The Alleged Origins of Chicken Vesuvio." http://www .lthforum.com/bb/viewtopic.php?t=3416.

Chinese

The first Chinese immigrants settled in Illinois around 1870, after the completion of the Transcontinental Railway. Discrimination in the western states, where they had

CHICKEN VESUVIO

Prep: 35 minutes

Cook: 50 minutes

Makes: 6 servings

Here is one version of the famous dish, based on those served at many Chicago restaurants, including The Italian Village and Gene & Georgetti's. If you have time, season the chicken several hours ahead and refrigerate. Some restaurants also use basil and thyme as additional seasonings.

   3 teaspoons dried oregano

   2 teaspoons salt, plus more to taste

   1 teaspoon freshly ground black pepper

   1 cut-up fryer chicken, about 2–3 pounds

   1/3 cup olive oil

   3 large russet potatoes

   4 cloves garlic, peeled, mashed

   1/2 cup dry white wine

   1/4 cup chopped parsley

1. Heat oven to 400 degrees. Mix 1 teaspoon of the oregano and the salt and pepper in a small bowl. Pat chicken dry. Sprinkle seasonings over all sides of the chicken. Heat the olive oil in a large, heavy skillet over medium-high heat. When oil is hot, add half of the chicken pieces. Brown, turning once, about 10 minutes; transfer chicken to a plate. Repeat browning with remaining chicken; transfer to the plate.

2. Meanwhile, peel potatoes; cut into thick wedges. Pat dry. When chicken is removed, add potatoes to the skillet. Fry, turning once, until golden, about 5–7 minutes. Remove; drain on paper towel. Sprinkle with salt to taste.

3. Return chicken to the skillet; transfer to oven. Cook, uncovered, until juices run clear, about 20–25 minutes. Remove from oven; place chicken on a large platter. Add cooked potatoes, garlic, wine, and the remaining 2 teaspoons oregano to the skillet; stir up browned bits. Return to oven; cook 5 minutes. Arrange potatoes around chicken; pour skillet juices over chicken. Sprinkle with parsley.

Gene & Georgetti's version of the classic chicken vesuvio. Photograph by Carol Mighton Haddix.

originally settled, and hard economic times drove them to seek lives further east.

T. C. Moy is thought to have arrived in Chicago in 1878 as the city's first Chinese citizen. He's said to have written to friends and relatives so enthusiastically about Chicago that 80 joined him within a year. By 1900, their numbers had grown to the point where Chinese immigrants ran 167 restaurants in the city, according to documents from the Chinese American Service League. Most of the Chinese in Chicago were Taishanese from southern Guangdong Province. Many set up their businesses around Clark and Van Buren Streets, including some upscale establishments boasting multiple floors, intricate architecture, and imported furniture.

By 1903, Chinese restaurants had become so established that the *Chicago Daily Tribune* published a story with the headline: "Chop Suey Fad Grows: Chicago's Appetite Is Becoming Cultivated to Chinese Dish of Mystery." The article described several Chinese restaurants downtown serving dishes that included chop suey and rice for 25 to 40 cents. A sample menu also featured mu gu chop, foo young dove, and rice for 30 cents. Boiled chicken was 25 cents and roast pork was 15–25 cents.

Some of Chicago's earliest Chinese restaurants included King Joy Lo, Mandarin Inn, and Joy Yen Lo, all located around Van Buren and Clark and all lavishly designed and decorated with furniture and accents from China. About 1913, some of the businesses started moving south to what is now known as Chicago's main Chinatown, near Wentworth Street and Cermak Road. Still, many restaurants stayed in the original downtown neighborhood. According to John Jung's book *Sweet and Sour*, of the more than 100 Chinese restaurants in Chicago in 1915, only 17 were located in Chinatown. Won How at 2237 South Wentworth, opened in 1928, is the oldest continuously operating Chinese restaurant in Chicago (and a favorite of Al Capone). Second oldest is Orange Garden at 1942 West Irving Park, founded in 1932.

The restaurants outside of Chinatown not only served chop suey, chow mein, and roast pork, but also a robust selection of American and Continental dishes. At the four-story Hoe Sai Gai on Randolph Street, these non-Chinese dishes took up two-thirds of the menu in 1933 and included frog legs, steak à la chasseur, lobster Newberg, lamb chops, fried halibut, whole squab, breaded pork tenderloin, and fried chicken on toast.

The large lavish downtown restaurants of this era, which included the Oriental Inn (at State and Randolph) and Hoe Sai Gai, often also featured floor shows, big bands, and extensive liquor selections that included fine wine and Champagne. Strangely, Chicago's Chinese

BEN MOY'S THE BIRD

For 25 years, the most unusual and acclaimed Chinese restaurant in the Chicago area was The Bird. In 1972, Ben Moy retired from the wholesale meat business and opened his restaurant in a small space at the Skokie Swift CTA station. It was packed by enthusiastic food connoisseurs from the start. Eventually, The Bird moved to a desolate strip mall in Melrose Park in the mid-1980s and became a destination for fans, including many members of the Chicago Symphony Orchestra. Moy's cuisine was based on the Cantonese principle that a dish should taste of "the thing itself," enhanced by the lightest touches of flavorings. Ingredients such as basil, two kinds of oregano, several types of wild garlic, rosemary, shallots, leeks, fenugreek, three kinds of chives, bourbon, Cognac, and gin were but a few of the ingredients he used. His famous dishes included boneless stuffed chicken wings (filled with chicken meat, black mushrooms, and water chestnuts); crispy skin chicken (boneless chicken, marinated, poached, deep-fried, cut into slices and served on a bed of lettuce); and mock squab (Cornish hen, marinated in Cognac, honey, and soy sauce, and then poached and deep-fried briefly). The Bird was destroyed when an errant car crashed into it in 1999. Already nearing 80, Chef Moy closed the restaurant and retired to tend his gardens.

—BRUCE KRAIG

restaurants of subsequent decades would never match this opulence. Instead, they became much more casual.

When George Tan, who ran many Chicago Chinese restaurants from the '40s through the '80s, was asked if the food was authentically Chinese, he replied, "No, of course, it wasn't. This was for white people." To the question of where Chinese people ate, the answer was "We had little places in basements in Chinatown." In his history of American family-run Chinese restaurants, Jung calls these restaurants in Chinatown *fan deems*. They were simple establishments where a worker could get a plain bowl of rice or noodles with a little vegetable and meat.

Despite the effects of the Chinese Exclusion Act of 1882, which severely limited Chinese immigration to the States, Chinese numbers kept rising in Chicago. With the repeal of the act in the post–World War II period, families started to be reunited, establishing more stable

CHOP SUEY JOINTS

Chicagoans were introduced to Chinese cuisine through the classic Americanized dish chop suey (and its sibling chow mein) at the end of the nineteenth century. The earliest restaurants serving this mixed vegetable and meat dish, also called "Chinese Irish stew," were small places in the Chinese community around Clark and Washington Streets and notably in the red-light levee district on 22nd Street. In addition to demimondaines, the earliest patrons were cabbies, policemen, and theatergoers who wanted a late meal at low cost. Restaurateur Sam Moy was a leading figure in setting up chop suey houses. By 1903, there were 35 in Chicago, located in the Loop and across the city. Dubbed by a newspaper as "the chop suey trust," many of the restaurants were owned by a conglomerate called the Hip Lung Company. Chop suey remains popular in Chicago, especially in low-income neighborhoods where small Chinese take-out places are common. There was a version called "Chicago Chop Suey," but because it has disappeared from city menus, its ingredients are a mystery.

—BRUCE KRAIG

communities in Chinatown. Chinatown would become a popular tourist destination, but its food selections went beyond the tourist favorites of chop suey and chow mein. These "more authentic Chinese" offerings reflected the almost entirely Cantonese makeup of Chicago Chinese. This included seafood dishes such as clams with black bean sauce, shrimp in lobster sauce, whole fish, and barbecued pork, all popular in that Southeast region of China. It also meant Hong Kong–style bakeries, featuring egg tarts, sticky rice in bamboo or lotus leaves, and *char siu bao*, barbecued pork buns. Chinatown also made room for large Hong Kong–style banquet halls and dim sum houses such as the Pagoda Inn, Won Kow, and Guey Sam.

Also in the post–World War II era, Cantonese restaurants found themselves capitalizing on the interest in the South Pacific (both from returning GIs and the musical by the same name). They gave their restaurants a Polynesian or tiki theme. Some of the most notable in Chicago were Trader Vic's in the Palmer House Hotel and South Pacific on Randolph near the Oriental Theater. These restaurants served tropical drinks along with barbecued ribs and a mix of fried treats and skewered meats dubbed a "pupu platter."

With the opening up to China during Richard Nixon's administration and the further easing of immigration restrictions, Chicago began to receive Chinese arrivals from beyond Canton (now Guangzhou), especially Taiwan. The first restaurant serving Northern Chinese food (so-called "Mandarin" cuisine) was Dragon Inn on the Far South Side, which opened in the late 1960s. It was soon followed by The Chinese Tea House (see sidebar, p. 73). In 1974, the House of Hunan opened at 3150 North Lincoln, the first restaurant to popularize the spicy fare of Hunan and Szechuan. It introduced such dishes as willow beef with a serious chili heat (warning diners with red underlining). Many new restaurants followed, and within a few years the Hunan/Szechuan revolution was well underway. Dishes such as scallion pancakes and moo shoo pork started appearing in Chinese restaurants all over the city.

Hoe Sai Gai restaurant menu, 1933. Courtesy of Monica Eng.

The 1970s also saw the relocation of the Hip Sing merchants' association to Argyle Street in Uptown. This became the anchor for a "new Chinatown" on the North Side. Although it continues to host some Chinese restaurants—including the banquet hall and dim sum restaurant Furama—the neighborhood has become increasingly Southeast Asian in the intervening years, with Chinese Vietnamese holding down major businesses along with Vietnamese.

As more mainland Chinese from areas outside Canton gained power and numbers in Chicago, the food also came to reflect their presence. In 1997, chef Tony Hu took over the Mandarin Chef at the west end of Chinatown Square, and started a revolution in Chicago Chinese dining. Serving Szechuan (Sichuan) dishes like Dong Po fried steamed pork elbow, fried pig intestines, *mapo* tofu floating in a half-inch of red oil, *ma la* cabbage, fatty twice-cooked pork, and his signature chili pepper chicken, Hu showed that a restaurant could survive without pandering to non-Chinese tastes. Hu would go on to take over many of the storefronts in Chinatown Square, serving regional specialties from areas including Beijing, Shanghai, Hunan, and Yunnan.

In a parallel development, an influx of highly educated Taiwanese established ad hoc Chinese communities in the Western suburbs around Oak Brook in the 1980s. This led to the opening of the International Mall Plaza, anchored by the Ding Ho Supermarket, in Westmont, in 1986. Its food court featured some of the most authentic Taiwanese and Northern Chinese dishes in the Chicago area. Patrons waited in long lines on the weekends to eat freshly fried *yu tiao* fritters, Northern style pancakes, and dumplings washed down with freshly made sweet or salty/spicy soy milk, *do jiang*.

In 2015, Tony Hu opened a Lao Sze Chuan location on Michigan Avenue. It attracts downtown shoppers but also draws heavily from the new crop of wealthy Chinese college students and recent grads who live downtown. These students have also spurred the growth of more regional restaurants in the Chinatown area. The most notable are those representing the northeast region of Dongbei with its wheat-based foods, including noodles, dumplings, and even bread.

It remains to be seen if Chinese restaurants ever will return to the social prominence they enjoyed 100 years ago.

Contributor: Monica Eng

BIBLIOGRAPHY

"Chop Suey Fad Grows: Chicago's Appetite Is Becoming Cultivated to Chinese Dish of Mystery." *Chicago Tribune*, July 19, 1903.

Day, Jennifer. "Won Kow's Past Interwoven with Chinatown's Story." *Chicago Tribune*. October 20, 2011.

Ho, Chumei, and Soo Lon Moy, eds. *Images of America: Chinese in Chicago 1870–1945*. Chicago: Arcadia Publishing, 2005.

CHEF INTRODUCED CHICAGO TO MANDARIN CUISINE

An influential Chinese chef, Peter Lo (birthday unknown; died 2013) was one of the first chefs to prepare northern Chinese cuisine (also called Mandarin cuisine) in the Chicago area. He first worked at Dragon Inn, which opened in 1964 in a shopping center in the south suburb of Glenwood Heights. It served such then-exotic dishes as hot and sour soup and moo shu pork—a significant departure from the usual chow mein and egg foo yung at most Chinese restaurants. In 1967, he left the Dragon Inn to open his own place, the Chinese Tea House on North Avenue east of Austin Boulevard. By the early 1970s, he was an owner of Cathay Mandarin and Peter Lo's, located first in Rogers Park, later on North Lincoln.

—COLLEEN SEN

Church, Ruth Ellen

Born in Humboldt, Iowa, Ruth Ellen Lovrien (1909–91) graduated from Iowa State University in 1933 with a degree in food and nutrition journalism. After a job as society editor for a small Iowa paper, she began a 38-year run in 1936 as food editor at the *Chicago Tribune*—one of the first American newspapers to have a test kitchen. She married Freeman Church, who later illustrated several of her cookbook covers.

Church wrote under the name of "Mary Meade," used by the newspaper for many previous food editors. She was one of the first food editors to write a wine column. During her career, Church won six Vesta Awards for excellence in food journalism. She wrote numerous cookbooks, among them one of her most well-known, *Mary Meade's Magic Recipes for the Electronic Blender*. Originally published in 1952, it sold more than 209,000 copies. Among her other cookbooks were *Mary Meade's Kitchen Companion* (1955), *Mary Meade's Country Cookbook* (1956), *The Burger Cookbook* (1967), and *Entertaining with Wine* (1970). She retired from the newspaper in 1974. She died tragically, killed during a home robbery.

Contributor: Kimberly Wilmot Voss

See also: Media, Print

BIBLIOGRAPHY

Voss, Kimberly. *The Food Section: Newspaper Women and the Culinary Community*. Lanham, Md.: Rowman and Littlefield, 2014.

Cocktails and Cocktail Lounges

Cocktails, which likely first appeared in the United States in the seventeenth or eighteenth century, are drinks comprising a blend of spirits, sugar, water, and bitters. While precursors to the cocktail date back as far as the 1500s (punch, for instance, was a popular quaffable beverage consumed in colonial England after being adopted from India), cocktails stand apart primarily due to the inclusion of bitters: potable, low-alcohol elixirs popularly used for medicinal purposes in the late eighteenth century. Trinidad-based Angostura and New Orleans–based Peychaud's are two of the surviving bitters producers of that era; nearly all other bitters production facilities were shut down after the ratification of the 18th Amendment to the United States. Constitution, known as the Volstead Act, or Prohibition (1920–33). Prohibition in the United States also meant that the manufacturing, transportation, and sale of intoxicating liquors became illegal, which in turn made illegal drinking all the more exotic, launching a second wave of popularity for the drink category.

Chicago's history with cocktails predates Prohibition, and ironically thrived during it. There were a rumored 20,000 speakeasies (underground cocktail bars) in the city by the middle of the 1920s, their existence largely ignored by then Mayor William Hale Thompson. When Prohibition was repealed in late 1933, the need for speakeasies dwindled, and Chicago's tens of thousands of taverns began shuttering. Many were replaced by drugstores and soda fountains that were more profitable because their customers did not linger, as they did in the old bars. A handful of the oldest, established prior to Prohibition, are still in operation, including Schaller's Pump, established in 1881, the city's oldest continually running tavern; Marge's Still, established in 1885; the Green Mill (frequented by Capone), established in 1907; and Twin Anchors (frequented by Frank Sinatra), established in 1910. These and other taverns and cocktail lounges continued to thrive into the second half of the twentieth century, plateauing with the popularity of highballs—simplified alcoholic drinks comprised of a spirit and a mixer (e.g., Cape Cod: vodka and cranberry juice; Screwdriver: vodka and orange juice)—then dwindled with increased consumption of wine and beer.

It was not until the 1990s that cocktails by definition began to resurface, following an ingredient-awareness movement established by television celebrity chefs, and

A PEACH OF A PUNCH

"There was the light furniture in the popular Swedish style, the brown carpet, the Chagall and Gris prints, the vines trailing from the mantelpiece, the bowl of Cohasset punch."

—SAUL BELLOW'S DESCRIPTION OF A CHICAGO COCKTAIL PARTY, FROM *DANGLING MAN*, 1944

Called the definitive Chicago cocktail, Cohasset punch was one of the city's most popular drinks until the 1950s. The invention of the drink, a sweet and fragrant rum concoction served over half a canned peach, is attributed to Chicago bartender Gus Williams, who created it for a famous comedian, William Crane, at Williams's summer house in Cohasset, Massachusetts. Returning to Chicago, Williams began serving the cocktail in his bar, Williams & Newman on Lake Street. When he retired in 1916, he is said to have sold the recipe to the owners of the Ladner Brothers Saloon at 207 W. Madison St. Until Prohibition, the drink was so popular that the owners called the saloon "Home of Cohasset Punch," began bottling it, and sold it for $2 a bottle. The bar was famous for its cages of birds, which led to endless jokes about "the more Cohasset punch one drank, the sweeter the birdies' songs became."

COLLEEN SEN

Cohasset Punch

Prep: 5 minutes
Makes: 2 drinks

Adapted from a recipe in Eric Felten's "Drinking the Chicago Way," *The Wall Street Journal*, December 20, 2008.

2 canned peach halves, syrup reserved
2 jiggers each: dark rum, sweet vermouth, orange brandy
Juice of 1 lemon
2 dashes orange bitters

Place the peach halves in 2 saucer-shaped or other short cocktail glasses. Fill each glass half full with shaved ice. Combine remaining ingredients in a cocktail shaker with more shaved ice; add a jigger of reserved peach syrup. Shake to chill. Strain into glasses.

embraced by increasingly health-conscious diners curious about where their food was coming from. Introduced by bartenders Tony Abou-Ganim at Harry Denton's Starlight Room in San Francisco and Dale DeGroff at New York's Rainbow Room, the third wave of cocktails in the United States married classic Prohibition-inspired recipes and proportions with modern, pure ingredients such as fresh juices and natural sugar and was manifested in cocktails such as the Cosmopolitan (popularized by DeGroff at the Rainbow Room, though he's denied inventing it) and the Cable Car (created by Abou-Ganim at the Starlight Room).

The modern wave of cocktails—eventually dubbed craft cocktails—was ushered into Chicago via the fine-dining scene by bartenders Bridget Albert (protégé of Abou-Ganim) and Adam Seger (protégé of DeGroff). Landing in Chicago independently after having spent the late-1990s in Las Vegas and Louisville, respectively, the pair established the Illinois chapter of the United States Bartender's Guild in 2005. Albert, as regional Director of Mixology for Southern Wine and Spirits and founder of the Academy of Spirits and Fine Service Illinois, a program for bartenders that covers the history of all spirits and pre-Prohibition cocktails, has trained hundreds of working Chicago bartenders, many of whom have since opened their own bars and consulting firms.

Chicago's best known craft-cocktail bar, The Violet Hour in Wicker Park, opened in 2007 with staff trained by the New York–based Alchemy Consulting group. Since then, Chicago has seen a boom of dozens of bars and lounges devoted to so-called craft cocktails created with fresh ingredients. Notable pioneers include Logan Square's Weegee's Lounge (opened in 2006) and The Whistler (opened in 2008) and The Drawing Room (2007–14) in the Gold Coast. Each introduced original cocktails that have since become modern classics, including The Violet Hour's Juliet & Romeo.

Another significant milestone in Chicago's cocktail history was marked in 2011 with the opening of Chef Grant Achatz's The Aviary, the city's first molecular-gastronomic cocktail lounge, in the Fulton Market District. The Aviary counts among its alums Diageo's 2014 World Class Bartender of the Year, Charles Joly. He bested nearly 50 international bartenders for the title while serving as The Aviary's beverage director. A handful of The Aviary's quixotic cocktails, such as opening Beverage Manager Craig Schoettler's In The Rocks (a classic cocktail presented in a hollow ice sphere that must be cracked to be consumed), have garnered national attention.

Contributor: Lauren Viera
See also: Bars, Taverns, Saloons, and Pubs; Prohibition

BIBLIOGRAPHY

Bensen, Amanda. "Did New Orleans Invent the Cocktail?" *Smithsonian*, February 24, 2009.
Cross, Robert. "Prohibition Begins." *Chicago Tribune*. http://www.chicagotribune.com/news/nationworld/politics/chi-chicagodays-prohibition-story-story.html.
Gentile, Jay. "The 10 Oldest Bars in Chicago." *Thrillist*, September 29, 2014.
http://www.thrillist.com/drink/chicago/oldest-bars-in-chicago.

Coffee and Tea

America's relationship with coffee and tea tipped in coffee's favor when Colonists dumped English tea into Boston Harbor in 1771; yet tea remained the most popular beverage in the United States until the 1820s. By the time Chicago was established in 1833, coffee had taken over, though tea continued to contribute to the city's growing economy. Rail lines radiating into Chicago brought both green coffee beans, coming from Central and South America, and leaf teas harvested from fields in Asia.

During the Civil War, soldiers relied on coffee. After the war, America's thirst for coffee increased. In the 1880s, The Great American Tea Company (later the Great Atlantic and Pacific Tea Company) started roasting its Eight O'Clock Breakfast Coffee in Chicago. In those early days, coffee and tea were sold by men traveling house to house with horse and cart. Salesmen enticed homemakers to buy their products with coupons that could be redeemed for household wares. Chicago became a hub of coffee innovation: In 1881, Steele & Price introduced cans made of paperlike strawboard, and, in 1884, the first paper and tin can that improved storage and freshness was patented by the Chicago Liquid Sack Co. The 1893 World's Columbian Exposition in Chicago introduced Turkish- and Viennese-style coffees, beans from Brazil and Mexico, and teas from British India.

In 1899, Dr. Sartori Kato, a Japanese chemist, brought a soluble tea to Chicago. The product was not a commercial success, but his dried coffee concentrate fared better, and in 1901 it was sold at the Pan-American Exposition in Buffalo, New York. By 1918, his company, the Soluble Coffee Company of America, supplied instant coffee to American soldiers fighting overseas.

Several coffee companies that would grow to be national brands began in Chicago. In 1913, William A. Stewart started a small coffee and tea company that supplied upscale hotels and shops, such as The Drake Hotel and Marshall Field's. In 1933, Stewarts was named the official coffee for the Century of Progress world's fair. Stewarts premium blended coffees and teas continue to be popular with drinkers into the twenty-first century. In 1908, 19-year-old Lithuanian immigrant Jacob Cohn started working with his brother in a business that supplied cafeterias and restaurants with coffee. By 1915, he branched off with his own company, Continental Coffee Co., and by the 1920s he had 15 employees. Twenty years later he had a national distribution network and hit $1 million in sales. By the 1980s, sales reached $1 billion. The company has changed hands through the years (it has been part of Sysco Corp., Quaker Oats, and, most recently, The Hillshire Brands Co.) and continues to produce private label coffee, tea, and cocoa for food service.

Coffee and tea continue to have a hold on Chicago. Numerous commercial coffee roasters and tea importers operate around the city and suburbs, and coffee and tea shops dot the landscape. In 2003, Argo Tea started as a Lincoln Park teahouse and within a decade had a network of shops around the world. High-end tea shops such as Adagio and Todd and Holland have found success with single-origin teas and eclectic blends.

According to the National Coffee Association, in 2013, 83 percent of U.S. adults drink coffee, with 63 percent of those drinking it daily. Chicago routinely ranks in the top 10 most caffeinated cities. It's no wonder, with modern roasters such as Intelligentsia, with six city coffee bars, and small-batch entrepreneur Metropolis Coffee Company. In 2011, the average Chicago household spent nearly three times the national average at coffee shops.

COFFEEHOUSES

Like the cafes in European cities, urban coffeehouses became social hubs, especially for Chicago's ethnic communities during the first half of the twentieth century. After the passage of Prohibition, coffeehouses flourished as gathering spots for businessmen, journalists, politicians, and intellectuals, providing a casual place where they could linger with a cup of something nonalcoholic and enjoy food and pastries and sometimes music and games from their home countries.

The German community favored The Knickerbocker Coffee Shop at 163 E. Walton Place (now the Millennium Knickerbocker Hotel). Glaser's Café, opened in 1918, at 3551 W. 26th St. (in what is now Little Village), attracted Czechoslovakian immigrants and Italian American politicians. Opera singers made their way to the open-all-night Amato's Café, 914 S. Halsted St. (in Little Italy).

With the influx of African Americans from the South and the introduction of jazz to Chicago, coffeehouses along State Street between 31st and 35th Streets (known as "the Stroll"), evolved into venues for rising jazz artists. New Orleans legend Jelly Roll Morton played for white audiences at The Royal Gardens Café (renamed Lincoln Gardens in 1920) at 31st and Cottage Grove.

The next evolution of coffeehouses brought students into the fold. Medici in Hyde Park, opened in 1958, was one of the city's first beatnik coffeehouses and became a popular spot for nearby law students, civil rights workers, and journalists. On the city's North Side, poets and folk musicians joined students at No Exit in Rogers Park.

As the beatnik generation aged, coffeehouses faded from streets and those seeking a cup of hot joe had to head to doughnut shops or diners. That landscape started to change in the late 1980s when Starbucks, a Seattle-based coffee shop, started its worldwide expansion. Now caffeine fiends can grab a cup of dark roast, a vanilla decaf, or a pumpkin-spiced latte at Starbuck's counters on city street corners and in hotel lobbies, airport concourses, and suburban strip malls. The public's thirst for coffee has meant growth for independent coffee shops as well, some that even roast their own beans. Today there are some 1,000 coffee shops in Chicago. Yet today's coffeehouse culture seems less about community interaction and more about Internet connectivity. Instead of students discussing health-care reform or Middle East peace over espresso, they're signed on to free wi-fi, researching movie quotes and posting photos of their foamy lattes to Instagram.

TEAHOUSES

The tradition of tea—a light afternoon snack intended to suppress hunger until dinner—began with English royalty in the early nineteenth century and soon became popular with American high society. Women would gather in their posh sitting rooms around a low table filled with small sandwiches and sweet biscuits or pastries. In the 1920s, the tea custom moved from private homes to hotels, department stores, and small teahouses. Restaurants of the day were the domain of men; tearooms, on the other hand, provided a place for women to socialize, and later organize, and many of them were run by women with female staffs.

In 1907, Marshall Field & Co. opened the first tea and lunch room in a department store. The Walnut Room offered women and their children a place to refuel so they could continue shopping (tearooms were the first eateries to offer separate menus for children). At one time there were six tearooms in the premier department store. The Walnut Room was the largest, and it continues to operate today on the seventh floor. When The Drake Hotel opened in 1920, it began afternoon tea service and quickly established a reputation as *the* place for tea, a reputation that has survived nearly a century.

In 1922, Mayme Clinkscale opened Chicago's first teahouse for African Americans at 3344 S. Michigan Ave. The Ideal Tea Room's menu included fried chicken, corn sticks, and lobster served on fine linens and with the best silverware. Through the 1930s and into the years of the Civil Rights Movement, teahouses served as hosts for social and political events.

Today's consumer embraces tea not so much for the tradition of it, but as a more healthful alternative to coffee and soda. That rise in popularity is leading to a renaissance in teahouses opening in and around Chicago. In 2012, Smashing Pumpkins frontman Billy Corgan opened a Chinese-French inspired spot, Madame ZuZu's, in Highland Park.

Contributor: Deborah Pankey

See also: Columbian Exposition; Coffee and Tea; Lutz's Café and Bakery; Manny's Coffee Shop & Deli

BIBLIOGRAPHY

"Coffee." *The Oxford Encyclopedia of Food and Drink in America.* Oxford: Oxford University Press, 2004.

"Guide to Tea in Chicago." World of Tea. http://www.worldoftea.org/chicago-tea.

Pendergrast, Mark. "Coffeehouses." *The Oxford Companion to American Food and Drink.* New York: Oxford University Press, 2007.

Rosenberg, Chaim M. *America at the Fair: Chicago's 1893 World's Columbian Exposition.* Bar Harbor, Maine: Acadia, 2008.

Columbian Exposition: The World's Fair

The Columbian Exposition was simultaneously an amusement park and encyclopedic display of new and exotic sights, sounds, and tastes held in a temporary and fantastic "White City" (so-called for its plaster architecture). The site lay seven miles south of Chicago's Loop in Jackson Park (extending east from S. Stony Island Avenue to Lake Michigan, and south from E. 56th to E. 67th Streets) and along the adjacent Midway Plaisance. Running for six months from May to October in 1893, the World's Columbian Exposition marked Chicago's entry onto a global stage as a city to be reckoned with. Notable for its ambitious architectural program, amusement-filled Midway Plaisance, and didactic exhibits, the Chicago World's Fair was also the greatest opportunity that modern food producers had ever had to win fairgoers over to the emerging industrial foodways that would come to feed America in the twentieth Century.

Outpacing in scope and scale the international fairs and expositions of London (1851), Philadelphia (1876), and Paris (1889), Chicago architect Daniel H. Burnham and famed landscape designer Frederick Law Olmsted created an almost 700-acre *de novo* urban environment of 200 buildings, interconnected waterways, and imposing statuary. Conceived as a commemoration of the 400th anniversary of the discovery of America, this Fair was to be a showcase of human progress in the intervening centuries. The 27 million ticketholders (almost half of the country's population) who passed through the Fair's gates experienced everything from fine art and novel invention to living exhibits of utterly foreign peoples and, if they dared, a seemingly death-defying ride on the world's first Ferris Wheel.

To fuel those visiting the Fair, Chicago's own Wellington Catering Company either ran themselves or provisioned some 35 restaurants and buffet-style lunch counters, serving an estimated 80–100,000 mouths per day. Items served at buffet counters were prepared daily in a centralized kitchen within the fairgrounds. Sit-down eateries in the "White City," with on-site kitchens, included the Banquet Hall, Big Tree Restaurant, French Bakery, Great White Horse Inn, Louisiana Kitchen, Japanese Tea House, Women's Building Café, Café de la Marine, New England Clam Bake, Philadelphia Café, Polish Café, and Swedish Café. Additionally, a seemingly endless array of international foods could be found on Sol Bloom's Midway Plaisance. Here the Irish and German Villages, Vienna Café, Turkish street vendors, Chinese Tea House, Log Cabin Restaurant, and French Cider Press tempted passersby with flavors from home and abroad.

Food was not only available for purchase at restaurants and stands, it was an important part of many exhibits at the Fair. Of the twelve official departments of the Fair, everyone had something to offer in relation to foodways. Exhibits in the Manufactures and Liberal Arts Building—then the largest structure in the world—included displays of cut-glassware and fine china for the table; silver knives, forks, and spoons; and cast iron kettles and pots. The Electricity Building showcased the latest appliances for efficient modern cookery, while the Rumford Kitchen cooked and served food to demonstrate how "scientific cooking" outside of the home could provide working-class families with supremely nutritious and economical meals. Meanwhile, the Board of Lady Managers responsible for this display compiled a souvenir cookbook of their own regional American recipes for the benefit of the home cook.

From the earliest stages of Fair planning, America's agricultural interests hoped to capitalize on the opportunity to teach the world the value and uses of their produce. The most productive and economical breeds of animals could be examined in the Stock Pavilion, with the dairy products of popular breeds on display nearby. Visitors to the Agricultural Building strolled countless aisles lined with vendors seeking to acquaint potential customers with their quality comestibles. Here, states visually proclaimed America's agricultural bounty with Gilded Age flair, from a life-size liberty bell rendered in California citrus to a map of the United States made of Pennsylvanian pickles.

Armour & Company, one of the largest meatpackers in Chicago's Union Stock Yards, advertised new processed

WORLD'S FAIR COOKBOOK

Many cookbooks were produced for the Columbian Exposition of 1893. One of them was a new edition of an earlier book by Adelaide Hollingsworth, with the following lengthy title:

The Columbia Cookbook, Toilet, Household, Medical, and Cooking Recipes, Flowers and Their Culture, Health Suggestions, Carving, Table Etiquette, Dinner Giving, Menus, Care of the Sick, Facts Worth Knowing, Etc., Etc. Embracing all the Points Necessary for Successful Housekeeping. A Complete Home Instructor. (Columbia Publishing Co. 1892)

The following recipe from the book was taken from Herbert Kinsley's The Cuisine—an example of unattributed quotation.

Spiced Beef

"For a round of beef weighing twenty or twenty-four pounds, take one-quarter pound of saltpetre, one-quarter of a pound of coarse brown sugar, two pounds of salt, one ounce of cloves, one ounce of allspice, and half an ounce of mace; pulverize these materials, mix them well together, and with them rub the beef thoroughly on every part; let the beef lie for eight or ten days in the pickle thus made, turning and rubbing every day; then tie it around with a broad tape, to keep it in shape; make a coarse paste of flour and water, lay a little suet, finely chopped, over and under the beef, enclose the beef entirely in the paste, and bake it six hours. When you take the beef from the oven, remove the paste, but do not remove the tape. If you wish to eat the beef cold, keep it well covered, that it may retain its moisture."

Welsh Rarebit

This recipe comes from Favorite Dishes, Carrie V. Shuman's collection of recipes from the Lady Managers of the Womens' Building at the Columbian Exposition in 1893. It was a popular dish at the time and a precursor of Kraft Company's many recipes using its version of American cheese, especially melted cheese sandwiches.

—BRUCE KRAIG

From MRS. COL. JAMES A. MULLIGAN, of Chicago, Lady Manager.

Take one pound of American cheese, cut up in small pieces, place in a chafing dish and season with half a salt-spoonful of red pepper; stir for ten minutes or until cheese is thoroughly melted; have ready six large pieces of toast on a very hot dish; cover each slice with the melted cheese; serve very hot as a relish.

food products like beef tea, Star ham, and condensed-meat pies. Other regional American products on display—like Gulden's mustard, Baker's chocolate, Heinz pickles, Rumford baking powder, and Pabst's beer—were awarded highly coveted, "scientifically" judged prizes that secured their futures in emerging national markets and American foodways. Meanwhile, smaller stands selling food and drink throughout the fairgrounds sought to win consumers over to Hygeia Mineral Water and Van Houten and Zoon Cocoa, and debuted iconic brands like Cracker Jack, Wrigley's Juicy Fruit gum, the ancestor of Vienna Beef Company, and Oscar Mayer sausage company products.

Even as they sampled delectable dainties, visitors to the "White City" consumed representations of the racial, ethnic, and gender ideologies that structured contemporary America. While traditionally attired "Dutch maidens" served patrons at the "cocoa school" in Jackson Park, African tribesmen on the Midway were depicted as savage cannibals whose foodways included eating their own kin. Meanwhile, in the Agriculture Building, ex-slave Nancy Green served pancakes in full "mammy" attire as the face of "Aunt Jemima," whose name and image had been lifted straight from the minstrel stage.

The totality of encounters that fairgoers had with food at the Fair carried with them implicit assumptions and overt messages about the past, present, and future of modern foodways. These experiences not only created consumer desires, they allayed consumer fears about new forms of food and modes of consumption that would dominate the twentieth century. Thus, the "food science" on display in the Rumford Kitchen spoke to the same concern for nutrition and home thrift that Chicago meatpackers tapped into in creating a market for their latest animal by-product–based commodities. Likewise, the racially stereotyped image of "Aunt Jemima" reassured consumers that highly processed, prepackaged foods were rooted in the "traditional' foodways, and social structures, of the American past.

Today, the Museum of Science and Industry (formerly the Palace of Fine Arts) stands as a physical vestige of the Fair, while archaeology has revealed what remains of the Fair below ground—but the prominence of processed foods, home economics, nutritionism, and agricultural science in the twentieth century are all testament to the impact that the Columbian Exposition had on modern American foodways.

Contributors: Rebecca S. Graff and Megan E. Edwards

See also: Armour & Co.; William Wrigley Jr. Company

BIBLIOGRAPHY

Bolotin, Norman, and Christine Laing. *The World's Columbian Exposition: The Chicago World's Fair of 1893*. Urbana: University of Illinois, 2002.

Harris, Neil, Wim de Wit, James Burkhart Gilbert, and Robert W. Rydell. *Grand Illusions: Chicago's World's Fair of 1893*. Chicago: Chicago Historical Society, 1993.

Community Gardens

A farmers market in a box. That is what people get when they subscribe to a program. The box usually includes fruits and vegetables, but also can include meats, eggs, honey, fish and seafood, dairy, woolens, and even goat's milk soap. These items can be collected at a pickup site, delivered to your home, or picked up at the farm. Many think of CSAs as an effective method for farms to sell their wares. The U.S. Department of Agriculture, in defining CSAs, writes, "Although CSAs take many forms, all have at their center a shared commitment to building a more local and equitable agricultural system, one that allows growers to focus on land stewardship and still maintain productive and profitable small farms."

The first CSAs in the Midwest began near Milwaukee and the Twin Cities in 1988. In 1990, John Peterson took over his family's dilapidated farm in Northern Illinois. He called his enterprise Angelic Organics and turned to the CSA model to serve the Chicago area. Over time, many other farms started CSAs for this market. In 2014, the *locavore* (locally grown) resource, The Local Beet, listed almost 90 CSA providers for the Chicago area.

Some CSAs provide year-round local produce. Most CSAs open their farms to their subscribers for potlucks or harvest days. CSAs are an excellent way of getting delicious food with less impact on the environment, but the real value lies in the ties it builds between those who produce food and those who consume food.

Contributor: Rob Gardner

See also: Agriculture, Urban; Wartime

BIBLIOGRAPHY

Carlson, Debby. "Tips for Joining a CSA." *Chicago Tribune*, September 15, 2013.

Gardner, Rob, "The Local Beet 2014 Guide to Chicagoland Community Supported Agriculture (CSAs)." *Local Beet Chicago*, March 10, 2014.

Consolidated Foods Corporation

The original Kitchens of Sara Lee were sold by the Lubin family to Consolidated Foods in 1956. Consolidated was created by Nathan Cummings, né Nathan Kaminsky (1896–1985), a Canadian with an unerring eye for food companies that would do well in local and national markets. Having made a fortune in Canada, he purchased C. D. Kenny Company, a grocery company in Baltimore in 1941 and turned it into a highly profitable company. In 1942, Cummings purchased Chicago's premiere wholesale grocer, Sprague, Warner & Company, which had been founded in 1864. Its house brands, Richelieu, Ferndell, and Batavia, were sold to grocers across the nation (Richelieu, now located in Massachusetts, is still in business). From 1909, Sprague, Warner was located in a large manufacturing and merchandising facility on Erie and Roberts Street along the North Branch of the Chicago River. After he created Sprague Warner-Kenny Corporation, the largest wholesale grocer in the country, Cummings was named by *Time* magazine as the "Duke of Groceries."

In 1945, the company's name was changed to Consolidated Grocers Corporation and later to Consolidated Foods. Because its Sara Lee division was so popular, the company became the Sara Lee Corporation in 1984. By then it was not only in the baking business, but also was one of the nation's largest meat processors and maker of other consumer products.

Contributor: Bruce Kraig

See also: Sara Lee Corporation

BIBLIOGRAPHY

"Consolidated Foods Corp." *Encyclopedia of Chicago*. http://www.encyclopedia.chicagohistory.org/pages/2623.html.

Warner, Mason. *Sprague, Warner and Company Incorporated*. Chicago: Sprague, Warner and Company, 1912. https://openlibrary.org/books/OL7217819M/Sprague_Warner_Company_incorporated.

Conte di Savoia

Since 1948, this food store has been an anchor in the Little Italy neighborhood. Now with two locations, 1438 W. Taylor St. and 2227 W. Taylor St., the retailer has provided authentic Italian delicacies for several generations.

Urban renewal rocked the area in the 1960s, when the University of Illinois at Chicago displaced large sections of Little Italy to build a campus. Stores such as Conte di Savoia were at the forefront of the legal and social battles that resulted from this renewal. The store moved east to Jefferson Plaza on Roosevelt Road, where it expanded into more "exotic" foods, such as Indian and Middle Eastern spices, as well as imported Italian products. It became a "go to" place for adventurous cooks. In 1989, the store returned to Taylor Street under the ownership of Michael Di Cosola.

Today, both stores serve fresh foods and sandwiches made to order. They sell authentic foods from Italy, such as parmigiano Reggiano, prosciutto, and mortadella and wines, pastas, and packaged goods that were difficult to find in Chicago until fairly recently, such as Colomba, the traditional Italian Easter cake in the form of a dove.

Contributor: Clara Orban

See also: Italians

BIBLIOGRAPHY

Conte di Savoia. http://www.contedisavoia.com/aboutus.html.

Spiselman, Anne. "The Only Guide to Italian Delis You'll Ever Need." *Crain's Chicago Business*, October 3, 2014.

Continental Coffee (See: Coffee and Tea)

Convito Café & Market

What was begun in 1980 as Convito Italiano, an upscale Italian market and cafe, has now transformed into Convito Café & Market, in the Plaza del Lago shopping center on Sheridan Road in Wilmette. Nancy Brussat created the market after many trips to Italy convinced her that the Chicago area needed a modern shopping experience for imported Italian food and wine. One of her goals was to educate customers about fine Italian products. It was one of the first markets to emphasize better, little-known wines from all over Italy. Brussat moved the store to Plaza del Lago and then opened a much larger Euro-style branch in downtown Chicago in 1984. However, a few years later, a fire forced her to close that store. In 1992, Brussat opened Betise, a French bistro, across the plaza from Convito. Then she consolidated the two operations in the Betise space and named it Convito Café & Market. Today, the café serves Italian and French dishes, and the market carries imported groceries, prepared sauces and pastas, cheese, and baked goods, in addition to wine. Brussat now is partner with her daughter Candace Barocci Warner and chef Noe Sanchez.

Contributor: Carol Mighton Haddix

BIBLIOGRAPHY

Vettel, Phil. "Trattoria Convito—A Less Pricey Version of Former Convito Italiano." *Chicago Tribune*, August 10, 1990.

Cookbooks (See: Books and Publishers)

Cooking Classes

Hundreds of cooking classes in the Chicago area today offer myriad topics, from meat butchering to elegant French pastries. Apart from the culinary schools for professional training, many classes for amateurs are found in cookware shops and department stores or offered by private instructors. But it wasn't always so.

Cooking classes didn't exist in Chicago's early days, when the only instruction came at the sides of mothers and grandmothers in their kitchens. Later, with the influx of immigrant labor in the late 1800s, many middle- and upper-class households in the city could afford to hire the new arrivals as cooks. There was no need for many women to learn the art. The days of such servants were numbered, though, as they found better jobs, and, into the 1900s, as the appearance of labor-saving tools and appliances helped homemakers (perhaps reluctantly) return to the kitchen. Cooking classes slowly began to appear.

One was the Chicago Training-School of Cookery, 2535 Prairie Avenue, with Mrs. Emma P. Ewing as superintendent. In 1882, she invited the press to the new school for a dinner cooked by her "lady pupils." Ewing's remarks were noted: "The (school) was opened last spring for the purpose of demonstrating, among other things that good cookery is economical cookery and economical cookery can be good cookery." The five-course meal cost 20 cents a person.

A notice in an 1892 newspaper advertised Hull House cooking classes. Settlement houses such as Hull House taught the poor economical ways to put nutritious meals on their tables. At the 1893 World's Fair, demonstration kitchens drew crowds who watched meals prepared under the latest nutritional guidelines.

The popularity of the domestic science movement also created more interest in cooking schools for amateurs, as evidenced by the well-known Boston Cooking School and its principal, Fannie Farmer. Her book, *The Boston Cooking-School Cook Book* (1896), sold all over the country.

At the Armour Institute at 31st and State Streets, women took classes in cooking and how to properly serve a meal, noted an 1894 article in the *Chicago Daily Tribune*. Boys could take the school's course in "Camp Cooking," geared to those in mining engineering courses.

Also in 1894, French chef Jean Bonnet demonstrated dishes such as veal stew and coq au vin to wealthy housewives at Mrs. Cotton's Cooking School in the Athenaeum Building on Van Buren near Michigan Avenue.

In 1895, under the auspices of the newly formed Domestic Science Association in Chicago, a cooking school "for married ladies," was opened at 140 N. Union St. In 1901, the School of Domestic Arts and Sciences opened at Fifth Avenue. It was an offshoot of the Armour institute, which had discontinued cooking classes due to lack of space, but club women of the community worked to open the new school, under director Isabel D. Bullard. As the new century progressed, home economics began to be taught in public schools, mostly with the goal of imparting rudimentary cooking skills.

Cooking classes became a form of promotion. In 1931, *Chicago Tribune* opened cooking class events, complete with entertainment, in four neighborhoods around the city under the direction of the paper's home economist, who wrote under the name Mary Meade. And the well-known restaurateur George Rector Jr. taught classes in 1935 for A&P markets at the Aragon Ballroom and the Trianon Ballroom. In March of 1943, a number of home economists from area food industry groups and firms joined with the Office of Civil Defense in a series of classes at the People Gas and Coke Co. on South Michigan Avenue. The title, "Good Cooking on 48 Points a Month," reflected the war shortages of the time.

After World War II and the postwar boom times, Chicagoans had more time for leisure and entertaining at home. Women wanted to learn more about how to re-create the foreign dishes that soldiers had tasted overseas and how to throw a gourmet dinner party. To the rescue came Antoinette Pope's School of Fancy Cookery, first begun in the late '30s in Antoinette's and husband François' home and later moving to an impressive site with kitchens, an auditorium, and reception rooms, at 316 N. Michigan Ave. The Popes brought their European background to their classes, teaching the basics as well as French and Italian classics. The popular school led the couple to write a series of cookbooks and create one of the first national television cooking shows in the 1950s.

In the 1960s, Chef John Snowden opened his school, Dumas Pere L'Ecole de Cuisine Française, on the North Side of the city and then moved it to Glenview in the 1970s, where he taught thousands of students the ins and outs of classic French food. Many of his students went on to become chefs themselves. Sears, Roebuck and Company began classes in 1968 in Chicago and brought in well-known chef Louis Szathmary of The Bakery restaurant to direct them.

With the growing popularity of food celebrities in the 1980s, area cooking shops and department stores invited famous cooks to teach classes and give demonstrations in Chicago. Especially popular were the Cook's Mart on LaSalle Street, run by Pat Bruno, who later became the *Chicago Sun-Times*' restaurant critic, and The Complete Cook in Glenview, owned by Elaine Sherman. James Beard, Julia Child, Diana Kennedy, and Jacques Pepin were just some of the national celebrities who came to

AN EDIBLE SPRING EXAM

In 1895, the graduating students in the Armour Institute's domestic science class prepared a final exam lunch—with a spring theme of green and white. The menu:

Green Pea Soup * Crackers
Olives * Salted Almonds
Sandwiches
Salmon with Hollandaise Sauce
Green Peas * Creamed New Potatoes
Biscuits
Lettuce Salad * Cucumber Salad
Pistachio Ice Cream
White Cake with Green Frosting *
Chocolate cake with Whipped Cream

town to teach, and often to sell their cookbooks. Later, national chains such as Williams Sonoma and Sur La Table continued the popular demonstrations. Two major stores also built demonstration kitchens: Carson Pirie Scott and Marshall Field's. However, as cookbook publishers reduced promotional budgets in the late 1990s and early 2000s, fewer and fewer food experts traveled to Chicago to sign books or teach a class.

Many institutions began adult education classes. They included Francis W. Parker, The Latin School, and the Alliance Française in Chicago, plus numerous community colleges in the city and suburbs. Supermarkets are a natural source for cooking demonstrations: Treasure Island was one of the first to build a demonstration kitchen, in its Clybourn Avenue store, and some Whole Foods stores offer occasional classes.

Meanwhile, a growing number of individuals offered classes in their homes or in community centers or food shops. Topics ranged from kids' cooking to gourmet French entrees. Among popular teachers were Ruth Law of What's Cooking, teaching mainly Asian techniques; Madelaine Bullwinkel of Chez Madelaine in Hinsdale; Elaine Gonzalez with her chocolate classes; and many more. Even the City of Chicago introduced lessons at its World Kitchen cooking school, under the direction of Judith Dunbar Hines. Newer locations for classes include The Chopping Block in the Merchandise Mart and on North Lincoln Avenue, Flavors Cooking School in Forest Park, and The Wooden Spoon on North Clark Street. About 100 classes are listed in August each year in the food section of the *Chicago Tribune* in print editions and on its website.

Finally, for dessert and, especially, cake decorating expertise, Chicagoans turn to The Wilton School of Cake Decorating and Confectionary Art, with classes at their suburban Woodridge headquarters and at many locations throughout the area.

Contributor: Carol Mighton Haddix

See also: Culinary Schools

BIBLIOGRAPHY

"Boys As Piemakers." *Chicago Daily Tribune*, May 6, 1894.

Owens-Schiele, Elizabeth. "100 Cooking Classes in the Chicago Area." *Chicago Tribune*, August 13, 2014.

"Scientific Cooking." *Chicago Daily Tribune*, April 16, 1882.

Cooperative Extension Service
(See: University of Illinois Extension)

Corner Bakery

A nationwide chain of casual dining restaurants with 188 locations (including 30 in the Chicago area), Corner Bakery began as a small neighborhood bakery. In 1991, Chicagoans Gary and Meme Hopmayer partnered with Richard Melman of Lettuce Entertain You and chefs Jean Joho and Jennifer Smith to open the European-style bakery serving artisan breads at 516 N. Clark St. It sold 28 kinds of Old World–style breads, all made with a sour starter and cooked in large ovens imported from Alsace. When customers began requesting sandwiches, the store started serving one or two types of sandwiches and continental breakfast. In 1996, the owners sold the restaurant to CBC Restaurant Corporation, an affiliate of Fornaio (American) Corp., which later sold it to a private equity group based in Atlanta. The chain now serves soups, breads, made-to-order salads, sandwiches, and pastas.

Contributor: Colleen Sen

BIBLIOGRAPHY

Pratt, Steven. "Loafing the Old World Way in the Corner Bakery." *Chicago Tribune*, December 5, 1991.

Rice, William. "It's All in the Right 'Start' at the Corner Bakery." *Chicago Tribune*, January 23, 1992.

Cracker Jack

Before C. C. Cretors introduced his popcorn machine at the 1893 Chicago World's Fair, corn usually was popped in wire baskets over live coals. While this method did pop the corn, it rendered a dry product that needed help. The most common remedy added something sticky. Popcorn balls were popular.

In 1872, Frederick and Louis Rueckheim, brothers from Germany, began operating a small candy and popcorn shop in Chicago called F. W. Rueckheim & Brother. Initially, they produced a "popcorn brick"—a rectangular block stuck together with corn syrup and molasses, essentially a variation on the popcorn ball. The brothers built their business through the 1880s but kept experimenting with molasses-based coatings. They began adding roasted nuts but, in 1893, switched to peanuts. By 1896, Frederick Rueckheim had developed a process that kept the coated kernels and peanuts from sticking together. A star was born.

It is not really known how the confection got its name, as the Rueckheims told several stories. However, the current company-approved tale is that a salesman, tasting the product, exclaimed, "That's a cracker-jack," which was slang at the time for "something excellent." However it happened, the name was trademarked in 1896. The new confection appealed to the public, and the Rueckheims were soon struggling to keep up with demand. The thing that moved Cracker Jack from success to American icon was its inclusion in the lyrics of Jack Norworth's popular 1908 song "Take Me out to the Ball Game."

In 1910, the Rueckheims began placing coupons on the packages, to be collected and exchanged for prizes. Then in 1912, they decided to place the prizes inside the package. In 1916, the Rueckheims began using a picture of a sailor boy and his dog, modeled on Frederick's grandson and his dog. All the pieces were finally in place.

By the 1950s, the company employed more than 1,000 people at its Chicago location. However, in 1997, Cracker Jack was purchased by Frito-Lay, and today the famous confection is made in Grand Rapids, Michigan.

Contributor: Cynthia Clampitt

See also: Popcorn

BIBLIOGRAPHY

"History & Lore," Cracker Jack Collectors Association. http://www.crackerjackcollectors.com/cjcahistory.htm.

Smith, Andrew F. *Popped Culture: A Social History of Popcorn in America*. Washington, D.C.: Smithsonian Institution, 2001.

Crate and Barrel

Today an international chain selling chic, contemporary household products, the first Crate and Barrel store was opened on December 7, 1962, on Wells Street in Old Town by Gordon and Carole Segal. (Segal's father, Sol Segal, owned Segal's Kosher Restaurant at Lake and Clark, for many years the only kosher restaurant in the city.) The

Segals's inspiration came during their honeymoon in the Virgin Islands where they found stores selling elegantly designed Scandinavian furniture and household products at reasonable prices. On returning, they decided to open a store for couples like them, "with good taste and no money."

Traveling to Europe, they sourced products such as stainless steel kitchenware, fabrics, and ceramics directly from artisans and small factories. In 1968, they opened their second store in Wilmette and a third in Oak Brook. In 1998, the world's largest privately held mail-order firm, Otto Versand, bought a majority stake in Crate and Barrel. Today, the company has more than 170 retail stores in the United State with outlets in Canada, Mexico, and Singapore.

Crate and Barrel's culinary products include glassware, dinnerware, cutlery, picnic and barbecue equipment, serving pieces, and even barbecue spices and rubs. The chain is known for its attractive store layouts, based on what it calls the "vignette" display, where a variety of products, such as wine glasses or coffee cups, are grouped together to create a unified look.

Online sales have been accounting for an increasingly large share of the company's sales: 36 percent in 2014, compared with 2 percent in 2009.

Contributor: Colleen Sen

BIBLIOGRAPHY

Eng, Dinah. "Crate & Barrel's 50-year 'Fun Run.'" *Fortune*, January 16, 2012.

Culinary Historians (See: Organizations, Other Culinary Groups)

Culinary Schools

The growing interest in culinary careers has seen a corresponding growth in the number of Chicago-area schools offering professional courses for future chefs and restaurateurs. The greatest concentration of culinary schools is within the city of Chicago.

Founded in 1937, Washburne Culinary Institute rates as the oldest professional culinary school in the nation. Always with long waiting lists for entry, the school has a national reputation for producing distinguished chefs and restaurateurs. It is one of several vocational schools funded by the city and trade unions, and it became part of the City Colleges of Chicago in 1994.

A number of community colleges in the surrounding suburbs followed suit and offered programs in culinary arts. Since the 1980s, private college and proprietary culinary schools also have been established in the Chicago area. All colleges hold accreditation as members of the North Central Association of Colleges and Schools, and some choose to pursue additional accreditation by the American Culinary Federation Education Foundation. Most schools are two-year programs, but some, such as Kendall College, have developed four-year baccalaureate programs in liberal arts in order to broaden students' professional opportunities.

The majority of schools are nonresidential and thus cost less than traditional colleges. Tuition costs vary, depending on whether the school is partially funded by state and local taxes. Chicago city and community colleges costs are much lower than privately operated for-profit schools. All schools offer financial assistance for students through grants, scholarships, loans (federal and private), and institutional financial plans. Culinary students can customize their training to their interests. Popular programs include:

- Culinary arts programs: Coursework is in a range of disciplines, including baking, knife skills, and business classes.
- Baking and pastry arts programs: Learning the art of baking and creating pastries. Often, pastry courses focus on the techniques of one particular region, such as France.
- Culinary and restaurant management programs: The business side of the culinary world, including personnel management, food safety laws, hospitality, and more
- Hospitality and hotel management programs: Business fundamentals specific to running a hotel or resort

A variety of degrees and certificates are available to students, including Culinary Arts—Associate in Applied Science, Culinary Arts—Bachelor in Arts, Culinary Management—Bachelor of Applied Science, Culinary Arts—Certificate, Baking and Pastry Arts—Certificate.

Most schools offer short-term continuing education courses for food enthusiasts and professionals. The teaching kitchens are equipped with commercial appliances identical to those in restaurant and hotel kitchens. Many culinary schools have integrated outlets to sell the food prepared in the training kitchens—a restaurant, delicatessen, or retail market. In addition to learning culinary arts, students practice dining room service, management, and customer hospitality.

Due to the high level of specialized skills necessary for teaching culinary arts and baking, faculty must have considerable experience working in the hospitality industry. Instructors typically have worked for a number of years in the culinary field and have held positions of responsibility as executive chef or pastry chef. Many faculty members pursue additional industry certification through the American Culinary Federation or similar certifying associations. All schools assist students to secure internships during their training and job placement upon graduation.

Culinary schools in the Chicago Metropolitan area include:

Washburne Culinary Institute (City Colleges of Chicago)
College of DuPage
Elgin Community College
Joliet Junior College
Moraine Valley Community College
Triton College
William Rainey Harper College
St. Augustine College
Robert Morris University
Kendall College
Illinois Institute of Art—Chicago

Contributor: George Macht

BIBLIOGRAPHY

"Culinary Schools In Illinois." *Education News.* www.educationnews.org/career-index/culinary-schools-in-illinois/.

Curtiss Candy Company

Founded in 1916, Curtiss is a chocolate candy company known for not only its chocolate but also for its innovative marketing techniques and the controversy surrounding the Baby Ruth bar. Curtiss's best known brands marketed today are Baby Ruth and Butterfinger. Baby Ruth was developed to compete with the Oh Henry! bar with the slogan, "Everything you want for a nickel." Other candies, now vanished, include Jolly Jacks, Earth-O-Nut Dipp, and Polar Bar.

The company was founded by Otto Young Schnering, nicknamed the "U.S. Candy Bar King" who was born and raised in Chicago by German immigrant parents. It was started in the back of a hardware store in 1916 when the chocolate candy industry in the United States was in its infancy. A University of Chicago graduate and former piano salesman, Schnering was considered to have a knack not only for making candies but also for marketing. Curtiss Company used slogans, circuses, hot-air balloons, airplanes, and sports events (Wrigley Field) to market the candies.

The Curtiss Candy Company was known for good working conditions, strong employee benefits, and above average pay for both men and women. In the mid–twentieth century, Curtiss developed the Curtiss Farm for the milk and butter, and later, Curtiss Breeding Services in Cary, Illinois.

By the mid-1960s Curtiss ranked among the top ten firms in the national candy industry. The company was also known for its involvement in many philanthropic and community services. The company was in Chicago for seven decades, part of the time on the same street as Wrigley Field. During the next forty years the company changed hands. In 1964, it was bought by Standard Brands; in 1981, by Nabisco; and in 1990, the Curtiss brands were sold to Nestle of Geneva, Switzerland, where it remains today.

Contributor: Geraldine Rounds
See also: Candy

BIBLIOGRAPHY

Chmelik, Samantha. "Otto Y. Schnering (1891–1953)." www.immigrantentrepreneurship.org.
Hughes, Jill Elaine. "When Candy Was Dandy." *Chicago Tribune.* www.chicagotribune.com. October 20, 2013.

Czechs and Slovaks

The Czech and Slovak immigrants who arrived in Chicago in the mid-to-late nineteenth century came with a love of sausages and beer, dumplings, and baked goods. They also brought their culinary skills and recipes seasoned by the regional flavors of Bohemia, Moravia and Silesia and influenced by countries bordering their homeland, from Austria and Germany to Hungary and Poland. In Chicago, they often were just called Bohemians. By 1910, about 100,000 were living in the city.

Butchers, bakers, and dumpling makers opened businesses in the neighborhoods where they settled, first around DeKoven Street before moving to the area clustered at 18th Street and Blue Island Ave. After a tavern owner opened a place there in the 1870s and named it after Plzen, the Czech town known for its beer, the name Pilsen stuck. But that was not the first Czech tavern in Chicago; Jan Slavic holds that honor with a place he opened in the 1850s near Clark and Chicago.

Many businesses then moved with their customers south and west, out along 22nd Street (renamed Cermak Road in 1933 for Czech-born Chicago Mayor Anton Cermak) and 26th Street, before heading to the suburbs of Berwyn, Cicero, Riverside, Brookfield, and points west. Several of those businesses still exist and continue to feed Chicago's appetite for Old World flavors, including *prasky, houska, kolacky,* and *knedliky.*

Crawford Sausage Company still is located at 2310 S. Pulaski Rd. (once known as Crawford) where, in 1925, a group of men established a link to their culinary traditions by making sausages. The garlicky *prasky* (the lunch-meat-style sausage is still one of its most popular items), *jaternice* (a pork-based sausage, in black or white and nicknamed "jet"), (*sulc)* headcheese, (*buchta*) a veal loaf, and cream sausage are among the 40 varieties of Crawford Sausages sold under the Daisy Brand.

Home bakers and commercial bakers these days get an assist, thanks to John A. Sokol, who arrived from Pilsen, Bohemia, in 1889. Sokol opened his first of several grocery stores in 1895 at 654 Polk St. He then moved into wholesale coffee, tea, and spices, before starting Sokol & Company in 1907. In the 1920s, he launched the Solo line of baking products that included prune and sweetened poppy seed fillings (crucial components of any platter of *kolacky*). Now located in Countryside, Sokol & Co. continues to offer those fillings, plus many more ingredients under the Solo, Baker, Borden, Chun's, and Simon Fischer brands.

For those with a hankering for Babi's (grandma's) rye to go with their *prasky*, Vesecky's Bakery still makes the caraway-studded bread as they did when the bakery was founded in 1929 a few blocks from where the shop now stands. And they also still bake *houska* (braided yeast bread studded with almonds and raisins) and *kolacky* as they have for 80-plus years.

No Czech or Slovak meal would be complete without a dumpling (*knedliky*) to accompany the roasted meats (pork, duck) or rich gravies (*omacka*), from the allspice-scented tomato gravy to fresh dill gravy (*koprova*). For proof, one need only open a booklet published by the Czechoslovak Society of America in Berwyn in the mid-1980s that boasted recipes for 12 types of dumplings, including yeast, raw potato, and boiled potato; a trio of fruit-filled; a farina-based version; and liver. And there is the Slovak *halusky*, a small dumpling made from a potato-based dough.

At least two businesses still sell dumplings. The Shotola family began selling dumplings based on their grandmother's recipe at their C. C. Shotola and Son meat market in the 1930s and 1940s in Cicero. Their dumpling dynasty expanded in 1949 when frozen food became a reality. They started Chateau Food Products, Inc., and began distributing yeast, potato, and liver dumplings to local grocers and then chain stores. Another dumpling maker is Josie's Home Style Bohemian Dumplings, originally based in Chicago, but in Stickney since the 1980s, selling bread, potato, liver, and fruit dumplings plus gravies.

The Atlas Brewery was opened in 1891 on Blue Island Avenue in Pilsen making Czech-style beers. It later became Atlas Prager Brewery and, after closing during Prohibition, it reopened and operated until 1962. Some of its brands included Magnet Beer, Atlas Prager Beer, and Atlas Prager Bock Beer.

Restaurants included the legendary Cafe Bohemia (at Adams and Clinton Streets). Opened by Joe Basek in 1936, it drew crowds and celebrities for the lion, bear, and other wild game, though roast duck was the most popular (reportedly, the one millionth order for roast duck was served in November 1970). The restaurant closed in 1986.

Other restaurants remain, serving liver dumpling soup, the pickled beef dish *svickova*, breaded pork tenderloin, roast duck with raw potato dumplings, and yeast dumplings with rich gravies. There's Klas, opened by Adolf Klas in Cicero, which retains its original stained-glass windows and rich wood interiors. Czech food is served Friday, Saturday, and Sunday. Others include Czech Plaza (Berwyn), which has been dishing up huge servings for more than four decades, and Riverside Restaurant (Riverside), Bohemian Crystal (Westmont), Bohemian Garden (Downers Grove), and a newcomer, Bohemian House (Chicago).

Thalia Hall was the center of cultural activity in the Czech-Slovak community in Pilsen. It recently was reborn as a music venue and restaurant, Dusek's. The menu is not Czech now, but it does have Czech beers on the menu.

With food so central to the Czech and Slovak culture, it is no surprise they have been celebrating the mushroom (*houby*) for some 40 years with the annual fall Houby Festival in Cicero. You would expect nothing less from folks who consider mushroom foraging a sport. In the 1930s, the Cicero Mushroom and Hunting Club held regular outings to search for the fungi.

Contributor: Judy Hevrdejs

BIBLIOGRAPHY

Blei, Norbert. "Bake Me a Houska as Fast as You Can." *Chicago Tribune*, January 24, 1971.

Lindberg, Richard. "Passport's Guide to Ethnic Chicago: A Complete Guide to the Many Faces & Cultures of Chicago." Second edition. 1997. Lincolnwood, Ill.: NTC Publishing Group, 109–22.

Sternstein, Malynned. *Images of America: Czechs of Chicagoland.* Chicago: Arcadia Publishing, 2008.

D

Dairy Industry

While nearby Wisconsin may be known as America's Dairyland, the Chicago metropolitan area long was a center of the dairy industry, providing fluid milk to area consumers and producing manufactured dairy products such as butter and canned condensed milk.

In early Chicago, fluid milk was provided by the family or a neighbor's cow. By the mid-1800s, however, the first large urban dairies had appeared, associated with distilleries. A herd of dairy cows was kept near the distillery, sometimes in the basement. They were fed "swill," the leftover grain from the distilling process. The cows often were kept in horrible conditions, and temperance activists also hated the link between distilling and milk, a food mainly fed to children. Activism around the subject was focused on New York but spread to Chicago. Swill dairies were outlawed in Illinois in the 1870s.

While Chicago milk production, outside of the swill producers, remained small-scale in the mid-to-late 1800s, less than 50 miles to the west, the "Elgin Dairy District," including portions of Kane, DuPage, McHenry, and northwestern Cook Counties, was a center for butter and cheese manufacturing beginning in the 1850s. The district was the first area in the western United States to produce butter at factories, called "creameries," rather than on the farm. Improved refrigeration allowed Elgin area producers to ship directly to faraway sites. They also set up the Elgin Board of Trade, which forced buyers of butter to come to Elgin rather than producers relying on "commission men" selling their products to buyers in Chicago. In 1874, Elgin producers also set up the Illinois Dairymen's Association to promote "progressive," scientific dairying. "Western

Bowman Dairy Wagon, ca. 1900. Courtesy of the Rogers Park / West Ridge Historical Society.

creamery butter," produced in the district, eclipsed the price of New York state grades.

While dairy manufacturers remained important in the Chicago region, as Chicago grew, the Elgin Dairy District, as well as adjacent areas such as Lake County, Illinois, and Walworth County, Wisconsin, switched their focus from manufactured and longer-term storage products such as butter and cheese to fluid milk production for the Chicago market. Chicago dealers utilized the extensive railroad network to procure milk. By 1903, 97 percent of the Chicago milk supply arrived by railroad, more than any other city with a population above 100,000. This milk was usually shipped in cans in nonrefrigerated boxcars to city dealers who picked it up, bottled it (or, early on, sold it "loose," dipped out of a container on a cart), and then sold it to street vendors, stores, or delivered it directly.

By the early 1920s, however, this method had declined, replaced by "country bottling": Farmers delivered milk to a plant in the country where the milk was pasteurized and bottled, and then shipped to the city for delivery. This method itself was soon replaced by larger city bottling plants, made possible by the innovation of glass-lined refrigerated tank cars, first on trains and then on trucks, which could ship large volumes of fluid milk into the city. The new technology also allowed city dealers to ship milk from longer distances. It also led to increased concentration of dealers. Between 1923 and 1935, the number of milk dealers in the city dropped from 352 to 236.

The 1920s and 1930s were times of great upheaval in the Chicago milk market, with technological changes and increased enforcement of pure milk regulations. At the same time, the Pure Milk Association, a cooperative focused on the Chicago milk market, organized Chicago-area dairy farmers to demand higher milk prices and protect the Chicago market from farmers outside the district. The cooperative went on strike in 1929, and procured an agreement for higher prices and exclusive rights to the Chicago market. This agreement broke down very soon, however, as dealers not affiliated with the cooperative began selling cheaper milk at stores on the outskirts of the city. Battles over milk prices and entry into the Chicago market continued throughout the 1930s and helped lead to the development of the federal milk marketing order program that governs milk prices in much of the country to the present day.

Bowman Dairy Company was Chicago's largest milk dealer during the first half of the twentieth century. Bowman's business model was based on home delivery of a "pure" product. In 1899, the company was the first in the city to deliver pasteurized milk. Bowman's business declined, however, after World War II, as consumers increasingly moved from home delivery of milk to store purchases. The Borden Co., the second largest milk delivery company in the area, was a national corporation that eventually got out of the milk delivery business and focused on its diversified dairy and other consumer products. Dean Foods began in 1925 and focused on supplying milk directly through stores. Dean, based originally in suburban Franklin Park, eventually became one of the largest dairy companies in the world. In 2001, it was acquired by Dallas-based Suiza who changed its name to Dean Foods. Dean maintains a large presence in Franklin Park.

Chicago also was a center of dairy manufacturing. While Borden was based in Connecticut, it opened a condensed milk plant in Elgin in the mid-1800s and, a century later, opened the largest dairy processing plant in the United States, in Woodstock. The Helvetia Milk Condensing Company, maker of PET products, was founded in 1885 in Highland Park. Kraft Foods was founded in 1903 as J. L. Kraft and Brothers, a Chicago wholesale cheese seller. Kraft has been the subject of many mergers and buyouts. The current version of Kraft Foods still markets cheese, macaroni and cheese, Parkay margarine, and other dairy-related products.

Contributor: Daniel Block
See also: Cheese

BIBLIOGRAPHY

Alvord, Henry E., and R. A. Pearson. *The Milk Supply of 200 Cities and Towns.* U.S. Dept. of Agriculture, Bureau of Animal Industry, Bulletin 46, 1903.

Block, Daniel R. "Public Health, Cooperatives, Local Regulation, and the Development of Modern Milk Policy: The Chicago Milkshed, 1900–1940." *Journal of Historical Geography* 35 (2009): 128–53.

Pegram, Thomas R. *Partisans and Progressives: Private Interest and Public Policy in Illinois, 1870–1922.* Urbana: University of Illinois Press, 1992.

Dairy Restaurants

During the late nineteenth century, many men working in Chicago's business district grabbed midday meals at inexpensive dairy lunch rooms or lunch counters. The name implied wholesome food, milk, and cheeses, as well as bakery goods always associated with milk products. By 1892, the *Chicago Daily Tribune* noted that such places were already a Chicago institution, with each establishment capable of feeding large numbers of people at the noon hour. Dairy lunch spots also were located in and around railroad depots, where disembarking passengers could grab fast, no-frills light meals.

These depot stands and counters eventually evolved into full-fledged dairy lunchrooms during the 1880s, such as those owned and operated by Herman H. Kohlsaat, who owned a large commercial bakery. Similar light repasts became so popular that they were served to fairgoers at the 1893 Columbian Exposition in the Dairy Pavilion. By 1906, chain restaurant companies, such as the Baltimore Dairy Lunch, also had opened lunchrooms in the city. In 1920, Charles Weeghman started a Chicago trend when he switched his "one-arm" dairy eatery (where waiters provided patrons seated in single-arm chairs with meatless lunches) over to a "serve yourself" dairy cafeteria.

Jewish dairy restaurants had other roots, specifically the kosher dietary restriction against mixing milk with meat. From 1927 until 1955, North Lawndale's Jewish People's Institute, with separate meat and dairy kitchens, was a fashionable venue for catered affairs, as well as for daily meals and sandwiches. The lower-level Blintzes Inn on the city's once Jewish West Side was even divided into two areas: the western half of the restaurant served meat dishes, while the eastern half served dairy. Jewish hospitals, such as the short-lived "Maimonides Kosher Hospital" and Mount Sinai, also had separate dairy and meat kitchens for their patients' meals. As Chicago's Jews migrated west and north from Maxwell Street and then out to the suburbs, many of the kosher dairy restaurants closed or moved along with their patrons. Kosher dairy lunches can still be purchased in some city Hillel Centers catering to Jewish university students. Today, because of changing demographics and other factors, there may be no kosher dairy restaurants operating within Chicago's boundaries, though other restaurants serve the iconic blintzes. Slice of Life in Skokie is one with a dairy section, and some ice-cream parlors with kosher certification, such as Dairy Star in Lincolnwood, can be considered purely dairy places.

Contributors: Ellen F. Steinberg and Jack H. Prost
See also: Cafeterias and Lunchrooms; Jews

BIBLIOGRAPHY

Whitaker, Jan. "Quick Lunch." *Gastronomica: The Journal of Critical Food Studies* 4, 1 (Winter 2004).

Delicatessens

A German word borrowed from French, *delicatessen* means *delicacies*. It initially applied to specific types of food: precooked, smoked, or cured sliced meats; poultry; and fish. Later, the term described stores selling those core items, along with sausages, cheeses, salads, soups, pickles, condiments, baked and fried goods, canned merchandise, beverages, snacks, and sandwiches made to order. Still later, a shortened version, "deli," applied to sandwich shops and restaurants offering precooked items, both hot and cold. Delis can be strictly takeout, eat-in, or a mixture of both.

Through the nineteenth and twentieth centuries, there were many delis throughout the city, reflecting the ethnic diversity of its population: German/Continental, Jewish, Polish, Swedish, Italian, Irish, Romanian, Greek, Czech/Slovak, Ukrainian, Lithuanian, Russian, and, most recently, Vietnamese-French, among others. As supermarkets opened and spread, many have installed deli departments stocking commercially produced generic foods.

Germans were one of the earliest and largest ethnic groups in Chicago. Kuhn's Delicatessen on North Lincoln Avenue became one of the primary food shops Germans patronized. Opened in 1929, it stocked imported hams, cheeses, stollen and lebkuchen, sausages and bratwurst, plus a selection of gourmet foodstuffs. Eventually, Kuhn's added a small café serving daily specials. The deli, along with other German establishments, moved to the suburbs as the neighborhood became less German. Another mainstay of Lincoln Square, Delicatessen Meyer, an old-world–style German deli, closed in 2007 after 55 years at the location. The 7,000-square-foot Gene's Sausage Shop & Delicatessen subsequently opened on the same site.

When Eastern European Jews poured into the Maxwell Street area, some entrepreneurs opened delicatessens. At first, they were kosher establishments adhering to Jewish dietary laws. Later, a number of "kosher-style" delis dotted the city wherever Jews lived. Among those early delicatessens was Lyon's Kosher Deli on Maxwell Street (1925). Ben Lyon sold out to Nate Duncan, a Yiddish-speaking African American. Renamed Nate's Deli, it was selected to be the "Soul Food Cafe" in the *Blues Brothers* film. Manny's Coffee Shop and Delicatessen on Jefferson Street near Roosevelt Road is another revered mainstay of the Jewish deli scene. Opened shortly after World War II, Manny's survived the shift from operating in a solidly Jewish neighborhood to anchoring the gentrifying area around the University of Illinois at Chicago. The newer Perry's Deli in the west Loop and Eleven City Diner in two city locations have traditional Jewish sandwiches, while Kauffman's in Skokie and Max and Benny's in Northbrook are much like old-time delicatessens.

Other delicatessens also are thriving. For example, both Milwaukee Avenue's Harrington's Deli and Norwood Park's O'Connor's Market and Deli offer corned beef, Irish bacon, and black pudding. Fiori's in West Town and Tony's Italian delicatessen in Edison Park are patronized by those desiring pasta salads that taste homemade, and submarine sandwiches. West Town's Kasia serves Podalski cheese and Krakus ham, along with other Polish treats. Lalich Deli in Albany Park is one of the few Serbian places remaining. Fairly new Vietnamese-French Ba Le Bakery and Deli in Uptown is known for its beef noodle soup and Vietnamese desserts. Yet, in Andersonville, Erickson's Deli, with its renowned limpa bread and Swedish meatballs, closed in 2014.

Delicatessens remain an integral part of Chicago's food scene. New iterations based on ethnic cuisines or current culinary fashions appear with regularity and will continue to do so in the future.

Contributors: Ellen F. Steinberg and Jack H. Prost

See also: Germans; Jews; Restaurants and Fine Dining

BIBLIOGRAPHY

Levy, Natalie. "Delis: Where Tradition—and Delectable Edibles—Are Still Carried Out." *Chicago Tribune*, May 6, 1977.

Sax, David. *Save the Deli: In Search of Perfect Pastrami, Crusty Rye, and the Heart of Jewish Delicatessen*. New York: Houghton Mifflin Harcourt, 2009.

Delivery Services

Enterprising peddlers provided delivery of basic foods from the early days of the city in the 1800s. As the growing population moved out from the city center into what became neighborhoods, home cooks often relied on these peddlers and their wagons for milk, ice, produce, and even kitchen tools. This rustic delivery system eventually disappeared as merchants set up more retail stores, including bakeries, produce markets, and butcher shops. Although many of the shops also took up delivering food, it mainly was to their prime customers on an occasional basis. One iconic delivery service that outlasted most was that of the milk man.

Today, Chicago cooks are taking food delivery to heart again, due to urban professionals' busy lives and the proliferation of online and mobile phone ordering. Once considered a luxury, home food delivery is now almost an everyday affair, with efficient and innovative on-demand services. Firms offer groceries, restaurant takeout, artisan food products, cocktails, and complete meals. The market is growing fast, and competitive national companies have entered the Chicago market in waves in recent years, including Amazon Fresh, Caviar, Door Dash, ebay, Foodler, Google, Home Chef, Instacart, Postmates, UberEats, and many more.

One unique firm, Artizone, began in Dallas and expanded in 2012 to Chicago. It focused only on local artisan food products such as breads from bakeries, produce, organic meats, cheeses, and patisserie-style desserts. Although it teamed in 2014 with Skokie-based pioneer Peapod, which added Artizone products to its online grocery offerings, the company closed down operations in early 2016. Peapod, founded in 1989 by two entrepreneurs, brothers Andrew and Thomas Parkinson, created a complete grocery store on home computers and, later, on mobile devices. In 2001, Peapod was bought by Royal Ahold, a worldwide grocery firm. Now Peapod's bright green trucks are seen all over the Chicago area and in other Midwest and East Coast cities, delivering groceries to businesses and homes. Irv & Shelly's Fresh Picks is a growing organic food delivery service, providing vegetables, meat and poultry, and other food products. Based in Niles, owners Irv Cernauskas and Shelly Herman search out local farmers and producers and deliver foods weekly around the city and suburbs.

Although some restaurants have always delivered food (especially pizza parlors and Chinese restaurants), it wasn't until computers came on the scene that separate delivery firms appeared. In 2000, Ceo Deliveries on South Wallace Street served about 80 restaurants and delivered mostly to downtown businesses and some homes. Later, it joined with Delicious Deliveries, then joined a Florida-based company, Delivery Wow. In the suburbs, Delivery-2You in Highland Park has offered delivery from gourmet restaurants on the North Shore since 2005, and Takeout Taxi in Schaumburg merged with the national Restaurants on the Run network in 2014.

But few have succeeded quite like GrubHub. Its Chicago founders, Matt Maloney and Mike Evans, were software engineers who found a way to make ordering food from restaurants easier via computer and mobile phones. In 2011 and 2012, the two won the Ernst & Young Entrepreneur of the Year Award. In 2013, they merged Grub-Hub with New York's Seamless, a similar delivery service. The firm was one of the most talked about IPOs in 2014. Through a series of acquisitions of other delivery services, such as AllMenus, Restaurants on the Run, and DiningIn, GrubHub Seamless now delivers food from more than 30,000 restaurants in the United States.

Apart from restaurant delivery, a more economical choice for Chicago families came with the rise of whole-meal delivery firms in the 2000s, offering packed, chilled dishes to be reheated at home. Some companies answered consumers' increased calls for more healthful options: Green Gourmet Chicago, and Cooked Chicago in Evanston are current examples. Kitchfix, founded by chef Josh Katt, delivers entrees centered on Paleo and anti-inflammatory diets.

The Chicago Fund on Aging & Disability raises and provides supplementary funding to three programs: The Holiday Meals Program, the Home Modification Program, and the Home Delivered Meals for Individuals with Disabilities Program, which is modeled after the National Meals on Wheels Program created in the 1960s.

Others offered simple, prepped ingredients plus recipes that customers could cook up in their own kitchens, such as Madison & Rayne from chef Josh Jones and Melanie Mityas. With their ready-to-cook ingredients, home cooks can create sophisticated dishes such as a couscous and kale salad or a crispy chorizo flatbread. Meez Meals, formerly an all-vegetarian service, now also offers responsibly sourced chicken, fish, or beef dishes. It has partnered with Common Threads in a Meals for Good Program, featuring recipes from well-known chefs.

Other chef-driven, app-enhanced companies include Radish, a San Francisco–based firm that arrived in Chicago in 2015, with former Baffo chef David Yusefzadeh creating three-course meals at affordable prices for delivery to downtown residents.

Contributor: Carol Mighton Haddix

See also: Catering

BIBLIOGRAPHY

Soper, Taylor. "A Tasty Trend Bubble? Why Investors and Entrepreneurs Are So Bullish on Food Delivery." Geekwire.com, July 23, 2014.

Lempert, Phil. "Top Food Trends for 2015 . . . Are You Ready?" *Huffington Post*, January 26, 2015. http://www.huffingtonpost.com/phil-lempert/top-food-trends-for-2015a_b_6225884.html.

Department Store Dining

"Give the lady what she wants" is the famous slogan coined by Marshall Field at his eponymous Chicago emporium. But in order to give the lady what she wants—especially if she didn't know what the "what" was yet—meant keeping her in the store. Serving food did just that. At Marshall Field & Co. on State Street, the idea was hatched by store manager Harry Gordon Selfridge (later of London's Selfridge fame) who wanted to attract middle-class women. A small tearoom run by Sarah Haring opened in 1890 and thrived.

In 1907, Marshall Field's become the first department store in the United States with a restaurant, the Walnut Room. Other dining options also were opened by Marshall Field's. "Six tea and grill rooms occupy the entire seventh floor of this great Chicago mercantile establishment," wrote John Drury in the 1931 guide, *Dining in Chicago*. "The Colonial Tea Room and the Mission Grill are for the convenience of the shopper whose time is limited."

Across the street, in Marshall Field's Store for Men, there was the Men's Grill. "It is usually crowded at noon with prominent business executives, physicians, and other professional men from surrounding office buildings," Drury wrote. Marshall Field's is now Macy's. But the Walnut Room survives in the State Street location along with an assortment of other dining options, including InFields and the Seven on State food court.

Duncan Hines, in the 1947 edition of *Adventures in Good Eating*, wrote that it was a "must" for anyone visiting Marshall Field's to visit "one of their attractive tearooms." But, as Hines's listing for Chicago makes clear, there were alternative stores in which to dine. He pointed to the tearooms at Carson Pirie Scott's store and its own Men's Grill at the Men's Store on Wabash and Monroe, which "is strictly for men except on Saturdays when ladies, if escorted, are welcomed into its club like atmosphere." The décor inside the Men's Grill was modeled on Haddon Hall, a sixteenth-century Tudor structure in England.

Drury's book lists now-vanished State Street stores such as Chas. A. Stevens, 17 N. State St., with its East Room, "devoted to more popular priced meals," and the elegant Persian Room with "colorful murals depicting scenes from the Arabian Nights"; the Boston Store dining room; the various rooms at Mandel Bros., at the corner of State and Madison streets; the Spanish Room with its music at The Fair; and the Davis Store, where booths bore the names of suburbs.

Today, fast-food dining options predominate just outside department stores in malls. A few major stores, such as Nordstrom's, Saks, Barney's, and Neiman Marcus offer restaurants ranging from casual cafes to upscale grills.

Contributor: Bill Daley

BIBLIOGRAPHY

Drury, John. *Dining in Chicago*. New York: The John Day Co., 1931.
Hines, Duncan. *Adventures in Good Eating*. New York: Duncan Hines Inc., 1947.

Depression Food

The Great Depression struck the nation in 1929 after the stock market collapse in October that year. This was not the first depression nor was it the last, and it was at least five years in coming. As factories became more efficient, unemployment became widespread from 1923 onward. Farm prices dropped, leading to a crisis that saw widespread bankruptcies. The financial disaster was the final shock, a catastrophe for all the working people of Chicago, as unemployment and underemployment reached 50 percent by 1933. Deflation set in, meaning that prices for everything fell, but so did wages. Even though food was cheap, people had so little money that hunger was widespread and worse in minority communities.

The first efforts to alleviate hunger were soup kitchens, also called "breadlines" by state and local governments and private organizations such as churches. Chicago was probably better off than other cities because of city and state action, but not by much. In 1931, an Illinois Emergency Relief Commission was set up to help the stricken poor, but by February 1932, it had run out of money. Cook County was broke because of a freeze on local taxes. The Commission called President Herbert Hoover in 1932 to say that half a million people in Chicago were on the verge of starvation unless funds were sent for relief feeding stations immediately. They had to make do until the next year with the passage of Federal Emergency Relief Act of May 12, 1933, in Franklin Delano Roosevelt's first term.

Soup kitchens had begun in churches and civic groups in 1929–30. In the South Side African American community, the Chicago Urban League working with city government set up a soup kitchen and shelters for homeless people. Others followed suit, the most celebrated being Al Capone whose soup kitchens served about 120,000 people in 1931–32 with breakfast, lunch, and dinner. Although "Big Al" was proud of a beef stew dinner served at one meal, the soup kitchen fare was Spartan. Soups and stews were made of whatever meats and vegetables could be garnered locally and cheaply, and in wintertime there were not many vegetables in Chicago. Bread was always served with meals, as was coffee. Milk and cheese were also occasionally on menus.

Once New Deal programs were in place, beginning in 1933, the specter of imminent starvation faded. Cook County families' relief payments went from $29.15 in December 1932 to $38.65 in June 1935. It wasn't enough to really fill a family of four's needs, but it kept them together. An "8 Cent Relief Banquet" held by the Illinois Workers Alliance of Cook County in May 1938, featuring potatoes, carrots, onions, and a small amount of meat per person, showed how hard it was for a family to survive on relief payments.

Despite mass privation, many people did have jobs; ate out in restaurants; drank beer, wine, and spirits; and had enough time and money to visit Chicago's Century of Progress in 1933 and 1934. Restaurants ranged from the old French-style elite places like Henrici's and many more inexpensive family-style restaurants such as Tofenetti's where a "tender round steak" dinner cost $1.40 and the famous "Spaghetti Special" made with meat sauce and parmesan cheese was 80 cents. The 1930s was the heyday of self-service cafeterias and lunch counters where sandwiches, such as BLTs, ham and cheese, and tuna or chicken salad, sold for 15–25 cents. The 1930s was a time

In 1931, notorious gangster Al Capone set up a soup kitchen to ensure good will with the public. Wikimedia Commons.

of major additions of cheap processed foods (now classics) to the American menu, such as Velveeta (introduced in 1927 but popular by 1931) and Kraft Macaroni and Cheese in its now familiar box.

Contributor: Bruce Kraig

See also: Soup Kitchens

BIBLIOGRAPHY

Maurer, David J. "The Great Depression in Illinois." *Illinois History*, May 1993. http://www.lib.niu.edu/1993/ihy930561.html.

Reed, Christopher Robert. *The Depression Comes to the South Side: Protest and Politics in the Black Metropolis, 1930–1933*. Bloomington: Indiana University Press, 2011.

Diet and Nutrition

Precise records of what ordinary people ate on a daily basis were compiled for the first time during the late nineteenth century. Chemists, interested in the composition of food and how much of it a person required, left their laboratories and visited kitchens and dining rooms throughout the country. In Chicago, they inventoried the food pantries of immigrant households, native-born members of the working class, and representatives of society's upper echelons. In the 1890s, when America's Gilded Age was in full flourish and Chicago rose to a world-class city, the disparities between rich and poor assumed proportions greater than ever before.

The day-to-day eating habits of Chicago's privileged families came to light in 1894 when the University of Chicago tested new menus for women who lived on campus. The idea was to model campus meals on the fare students were accustomed to at home. A report on the project detailed menus for the first three weeks of March. Breakfast on March 1, for example, consisted of grapefruit, Farinose (a packaged breakfast cereal), creamed codfish, and baked potatoes. For lunch, the staff served cold ham, sausages, and corned beef accompanied by creamed potatoes and peaches. Dinner began with beef soup and a lettuce salad, followed by boiled lamb in caper sauce, mashed potatoes, and corn. The menu concluded with "delicate" pudding. Butter, milk, cream, sugar, bread, and rolls appeared on the table at every meal, and students always had a choice of coffee, tea, or cocoa to drink.

A second study of the eating habits of Chicagoans in comfortable circumstances was carried out in 1895 under the direction of the USDA's Office of Experiment Stations. The investigation involved upper-middle-class households, one located in the city, the other two in unnamed suburbs. Food purchases were inventoried daily in midspring, several weeks later in the year than the study conducted at the University of Chicago. Consequently, veal, chicken, and eggs (back then more plentiful during spring than during winter) appeared as core constituents of the diet. On the vegetable side, asparagus, lettuce, and peas emerged as core items in place of the cabbage and parsnips listed on the coeds' menus.

Investigators calculated the macronutritional contents of the foods their subjects consumed (vitamins and minerals were not within their purview as yet). Intakes among the university women amounted to 108 grams (g)/day (d) protein, 103 g/d fat, 387 g/d carbohydrate, yielding in total 2,953 Calories (kcals)/d. Values among upper-middle-class householders averaged a bit more, but mainly because the researchers did not account for waste.

Energy intakes reported during the Gilded Age appear high by today's standards (consumption per capita currently averages about 2,700 kcals, according to the USDA). This makes sense because, at the time, walking ruled as the primary means of transportation, and most folks were less sedentary than people are today.

Consider, too, that Americans wanted to appear more full-bodied than is fashionable nowadays. A man could take pride in having a big belly. A woman wanted a body possessing a "florid plumpness" like that of the popular entertainer Lillian Russell. Nature, of course, did not always oblige. For those who needed help, Chicago physician T. C. Duncan wrote *How to Be Plump: Or Talks on Physiological Feeding*. Duncan's lessons, first published in 1878, equated thinness with various morbid conditions. He advised the woman of slender physique to begin each day with a substantial breakfast of potatoes, meat, fried mush, oatmeal, bread, butter, and well-milked tea or coffee. Four or five hours later she needed to sit down to a hearty dinner featuring plenty of vegetables and accompanied by a glass of milk or chocolate. Only in the evening, so as not to disturb sleep, did Dr. Duncan permit a light meal.

Scientists began paying attention to Chicago's working-class diets during the spring of 1892 when Ellen H. Richards and Amelia Shapleigh, with the help of Hull House, initiated dietary studies on the West Side. This undertaking, in addition to recording the diets of many immigrants, listed the foods consumed by the members of 13 all-American households. Most of these enjoyed a decent standard of living. Still, their diets differed substantially from those consumed by upper-class Chicagoans.

Compared to the diets of the privileged classes, Chicago's working-class diet was rich in macronutrients but short on variety. Average energy intake, calculated at 3,566 kcals/d, exceeded elite averages by a considerable margin. This comes as no surprise considering the demands of manual labor. The USDA's late-nineteenth-century estimate placed the energy requirement of a moderately active man at 3,500 kcals/d. The significance of dietary variety relates to completeness and balance. As variety increases, so does the probability of nutrient adequacy. The working-class diet on Chicago's West Side typically provided householders with 22 different sorts of food per week. During winter, however, a week's meals might consist of just 17 foods. Considering the late-winter table at the University of Chicago, where the daughters of the well-to-do routinely dined on more than 60 different foods per week, the contrast between the advantaged and the working class appeared especially stark.

Contributor: Robert Dirks

BIBLIOGRAPHY

Atwater, W. O., and A. P. Bryant. "Dietary Studies in Chicago in 1895 and 1896." In Department of Agriculture, Office of Experiment Stations—Bulletin No. 55. Washington: Government Printing Office, 1898, 7–76.

Richards, Ellen H., and Amelia Shapleigh. "Dietary Studies in Philadelphia and Chicago." In *Dietary Studies in Boston and Springfield, Mass.* Philadelphia and Chicago. U.S. Department of Agriculture, Office of Experiment Stations—Bulletin No. 129. R. D. Milner, ed. Washington: Government Printing Office, 1903, 37–99.

Richards, Ellen H., and Marion Talbot. *Food as a Factor in Student Life.* Chicago: The University of Chicago Press, 1894.

Distilleries (See: Spirits and Distilleries)

Domestic Servants

The economy of Chicago experienced massive growth in the second half of the nineteenth century. The city's economic expansion led to a large influx of European immigrants and the growth of a middle and upper class seeking domestic servants to help with everyday activities, such as cleaning, childcare, and cooking. Many German, Irish, and Scandinavian women sought employment in the field of domestic service.

Most domestic servants were single women who stayed employed until they married. Domestic servants were provided room and board, meals, and meager pay for their services. As the economy grew, new opportunities opened in fields such as sales and clerical work, leading many working-class women to choose to leave domestic service for other jobs. After World War I, domestic service increasingly became an avenue of employment for many African American women migrating from the South.

While many middle-class families had one servant who took care of daily housekeeping tasks, new industrial and commercial giants in Chicago—men such as Marshall Field, George Pullman, and Philip Armour—employed many domestic servants. Housekeepers, cooks, laundresses, butlers, and stablemen worked to maintain the households of Chicago's growing upper class. Many of Chicago's wealthy citizens resided on Lakeshore Drive, Astor Street, and Dearborn Parkway on Chicago's North Side and Michigan Avenue, Dexter Boulevard, and Prairie Avenue on Chicago's South Side.

The kitchen was the center of domestic service. Kitchens were usually located in the basement of wealthy homes. Cooks were responsible for feeding both the employers and their guests, as well as the other domestic servants living within the household. The kitchen staff went unseen by guests to the home, and food was delivered via dumbwaiters to housemaids serving the food.

Cooks worked long hours. A typical day saw a cook rise at 6 a.m. to have breakfast made by 8 a.m. Dishes, cleaning, and food prep followed, and lunch was expected by 1 p.m. More dishes and cleaning as well as additional food preparations were needed to have dinner ready by 6 p.m. Cleaning and dishwashing kept many kitchen servants busy until well past 9, leaving little time for cooking and feeding the other servants.

Cooks often presented menus to employers and, for special occasions, cooks and employers checked the larder together to decide what to prepare. Extravagant multicourse meals were common for dinner parties in Chicago's wealthy homes. Soups, followed by pairings of fish/fowl with wine, beef and vegetables with champagne, and desserts of sorbet, pudding, and ice cream. But the domestic servants who prepared the feast ate modest, unadorned foods and rarely, if ever, ate the leftovers of their employers.

The long hours, lack of leisure time, and the amount of supervision and constant work led to a "servant problem" in Chicago and other major cities from the 1870s into the twentieth century. Families found it difficult to find and keep servants. Employers felt kitchen help lacked training in the culinary arts, focusing too much on simple soups and boiled dishes. Some Chicago residents sought to professionalize domesticity and turn it into a science. Institutions like the School of Domestic Arts and Science of Chicago begun in 1899 were meant to provide training in domesticity, especially cooking, to provide Chicago's wealthier families with answers to the "servant problem." Modern appliances eased the burdens of cooking and housekeeping, eventually phasing out the need for many domestic servants after World War I.

Contributor: Joshua Evans

BIBLIOGRAPHY

Callahan, Helen C. "Upstairs-Downstairs in Chicago 1870–1907: The Glessner Household." *Chicago History* 6.4 (1977): 195–209.

Molloy, Mary Alice. *Prairie Avenue Servants: Behind the Scenes in Chicago's Mansions, 1870–1920.* St. Clair Shores, Mich.: Palindrome, 1995.

"Rights and Duties of Servants: Questions Should Be Many. Management." *Chicago Daily Tribune,* April 20, 1902.

Dominick's Finer Foods

The former Chicago supermarket chain of 116 stores, known for its innovations, was originally a family-owned local grocery store founded in 1918 by Sicilian-born Dominick DiMatteo. Located at 3832 W. Ohio St., Dominick's specialized in fresh quality produce, meat, and personalized neighborhood service. A second store was added in 1934, and in 1950, the first Dominick's supermarket opened as Dominick's Finer Foods, offering new ideas such as adding a delicatessen and frozen foods.

The family business was taken over in 1968, by his son, Dominick Jr., who sold it to Fisher Foods, Cleveland. Unhappy with operations, the family bought it back in 1981. During the 1980s, expansion occurred, especially in the suburbs, where Dominick's opened floral and cosmetic departments, enlarged the deli and fish departments, and added one-hour photo processing, liquor stores, and pharmacies. Some stores even had a dry cleaner on the premises. CEO James DiMatteo took over from Dominick Jr. in 1985. Prepared foods and Starbucks bars became draws.

Dominick's was bought by Burkle (Yucaipa group 1994–98). In the 1990s, the stores included in-store dining, takeout foods, upscale meat and produce, specialty bakeries, and floral shops. Private Selection replaced the old Heritage House Brands, and 1995 saw the first in-store bank. Safeway acquired the chain in 1998 and based its operations in California with centralized ordering (Safeway Brands), thereby replacing the neighborhood store concept. Despite rebranding campaigns ("Fresh Food" in 1998; "Ingredients for Life" in 2005), and after closing 20 stores in 2003, all stores were closed by December, 2013. Many locations were taken later by local chains such as Caputo's and Pete's Fresh Foods.

Contributor: Geraldine Rounds

See also: Supermarkets and Grocery Stores

BIBLIOGRAPHY

Channick, Robert. "Dominick's: From a Corner Grocery to a Chicago Institution." *Chicago Tribune,* October 10, 2013.

Gallagher, Mari. "Why Dominick's Sputtered Out." *Crain's.* http://www.chicagobusiness.com. October 14, 2013.

Dormeyer

Albert F. Dormeyer pioneered the electrical food mixer and produced small kitchen appliances from the 1920s to the 1960s. Dormeyer introduced the world's first mass-produced handheld mixer in 1921 while working for the MacLeod Manufacturing Company. After buying MacLeod, he renamed it the A. F. Dormeyer Company by 1930. Dormeyer used the reliable and cost-effective Hamilton-Beach universal motor to drive its mixers on AC or DC current.

Dormeyer adapted his handheld beater to make the first mass-produced tabletop mixer in the early 1920s. Although other manufacturers soon made mixers of their own, the basic concept of this device was used for all later iterations of kitchen mixers, including the iconic Mixmaster that appeared a decade later.

A. F. Dormeyer introduced an innovative handheld mixer in the 1930s that could stand independently in a bowl and mix much like a stand mixer.

Dormeyer also produced countertop broilers, percolators, fryers, toasters, electric skillets, and knife sharpeners from the 1940s to the 1960s. Its "Powerchef" stand mixers and "Dormey" hand mixers remained the most popular products. Pop artist Claes Oldenburg replicated four "Dormey" mixers in soft plastic in a 1965 sculpture "Soft Dormeyer Mixers."

Throughout its history, Dormeyer listed multiple locations for its manufacturing headquarters, including 2540–2640 Greenview Ave. in the 1920s and 1930s, 4300 N. Kilpatrick Ave. in the 1940s, and the intersection of Kingsbury and Huron Streets in the 1950s and 1960s. Dormeyer shuttered its doors in 1970.

Contributor: Stefan Osdene

See also: Equipment, Home

BIBLIOGRAPHY

"Dormeyer Mixers." http://www.jitterbuzz.com/indkit.html#dorme.

Snodgrass, Mary Ellen. *Encyclopedia of Kitchen History.* Abingdon, U.K.: Routledge, 2004.

Doughnuts

Originating in Colonial Dutch New York, Doughnuts migrated along with settlers from New York to early Chicago. Deep-fried rings of batter, they became fixtures in home cooking, in local bakeries, and then became industrial-scale products sold in franchises and supermarkets. Still, the city has prized local artisanal products.

Traditionally, doughnuts were made by family bakeries, especially after German and Polish immigration in the nineteenth century. Lakeview's Dinkel's Bakery, launched in 1922 by a Bavarian immigrant, wins nods on national lists. Scafuri Bakery in Little Italy dates to 1904, and Swedish Bakery, which closed in 2017, in Andersonville to the late 1920s. More recently (1998), Delightful Pastries in Jefferson Park is reputed for its Polish-style *paczki* (filled doughnuts). Paczki are deep-fried spherical donuts traditionally filled with jam, custard, and other sweet fillings and covered with powdered sugar. They are popular among all Chicagoans on the first day of Lent, known as Paczki day. One bakery, Clyde's in Lincoln Park became so successful that it moved to Addison, where it supplies 20 states with frozen doughnuts.

Although the metropolitan area is peppered with Dunkin' Donuts, franchises of the Massachusetts chain, gourmet doughnut shops from local restaurateurs have made inroads. In the shadow of the Merchandise Mart, people line up in all weather outside The Doughnut Vault from Brendan Sodikoff. Firecakes, Stan's, Glazed and Infused (from the Mia Francesca chain), and Do-Rite Donuts (from Lettuce Entertain You) specialize in big, bold cake and yeast doughnuts with vibrant glazes such as chestnut or cranberry, often punctuated with bacon. Beaver's was the first doughnut truck to hit the streets, in 2011, deep-frying each batch in the truck.

NEW-GUARD FLAVORS

Whether cake or yeast, glazed or filled, Chicagoans never lack for doughnut deliciousness. But the new guard of doughnut shops are elevating flavors and combinations. Glazed & Infused serves up a Maple Bacon Long John, Do-Rite makes the case for pistachio–meyer lemon or vegan chai, and Firecakes has one with Valrhona chocolate and espresso cream. Beaver's Coffee and Donuts will top with marshmallow sauce, graham crackers, or Nutella (for a start). And will put them in a milkshake. A number of shops dish up gluten-free doughnuts to make them "healthier."

—JANINE MACLACHLAN

Dat Donuts in the Chatham neighborhood has the added benefit of being open 24 hours. But it is Old Fashioned Doughnuts on Michigan Avenue at 112th Street in Roseland that enjoys status as the destination for some of the best doughnuts in the city. Owner Buritt Bulloch founded the shop in 1972 and still makes the doughnuts in the store window, dropping hot dough into seething oil, flipping them with oversized chopsticks and then coaxing them onto a dowel. He walks the dowels over to the frosting vat and ladles on sugary goodness. His apple fritters are the size of a dinner plate.

Contributor: Janine MacLachlan
See also: Baking and Bakeries

BIBLIOGRAPHY

Clyde's Donuts. http://www.clydesdonuts.com/aboutus.html.

Dove Bar

One of America's premium confections, Dove Bar is ice cream on a stick, covered in high-quality chocolate. The product was developed in 1956 by Leo Stefanos at his Dove's Ice Cream and Candy shop at 60th and South Pulaski Road in Chicago. Part of an extended family of confectioners who own Cupid Candies now in Orland Park, Stefanos opened his shop in 1939. Chocolate-covered ice-cream bars were common, but Stefanos decided to make a superior version and took many months to develop the formula and technique. Dove Bars went national: by the late 1970s, more than a million bars were sold annually. Candy giant Mars, Inc., bought Dove Bars in 1986, keeping Leo's son Mike as a consultant. Dove Bars in several flavors are now found in supermarkets and drugstores across the nation. Dove's original store has been long closed; the company is now headquartered in Burr Ridge.

Contributor: Bruce Kraig
See also: Candy; Greeks

BIBLIOGRAPHY

http://www.indianprairielibrary.org/localhistory/wp-content/uploads/2010/08/06–30–2010SubLifeDove-Ice-Cream1.pdf.

Dressel's Bakery

Luscious Danishes and dreamlike whipped cream cakes in red and white Dressel's boxes are still fond memories for many Chicago shoppers. German brothers Joe and Bill Dressel opened their neighborhood bakery in 1913 in Bridgeport and soon were joined by younger brother

Herman. They built a second location in Cicero, and then a factory, and were making 3,000 cakes an hour by the 1950s. Herman created a frosting that could freeze well, and soon Dressel's cakes could be found in grocery store bakeries and freezer cases. Chicagoans no longer had to travel to the corner bakery for a delicious celebration cake, such as the popular chocolate fudge whipped-cream cake. American Bakeries purchased Dressel's in 1961, and soon airlines and fast-food restaurants served the bakery items. In 1987, Pain Lacquet, France's largest baked-goods operation, purchased Dressel's. Sales reached $13 billion annually. But the firm ended up in bankruptcy, and that was the demise of Dressel's.

Contributor: Jenny Lewis

See also: Baking and Bakeries

BIBLIOGRAPHY

Healy, Vikki Ortiz. "Whatever Happened to Dressel's Bakery in Cicero?" *Chicago Tribune*, January 8, 2010.

Lost Recipes Found. http://www.lostrecipesfound.com.

Drury, John

Drury (1898–1972) was a Chicago newspaperman and food writer, best known for his 1931 book, *Dining in Chicago*. During a brief stint with City News Bureau followed by a long tenure as a *Daily News* reporter (1926–44), he became familiar with all the neighborhoods and social strata of Chicago. His *Chicago in Seven Days* (1928) comprises a series of wide-ranging tours of the city.

Several years later, he turned his all-inclusive approach to the city's restaurants: *Dining in Chicago* includes almost 300 establishments, from temples of haute cuisine and hangouts of politicians and writers to cafeterias and sandwich counters. Coverage of ethnic restaurants—Mexican, Japanese, Turkish, Filipino, African American, and more—was especially strong, and quite unusual for the time. In 1933, Drury covered the Century of Progress World's Fair for the *Daily News* and in a guidebook containing concise but well-chosen restaurant reviews.

In the mid-1940s, Drury and his wife moved to Chesterton, Indiana, where he continued his writings on midwestern architectural history begun more than a decade earlier. Commuting by train from Indiana, he researched *Where Chicago Eats* (1953), his successor to *Dining in Chicago*. Unfortunately, his easy familiarity with Chicago's restaurants was lacking in this later work and the book didn't sell well.

For most of the 1950s and into the '60s, he wrote a series of articles for *The Butcher Workman*, the monthly magazine of the Amalgamated Meat Cutters union, on historical topics as diverse as Native American meat cookery and the development of the refrigerated railcar. In 1966, a collection of these essays made up his last published work.

Contributor: Peter Engler

See also: Restaurant Critics

BIBLIOGRAPHY

Drury, John. *Dining in Chicago*. New York: John Day Company, 1931. https://archive.org/details/dininginchicago00drur.

Duffy, Curtis

The award-winning chef and co-owner of Grace Restaurant, Duffy was born in Columbus, Ohio, in 1975. A teacher encouraged his love of cooking, and at the age of 14, he began working at a local diner. Duffy entered Columbus State Community College's culinary program and, at the age of 16, began cooking at an exclusive golf club. In 1994, he took first place in a statewide cooking competition.

After coming across a cookbook by Charlie Trotter, Duffy left his job as chef de cuisine at another golf club and drove to Chicago, where he volunteered in Trotter's kitchen and then was hired in 2000. There he met Grant Achatz and eventually followed him to Trio restaurant as pastry

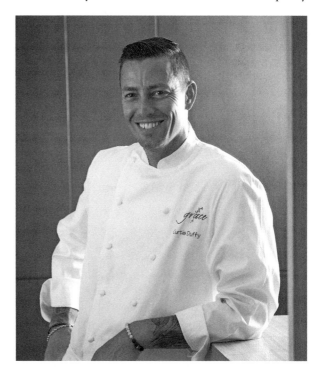

Curtis Duffy, chef/owner of Grace Restaurant. Courtesy of Grace Restaurant. Photograph by Huge Galdones.

chef. In 2005, he became chef de cuisine at Achatz's Alinea and subsequently took the position of chef de cuisine at Avenues in the Peninsula Hotel, where he won 2 Michelin stars. In July 2011, he announced he was leaving Avenues to open the best restaurant in the country, a goal he said was as much about personal validation as financial security. Grace opened in late 2012 on West Randolph Street and won first 2 and then 3 Michelin stars. In 2014, Kevin Pang and Mark Helinowski directed a film, "For Grace," about Duffy's life and the opening of the restaurant.

Contributor: Colleen Sen

See also: Chefs; Grace; Restaurants and Fine Dining; Restaurateurs and Restaurant Groups

BIBLIOGRAPHY

Pang, Kevin. "His Saving Grace." *Chicago Tribune*, February 14, 2013.

Eataly

Chicagoans flocked to this emporium of Italian edibles and wine when it opened in 2013 on East Ohio Street just off the Mag Mile. One of 27 Eataly locations around the world, and the second U.S. location after New York City, the store contains two floors of imported Italian foods, wine, and cookware as well as fresh breads, seafood, meats, vegetables, cheeses, pastries, chocolates, gelato, a mozzarella bar, a Nutella bar, and a brewery. With 63,000 square feet of marketing pizazz, no other specialty market in Chicago can compare as a shopping experience.

Sit-down restaurants plus eating bars are scattered throughout the building. Wine tastings and cooking classes aim to educate locals and tourists alike. Some adjustments have been made since opening, such as combining the menus of some of the restaurants to simplify options. Partners in Eataly include celebrities Mario Batali, Joe and Lydia Bastianich, Adam and Alex Saper, and Oscar Farinetti, who founded Eataly in Turin, Italy, in 2007. Eataly Chicago earned an estimated $50 million in revenue in 2015.

Contributor: Carol Mighton Haddix

See also: Italians; Restaurants and Fine Dining

BIBLIOGRAPHY

Ankeny, Jason. "Eataly Elevates Food Retail, Tastes Success. What's Next?" *Entrepreneur*, November 2014.

Eddington, Jane

With a pen name of Caroline Shaw Maddocks, Jane Eddington (1866–1938) was the food columnist for the *Chicago Tribune* from 1910 to 1930. Her nationally syndicated column, "The Tribune Cook Book," included daily menus; articles on exotic (for the time) items like mangoes, garlic, and kumquats; short restaurant reviews; and instructions for making everything from strawberry shortcake to Indian curries. She often included recipes for vegetarian readers, recommending, for example, eggplant as a versatile substitute for meat. After her retirement, she was succeeded by five food editors, all of whom, until 1974, wrote under the name Mary Meade. She bequeathed her extensive library to her alma mater, Wellesley College.

Contributor: Colleen Sen

See also: Media, Print

BIBLIOGRAPHY

Eddy, Kristin. "Serving Food News for 150 Years." *Chicago Tribune*, July 6, 1997.

EKCO Housewares

In 1888, 25-year-old Edward Katzinger founded a company to produce baking pans for Chicago's burgeoning commercial bakers. He chose the name EKCO, based on his own initials combined with the word *Company*. The pans were not only successful in mass-production bakeries, but also later in homes and restaurants. Katzinger took advantage of the new stamped aluminum, which was first manufactured for cookware in 1892 in Lemont, Illinois, by Illinois Pure Aluminum Company.

By the mid-1960s, EKCO evolved as the country's largest nonelectric housewares manufacturer, and its muffin and cake pans were staples in most American kitchens. In 1994, a subsidiary company helped the firm expand into the upscale housewares market.

The company was purchased by Corning and then by Borden in 1999, and finally by World Kitchen LLC, a privately held housewares maker and distributor, based in Rosemont Illinois. World Kitchen distributes a wide range of home goods and kitchenware around the world, employing about 3,000 people. It still sells bakeware under the EKCO brand name.

Contributor: Judith Dunbar Hines

BIBLIOGRAPHY

International Housewares Association. http://www.housewares.org/
HousewaresConnect365/Detail?com_uid=1563.

Eli's Cheesecake

In the late 1970s, Eli Schulman decided to try his hand at creating a great cheesecake for his restaurant, Eli's the Place for Steak. During the restaurant's downtime, he baked cheesecakes, using his customers as tasters. By early 1980, Schulman finally put his Eli's Chicago's Finest Cheesecake on the menu. The original cake was plain, but richer and creamier than the New York version, and it was followed by chocolate-chip, cinnamon-raisin, and Hawaiian flavors.

The cheesecake's popularity grew by word of mouth. Schulman was credited with putting "Chicago-style" cheesecake on the map. When he decided to offer it at the first Taste of Chicago on July 4, 1980, hundreds lined

Eli Schulman worked on many versions of cheesecake at his steak restaurant. Photograph by Steve Leonard.

up to get a slice. Other leading restaurateurs wanted to serve Eli's Cheesecake, so Eli's son, Marc Schulman, joined his father full time in 1984 to help expand and has led the cheesecake business since. The cheesecake's popularity grew as it became tied to Chicago's milestone events, such as mayoral and presidential inaugurations and Abraham Lincoln's Bicentennial celebration. The company built a state-of-the-art bakery, café, and visitors' center on Chicago's Northwest side in 1996. Today, Eli's Cheesecake bakes more than 15,000 cheesecakes and desserts daily. In 2015, Eli's celebrated its 35th anniversary by publishing *The Eli's Cheesecake Cookbook: Remarkable Recipes from a Chicago Legend*.

Eli Schulman died in May 1988, but Eli's the Place for Steak continued in business (under the leadership of Eli's wife, Esther), until it closed permanently in 2005 to make way for the development of the new Lurie Children's Hospital.

Contributor: Scott Warmer

See also: Baking and Bakeries

BIBLIOGRAPHY

Davis, Kevin, "A Global Empire Built on Cream Cheese and Graham Cracker Crust." *Crain's Chicago Business*, April 10, 2013

Equipment

HOME

Chicago emerged as a manufacturing hub for the production of consumer durables in the late nineteenth and early twentieth centuries. The presence of major retail outlets such as Sears and Roebuck and the ease of access to transnational markets via railway and waterway spurred the growth of a varied manufacturing base. The emergence of steel mills on the outskirts of Chicago and its geographical location in the Midwest made access to raw materials relatively inexpensive. Expansion of electrical power networks and gas supply lines in the 1890s stimulated the growth of industries dedicated to the production of domestic technologies. Manufacturers also relied on a steady influx of immigrant laborers who began arriving in Chicago, en masse before the turn of the twentieth century.

Between 1900 and 1930, many of the nation's biggest makers of appliances established their bases of operations in Chicago, producing iconic brands such as Sunbeam, Kenmore, Dormeyer, General Electric, Hotpoint, Edison Electric, Handyhot, White Cross, Montgomery Ward, and Universal Stoves by Cribben and Sexton.

Early electrical heating manufacturers such as D. C. Hughes in Ravenswood pioneered the sales of mass-produced electric stoves in the 1910s. General Electric, the behemoth of the appliance industry, recognized the commercial possibilities of the electrical stove market and purchased D. C. Hughes around World War I. The combined firm became the G.E.-Hotpoint Company, an enterprise with many factories in Chicago. It became one of the three largest makers of small heating appliances and electrical stoves between World War I and World War II.

The development of universal electric motors operable on AC or DC current made the small electric mixer a formidable presence in the home appliance market by the 1920s. Dormeyer and Sunbeam became the leaders in this segment of the market during the Great Depression, continuing their dominance well into the postwar era. Chicago became the center of mixer production in the United States.

Economic concerns during the Great Depression led to the development of inexpensive household appliances that could be purchased for a fraction of the price of previous models. Cheaply made toasters, heating appliances, blenders, and other motorized appliances made of inexpensive painted or plated drawn steel became de rigueur in the 1930s. Chicago firms such as Bersted, Vidrio Manufacturing, Chicago Electric/Handyhot, Miracle Products, Club Metals, and Great Northern Manufacturing became market leaders. The inexpensive nature of their Depression-era products helped to democratize access to home appliances for the masses despite bleak economic circumstances.

In their heyday in the 1920s and 1930s, many of Chicago's appliance manufacturers had adopted the streamlined designs of industrial designers such as Raymond Loewy and Harold Van Doren. Products such as the iconic Sears Coldspot refrigerator represented the pinnacle of modernity in industrial design. Chicago manufacturers brought high-style manufactured goods to the broad public at cost-effective prices. The trend continued well into the 1960s and 1970s, stymied only when outsourcing began to erode America's largest regional base of appliance manufacturing. A few Housewares manufacturers remain in the metropolitan area, notably Chicago Metallic, headquartered in Lincolnshire.

Contributor: Stefan Osdene
See also: Dormeyer; Home Cooking and Kitchens; Sunbeam Corporation

BIBLIOGRAPHY

Matranga, Victoria Kasuba, and Karen Kohn. *America at Home: A Celebration of Twentieth-Century Housewares*. Rosemont, Ill.: National Housewares Manufacturers Association, 1997.

COMMERCIAL

During the late nineteenth and early twentieth centuries, Chicago, like other midwestern cities, benefited from an influx of ambitious newcomers who established successful food businesses. But the transition from neighborhood shop to regional and national food enterprises required new methods for increased production and transportation. In these components, Chicago outpaced its rivals.

Cyrus McCormick had moved reaper manufacturing to Chicago in 1847, thereby expanding crop production all the way to the Great Plains. The first farm silo was invented in 1873 by Fred Hatch of Spring Grove, Illinois; it eliminated the spoilage caused by the common practice of storing grains in ditches. Gustavus Swift developed the refrigerated railcar (though his company did not invent it) to allow shipping of fresh meat products to the East Coast and provided the equipment blueprint for the shipping of fresh dairy, fruits, vegetables, and later, candy.

With Chicago as a great railroad hub by the end of the 1850s, it could now ship and receive agricultural products with ease. Forrest Mars claimed to have initiated the move of Mars Candy to Chicago in 1929 by telling his father Frank, "The freight rate in Chicago is half of Minneapolis . . . with this rate we can really make some money." Naturally, Chicago became a center for railroad manufacturing and repairs. By 1890, 12,000 people were employed in this industry. From Pullman cars to the more than 20,000 refrigerated cars owned by meatpackers, Chicago was a world leader in railroad manufacturing. It remained so well into the twentieth century.

As the nation's confectionary center from the late nineteenth century, Chicago was the candy manufacturing equipment center. The basic steps of candy-making include cooking, panning (for round, layered candies), coating (for outer layers of chocolate or caramel), and packaging. Early candy-makers tended to design and sometimes build their own equipment. Frederick and Louis Rueckheim invented process equipment in the early 1890s to keep their sticky Cracker Jack product from clumping together and developed a wax-sealed, foil package to keep it fresh.

Emil J. Brach built the largest candy plant in the country filled with high-speed equipment that allowed him to sell candy for 20 cents per pound versus the normal 50-cent retail price. Bunte Brothers pioneered machinery that produced hard candies with soft fillings.

The Williamson Candy Company replaced hand-dipping of its Oh Henry! bar with enrobing machines that coated chocolate in a "waterfall" process and sent the bars speedily to cooling and packing rooms. The Curtiss Candy Company adapted "pulling" machines from taffy and gum production to make its Butterfinger bars chewy and introduced machines that injected air to open wrappers for inserting and then sealed them.

Packing Brach's Candy Boxes, 1950s. Courtesy of the Chicago Public Library, Special Collections and Preservation Division.

At its height in the first three-quarters of the twentieth century, one-third of U.S. candy production was based in Chicago, but acquisitions by non-Chicago companies led to a decline in candy leadership. However, the Chicago area is still home to unique companies such as Wilton Industries, a leader in candy and cake decorating, whose founder Dewey McKinley Wilton combined an assortment of homemade tools to create "pulled" and "spun" sugar creations. Chicago is also headquarters for the Knechtel Company, founded by a veteran of Marshall Field's candy kitchen, which designs equipment worldwide for confectionary, food, and pharmaceutical manufacturing.

Chicago had a direct effect on the nation's hamburger industry. Chains such as White Castle and White Tower in the 1920s made cheap hamburgers popular; later Chicago-area McDonald's made them ubiquitous. Chicago became the leader in creating hamburger manufacturing machinery when Harry Holly, a tinkerer, invented the Hollymatic machine in the 1930s. His machines stamped out hamburgers in the exact size and weight proportions required by the McDonald's System. Holly's former employee, Lou Richards, superseded the Hollymatic with the Formax press that used hydraulics to meet the volume required by the fast-growing burger chains.

Sausage making always was limited by the supply of animal intestines. In 1925, Erwin O. Freund, founder of Viskase Corporation, discovered a process for making sausage casings from cellulose. This greatly expanded sausage production, especially for "skinless" wieners, making the hot dog ever-present at venues such as ballparks, church picnics, and school cafeterias. Viskase, headquartered in the Greater Chicago area, remains a world leader in food-service manufacturing, making cellulose and plastic casings for many food applications.

A food equipment salesman, Augie J. Antunes, developed a revolutionary roller system for grilling hot dogs that he named Roundup in the mid-1960s. Other A. J. Antunes & Company products, including toasters, steamers, and counter equipment, have become mainstays for some of the largest chains in the quick-service industry.

Chicago remains a major player in food equipment manufacturing from food processing to ovens and controls.

Contributor: Michael Rossmeier

See also: Candy; Faulds Ovens; Fish Oven Company; Hot Dogs; Middleby-Marshall Company

BIBLIOGRAPHY

Kimmerle, Beth. *Sweet Times: 100 Years of Making Confections Better*. Chicago: PCMA, 2007.

Smith, Andrew F. *Hamburger: A Global History*. London: Reaktion, 2008.

Stover, John F. *American Railroads*. Chicago: University of Chicago Press (2nd Edition), 1997.

European Imports, Inc.

Founded in 1978 by Seymour and Beverly Binstein, this firm specialized in cheese in its early years in Chicago and gradually expanded to about 4,700 imported food products. Now headquartered in Arlington Heights, the company supplies retail and food-service accounts around the country. The firm acquired many small firms, including Wild Game Inc. in 1997, expanding its line with exotic meats and charcuterie items. It also carries European lines of pasta, pastry, oils, vinegars, preserves, and more. In 2012, it was purchased by Sysco Co. but still operates under its own name and the Binstein family.

Contributor: Carol Mighton Haddix

Evans Food Products Co.

That loud crunch you hear is America munching on pork rinds. No matter how you like them, plain or seasoned (barbecue, jalapeno-cheddar, spicy hot), the puffy snacks helped build Evans Food Products Co. of Chicago into one of the world's largest producers of fried pork rinds and their kin, cracklins, *sancochos*, and pellets. Evans's fried pork rinds come in several sizes and flavors, as do the meatier, thicker cracklins. *Sancochos*, larger fried pork rinds, are used throughout Latin America for the bacon flavor they give soups and stews. Pellets are cooked pork rinds sold to companies or organizations to pop on their own.

Founded by Lester Olin and his first partner (last name Evans, first name unknown) in 1947, the company initially made potato chips and pork rinds. Rinds ruled, though, and chips were dropped. In 1985, the company was purchased by brothers Alejandro and Carlos Silva and Jose Garza. (Lester Olin died in 1992.) In 2016, the firm was bought by private equity firm Wind Point Partners. The company distributes products to 15 countries worldwide from facilities around the United States. Headquartered at 4118 S. Halsted St., the firm sells fried pork rinds under the brand names Mac's and La Tonita (as chicharrones). Cracklins are sold under the Porkies and Bill's brand names.

Contributor: Judy Hevrdejs

BIBLIOGRAPHY

Burleigh, Nina. "Rindmaker to the World: A Chicago Firm Is the World's Largest Producer of That Ultimate Pigout Food: The Fried Pork Rind." *Chicago Tribune*, April 7, 1991.

Everest

Consistently one of the most awarded restaurants in Chicago, Everest has been serving fine French fare with an Alsatian flavor since 1986. Chef Jean Joho, in partnership with Lettuce Entertain You Enterprises, created a quiet, elegant, art-filled atmosphere on the 40th floor of the Chicago Stock Exchange in the South Loop. With breathtaking city views facing to the west, Everest has become a romantic, special-occasion destination. Its tasting menu is known for perfectly prepared locally sourced ingredients, including Alsatian-inspired house-smoked salmon, venison with wild huckleberries, lobster in gewurztraminer sauce, marinated cabbage, pear William souffle, and chestnut and chocolate beignets.

Joho and the restaurant have won almost every dining award possible, from the James Beard Foundation's Best New Restaurant and Best American Chef Midwest awards to *Travel & Leisure* magazine's salute as one of America's most romantic restaurants. The restaurant is a member of the prestigious Chateaux & Relais group.

Contributor: Carol Mighton Haddix

See also: Lettuce Entertain You Restaurants; Restaurants and Fine Dining; Restaurateurs and Restaurant Groups

BIBLIOGRAPHY

Vettel, Phil. "Revisiting Everest, Les Nomades." *Chicago Tribune*, July 11, 2013.

Fannie May

While Fannie May has enjoyed some sweet success in its nearly 100-year history, the renowned candy maker has also tasted bittersweet times. H. Teller Archibald, a Chicago real estate executive and his wife, Mildred, opened the first Fannie May retail store in 1920 at 11 N. LaSalle St. in Chicago. It was their vision to create delicious tasting, handcrafted chocolates. By 1935, Fannie May had nearly four dozen retail stores in Illinois and surrounding states, and the parent Archibald Candy Corp. established itself as one of Chicago's leading manufacturers and retailers of confections and chocolates.

During World War II, while other companies decided to change their recipes when ingredients became scarce, Fannie May retained its recipes but made only what it could, which often meant closing shops early. In 1946, the company introduced its signature pecan-caramel chocolate confection, the Pixie.

In the postwar period, the company grew steadily to more than 180 stores. Fannie May then embarked on a period of changing ownership, bankruptcy, and renewal. The Thorne family took over the company in the late 1970s and ran it until patriarch Denton Thorne died in 1980. His wife Jean Thorne and financial partner John Hughes assumed control and ran it until 1991, when Archibald Candy Corp. was acquired by Jordan Co., a private equity group., In 1992, Archibald acquired Fanny Farmer, a similar company that had 200 retail stores in the northeastern and midwestern United States. It became the largest chain of candy retailers in the country.

FROM A HANDFUL OF CHOCOLATES . . .

In 1946, shortly after World War II, Fannie May created its most well-known candy to date, the Pixie. Caramel was poured by hand over nuts and then drenched in chocolate. The company continued to develop new candy flavors. In 1970, it introduced the Trinidad (crunchy, coconut-and-white-chocolate-covered dark chocolates), which became its most popular candy to date. The beauty of a Trinidad lies in its decadent layers of rich, creamy real dark chocolate, covered in a golden toasted coconut shell. Other Fannie May mainstays are Mint Meltaways, along with vanilla buttercreams and chocolate truffles. Fannie May now makes more than 100 different confections.

—SCOTT WARNER

Fannie May Loop storefront, ca. 1940. Courtesy of Fannie May.

Archibald also acquired a crushing debt load and filed for Chapter 11, seeking bankruptcy protection. The company ultimately shuttered Fannie May's 228-store candy empire in 2004. But the iconic chocolate maker was reborn that same year when Alpine Confections, Inc., bought Fannie May and Fanny Farmer. Both companies became wholly owned subsidiaries of Alpine.

While Fannie May's corporate headquarters remained in Chicago, Alpine moved the production of Fannie May chocolates to Harry London Candies in North Canton, Ohio. Ownership changed again in 2006 when Fannie May was purchased by the Internet retailer 1–800-Flowers .com. Today, Fannie May candies are sold in more than 100 retail locations in six states and Canada.

Contributor: Scott Warner

See also: Candy

BIBLIOGRAPHY

Fannie May Confections Brands, Inc. *Reference for Business*. http://www.referenceforbusiness.com/history2/31/Fannie-May-Confections-Brands-Inc.html.

Marton, Renee. "Fannie May." *The Oxford Companion to American Food and Drink*. New York: Oxford University Press, 2007.

Farmers Markets

"Get out and shake the hand that feeds you" may be the motto of farmers market shoppers, who now enjoy many choices for fresh, local food direct from Midwest growers. It was not always the case. Although farmers markets have existed almost as long as there have been farmers, a move to keep food in the sterile indoors was the order of the day with the advent of the supermarket in the early twentieth century. The Farmers-to-Consumer Direct Marketing Act,

1976, made it easier for farmers to sell directly to consumers, resulting in a boom in farmers markets. In 1994, the U.S. Department of Agriculture (USDA) documented 1,775 markets in the United States; 2014 saw 8,268.

As of 2015, about 150 farmers markets existed in Chicago and suburbs. The City of Chicago operated 22 farmers markets and collaborated with other organizations to foster even more. For example, grants from the USDA Farmers Market Promotion Program (FMPP) were used to start markets in the Pullman, Austin, and Englewood neighborhoods. The aim was to transition operations to nonprofit or community groups to sustain them, thus expanding the reach of the program as the city moves on to identify other neighborhoods ripe for new markets. The downtown marquee markets, including Daley Plaza, Federal Plaza, Museum of Contemporary Arts, and Willis Tower Plaza, are all producer markets, meaning the farmer must be present to sell there. Neighborhood markets have a little more latitude to sell products such as prepackaged foods created by restaurants, local businesses like bakeries, and artisan products, such as handmade soaps and lotions.

Farmers market pioneers launched them in affluent areas, such as Oak Park, in response to new ideas about health and nutrition and essentially to help the farmers stay in business. As the movement grew, efforts increased to bring fresh food to underserved people, and now markets operate in areas with more economic diversity. Market organizers work to help underserved people use benefits provided by the Supplemental Nutrition Assistance Program (SNAP), formerly known as food stamps. City-run markets accept Link cards, the swipe cards that Illinois residents use for SNAP benefits, and most independent markets have followed suit. The 61st Street Farmers Market, run by the nonprofit Experimental Station, gives grants to double what SNAP recipients can spend on fresh food. Such grant programs are run by organizations such as the Fair Food Network and the Wholesome Wave Foundation.

Chicago's Green City Market, the grande dame of the Chicago farmers market scene, reigns twice a week in leafy Lincoln Park, a far journey from its humble start. Founded by Abby Mandel in an alley behind the Chicago Theater on State Street, the fledgling market had six farmers and not many shoppers. But Mandel wanted a chef-driven market, with higher standards for vendors, and grew the market over time, moving it to its current location and raising funds to hire permanent staff. A second location opened in 2015 in the West Loop. Green City is one of few markets that requires all vendors to be certified in sustainable farming practices.

Fledgling businesses find Chicago farmers markets great places to build clientele, test new products, and then eventually open their own shops. Examples include

Hoosier Mama Pie Company and Floriole Café and Bakery, both started at Green City Market. The Logan Square Farmers Market hosts a large proportion of vendors who manufacture artisan products, including Chicago Honey Co-op, Katherine Anne Confections, Spencer's Jolly Posh Foods, and Lucila's Homemade, which sells *dulce de leche* sandwich cookies, and *alfajores*, inspired by Argentina.

Contributor: Janine MacLachlan

See also: Agriculture, Urban; Green City Market

BIBLIOGRAPHY

Illinois Farmers Market Association. http://ilfarmersmarkets.org/.
MacLachlan, Janine. *Farmers' Markets of the Heartland.* Urbana: University of Illinois Press, 2012.

Farming (See: Agriculture, Urban)

Fasano Pie Company

"As good as Mother's and better than others." That was the assured slogan of the Fasano Pie Co., once the largest pie maker in the Chicago area, with a reach that extended to 48 states. Joseph Fasano Sr. opened Fasano and Sons Bakery in 1946. By the 1960s, the company had changed its name and was doing $8 million in annual sales, supplying fresh and frozen pies to retail clients from its Bedford Park bakery at 6201 W. 65th St. The firm folded in 1985 amid declining sales and a rise in convenience foods. In 2011, grandson Peter Fasano revived the business using the original recipes. Fruit pies and cream pies are sold in grocery stores, in restaurants, and via a "Pies by Fasano" food truck.

Contributor: Janet Fuller

See also: Bakeries and Baking; Italians

BIBLIOGRAPHY

Vickroy, Donna. "Fasano Pies Making a comeback." *Chicago Sun-Times Media*, December 28, 2011.

Fast Food/Quick Service

Chicago's fast-food tradition reflects the city's ethnic and culinary history, from the sausages and pork chops of the old Maxwell Street market to the multinational chains of today. Fast food or quick-service food began with food carts and wagons in the nineteenth century and extended to fixed-location lunch counters and later hot dog stands. Among the early dishes is the first credible mention of a "hamburger sandwich" in 1894, along with hot dogs, ham, and cheese sandwiches. The terms *fast food* and *quick service* were first used in professional food-service journals in the 1950s. The city has played a significant role in the development of American fast-food culture. The king of national and international fast-food chains is McDonald's Corporation, founded by Oak Parker Ray Kroc and headquartered in Oakbrook, Illinois.

In addition to national chains, Chicago also has a number of fast-food restaurants unique to the area. They typically feature a menu with one or more of the dishes traditionally associated with Chicago—hot dogs, Italian beef, gyros, and grilled or fried chicken. During lent, fried and grilled fish sandwiches are popular menu items, as are bell pepper and egg sandwiches served on an Italian sub roll.

Al's Beef was founded in 1938 by Al Ferrari and his brothers-in-law Frances and Chris Pacelli. It started as a food stand before moving to a restaurant space at 1079 W. Taylor St., still in operation. The menu grew to include hot dogs, Italian sausages, and Polish sausages. Franchise rights were purchased in 1999 by Chicago Franchise Systems, and

THE BURGER BOOM

Yes, Chicago is "hot dog city." But burgers in this town also do a bang-up business, and no more so than lately, as new burger restaurants compete for Chicagoans' loyalties. Chains—such as the New York phenomenon Shake Shack, or Five Guys, Epic Burger, and Umami Burger—have invaded the city.

Locally owned burger joints amp up the competition: Burger Bar, Butcher & the Burger, DMK Burger Bar, Edzo's Burger Shop, Grange Hall Burger Bar, Kuma's corner, M Burger, Spritz Burger.

Even full-menu restaurants have joined the burger wars. Top burger honors have gone to such fine-dining venues as Naha, David Burke's Primehouse, and Nico Osteria. And, in a surprise choice by television's The Food Network, Au Cheval's double-patty cheeseburger won as top burger in the United States. The burger, made with three patties topped with cheddar, maple-glazed bacon, and homemade Dijon mayo (fried egg, optional) was praised for its "perfect burger-to-cheese ratio."

—CAROL MIGHTON HADDIX

An early version of quick-service places on the Chicago docks, 1880s. Courtesy of the Chicago History Museum, DN-0003793.

the chain began expansion in 2001 with a stand in Tinley Park, Illinois. It now includes 12 Illinois locations, as well as locations in Las Vegas, Dallas, and California.

Harold's Chicken Shack Inc. is a chain of fried chicken restaurants prominent on the South Side and in the south suburbs. It was founded as Harold's the Fried Chicken King in 1950 by Harold Pierce at 47th and Greenwood. Harold's served chicken fried to order within 15 minutes in a mixture of beef tallow and vegetable oil. Pierce franchised the concept, which expanded to locations (numbered individually) primarily on the South and West Sides. Some locations still carry the original name, and all feature some version of a logo depicting a cook chasing a chicken with a cleaver. It was one of the few fast-food chains at the time to cater to an African American clientele. Pierce died in 1988, and his children now run Harold's; they introduced a par-cooking process that halved the preparation time. The chain has since grown to include locations in North Side neighborhoods, as well as Indiana, Michigan, and Georgia.

James J. Green founded J & J Chicken and Fish in March 1982 (as J & J Fish) at 35th Ave. and Martin Luther King Drive. It expanded to more than 130 restaurants in the Chicago metro area, southeast Wisconsin, Detroit, and the San Francisco Bay Area. The menu features batter-fried fish, shrimp, and chicken.

Pepe's Mexican Restaurants began in 1967, with owners Mario Dovalina and Edwin Ptak offering an early take on Mexican-influenced fast food. In addition to about 40 locations in Chicago and northwest Indiana, the Pepe's chain produces private label Mexican foods for clients worldwide.

Pockets opened in 1989 as a health-oriented fast-food storefront in Lincoln Park. The chain, founded by former options trader David Lichtman, offers sandwiches served on multi-grain bread baked in house, along with calzones, pizza, and salads. There are nine locations throughout Chicago, as well as two suburban locations in Aurora.

Portillo's began in 1963 as The Dog House, a catering trailer in Villa Park with no running water, operated by Dick Portillo. After finding success and a building with utilities in 1967, the restaurant expanded to include 38 locations in Chicagoland, Indiana, Arizona, and California, as well as catering that ships to all 50 states. As the single largest buyer of Vienna Beef hot dogs in the country, Portillo's has some leverage in purchasing, switching to a secret proprietary blend at one point during the mid-2000s before going back to the original Vienna franks. In 2015, Portillo's was sold to the private equity firm Berkshire Partners, but the founder remains involved in the business.

Contributor: John Carruthers

See also: Fast Food/Quick Service; Hot Dogs; Italian Beef

BIBLIOGRAPHY

"Best-of-Chicago." *Chicago Magazine*, August, 2008.

Sula, Mike. "The First Family of Fried Chicken." *Chicago Reader*, April 14, 2006. http://www.chicagoreader.com/pdf/060414/060414_harolds.pdf.

Faulds Ovens

Faulds Ovens have been an iconic part of Chicago's culinary landscape since the mid-1930s. They continue to play a key role in pizzerias and bakeries even though they have not been manufactured for several decades. These large rotating ovens first began appearing in large-scale baking operations after John Faulds left his position as a designer at the Middleby Oven Company in the late 1890s and started his own manufacturing company at 4256 West Diversey Ave. Faulds worked alongside lead engineer John I. Marshall at Middleby, creating some of the most mechanically advanced ovens in the United States prior to the Great Depression. Features such as cool-to-the-touch exterior panels, illuminated interiors, and electrically operated rotating racks became hallmarks of his designs. These early Faulds ovens for Middleby used a Ferris Wheel–like rotating rack that circulated the baked goods throughout the different temperature zones in the oven. This allowed for a more even cooking process, a feature that can be seen as the forerunner of the modern convection oven.

John Faulds continued to improve upon those basic design elements at his own firm. Faulds ran a small operation that catered to midwestern pizzerias and bakeries. He offered custom-designed ovens, including one from 1957 still in use at John's Pizzeria on 2104 N. Western Ave. in Chicago. This unit, coated in vitreous white enamel with black accents, has a custom enameled inlay that reads "Faulds Oven Designed for John's Pizzeria." The owner of State Line Pizzas in Hammond, Indiana., continued to use a Faulds oven well into the 1990s, despite the fact that traditional deck ovens could cook pizza in twice the time. In his estimation, the indirect heat and relatively low cooking temperature made the Faulds oven ideal for Chicago-style pizza.

Moskal Industries acquired Faulds in 1975 and relocated its factory to 3126 N. Clybourn Ave. Faulds ceased to manufacture ovens in the late 1990s. Faulds Ovens represent an early attempt to mechanize the process of pizza and bakery production, while also offering a greater capacity than a static oven. They continue to be a preferred choice for restaurants that create the breadlike deep-dish and stuffed pizzas that have become a Chicago hallmark.

Contributor: Stefan Osdene
See also: Equipment, Commercial

BIBLIOGRAPHY

Gebert, Michael. "Great Unknown Pizzas of the South Side, Part 1." http://skyfullofbacon.com/blog/?p=4322.
Pizza Today, Vol. 9. Santa Claus, Ind.: Pro Tech Publishing and Communications, 1991.

Atomic Fireballs, one of Ferrara Pan's best known "hot" candies. Courtesy of Lake County (Ill.) Discovery Museum, Curt Teich Postcard Archives.

Fegan, Patrick

After graduation from the University of Illinois at Chicago, Patrick Fegan (1948–2016) traveled to France to learn about wine. He ended up working the 1971 harvest in Bordeaux and then taking a technical wine course at Université de Bordeaux à Talence. He since traveled to every wine region in the world, across five continents.

His interest in wine developed into a career teaching others back in his hometown, starting in 1975. He opened the independent Chicago Wine School (CWS) in 1984, offering beginning and advanced courses plus workshops and seminars. He taught more than 22,000 people the basics, from how to taste wine to the importance of soil composition for vine growth. Fegan also wrote about wine for the *Chicago Sun-Times*, *Chicago Tribune*, and national publications. He wrote two books: *Vineyards and Wineries of America: A Traveler's Guide* (1982) and *The Vineyard Handbook: Appellations, Maps and Statistics* (1992, revised 2003). He also passed the world's most difficult wine-tasting exam from the Institute of Masters of Wine in London and earned the Wine Educator of the Year award by the European Wine Council. CWS was named one of the top five schools in the country to learn about wine by *Food & Wine* magazine. Fegan died in March 2016.

Contributor: Carol Mighton Haddix
See also: Wine and Wineries

BIBLIOGRAPHY

"Patrick W. Fegan." *Appellation America*. http://wine.appellation america.com/wine/writer/Patrick_W. Fegan.html.

Ferrara Pan Candy Company

The geography of the Chicago area can be mapped by its food aromas. Travel west on the Eisenhower Expressway, and if you notice the pungent aroma of cinnamon, no doubt you are near Harlem Avenue and the Ferrara Candy Company, where one of their signature candies, Red Hots, are most likely coming off the production line.

In 1908, Salvatore Ferrara, originally from Nola, Italy, founded the Original Ferrara Pastry and Bakery on Taylor Street, where he made not only pastries, but also candy-covered almonds that are traditional favors of good luck at Italian weddings. In 1959, as the company grew, the factory moved to Forest Park.

Salvatore's son, Nello Ferrara, originated Atomic Fireballs in 1954 after serving in Occupied Japan in the post–atomic bomb era. The fiery sensation in the candy comes from capsicum clocking in at 3500 Scoville units. Other signature hard candy favorites include (besides Red Hots)

Lemonheads and Boston Baked Beans. Nello died in 2012 at age 93.

When Nello's son Salvatore II became CEO, the company expanded into gummy lines, chocolate-covered panned nuts and raisins, and private label items for large candy and cereal companies. The company became Ferrara Candy Company when it merged with Farley & Sathers Candy Company in 2012 and continued to be managed by Salvatore II until 2014. Salvatore II is responsible for taking the company international. Nello and Salvatore II each received the candy industry's highest achievement: The Kettle Award.

Invariably, the question arises, "What is the Pan in Ferrara Pan Candy?" The manufacturing process known as panning can best be visualized as the creating of a snowball or cultured pearl. A grain of sugar or other center such as a nut, candy, or piece of fruit is tossed into a rotating pan as granulated sugar and other flavoring and ingredients are added. The layers build, increase in size, and the candy is formed.

The Original Ferrara Pastry and Bakery is at 2210 W. Taylor St. in Chicago. The company's outlet store is at the 7301 Harrison St. plant in Forest Park. Both locations feature honorary street signs, in Chicago for Salvatore's wife, Serafina Ferrara, and in Forest Park for Nello Ferrara.

....

Contributor: Eleanor Hanson

See also: Candy; Italians

BIBLIOGRAPHY

Candy Alliance LLC: Ferrara Pan. http://www.ferrarausa.com/.

O'Donnell, Maureen. "Nello Ferrara, 93, Invented Lemonheads, saw MacArthur in Occupied Japan, Sang with Sinatra." *Chicago Sun Times*, February 7, 2012.

Festivals

Judging by Chicago's food festivals, it is hard to imagine a more food-oriented city. In addition to the famed Taste of Chicago and the barbecue/rib fests, there are countless other food festivals. Many raise money for good causes; others celebrate neighborhoods, ethnic cuisines, and religions.

At the peak of the culinary ladder is Chicago Gourmet, begun in 2006. It was billed as "a celebration of wine and food" and held over a weekend in September in Millennium Park. Considered a top-drawer version of Taste of Chicago, Chicago Gourmet features more than 150 of the city's best restaurants, sommeliers, and winemakers. Tickets for a day cost more than $180.

A similar event to benefit Chicago's Green City Market, the Chef's BBQ, takes place in Lincoln Park in mid-July and includes over 90 of the city's top chefs. They use sustainably raised products from the market's vendors to provide a taste of everything from Rick Bayless's tacos to Sarah Stegner's honey ice cream.

Neighborhood food festivals usually combine music and food from restaurants in the immediate area. June's Taste of Randolph Street features both music and food along the famed Randolph Street Restaurant Row, including BellyQ, La Sardine, and Publican. Randolph Street is part of the city-designated Fulton Market District, intended to highlight the traditional wholesale meat and produce district west of Chicago's Loop.

The three-year-old Taste of Lakeview has a deep-dish pizza and gelato vibe, catering to the musical tastes of its majority single attendees. With a $5 requested admission, it has attracted upward of 35,000 participants.

Also in July, the Taste of River North highlights the diverse restaurant options in this hip Chicago neighborhood, home of the East Bank Club. Previous fests have featured food from Farmhouse, Starfruit, The Kerryman, and Kinzie Chop House.

Fiestas Puertorriqueñas in Humbolt Park celebrates the neighborhood's Puerto Rican heritage. Held over a June weekend, the area's Puerto Rican restaurants produce such traditional foods as *arroz con gandules* (yellow rice with pigeon peas), *alcapurrias* (meat-stuffed fritters), *plátanos maduros* (sweet fried plantains), and *lechón* (pulled roasted pork). Following the traditional Puerto Rican Day Parade, the festival is run by the Puerto Rican Parade Committee, founded in 1965, to present events of relevance to Puerto Rican culture.

A broader Latin beat drives August's Taste of Latin America in Logan Square. Launched in 2012, the festival features music, art, and food from Central and South America. Participating restaurants have included El Veneno de Nayarit, La Bomba, Mekato's Colombian Bakery, and Cemitas Puebla.

A dramatically different ethnic flavor profile is found at the Ginza Festival, a 60-year August tradition at the Midwest Buddhist Temple in Old Town. Sushi, tempura, and Japanese beer refresh attendees who watch Japanese martial arts and decorative arts demonstrated on the spot.

Moving around the globe, the Taste of Greektown, also in August, takes place in Chicago's historic Greektown neighborhood on Halsted Street, west of the Loop. Such traditional Greek foods as baklava, souvlaki, and gyros sustain visitors, who also enjoy the Greek dancing and art.

Although Chicago's Little Italy on Taylor Street was largely replaced by the University of Illinois Circle Campus, the Taylor Street Festa Italiana brings back the old energy and spirit of the neighborhood. In addition to the expected pizza and meatballs, vendors offer *arancini*, *cannoli*, and Italian ices.

Neighborhoods are not the only organizing strategy for Chicago food festivals. A new specialty food festival launched in June of 2015 is the Chicago Food Truck Fest, paying tribute to the recent food truck expansion in Chicago. Chicago has a contentious history of food truck regulation designed to protect existing restaurants. Trucks like Fat Shallot and Bombay Wraps demonstrate the range of food truck offerings in Chicago.

Burgers of all kinds characterize the Roscoe Village Burger Fest. Over a dozen of Chicago's best burger-focused restaurants compete for the Critic's Choice Award for the Best Burger. Music on two stages and a kids' area add to the July festivities.

A relative newcomer, the Chicago Hot Dog Fest is held in August at the Chicago History Museum. Following the pattern of neighborhood festivals, the activities include a music stage and kids' activity area in addition to a wide range of vendors of Chicago's beloved summer staple.

Although far from the coast of Maine, modern transport permits Chicago to host the Great American Lobster Fest on Navy Pier. In addition to music and the Air and Water Show going on at the same time, the festival provides fireworks to underscore the special treat delivered by the sweet crustacean.

Lakeview Taco Fest, Berghoff Octoberfest, and Schock Top Oyster Fest, with their self-evident food specialties, round out the list of leading food fests in Chicago.

....

Contributor: Elizabeth D. Richter

See also: Chicago Gourmet; Green City Market; Taste of Chicago

BIBLIOGRAPHY

"Chicago Festivals." City of Chicago. www.cityofchicago.org/city/en/depts/dca/provdrs/chicago_festivals.html.

"Taste of Latin America." Special Events Management. www.chicagoevents.com/event.cfm?eid=251.

Filipinos

The first Filipino immigrants to Chicago came in the early 1900s and, unlike the large waves of agricultural laborers who came to California and Hawaii, they were young men from wealthy families who attended universities on government scholarships. Their legacy attracted subsequent waves of working students, who came without government assistance and with varying degrees of wealth, from the 1910s through 1930s.

In the 1920s and 1930s, a Filipino enclave settled between Oak Street and Chicago Avenue. An early restaurant, the Manila Village Cafe, was in the basement of the Filipino Community Center. Although the number of Filipino immigrants was not large in those early years,

they formed social clubs such as the Filipino Association of Chicago, based in the Garfield Park neighborhood. Other clubs organized themselves around regional and provincial origin, such as the Nueva Vizcaya Association of Chicago, the La Union Association, and the Ilocos Sur Club. These groups provided assistance with employment and housing and reinforced cultural ties with banquets and picnics of Filipino foods.

Unlike other immigrants to the area or Filipino migrants to other parts of the United States, Chicago's Filipinos did not form into an ethnic enclave, "ghetto," or a centralized hub for commerce and residences. Some Chinese and South Asian markets offered ingredients for Filipino home cooks, including imported dry goods and frozen produce. In the early days, Filipinos also could secure offal or variety meats for free from some grocers, butcher counters, and fishmongers. Filipinos also bought direct from the butchers in Fulton Market on the city's Near West side.

The Exchange Visitor Program in the 1960s brought English-speaking Filipino nurses (almost all female) on two-year exchange programs to the United States. When the Immigration Act of 1965 gave preference to potential immigrants based on profession and family ties, waves of Filipino immigrants came to Chicago, largely health-care professionals and family members.

The market for Filipino food grew, and selling prepared Filipino food to other Filipinos became a viable enterprise. Many, such as nurses, opened catering businesses, moonlighting in their spare time, a practice that continues today.

In the 1970s, Filipino-owned grocery stores, called *sari-sari*, opened in Chicago and surrounding suburbs. They carried Philippine-made dry goods and specialty ingredients. Some carried Asian produce such as bitter melon from local Filipino-owned farms. Larger Filipino grocery stores such as the chain Uni-Mart housed the first *turo-turo* ("point-point") counter service restaurants. With the 2008 economic downturn and the competitive grocery chains, many of the smaller Filipino grocery stores have closed.

One of the first restaurants, Little Quiapo, opened in the 1980s on Clark near Montrose. A few more Filipino restaurants appeared in the 1990s, including Feliz on Belmont Avenue, Ovenmaid Bakery in Evergreen Park, Cebu in Downers Grove, and the fine-dining establishment, Rambutan, in Chicago's Wicker Park, which closed in 2002. In the 2000s, came Isla Filipina in Lincoln Square; and in West Town, Uncle Mike's, a longtime American diner that added a Filipino breakfast menu. The 200-seat high-profile Sunda in the tony River North neighborhood started serving

Filipino and other Asian cuisines in 2009. In 2012, Chef Chrissy Camba, a Filipina American, competed on the reality TV show, *Top Chef.* Camba opened a modern Filipino restaurant in Lincoln Square, which closed in less than 6 months. She continued to cook a pop-up dinner series under the name Maddy's Dumpling House. Chef Joaquin Soler, a former sous chef at Rambutan, opened smalls, a barbecue joint that featured Filipino-style barbecue and house-made *longganisa* in 2013 in Old Irving Park. In 2014, Chef Kristine Subido closed her Uptown restaurant, Pecking Order, after two years but continued to cater at the Logan Square Farmers Market and Nosh.

In The Philippines, food is usually served family-style, with all the dishes on the table at once or, during *piyesta* (fiesta), in a long buffet spread. Typically, U.S.-based Filipino restaurants divide the menu into Western-style courses, though the *turo-turo* will offer a few specials a la carte. A common appetizer, *lumpia shanghai*, a meat- and/or vegetable-filled, deep-fried eggroll, is served at home during special occasions rather than on a regular basis. Soup is always *sinigang*, a tamarind- or guava-soured broth with pork, head-on prawns or shrimp, and vegetables. Popular entrees are *kare-kare* (oxtail, eggplant, green beans in a peanut stew with a side of fermented shrimp paste) and *adobo* (a vinegar-soy braise of pork or chicken with bay leaves and black peppercorn). Older generations try to get their youngsters to taste *dinuguan*, a variant of adobo with pork blood added, sometimes called "chocolate meat."

Tradition dictates that the stir-fried noodle, meat, and vegetable dish *pancit* be eaten on one's birthday, and often both *pancit* (egg noodles) *canton* and *bihon* (rice noodles) are on the menu. Entrees usually come with steamed jasmine rice. Many offer *sisig*, pig's cheek, ear, and brain (more often with mayonnaise in place of brain), minced fine with Thai chilies, served slightly crispy on a sizzling platter with an over-easy egg on top. Desserts include *leche flan*, the Spanish egg custard with caramelized sugar syrup, and *halo-halo*, the kitchen sink of shaved ice desserts: condensed milk, ice creams like *ube* (purple yam), avocado, and/or *mais con queso* (corn and cheese); agar-agar gelatin; *kaong* (sugar palm fruit); *pinipig* (pounded rice flakes); red beans; and fruit such as jack fruit, bananas, or whatever is available and delicious. In 2015, Filipino Kitchen, a Chicago-based food media and events group, launched Kultura, an annual Filipino-American food and arts festival.

Contributor: Sarahlyn Pablo

BIBLIOGRAPHY

Alomar, Estrella Ravelo, and Willy "Red" Buhay. *Filipinos in Chicago*. Chicago: Arcadia Publishing, 2001.

Futterman, Lisa. "The Next Asian Cuisine," *Food & Wine*, June 2001. http://www.foodandwine.com/articles/the-next-asian-cuisine.

Lau, Yvonne M. "Re-Visioning Filipino American Communities: Evolving Identities, Issues, and Organizations," John Koval, Larry Bennett, Michael Bennett, Fassil Demissie, Roberta Garner, and Kiljoong Kim, eds. *The New Chicago: A Social and Cultural Analysis*. Philadelphia: Temple University Press, 2006.

Fine Dining (See: Restaurants and Fine Dining)

Fingerhut Bakery

Bohemian immigrant Frank Fingerhut opened his bakery in 1895 at 18th and May Streets. His baked items were like those in the "old country." *Babi* (the Bohemian word for grandmother) was a rye bread. *Kolacky*, a soft and sweet cookie filled with jam, and *houska*, a sweet yeast bread with raisins and dried fruits, also were staples.

In about 1915, Frank's son Charles purchased land at Cermak and Central (5537 W. Cermak) and built the Charles Fingerhut Bakery. Another store, Fingerhut's Oven Fresh Bakery, opened in Brookfield, Illinois. Herb Fingerhut, a grandson and a seventh-generation baker, later ran the bakery firm until it closed in 2004.

Contributor: Jenny Lewis

See also: Baking and Bakeries; Czechs

BIBLIOGRAPHY

Cantrell, Wanda. "Family Bakery Part of the Neighborhood." *Chicago Tribune*, July 25, 1990.

Fingerhut was founded in 1893 at May and 18th Streets. Courtesy of Herb Fingerhut.

Fish and Seafood

Chicago's economy was built in the nineteenth century, based on lumber, meat, and grain—not fish. Railroad transportation could sustain trade in the other items, but fish would rot. However, Lake Michigan was full of lake whitefish (a freshwater salmonid), varieties of lake trout, and walleye. These were fished for local consumption by native people and later by European settlers. Oysters, one of the first seafoods to travel well, were brought, alive, in iced barrels from the East Coast, except in the four warm months that had no "R" in them, and eaten in quantities that would seem gluttonous today.

Discussion of fish in histories of early Chicago is rare, crowded out by talk of settlements, architecture, politics, and trade. But a widely seen benefit to Chicago's new (and still standing) romantic water tower of 1869 was that it left the municipal water drawn from Lake Michigan free of fish for the first time.

Refrigerated rail transport did not lead to much change in how Chicago's seafood was marketed or how far it traveled, because there was no great inland market for saltwater fish. The local focus remained on whitefish and lake trout until refrigerated transport became developed enough to carry ocean fish from the East. This seems to have begun as a taste for novelty or sophistication, a trend that continued in the early age of air transport when suddenly restaurants began identifying their seafood with the proud slogan, "just flown in."

Before World War II, Chicago was home to nearly two-dozen large seafood wholesalers, who operated along the Chicago and Calumet Rivers. Lake Michigan trout was bountiful in the 1930s and 1940s. But by the time WWII ended, the lake trout population had dwindled.

Perch was more abundant: On April 6, 1951, one fishing boat, the Iva T, hauled in a ton of perch, bringing it to Lawrence Schweig's Fish Company at 2120 S. Canal St. Schweig's crews were the last to have local boats on the water.

Commercial fishing all but disappeared. The popular explanation was that the 1959 opening of the St. Lawrence seaway, which connected the Great Lakes directly to the Atlantic Ocean, had let in sea lampreys, an invasive species that remain a major challenge in management of the fishery today. However, Great Lakes native fish populations had been in decline decades before from overfishing, environmental neglect, and pollution. Even sea lampreys had made their way through the Erie Canal into the lower Great Lakes much earlier.

Ireland's restaurant on LaSalle Street specialized in seafood and merited prominent mention in John Drury's 1931 *Dining Guide to Chicago*. Jory Graham cautioned her readers in 1968 that visitors from the coasts to Chicago's seafood restaurants should interrogate their waiters about whether their fish was "fresh" or frozen. Freshness, of course, is a slippery concept, and "flown-in" fish can vary in quality depending on how it is processed and handled.

By this time, whitefish from Lake Michigan had become nearly extinct. Local connoisseurs who admired the fish began to focus on the term, "Lake Superior whitefish," which was proudly served sautéed, with butter and parsley, as a local specialty at the Berghoff, Binyon's, and city and country clubs. Since that time, whitefish stocks have recovered, possibly because of campaigns to "manage" the sea lampreys and to stock a predatory fish, Coho salmon. In spite of challenges from new invasive species, mainly zebra mussels, Northern Lake Michigan has become a renewed source of whitefish, while stocks have declined in Lake Superior.

However, the seafood focus in Chicago is no longer local. Gradually, the world market has taken hold. Burhops, Chicago Fish House, and Isaacson & Stein were early fish stores operating as middlemen to a national and then international market; Isaacson & Stein exists now as a sort of hybrid between old-style wholesale and retail. A wave of improvement was brought on by the explosion of Japanese restaurants in the 1980s, with sushi chefs insistent on a level of quality not always seen in Chicago's wholesale distributors downtown.

Around the world, ports have become less important to fresh-fish distribution and airports more important. Chicago's fresh fish distribution system now centers around O'Hare Airport. Fortune Fish, Supreme Lobster, and Seafood Merchants are the leading local distributors, and the giant Korean-owned True World Foods also looms large. High-quality specialty retailers, such as Dirk Fucik's Dirk's Fish and Bill Dugan's The FishGuy Market, opened, along with, more recently, Oscar Farinetti's worldwide Italian specialty shop, Eataly. These emporia have set new standards for selling seafood of high quality to the public. Bob Chinn's Crab House, one of the highest grossing independent restaurants in the United States, lists the flight numbers for the arrival of each fish on its "jet fresh" board. Nico Osteria, opened in 2013, achieved a nationwide following for its care and selection of seafood, and its chef, Erling Wu-Bower, has said a secret to being a seafood chef in Chicago today is being "a FedEx expert . . . an airline-schedule expert."

Contributor: Richard Warren Shepro
See also: Seafood Restaurants

BIBLIOGRAPHY

Bogue, Margaret Beattie. *Fishing the Great Lakes: An Environmental History, 1783–1933*. Madison: University of Wisconsin Press, 2000.

Ebener, Mark P., et al. "Management of Commercial Fisheries for Lake Whitefish in the Laurentian Great Lakes of North America." In *International Governance of Fisheries Ecosystems*. Bethesda: American Fisheries Society, 2008. http://www.miseagrant.umich.edu/downloads/research/journals/08–310.pdf.

Gebert, Michael. "Nico Osteria's Erling Wu-Bower Talks His World of Seafood." *Chicago Reader*, February 25, 2014.

Fish Oven Company

Brick mason A. J. Fish purchased the rights to a rotary pastry oven patented by Joseph Vale in 1868. Fish took over Vale's fledgling Chicago factory in 1874, renamed it the Fish Oven Company, and became a pioneer in the development of the rotary bake oven.

The rotating oven set a technological precedent in automated baking equipment and the mass production of baked goods. The earliest Fish Ovens consisted of multi-tiered rotating cylindrical shelves within a baking cavity. By rotating the food through different heat zones in the oven, the machines ensured even baking, free from the hot spots found within static ovens. Their large size also enabled big-batch baking that saved time and reduced production costs.

For almost two decades, Fish remained the nation's only maker of rotating bake ovens—a market segment that attracted the attention of other firms such as Middleby-Marshall, Faulds, and Clauss Ovens of Cincinnati after the turn of the twentieth century.

One of the earliest Fish factories stood at 159 Lake St. in Chicago. After several moves back and forth to Wisconsin in the early 1900s, the company settled in Wauconda, Illinois, in the 1980s, at 120 W. Kent St. It continues to produce rotating tray ovens for bakeries and pizzerias throughout the United States.

Contributor: Stefan Osdene
See also: Baking and Bakeries; Equipment, Commercial; Pizza

BIBLIOGRAPHY

http://www.fishoven.com/history.html.

Fisher Nuts

Sam Fisher was a young boy when his family emigrated from Russia to St. Paul, Minnesota. As a U.S. soldier stationed in France during World War I, he became enchanted with French roasted nuts. Upon returning to St. Paul, he started making salted in-shell peanuts and in 1920 established Fisher Nuts. In 1989, Proctor & Gamble bought Fisher Nuts and later sold it to John B. Sanfilippo and Sons, Inc.

In 1922, John B. Sanfilippo, an immigrant from Sicily, had started a small pecan-shelling factory on Larrabee Street in Chicago. In 1963, son Jasper took the helm and stepped up diversification to include almonds, walnuts, and peanuts. At retail outlets, Sanfilippo sold products under the Prairie State label. In 1974, Sanfilippo acquired competitor H. H. Evon Co.'s brand name and assets, allowing Sanfilippo to expand its reach throughout the Midwest. In 1994, Sanfilippo, now based in Elk Grove Village, started handling production of Fisher Nuts for Procter & Gamble, and by 1995, had acquired the Fisher Nuts line. The company, headquartered in Elgin since 2007, offers raw and processed nuts in a variety of styles, as well as peanut butter, snack mixes, dried fruit, baking ingredients, and a number of other food products. In 2013, net sales reached $734.3 million.

Contributor: Deborah Pankey

BIBLIOGRAPHY

"Fisher Nuts." *International Directory of Company Histories, Vol. 14*. St. James Press, Mo.: St. James Press, 1996.

Fisher Nuts/John B. Sanfilippo and Sons. http://www.jbssinc.com/jaboutus-ourstory.

Flavorings

Chicago has a flourishing food science community and is home to a number of companies that marry taste with technology to create flavorings, many of them custom, for makers of foods and beverages found in foodservice products, and on grocery store shelves. Chicago's major flavorings manufacturers include Prinova, Flavorchem, FONA (Flavors of North America), Heller Seasonings & Ingredients (owned by Newly Weds Foods), and Sensient Beverage Flavors in Hoffman Estates (a branch of Sensient Technologies in Milwaukee). Some flavoring companies have been in the field for more than 100 years. Weber Flavors dates to 1902. Bell Flavors & Fragrances began as the William M. Bell Company in Chicago in 1912 and specializes in natural food extracts for bakery, confections, and dairy. B. Heller and Company, begun in 1893, specialized in dry spices used in the preparation of meat products. Its famous Zanzibar Mixes were used extensively in the Chicago meat industry and remains a major supplier to meat companies.

One of the world's largest flavoring companies is Newly Weds Foods with headquarters on Fullerton Avenue. The company originated as a bakery whose owner Paul Angell invented the ice-cream cake roll in 1932. In

1952, the company began making food coatings such as batters and got into the flavorings business in the 1980s. Today, it operates in 68 countries selling food coatings and flavorings.

....

Contributor: Janine MacLachlan
See also: Food Technology; Nielsen Massey

BIBLIOGRAPHY

http://www.newlywedsfoods.com.

Flying Food Group

Sue Ling Gin founded Flying Food Group in 1983 with one commercial kitchen at Midway Airport to supply Midway Airlines with passenger meals. From that small beginning, she grew the catering firm to serve more than 70 international airlines with 20 kitchens around the United States and China and earn $435 million in revenue in 2013. Clients include British Airways, Air France-KLM, Qantas, and Royal Jordanian, as well as retail outlets such as Starbucks.

In 1996, Gin began to diversify beyond airlines by adding a new segment to the business, Fresh Food Solutions. Chilled meals and heat-and-serve dishes were created to sell to grocery stores and food-service operations. The firm also makes Sano parfait, a yogurt, granola, and fruit layered snack now sold across the United States.

The downturn in air travel after 9/11 terrorist attacks hurt the firm, but foreign clients and the nonairline accounts helped it bounce back. Today, a multiethnic staff of chefs create airline dishes for American, French, German, Halal, Italian, Indian, Japanese, Korean, Malaysian, Thai, and Turkish cuisines. Gin died in 2014, and Milt Liu took over as CEO. Flying Food Group is headquartered at 212 N. Sangamon St. in the West Loop.

....

Contributor: Carol Mighton Haddix
See also: Catering; Gin, Sue Ling

BIBLIOGRAPHY

Strayler, Steven R. "Sue Gin, Pioneering businesswoman, Has Died." *Crain's Chicago Business.* http://www.chicagobusiness.com/article/20140926/NEWS07/140929854/sue-gin-pioneering-chicago-businesswoman-has-died.

Foie Gras

In April 2006, the Chicago City Council voted 48 to 1 to outlaw the sale of foie gras by restaurants and retail stores. Foie gras is the fatty livers of geese and ducks produced by force-feeding them with grain, a practice some consider inhumane. The reaction was swift and multifaceted. A group of chefs formed an organization called Chicago Chefs for Choice to overturn the ban, while the Illinois Restaurant Association sued the city, arguing that the council overstepped its authority. Several restaurants, including a pizzeria, began to serve foie gras at no charge. Others developed substitutes: Spiaggia, for example, created a vegetarian foie gras terrine, while Tru created a "faux gras" made of sautéed chicken livers and pork fat in a gelatin coating. The only restaurant owner to be penalized under the ordinance was Doug Sohn of Hot Doug's, who was fined $250 in March 2007. In May 2008, the city council voted 37 to 6 to overturn the ban.

....

Contributor: Colleen Sen

BIBLIOGRAPHY

"Chicago City Council Overturns Foie Gras Bah." *Fox News*, May 14, 2008.
DeSoucey, Michaela. "Gullet Politics: Foie Gras in the U.S." PhD dissertation, Northwestern University, 2010.
Ruethling, Gretchen. "Chicago Prohibits Foie Gras." *New York Times*, April 27, 2006.

Foley, Michael

Chef and restaurateur Foley was at the forefront of the new American cuisine in the late 1970s and early 1980s, and one of the first chefs to embrace farm-to-table menus before that term became as ubiquitous as ham-and-eggs. His Chicago restaurant, Printer's Row, in the South Loop neighborhood of the same name, became a fine-dining destination in a marginal neighborhood of pioneer loft dwellers. And Foley was a pioneer, too, with his French-influenced, but wholly American, cuisine that emphasized local midwestern ingredients, including plenty of game (venison, grouse), local fish (pike, walleye), cheeses, and vegetables.

Foley grew up in the restaurant business (his grandparents started Ray Foley's in Chicago), but went to Georgetown University to study history and government. While in Washington, D.C., he worked at an Indian restaurant and then traveled to France to work in several restaurants. Upon return, he earned a master's degree in restaurant and hotel administration at Cornell University. Returning to Chicago, he worked in various restaurants until he opened Printers Row with his father, Robert Foley, in 1981.

Foley's cooking earned him honors as one of 1985's top American chefs from *Food & Wine*, a 1987 award as one of the best American chefs from Cook's Magazine, and the White House Golden Plate Award, presented by President Ronald Reagan. He opened two more restaurants, First Street and Foley's on Ohio, and brought back

Le Perroquet on Walton Street, but he did not have the same success with them as with Printers Row.

Foley also worked to revitalize the Printers Row area and was involved with the city's efforts to expand farmers' markets throughout Chicago neighborhoods. Later he helped create the sustainable-foods farmers market, Green City. After 23 years, he closed Printers Row and turned to consulting and developing menus and products for restaurants and food companies.

Contributor: Carol Mighton Haddix

See also: Printers Row Restaurant; Restaurants and Fine Dining

BIBLIOGRAPHY

Fonda, Daren. "Printers Row, Chicago, Ill." *Cigar Aficionado.* November-December 1998.

Mandel, Abby. "Michael Foley's Midwest Quest." *The Midwestern Table.* November-December 1996.

Food Deserts

The term was first used by a British health researcher in 1996, but it didn't come into common American parlance until a decade later when Chicago researcher Mari Gallagher published a report about food deserts in Chicago and their possible connection to negative public health outcomes. She noted that almost all food deserts in Chicago were majority African American neighborhoods. Diet-related health outcomes there were very poor, but Gallagher was quick to note that lack of accessibility to food was only one factor that contributed to the poor health.

Broadly defined, a food desert is a geographic area with little or poor access to fresh, healthful food. But the city of Chicago, under Mayor Rahm Emanuel in 2011, created a more precise definition. Under the city's definition, any resident who lived more than a mile from a large retail food establishment (more than 10,000 square feet) technically lived in a food desert.

In that same year, Emanuel's administration pledged to reduce the number of those in a food desert. Through a number of tax incentive and other programs that brought grocery stores to underserved neighborhoods, the city claimed to have reduced the number of citizens living in food deserts from 100,159 to 79,343—within two years of the mayor's pledge.

Contributor: Monica Eng

BIBLIOGRAPHY

Moser, Whet. "Challenges to the Concept and Effects of the Food Desert." *Chicago Magazine*, April 18, 2012.

Wehent, Jennifer. "The Food Desert." *Chicago Magazine*, August 11, 2009.

Food in Literature

Chicago has been the subject matter of a number of America's most influential authors, many of whom lived in the city. And food often has appeared in their literary works, reflecting Chicago's earthy character and its central role in supplying America's food.

One early example came from Chicago journalist Peter Finley Dunne and his fictional Mr. Dooley, who skewered corrupt politicians, lampooned imperialistic presidents, and chronicled the lives of the working poor in more than 700 syndicated newspaper columns appearing from the 1890s onward. The Bridgeport saloon-keeper, sage, and survivor of Ireland's Great Famine wrote that while he doesn't know

A CHICAGO VIEW

Carl Sandburg's 1913 *Chicago Poems* sticks up for the little guy, as in his poem "Child of the Romans."

The dago shovelman sits by the railroad track
Eating a noon meal of bread and bologna.
A train whirls by, and men and women at tables
Alive with red roses and yellow jonquils,
Eat steaks running with brown gravy,
Strawberries and cream, eclairs and coffee.
The dago shovelman finishes the dry bread and
 bologna,
Washes it down with a dipper from the water-boy,
And goes back to the second half of a ten-hour day's
 work
Keeping the road-bed so the roses and the jonquils
Shake hardly at all in the cut glass vases
Standing slender on the tables in the dining cars.

Carl Sandburg's 1914 "Chicago" poem takes inventory of the city's stockyards, rich farmland, and enviable transport that make it "Hog Butcher for the World . . . Stacker of Wheat . . . the Nation's Freight Handler . . . City of the Big Shoulders"—all amid the "wanton hunger" of its inhabitants. Sandburg's 1922 *Rootabaga Stories* for children are peppered with references to the Village of Liver-and-Onions, Village of Cream Puffs, Corn Fairies, and Potato Face Blind Men.

In Ring Lardner's 1916 book, *You Know Me Al*, newlywed Chicago White Sox pitcher Jack Keefe frets about meal expenses at a Cottage Grove Avenue restaurant, ponders his wife's fondness for dessert, and adjusts to life in the major leagues.

Edna Ferber's 1924 Pulitzer Prize–winning novel, *So Big*, has the penniless and newly orphaned Selina Peake DeJong leaving Chicago for High Prairie, a stand-in for South Holland, Illinois. Selina sees beauty in a cabbage patch; adjusts to greasy pork and potato dinners, a contrast with the Palmer House's elegant dishes of chicken and quail; and learns to farm. Taunted for doing men's work as she travels the Halstead Road with produce bound for Randolph Street's Haymarket, Serena soon commands a premium price for DeJong asparagus and hothouse tomatoes from the South Water Street commission merchants.

Ben Hecht and Charles MacArthur's 1928 play, "The Front Page," depicts Chicago as a "town festering with corruption," where "everyone aspires only to scrabble to the top of the dung heap," including hacks in a Chicago newsroom. When journalist Bensinger reports that a condemned prisoner's last supper consists of mock turtle soup, chicken pot pie, hashed brown potatoes, combination salad, and pie a la mode, noting that the meal was supplied by restaurant proprietor Charlie Apfel, a colleague remarks that somebody is assured of a new hat (meaning that his hat is likely to be stolen).

James T. Farrell's *Studs Lonigan* trilogy (1932) finds Studs and his friends stealing ice cream and candy from Schreiber's ice-cream parlor, located between Prairie and Indiana on 58th Street, after the owner is carted away to jail. They are not permitted to eat supper for a week afterward. Farrell's O'Neil-O'Flaherty family pentalogy set from 1909–29, beginning with *A World I Never Made*, has a good deal of home cooking, mainly plain roasted or baked meats and potatoes, and the characters often eat street food, especially hot dogs.

Richard Wright remarked that "men can starve from a lack of self-realization as much as they can from a lack of bread." In his 1940 novel, *Native Son*, Bigger Thomas is consumed with a bodily hunger and rage against a segregated society that cannot nurture or feed him physically,

many who would steal a ham and shoot a policeman, he knows plenty who would steal the whole West Side of Chicago and fix the jury. When asked what should be done with the fruits of America's victory in the Spanish-American war, he replied, "if 'twas up to me, I'd eat what was r-ripe, an' give what wasn't r-ripe to me inimy."

In Theodore Dreiser's 1900 novel, *Sister Carrie*, the teenaged Carrie Meeber leaves Wisconsin to seek her fortune in Chicago, hooking up along the way with Charles Drouet, to whom she is nothing but a "delicious conquest." Soon Carrie is ensconced in his furnished rooms on the West Side, near Union Park; memories of her flour-covered father, a miller from "the underworld of toil," fuel her hunger for a different life. The novel has a number of restaurant scenes, notably Rector's and Fitzgerald and Moy's fabulous bar.

In Upton Sinclair's 1906 exposé of the meatpacking industry, *The Jungle*, unsavory meat-canning factories serve up a piquant recipe to an unsuspecting public: one part rotten meat, one part bread saturated with rat poison, and one part rats. The novel influenced the passage of the 1906 Meat Inspection Act and the Pure Food and Drug Act, the latter a forerunner of the Food and Drug Administration. Both acts were signed into law by President Theodore Roosevelt, who, according to Peter Finley Dunne's Mr. Dooley, flung his sausages out the window after reading *The Jungle*.

emotionally, or spiritually. In Wright's autobiographical novel, *Black Boy (American Hunger)*, he writes of a childhood hunger for food, love, and social justice, and says that because "my environment had failed to support or nourish me, I had clutched at books."

"I am an American, Chicago born," says Augie March in Saul Bellow's 1949 *The Adventures of Augie March*. Augie's depression-era journey of self-identity and soul formation takes place in an idolatrous Chicago that is an "Ezekiel cauldron of wrath stoked with bones." It involves a surrogate mother who feeds him a huge meal of macaroni, brain and lung stew, calves' foot jelly with bits of calves' hair and sliced egg, and pickled fish and tripe, and a father-figure who warns him not to be a sap and to stay out of prison: "what the state orders bread and beans long in advance for." In Bellow's 1973 Pulitzer Prize–winning novel, *Humboldt's Gift*, writer Charlie Citrine notes that his biographies of the dead were his bread and butter and delves into Rudolf Steiner's theosophy, where biodynamic vegetables are grown for both spiritual and physical nourishment and transcend any "dog-food level of things." Charlie has some notable meetings in Chicago restaurants.

Nelson Algren observes that the "city's arts are built upon the uneasy consciences that milked the city of millions on the grain exchange . . . and sausage stuffing . . . with never a harvest in sight hereabouts for humanity's spirit" in his 1951 essay, "Chicago: City on the Make."

Investment in a liquor store turns into a sham deal in Lorraine Hansberry's 1958 play, "A Raisin in the Sun." The character Beneatha Younger is renamed Alaiyo, a Yoruba name meaning "One for Whom Bread—Food—Is Not Enough." And in "cool, quiet-looking restaurants," white boys put together million-dollar deals. Both underline Hansberry's themes of hunger, race, and redemption.

In Gwendolyn Brooks's 1960 poem, "The Lovers of the Poor," ladies from Glencoe and Lake Forest, members of the North Shore Ladies' Betterment League, travel to the Chicago slums to give money to the poor. They are disturbed to encounter "cabbage, and dead beans, dead porridges of assorted dusty grains . . . and, they're told, something called chitterlings."

The Greek American immigrant community depicted in the 1963 book *The Odyssey of Kostas Volakis*, by Harry Mark Petrakis, suffers through 18-hour days, working in rat-infested restaurants in pursuit of the American dream. They make food "fit for the palates of kings and gods and serve it to beggars and boors" and admit that while their food hasn't poisoned or killed anyone, it hasn't made anyone healthier. They open the Parthenon, a new restaurant in Greektown, fortuitously located near a funeral parlor, at the ready to feed the friends and family of the deceased.

Throughout a series of books, Sarah Paretsky's private detective V. I. Warshawski drinks Armagnac, Johnny Walker Black Label, and Torgiano; fortifies her sleuthing forays with extra-cheesy pasta, meatball subs, steaks, cheese sandwiches, and a Skokie deli's jumbo corned beef; cooks spaghetti and frittatas at home; and cherishes her late mother's red Venetian wine glasses with the twisted stems.

In Sandra Cisneros's *The House on Mango Street*, neighborhood kids fling about food-related insults, telling each other they're the lumps in Cream of Wheat cereal or cold frijoles, while Rafaela, kept prisoner in the house by a jealous husband, lives for coconut and papaya juice, delivered weekly via a clothesline pulley.

Studs Terkel's 1986 *Chicago* tells of a 1923 William E. Dever mayoral campaign rally at the Ashland Auditorium, where Terkel gleefully chowed down on hot dogs, soda, and two popular confections that helped make Chicago the candy capital of the world: Crackerjack and Baby Ruth.

Stuart Dybek's 1990 *The Coast of Chicago: Stories* features a girlfriend "packing Popsicles, Fudgesicles, Creamsicles, and Dreamsicles into freezer cartons" in a one-room Halsted Street apartment over a Greek restaurant, and "nuts, cheeses, dried cod sold in the streets."

In Aleksandar Hemon's 2008 novel, *The Lazarus Project*, Sarajevo immigrant Vladimir Brik chronicles the early 1900s life of Lazarus Averbuch, a malnourished escapee from the Russian pogroms. Brik frequents Chicago coffeehouses, including the North Side's Kopi Cafe, "a venue reeking of patchouli and former-colony teas." Lazarus packs eggs at the South Water Street Commission House, assuaging his hunger with bitter lozenges from Ludwig's Supplies on Clark and Webster, too poor to buy the fresh-baked bread, potatoes, or sausages.

....

Contributor: Mary La Plante

BIBLIOGRAPHY

Ahearn, Edward J. *Urban Confrontations in Literature and Social Science, 1848–2001: European Contexts, American Evolutions.* Surry, U.K.: Ashgate Publishing, 2013.

Fanning, Charles. *The Irish Voice in America: 250 Years of Irish-American Fiction.* Lexington: The University Press of Kentucky, 1999.

Goldman, L. H. *Saul Bellow's Moral Vision: A Critical Study of the Jewish Experience.* New York: Irvington Publishers, 1983.

Food Pantries

The notion of those more fortunate helping out those in need is part of human nature, but in Chicago that notion solidified into organized action in 1857. In that year, the members of the Paris-based Society of St. Vincent DePaul started an outpost in Chicago to help Chicago's immigrants during the economic depression. Members, all men, provided material aid, sometimes in the form of grocery vouchers, to families in need. In the 1870s and 1880s, as economic recession and immigrant waves collided, formal soup kitchens and breadlines were established by a variety of faith-based organizations. During the Great Depression, mobster Al Capone ran a soup kitchen in Chicago in an effort to clean up his image. Unemployed men in suits would line up daily for free coffee, doughnuts, and soup. Yet these private efforts alone couldn't meet demand, so New Deal programs provided additional relief.

In the 1960s, a modest food stamp program was enacted by Congress, but hearings and studies by impartial organizations showed that only 18 percent of the poor received assistance and many of them not enough of it. In 1969, President Richard Nixon announced a White House Conference on Food, Nutrition and Health, organized by nutritionist Jean Mayer and, in 1974, the Senate Committee on Nutrition and Human Needs heard stories that in poor urban areas one-third of the dog and cat food sold was for human consumption. As a response to an ongoing food crisis, the nonprofit Greater Chicago Food Depository was formed in 1979. It works with farmers, food manufacturers, food retailers, and neighborhood volunteer groups to stock its 268,000-square-foot distribution center. One of its biggest annual donations comes after the National Restaurant Association's spring convention. Since 2001, the show has donated 1 million pounds of food, left over from exhibitors, to the depository. Through its relationships with some 650 food pantries, shelters, and similar hunger relief agencies in Chicago and Cook County, the depository in 2013 distributed 67 million pounds of non-perishable foods, fresh produce, dairy products, and meat that equated to 154,000 meals each day.

In 1983, the Northern Illinois Food Bank started in suburban DuPage County. The Geneva-based nonprofit works with 600 partner agencies. In 2013, it provided 35 million pounds of food to food-insecure neighbors.

Over the past century, soup kitchen and shelter meals have evolved from basic broth and bread fare. Volunteers prepare Friday night pasta buffets at homeless shelters, barbecued pork under tents in tornado-devastated towns, and roast turkeys for holiday feasts—complete with mashed potatoes, green beans, and fresh cranberries—in church basements and veterans' halls.

Contributor: Deborah Pankey

BIBLIOGRAPHY

Greater Chicago Food Depository. www.chicagosfoodbank.org/site/PageServer?pagename=lb_about.

Northern Illinois Food Bank. solvehungertoday.org/about-us/who-we-serve/.

Pyke, Marni. "Food Pantries Challenged by Growing Demand." *Daily Herald*, November 25, 2008.

Food Reform Legislation of 1906

The rapid expansion of American industry in the late nineteenth century created explosive growth in the American workforce. The Progressive Movement (1901–17) was initiated as a response to this unchecked growth and the resulting corporate and political abuses. Embraced by religious groups, members of the press and radical political groups, the Progressive Movement sought government oversight and reform in areas of social work, industrial workplaces, corporate monopolies, and the political arena. Reformers attacked the social ills and corporate abuses that negatively affected U.S. society.

The Chicago meat-processing industry became the subject of an intensive seven-week study by muckraking journalist Upton Sinclair. Sinclair was paid $500 by a socialist newspaper to enter into the workforce of a Chicago meatpacking facility to uncover the squalid working conditions of the American laborer. Sinclair succeeded. More important, Sinclair discovered the unsanitary conditions involved in the manufacturing of meat intended for consumption by the American public.

Upton Sinclair published the interviews he gathered from meatpacking workers and union organizers in his 1906 novel, *The Jungle*. This powerful book tells the story of Lithuanian immigrant Jurgis Rudkus, who brings his family to America for a better life, ultimately succumbing to the brutal life conditions forced upon him through employment in the Chicago meatpacking industry. Sinclair details the meat company's business practice of blending rancid meat shipped in from Europe with good meat in the processing of meat products. He describes in sickening detail the common occurrence of rats falling onto production lines, and rat feces covering piles of stored meat products later to be used in the production of sausage. There are allegations in his book that workers who fell into the giant vats of meat were ground up and packaged for human consumption.

The commercial success of *The Jungle* was immediate and reinforced the long campaign for reform by the Department of Agriculture's chief chemist, Harvey Washington Wiley. The American public outcry in response to the book incited President Theodore Roosevelt to dispatch Labor Commissioner Charles Neill and Assistant Secretary of the Treasury James Reynolds on surprise inspections of meat-processing facilities in Chicago. The 23-page Neill-Reynolds report produced for President Roosevelt by the two inspectors affirmed the allegations presented in Sinclair's novel and helped in the passage of two important pieces of federal legislation in 1906.

The first was the Pure Food and Drug Act effective on June 30, 1906, enforcing laws given to the existing

Bureau of Chemistry in the Department of Agriculture. The Bureau's name was changed to the Food, Drug, and Insecticide Administration in July 1927 and, in July 1930, the name was shortened to the present-day Food and Drug Administration. The Bureau/FDA's main purpose was to ban foreign and interstate traffic in adulterated or mislabeled food or drug products. The second piece of legislation was the Federal Meat Inspection Act, which created Federal guidelines for the sanitary slaughtering and processing of meat and meat products. Ironically, it was a Chicago packer famous for its sausages that received the first Federal Meat Inspection Certificate license: the Oscar Mayer Company.

Contributor: Philip V. Wojciak

See also: Meat and Poultry; Union Stock Yards

BIBLIOGRAPHY

"Meat Inspection Act." Federal Laws. http://federal.laws.com/meat-inspection-act.

Sinclair, Upton. *The Jungle*. New York: Doubleday, Page and Co., 1906.

Food Safety

As populations grew, especially in urban centers, the complex problem of food safety increased. Chicago's population from 1850 to 1860 surged from 30,000 to 109,000, and there were few systems of food distribution or food safety. Trust was essential between vendor and shopper. Because of the lack of refrigeration, Chicagoans had to shop on a daily basis. Eventually, public food markets gave way to the corner store where food could be dispersed more conveniently. New rail systems brought in perishables with longer and different growing seasons from further away.

That everyday commodity, milk, was a central cause of alarming deaths among children in Chicago in 1867 due to unsanitary practices. The first dairy inspections began that year because of those tragic deaths. Then dangerous chemicals were found in a range of food items, from sugar to nuts, cider to honey. Food reform became the watchword in the late 1800s.

The Woman's Canning and Preserving Company was founded in a response to the suspicion about food quality. The firm processed foods under a new low-temperature method, invented by Amanda T. Jones of Chicago.

Polluted water also brought about a state of emergency: In 1891, the typhoid death rate was 174 per 100,000 residents. Reversing the Chicago River became a priority for human safety and, ultimately, food safety as well. Water was necessary to cook food, as well as for drinking. Industrial

and human waste flowed directly into the Chicago River and Lake Michigan. In 1889, the State of Illinois enacted a law creating a Sanitary District of Chicago for safeguarding Chicago's water supply. A canal was cut to reverse the flow of branches of the Chicago River toward the Mississippi River and Gulf of Mexico, diverting sewage away from the Lake Michigan supply. Opened in 1900, the Chicago Sanitary Canal was an engineering marvel, but not for the towns downstream that received Chicago's bacteria-laden waste.

The Pure Food and Drug Act, passed by Congress in 1906, established the federal government's duty to regulate foods other than poultry and meat and to prohibit the interstate sale of food adulterated or misbranded with chemical preservatives. This was the first of more than 200 laws dealing with consumer protection and public health. Upton Sinclair's novel *The Jungle* catapulted the Chicago's meatpacking industry into the limelight. Lawmakers passed the Meat Inspection Act of 1906, setting sanitary standards for butchering and leading to daily U.S. Department of Agriculture inspections in slaughterhouses.

Today, the large global food system brings food products to Chicago that may or may not have been held to the same sanitary conditions for production as expected in the United States. U.S. consumers demanded country-of-origin labels on food in 2002 and 2008. Sellers must disclose where products are grown or raised. These rules were challenged in the World Trade Organization, and the United States lost every challenge and appeal. Rather than face massive retaliatory tariff increases by Mexico and Canada, the Country of Origin Labeling law (COOL) was repealed when Congress passed, and Obama signed, the Omnibus Appropriations bill in December 2015. Nonetheless, the federal and state governments have a number of food safety agencies that have units in and around Chicago. These range from the Environmental Protection Agency to the Illinois Department of Agriculture Bureau of Meat and Poultry Inspection.

Contributor: Jenny Lewis

See also: Ice Houses; Meat and Poultry; Refrigeration; Sanitation

BIBLIOGRAPHY

Drexler, Madeline. *Food Safety: A Historical Look*. Schuster Institute for Investigative Journalism, Brandeis University. September 17, 2011. http://www.brandeis.edu/investigate/food.

"Regulatory Information." *Legislation*. U.S. Department of Health and Humans Services, 2012. August 29, 2014. http://www.fda.gov/RegulatoryInformation/Legislation/default.htm.

Food Styling and Photography

Chicago long has been a major center for food photography. Located at the edge of the wheat belt, surrounded by good midwestern farmland, at the center of an extensive transportation network reaching coast-to-coast, and home to the Union Stock Yards, Chicago quickly became a hub to developing corporate food giants and their advertisers. Companies such as Swift & Company, Quaker Oats, Oscar Mayer, Kraft Foods, Armour, Sara Lee, William Wrigley Jr., and Minnesota Valley Canning had their corporate headquarters in Chicago by the early 1900s.

Lord & Thomas, founded by Albert Lasker in 1898, was one of the first prominent advertisers in Chicago. Lasker later sold Lord & Thomas to three of his employees, creating the agency Foote, Cone and Belding, which remains a force today. Leo Burnett added to the concentration of food advertising talent when he arrived in Chicago in 1930. By the early twentieth century, Chicago was considered to be "the heart and soul of American advertising."

Chicago emerged as a center for large-scale print advertising and food packaging photography. The presence of R. R. Donnelley and Sons Company, founded in 1864 and soon to become among the largest printers in the world, might have been a factor in the development of Chicago as a print advertising mecca, as studios, companies, and agencies were drawn to easy local printing.

The earliest food photography took place within ad agency test kitchens, where staff created recipes and new products for the clients and where the photography happened. By the 1930s, most Chicago ad agencies had their own test kitchens, all "manned" by women who did the product and recipe development, as well as copywriting. In 1918, Arthur Brisbane, founder of the *Chicago Herald*, said, "Use a picture. It's worth 1,000 words." Ad men and women took that to heart and began including photography in nearly every food ad. At the time, photography was viewed as somehow trustworthy: an objective truth about the product. The public came to know better when investigations by the Federal Trade Commission revealed doctored food photographs in 1968.

In the 1950s, as food corporations such as Kraft and Sara Lee began to grow and consolidate, they built their own test kitchens and photo studios. When aerial photographer Fitz Lee returned home from World War II, he started working in the mailroom at Kraft. Soon after, he was using his wartime photography skills to shoot new products and recipes in the test kitchen there. By the mid-1960s, Lee had a team of six photographers at the Peshtigo Court headquarters in Chicago.

By the late '60s and '70s, test cooks and food stylists, nearly all women, were professionally trained in nutrition, home economics, or food science. They were responsible for creating and testing new products to present to executives and would then work with the agency and the photographer over several days to create a print ad.

The 1970s and '80s were the heydays of Chicago food photography. Independent photographers known for specific skills were sought after. Beverage splashes, mood lighting, and slick dessert photography were in. Denis Dubiel exemplified the independent food photographer of Chicago in the 1970s. He opened his own studio in 1972, drawing big budget ad agencies from around the country. Through his relationship with American Photographic Artists (APA), he drew together the Chicago food photography scene into a close-knit network, intent on drawing big-name clients to Chicago. Clients had big budgets; photo shoots were a glamorous and exciting culmination of months of work. The APA cosponsored lavish parties for the Chicago food photographers and stylists at locations such as the Field Museum, where horse-drawn carriages brought guests to the door.

The development of digital photography produced a seismic shift, dramatically changing the process for all aspects of the business. Photo studios no longer had to run their own photo labs, or wait for hours for the film to come back from the lab to see if they got the shot they needed. Stylists no longer needed to specially treat food to last for hours under hot lights. They could work with food in its natural state, positively altering the aesthetic of food and what is considered to be appetizing.

A new democratization of food photography arrived with social media. People armed with a smartphone now believe that they can be food photographers. They are wrong, and respect for the skills and professionalism of the commercial food photographers and stylists in Chicago has remained.

Contributor: Mary Valentin

See also: Advertising; Media

BIBLIOGRAPHY

5 Giants of Advertising. Paris, France: Assouline, 2001.

Schultz, Quentin. "Advertising." *Encyclopedia of Chicago*. http://www.encyclopedia.chicagohistory.org/pages/24.html.

Food Technology

Food technology or food science is both an academic discipline and a profession in which the sciences of chemistry, microbiology, nutrition, engineering, and psychology are applied to the creation of safe, nutritious, and economical foods and food processes. As an academic discipline, it is taught in about fifty departments in the United States and scores of other countries around the world. Academic departments have curricula approved by the Institute of Food Technologists (IFT), based in Chicago.

The IFT was formed in 1939 as a nonprofit scientific society committed to advancing the science of food. There were about 18,000 members from 100 countries in 2014. The Institute's publications include *Food Technology*, sent monthly to all members; the *Journal of Food Science*, available by subscription; the *Journal of Food Science Education*; and *Comprehensive Reviews in Food Science and Food Safety*. In addition, IFT publishes books in partnership with Wiley-Blackwell.

IFT holds an Annual Meeting and Food Expo, frequently in Chicago at McCormick Place, and in select other cities capable of accommodating the very large Expo. The Expo is one of the largest displays of food ingredients, services, and process equipment in the world.

Chicago was a logical site for the formation of the Institute because of the city's historic importance to the food industry. In addition to the Union Stock Yards, where as many as 40,000 people were once employed and all the major meat companies had plants (Swift, Armour, Cudahy, and others), Chicago was a center of confectionery manufacture (Brach, Tootsie Roll, Wrigley, Fannie May, Ferrara Pan Candy, Mars, and others) and had major plants for Nabisco, General Foods, Campbell Soup, Sara Lee, and Continental Baking, among others. The local section of IFT is the first one formed and still the largest in the United States. In addition to hosting the annual meeting and Expo, the local section presents a suppliers' night in November that is second only to the Expo as a showcase for ingredients.

Academic departments of food science are mostly found in the College of Agriculture at land grant universities. Every state has a land grant university, so named because they were originally endowed with rights to federal land retained when the transcontinental railroads were granted land as an inducement to build their systems. Every other section along the right of way was retained by the government while the alternate sections were sold by the railroad to fund their construction.

There are a few departments in private universities, of which a notable case is the Illinois Institute of Technology (IIT), formerly the Armour Institute of Technology. IIT was formed in 1940 by the merger of the Armour Institute and Lewis Institute. For many years, IIT has offered a graduate program, usually taught in the evening, of food engineering, mostly taught by industrial practitioners.

Since 2011, IIT has supported the Institute for Food Safety and Health (IFSH), which built upon and expanded the 20-year-old National Center for Food Safety and Technology (NCFST). Both organizations are (or were) collaborative research centers involving the U.S. Food and Drug administration (FDA), IIT, and industry members. The physical facilities are the former research center for Corn Products Company (CPC) in Argo-Summit, Illinois.

The center was donated to IIT as CPC was reorganizing. CPC is now part of Ingredion, the result of a merger between CPC and National Starch.

Food science as an academic major can be challenging because of its heavy emphasis on several of the life sciences, including microbiology, nutrition, and chemistry. Compared with engineering, it uses less mathematics, though each academic department is expected to require at least one course in food engineering and food processing. Degrees offered include bachelors, masters, and doctorates. Often, there are masters options that do not require a research thesis but rather a significant project that may be more convenient for students who hold full-time jobs.

In the Chicago area, the University of Illinois–Urbana Champaign offers such a distant learning option tailored to the significant population of practicing food scientists working for Kraft, Tate & Lyle, Hillshire (previously Sara Lee), and other local food companies.

Other departments of food science in the general area include the University of Wisconsin at Madison, Purdue University in West Lafayette, Indiana, and Dominican University in River Forest, Illinois. Dominican is an example of a previously existing department of nutrition and dietetics expanding into food science. Around the country, other institutions have attempted the same path of growth. A frequent challenge is the absence of a pilot plant, which is necessary to teach the elements of food processing and engineering as is required for a complete degree program in food science or technology.

Food science graduates are in great demand and earn good salaries, not far behind engineering graduates. The majority of practicing food scientists work in food product development. Other responsibilities include regulatory affairs, quality assurance, sensory evaluation, and food manufacturing.

Product development encompasses most of the profession's skills. Typically, the marketing function identifies a consumer need—an extension of an existing product line, a totally new concept, or a match to a competitive product. There are always cost constraints and, often, what seem unreasonable time demands. Product development usually proceeds by teams that include, besides food scientists, process engineers, culinary experts, and marketing experts. In addition to time and cost constraints, a new product must be safe, must be capable of being produced in the existing facilities (if possible), and must also satisfy nutritional and label requirements.

Food scientists have an extensive tool box at their disposal, including natural and artificial flavors, functional ingredients, and numerous processing techniques. Through education and experience, they apply these to the formulation and preservation of products that are then evaluated by various sensory techniques, ranging from informal in-house panels to full-blown consumer market trials. Despite some controversy, thanks to the advances of food technology, the United States enjoys the least expensive and arguably safest food supply in the world.

Contributor: J. Peter Clark
See also: Flavorings

BIBLIOGRAPHY
www.IFT.org.
www.iit.edu.

Food Trucks and Carts

Food carts have been a part of the Chicago food scene for all of the nineteenth and most of the twentieth century, although not nearly to the extent they have been in other cities. And through the years, they have met with unpredictable law enforcement and regulations.

After the Great Fire of 1871, mobile food became a necessity. On State Street and other major thoroughfares, horse carts were pressed into service serving simple lunches, sandwiches, and coffee. One of the most famous was the Little Grand Pacific, named after a downtown hotel that had burned down. However, by the mid-1880s most of what a newspaper called "peripatetic lunch houses" had closed down, largely because of the availability of free lunches served by many taverns and because of the rise of lunchrooms and lunch counters.

The aftermath of the Great Fire also saw the appearance of walking street vendors. Many sold fruit that they bought at the city's Water Street market. Toward the end of the century, Greek and Italian immigrants became the fruit and candy street vendors. They later moved into fixed stores and wholesaling. Other street vendors cooked simple dishes over gasoline stoves, such as popcorn, waffles, red hots, and tamales. The first lunch wagon cooking food to order appeared around 1890 and soon had a fleet of imitators. Regulation was light, and the quality of meals was considered superior to that of restaurants. The 1893 World's Fair created a new market for street food for the swarms of visitors. By 1895, there were hundreds of roving food vendors and some 100 lunch wagons. This led to a backlash from restaurants, who complained of unfair competition and, by the late 1890s, city ordinances restricted their operation.

In response to discrimination and what they said were unfair fines and licensing requirements, Chicago street vendors moved to unionize in 1908, forming the Peddlers' Union of Chicago. The Greek and Jewish vendors of the early part of the century gradually gave way to largely Mexican popsicle and corn vendors by the 1980s.

Apple seller Mary, photographed in 1890, was typical of street vendors before and after the Great Fire. Courtesy of the Chicago History Museum, DN-0004666; Chicago Daily News, Inc.

Complaints from brick-and-mortar business owners caused the city council to pass legislation excluding carts from all but about 15 wards (most with a largely Latino population). Those who strayed outside the boundaries (and sometimes those who remained inside but were reported by other businesses) could face fines of $500. By the mid-1990s, the Asociación de Vendedores Ambulantes (AVA), also known as the Chicago Street Vendor Association, had been established in the city to organize and create a pathway to licensing for the vendors.

In 1997, according to the *Chicago Tribune*, "Ald. Margaret Laurino (39th) proposed legislation that would add new penalties for violations and provide for confiscation of carts. Even though the legislation was never passed, police began enforcing it, seizing four carts, before a judge ruled that, even in Chicago, enforcing a law before it has passed puts the cart before the horse."

Plans to regulate and create uniform sanitation standards for the carts (which now sell fresh cut fruit, corn, chips, shaved ice, tamales, porridge, and popsicles) have been proposed over the years, but none have ever met with the approval of the Chicago Health Department.

A 2010 effort to amend the municipal code to allow cooking food trucks to operate in Chicago initially included food carts in its language, but that aspect fell away by the time it was presented to the City Council. Even so, the proposed amendment stayed stuck in committee for nearly two years before two powerful alderman came up with a new version.

In the meantime, dozens of food trucks popped up all over the city and operated under already passed provisions that allowed for the sale of prepackaged foods cooked in a licensed kitchen. This was the kind of food already served from construction-site lunch trucks and by West African vendors who often catered to taxi drivers. The food was cooked and held at warm temperatures and then served from plastic containers into foam boxes.

By July 2012, a revision of the proposed amendment was crafted by restaurateur and alderman Tom Tunney, along with Proco "Joe" Moreno. This version seemed to favor brick-and-mortar restaurants, with a provision that would not allow trucks to operate within 200 feet of any retail food establishment, as well as the requirement that each truck keep a GPS on board that would allow the city to monitor where it parked. Violation of these provisions could result in a $1,000 fine. This angered truck owners, who fought in vain to get the provisions revised. One concession to the truck operators was that the city would establish so-called food truck stands in areas around the city. Operators could park for two hours at a time, even if they were within 200 feet of a retail food-service establishment. This has worked out fairly well for many truck operators. Although the new ordinance finally did allow onboard cooking, it took more than five months before the first truck got a license to do so. Regulations in Chicago remain some of the strictest in the nation, and operators blame them for the lack of growth in the market, especially among those who cook on board. In September 2015, the City Council passed a measure authorizing pushcarts in the city. Chicago's 2,000 vendors of hot dogs, tacos, tortas, and other items were licensed as of November 2015.

Contributor: Monica Eng
See also: Hot Dogs; Mexicans; Sandwiches

BIBLIOGRAPHY

Phan, Kim, Phillip Shen, and Terri Phillips. *Food Truck Road Trip*. Salem: Page Street Publishing, 2014.
Shouse, Heather. *Food Trucks*. Berkeley: Ten Speed Press, 2011.

Foraging

An ancient practice, foraging is the harvesting of local wild plants and fungi for medicinal or culinary purposes.

Foraging became fashionable in the culinary world in the early twenty-first century after chef Rene Redzepi opened his restaurant Noma in Copenhagen, Denmark, in 2003. Redzepi uses local and seasonal ingredients foraged from the seashore and forest to create a "new Nordic cuisine." From 2010–14, Noma was ranked Best Restaurant in the World by *Restaurant* magazine.

In Chicago, foragers search alleyways, abandoned properties, and rail lines for plants such as dandelions (traditionally picked by Koreans and other ethnic groups), purslane, wild ferns, garlic mustard, cattail shoots, pine cone seeds, wild chives, wood sorrel, berries, nettles, and many mushroom varieties. Since 2009, Skokie forager David Odd, owner of Odd Produce, has supplied more than 500 foraged ingredients to about 200 Chicago restaurants, including Alinea, Brindille, Frontera Grill, Blackbird, and Lulu Café.

The epitome of restaurants using foraged ingredients is Elizabeth restaurant, opened in 2012 at 4835 N. Western Ave. by former underground chef Iliana Regan, who calls her food "new gatherer's cuisine." The décor is rustic, and the menu, which changes seasonally, was originally divided into The Farm, Ponds, Lakes and Seas, and The Woodlands sections, each with its own sequence of dishes. Foraged ingredients may include lamb's quarters, made into a foamy sponge, with gel from wild carrot flowers. The complex dishes incorporate many "molecular gastronomy" techniques; for example, white chocolate and hibiscus spheres filled with tomato water, or a buttermilk breadstick topped with bits of candied lime, trout roe, and lime basil. Since 2013, Elizabeth has received a Michelin star. *Food and Wine* magazine named Iliana Regan The Best New Chef of 2016.

Another type of forager deals with farmers, not forests. The City of Chicago and the Green City Market partnered to create the position of farm forager for city farmers markets in the early 2000s. A farm forager searches out quality, small-scale farmers and food producers in the Midwest and convinces them to sell their foods at the farmers markets. The forager also checks farm operations to make sure they follow guidelines set up by farmers markets. They also can link farmers with local chefs or retail food markets, such as Whole Foods. One such forager, Dave Rand, worked with Green City Market and then helped start a business called Local Foods, a wholesale and retail firm that "sources" meats and produce from within a 350-mile range of Chicago.

Contributor: Colleen Sen
See also: Farmers Markets

BIBLIOGRAPHY

Ruby, Jeff. "Review: Elizabeth Restaurant." *Chicago Magazine*, January 14, 2015.

Sacks, Katherine. "Urban Foraging Tips: How to Find Your Dinner in Chicago's Wild." *Chicago Magazine*, August 2011.

Vettel, Phil. "A Second Look at Elizabeth." *Chicago Tribune*, August 8, 2013.

Frango

Frango mints, an iconic Chicago candy that was popularized by the Marshall Field & Company department store, actually had its origins at Frederick & Nelson department store in Seattle, Washington, in 1918. The name originally was "Franco" (for Frederick and Nelson Co.) and referred to a frozen maple- or orange-flavored dessert sold in the store's elegant Tea Room. The name was later extended to other products. In 1927, Ray Alden, who ran Frederick & Nelson's in-store candy kitchen, developed a Franco mint meltaway chocolate candy. Alden's coveted recipe used chocolate made from South American and African cocoa beans, along with triple-distilled oil of Oregon peppermint and local butter. In 1929, Marshall Field's took control of Frederick & Nelson and brought the company's candy makers to Chicago to introduce Franco mints. When Generalissimo Francisco Franco came to power in Spain in the 1930s, the company changed the name to Frango.

For the next 70 years, Marshall Field's candy kitchen produced its own hand-dipped version of the Frango recipe and a line of Frango products evolved: truffles, coffee, cookies, and cheesecake. In 1999, Field's corporate owner, Dayton-Hudson Corp., closed the Field's candy kitchen, and turned over the Frango production to Gertrude Hawk Chocolates in Pennsylvania. The move angered Chicago Mayor Richard M. Daley, who pushed to have the beloved chocolates made by a local Chicago company. In 2005, Macy's of New York acquired Field's, and changed the store's name to Macy's. In 2009, Macy's acceded to the mayor's wishes, and hired longtime Chicago candy maker Cupid Candies to produce Frango mint chocolates for its Chicago-area stores.

....

Contributor: Scott Warner

See also: Candy; Marshall Field's

BIBLIOGRAPHY

Chandler, Susan. "Mints May Again Be Chicago-made." *Chicago Tribune*, September 21, 2005.

French

The French were the first colonial power in the Midwest, but by the time Jean-Baptiste Point du Sable, a Frenchman of African descent, settled in Chicago, Illinois was already a territory of the United States. Du Sable left no culinary footprint in Chicago, nor did French (actually French-Canadian) immigrants who settled in Chicago in the early twentieth century. French cooking in Chicago was never "ethnic" food.

Before the 1960s, French cuisine had a limited impact in Chicago. A few restaurants had French names and, even more occasionally, French chefs, but in the 1960s a number of authentically French restaurants opened, including Café French Market, Maxim's, L'Escargot, and Le Bordeaux. The timing corresponded roughly with the appearance of Julia Child's television program, *The French Chef*, in 1963, but also with the growing transformation of Chicago into a world-class cosmopolitan city. For example, Chicago's International Film Festival began in 1965.

The consecration of French cuisine in Chicago was marked by the arrival of Jean Banchet, who opened Le Français in Wheeling in 1973. Banchet, as a culinary superstar with an international reputation, brought French *haute cuisine* to Chicago. Some of Chicago's prominent restaurateurs—Roland Liccioni, Carlos Nieto, Mark Grosz, and Michael Lachowicz—originally trained at Le Français. Around this time, Jovan Trboyevic opened Le Perroquet in downtown Chicago, Pierre Pollin Le Titi de Paris in Arlington Heights, and Bernard Cretier Le Vichyssoise in Lakemoor. Other prominent chefs—for example Jean Joho of Everest—left France to work in restaurants in Chicago. Banchet was a role model for subsequent generations of superstar chefs in Chicago, such as Charlie Trotter and Grant Achatz, who, even if they did not cook explicitly French food, prepared their own varieties of haute cuisine profoundly influenced by French cooking.

Alongside such expensive French restaurants featuring haute cuisine, an increasing number of midpriced restaurants opened serving what is known in France as *cuisine bourgeoise*, somewhat less elaborate food but often of very high quality: pommes frites, moules, and coq au vin. These restaurants would be called bistros in France, and a spate of French restaurants included the word in their names—for example, Kiki's Bistro, Bistro Zinc, Bistro 110, Bistro Campagne, Bistronomic, and Bistro Margot, to name only a few. In 1972, La Crêperie opened on Clark Street, featuring an even more affordable, casual French cooking. Many such restaurants featured chefs from France, such as Didier Nolet, Dominique Tougne, or Martial Noguier. But an increasing number of American chefs, some trained in France and some in the United States, demonstrated their ability to cook authentic French food.

French restaurants, because they served food which was neither American, generically "continental," nor "ethnic," supplied a model for restaurants featuring fine dining from other national traditions, including Italian, Japanese, and Mexican. More recently, some of these restaurants have explicitly featured a "fusion" of French and other traditions, with names such as Mexique or Japonais.

In 2006, French (and French-inspired) cuisine was at the center of controversy when the city council voted to ban the sale of foie gras. The controversy pitted two emerging middle-class food ideologies against one another. The first centered on the ethics of food production and consumption, while the second was focused on culinary experimentation and variety. Opponents of foie gras contended that the forced gorging of ducks and geese, a necessary feature of its production, was intrinsically inhumane, but they also appealed to populist (and often francophobe) biases, implying that such expensive French delicacies appealed to a small and snobbish elite. In any case, the ban attracted mostly unfavorable national and international publicity and was repealed two years later.

Over the years, a number of French bakers and pastry chefs have either opened shops or taught classes in Chicago. Michel Tournier owned a French bakery in Winnetka in the 1980s. Pierre Zimmerman opened La Fournette at locations in Old Town and Lincoln Park. Increasingly, American bakers have opened stores such as Vanille, which prominently feature French specialties. Jacquy Pfieffer opened the French pastry school, while both French cooking and baking are taught in all the city's culinary schools. In addition, the Alliance Française, which holds classes in French language and culture, occasionally offers French cooking classes for children and adults.

Contributor: Robert Launay

See also: Baking and Bakeries; Banchet, Jean and Doris; Chefs; Foie Gras; Le Français; Restaurants and Fine Dining; Trotter, Charlie

BIBLIOGRAPHY

http://www.timeout.com/chicago/restaurants/best-french-food-best-french-restaurants-in-chicago.

https://www.zagat.com/l/chicago/top-french-restaurants-in-chicago.

Fritzel's Restaurant:

One of Chicago's glamour restaurants for more than 20 years, Fritzel's attracted the city's elite, a power-wielding mix of business execs, sports figures, politicians, and entertainers. Its downtown location made it an especially popular gathering spot for the after-theater and late-night crowd. This was a jacket-and-tie kind of place at a time when dress codes were important.

Partners Joe Jacobson and Mike Fritzel, the owners of Chicago's celebrated Chez Paree nightclub, opened Fritzel's restaurant at the corner of State and Lake in 1947.

Fritzel retired in 1953, but Jacobson, who was partial to long black cigars, continued to run the restaurant until 1968. Fritzel's closed in 1972.

Of the hundred items on Fritzel's menu, none was more popular than Shrimp de Jonghe, an uber-rich dish made with premium shrimp, garlic, and lots of butter. One of the first dishes to be specifically linked to Chicago, Shrimp de Jonghe is attributed to the DeJonghe brothers (Henri, Pierre, and Charles), Belgian immigrants who ran DeJonghe's Hotel and Restaurant at 12 E. Monroe from 1899–1923. Fritzel's didn't invent the dish, and it wasn't the only restaurant that served it, but even so, the two are inextricably linked.

Contributor: Barbara Revsine

See also: Shrimp de Jonghe

BIBLIOGRAPHY

Drury, John. "Fritzel's," Where Chicago Eats. Chicago: *Rand McNally Guide*, 1953, 21.

Frontera Grill

Celebrity chef and cookbook author Rick Bayless and his wife, Deann Groen Bayless, opened their flagship Mexican restaurant in the city's River North neighborhood in January 1987, upon returning from an extended trip to Mexico where they were researching their first cookbook.

Adorned with vibrant Mexican art, the bustling, tiled dining room is the backdrop to what is billed as "real" Mexican food. Frontera Grill's Chef de Cuisine is Richard James, and Jennifer Jones is its pastry chef. The menus are highly seasonal and oft-changing, drawing from local ingredients sourced from small, midwestern farms when possible. The menu takes Mexican cuisine to a high level, with steak moles, tacos, and ceviches. Handcrafted cocktails—some made with local, small-batch spirits, others with mescal—are also of note. Frontera Grill's wine list emphasizes biodynamic labels, and the purchase of bottles benefits a culinary education scholarship fund at Kendall College.

In 2007, Frontera Grill received an Outstanding Restaurant award from the James Beard Foundation. The restaurant received the *Michelin Guide*'s Bib Gourmand designation from 2011–16. Frontera is the casual, next-door sibling of Mexican fine-dining destination Topolobampo.

Contributor: Jennifer Olvera

BIBLIOGRAPHY

Chicago Gourmet. http://www.chicagogourmet.org/?page=224.

"Frontera Grill." *Chicago Magazine*. http://www.chicagomag.com/dining-drinking/November-2013/Frontera-Grill-Updated-Listing/.

G

Gand, Gale

One of Chicago's best-known pastry chefs, Gand also is an author and national television personality. In 1999, she partnered with Rich Melman of Lettuce Entertain You and her former husband and chef Rick Tramonto to open the acclaimed restaurant, Tru, 676 N. St. Clair St. In 2001, she was named Pastry Chef of the Year by the James Beard Foundation.

While attending college on her way to a fine arts degree, Gand worked in a restaurant and became interested in cooking. After graduation, she attended La Varenne cooking school in France and discovered a love for creating pastries. After a job cooking at Stapleford Park, a country house hotel in England, Gand and Tramonto worked at Trio in Evanston and then opened Brasserie T in Northfield. More recently, Gand became a partner in the new SpritzBurger restaurant in Lakeview.

Gand has written eight cookbooks, including three with Tramonto: *American Brasserie* (1997), *Butter Sugar Flour Eggs* (1999), and *Tru: A Cookbook from the Legendary Chicago Restaurant* (2004). Her other books include *Just a Bite* (2001), *Short and Sweet* (2004), *Chocolate and Vanilla* (2006), *Gale Gand's Brunch* (2009), and *Gale Gand's Lunch!* (2014).

In 2000, Gand starred in her own show, the Food Network's *Sweet Dreams*, the first television show devoted to desserts. It ran for eight years. She also competed on *Iron Chef America* and appeared on *Baking with Julia* and *Oprah*, among many others. As a celebrity judge, she appeared on *Food Network Challenge*, *Last Cake Standing*, *Top Chef*, and *Top Chef Just Desserts*. In 2014, Gand was inducted into the Chicago Chefs Hall of Fame. In her spare time, Gand also makes root beer. Gale's Root Beer is a vanilla-, cinnamon- and ginger-flavored soda that is sold nationally.

Contributor: Carol Mighton Haddix
See also: Restaurants and Fine Dining; Soft Drinks

BIBLIOGRAPHY
Hensel, Kelly. "Chef Gale Gand's Sweet Success." Institute of Food Technologists. http://www.ift.org/Food-Technology/CPOV/Gale-Gand.aspx.

Gangsters

Organized crime figures owned wining and dining establishments in Chicago, even before Prohibition. The notorious First Ward Alderman and vice lord Michael "Hinky Dink" Kenna opened a saloon, Hinky Dink's Place, in 1897. It was followed by a bigger saloon at 427 S. Clark St., nicknamed "The Workingman's Exchange," because it offered free lunches to poor people and potential voters of the district. The saloon had a 30-foot walnut bar and served 10,000 drinks a week. A bowl of beer cost a nickel.

Giacomo ("Big Jim") Colosimo (1878–1920) was a Hinky Dink protégé who owned about 200 brothels as well as gambling and racketeering operations. In 1909, he opened Colosimo's Restaurant, Café and Cabaret, 2126–2128 S. Wabash St. It featured a mahogany and glass bar, a huge dining room papered in green velvet wallpaper, solid gold chandeliers over the dance floor, and showgirls and an orchestra on a rising stage. Guests included Enrico Caruso, Clarence Darrow, and Al Capone. Colosimo was always at the restaurant, personally overseeing the music and menu. He opened a branch called Colosimo's Arrow Head Inn in suburban Burnham, a community of resorts and gambling dens. Customers could enjoy a fish ($1), frog leg ($1.25), or chicken ($1.50) dinner, all including appetizer a la Colosimo and spaghetti a la Colosimo. When Prohibition went into effect in 1920, Colosimo refused to join other mobsters in bootlegging and was shot to death in front of his restaurant. It continued under different owners until it closed in 1945.

Giuseppe (Joe) Aiello (1891–1930) (once considered the most dangerous criminal in the United States) and his brothers opened a grocery in the Little Sicily neighborhood on the Near North Side. Later, he started Aiello & Co. on W. Division St., a wholesale bakery specializing in wedding cakes and Italian bread. He also was part-owner of a candy store and, together with gangster Tony Lombardo, ran a cheese importing business. With the advent of Prohibition, grocery stores became valuable assets for mobsters because they could buy and store sugar and grapes.

Aiello and Capone battled for control of the bootlegging business and were sworn enemies: Aiello even offered money to the chef of Diamond Joe Esposito's Bella Napoli Café, Capone's favorite restaurant, to put prussic acid in Capone's soup. However, the cook squealed and the plot was averted. The N. Halsted St. café was a popular meeting place for political figures of the 19th ward, where Esposito was ward boss. Another famous mobster, Paul "The Waiter" Ricca, worked at Bella Napoli. Ricca hated this nickname and would bark at reporters, "I was a manager not a waiter, but the truth really doesn't matter to you people, does it?"

After the St. Valentine's Massacre of his North Side rivals on February 14, 1929, Capone and his gang adjourned to the Idle Hour Cafe, on W. Ogden Ave., in Lyons. The Idle Hour promised "steaks, chicken dinners and sandwiches of all kinds" but was a bootlegging delivery spot for Capone during Prohibition. The Idle Hour also used Prohibition code words such as "ice cream" (which denoted beer) and "soft drinks" (which stood for hard liquor.)

Another of Capone's North Side rivals was Charles Dean O'Banion, who worked as a waiter at McGovern's Brothers Tavern (later renamed the Liberty Inn), on N. Clark St., a favorite watering hold of his confidant, Bugs Moran. O'Banion sang Irish folk ballads on the restaurant floor while his gang members were going through coatroom belongings. O'Banion also had his bartender spike the drinks of his customers, which popularized the term "Slipping a Mickey Finn." As drunk customers stumbled out of the club, O'Banion and his gang would rob them. The gangster's legacy was introduced to a new generation in 1978, when the popular O'Banion's punk and dance club opened on the site; it closed in 1982.

Capone also frequented the 226 Club, on S. Wabash Ave., later known as the Wonder Bar and then the Exchequer Restaurant and Pub. Capone's personal chef, Joseph Di Buono, was the founder of Tufano's Vernon Park Tap.

Today, the most visible reminder in Chicago of the Prohibition era is the Green Mill Cocktail Lounge, located on N. Broadway. The jazz club opened in 1907 as Pop Morse's Roadhouse. By the time Capone was a regular in the club, it was known as The Green Mill Gardens. Jack "Machine Gun" McGurn, one of the architects of the St. Valentine's Day Massacre, was a part-owner. Capone's favorite booth was said to be west of the short end of the bar so he could see the club's doors. A trap door still exists behind the bar where Capone could exit and go through a series of tunnels that wound all the way to the Aragon Ballroom, a block away on W. Lawrence Ave.

Over the years, restaurants have attempted to capture the legacy of the gangster era. In 1999, Chicago restaurateur Jerry Kleiner opened Gioco ("The Game"). Kleiner retained the original brick and plaster walls of the 1890 building. The former speakeasy had a walk-in safe, which is still in the restaurant. He also opened Room 21, and later Via Ventuno (now closed) on S. Wabash Ave. Capone ran the city's largest brewery and speakeasy at the site, which was walking distance from his Chicago headquarters at the now-demolished Lexington Hotel, located on S. Michigan Ave. Tommy Gun's Garage is a re-creation of a speakeasy. It serves "gangland feasts," with dishes such as "Big Jim Colosimo" and "Don't Call Me Chicken," and a live performance that includes a raid by cops.

Contributors: Dave Hoekstra and Colleen Sen

See also: Prohibition; Speakeasies; Supper Clubs and Roadhouses

BIBLIOGRAPHY

Lindberg, Richard. *Chicago by Gaslight (A History of Chicago's Netherworld 1880–1920)*. Chicago: Chicago Review Press, 2005.

Sawyers, June. "The Vice Lord Who Fell in Love with a Choir Singer." *Chicago Tribune*, July 26, 1987.

Tuohy, John William. *Chicago's Mob Bosses, from Accardo to Zizzo*. Chicago: *CreateSpace*, 2011.

Garrett Popcorn (See: Cracker Jack; Popcorn)

Geja's Café

Consistently ranked as one of Chicago's most romantic restaurants, Geja's Cafe is a fondue spot that originally opened on Wells Street in 1965. In 1971, owner John Davis moved to a former grocery store on Armitage Avenue in the Old Town neighborhood, where it has remained ever since.

Dining here is a DIY experience, during which a cast-iron fondue pot is placed in the center of the tables. The dining room is set within a dark, moody, subterranean space. Typically, meals are enjoyed in courses and include a choice of cheese fondue; a main course offering that includes a mixture of vegetables, meat, and seafood with a series of dipping sauces; and chocolate fondue, which may be flamed with liqueur and is served with fruits, pound cake, and marshmallows for dipping. The restaurant features three private-label wines as well as an extensive, global wine list. It often hosts wine dinners, an annual wine tasting competition, and other events, as well as live flamenco guitar. It's a popular destination for engagements.

Contributor: Jennifer Olvera

BIBLIOGRAPHY

Borrelli, Christopher. "Lovers, Family, First Dates Dip into Geja's." *Chicago Tribune*, December 27, 2012.

Gene and Georgetti

Now in its eighth decade, Gene and Georgetti, 500 N. Franklin St., is Chicago's oldest steakhouse. It was founded in 1941 by partners Gene Michelotti and Alfredo Federighi, who was nicknamed "Georgetti" after a famous Italian cyclist. The Italian-style, family-owned restaurant serves only prime aged beef, all broiled to order. In addition to the steaks, the menu includes lamb, pork, and veal chops, along with pasta and entrees like Chicken Vesuvio, Greek-style chicken, and fried shrimp.

Built with wood salvaged from the Chicago Fire, the restaurant exudes a strong sense of place. Much of the waitstaff has worked at the restaurant for years, and while "regulars" often ask to be seated in a particular server's section, newcomers receive the same level of service. The owners are planning to open a branch in Rosemont.

Contributor: Barbara Revsine
See also: Steak and Chop Houses

BIBLIOGRAPHY

http://www.chicagoreader.com/chicago/gene-and-georgetti/
    Location?oid=1025349.

Germans

During the mid-to-late nineteenth century, German immigrants who came to Chicago arrived from the many countries in Europe where enclaves of German-speakers lived. Prior to 1871, when Germany was united, German-speakers sometimes passed through immigration listing themselves as "German," whether they had lived within the borders of what would become Germany-proper or not. Doctors, lawyers, entrepreneurs, artisans, teachers, merchants, and brewers were among the first sets of migrants; later settlers were primarily rural people. Most of them arrived with their Old World recipes and food traditions. In addition, the brewers brought their lager beer and malt liquor recipes along with their specialized brewing techniques, which they immediately put to work.

The Winzer and Meine families stand in front of their grocery store in the 1880s. Note the signs for English and American products as the family assimilated. Courtesy of the Chicago History Museum, ICHi-85013.

Although a few Germans may have passed through Chicago earlier than the 1840s, the bulk of them arrived in the city after 1848. They came largely in four waves: the first group, called "Forty-Eighters," many of whom were well-educated, found their way to Chicago between the 1840s through the 1850s, following social unrest in their homelands; the second wave occurred during the 1870s, in response to Bismarck's anti-Catholic and antisocialist laws; the third onslaught, during the next decade, consisted overwhelmingly of young men fleeing conscription, artisans, tradesmen, farmers seeking land outside the city, and the employment-seeking poor, who had been provided with free one-way tickets. A fourth influx of Germans followed the Second World War.

Numerically, the brewers hailed from Bavaria and Bohemia. The rural people and others mostly came from Central and Southwest Germany and a smattering of others from regions such as Lower Saxony, Westphalia, the Rhineland, Switzerland, Alsace-Lorraine, Luxembourg, Prussia, Austria-Hungary, Belgium, Russia, and even Poland. The 1890 census of the Chicago population showed that the 490,542 who called Chicago home were from the countries and regions mentioned earlier. It quickly became known as a "German city." By 1977, the numbers of self-identified Americans of German heritage in Chicago was estimated at about 600,000; by 1990, their numbers had reached about 700,000.

It has been said that Germans were initially slow to assimilate, reluctant to abandon their "home" language, and loathe to adopt new foods. At one point early on, sections of Chicago where the German-speakers settled might have been mistaken for the Old Country instead of a burgeoning city in the American Midwest. The German language, both High and Low, was spoken in homes, stores, restaurants, schools, theaters, churches, and synagogues. Newspapers and books were also printed in German. It was possible to survive in Chicago's German areas, collectively called *Kleindeutschland*, without learning or speaking a single word of English.

Well into the twentieth century, German-speaking home cooks, chefs, bakers, and their descendants continued to make foods reflecting their own or their families' points of origin. Among the foods that graced their tables and restaurant menus and filled their delicatessens were meats: Central German thüringer, würsts, salted ham, pigs' knuckles, Rhenish *wammerl* (pickled pork belly), *kassler rippchen* (smoked pork chops), *buletten* (meat patties), *königsburger klopse* (Prussian meatballs), meat loaf, Russian *bierocks* (meat-filled pastries, a take on Polish pierogis), *hackpeter* (steak tartar), sauerbraten, wienerschnitzel, Frisian corned beef, Mecklenburg and Pomeranian-style goose, duck and other game birds, and hasenpfeffer (rabbit). Dumplings of various kinds were common, including liver, fruit, and wheat dumplings, and Swabian spätzle. Side dishes were often potato salad, *kartoffel pfann kuchen* (potato pancake), Franconian *pickelsteiner*, bean salads, red cabbage, sauerkraut, and gherkins. Cheeses in German styles (including stinky Limburger introduced in the 1860s), fish, sorrel, green pea, and cream soups; wine and cream gravies; pretzels; pumpernickel, raisin, and black breads; rolls, *schnecken*; stollen; strudels; cookies of all sorts; doughnuts, pastries, and cakes were all on the German American menu. All were staples of Chicago's German restaurants.

In 1962, Chicago's version of Oktoberfest, a celebration begun in Munich in 1810, was apparently mentioned in the press for the first time. Unlike the 16-day celebration in Germany, it was a 1-day affair sponsored by Lufthansa German Airlines at the exclusive Germania Club on the Near North Side. Five brands of German beer, locally made Munich *Weisswürst*, German potato salad, and pretzels from Kuhn's Milwaukee Avenue delicatessen were served. Approximately 1,200 people attended. In 1977, Chicago also began a tradition of holding a weekend-long ethnic Folk Food Fair, precursor to the Taste of Chicago, where German sauerbraten and knockwürst were sold. Inspired by the centuries-old Christkindlesmarket in Nuremberg, Germany, in 1996 the City of Chicago held the first Christkindlesmarket Chicago in downtown Chicago. Vendors sell such typical German dishes as sausages (including currywurst), potato pancakes, strudel, and Gluhwein, a hot spiced wine traditionally sold at markets.

By the twentieth century, most German immigrants were well integrated into Chicago's mainstream. Their foods also blended into the culinary traditions of the city: hot dogs, hamburgers, bratwursts, meat loaf, three bean and potato salads, sauerkraut, rye breads, and cheesecakes. Also adopted from the Germans are what have come to be seen as quintessentially "American" habits: preferences for hearty breakfasts, afternoon snacks, and after-dinner sweets. Embraced was the German standard of meat, potatoes, and a vegetable for the largest meal of the day, whether it was eaten at noon or in the evening.

At one time in Chicago, there were more than 140 German restaurants, or enterprises serving German-style foods, and 60 or more breweries making lager and/or malt liquor beer. However, because of Prohibition, the Great Depression, two world wars, urban renewal, escalating prices, shifting demographics, and changing tastes, most of these restaurants went out of business. By the 1980s, there were a mere seven "top German restaurants" operating in the city; by the 1990s, fewer than a handful remained, including Berghoff Restaurant on West Adams, Laschet's Inn on Irving Park, Chicago Brauhaus in Lincoln Square, The Radler on North Milwaukee, Resi's Bierstube on Irving Park, and others. This decline also was reflected among German bakeries. The same factors coalesced to close the local breweries, but contributing to their demise was additional pressure from large breweries with national markets, state and local laws, taxes, and distribution issues.

Contributors: Ellen F. Steinberg and Jack H. Prost

See also: Beer, Breweries, and Brew Pubs; Beer Gardens; The Berghoff; Delicatessens; Sausages; Schlogl's

BIBLIOGRAPHY

Heinen, Joseph C., and Susan Barton Heinen. *Lost German Chicago*. Mount Pleasant, S.C.: Arcadia Publishing, 2009.
Hofmeister, Rudolf A. *The Germans of Chicago*. Champaign, Ill.: Stipes Publishing, 1976.
Knoblauch, Mark. "Eats: Deutsch Treat. Chicago's Top German Restaurants, from Chops to Schnapps." *Chicago Tribune*, March 14, 1980, C1.

Gin, Sue Ling

A real estate maven, restaurateur, CEO, and one of the most powerful business women in the Chicago area, Gin began her career in the 1980s. After taking odd jobs following college at DePaul University, including a short stint as a Playboy Bunny waitress, she eventually found a career in real estate, including owning several restaurants such as Cafe Bernard in Lincoln Park. She was a pioneer investor in loft properties in the now-hot Randolph Street Market area where restaurants are thriving.

But it was an encounter with a bad, half-frozen sweet roll on a business flight in 1982 that launched her journey to CEO of a multimillion-dollar firm, Flying Food Group, Inc. As she related to *Crain's Chicago Business*, she felt airline food could be better, so she wrote to the chairman of Midway Airlines to say so, and ended up with a contract to supply meals to the airline. Some 30 years later, Flying Food serves more than 70 international airlines, including British Airways, Air France-KLM, Qantas, and Royal Jordanian, as well as retail outlets such as Starbucks. Crain's reports her firm had $435 million in revenue in 2013.

Coming from an immigrant family (her parents owned a Chinese restaurant in Aurora), Gin was interested in immigrant issues and sat on the board of the Chicago Council of Global Affairs. She also served on the boards of many charities and businesses. She headed the board of the William G. McGowan Charitable Fund, which advances the legacy of her late husband, who was chairman of MCI Communications. She died in 2014 at age 73, after suffering a stroke.

Contributor: Carol Mighton Haddix

See also: Catering; Flying Food Group

BIBLIOGRAPHY

Strahler, Steven R. "Sue Gin, Pioneering Chicago Businesswoman, Has Died." *Crain's Chicago Business*, September 26, 2014.

Glessner, Frances and John

Sarah Frances Macbeth married John Jacob Glessner (1843–1936) in 1870. He was involved in the agricultural equipment business and later became vice president of International Harvester.

For decades, their primary home at 1800 S. Prairie Ave., designed by H. H. Richardson in 1887, was the site of hundreds of social engagements. Dinner at the Glessners' was so renowned, the story goes, that a policeman, stopping a couple in a speeding car, waved them on when he was informed that they were "going to Mrs. Glessner's for dinner and we're late."

The Glessners hosted dinner parties around the table built for 18. Or they could accommodate 100 by using the library and entry hall and pulling beds from bedrooms to make room for tables for guests. Mrs. Glessner regularly hosted a Monday morning Reading Class for discussion, and followed it with lunch, and usually musical entertainment, for 30 to 40 women. The couple's support of the Chicago Symphony Orchestra provided the impetus for many significant musical events, including dinner for the entire 96-piece orchestra and recitals by visiting artists.

In addition to her hostess responsibilities, Frances Glessner was active in many pursuits, not the least of which were beekeeping (producing over 1,000 pounds of honey each year to use as gifts and at the table), metal work (examples of her silverwork tableware are on display at the Glessner House Museum), and writing, with her husband, an extensive article on etiquette and entertaining, published in the *Saturday Evening Herald* in 1889.

Her most historically significant act was leaving behind all of her daily journals and menu books, describing each tea, luncheon, and dinner, including who was in attendance, what was served, and how the table or house was decorated, as well as a 100-volume cookbook collection. Those records are available today at the Glessner House Museum and the Chicago History Museum.

The couple had two children, George (1871–1929) and Frances (Franny, 1878–1962).

Frances Glessner died in Chicago October 19, 1932, at the age of 84.

Contributor: Judith Dunbar Hines

BIBLIOGRAPHY

Callahan, Carol. *Prairie Avenue Cookbook.* Carbondale: Southern Illinois University Press, 1993.

Glessner House Museum. http://www.glessnerhouse.org.

Sarah Frances Macbeth Glessner in her family mansion on Prairie Avenue. Courtesy of the Glessner House Museum.

Gonnella Baking Company

Perhaps the most impressive aspect of the Gonnella Baking Company, besides their bread and buns, is that after more than 125 years, it continues to be a family-owned-and-run business. Current President Nick Marcucci is one of more than 30 relatives of founder Alessandro Gonnella who are part of the organization.

Gonnella bought his first bakery on DeKoven Street in 1886, and gives fair claim to the title of oldest baker in Chicago. By the early 1900s, Gonnella's wife, Marianna Marcucci, and his young brothers-in-law joined him in Chicago from their native Italy. In 1915, the bakery moved to Erie and Damen and, for decades, Gonnella delivery trucks could be seen all over the city and suburbs delivering fresh breads and rolls.

But the business has prided itself on staying tuned in to the times. By the 1970s, the family realized that store-direct delivery limited the potential for significant company growth. In order for Gonnella to transition from a local to national presence, the company entered the frozen dough market, selling to the expanding system of in-store bakeries and food-service entities.

Fresh bread and rolls still are an important presence. Gonnella supplies the hot dog buns at Wrigley Field, and odds are good that the juice on Chicago's Italian beef sandwiches soaks into a Gonnella roll.

Contributor: Eleanor Hanson

See also: Baking and Bakeries; Italians

BIBLIOGRAPHY

Fuller, Janet Rausa. "Gonnella Bakery Marks 125 Years in Chicago." *Chicago Sun-Times*, March 7, 2011.

"The Gonnella Story." htttp://www.gonnella.com.

Grace

Less than a year after it opened in December 2012 at 652 West Randolph, Grace was awarded 2 Michelin stars for what the *Michelin Guide* called "its contemporary seasonal tasting menus that are as modern and stylish as the setting in the West Loop." The following year it won its 3rd star. Its many other accolades include a James Beard Award for Best Restaurant Design, *Chicago Magazine*'s Best New Restaurant, and *Chicago Tribune*'s Chef of the Year for chef/owner Curtis Duffy.

After a career that included working for Charlie Trotter and Grant Achatz, Duffy joined wine director Michael Muser and investor Mike Olszewski to launch Grace in an old frame shop, The elegant neutral-toned dining room has 64 white leather seats. Grace has two seasonal menus, vegetarian (flora) and nonvegetarian (fauna), each consisting of 9 to 13 courses. Each intricately plated dish is intended to be consumed in six bites or less.

Distinctive features include unusual serving dishes— for example, curved bowls imported from France that look like fat inner tubes or a charred whiskey barrel stave— and esoteric ingredients, such as African blue basil, Iranian pistachios, or Satsuma oranges. Dishes have included chestnut puree with truffle shavings, roasted almond milk, and red sorrel (flora) and veal cheeks with wine braised endive, black mint, and tempura anchovies (fauna).

The restaurant's name reflects Duffy's cooking style, elegant and delicate, and his spiritual connection with cooking. "It's all about grace," he writes when signing menus.

Contributor: Colleen Sen

See also: Duffy, Curtis; Restaurants and Fine Dining

BIBLIOGRAPHY

"Grace." *Chicago Magazine*, April 8, 2013.

Vettel, Phil. "Four Stars for Grace." *Chicago Tribune*, February 7, 2013.

The Greater Chicago Food Depository

Chicago's food bank has been working to end hunger in the Chicago area since 1978, based on a model developed in Phoenix. The nonprofit 501(c)(3), located at 4100 W. Ann Lurie Pl., is a food distribution and training center providing food for hungry people while striving to deal with the causes of hunger in the area.

Through a network of more than 650 pantries, soup kitchens, shelters, mobile programs, children's programs, and programs for older adults, the Food Depository serves more than 800,000 adults and children a year. It delivers more than 67 million pounds of food, including 22 million pounds of fresh produce, annually. Specific recipients include Kids Cafes and Chicago Public Schools, low-income older-adult residences (CHA and HUD), and local nonprofit organizations. More than 232,100 households are served each year.

Donations to the Food Depository come from wholesalers and food-service organizations, retailers, individuals, and organizations through food drives and governmental programs.

In addition to nearly 60,000 donors and 500 corporations and foundations, the Food Depository runs a volunteer program for about 20,000 people giving 99,000 hours a year. Millions of pounds of healthful food are contributed by 350 food companies.

The growth of the Food Depository was helped significantly in 1982 when Illinois legislators passed a Good Samaritan law. Written to protect food contributors from legal liabilities, the bill helped support similar national legislation passed by Congress in 1996. Today, the Food Depository operates from a 268,000-square-foot warehouse and training center opened in 2004, following a successful $30 million capital campaign. In keeping with its goal to end hunger, the Food Depository launched its Chicago's Community Kitchens program to provide culinary training programs for unemployed and underemployed adults.

Contributor: Elizabeth Richter

See also: Food Pantries

BIBLIOGRAPHY

http://www.chicagosfoodbank.org/site/PageServer.

Greeks

Greek settlement in the United States was negligible before the great wave of immigration from southern and eastern Europe that started about 1880. Between 1890 and 1930, more than 450,000 Greeks came to the United States. Early arrivals included a high proportion of single, young men seeking to earn money and then return to their families back home. Difficult labor conditions (often including seasonal work in construction) were the norm, though many Greeks soon managed to save enough money to be able to start their own modest businesses. Only gradually during this first period of immigration did the number of women rise and allow for the development of full-fledged Greek American communities. After World War II, immigration resumed, with more than 200,000 arriving between 1950 and 1980; many of the postwar immigrants settled in those same areas with established Greek American communities.

The most concentrated settlement in the city—and for several decades the largest Greek American community in the United States—developed on the Near West Side. Commonly called "the Delta," this area was roughly bounded by Halsted, Harrison, Polk, and Blue Island Streets and lay immediately to the north of the predominantly Italian Taylor Street neighborhood. The Delta, or "Greektown," thrived from the 1920s to the early 1960s, when it was largely demolished to make way for the University

of Illinois' new Chicago campus. Chicago's current and popular Greektown on Halsted from Van Buren north to Madison is a vestige of the old neighborhood. It supports a concentration of Greek restaurants and other businesses, but without much of a resident Greek population in the area. Many moved to Lincoln Square or suburban areas.

As an immigrant community, the Greeks were well-known for their hard work and entrepreneurship. In Chicago, as elsewhere in the United States, one of the first fields of opportunity for them was the food industry. Many Greeks became fruit and produce peddlers in the early years and, of these, a remarkable number managed to found successful grocery shops or wholesale food businesses. Eventually, Greeks came to control a major share of the wholesale food industry at the central-city markets on Randolph and South Water streets. Another niche was in confections and ice cream, as Greeks became owners of candy stores and soda shops, such as Margie's on Western, founded in the 1920s. A nationally popular ice-cream product, the Dove Bar, was the creation of Leo Stefanos, the proprietor of one sweets shop, in the 1950s. So popular

Constantine Pergantic and customers in his confectionary store, 1950s. From the National Hellenic Museum's Photography Collection.

were Greek confectioners that people came from across the country to be trained in the art and craft of candy making and "dairy creations" such as sundaes and milkshakes. It has been said that between the 1920s and about 1970 most of America's candy shop owners had been trained or influenced by Chicago's Greek confectioners.

The most striking aspect of Greek American participation in the U.S. food industry is the community's role in the restaurant business. Prior to its shrinkage, Greektown was home to 30,000 Greeks who were served by food stores, coffee shops, restaurants, and a pool hall or two. The Pilafas Greek Grocery Store, Sarantakis Greek Grocery Store, and Deligiannis Greek Grocery Store were side by side with eight coffeehouses, a half dozen bakeries, and a dozen restaurants (one of which was the El Paso Mexican Tavern). All served Greek baked goods and plenty of "Turkish" coffee. Some groceries and restaurants remained, notably Diana's run by the effervescent Petros Kogiones. Made into a restaurant named Diana's Opaa in 1961, the restaurant became a magnet for Chicagoans wanting a taste for more-or-less authentic Greek food and to be entertained by the dance-loving owner.

Greektown restaurants were only a small number of many more throughout Chicago. Unlike other immigrants with restaurants that featured their own food traditions, most Greek American restaurateurs created menus with the broadest appeal. They served mainstream American breakfast fare, hamburgers, club sandwiches, basic dinner plates (roast turkey, meatloaf, roast beef, and so forth), and some particularly popular ethnic dishes (spaghetti and meatballs, chicken parmigiana, and fajitas). Usually only a few overtly Greek items were included (Greek salad with feta, Greek-style roasted chicken, and gyros). Typically, these establishments, many of which were "diners," had long hours of operation. Some notable examples that date back to the mid–twentieth century are the White Palace Grill (Canal at Roosevelt), the Palace Grill (Madison and Loomis), and Lou Mitchell's (Jackson near Jefferson).

Greek Americans also have been involved in the fast-food business nationally and locally, where the gyros sandwich takes its place alongside the Chicago-style hot dog and Italian beef as a local specialty. Greek-owned fast-food stands serve all three, as well as hamburgers. On the Southwest Side, a two-patty style of hamburger called "the Big Baby" is widespread and has its origins in a Greek-owned stand. Including fast-food stands, diners, and other, more formal eateries, it has been claimed that, in the 1950s, Greek Americans owned about 85 percent of all restaurants in the Loop; it seems likely very few, if any, specialized in Greek cuisine.

Full-fledged Greek restaurants are found here and there throughout Chicagoland, with one particular

WHERE TO BUY GREEK INGREDIENTS

While Greek cuisine remains largely outside the American mainstream, the current fascination with the Mediterranean diet has increased its popularity and also brought a demand for many of the staple products used in Greek cookery. The once numerous specialty shops serving the Greek American community now are a mere handful (Elea in Greektown, Spartan Bros. in Edison Park, Minos in Addison), but these remain important sources for such items as Greek olive oils, cured olives, wines and liqueurs, aged and fresh cheeses, pasta, *paximadia* (barley rusks), giant beans, *volvi* (hyacinth bulbs), dried oregano, and sweets. Increasingly, many of these items are on offer in mainstream groceries, especially those owned by Greek Americans (Treasure Island, Pete's Fresh Market).

—ANTHONY BUCCINI

concentration in Greektown, where, within a span of a few blocks along Halsted, there were six left in the early twenty-first century: Artopolis, Athena, Greek Islands, Pegasus, Roditys, and Santorini. All are moderately priced. All offer an array of *mezedes* (appetizers), including feta cheese and olives, spreads such as *taramosalata* (fish roe), *melitzanosalata* (eggplant), *tzatziki* (cucumber and yogurt), grilled and sautéed seafood (octopus, squid, shrimp), *keftedes* (meatballs), *dolmades* (rice-stuffed grape leaves), *spanakotiropita* (spinach-cheese pies), and flambéed saganaki, a traditional dish of fried cheese, which was reportedly first served flambéed at the Parthenon restaurant, which closed in 2016. Grilled, roasted, and braised meats are a mainstay, with lamb particularly featured in various traditional recipes. Fresh seafood forms an important part of each of these restaurants' offerings, as well as traditional dishes such as moussaka (eggplant-potato-lamb casserole), pastitsio (baked pasta with ground meat sauce and béchamel), spaghetti with browned butter and cheese, and *bakaliaros* (salt cod, often fried and served with *skordalia*). Meat or fish dishes are accompanied by one or more starches (oven-roasted potatoes, rice, and *kritharaki* [orzo pasta]). Always on offer are also *horta* (boiled dandelion greens) and other vegetable preparations (artichoke, zucchini, green beans) and various salads (*horiatiki* "village salad" with feta). Common desserts are baklava (nut-stuffed phyllo), *galaktoboureko* (custard in phyllo), and yogurt dressed with honey. All these restaurants feature Greek wines, including retsina, and Greek-style coffee.

In recent years, more upscale Greek restaurants have begun to appear, such as Avli Estiatorio in Winnetka and Taxim in Chicago's Wicker Park, which serves chef-driven food taking its inspiration from the cuisine of the eastern (Anatolian) Greeks.

Contributor: Anthony F. Buccini

See also: Candy; Dove Bars; Lunch Wagons and Diners

BIBLIOGRAPHY

Ganakos, Alexa. *Greektown Chicago. Its History—Its Recipes*. St. Louis: Bradley, 2005.

Kochilas, Diane. *The Glorious Foods of Greece*. New York: Harper-Collins, 2001.

Kopan, Andrew. "Greek Survival in Chicago." In *Ethnic Chicago. A Multicultural Portrait*, Melvin G. Holli and Peter d'A. Jones, eds, 260–302. Grand Rapids: Eerdmans, 1995.

Green City Market

Founded in 1998 by cookbook author and columnist Abby Mandel, the market is an independent, 501(c)(3) farmers market in Lincoln Park. Mandel's mission was to improve the availability of high-quality local and sustainably grown food, connecting local farmers to chefs and customers and promoting a healthier society. Mandel was inspired by her visits to European markets, and by Julia Child and Alice Waters, who celebrated local, sustainably grown food.

The outdoor market, on North Clark Street just north of LaSalle, features more than 65 farmers and vendors who offer fresh, sustainable and locally grown produce and products. All are carefully vetted and must be certified by a third party to ensure sustainable growing practices. In winter, the market moves to the Peggy Notebaert Nature Museum. An estimated 456,000 people shop at Green City Market each year.

Educational initiatives include the Sprouts program, introducing children to fresh fruits and vegetables; the Edible Gardens, demonstrating how market produce grows; and chef demonstrations of using market products. In 2014, the market published *The Green City Market Cookbook*, with seasonal recipes from the community of chefs, farmers, and customers. A featured event each year is the Annual Green City Market Chef's BBQ, a fundraiser for Market programs that features 80 or more of Chicago's best chefs. They create dishes entirely from products sold in the market. Because of its popularity, the Market is exploring options for a permanent indoor-outdoor location, including the historic Fulton Market wholesale district.

Contributor: Elizabeth Richter

See also: Agriculture, Urban; Festivals

BIBLIOGRAPHY

Green City Market. http://www.greencitymarket.org/.

Green City Market, ed. *The Green City Market Cookbook*. Evanston, Ill.: Agate Midway, 2014.

Green River Soda

Green River was first manufactured in Chicago in 1919 by the Schoenhofen Edelweiss Brewing Company at 18th Street and Canalport in what is now Chicago's Pilsen neighborhood. The verdant bubbly soda was packaged into recycled beer bottles, and the product kept the brewery afloat during Prohibition.

But the soda did not start in Chicago. Like many bottled sodas, it began as a syrup to be mixed at soda fountains. The syrup was developed in 1914 in Davenport, Iowa, by inventor Richard C. Jones, who ran a candy store. He conjured up a sparkling green, caffeine-free, lime-based soda to attract students from the nearby high school to his store. Those students dubbed the drink "Green River." The river referenced is the Mississippi River, not the Green River that cuts through northwestern Illinois, nor the Chicago River, which is dyed green in celebration of St. Patrick's Day.

Jones was not a marketer, but he knew some men at a flavor house in Chicago who connected him with the Schoenhofen Edelweiss brewery to produce the drink in quantity. From the 1930s to 1950s, Green River was second only to Coca-Cola in Midwest sales, and into the 1960s, Green River was a staple at corner soda fountains.

Green River became a nationally known Chicago icon. In 1969, the rock band Creedence Clearwater Revival had a popular song and album called "Green River." Songwriter John Fogerty says he took the name of the song from the soda, but the river he sings about isn't a river at all but Putah Creek in Winters, California.

WIT Beverage Company purchased Green River in 2011 and rolled it into its specialty soda portfolio. The drink still is produced in Chicago with natural lime flavoring and cane sugar, but the soda is bottled in Oak Creek, Wisconsin. In 2013, sales of Green River generated $15 million for WIT.

Contributor: Deborah Pankey

See also: Soda Fountains, Soft Drinks

BIBLIOGRAPHY

Hwa-shu, Long. "Green River Success Runs Deep for Beverage Company Owners." *Chicago Sun-Times*, August 9, 2013.

Grocery Stores (See: Supermarkets and Grocers)

Gunther, Charles F.

German American confectioner, politician, and collector, Gunther (1837–1920) was known as "The Candy Man." Born in Wurttemberg, Germany, he immigrated to Pennsylvania, then moved to Peru, Illinois, and finally Chicago. Gunther founded a candy company in 1868 at 125 N. Clark St. that occasionally is credited with introducing caramel to the United States. Gunther rebuilt his operations at 212 S. State St., following the 1871 Great Fire. He found financial success selling to wealthy socialites (including Bertha Palmer) and shipping caramels nationwide. Politically active and civic-minded, he served as alderman of Chicago's second ward from 1897–1901, and as city treasurer from 1901–05.

As he found business success, Gunther began to purchase and display historical artifacts in a private museum he maintained above his candy store on State Street. The collection grew to include notable Civil War artifacts, such as the table at which Robert E. Lee surrendered at Appomattox, and the deathbed of Abraham Lincoln. Gunther also purchased the Libby Prison, which held Union Army soldiers in Richmond, Virginia, and reassembled it in its entirety as a museum on the 1400–1600 blocks of S. Wabash Ave. Though an avowed Unionist, Gunther was arrested (and later released) by the Union Army in 1862 while serving as the purser of a Confederate steamship.

After Gunther's death, the Chicago Historical Society purchased most of his collection. This acquisition formed much of the early collection of the Chicago History Museum, which opened in 1932 at 1601 N. Clark St. and has remained in operation since.

Contributor: John Carruthers
See also: Candy

BIBLIOGRAPHY

"Charles F. Gunther. 1837–1920." *Journal of the Illinois State Historical Society (1908–1984)* 13, 1 (April 1920): 141–42.

Gyros (yee-ros)

A Greek-style sandwich made of meat wrapped into a cone around a skewer and roasted vertically. The meat, usually ground lamb or beef, is sliced off the skewer and served in pita bread with vegetable garnishes and perhaps some *tzatziki*, a cucumber and yogurt sauce.

The Parthenon restaurant in Greektown was one of the first places to sell gyros in the city. Other restaurants and gyros makers followed, flourishing to such a degree that Chicago was called gyros capital of the world in a 1993 *Chicago Tribune* article. Greek-born Chris Tomaras gets much credit for that. Sensing gyros could be a big trend, he opened Kronos Foods in 1975. By 1979, he reportedly supplied meat cones to 60 percent of the gyros market in Chicago. Tomaras sold his controlling interest in 1994; he died in 2015. Kronos now is based in Glendale Heights, IL. Called the world's largest manufacturer of gyros in 2009, the company makes a variety of Mediterranean food products for restaurant and consumer use.

Contributor: Bill Daley
See also: Greeks

BIBLIOGRAPHY

Lavin, Cheryl, "The Hero of Gyros: Chris Tomaras' Spartan Work Ethic Builds a Dining Empire." *Chicago Tribune*, July 22, 1993.

Segal, David, "The Gyro's History Unfolds." *New York Times*, July 14, 2009.

Harding's Colonial Room

Back when going downtown was a major event, lunch at Harding's Colonial Room was the icing on the cake. The restaurant, which was owned by the Harding Restaurant Company, was on the second floor at 21 South Wabash, just a short walk from both Marshall Field's and Carson, Pirie, Scott & Co.

Complete with servers dressed in costumes typical of the Colonial Era, the restaurant had a kid-friendly menu. Prices topped out at $1 for the Captain Kidd Special: a two-course lunch that included a glass of white or chocolate milk and ice cream for dessert. At the end of the meal, children were entitled to pick out a nicely wrapped gift from the restaurant's Treasure Chest.

Harding's was especially famous for its corned beef cabbage, which was also served at several other Harding lunch rooms in the city.

Contributor: Barbara Revsine

BIBLIOGRAPHY

Drury, John. "Harding's Colonial Room." *Dining in Chicago*. New Your: John Day Co., 1931.

Harold's Chicken Shack (See: African Americans; Fast Food/Quick Service)

Harris, Scott

After earning a culinary degree from Joliet Junior College, Harris worked at many Chicago-area restaurants, including The 95th, Avanzare, Ambria, and Trattoria L'Angolo di Roma. He then opened his own place in 1993 on North Clark Street, Mia Francesca. It was a friendly neighborhood restaurant with fresh Italian fare and so successful, it led to 23 more Francesca locales across the country. In 2009, he opened a new Italian concept in Little Italy called Davanti Enoteca, with an emphasis on affordable wines. He also was a partner in The Purple Pig on Michigan Avenue, but after financial disagreements, he filed a lawsuit against his partners, which was settled amicably in 2016. He is no longer associated with the restaurant.

Contributor: Carol Mighton Haddix

BIBLIOGRAPHY

Coburn, Marcia Froelke. "Scott Harris: The Most Underrated Restaurateur in the Country?" *Chicago Magazine*, August 25, 2011.

Hart Davis Hart Wine Company

Perhaps the premier wine auction house in America, Hart Davis Hart (HDH) was formed in Chicago in 2004 when fine wine merchant John Hart partnered with virtuoso wine auctioneers Michael Davis and Paul Hart (no relation to John).

John Hart previously owned the Chicago Wine Company and John Hart Fine Wines; auctioneers Davis and Hart are known for their über high-end wine auction work for both Christie's and Sotheby's. All three are considered experts in the field, and HDH is renowned for its fine customer service and the delicate care it takes with fine wine storage.

HDH is both a wine auction house and an online retail resource. Live auctions are held at TRU restaurant seven times per year; bids can be made in person or online. The firm leads the market in wine consignment for auction from fine wine collectors around the world. In addition, HDH holds many special events (such as winemaker dinners and wine tastings) each year. The offices and cellar of HDH relocated in February 2015 from the River North neighborhood to 1511 W. 38th St. in Chicago.

Contributor: Julie Chernoff

BIBLIOGRAPHY

"U.S. Wine Auction Market Enjoys Banner Year as Hart-Davis-Hart Again Takes Top Spot. *Shanken News Daily*. http://www.shankennewsdaily.com/index.php/2015/01/15/11523/u-s-wine-auction-market-enjoys-banner-year-as-hart-davis-hart-again-takes-top-spot/.

Health and Natural Foods

The movement toward a healthier and more holistic approach to eating goes by many names: health food, natural food, organic food, locavorism, sustainability. But all are related to the effects of food on the body and on the world at large. Vegetarian diets had been popularized by Sylvester Graham, other vegetarians, food reformers, and religious groups, but the most famous was the renowned Battle Creek Sanitarium in Michigan (founded in 1866 by the Seventh Day Adventist Church). Its superintendent from 1876, Dr. John Harvey Kellogg popularized a diet low in fat and protein and high in whole grains and nuts that became the basis for the modern breakfast food industry.

Many early health food movements were mainly concerned with getting enough vitamins and other nutrients, but did not connect the health of the soil to the amount of nutrients in vegetables and fruits. Once the movement began to grow in Chicago in the 1960s, it helped spawn the broader environmental movement and was connected closely to animal rights issues. The natural foods movement of the late twentieth century emphasized eating foods that are minimally processed, such as vegetables and whole grains, and livestock that are not fed antibiotics or hormones or confined to cages.

The natural food movement is inextricably bound up with vegetarianism. An interest in healthful eating often leads to vegetarianism. Conversely, as vegetarians become more involved in the broader movement, they often learn about the health and environmental hazards of industrial food production and begin to eat more organically grown, less processed foods.

Kramers, a health food store that opened in 1927 on West Adams, is still open, albeit on South Wabash and with a different owner. In 1948, the family-run Southtown Health Foods store opened on 63rd and Halsted, later moved several times, and now operates at 95th and Hoyne. By the 1960s, many more health food stores had opened in Chicago, mainly downtown. Most of them sold packaged products and mixes, vitamins, and other nutrients, and often fresh, whole organic chicken on the weekend.

Between the 1960s and 1980s, Chicago had a chain of health food stores called Nature's Foods. Other stores included the House of Nutrition on State Street, It's Natural on Michigan Avenue, the Golden Carrot on Chicago

Avenue, and Aides by Paige on Broadway in Uptown. These stores were small precursors to the arrival of national chains, such as Whole Foods and Trader Joe's, in the 1990s. The city also hosted the National Health Federation's yearly health food convention for many years at the Congress Hotel on Michigan Avenue.

Rogers Park's Heartland Café, opened by Michael James and Katy Hogan in 1976, was Chicago's first health food restaurant, serving brown rice, beans, and a number of vegetarian entrees, along with chicken, fish, and buffalo meat. It also served as a community center.

One health food store that opened in the late 1960s heralded a different approach to eating. Food for Life, on North Halsted Street, had dozens of barrels of bulk whole grains, beans, flours, nuts, and seeds. Although it might not have carried meat, the store was macrobiotic and promoted eating fish. It had an ecological consciousness, which was manifested in a small index card taped to the top of the cash box (no cash register for several years). The card stated, "1 grain: 10,000 grains," a message to not waste, as one grain of rice will transform, in time, to 10,000 grains of rice.

Contributor: Kay Stepkin

See also: Vegetarianism

BIBLIOGRAPHY

Dobrow, Joe. *Natural Prophets: From Health Foods to Whole Foods— How the Pioneers of the Industry Changed the Way We Eat and Reshaped American Business.* Emmaus, Pa.: Rodale, 2014.

"Kramer's." Vegguide.org. https://www.vegguide.org/entry/1547.

Henrici's (See: Restaurateurs and Restaurant Groups)

Hirsch, Gerald

The founder of Heritage Wine Cellars Ltd., in 1981, Hirsch (1928–2008) became known as one of the most knowledgeable wine experts in Chicago. He started out helping his mother at a liquor shop on Madison Street after the death of his father. He moved on to work at area wine distributors, including Wines Unlimited and then opened Heritage in suburban Niles. His expertise led to supplying fine wines and consulting with many of the top restaurants in town through the 1980s and 1990s. He traveled to vineyards in California and Europe, taught classes and seminars, and was recognized by France and Italy for his wine industry contributions. Heritage still imports and distributes wine and craft spirits under the direction of Hirsch's son, Steven.

Contributor: Carol Mighton Haddix

See also: Wine Distribution and Sales

BIBLIOGRAPHY

Jensen, Trevor. "So Passionate about Wine." *Chicago Tribune*, October 15, 2008.

Home Cooking and Kitchens

In Chicago's early days, the kitchen was the heart of the home. It was the room with the fireplace that heated the cooking pots and the rest of the house. Families gathered around the kitchen table for meals; this was where children played and studied and household accounts were reconciled. It was not easy work to prepare meals: hauling water in, chopping wood to stoke the wood-burning stove, dispatching chickens for the evening meal. It is little surprise that, as immigrants poured into Chicago in the 1870s, one in five households included a domestic worker, typically a woman of Irish, German, Polish, or Scandinavian descent. By the early 1900s, African American women joined the ranks of kitchen help.

During the late 1800s, Chicago built a water network that brought running water to more kitchens and improved food safety and cleanliness. The 50-some homes built on the city's Near North Side by Chicago businessman and developer Potter Palmer from 1889 to 1891 were the first to include indoor plumbing. By 1910, plumbing fixtures became more affordable and indoor running water was within reach of more Chicagoans. A photograph taken that year for the *Chicago Daily News* of a modern kitchen in suburban Park Ridge shows a tidy room with a sink and a wood-burning stove. During the "bungalow boom" of the 1920s, running water for kitchens, laundry, and bathrooms became a standard feature. It wasn't until that decade, when refrigerators also became more widely available, that food storage and meal preparation were separated from the dining room in most homes.

An all-electric kitchen was first shown at the Columbian Exposition in 1893, but it was only for wealthy families. Society maven Frances Glessner bought one immediately after seeing one demonstrated at the Exposition (her Irish cook quit rather than be forced to cook on the new-fangled apparatus). By the late 1930s and early '40s, electric stoves and refrigerators with freezers, many manufactured in Chicago, would become common in most kitchens.

After World War II, Midwest homes, like those built by Kimball Hill in northwest suburban Rolling Meadows, included built-in cupboards and countertops (as opposed to freestanding Hoosier-style cabinets); a functional feature that remains integral in today's kitchens. Often those cabinets were made of steel and manufactured in west suburban St. Charles. The St. Charles brand, launched in 1935, was considered the top of the line. The brand was purchased by Viking in 2001, but the line was discontinued about 10 years later.

Kitchen design started to formalize with the concept of the work triangle: that your refrigerator, stove top, and sink—the three points of a triangle—had to be arranged as such for maximum efficiency. The idea was later formalized by the University of Illinois School of Architecture and became the standard construction model for homes throughout the suburbs.

Refrigerators and stoves remain key components in the kitchens of the twenty-first century, but cooks also are likely to use countertop electrics including slow cookers, blenders, grills, food processors, pizza cookers, and quesadilla makers for meal preparation. And, of course, they need space to put all that stuff. Kitchens have grown to accommodate all that and now are sometimes the biggest room in the house, with restaurant-sized high-temperature ovens and double-doored refrigerators. Open floor plans, in which the kitchen space flows into the family room or dining area, allow the cook—just as likely to be the male head of household—to be with the family during meal preparation.

What families cooked in those kitchens was ever-changing. Immigrants in the mid-to-late 1800s brought their culinary traditions with them to Chicago: Polish families made pierogies, Italian families made pasta and wine, Asian families made dumplings. They made do with ingredients from Chicago's early markets or from their own small gardens, substituting for the Old World foodstuffs they were used to. Until the transportation systems improved and more exotic ingredients became available, Chicago cooks were forced to prepare simple, basic meals for their families, often using their own preserved foods through the winter months.

In the mid–twentieth century, food manufacturers flooded grocery stores with convenience foods, including canned vegetables, boxed seasoned rice, and macaroni made with dehydrated cheese. More high-end foods arrived in supermarkets and specialty stores for home cooks to try. An interest in natural, organic ingredients began to influence their cooking. As the century drew to a close, the popularity of the Food Network and the cult of the celebrity chef (such as Charlie Trotter, Rick Bayless, Gale Gand, and Grant Achatz in Chicago) had cooks stretching their boundaries and attempting to replicate restaurant dishes at home (as well as spurring more restaurant visits). Consumers spent increasing amounts of money on specialty kitchen electrics, such as immersion blenders, commercial-grade mixers, and high-quality knives, so they could cook like those chefs they watched on TV.

After the terrorist attacks of September 11, 2001, the pendulum started to swing back to comfort food in Chicago as in the rest of the nation. The popularity of cooking blogs and recipe databases on the Internet opened up a worldwide network of recipe sharing. Cooks no longer were putting all their trust in professional chefs and culinary institutions; they were turning to each other for recipes, emailing links, posting cooking videos to YouTube, and "tweeting" recipes in 140 characters or less. It became the modern-day equivalent of passing recipes over the backyard fence while hanging laundry.

By 2013, Americans ate 8 out of 10 of their meals at home, according to Rosemont-based NPD's 29th annual "Eating Patterns in America Report." The drop in restaurant visits (a side-effect of the recent recession) and the increase in meals in the home is one of the single biggest changes in eating patterns in America in the last five years.

Contributor: Deborah Pankey

BIBLIOGRAPHY

Houston, Lynn Marie. "Kitchens, 1800 to Present." *Oxford Encyclopedia of Food and Drink in America* Vol. 2. New York: Oxford University Press, 2004.

Jones, Rob. "The Life and Times of the Modern Kitchen: A Long Form Read." BuildDirect Blog. http://blog.builddirect.com/the-life-and-times-of-the-modern-kitchen-a-long-form-read/.

Poe, Tracy. "Foodways." *The Encyclopedia of Chicago*. Chicago History Museum, 2005. www.encyclopedia.chicagohistory.org.

Home Economists

The hundreds of women who worked as home economists in food, appliance, and utility companies; schools; trade associations; retailers; or magazines and newspapers in mid-twentieth-century Chicago probably didn't think of themselves as activists. But social reform was very much a part of early home economics. The first generation of home economists were equal rights advocates, chemists and public health advocates, labor reformers and innovators. Ellen Swallow Richards, generally considered the founder of the profession, was the first woman admitted to MIT. She received a degree in chemistry in 1873 and later became the institution's first female instructor. Richards passionately believed that domestic work within the home was a vital part of the economy and lectured on the subject at Chicago's Columbian Exposition in 1893. Jane Addams and other activist women were influenced by Richards's work and talks.

Home economics in the early 1900s provided a pathway to higher education for women. Isabel Bevier created the program of Household Science at the University of Illinois in Urbana-Champaign in 1900, providing college degrees for thousands of women. Bevier, who had studied with Richards at MIT, was at the forefront of the professionalization of home economics.

Another MIT graduate was Marion Talbot, who became dean of women at the University of Chicago in 1895 and established the Department of Household Administration in 1904. However, land grant institutions such as the University of Illinois seemed to fare better with financial support. The U. of C. program dwindled and was discontinued in 1956.

By the mid–twentieth century, home economists in Chicago were not viewed as crusaders but as an integral part of a variety of institutions. From the 1920s through the 1970s, home economist positions provided some of the scant opportunities for women to have professional careers. Especially in companies populated almost entirely by men, home economists' ideas and opinions in their areas of expertise were well regarded.

By the late twentieth century, women were succeeding in a wider range of professions. The generalized teachings of home economics were spinning off into areas of specialization. Universities redefined Home Economics departments as Consumer Sciences or Human Ecology. Home Economics courses were dropped from secondary school curriculums. Today, one would be hard pressed to find anyone younger than 50 with a home economics degree.

For decades, home economists had wide-ranging impacts on Chicago food life. A representation of notable mid-twentieth-century home economists in Chicago includes Jane Armstrong (Jewel Foods), Thora Campbell (Swift), Doris Christopher (The Pampered Chef), Ruth Ellen Church (*Chicago Tribune*), Mary Dahnke (Kraft), Marguerite Gustafson (American Dairy Association), Dorothy Holland (Kraft), Lois Ross (Quaker Oats), Reba Staggs (National Live Stock and Meat Board), Marion Tripp (J. Walter Thompson), and JoAnn Will (J. Walter Thompson, *Chicago Tribune*).

Contributor: Eleanor Hanson

See also: Columbian Exposition; Media; Hull House

BIBLIOGRAPHY

McCurdy, Christen. "What Happened to Home Economics?" *Bitch Magazine*. http://bitchmagazine.org/article/what-happened -to-home-economics-history-feminism-education.

Stage, Sarah, and Virginia B. Vincenti. *Rethinking Home Economics: Women and the History of a Profession*. Ithaca: Cornell University Press, 1997. http://www.uic.edu/.

Hot Dogs

Of all foods commonly perceived to be Chicago icons, none is as important as the hot dog. With about 2,500 locations, the Chicago area has more fixed-location hot dog restaurants than any other city in the world. The hot dog stand has cultural cachet, and the modern Chicago hot dog is a unique regional style that is known across the world.

Hot dogs are sausages descended from several varieties brought by German immigrants, beginning in the 1850s. The other terms for hot dogs are *frankfurters* and *wieners*, named for two German cities, and still used interchangeably with the name *hot dog*. As German food became incorporated into Chicago's culinary lexicon, sausages became mainstream.

Three trends brought hot dogs to the fore in Chicago. From its inception as a tiny village, the city grew to a million people in 1890, three million by 1930. People packed into the central city for work and also to visit entertainment venues such as baseball games, theaters, and the lakefront. With them came street food vendors, who served, among other things, cooked German-style sausages. By the 1880s, vendors were everywhere calling out for customers to get their "red hots." By the 1890s, the sausages also were called "hot dogs," a joke referring to unsavory meat ingredients: the city's meatpacking firms did little to help the hot dog's reputation. Sausages were made from the leftover scraps from butchering, with unsavory bits getting into the products. But hot dogs were a source of cheap protein for impoverished Chicagoans, many of whom worked for the self-same packers. Hot dogs also could be eaten on the run, and soon they became part of the exciting new sport that gripped the city: baseball.

Finally, immigration helped the hot dog's popularity. In the late nineteenth and the early twentieth centuries, massive migration from eastern and southern Europe brought new foods to Chicago. By 1900, 270,000 Ashkenazi Jews lived in the city, many in the Maxwell Street area near Halsted and Roosevelt Road. This enclave adjoined Italian and Greek communities. Many from all three groups went into the street vending business, and later into food manufacturing and distribution. Because Jews did not eat pork, and beef was so plentiful, all-beef sausages became the default hot dog in their area. The modern Vienna Beef Company, whose origins were on Halsted near Maxwell Street, is a prime example. By the 1920s, the Jewish hot dog makers' reputations for quality were so good that the all-beef hot dog became the sausage of choice for street vendors and the growing number of hot dog stands.

Street food from carts and wagons was severely restricted by city ordinances after 1902 and in subsequent legislation into the 1960s. In the 1920s, mobile food selling operations settled into permanent stands in neighborhoods all over the city, though many unlicensed street vendors existed. Stands could be simple wooden shacks or more

Women eating hot dogs at White City Amusement Park, 1920. Courtesy of the Chicago Public Library, Special Collections and Preservation Division.

onions, sliced tomatoes, dill pickle spears, mildly hot pickled "sport" peppers and, optionally, a sprinkling of celery salt. French fries are an expected accompaniment. And never, ever is ketchup allowed on the hot dog, though it might be available for the fries. Several purveyors claimed to have invented this superb creation, notably Abe Drexler who operated Fluky's in the old Jewish section of Roosevelt Road in the 1920s. This assertion has never been proved. The earliest mention of condiments such as piccalilli (relish) appeared at a Cubs–White Sox game in 1928. The style certainly took root in the post–World War II stands. And today, the Vienna Beef Company, the dominant hot dog maker in the Chicago market, still promotes this Chicago hot dog through its advertising and colorful stand signs.

Contributor: Bruce Kraig

See also: Ballpark Food; Sausages; Jews

BIBLIOGRAPHY

Kraig, Bruce, and Patty Carroll. *Man Bites Dog: Hot Dog Culture in America*. Lanham, Md.: Rowman and Littlefield, 2012.

Schwartz, Bob. *Never Put Ketchup on a Hot Dog*. Chicago: Chicago's Books Press, 2008.

Hot Doug's

Located on Chicago's Northwest Side, Hot Doug's was arguably THE most celebrated hot dog stand between New York and California. Food authority Anthony Bourdain declared Hot Doug's as "one of the thirteen places to eat before you die."

The restaurant had two incarnations. It opened as a small eatery in Roscoe Village in 2001, which was destroyed by fire in 2004, and then reopened at a larger location in 2005 at Roscoe and California, "near my home, so I could walk to work," owner Doug Sohn said. With write-ups in the likes of *Bon Appetit* and the *New York Times*, and TV coverage as well, this "encased meat emporium," as Sohn preferred to call it, brought lines of customers. They went into ecstasy over the cornucopia of hot dogs and fresh-cut fries, served up with a healthy dose of Sohn's humor and friendly manner.

The compact eatery, painted in mustard yellow and ketchup red, featured Sohn behind the cash register, writing down every order, kibitzing with customers, and making suggestions, especially for first-timers. Many of his dishes were named after celebrities: the Elvis Polish Sausage, "smoked and savory, just like the King"; the game sausage of the week, which might include rattlesnake, 'gator, or rabbit; or a gourmet Cognac-infused smoked pheasant sausage with sauce moutarde. One of his sausages, concocted of foie gras and duck meat, gained Sohn

well-built structures, but the model was the same: a box with a service window on one side. They served hot dogs heated in a hot water bath (grilling was deemed a fire hazard), with steam-heated buns and simple condiments such as mustard, chopped onions, relish, and perhaps pickled peppers. Called "Depression Dogs," these simpler versions of the now-standard dog "dragged through the garden" were the mainstays of the business until the 1950s.

After World War II, hot dog stands grew more sophisticated in décor, foods, and numbers. Veterans returning to Chicago looked for businesses to start, and what better than the familiar and beloved hot dog? One example is Maurie and Flaurie Berman, who opened the celebrated Superdawg in Norwood Park in 1948. Stands became canvases for vernacular art and described the social character of neighborhoods. To this day, Chicagoans are attached to their local stands, often arguing with fellow citizens about the merits of each place.

Chicago-style hot dogs are defined by an elaborate style of toppings. An all-beef hot dog, preferably natural casing, heated in a hot water bath, placed on a steamed bun (poppy seed or plain), then topped with a smear of yellow mustard, a trail of bright green relish, chopped fresh a $250 fine and headlines during the Chicago City Council's short-lived ban on selling foie gras.

Sohn, whose career path included a culinary degree from Kendall College, also worked as a cook, caterer, and cookbook editor. He documented his success with *Hot Doug's: The Book*, published in 2013. Sohn closed his restaurant the following year. "I'm not burnt out. I also don't want to be burnt out. It's just time," he told the *Chicago Tribune*. In the summer of 2015, Sohn opened a Hot Doug's concession stand at Wrigley Field where he shows up at some games to meet and greet.

Contributor: Scott Warner

See also: Hot Dogs

BIBLIOGRAPHY

Sohn, Doug, and Kate Devivo. *Hot Doug's: The Book*. Chicago: Agate, 2013.

Warner, Scott. "Dr. Herb Sohn Relishes Son's Wienie Success." *Chicago Medicine*, Spring 2006.

House of Glunz

Louis Glunz arrived in Chicago from Westphalia, Germany, in 1888. Glunz operated a Schlitz Beer concession at the 1893 Columbian Exposition. He soon enlisted family members to help start a company to bottle and distribute Schlitz and other beers as well as spirits and wines, which were sold by the cask and delivered by horse-drawn carriage. Later, Louis Glunz Beer was spun off and remains the country's oldest beer distributor. With a loan from Charles Wacker, also from a German brewing family, he opened Glunz Tavern (1202 N. Wells St.) in one of the first brick buildings to be constructed after the Great Fire of 1871 (postfire ordinances dictated that flameproof brick had to be used instead of wood to avoid another disaster). Glunz Tavern operated until just before Prohibition, and then it closed for about 80 years.

Next door to the tavern is House of Glunz, the small retail shop that was allowed to remain in business during Prohibition selling wine to the Catholic church, as well as medicinal elixirs and soda pop. Today, it features a well-curated wine selection and a gorgeous period-style tasting room. House of Glunz was the first wine shop in Chicago to champion California wine.

In 2013, the tavern reopened in a remodeled space that features vintage appointments salvaged from historic Chicago restaurants such as Red Star and The Berghoff. The tavern also serves food that reflects the German tradition, with dishes such as spaetzle Uberbacken, bratwurst, and Thuringer, prepared under the direction of chef Allen Sternweiler.

House of Glunz proprietor Barbara Glunz (granddaughter of Louis) operates the tavern and shop with her son, Christopher Donovan, while maintaining the retail side of the business. The Glunz family also opened the Glunz Family Winery and Cellars in Grayslake in 1992, and a *bierstube*, Glunz Bavarian House, in North Center in 2003.

Contributor: David Hammond

See also: Bars, Taverns, Saloons, and Pubs; Germans; Wine Distribution and Sales

BIBLIOGRAPHY

The House of Glunz. http://thehouseofglunz.com/about-us.aspx.

Louis Glunz Wines. http://www.glunzwines.com/aboutglunzwines .html.

Viera, Laura. "Glunz Tavern to Reopen after 80 Years." *Crain's Chicago Business*. http://www.chicagobusiness.com/article/ 20120804/ISSUE03/308049986/glunz-tavern-on-tap-to-reopen -after-80-years.

Hull House

Chicago's most famous Settlement House (1889–1963), on Halsted Street near Polk Street on the Near West Side, was founded by Jane Addams with school friend Ellen Gates Starr in what had been a mansion built in 1856 by merchant Charles J. Hull. Like its neighborhood, the house had deteriorated; on either side were a saloon and an undertaker. But it satisfied Addams's desire—consistent with the new "settlement" concept—to move into the city among people needing help coping with the hard realities of life in an industrial town. On September 18, 1889, Hull House opened its doors.

The one building would become 13, providing a dining hall, women's residence, gymnasium, and schools. It was a community center that in any given week could welcome 2,000 people, many with nowhere else to go. (Benny Goodman played clarinet for the Hull House band.) It would serve waves of immigrants: Italians, Russian Jews, Greeks, and Poles and then Mexicans and African Americans migrating from the South.

Addams was influenced by the New Nutrition movement she learned about at the 1893 World's Fair. She installed a "healthy" soup kitchen for immigrant families, but it eventually failed because Italians, for example, liked their own cooking better.

The Hull House complex is mostly gone now, taken down in 1963 to make way for the University of Illinois' Chicago campus, but the restored mansion and dining hall remain, as the Hull House Museum.

Contributor: Alan Solomon

See also: Addams, Jane; Settlement Houses

BIBLIOGRAPHY

Commager, Henry Steele. Foreword to *Twenty Years at Hull-House*, by Jane Addams. New York: Signet Classics, 1961.

Grove, Lori, and Laura Kamedulski. *Chicago's Maxwell Street*. Mount Pleasant, S.C.: Arcadia Publishing, 2002.

Jones, Anita. "Conditions Surrounding Mexicans in Chicago," PhD dissertation, University of Chicago, 1928.

Hungarians

Hungarians began to immigrate to the Chicago area in the 1870s. The first Hungarians arrived escaping the Revolution of 1848 and were tradesmen and shopkeepers. Successive waves of immigrants arrived to work in the Chicago steel mills, to escape the Nazi invasion and Holocaust during World War II, and then to escape after the failed Revolution of 1956. Newcomers in the 1990s and the new millennium arrived to take advantage of economic opportunities.

Hungarians moved to the South Chicago, Burnside, West Pullman, and Roseland areas at first, congregating around parishes that catered to Hungarian immigrants. Over the course of the twentieth century, the traditional communities scattered and intermarried, with most Chicagoans of Hungarian descent now living in the western suburbs. The 2012 census registers almost 50,000 citizens of Hungarian descent in Illinois.

Hungarian food has not been as prominent in Chicago as in cities such as Cleveland or Toronto. Still, important Hungarian food and pastry stores such as Kenessey's, Lutz, Bende, and the Hungarian Kosher Supermarket (in Skokie), were and sometimes still are, fixtures. Hungarian cuisine is best known in Chicago for the ubiquitous "paprikash" (usually chicken) stew, and goulash, both served in non-Hungarian restaurants. Hungarian pastries (*dobosh*, *Esterhazy*, *kremes*), deservedly world famous, can be found at Café Lutz, Café Vienna, and Meinl, an Austrian pastry shop with Chicago locations.

Contributor: Clara Orban

BIBLIOGRAPHY

"Bende." http://www.bende.com/aboutus.php. Retrieved June 16, 2014.

"Hungarians." *Encyclopedia of Chicago*. http://www.encyclopedia.chicagohistory.org/pages/618.html.

Ice Cream

It is as American as apple pie. Ice cream was made in colonial America, churning machines having been owned by George Washington and Thomas Jefferson. By the time of Chicago's incorporation, ice cream was a staple of fine-dining menus, including that of the first freestanding restaurant, The Exchange Coffee House on Clark Street in 1844. Within the next decade freestanding ice-cream places had popped up nearby. One of the earliest mentions is a classified ad from May 28, 1853, in which "Mr. J. P. Heth would respectfully inform the citizens of Chicago that he has fitted up and opened his Soda Water and Ice Cream Saloon, for the reception of those who wish to imbibe the luxuries and delicacies the season affords . . . at No. 163 Randolph St." Five years later, on June 16, 1857, another ice-cream purveyor was using the weather as a reason to come on in: "COOLING—No matter how sultry the weather, the delicious ice cream at Anderson's, opposite the Court House, will make everything cool and pleasant."

Around the time of the 1893 World's Fair, a number of ice-cream parlors, or "Ladies' Cafes, "opened along State Street. Gunther's was a large cafe with counters running down both sides, opened by Charles F. Gunther, a candymaker. Plow's was another popular spot. In addition to ice cream, the cafes also sold special drinks, often with a good measure of alcohol, as in one concoction called the Yum Yum.

But by the turn of the twentieth century, ice-cream "saloons" were being viewed in a more sinister, and xenophobic, light. "The ordinary ice-cream parlor is very likely to be a spider's web for her entanglement," warned Ernest A. Bell in *Fighting the Traffic in Young Girls or War on the White Slave Trade*, published in 1910. He noted police reports of the day singled out ice-cream parlors as the scene of many tragedies. "The only safe rule is to keep away," he wrote.

Obviously, people did not steer clear of ice-cream parlors, in Chicago or elsewhere. A number of well-beloved vendors sprang up, such as Gertie's Ice Cream, which opened in 1901 on South Kedzie Ave. and is now teamed with Lindy's Chili in many locations on the South Side.

Also there was Petersen's Ice Cream, founded in 1919 in Oak Park; Gayety's Chocolates and Ice Cream Co., established in 1920 in South Chicago and now located

Ice cream vendor serving children on the South Side, ca. 1960. Courtesy of the Chicago History Museum, ICHi-85006; Pauline Campbell.

in Lansing and Schererville, Ind.; Margie's Candies at N. Western Ave. and W. Montrose Ave., opened in 1921; Oberweis Dairy, based in Aurora and launched in 1927, which makes ice cream and operates many ice-cream parlors in the Chicago area; Mitchell's Ice Cream of Homewood, founded in 1930 on Chicago's South Side; Homer's Homemade Gourmet Ice Cream, open since 1935 in Wilmette; and The Plush Horse, serving ice cream in Palos Park since 1937. One of the best-known spots for ice-cream cones was The Original Rainbow Cone, begun in 1926 on Western Avenue near 92d Street by Joseph and Katherine Sapp, who came up with a winning mix of many flavors layered in one large cone. One flavor was called Palmer House, named after the downtown hotel, combining vanilla ice cream with cherries and walnuts.

Newer operations featuring more artisanal ice creams have joined the scene. Among the notable are: Bobtail Ice Cream; Black Dog Gelato, with several locations; George's Ice Cream & Sweets on N. Clark St.; Lickity Split Frozen Custard & Sweets with spots on N. Broadway St. and N. Western Ave.

The Chicago area also has been home to ice-cream innovation. Soft-serve ice cream was invented by a father-and-son team living in Green River and first sold in Kankakee in 1938, which led to the opening of the first Dairy Queen store in Joliet in 1940. The American Dairy Queen Corporation is now a subsidiary of Berkshire Hathaway, Inc., and DQ franchises are found worldwide. Another Chicago success story is the Dove Bar, which was created in 1956 by Leo Stefanos, a South Side candy merchant. Dove Bars took off in the 1980s as Michael Stefanos,

the founder's son, joined others to expand operations from premium, hand-dipped bars sold in specialty stores to a wider distribution. DoveBar International, Inc., was acquired in 1986 by Mars Inc., the candy giant.

Contributor: Bill Daley

See also: Dove Bar; Gunther, Charles F.

BIBLIOGRAPHY

Borrelli, Christopher. "Ice Cream in Chicago Finally Raising Its Game, Thanks in Part to Emerging Artisans Who Craft the Delicious Dessert Staple with Spoonfuls of Love." *Chicago Tribune*, July 22, 2010.

Phillips, Richard. "Ice Creammakers Savor the Sweet Taste of Success." *Chicago Tribune*, June 19, 1986.

Weiss, Laura B. *Ice Cream: A Global History*. London: Reaktion Books, 2011.

Ice Houses

The primary contribution of ice to American cuisine was to prevent food from spoiling. The first companies began to cut ice from the Chicago River and other neighboring bodies of water during the 1840s. Breweries were the first customers for the city's ice industry, but as meatpacking grew in importance, its demand for ice outpaced all other users.

While Gustavus Swift became rich, setting up icing stations on the route between Chicago and the East Coast, packers of all kinds needed ice to do business during the warm summer months before reliable mechanical refrigeration appeared in the 1890s. Pork packers could keep their facilities operating at full capacity year-round. Beef packers used ice in summer to cure the cattle they slaughtered before preserving them with salt. By ensuring that fresh meat would not go bad, this innovation made it possible for Chicago to develop as the center of meatpacking for America.

Chicago's residential ice trade grew like those in other cities around the country during the nineteenth century. As the city's population grew, ice companies that delivered to homes had to go further and further away to find sources of ice that were not tainted by pollution. By the late 1870s, much of Chicago's ice came by rail from as far away as northern Wisconsin. The ice, cut into large blocks, was shipped packed with wood shavings, sawdust, or straw between and around the blocks. Within ice houses, large, dark, well-sealed rooms kept the blocks, still insulated in their packing, through the summer months, typically until November. While industrial users could employ tainted local ice because it never touched the food, residential consumers preferred ice that appeared clean and therefore pure. Ice houses were once common features of the city.

Competition between these two kinds of customers and the long trip from Wisconsin meant that Chicago tended to have higher ice prices than the rest of the country. When the national Ice Trust bought out many Chicago firms during the 1890s, prices stayed high. Local equipment firms began making ice-making machines, which ultimately destroyed the natural ice industry during World War I. These machines would, in turn, become obsolete after the development of household refrigeration during the 1920s.

Contributor: Jonathan Rees
See also: Refrigeration

BIBLIOGRAPHY

Duis, Perry R., and Glen E. Holt. "Cold Times in the Ice Trade." *Chicago Magazine*, August 1979, 82–84.

Rees, Jonathan. *Refrigeration Nation: A History of Ice Appliances and Enterprise in America.* Baltimore: The Johns Hopkins University Press, 2013.

Irish

"Bland" might be the word most often used to describe a typical Irish meal of potatoes, boiled meat, potatoes, and more potatoes. In fairness, though, the Irish seldom learned to cook, in large part because they barely had access to food. From the seventeenth century until the early twentieth century, much of the land in Ireland was owned by absentee English landlords. Cash crops produced by native tenant farmers were mostly sent back to England. Even the fish in the streams were off limits. That is why the Irish lived on potatoes—they were easy to grow and, being mostly starch, filled the bellies of hard-working

peasants. When a recurring blight destroyed potato crops in the middle 1800s, the Irish, with no food left to eat, died or emigrated by the millions. In just 15 years, the Irish population dropped by 30 percent.

Many Irish immigrants landed in Chicago, lured first by the promise of a burgeoning midwestern city and then, after the Great Fire, by the seemingly endless opportunities rebuilding that city. Unlike many other immigrant groups who arrived with little to no English, the Irish were able to move quickly into the ranks of public service and leadership positions through the late 1800s and into the 1900s.

Today, more than 200,000 Chicagoans identify themselves as Irish or Irish American, according to the *U.S. Census American Community Survey*. While the Irish are distributed across the city and suburbs, the two main communities often are described as being "North Side" and "South Side."

Because Irish immigrants left behind little but famine and starvation, the idea of "traditional Irish" food never played a role in most Irish American households. Irish immigrants often desired nothing more than simple, filling meals of meat and, of course, potatoes. Certain Chicago public houses in the 1900s became popular with the Irish community, not just because of such filling cuisine, but also because of their Irish or Irish American management.

In the 1960s and 1970s, South Side places such as the Glendora House, founded by Mike Keane of Glendora, County Clare, and Fox's, founded in 1964 by first-generation Irish Americans Therese and Tom Fox, regularly catered to an Irish clientele but served standard American food. Fox's has expanded over the years to six locations on the South Side and south suburbs and often features live Irish music. Still, their menu contains only passing

GREEN BEER AND A GREEN RIVER

In Chicago, everyone is Irish on St. Paddy's Day, at least gauging by the often rowdy activity of every neighborhood bar, tavern, and pub. From Fadó to The Kerryman, from The Curragh to Poag Mahone's, Irish and honorary Irish alike dine on corned beef and cabbage, Irish stew, colcannon, and Irish soda bread—and of course, drink green beer.

The Feast of Saint Patrick (Lá Fhéile Pádraig), patron saint of Ireland, is traditionally celebrated each year on March 17, the date attributed to his death. In Chicago, as elsewhere, it is both a religious and cultural celebration, but only in Ireland is it a national holiday. After all, Saint Patrick did rid the Emerald Isle of snakes with just his trusty wooden staff.

As part of the cultural nature of the holiday, "the wearing o' the green" is traditional. In Chicago, green is taken to the next level with the dyeing of the Chicago River, which happens the Saturday of or before March 17. The nontoxic formula for the green dye itself is the well-kept secret of the Chicago Journeymen Plumbers (Local 130 U.A.), who dye the river each year. Mysteriously, the dye appears orange when first distributed, and then the river slowly turns a bright emerald green to the cheers of tens of thousands of Chicagoans gathered along the river's edge.

—JULIE CHERNOFF

references to their Irish heritage with items such as "Irish nachos" and "Paddy melt."

In the 1990s, interest in Irish cultural traditions exploded with the worldwide success of the dance and music show "Riverdance" (starring Chicago's own Michael Flatley, whose family owned a pub for many years on South Western Ave.). Since that time, several restaurants and pubs have expanded their Irish concept beyond their name to include more traditional fare in their menus.

Chicago establishments where Irish classics are likely to be found include Chief O'Neill's Pub and Restaurant and The Abbey Pub, both in the Avondale neighborhood; The Galway Arms in Lincoln Park; Fado, downtown; Mrs. Murphy's Irish Bistro in North Center; and the Curragh, with locations on the Northwest Side and in the suburbs. Other suburban outposts of quintessentially Irish fare include The Kerry Piper in Willowbrook, The Irish Times in Brookfield, and Tommy Nevins' Pub, with locations in Evanston, Naperville, and Frankfort.

Two main Irish cultural institutions serve as meeting places for Chicago's North Side and South Side Irish populations. Located in a refurbished Chicago public school, the Irish American Heritage Center in Mayfair hosts Irish cultural events and dinners along with food in the pub. On the Far South Side, Gaelic Park in Tinley Park also offers food, drink, and cultural events, along with traditional Irish sporting competitions such as Gaelic football.

Not surprisingly, given the dearth of true Irish cuisine, the fare in all of these establishments includes many of the same dishes. The food is heavy on meat and potatoes, with occasional fish dishes (fish and chips and lots of salmon, partly because of its general popularity among American diners but also because it is plentiful in Irish rivers). Oysters and mussels are common, owing to their abundance in the waters off Ireland's coasts.

Other popular dishes associated with Irish cuisine include bangers and mash (mild pork sausages served over mashed potatoes), beef and Guinness stew (classic beef stew is made Irish with the addition of Guinness stout, a night-black porter brewed in Dublin), bridies (ground, seasoned meat encased in a pastry crust, found more often at festivals than in pubs and restaurants), shepherd's pie (casserole-style dish of ground meat in a savory sauce over cooked carrots and peas, topped with mashed potatoes), and soda bread. Corned beef and cabbage, perhaps the single dish most associated with the Irish, is not an Irish dish. The Irish would have eaten bacon and cabbage instead, using bacon cured from the loin rather than the belly. In Ireland, beef typically was costlier than pork. Irish immigrants started using corned beef when

bacon, prohibited by kosher laws, was not available in Jewish delis in crowded New York.

While many Irish emigrated with few yearnings for native foodstuffs, there are items that Irish transplants still crave. Barry's Tea, Bird's Custard (a powdered, egg-free custard mix), and McCann's Irish Oatmeal are just a few items that, through globalization and relaxed trade regulations, now are available at many chain grocers, but once were available only through Irish importer shops. For years, places such as The Irish Shop in suburban Oak Park and Gaelic Imports on West Gunnison, were the only options for homesick immigrants to find the flavors of home.

While items such as tea and powdered custard travel well, meat is harder to transport across the ocean. Fortunately, Chicago boasts two sausage factories that produce, among other things, traditional "bangers" that are beloved across Ireland. Since 1967, Winston's Sausages on the South Side, founded by County Roscommon, Ireland, native, Michael Winston Sr., has been providing sausages, corned beef, black and white puddings, and other Irish foods to patrons yearning for a taste of home. In 1983, Galway native John Diamond began a wholesale sausage business, and his products are available in many restaurants and groceries.

At the start of the third millennium, Irish food is not difficult to find in Chicago. Truthfully, however, as food influences from around the world find their way into restaurant kitchens across Ireland, Ireland's cuisine is changing, and it's quite possible that Irish food in Chicago is as much Chicago as it is Irish.

....

Contributor: James P. DeWan

See also: Bars, Taverns, Saloons, and Pubs

BIBLIOGRAPHY

Diner, Hasia, R. *Hungering for America: Italian, Irish and Jewish Foodways in the Age of Migration*. Boston: Harvard University Press, 2003.

"Irish." *Encyclopedia of Chicago*. http://www.encyclopedia.chicago history.org/pages/652.html.

Italian Beef

The Italian Beef sandwich, or simply "beef," is an iconic dish for Chicagoans. It enjoys enormous popularity as a quick meal in fast-food restaurants throughout the area, most particularly in "beef stands." It also is commonly featured in buffet-style meals at celebratory gatherings, such as birthday parties, either catered by restaurants or prepared at home. Italian beef is also offered at lunch in many sit-down restaurants, especially those featuring Italian American food.

GIARDINIERA

Order a "Beef, hot" and chances are your sandwich will be topped with a few spoonfuls of a spicy vegetable relish. Though giardiniera isn't unique to Chicago—it's often called *giardiniera sottaceto* in Italy—the condiment has established a foothold here like nowhere else in the country, largely because of its association with Italian beef. Most recipes call for chopped vegetables—often including fresh green chilies (sometimes supplemented with crushed dried red peppers), celery, cauliflower, or carrots—to be salt brined or pickled in vinegar and then submerged in vegetable oil. Variations abound: some versions are fresh and crunchy while others are fermented and softer; texture can be chunky or fine; and heat levels range from mild to challenging. Many beef stands prepare their own giardiniera, but plenty of locally packed brands can be found. A well-stocked supermarket or Italian delicatessen might carry a dozen or more varieties.

—PETER ENGLER

Both the method of cooking the meat and the manner of serving the sandwich are essential to the authenticity of a proper "beef." The meat typically is seasoned with dry herbs (oregano, basil) and spices (red pepper, black pepper, sometimes nutmeg or cloves) and fresh garlic or garlic powder. Then it is roasted slowly, partially submerged in beef stock. Once cooked, the beef is cooled to facilitate slicing; then the thinly sliced meat is bathed in the reheated broth and cooking juices (called au jus, juice, or gravy). To form the sandwiches, forkfuls of the soaked beef are placed inside French bread (cut lengthwise). According to individual preferences, a ladleful of juice may be added (thus served "wet") or the entire sandwich may be plunged into the juice to soak the bread thoroughly ("dipped"). The traditional additions are hot peppers (*giardiniera*) and/or sweet peppers (fried or roasted mild bell peppers). The best beef stands prepare the meat and condiments in-house. Beef sandwiches are often eaten along with French fries: many well-regarded stands offer freshly cut, twice-fried potatoes.

Variants of the sandwich include the "combo": a normal beef to which is added a link of grilled Italian sausage; "cheesy beef": a normal beef with slices of low-moisture mozzarella or provolone added; "gravy bread" or "soaker": the bread served without the beef, wet or dipped; and "potato sandwich": meatless, filled with French fries and dressed with juice.

The bread used for beef sandwiches is the type that old Italian bakeries in Chicago called "French bread" and is distinguished from basic Italian bread in having a longer, narrower shape, thinner crust, and a softer, hole-less crumb. Small- and large-scale Italian bakeries (Turano, Gonnella, and D'Amato's) are favored sources for this bread.

Though some businesses claim to have invented Italian beef (Al's, Scala), its origins clearly lie in Italian American home cooking. The key stage in the development of the sandwich was its use in so-called "peanut weddings" (attested from the 1920s). Working-class Italian American families would rent halls and supply their own food for the event, commonly including roasted peanuts and sandwiches filled with slices of wet-roasted beef. Given the volume of food required for such gatherings, families would prepare the beef and often take it to a local Italian bakery for cooking in a large oven, with the bakery supplying the bread. Similar weddings were common elsewhere (New York's Italian "football weddings" with sub sandwiches), but beef sandwiches are specific to Chicago. Out of this peanut wedding tradition emerged the beef stand business before World War II, mainly in the Taylor Street neighborhood. Parallel to the pizza business, beef stands proliferated greatly after the war, soon gaining popularity outside the Italian American community.

Contributors: Anthony F. Buccini and Michael Stern
See also: Fast Food/Quick Service; Italians

BIBLIOGRAPHY

Gentile, Maria. *The Italian Cookbook. The Art of Eating Well; Practical Recipes from the Italian Cuisine.* London: Forgotten Books, 2012 [orig. 1919].

"ItalianBeef.com FAQ's, Here Are Facts, Trivia & Knowledge about Italian Beef!" http://www.italianbeef.com/faq.php.

Italian Ice

Italian Ice, a sweetened frozen dessert made from sugar, water, and fruit (juices, concentrates, or purees), may use artificial colors or flavors. Similar in consistency to sorbet rather than ice cream, it is made by freezing ingredients while mixing them. Italian Ice usually comes in fruit flavors such as lemon, lime, orange, strawberry, cherry, raspberry, and watermelon.

Italian Ice developed from the Italian granita frozen dessert, also a mixture of water, usually fruit flavors, and sugar. Granita has a more crystalline texture than Italian Ice, but varies from region to region in Italy. Native to Sicily, granita is now common in all of Italy. Given the large Sicilian immigration to Chicago, granita morphed into Italian Ice in the early part of the twentieth century.

Italian Ice is associated primarily with Italian street vendors in the Little Italy neighborhood on Taylor Street. It then became common in other establishments such as Italian beef joints. Italian Ice is also available commercially, with notable brands such as Wyler's, Luigi's, and Mazzone (which is made in Chicago). One of Chicago's best-known Italian Ice stands is Mario's, 1066 W. Taylor St., still in the "old neighborhood." But Mario will not let you call it "ice": it is "Italian lemonade." Other places that specialize in Italian Ice: Johnny's Beef in Elmwood Park, Carm's Beef and Italian Ice, and Anthony's Italian Ice.

Contributor: Clara Orban

See also: Italians

Italians

Chicagoans of Italian descent make up one of the largest ethnic sectors of the population of the city and suburbs and have influenced the city's food landscape commensurate to their presence. According to the latest census, Illinois citizens of Italian ethnicity are just more than 800,000. Italian food is among the most prevalent and prized in Chicago, with pizza, pasta, and other dishes part of the culinary landscape. This has been true practically since the arrival of the first Italians.

Italy is a patchwork of regional identities with sharp contrasts between those in the north and those in the south. The first Italian immigrants to Chicago came from the Liguria region in the northwest, mainly escaping the aftermath of Italian Unification in the late 1860s. Italian immigration increased dramatically during the end of the nineteenth and beginning of the twentieth century as economic difficulties drove Italians to emigrate to North or South America. But subsequent Italian immigration to Chicago was largely from southern Italy, Naples, Calabria, Bari, and Sicily in particular. After World War II, Tuscans and other Central and Northern Europeans arrived, escaping the ravages of war in their native areas.

In 1920, with 60,000 strong, Chicago had the third largest Italian population in the country, behind New York and Philadelphia. Italians created the Little Italy neighborhood around Taylor Street. Churches, shops, and benevolent societies all catered to the Italian population. During the early years of the twentieth century, one could grow up in Chicago speaking only Italian in these areas. Little Italy has largely disappeared after the controversial building of the University of Illinois at Chicago campus in the 1960s. Migration to the suburbs had already begun, and it increased rapidly as the land in the area was appropriated for the campus. An area along Harlem near Grand Avenue in Chicago and Elmwood Park became heavily Italian and

remains so. However, some Italian businesses continued in the Taylor Street area, and it still is considered "Little Italy."

The Italian communities encountered difficulties from the German and Irish populations already established in the city. Italians formed societies for protection and for work opportunities. Many workers were exploited by "bosses" or "padroni," who forced them to give up a portion of their wages for protection. This hearkened back to a quasi-feudal system still in force at that time in many areas of southern Italy. Jane Addams's efforts to materially help and integrate immigrants into American life were strongly focused on the women in the nearby Italian community.

With Prohibition, Italians again were under suspicion, because the Italian Mafia wrested control of underworld activities from the Jewish and Irish gangs that had dominated the city. Even today, Chicago often is associated with its gangster (aka Italian Mafia) past with the likes of Alfonse "Al" Capone being the most notable. Italian Americans also came under suspicion during World War II because of their presumed ties to the fascist motherland. Eventually, Italians became part of the fabric of the city and one of the most prominent and important ethnic groups in the area. One means of acceptance was food.

Italian food has penetrated American culture, becoming Italian American in the process. It has continued to be the top-selling "ethnic" food in the United States. Italian American cuisine was created by the first immigrants largely from southern Italy. Americans became very familiar with the food evolved from the southern Italian cuisine, which became synonymous with "Italian food." Dishes such as spaghetti and meatballs smothered in tomato sauce and eggplant Parmesan became well known in Chicago restaurants. Fresh Italian sausages leapt from Italian butcher shops to supermarket meat counters everywhere. One of the top-selling foods in the United States is pizza, and the popular deep-dish pizza is peculiarly Chicagoan. Italian pizza made in Italy (and New York) is thin crust. Chicago's deep-dish and stuffed versions are spin-offs, with thicker crusts and more toppings than Italian pizza. Other influences can be seen in the Italian beef stands and the ice stands dotting the city. Italian Ice, reminiscent of Italian granita, now has become common in supermarkets.

Today, many Italian restaurants all over Chicago feature this "old school," Italian American cuisine, but changes came starting in the late twentieth century: Italian cuisine in Chicago and the United States underwent a transformation. Menus more typical of northern regions were featured at restaurants owned and operated by immigrated Italian chefs or Italian-trained American chefs. Award-winning restaurants, such as the Loop's Italian Village or the upscale Spiaggia in Chicago's Gold Coast, offer dishes with artisanal ingredients, homemade pasta, and touches common to cities such as Bologna or Parma in Emilia-Romagna.

Alpe Foods and Conte di Savoia market provide Italian-style breads and imported products. Caputo Food Store, which began as a small storefront in Elmwood Park, has expanded its locations to Chicago and other suburbs. Initially a store that provided Italian imported foods, it now has wide selections of ethnic products from Poland, Mexico, and other parts of the world that reflect its diverse customer base. Racconto is a Melrose Park Italian importer that featured foods from founder Andrea Mugnolo's home city of Naples. Begun in 1973 as a small business, it now has national distribution of its pasta, olive oils, canned tomatoes, and more. More recently, modern Italian shops have arrived, such as Convito Italiano in Wilmette and Eataly, the Italian-based megastore and dining emporium that counts Mario Batali as a partner.

Italian pride manifests itself in numerous festivals and traditions, including the Columbus Day Parade in October. Chicago's St. Donatus festival in Blue Island has been a major gathering of Italians, with pizza bread and cannoli among the culinary highlights. Melrose Park, with its large Italian population, hosts an Italian Festival of Our Lady of Mt. Carmel, with delicacies such as *arancini* and *pizzette* on the menu.

Contributor: Clara Orban
See also: Italian Beef; Italian Ice; Pizza

BIBLIOGRAPHY

Italian American Women's Club. *Italian-American Women of Chicagoland*. Chicago: Arcadia Publishing, 2003.
"Italians." *Encyclopedia of Chicago*. http://www.encyclopedia.chicago history.org/pages/658.html.
Nelli, Humbert S. *Italians in Chicago. A Study in Ethnic Mobility 1880–1930*. New York: Oxford University Press, 1973.

Izard, Stephanie

The first woman to win Bravo's TV competition "Top Chef" (in 2007), Izard was born in Evanston, Illinois, in 1978, grew up in Stamford, Connecticut, and studied at the University of Michigan and Le Cordon Bleu College of Culinary Arts in Scottsdale, Arizona. Returning to Chicago in 2001, she worked under chefs such as Jean-Georges Vongerichten at Vong and Sean McClain at Spring. In 2004, she opened her first restaurant, Scylla, with a menu emphasizing seafood. It closed in 2007.

In mid 2010, Izard opened Girl & the Goat, 809 W. Randolph St., with partners Rob Katz and Kevin Boehm of BOKA Restaurant Group. The 130-seat restaurant features "nose-to-tail" cooking, which uses all parts of an animal. Characteristic dishes include goat belly confit and panfried duck tongues with pickled watermelon rind. In 2012, she opened Little Goat Diner, featuring a bakery, deli sandwiches, and all-day breakfasts. She won the James Beard Award for Best Chef: Great Lakes in 2013. In March 2016, Izard opened a Chinese-inspired restaurant, Duck Duck Goat, on the newly gentrified W. Fulton St. (The "goat" in the restaurants' names comes from her surname, Izard, a breed of Pyrenees goat.)

Contributor: Colleen Sen
See also: Chefs; Restaurateurs and Restaurant Groups

BIBLIOGRAPHY

Bowen, Dana. "Girl & the Goat: Architect of Flavor." *Saveur*, February 24, 2011.
Walker, Cassie. "Stephanie Izard on the Girl & the Goat, Top Chef, and More." *Chicago Magazine*, April 2010.

Japanese

Japanese emigration to the United States was sparked by the country's Meiji Restoration of 1868 and the Chinese Exclusion Act of 1882, both of which saw Japanese immigrants landing in Chicago and other cities by way of Hawaii and the West Coast. During the World War II internment of Japanese Americans, more than 100,000 on the West Coast were forcibly transferred to camps. Chicago played a unique role as home to the first field office of the War Relocation Authority, which helped Japanese

Americans transition out of the camps. Some 30,000 Japanese Americans were relocated to Chicago.

Of the 2010 census' estimated 1.3 million Japanese Americans in the United States, Illinois counts about 28,500, mostly spread among Chicago's metro and suburban areas. Pockets of Chicago's Japanese American population live on the city's North Side in neighborhoods including Edgewater, Lakeview, and Uptown, and in the northwest suburbs, including Arlington Heights, Skokie, and Hoffman Estates. Arlington Heights is home to a community of Japanese expatriate businessmen and their families and is the site of the Midwest's largest Japanese supermarket, Mitsuwa, which has eight other locations in California and New Jersey. Mitsuwa is primarily known for Japanese supermarket provisions, but also boasts an impressive food court, serving a variety of traditional Japanese foods such as noodles, tempura, and sushi.

Chicagoans' first experience of Japanese food came at the Columbian Exposition of 1893 when cups of tea and rice cakes were served at the Japanese teahouse. One of the city's first Japanese restaurants was Mrs. Shintani's at 3725 Lake Park Ave., which specialized in sukiyaki. Sukiyaki, prepared tableside, was the most popular Japanese dish in Chicago before the arrival of sushi. Customers included the Crown Prince and Princess of Japan, who visited Chicago during their honeymoon. In 1939, Mrs. Futaba opened a Japanese restaurant on Oak Street that served special fish dinners "marinated in an exotic sauce." Other early restaurants were Wisteria Tea Room on Ohio Street, opened in the mid 1940s, and the elegant Naka-No-Ya on Lincoln Park West, which had sushi on its menu, prepared tableside. In 1967, Marion Konishi opened Kamehachi of Tokyo on Wells St. in Old Town, perhaps the first in the city to serve mainly sushi. It moved further south on Wells and, by 2014, had four other locations in the city and suburbs. By the early 1970s, Chicago had a half-dozen sushi bars. In 1980, Hatsuhana, part of a New York chain, opened on East Ontario Street and garnered glowing reviews for its well-prepared sushi.

Another category of restaurant, Japanese steak houses, featured knife-wielding chefs preparing steak and other dishes at tables or counters equipped with grill tops where seated diners watched. Ron of Japan and New York–based Benihana of Tokyo both opened branches in downtown Chicago in the late 1960s and later expanded to the suburbs.

Sushi restaurants are ubiquitous in Chicago and suburbs. It seems every neighborhood in the city has a small storefront devoted to the popular Japanese raw-fish specialty. Many are run by Japanese chefs. Some, especially in northwest Chicago, are owned by Koreans, and many Thai restaurants also offer sushi. American chefs, too, are following the sushi craze.

Chicago's oldest operating sushi bar is Kamehachi on Wells Street, which opened in 1967. Hashikin on Clark near Fullerton opened in the early 1970s. By the end of the decade, Chicago had half a dozen sushi bars, including Hashikin, Happi Sushi Kabuki, Kamehachi, Mikado, and Tokyo.

As sushi-grade fish became more available, the quality of sushi in the city rose. Today's standout sushi spots include Katsu in Rogers Park (opened in 2006), which specializes in super premium sashimi; West Town's Arami (2010), well known for its ramen as well as sushi and nigiri; and relative newcomer Kai Zan in Humboldt Park (2012), which offers a traditional *omakase* (chef's choice) tasting menu. Inventive, Americanized takes on sushi rolls are the specialty at the city's popular trifecta of Coast Sushi restaurants, established in the early 2000s. Wicker Park's seminal Mirai (opened in 1999), known for its sushi as well as its modern Japanese entrees, expanded in 2014 to the Gold Coast. And the newer Juno on N. Lincoln Ave. rated a 3-star review by the *Chicago Tribune*.

Another well-known restaurant, Takashi—the eponymous fine-dining restaurant of *Top Chef Masters* alum Takashi Yagihashi—closed in early 2015 after eight years and multiple Michelin stars. Yagihashi's casual comfort food restaurant, Slurping Turtle (established 2011), continues to operate in downtown Chicago and Ann Arbor, Michigan. He also owns Noodles By Takashi (at Macy's) and Tabo Sushi (Plum Market) in Chicago.

One popular, fine-dining restaurant was Japonais (established 2003), located on the North Branch of the Chicago River in the old Montgomery Ward warehouse. It was revamped and reopened in 2014 as Japonais By Morimoto, under renown celebrity *Iron Chef* Masaharu Morimoto but then closed in 2015.

A more recent notable addition to the city's Japanese dining scene is chef Matthias Merges, an alum of Charlie Trotter's, who opened Yusho in Logan Square in late 2011.

Japanese American Grocery Store in Chicago, 1949. Courtesy of the Japanese American Service Committee Legacy Center in Chicago, Ill.

Following the Japanese *yakitoriya* tavern model, Yusho specializes in sharable skewered plates and a full drink menu of sake, beer, and cocktails. Two more locations of Yusho opened in 2014: one in Las Vegas, and a second Chicago location in Hyde Park. Momotaro opened in 2014 and included three floors of dining on West Lake Street, offering sushi, tempura, and grilled foods in a basement tavern.

Tavern-style dining coincided with a surge in ramen shops citywide, including Japanese chain Ramen Misoya (opened in Mount Prospect in 2013) and local restaurateur Brendan Sodikoff's High Five Ramen (opened in West Loop in 2014).

Sushi restaurants round out Chicagoland's Japanese offerings, many of which include a handful of pan-Asian entrees on their menus as well.

Contributors: Lauren Viera and Colleen Sen

BIBLIOGRAPHY

Kramer, Julia. "Best Japanese Restaurants in Chicago." *Time Out Chicago*, July 22, 2013. http://www.timeout.com/chicago/restaurants/best-japanese-restaurants-in-chicago-sushi-ramen-and-more.

Loring, Kay, "Japanese Restaurants—Tea Rooms to Sushi Bars." *Chicago Tribune*, February 7, 1971.

"A Portrait of Japanese Americans in the Chicago Metropolitan Area." Chicago Japanese American Historical Society. http://www.cjahs.org/CJAHSDiscoverNikkeiCensus2000.pdf.

Jays Potato Chips

The jingle "Can't stop eating 'em!" has powered the classic chip and its assorted crunchy cousins for a good part of Jays Foods, Inc.'s history and kept its snacks in midwestern fans' hands for almost 90 years. The company was founded in 1927 by Leonard Japp, a Minnesota native who rode the rails to Chicago and then worked a variety of jobs (as a steeplejack and a lifeguard at Oak Street Beach alongside Johnny Weissmuller, for example) before teaming up with George Gavora to sell snacks to the city's speakeasies from a truck.

Initially, they sold snacks such as pretzels and nuts, but when customers requested potato chips, they added chips to their snack line. They used several potato chip suppliers until 1940 when they opened their first manufacturing plant in Chicago and called their snack Mrs. Japp's Potato Chips. Following the 1941 Pearl Harbor attack, anti-Japanese sentiment prompted a name change.

By 1950, the company had come up with their slogan: "Can't stop eating 'em!" O-ke-doke (ready-to-eat popcorn) and Krunchers (kettle-cooked snacks) were added to the line. The company changed hands several times during its history and closed its Chicago manufacturing plant in December 2007. It is currently owned by Snyder's-Lance, a Charlotte, North Carolina, company, which continues the snack tradition with a dozen Jays Potato Chip iterations, plus Krunchers! (eight varieties) and O-ke-doke (seven flavor variations).

Culinary credit must be given to Japp's wife Eugenia. She insisted Leonard put a recipe on the package and gave him her recipe for tuna fish casserole topped with potato chips.

Contributor: Judy Hevrdejs

BIBLIOGRAPHY

Gorman, John. "Jays Founder Japp Wasn't Always in the Chips." *Chicago Tribune*, November 25, 1985.

Mueller, Jim. "Still Chipper at 92: Meet Leonard Japp Sr., the Man Who Dreamed Up Jays Potato Chips." *Chicago Tribune*, October 13, 1996.

Jeppson's Malort

This notoriously bitter, amber-colored, wormwood-based liqueur is descended from Swedish *besk*, or bitters that are commonly taken as digestive aids. In the late 1930s, Chicago attorney George Brode purchased a recipe from Swedish immigrant Carl Jeppson, and began marketing the spirit on its powerful malignance. "Are you man enough to drink our two-fisted liquor?" read one of Brode's advertisements. Over the years it grew in popularity among Chicago's Polish and Latino communities and in dive bars, where it was frequently taken in shots as a test of one's capacity for suffering or poured as a prank for unsuspecting drinkers.

In the early part of the twenty-first century it began to achieve cult status among a young generation of Chicago bartenders and drinkers, who began experimenting with it in complicated cocktails or creating their own *besk*-style liqueurs. Some taverns, such as Logan Square's Scofflaw, began offering it on tap. Jeppson's, which is made from dried wormwood macerated in grain neutral alcohol, is produced in Florida, but throughout much of its existence it was sold only in Chicago and surrounding suburbs. As its popularity grew, it began appearing in other cities, such as Milwaukee and Washington D.C.

Contributor: Mike Sula

See also: Cocktails and Cocktail Lounges

BIBLIOGRAPHY

Sula, Mike, "Shot of Malort, Hold the Grimace." *Chicago Reader*, April 9, 2009. http://www.chicagoreader.com/chicago/shot-of-malort-hold-the-grimace/Content?oid=1098569.

Jewel-Osco

Frank Rossi and his brother-in-law Frank Skiff founded the Jewel Tea Company in 1899 with $700 and a secondhand buggy and wagon. They sold tea, coffee, and groceries

A Jewel store's self-serve meat case, 1950s. Courtesy of Jewel-Osco.

door to door. By 1915, the company had 850 routes and $8 million in annual sales. In the 1930s, the company moved from Chicago to Barrington, Illinois, and continued to grow and expand through the 1950s, merging a separate unit of grocery stores called Jewel Foods with Jewel Tea Company and introducing a catalogue mail service.

In its expansion in the 1960s, Jewel bought Osco Pharmacies and became Jewel-Osco, combining these stores under one roof in the 1980s. American Stores, based in Salt Lake City, Utah, purchased Jewel in 1984. In turn, the privately held Boise, Idaho, grocery company, Albertson Inc., took over in 1999.

Jewel-Osco, consisting of 185 stores, had approximately 45 percent of the Chicago market by 2010. Jewel has been credited as the first chain to offer generic brands, in 1977. In 2008, Jewel opened a LEED certified store in Chicago at Kinzie Street and DesPlaines Avenue, complete with rooftop garden. Jewel-Osco's midwestern operations are headquartered in Itasca, Illinois.

Contributor: Geraldine Rounds
See also: Grocery Stores

BIBLIOGRAPHY

http://www.encyclopedia.chicagohistory.org/pages/2727.html.
Jewel-Osco. www.jewelosco.com.

Jews

The first Jew documented to have settled in a small outpost situated on the shores of Lake Michigan, which later became the city of Chicago, was German-born Morris (Moritz) Baumgarten. Arriving in 1832, he worked as a carpenter. A decade later, large numbers of other German-speaking Jews, called the '48ers, made their way west to Chicago. They were economic, social, political, and ideological refugees, primarily from South, West, and Central Germany—Bavaria, Bohemia, and Austria-Hungary—fleeing the aftermath of the failed 1848 revolution. Not all were observant Jews and did not maintain all of their ages-old religious customs and practices. To Reform Jews, who comprised 90 percent of the German Jews in the United States at that time, strict observance of dietary laws epitomized an archaic orthodoxy. They wanted to blend in and acculturate to American society; if this meant they had to eat nonkosher American foods and cook American dishes to accomplish those goals—except perhaps around the big Jewish holidays—then they would do that.

On the other hand, they maintained their German cultural ties and language long after settling in the city. Except for their religion, not much distinguished them from their gentile German neighbors. In many cases, especially among the Reform Jews, not even their foodways were very different; after all, they were German. A Friday dinner table might have chicken soup, roast goose or chicken, roasted potatoes, cabbage, and good German breads. It would also have German-style pastries and tortes such as *lebkuchen* (a light pastry with caramel sauce).

Eastern European Jews arrived in droves during the latter nineteenth century. Unlike their German coreligionists, they had no particular national ties. They had never been considered true citizens of any specific country no matter how long their families had lived within the borders of the various eastern European regions from which they eventually emigrated. Their common language was Yiddish, and their identity was strongly tied to their shared religion. While they sought to become good Americans, they seemed determined to maintain the customs and traditions of Judaism, a way of life and a culture—which some refer to as "Jewishness"—that had set them apart from others for centuries. It was their culinary traditions and foods that have come to be identified in America's collective mind as "Jewish." Bagels, bialys, sour rye bread, challah, chicken soup, matzo balls, kneidlach (dumplings), kugels (noodle or potato puddings, either savory or sweet), potato latkes fried in schmaltz (pancakes cooked in rendered chicken fat), gefilte fish, pickled herring, and lox are dishes that have become familiar to American diners.

Like the Eastern European Ashkenazi Jews, the bulk of Chicago's small number of Sephardi, mostly from Syria, Persia, and Turkey, arrived between the 1890s and the First World War. These Jews, never numbering more than 4 percent of the Jewish population in the city, also placed their roots in their religion and their practice of

THE MEANING OF KOSHER

Kosher, meaning *proper* or *right*, refers to articles of food that are permitted to Jews and have been prepared in accordance with the dietary laws (kashruth) laid down in the Hebrew bible and expanded by rabbinical commentary. The laws are complex, but generally prohibit the consumption of blood and certain categories of animals (including pigs and fish without scales), and the combination of meat and dairy products in a dish or meal. Animals must be slaughtered in a humane fashion under rabbinical supervision.

There are four kosher certifying agencies in Chicago, each with its own symbol that is placed on qualifying food products.

The largest and best known nationally is the Chicago Rabbinical Council. It offers a wide variety of Jewish services including kosher supervision of many products.

In Chicago's West Ridge neighborhood, which has one of the largest orthodox communities in the country, the local Jewel supermarket has an extensive kosher section under the supervision of an in-store rabbi. Dozens of restaurants in the Chicago area serve only kosher food, including a sushi bar and a barbecue restaurant.

—BRUCE KRAIG

it. Multinational and multilingual by culture and practice, instead of speaking German or Yiddish as did most of the Ashkenazi, many Sephardic Jews spoke, wrote, and prayed in Ladino. Their religious practices, somewhat different from the German and Eastern European Jews, also set them apart. In general, they tended to form groups according to the countries from which they came. Their culinary traditions included many dairy dishes as well as the use of spices unfamiliar to Northern or Central Europeans.

In the aftermath of World War II, thousands of Jewish refugees seeking a better life free from persecution settled in the area, bringing with them culinary traditions from Greece, Northern Africa, and Europe. More recently, Middle Eastern Jews, oftentimes lumped together with the Sephardi, have swelled the numbers of Chicago's Jews to

Postcard of shoppers on Halsted Street in the Jewish neighborhood ca. 1905. Courtesy of Lake County (Ill.) Discovery Museum, Curt Teich Postcard Archives.

Section of a supermarket catering to religious and cultural heritages. Photograph by Colleen Sen.

a total population of just more than a quarter of a million, second only to New York.

Those who kept to Jewish dietary laws (*kashrut*) had no hardships finding what they needed to prepare meals in Chicago. Large, commercial meatpackers headquartered at the Union Stock Yards, such as Swift, Armour, and Wilson, all provided kosher meats to kosher butchers and, thence, to their customers. Fresh poultry from farms outside the city limits was readily available. Milk, direct from bottling plants or kosher-run dairies, was delivered to their doors daily, or even picked up from the Pure Milk stations that dotted the Near West Side. Inexpensive flour of wheat, corn, rice, or other grains was easily found in stores. In nineteenth-century Chicago, Jewish matzo bakers did a good business meeting the demand for the crackers required during the feast of Passover (and eaten year-round). The city's South Water Market provided locally grown fresh fruits and vegetables

to greengrocers, neighborhood retailers, and even peddlers. Huge amounts of fish were caught daily in Lake Michigan and its associated rivers. Once refrigerated railcars became the norm, Chicago stores handled additional varieties of produce, while local fish markets sold catches from both coasts. Commercially canned goods, arriving by various transportation means, were stocked high on local grocery shelves.

This was abundance rarely seen in the Old Country, whatever it might have been, and Chicago's Jews took advantage of the plentitude. Meat dishes of beef and lamb were, perhaps, more frequently consumed than they had been elsewhere in the world. Diets, also, were greatly improved by the addition of relatively cheap fruits, vegetables, and legumes. Fish, meeting kosher requirements by having both fins and scales, were welcome alternatives to a meat menu.

When, in rare instances, certain ingredients needed for traditional dishes might not have been available, substitutions easily could be made; recipes were borrowed, tried out, assessed, perhaps "tweaked" a bit, and then passed along. And in the passing, some of these hybrid dishes became traditions. Eventually, kosher-certified restaurants, delicatessens, or takeouts, whether meat, dairy, or vegetarian, filled the needs of observant working Jews as well as those who wanted a break from daily meal preparation. For Jews who did not keep kosher, delis and restaurants serving nonkosher dishes sprang up around the city in Jewish neighborhoods. Bagels, lox, cream cheese, and blintzes were among the dishes that crossed cultural boundaries onto American menus.

A common thread runs through the food history of Chicago's Jews, whether they were, or are, Reform, Reconstructionist, Conservative, Orthodox, Ultra-Orthodox, culturally Jewish, or culturally secular: Cooks celebrated, and continue to celebrate, in a myriad of artful and imaginative ways, their identity as American Jews.

Contributors: Ellen F. Steinberg and Jack H. Prost

See also: Delicatessens; Germans; Maxwell Street Market; Russians

BIBLIOGRAPHY

Deutsch, Jonathan, and Rachel D. Saks. *Jewish American Food Culture*. Lincoln: University of Nebraska Press, 2009.

Steinberg, Ellen, and Jack Prost. *From the Jewish Heartland: Two Centuries of Midwest Foodways*. Urbana: University of Illinois Press, 2011.

Jibarito

Jibarito means country bumpkin in Puerto Rican Spanish. But in Chicago dining circles, starting in 1996, it came to mean something more—specifically, two smashed and fried green plantains sandwiching seared steak, mayonnaise, American cheese, lettuce, and tomato. The whole thing is topped with a smear of fragrant garlic oil and eaten hot.

Although dozens of restaurants around the country now serve the jibarito, or *jibaro*, its origins stem from a small restaurant in Chicago's Humboldt Park neighborhood called Borinquen. This original California Avenue location closed in 2014, but other Borinquens remain around the city.

As Borinquen's owner Juan C. Figueroa tells it, he had run a series of failed liquor stores and was ready to call it a day on Borinquen as well. But then one day, he was leafing through a Puerto Rican newspaper where he saw a recipe for a sandwich using fried green plantains (or large tostones) for the bread. He cooked one for his visiting father, who requested another and another over the following days, and suggested Figueroa put it on the menu. When he did, it became an instant hit with customers, baseball players, and foodies all over the city. When competitors duplicated the sandwich, complete with the name, Figueroa started serving it with extras, a side of rice and pigeon peas, which he continues to do today.

Contributor: Monica Eng

See also: Caribbeans; Sandwiches

BIBLIOGRAPHY

Moser, Whet, "In Praise of the Jibarito, Chicago's Great Food Invention." *Chicago Magazine*, November 15, 2011.

Jim Shoe

The *Jim Shoe* (sometimes with alternate spellings of *Gym* or *Shoo*) is a large submarine sandwich filled with corned beef, roast beef, and gyros meat—sometimes chopped and cooked on a flat-top griddle, sometimes simply sliced. Lettuce and tomato are almost always included, and onions, cheese, *tzatziki*, mayonnaise, mustard, and *giardiniera* are common additions. It originated several decades ago in the African American neighborhoods of Chicago's South and West Sides and is still found mainly there, although in the last several years, more examples have been appearing on the North Side and even in other cities such as Milwaukee and Indianapolis. The many dozens of sub shops featuring the Jim Shoe are almost always Pakistani-owned and feature large menus

without pork products. Many of these shops are located in "food deserts," underserved by both food stores and restaurants, and often are among the areas' few sources of prepared hot food.

Contributor: Peter Engler

See also: Sandwiches

BIBLIOGRAPHY

Kindelsperger, Nick. "Standing Room Only: In Search of the Gym Shoe, Chicago's Unsung Sandwich." Serious Eats, June 22, 2012. http://chicago.seriouseats.com/2012/06/standing-room-only-in-search-of-the-gym-shoe.html.

Joho, Jean

A veteran restaurateur, Joho is the chef/owner of Everest, Paris Club Bistro & Bar, Studio Paris, M Burger, and Nacional 27 in Chicago, as well as Las Vegas's The Eiffel Tower Restaurant and Brasserie JO in Boston. Additionally, he is the cofounder of the Corner Bakery and a managing partner at Lettuce Entertain You Enterprises, a Chicago-based restaurant group.

Joho was born in Alsace, France, and he began helping his aunt peel vegetables in her restaurant kitchen at the age of six. By 13, Joho was training at L'Auberge de l'Ill under Paul Haeberlin. By the age of 23, he was a sous chef at a Michelin 3-star restaurant where he oversaw a staff of 35 people.

After his move to Chicago, and a stint as chef at Maxim's de Paris, Joho rose to public acclaim after opening Everest, an elegant, panoramic French dining room perched on the 40th floor of the Chicago Stock Exchange. The Lettuce Entertain You venture features a large, award-winning wine list and a seasonal menu that changes frequently. It has been called one of the most romantic restaurants in Chicago, and has received many accolades, including a 4-star review in 2013 from the *Chicago Tribune*'s Phil Vettel. Joho also has received numerous accolades, including "Who's Who," "Best New Restaurant" and "Best American Chef: Midwest" from the James Beard Foundation and has one Michelin star.

Contributor: Jennifer Olvera

See also: Chefs; Restaurants and Fine Dining; Restaurateurs and Restaurant Groups

BIBLIOGRAPHY

Vettel, Phil. "Revisiting Everest, Les Nomades." *Chicago Tribune*, July 11, 2013.

K

Kahan, Paul

Co-owner and executive chef of a growing restaurant chain, One Off Hospitality Group, Kahan is one of Chicago's most applauded chefs/restaurateurs. Beginning with Blackbird restaurant in 1997, he has helped build a successful, eight-restaurant business that has earned him a national Outstanding Chef award from the James Beard Foundation in 2013, Michelin stars since 2011, and 3-star reviews in area newspapers and magazines.

His father owned a deli and a smokehouse, but Kahan studied computer science at Northern Illinois University. After graduation, he worked for a time in the computer field, but liked cooking better and ended up training with chefs Erwin Drechsler and Rick Bayless. Using midwestern ingredients with a French and Mediterranean approach, Kahan is known for what he calls "minimal, but developed flavors." In addition to the sophisticated Blackbird, which has one Michelin star, his varied restaurants include avec (Mediterranean small plates), The Violet Hour (Cocktails), Big Star (Mexican street food), Publican (beer hall), Publican Quality Meats (butcher shop fare), Nico Osteria (Italian seafood), and Dove Luncheonette (upscale diner).

Contributor: Carol Mighton Haddix

See also: Restaurants and Fine Dining; Restaurateurs and Restaurant Groups

BIBLIOGRAPHY

Rousseau, Caryn. "Why Acclaimed Chicago Chef Paul Kahan Wants Nothing to Do with the Spotlight." Huffington Post. http://www.huffingtonpost.com/2014/03/26/paul-kahan_n_5037872.html.

Keebler Company

What would summer be without ice-cream cones? Chicago's contribution to this seasonal essential comes from the Keebler factory at 10839 S. Langley Ave. The world's largest bakery of ice-cream cones, the plant produces sugar cones, waffle cones, waffle bowls, vanilla cups, vanilla cones, and fudge-dipped cups. The plant's 28 ovens bake more than 3 million items daily. From 1966 through 2004, Keebler Co., one of America's largest manufacturers of cookies, crackers, and other baked snacks, was headquartered at One Hollow Tree Lane, Elmhurst, Illinois. The address is part of Keebler's advertising campaigns and logo that feature elves who live in a hollow tree.

The Keebler firm resulted from many mergers and acquisitions, including the Illinois Baking Corp., established by Max Goldberg in 1931, and Chicago-based United Biscuit Co., itself a conglomerate of regional bakeries formed in 1927. The company ultimately took its name from its oldest unit, a bakery opened by Godfrey Keebler in Philadelphia in 1853.

Kellogg Co., which bought Keebler in 2001 for a reported $3.86 million, kept the brand name but moved the head office to Michigan three years later. However, Keebler still maintains an Illinois Baking Division with two Chicago plants.

Contributor: Leah A. Zeldes

BIBLIOGRAPHY

Catlin, Kay, "Keebler Has Magic but No Elves." *Chicago Tribune*, February 13, 1985.
Zeldes, Leah A. "We Are the Cone Home." *Intercity Intelligencer*, June 11, 2013.

Kinsley, Herbert M.

In the last quarter of the twentieth century, Herbert M. Kinsley (1831–94) was Chicago's leading restaurateur and caterer. His restaurant, Kinsley's, was nationally known and was described in the *New York Times* as holding "first rank as an eating house in all the West," the Delmonico's of Chicago.

Kinsley was a native of Massachusetts. Largely unschooled, he left home as a teenager, working in hotels across the country and Canada and ending up in Chicago in 1865. He opened several restaurants, catered the first Pullman railway cars—including the special car for dignitaries going to Utah for the linking of the transcontinental railroad in 1869. His first major restaurant fell victim to the Chicago fire in 1871, but his catering business remained strong. Finally, he opened Kinsley's in 1884 at 105 W. Adams Street. A Moorish style five-story building, it housed several restaurants including a beer hall, lavishly decorated dining rooms, and a massive catering operation: 2,500–3,000 meals per day with 250 employees.

Kinsley was asked to plan the dining areas for the Columbian Exposition and hosted banquets held by the Fellowship Club. Composed of the leading social and economic lights of the city, members of the Club supported the Fair and feted visiting dignitaries, such as former president Benjamin Harrison, the vice president, cabinet secretaries, and everyone who was anyone in Chicago. They ate dishes typical of Kinsley's menu, beginning with his specialty, bluepoint oysters. He was the first

BEEFSTEAK A LA 1894

The great restaurateur, H. M. Kinsley, wrote one cookbook: *One Hundred Recipes for the Chafing Dish*, published in 1894 by the Gorham Company, maker of chafing dishes and silverware. This dish represents the fine dining at Kinsley's and other fin de siècle restaurants.

—BRUCE KRAIG

Beefsteak with Oysters

Put a pat of butter in Chafing Dish and let thoroughly melt; have nice rump or sirloin steak, one pound in two pieces, about one-inch thick prepared by being nicely trimmed, put in dish; cook on one side for ten minutes, turn and cook for five minutes over hot water, cover on. Season to taste. Can be served plain or with a little chopped parsley. A little paprika makes a delicious seasoning.

Once the steak is cooked put it on a hot platter.

Put juice of twenty-four large oysters in a Chafing Dish over open fire, let it come to a boil, then skim off the froth and add two pats of butter and the oysters. When the oysters are shriveled, season to taste, pour them over the steak and serve.

to import them fresh to the city. He also served terrapin soup, planked whitefish, filet of turkey *au marron*, breast of prairie chicken, roasted saddle of venison, breast of red-headed duck, asparagus vinaigrette, Parisienne potatoes, and glaces and pastries. Mayor Carter Harrison Jr., abroad in retirement, recalled Kinsley's fondly, especially the tall "Negro" chef who stood at a station in the great dining room carving huge joints of roasted beef. Kinsley was notable in his era for his employment of African American staff and for serving black patrons in the same manner as whites.

A stout, jovial man beloved by all, Kinsley died during an operation for a hernia in New York City in 1894. He was there to oversee his new Holland House restaurant, built for an unheard of $2.5 million and meant to rival the great Rector's and Delmonico's. Kinsley's in Chicago carried on with new owners but closed in 1906. The building was later torn down to make way for an 18-story apartment and retail complex.

Contributor: Bruce Kraig
See also: Catering; Restaurateurs and Restaurant Groups

BIBLIOGRAPHY

Cropsey, Eugene H. *Crosby's Opera House: Symbol of Chicago's Cultural Awakening*. Madison, N.J.: Fairleigh Dickinson University Press, 1999.

"Herbert M. Kinsley Dead." *New York Times*, September 23, 1894.

Kleiner, Jerry

A fashion-design major in college, Kleiner was one of the first to recognize the potential of the grungy Randolph Street Market area for bars and restaurants. He opened two trendy nightclubs, Cairo and Shelter, in that marginal part of the city, which was home to warehouses, wholesale butchers, produce firms, and food distributors. Then, along with Dan Krasny and Howard Davis, he created the KDK Group, and opened Vivo restaurant on Randolph Street in 1990.

Kleiner brought his design sensibility to Vivo and to each succeeding restaurant the group opened. His signature was bright colors on the walls and banquettes, oversized hanging lamps and whimsical wall decorations. The restaurant kickstarted the now-booming restaurant row neighborhood along Randolph St. The popular Marche came next, followed by Red Light. But the group split up over disputes while opening Red Light. Krasny took Vivo, Kleiner and Brown took Marche and Red Light, and the two proceeded to open more restaurants such as Gioco (Italian), Opera (Chinese), and Saiko (Japanese), all in the South Loop. All closed due to the economic downturn and resulting tax problems, and Kleiner and Davis parted company in 2011.

Meanwhile, on his own, Kleiner opened Room 21, a restaurant and event space located in a former Al Capone brewery at 2110 S. Wabash Ave., plus Carnivale, Victor Hotel, Park 52, 33 Club, Il Poggiolo in Hinsdale, and Barbakoa in Downers Grove.

Contributor: Carol Mighton Haddix
See also: Restaurateurs and Restaurant Groups

BIBLIOGRAPHY

MacArthur, Kate. "Restaurant Partnership KDK Falters as Last Venues Are Shuttered." *Crain's Chicago Business*, April 2, 2011.

Koreans

As of 2013, there were 1,446,592 Koreans living in the United States, according to the U.S. Census Bureau. Chicago's population of Koreans, at around 40,000, ranks third behind Los Angeles and New York City. Some 66,397 Koreans live in Illinois.

The first Korean came to Chicago in 1916. Kyung Kim was an architect who designed houses but later became a restaurateur, opening a number of cafeterias around town. The first Korean business in Chicago was the Diversey Cafeteria, which operated at the corner of Clark and Diversey Streets in the '20s. The Korean population jumped in the 1960s, concentrating in Lincoln Park and Lakeview, but in the 1980s spread out to North Park, Irving Park, West Ridge, Lincoln Square, and primarily Albany Park, which became known as Koreatown. Bounded by Pulaski, Montrose, Foster, and Clark Streets, the area saw the number of businesses jump from about 30 in 1978 to 428 in 1999.

Lawrence Avenue, where rents were lower than further south, became the main commercial area. It was dense with Korean restaurants of all varieties—barbecue restaurants, bakeries, and soup specialists, like the late Han Bat, which purveyed the milk beef-bone soup *seolleontang*, and Ssyal Ginseng, which serves the restorative soup known as *samgyetang*: the original owners once fortified the latter with ginseng grown on their own farm. Many restaurants opened on Bryn Mawr between California and Kimball Streets, where the yearly Chicago Korean Festival is held. Vendors set up stands there selling traditional street foods not often encountered in restaurants, such as blood sausage (*soondae*), tempura-fried vegetables and seafood (*twigim*), skewered fish cakes simmered in broth (*odeng*), and rice and fish cakes in sweet spicy sauce (*tteokbokki*).

Barbecue restaurants are among the most popular and often act as a gateway food for non-Koreans. Barbecue typically is eaten communally; diners gather around a gas or charcoal fired grill set in the middle of the table and cook pieces of marinated meats, such as *bulgogi*, *galbi*, and *samgyeopsal*, which are then wrapped in lettuce and dipped in salted sesame oil, red pepper paste (*gochuchang*), or bean paste (*deonjjang*). These meals, like most Korean restaurant meals are supplemented by an array of small side dishes called *banchan*, which can range from various kinds of kimchi, to fish cakes, bean sprouts, seasoned seaweed, dried anchovies, seafood pancakes (*pajeon*), and always rice.

A subset of Chinese-Korean restaurants specializes in a particular form of Chinese food acculturated to Korean tastes. Dishes include *ja jiang mian*, fresh noodles in inky black bean sauce; *jjam pong*, spicy seafood noodle soup; and *gampongi*, sweet, spicy, and sticky fried chicken wings.

In the 1990s, four large Korean groceries operated within the boundaries of Koreatown, and at least three kimchi factories. But beginning in the later part of the decade, the city's Korean population began to diminish, as it migrated to northwestern suburbs such as Niles, Arlington Heights, and Morton Grove. This follows a national trend seen in other cities, where Koreans move out of large cities into smaller towns and suburbs in search of cheaper living costs, better jobs, and better schools. Restaurants and businesses in the city began to close. Today, only one large food market remains in the city limits, Joong Boo. It now competes with two large suburban outposts of the mega supermarket chain, Hmart.

Restaurants flourished in the suburbs, including those that specialize in *soondae*, the invigorating goat stew know as *yumso tang*, or *bossam*, a popular drinking food that includes boiled pork, kimchi, and a number of side dishes. In 2013, a *makkeolli* brewery opened in Niles, the first in the United States to produce this fermented Korean rice drink.

Just as Koreans began emigrating from the city, Korean food's popularity was on the rise. Well-known Korean American chefs began cooking Korean fusion food. Chefs such as Bill Kim of BellyQ, Beverly Kim of Parachute, and Edward Kim of Ruxbin and Mott St. all earned national reputations by blending Korean culinary traditions with those of France, Puerto Rican, Italian, and American fast food. At a lower price point, fast-casual restaurants such as BopNGrill and Del Seoul were serving Korean takes on burgers and fries and tacos, all contributing to a greater awareness and popularity of Korean food in Chicago.

Contributor: Mike Sula

See also: Barbecue; Festivals

BIBLIOGRAPHY

Eng, Monica. "Koreans Celebrate 100 years in Chicago." *Chicago Tribune*, March 14, 2013.

http://articles.chicagotribune.com/2003–03–14/features/0303140028 _1_korean-immigrants-south-koreans-korean-community.

http://koreatimes.co.kr/www/news/biz/2010/03/602_62780.html.

Youn-jin Kim. "Korean." *Encyclopedia of Chicago*. http://www .encyclopedia.chicagohistory.org/pages/694.html.

Kornick, Michael

An acclaimed Chicago chef, Kornick has recently become one of the city's top restaurateurs. He partnered in 2009 with Peter Morton to create the DMK Restaurant Group, which in the following years opened three DMK Burger Bars, plus Fish Bar, Ada Street, County Barbecue, DMK Burger & Fish, and Henry's Swing Club.

At the start of his career, after graduating from the Culinary Institute of America, Kornick trained with top chefs/restaurateurs such as Barry Wine at the Quilted Giraffe, New York City, and Gordon Sinclair and Richard Melman in Chicago. He was opening chef for Marche and Red Light and then opened his own place, mk The Restaurant, with his wife Lisa in 1998. His fresh seasonal cuisine at mk earned 3-star reviews from local newspapers, plus accolades from *Esquire, Conde Nast Traveler*, and the James Beard Foundation. Kornick also was cocreator of nine steakhouses in Chicago and Las Vegas.

Contributor: Carol Mighton Haddix

See also: Chefs; Restaurateurs and Restaurant Groups

BIBLIOGRAPHY

"Chef Michael Kornick, Legendary Chef." *Chicago Culinary Museum and Chefs Hall of Fame, 2014.* http://www.thechicago culinarymuseum.org/2014-chefs-hall-of-fame-event.html.

Kraft, James L.

"What we say we do, we do do." For thousands of Kraft employees, both past and present, this rather awkwardly worded imperative is the company motto as coined by J. L. Kraft (1874–1953). Born in Canada, Kraft ended up stranded in Chicago in 1903 without a job. Already tuned in to customer needs, he saw that he could provide a convenience and service to small storekeepers by delivering cheese directly to them from the wholesale suppliers. Thus, he acquired a wagon and his horse "Paddy," company icons to this day.

Cheese, of course, is perishable. Kraft knew that developing a product with a longer shelf life could revolutionize the business. In 1916, he received a patent for his method of blending and pasteurizing cheese in order to extend its shelf life. Processed cheese was born. His timing was propitious. WWI was escalating. The U.S. Military bought millions of tins of Kraft's new cheese during the war and remained a key customer for many decades thereafter. The most famous of these cheese products is Velveeta (1927) and Cheese Whiz (1952–53).

During the Great Depression, Kraft also saw the advantage of low-cost, good-quality food products. Miracle Whip, Mayonnaise, and Kraft Macaroni and Cheese Dinner were all introduced in the 1930s.

Mr. Kraft was deeply religious and loved collecting jade. He combined these two passions by donating a

James L. Kraft, the founder of Kraft Foods. Courtesy of Kraft Foods.

leaded jade window to the North Shore Baptist church where he was an active member. From 1933 until 1994, a Jade Ring was presented to select Kraft employees for meritorious service.

Contributor: Eleanor Hanson

See also: Kraft Foods

BIBLIOGRAPHY

Kass, John. "Kraft a Jewel to Those Jaded by Big Business." *Chicago Tribune*, January 31, 2003.
Kraft, James L. http://www.kraftfoodsgroup.com/.

Kraft Foods

Since 1903, when Canadian-born James L. Kraft began selling cheese from a wagon in Chicago, Kraft has gone through many transformations. But cheese remains a core business throughout all of the corporate acquisitions and mergers (National Dairy Products, Philip Morris), name changes (Kraft Phenix Cheese, Kraft Cheese, Kraftco, Kraft General Foods, Kraft Foods Inc.), and company acquisitions (RJR Nabisco, Oscar Mayer, Cadbury). Most recently, in 2012, Kraft split into the Kraft Food Group and the newly named Mondelez International.

J. L. Kraft's development of processed cheese in 1915 revolutionized the industry. As the company grew, other products were added. Kraft introduced its version of Velveeta in 1927, and Philadelphia Cream Cheese became part of the company in 1928, after a merger with Phenix Cheese Corporation. Appealing to Depression-era consumers, Kraft Mayonnaise, Miracle Whip, Kraft Macaroni and Cheese Dinner, and Pourable Dressings all were introduced in the 1930s. The 1950s heralded Cheez Whiz and Deluxe processed cheese slices, the first commercially packaged sliced cheese. In 1965, Kraft Singles came to market as the first individually wrapped process cheese slices. Products continued to be developed, added, and divested, through acquisitions and mergers. Today Kraft markets myriad products under some 30 brands, including many from the acquisitions of General Foods, Oscar Mayer, and Nabisco. But more than 20 percent of its business is still devoted to cheese.

Kraft long has been a presence in the Chicago area, starting with the 1905 headquarters on Kinzie Street. A move to River Street in 1911 was followed by one to 400 Rush St. in 1921. In 1938, the then Kraft Phenix Cheese Company moved to its newly built location at 500 Peshtigo Court, which housed both manufacturing and head offices. Kraft remained at the Peshtigo location until 1980, when it consolidated operations in Glenview. After merging with H. J. Heinz in 2015, the company announced that it was moving its Chicago offices to the Aon Center in the heart of the city.

Through the decades, most Americans have been familiar with Kraft Foods' "For Good Food and Good Food Ideas" from the Kraft Kitchens. The Kraft Kitchens forerunner, the Consumer Services Department, was established in 1924, with Marye Dahnke as the company's first home economist. She traveled around the country demonstrating cheese recipes, developed and tested recipes first in her home and later in a newly built kitchen in the Rush Street headquarters, and with her staff, answered any and all consumer requests for recipes and product information.

With the move to Peshtigo Court, new state-of-the-art kitchens were built and, by 1953, occupied the entire ninth floor. In 1962, the now named Kraft Kitchens along with the photo studio were relocated to the top of the sixth-floor wing of the building. Marye Dahnke retired in 1962. Dorothy Holland joined the company in 1950 and was director of the Kraft Kitchens from 1958 until her retirement in 1984. In 1972, the Consumer Affairs Department was formed and Holland was named the first female vice president of the then Kraftco Corporation. Kraft was a pioneer as an early television advertiser. Many Americans of a certain age associate Kraft with the television "hands" commercials. First airing in 1947, the

CREAM CHEESE DISAPPEARING ACT

The oft-repeated "clam dip" story exemplifies the strength of Kraft's recipe strategy. Two days after a national commercial aired featuring a recipe for clam dip prepared with Philadelphia Cream Cheese, grocery stores everywhere sold out of canned clams.

—ELEANOR HANSEN

Clam appetizer dip

Prep: 10 minutes
Makes: 6 servings
Adapted from the kitchens of Kraft Foods

1 package (8 ounces) cream cheese, softened at room temperature
1 can (6 1/4 ounces) minced clams
2 teaspoons lemon juice
1 1/2 teaspoons Worcestershire sauce
1/4 teaspoon garlic salt
Dash freshly ground black pepper

Place cream cheese in medium serving bowl; beat with wooden spoon until fluffy. Drain clams, reserving 1/4 cup of the liquid. Add clams, reserved liquid and remaining ingredients to the cream cheese; mix until well blended. Cover; refrigerate several hours or until chilled. Serve with cut-up vegetable dippers or potato chips.

recipe-themed commercials focused on a pair of woman's hands preparing a recipe. Weekly Kraft programs using the "hands commercial" advertising format continued until the early 1970s. From then until the late 1980s, television specials airing several times a year replaced the weekly programming and featured four to six 90-second how-to commercials. Each commercial showcased four recipes appropriate for a meal or other occasion and paid homage with a few frames of "hands" preparation.

Kraft was split into two companies in 2012: Kraft Foods Group and Mondelez International. In 2013, 110 years after J. L. Kraft began selling from his wagon, sales for the Kraft Foods Group topped $18 billion. In 2015, Kraft was acquired by H. J. Heinz. But a still significant portion of sales continues to be cheese-related.

Contributor: Eleanor Hanson
See also: Kraft, James L.

BIBLIOGRAPHY

Bucher, Anne and Melanie Villines. *The Greatest Thing Since Sliced Cheese, Stories of Kraft Foods Inventors and Their Inventions.* Northfield, IL: Kraft Foods Holdings, Inc., 2005.

Kraft Foods Corporate Timeline/History. http://www.kraftfoods group.com/.

Kroc, Ray

McDonald's Corporation founder Ray Kroc (1902–84) was born in Oak Park, Illinois. After serving as an ambulance driver in WWI, Kroc sold Multimixers, which were used to whip multiple milk shakes. In the early 1950s, he visited the McDonald's quick-service restaurant in California.

The owners, the McDonald brothers, had purchased eight mixers, and Kroc wanted to know why they needed so many. After visiting the bustling drive-in, Kroc became national franchiser for what would become the world's largest restaurant chain. In 1955, he founded McDonald's Corporation. During his lifetime, Kroc contributed to many philanthropic causes and was the owner of the San Diego Padres.

Contributor: David Hammond

See also: Fast Food/Quick Service; McDonald's Corporation

BIBLIOGRAPHY

Kroc, Ray, and Robert Anderson. *Grinding It Out: The Making of McDonald's.* Chicago: H. Regnery, 1977.

La Preferida Foods

The giant family-owned producer of Hispanic specialty foods was born in the Pilsen neighborhood, nurtured by the Steinbarth family, and grew to international prominence with help from a chile-pepper–spiced, garlicky, reddish sausage called chorizo.

Henry Steinbarth, a German American, opened a grocery-butcher shop in the 1920s, making sausages for the Central Europeans who settled in Pilsen. When an increasing number of immigrants from Mexico moved into the area, his son, Ralph Steinbarth, decided in 1949 to introduce Chicago to the city's first packaged links of chorizo.

These days, La Preferida is headquartered at 3400 W. 35th St., but the red, green, and white logo can be found around the world on food cans, bottles, bags, and those packages of chorizo. The firm began manufacturing its own food products in 1952, and today there are more than 300 items, including canned and dried beans, salsas, marinades, tamales, and tortillas. Its canned refried beans come fat-free, vegetarian, and chipotle-spiced, among other variations.

La Preferida translated means *the preferred*. And that has been the focus for four generations of the Steinbarth family. Rich Steinbarth now is president and COO.

Contributor: Judy Hevrdejs

BIBLIOGRAPHY

Harris, Jim. "The Preferred Choice: With Its Focus on Producing the Finest Quality Products, La Preferida Remains a Staple in the Mexican Food Market Nationwide." *Food & Drink* Winter 2010.

Meade, Mary. "Let's All Enjoy Pan-American Foods Now!" *Chicago Tribune,* August 28, 1959.

Labor and Unions

In 1914, the poet Carl Sandburg famously described Chicago as "the Hog Butcher for the World" and "Stacker of Wheat." Chicago became the center of the "everything but the squeal" method of livestock disassembly after the Civil War. By 1899, meatpackers were the largest employer in Chicago, but the 25,000 employees in the industry had little say over the nature of their employment. Reformers such as Upton Sinclair hoped for better days, but the reality remained bleak. The response to Sinclair's sensational exposé, *The Jungle*, disappointed reformers because, although it led to government food inspection standards, it offered no help for workers, whose major strikes in 1904 and 1921 ended in failure.

In the 1930s, organized labor finally came to meatpacking workers' aid with the formation of the Congress of Industrial Organizations (CIO) in 1935 and its subsequent backing of the Packinghouse Workers Organizing Committee (PWOC) two years later. This industrial union succeeded where others failed by building interracial and ethnic unity among the workers, and it gained the protection of the Wagner Act and other New Deal labor legislation. By 1943 the union was established as the United Packinghouse Workers of America (UPWA) and boasted 40,000 Chicago members. For the next three decades, the UPWA brought some dignity to work in the packing houses by improving conditions, giving better pay, recognizing seniority, and establishing grievance procedures while inspiring civil rights demands beyond the shop floor. Decentralization of meatpacking led to the close of the Union Stock Yards in 1971 and with them the old unions. The UPWA merged with other unions, namely the Amalgamated Meat Cutters and Butcher Workmen of North America (an American Federation of Labor union founded in Chicago in 1897), eventually becoming the United Food and Commercial Workers International Union (UFCW) headquartered in Washington, D.C.

Wheat and grain workers multiplied as grain corporations and commodity markets took root in Chicago. In the 1840s, Cyrus Hall McCormick made grain harvesting easier with the invention of the mechanical reaper. It sold well to farmers, and McCormick's Chicago factory employed hundreds of workers who, in the 1880s, increasingly sought to organize against labor abuses. On May 3, 1886, the confrontations between striking workers, strikebreakers, and police came to a head as the police shot and killed two workers outside of the factory gates. This violent act led to the famous Haymarket "riot" and subsequent trial and execution of several innocent Chicago labor leaders.

Farmers also brought their wheat to Chicago for storage, sale, and processing. Chicagoans boasted steam-powered grain elevators in the 1840s. The mixing of different farmers' grain and the necessity of grading grain quality created the need for a commodity market. The Chicago Board of Trade (CBOT) filled this role, employing hundreds of workers. But the futures market had a concomitant physical labor market for the processing of grains for much of the twentieth century. Workers processed corn products at Argo, oats and cereals at Quaker Oats, and crackers at United Biscuit Company beginning in the 1910s, and the Libby, McNeill, and Libby Canning Company in Chicago was the second largest canner of food in America after World War I.

Dressed cuts of meat often ended up at local markets, and Chicago's neighborhoods by the 1910s had 1,800 meat markets 7,400 grocery stores, and hundreds more fruit and vegetable stands and bakeries. By the 1920s and 1930s, chain stores challenged the independent food sellers that had long dominated the ethnic neighborhoods of Chicago. Chicago's bakers, for example, operated 280 bakeries in the 1880s but experienced a sharp decline by the 1930s. This shift cost many Chicago food artisans and family businesses their jobs, but it had a positive impact on workers' overall ability to organize. The Retail Clerks International Union succeeded between the late 1930s and 1950s in organizing many chain food stores, though an increasingly hostile union environment since the 1980s has diminished this strong level of organization in recent decades.

Since the 1840s, Chicago has been labeled a great "expense account town" for businessmen as well as the tourists and locals who have sought culinary experiences in its restaurants. The hospitality industry has employed thousands of cooks, waiters, dishwashers, and other restaurant employees. In the late nineteenth century, African American men made up over half of the waiters in Chicago, but they had to form their own unions because of racist exclusion from the American Federation of Labor. In 1890, Chicago's white and black waiters—furious with low pay, no job security, and long hours—formed an interracial Culinary Alliance. The Alliance waged strikes against some of Chicago's restaurants, but it fell apart due to employer resistance, especially the hiring of female strikebreakers. After the end of Prohibition, unions had more success among bartenders than waiters. Although rumored to be connected to the mafia, Chicago's Bartenders Local 278 boasted more than 3,000 members and was the largest such local in the nation in the 1930s.

Waiters increasingly gave way to waitresses as many of these food-service positions became feminized jobs, especially in new "cheap eats" and cafeteria-style restaurants. In the 1910s, the Women's Trade Union League organized waitresses' strikes, and in the post–World War II era the Hotel Employees' and Restaurant Employees' International Union (HERE) unionized about one-quarter of this female-dominated labor force. But these workers still relied largely on tips to survive given that the wages were often the lowest of any occupational group. For example, Dolores Dante, a single mother of three, had worked as a server six days a week from 5 p.m. to 2 a.m. since the 1950s when Studs Terkel interviewed her for his 1974 book, *Working*. Her story personifies the harsh yet skilled and even artful work provided by Chicagoans serving food. "Everyone wants

Women workers employed as wipers in the roundhouse enjoy lunch at Northwestern Railroad in 1943. Library of Congress.

to eat, everyone has hunger. And I serve them," she said about her Chicago waitress job. "I can't be servile. I give service. There is a difference," she explained, because "to be a waitress, it's an art."

In the twenty-first century, even as its manufacturing and disassembly of raw food products has diminished, Chicago remains a central culinary destination and huge employer of food-service workers. The more than 250,000 Chicago region restaurant workers have sought out traditional labor unions as well as new labor groups such as Workers' Centers to fight for better wages, sick days, and improved conditions. The Restaurant Opportunity Center, founded in Chicago in 2008, has demanded "high-road" practices among restaurant owners, especially since the area's food industry generated $12.7 billion in 2008 while its workers earn only half the minimum wage of other Chicago workers. Chicago grocery store chains such as Jewel-Osco and Mariano's have remained organized by the United Food and Commercial Workers (the UPWA and the Retail Clerks International Union merged into this union in 1979). But other large corporate grocers such as Whole Foods, Target, and Wal-Mart have recently opened stores in Chicago with explicit antiunion policies. In addition, Chicago workers have made strides in efforts to organize the fast-food industry. With the rise of franchised food operations and low-wage work, the Workers' Organizing Committee of Chicago formed the "Fight for 15" campaign, engaging in its first strike in April, 2013, to demand living wages for these food-service jobs. While the success of these campaigns is yet to be determined, one thing is certain: Chicago's food laborers have continued to make their city a global force in all of its edible commodities.

Contributor: Erik S. Gellman
See also: Food Reform Legislation; Sinclair, Upton; Union Stock Yards

BIBLIOGRAPHY

Barrett, James. *Work and Community in the Jungle: Chicago's Packinghouse Workers, 1894–1922*. Urbana: University of Illinois Press, 1987.

Horowitz, Roger. *"Negro and White: Unite and Fight!" A Social History of Industrial Unionism in Meatpacking, 1930–1990*. Urbana: University of Illinois Press, 1997.

Newell, Barbara. *Chicago and the Labor Movement: Metropolitan Unionism in the 1930's*. Urbana: University of Illinois Press, 1961.

Lach, Alma

Born in 1914 in Petersburg, Illinois, near Springfield, Lach grew up on a farm and learned to cook at an early age. Her skill at the wood-burning stove perhaps led her years later to become one of Chicago's best-known food experts—an editor, author, and consultant. She attended the University of Chicago in 1939, where she met Donald F. Lach, a graduate student in history. They married and then, in 1949, Donald earned a scholarship to study in France. Alma followed and also studied at Le Cordon Bleu, where she earned the Grand Diplome, one of the first Americans to do so. Returning to Chicago, she became the food editor at the *Chicago Sun-Times* from 1957 to 1965. She created and starred in one of the first television cooking shows for children, *Let's Cook*.

She also wrote cookbooks, including *A Child's First Cookbook* (1950) and *Cooking a la Cordon Bleu* in 1970. But it was the *Hows and Whys of French Cooking* in 1974 (University of Chicago Press) that brought her accolades. It was the first general-interest book printed by the academic publisher, and it offered home cooks a clear-cut guide to French cooking. Many called it a more accessible guide than the famed Julia Child's *Mastering the Art of French Cooking*.

She also worked as a consultant for Midway Airlines and Lettuce Entertain You. She was a founding member of the professional group, Les Dames d'Escoffier Chicago. In 2007, Lach was honored by the group as a "Dame of Distinction." She died at 99 in 2013. Her more than 3,000 cookbooks and papers are now part of the Special Collections Research Center of The University of Chicago Library.

Contributor: Carol Mighton Haddix
See also: Books and Publishers; Media, Print

BIBLIOGRAPHY

Station, Elizabeth. "Food Life." The Core. http://thecore.uchicago.edu/Summer2014/departments/forgotten-history.shtml.

Le Français

Transplanted French chef Jean Banchet was having a successful run at the tony Playboy Club in Lake Geneva, Wisconsin, when he and his wife/partner Doris decided to open their own restaurant. It was 1973 and, unable to afford a suitable location in the city, the Banchets eventually found a satisfactory spot in Wheeling north of Chicago. Banchet opened Le Français in February 1973. The original building burned down in 1975 and was rebuilt deeper into the property and designed along the lines of a French auberge, or country inn. Le Français garnered rave reviews from the start. In addition to being widely acknowledged as the best restaurant in the Chicago area, many considered it the best restaurant in the country.

The restaurant's menu featured a dozen entrees and appetizers, augmented by daily specials and often using luxurious ingredients, especially lobster and truffles. A typical entree would be a warm terrine with large pieces of lobster meat and other shellfish and fin fish in a cream sea urchin and butter sauce. A featured entree was wild bass with lobster and truffle vinaigrette topped with caviar and shaved truffle. Le Français was famous for its game dishes, such as stuffed quail with verjus, rabbit saddle, and guinea hen with truffle sauce decorated with noisettes of Scottish venison. Service was elaborate and ceremonious.

Banchet was a perfectionist and, by 1989, he needed a break. He leased the restaurant to chef Roland Liccioni and his wife, pastry chef Mary Beth Liccioni. The duo had been in charge of the kitchen at Carlos', a top-tier restaurant owned by Carlos Nieto, who had worked at Le Français, and his wife Debbie.

When the Liccioni's 10-year lease ended, Banchet came back and ran it until he retired in 2001. Banchet eventually sold the restaurant to chef Don Yamauchi and his business partner Phil Mott. In 2003, buffeted by the downturn that followed 9/11, Yamauchi and Mott shuttered Le Français. It was truly the end of an era.

Contributor: Barbara Revsine
See also: Banchet, Jean and Doris; French; Restaurants and Fine Dining

BIBLIOGRAPHY

Revsine, Barbara. "Sad Good-Bye: Jean Banchet." *Food Arts*, January/February 2014.
Vettel, Phil, "Le Français Soars with Jean Banchet." *Chicago Tribune*, March, 2000.

Le Perroquet

Long considered one of Chicago's top dining spots, Le Perroquet (The Parrot), an elegant restaurant on Walton Street, was restaurateur Jovan Trboyevic's second restaurant. The third-floor dining room was an oasis of quiet and refinement and the service was impeccable. Featured were such dishes as mussels in Calvados cream and duck Perroquet with tarragon-cognac sauce. Perroquet may have been the first restaurant in Chicago to have an espresso machine. Trboyevic ran the restaurant from 1973 to 1985, when he sold it to brothers Gerard and Jean-Pierre Nespoux, the restaurant's long time maître d'.

Although Le Perroquet retained its identity, its ratings slipped, and the restaurant closed in February 1991. The following year Michael Foley, chef/owner of the top-rated Printer's Row restaurant in the South Loop, bought Le Perroquet. To head up the kitchen, Foley hired Didier Durand, a French chef who had worked for Carlos Nieto (Carlos'), Gordon Sinclair (Gordon), and Jacques Barbier

(La Boheme). The cuisine was lighter, the price point more approachable, and the menus a mix of French and English terms, complete with a la carte options. Le Perroquet closed in 1994, but Foley, who presided over the restaurant's 25th anniversary, says "the parrot is just sleeping." The name was later borrowed for the training place at the Washburn Culinary Institute in the South Shore Culinary Center.

Contributor: Barbara Revsine
See also: Restaurants and Fine Dining; Restaurateurs and Restaurant Groups

BIBLIOGRAPHY

Rice, William. "Au Revoir, Perroquet." *Chicago Tribune*, February 7, 1991.

Lettuce Entertain You Restaurants

Lettuce Entertain You is one of the nation's largest multiconcept restaurant companies, with annual revenues of about $400 million and a diverse portfolio of more than 95 restaurants in nine states. Founder and chairman Richard Melman got his first restaurant job at age 14, and a taste of rejection in his early 20s when his father declined his offer to buy into the family's deli business.

In 1970, Melman met real estate agent Jerry Orzoff, who would become his business partner and confidante until Orzoff's death in 1981. On June 10, 1971, with $17,000, the duo opened R. J. Grunt's at 2056 N. Lincoln Park West. The menu was eclectic and the music loud. The salad bar ("splendrous," the menu declared) with its dozens of toppings was like none other. In a way, it was the precursor of now popular fast-casual restaurants.

Melman and Orzoff opened their next restaurants in rapid succession from 1973 to 1976, each with a punny name and distinct theme: Fritz That's It! in Evanston; The Great Gritzbe's Flying Food Show, Jonathan Livingston Seafood, 5419 N. Sheridan Rd. (now company headquarters), and Lawrence of Oregano.

In 1975, they bought the historic, and failing, Pump Room in the Ambassador East Hotel and turned it around under chef Gabino Sotelino. That run lasted 22 years until new owners took over. The partnership with Sotelino continued with the 1980 opening of the upscale Ambria in the Belden-Stratford Hotel, the 1981 opening of Un Grand Café (now Mon Ami Gabi) in the same hotel, and the 1986 opening of Café Ba-Ba-Reeba! Ambria, which closed in 2007, was replaced by L20, a fine-dining seafood restaurant that in 2013 earned 2 Michelin stars.

The 1980s also saw the opening of the first Lettuce restaurants outside of the Chicago area: Don & Charlie's American Rib and Chop House in Scottsdale, Ariz., still

HOW R. J. GRUNTS GOT ITS NAME

When Richard Melman and Jerry Orzoff became partners and opened their first restaurant in 1971 in Lincoln Park, they wanted the restaurant to reflect their identities and their sense of humor. They chose their first initials, and then added a word for the piglike sounds one of Orzoff's dates made when she ate. R. J. Grunts was born, and after only a month became one of the hottest restaurants in the city. Melman has said Grunts is the most meaningful of all his restaurants: he started it with his best friend; he met his wife Martha there; and he named his first son R. J., who ultimately served as manager of his namesake eatery.

—SCOTT WARNER

in operation, and the 1950s-themed diner Ed Debevic's in Phoenix, known for its sass-talking waitstaff. Melman later opened Debevic's in Beverly Hills, New York, and even Japan. All, including the original Ed Debevic's at 640 N. Wells St., are now closed.

The 1990s brought Maggiano's Little Italy (Brinker International now operates Maggiano's and Corner Bakery restaurants in 28 states), Ben Pao, and another fine-dining restaurant, Tru, with chefs Rick Tramonto and Gale Gand. Melman redefined the mall food court with the opening of Foodlife and Mity Nice Bar & Grill in Water Tower Place on N. Michigan Ave.

Additions in the 2000s included the 1940s-style steakhouse Petterino's on N. Dearborn St.; Wow Bao, specializing in Asian steamed buns (now with six locations, a food truck, and a frozen product line sold in more than 30 grocery stores in Illinois and Michigan); and M Burger with four locations.

Key to Lettuce's formula is staff training and development and partnerships with chefs and longtime employees, including chef Jean Joho (Everest, Eiffel Tower, Paris Club) and president and CEO Kevin Brown, creator of several popular concepts, including Big Bowl and Shaw's Crab House.

Melman's sons, R. J. and Jerrod, and daughter, Molly, have joined the business. Since 2008, they have opened several concepts, including HUB 51, RPM Italian in the old Ben Pao space, and the tiki lounge Three Dots and a Dash. R. J. Grunt's remains open in Lincoln Park, with much of the original décor—and the salad bar—intact.

Contributor: Janet Fuller

See also: Melman, Richard; Restaurants and Fine Dining; Restaurateurs and Restaurant Groups;

BIBLIOGRAPHY

Mautner, Julie. "Grilled in a Minute: Rich Melman." *Food Arts*, August 29, 2012.

Samors, Neal, and Eric Bronsky. *Chicago's Classic Restaurants: Past, Present & Future*. Chicago: Chicago's Books Press, 2011.

Levy Brothers

In 1978, a Chicago restaurant dynasty was born in a humble deli. That was the year brothers Larry and Mark Levy bought the struggling D. B. Kaplan's Delicatessen at Water Tower Place. Six months into the venture, business was not as strong as they had hoped, so they brought in a lady they knew could command the kitchen and produce Jewish food to match their vision—their mother Eadie. The restaurant flourished, and within a few years, the pair had opened three more restaurants (The Chestnut Street Grill, Dos Hermanos, Laura's) at the shopping mall.

The brothers—Larry is older by three years—grew up in St. Louis, the sons of a music promoter who brought entertainers by the house for a home-cooked meal. That was the brothers' first lessons about the positive impression heartfelt hospitality had on people. Larry traveled to the Chicago area to study (receiving a degree from the Kellogg School of Business Management in 1967) and got into the real estate business. His brother followed him to Chicago and settled into the insurance industry before taking over daily oversight of the deli.

In 1982, Levy Restaurants brought "fine dining" and the first dessert cart to the corporate skyboxes at the now-demolished Comiskey Park and provided concessions at Ravinia Festival, an outdoor concert venue in Highland Park. Spiaggia, a high-end Italian restaurant on the Magnificent Mile, opened in 1984, and more than 30 years later continues to command the attention of national restaurant critics. The pair also won a contract to open the first independent restaurants at Walt Disney World. As the late 1980s ushered in a new breed of ballparks, the company jumped further into the stadium hospitality market, and by the end of the century, Levy Restaurants provided catering and concessions to numerous stadiums, convention centers, and entertainment venues around the United States.

In 1998, Mark left the business (worth $165 million at the time) to form an investment firm; Larry, who was more comfortable as the "face" of Levy Restaurants, grew the concessions side of the business. In 2000, Levy Restaurants sold half of the business to U.K.-based Compass Group, and in 2006, Compass Group bought the remainder of the business. In 2014, Larry served on the boards of Kellogg

Business School and a handful of charitable organizations around Chicago. Mark is the CEO of Mastro Restaurants.

Contributor: Deborah Pankey

See also: Restaurants and Fine Dining; Restaurateurs and Restaurant Groups

BIBLIOGRAPHY

"Levy Restaurant Founders Split Up." *Crain's Chicago Business*, July 25, 1998.

Shefsky, Lloyd. "Invest, Reinvent, Thrive" excerpt. New York: Mc-Graw Hill, 2014. http://insight.kellogg.northwestern.edu/article/book_excerpt_from_invent_reinvent_thrive/.

Libby, McNeill & Libby

Archibald McNeil and two brothers, Arthur and Charles Libby, founded a meatpacking company in 1868. Their main product was beef preserved in brine. After a good deal of experimentation, the company developed brined (corned) beef that was placed in a pyramid-shaped can in 1875. It became the standard shape of many other companies' beef for years to come. In 1875, they moved the company to the Chicago stockyards and, within 20 years, Libby employed 1,500 people at their processing plant and were slaughtering 200,000 cattle per year. A bustling hotel trade and fresh tenderloins for the restaurant industry were also part of their product lines. Sales for Libby's canned corned beef and roast beef soared, not only in the United States, but also in Europe.

Swift & Company purchased Libby in 1920. Fruits and vegetables were added to the line; a pineapple cannery in Hawaii and a cannery for tomatoes in California were built. By 1960, Libby's employed 9,000 Chicagoans, and by 1970 the firm had $500 million in sales. Nestle became the new owner but sold off parts of Libby to other firms. Nestle still maintained its pumpkin and juice products. Conagra Foods purchased the canned meats

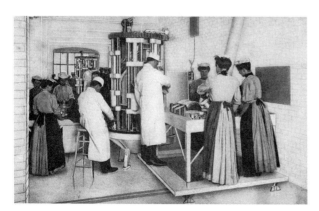

In 1898, Libby's created its iconic corned beef tin. Wikimedia Commons.

LIBBY'S SHAPELY CANS

In a time when few people had refrigeration, canned foods became popular. Seeing an opportunity, Chicago's Libby, McNeil, & Libby began experimenting with canning corned beef in 1872. After many experiments, Libby came up with a tapered tinned can in 1875 that made the meat easier to remove in one piece for slicing. It was so successful that the tapered can shape remains the standard to this day.

—CAROL MIGHTON HADDIX

division. Many of Libby's products live on outside North America, mainly in Europe and the Latin American market. From canned meats, fruits, vegetables, and juices, this household name continues to resonate under the umbrella of Nestle. As an old Chicago company, it is appropriate that its papers are housed at the Chicago History Museum.

Contributor: Jenny Lewis

BIBLIOGRAPHY

Duis, Perry. "Part Three: Food." *Challenging Chicago: Coping with Everyday Life, 1837–1920*. Urbana: University of Illinois, 1998.

Wade, Louise Carroll. *Chicago's Pride: The Stockyards, Packingtown, and Environs in the Nineteenth Century*. Urbana: University of Illinois, 1987.

Liccioni, Roland

Born in Saigon when it was part of French Indo-China, Roland Liccioni grew up in France, where his parents had a small restaurant. His Vietnamese mother gave him a thorough grounding in her native cuisine, and the flavors and techniques he learned from her continue to influence his cooking.

He left for culinary school when he was 15 and, three years later, headed to Paris to work at Brasserie Bofinger. A stint in London, working with the Roux Brothers, came next, followed by a trans-Atlantic hop to suburban Highwood. He worked there for six months at a friend's restaurant before signing on as executive chef at Carlos' restaurant in Highland Park, a newcomer that quickly became a superstar.

Roland and his wife at the time, pastry chef Mary Beth Liccioni, leased the famed Le Français from Jean Banchet in 1989 and ran it for 10 successful years. In 2000, they relocated to Les Nomades, where—once again—they garnered rave reviews. Roland left Les Nomades in 2004 and, for a decade, he headed up kitchens at various restaurants in the area. While the surroundings changed, Liccioni's cooking was never less than excellent. In 2011, Liccioni returned to Les Nomades. In 2015, he and chef Matt Ayala (Schwa, Moto) opened a French brasserie, Le Cochon Volant, inside the Hyatt Centric Hotel in the Loop.

Contributor: Barbara Revsine

See also: Le Français; Restaurants and Fine Dining; Restaurateurs and Restaurant Groups

BIBLIOGRAPHY

Vettel, Phil. "Roland Liccioni Returns to Les Nomades." *Chicago Tribune*, November 8, 2011.

Lithuanians

In 1870, 18 workers came from Lithuania to lay track for the railroads. One would die in October 1871 in the Great Fire—a fire that generated construction jobs that would lure more Lithuanians. Later, the Union Stock Yards, which had created jobs too miserable for the resident Germans, Scandinavians, and Irish, attracted immigrants from Poland, Slavic countries, and Lithuania desperate to begin a new life in this still-new world. More came to help build the 1893 World's Columbian Exposition—and they stayed, too. They brought with them their culture, their language, their church—and their *koldunai* (dumplings), *cepelinai* (filled potato dumplings), *kugelis* (potato pudding), *balandiniai* (stuffed cabbage), and other good things.

By 1910, when the city's Lithuanian population approached 30,000, one observer boasted "there are more Lithuanians living here than in any other city in the world"—including Lithuania. That number would triple by the 1930s. The stockyards would come to be identified so strongly with Lithuanians that when Upton Sinclair wrote his landmark novel about the yards, *The Jungle*, his main character would be Jurgis Rudkis, a Lithuanian who "could take up a two-hundred-and-fifty-pound quarter of beef and carry it into a car without a stagger, or even a thought."

Chicago's Lithuanians settled near that workplace, primarily in the Bridgeport neighborhood and in the Town of Lake, home of the stockyards, and annexed by the city in 1889. Later, the growing community also populated much of the Marquette Park neighborhood on the city's Southwest Side—and here could be found the city's best Lithuanian restaurants: Nida, Ruta, Tulpe, Neringa, Palanga, and the still-standing Seklycia on West 71st Street—along with

bakeries and delis. The Healthy Food Restaurant (since 1938), on Halsted Street in Bridgeport, would become an icon.

But neighborhoods change. The few Lithuanian restaurants still in the area are on the edge of the city and in the suburbs, such as the Grand Duke's Restaurant in Summit, with its sampler platter of sausages, potato dumplings, and sauerkraut, or pork with mushrooms, or cottage cheese blintzes.

Contributor: Alan Solomon

BIBLIOGRAPHY

Fainhauz, David. *Lithuanians in Multi-Ethnic Chicago until World War II*. Chicago: Lithuanian Library Press and Loyola University Press, 1977.

"Seklycia," LTH Forum. http:/www.lthforum.com.

Lou Mitchell's Restaurant

In 1923, Greek immigrant William Mitchell opened his family restaurant on Jackson Boulevard in Chicago. His son Louis joined his father there some 13 years later. By 1949, Lou had moved the restaurant across the street to 565 W. Jackson Blvd. He added his name and neon signs proclaiming Lou Mitchell's served "the World's Best Coffee," as well as "We Do Our Own Quality Baking." City fathers worried the signs would affect the "esthetics of the boulevard," the legendary Mother Road, Route 66.

Those signs drew drivers cruising along Route 66, commuters from nearby Union Station, U.S. presidents, and movie stars. They weren't the restaurant's only draw. There were omelets served in skillets, fresh-squeezed orange juice, thick slices of sesame-seed-topped Greek toast, and "Uncle" Lou, who greeted customers and dispensed Greek philosophy for 50-plus years. In 1958, he began offering freshly made doughnut holes and, to children and women, tiny boxes of Milk Duds to those waiting in line for a seat. Lou Mitchell, who retired in 1988, died in March 1999. The restaurant, added to the National Register of Historic Places in 2006, is now run by the Thanas family, who continue Lou's doughnut-and-Milk-Duds tradition, as well as the orange-wedge-and-a-prune welcome served each diner.

Contributor: Judy Hevrdejs

BIBLIOGRAPHY

"City Is in Dark about Signs." *Chicago Daily Tribune*, January 22, 1959.

National Register of Historic Places. www.nationalregisterofhistoric places.com/il/state.html.

Struzzi, Diane, "Restaurateur Louis Mitchell, 90." *Chicago Tribune*, March 30, 1999.

The Berghoff, founded 1878. Library of Congress.

Alinea's steelhead roe, carrot, coconut, and curry. Wikimedia Commons.

Exterior of the Orange Garden Restaurant with the oldest working neon sign in Chicago. Photograph by Stefan Osdene.

A poster celebrating the unique and world-famous Chicago hot dog. Courtesy of Vienna Beef.

The Mother-in-Law, a unique Chicago sandwich. Photograph by Peter Engler.

The Green City Market is the largest and best known of Chicago's farmers' markets. Photograph by Cindy Kurman.

Markets on the South and West Sides catering to African-American communities. Photograph by Peter Engler.

Postcard of the Klas Czech restaurant in Cicero, Ill., 1950s. Courtesy of Lake County (Ill.) Discovery Museum, Curt Teich Postcard Archives.

Poster for Southern California Citrus Fair, Chicago, 1886, showing rail lines from California to Chicago. Courtesy of William L. Clements Library, University of Michigan.

Paul Bunyan statue with a hot dog. Courtesy of Patty Carroll.

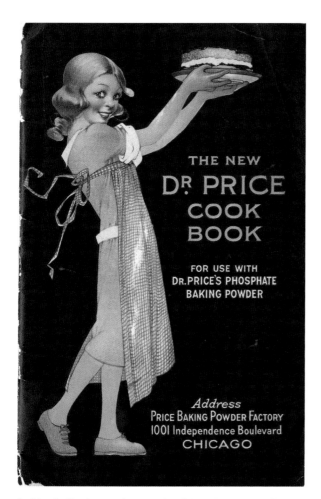

Dr. Price Cookbook, 1920s. Courtesy of the Chicago Public Library, Special
Collections and Preservation Division/Clabber Girl Co.

Gordon's popular artichoke fritters. Photography by
Pam Haller. Art Direction by Rich Nickel.

BIRD'S-EYE VIEW OF THE WORLD'S COLUMBIAN EXPOSITION, CHICAGO, 1893.

Bird's-eye view of the Columbian Exposition, 1893. Library of Congress.

Shanghai lumpia eggrolls at UNI-MART Original Baker's Delight. Courtesy of UNI-MART OBD.

Grace restaurant's king crab appetizer with cucumber and lemon balm. Courtesy of Grace Restaurant. Photograph by Huge Galdones.

Mithai Bangladeshi restaurant. Photograph by Ashish Sen.

Iconic hot dog stand, Superdawg, founded in 1948. Photograph by Patty Carroll.

Panoramic view of the Century of Progress fair by Durkee Foods. Courtesy of the Chicago Public Library, Special Collections and Preservation Division/Durkee Foods.

Chicago was a major center for baking products such as Jacques Baking Powder. Courtesy of the Chicago Public Library, Special Collections and Preservation Division/Calumet Baking Powder.

Chef Jean Joho of Everest. Courtesy of Lettuce Entertain You Restaurants.

Deep-dish pizza from the Bacino's chain. Courtesy of Meathead, AmazingRibs.com.

Bibimbap, an iconic dish in Chicago's Korean restaurants. Courtesy of Meathead, AmazingRibs.com.

Shrimp de Jonghe, a classic Chicago dish, created in the late 1800s. Photograph by Chris Cassidy.

Charlie Trotter was a pioneer in farm-to-table cookery. Photograph by Tim Turner.

Food as art: Charlie Trotter's asparagus terrine. Photograph by Tim Turner.

Grant Achatz preparing a dish at Alinea. Wikimedia Commons.

Jim Shoe sandwiches are found mainly on Chicago's South and West Sides. Photograph by Mary Valentin.

The soda Vin Fiz marked the first continental airplane flight in an advertisement. Wikimedia Commons.

Lunch Counters

A popular fixture of Chicago's five-and-dime stores, lunch counters were found at Kresge's (precursor to K-Mart), Walgreens, and Woolworth's. The counters provided inexpensive American standards—roast beef, patty melts, grilled cheese, and ham salad sandwiches. The aim of adding lunch counters was to provide enticement for customers to visit more often and to hedge against the seasonal nature of soda fountains by making use of the space year-round.

When Charles Walgreen opened his first store on the South Side in 1901, the store served hot-plate lunches and sandwiches prepared by his wife, Myrtle. Later, employee Ivar "Pop" Coulson began to add ice cream to the malted milk recipe in 1922, selling the item as Horlick's Malted Milk. He is widely credited with the invention of the milkshake. In the 1980s, Walgreens briefly expanded into stand-alone 24-hour casual restaurants, called Wag's, before selling the business to Marriott Group in 1988. In 2012, the company resumed food service in select urban stores branded Walgreens Upmarket. In addition to packaged and prepared foods,

Perfect Eat Shop, 1942. Library of Congress.

these locations feature freshly prepared food, including sushi, espresso, and smoothies.

Lunch counters, along with the five-and-dimes and affordable department stores that housed them, began to decline in the 1950s and 1960s as many shoppers moved to the suburbs. The prominent chains either adapted or ceased to exist. Walgreens became the largest drug retailer in the United States. Kresge's focused on the suburban department store and became K-Mart, now part of Sears Holdings. The 22 Woolworth's stores in the Chicago area closed in 1997 with the rest of the company's U.S. stores. The flagship downtown store at 18 N. State was converted into loft condos in 2003.

Contributor: John Carruthers

See also: Malted Milk Shake; Soda Fountains; Walgreen, Myrtle and Charles

BIBLIOGRAPHY

Kilian, Michael. "Counter Culture." *Chicago Tribune*, June 27, 1997.

F. W. Woolworth menu, ca. 1950. http://curly-wurly.blogspot.com/2006/12/woolworths-menu.html.

Lunch Wagons and Diners

As Chicago businesses and manufacturing grew, so did the need to feed the people who worked in them. By the mid-to-late nineteenth century, city streets and alleyways were filled with pushcarts selling such items as sausages, roasted corn, popcorn, fruit, peanuts, and ice cream. By the 1890s, pushcarts were augmented by numbers of horse-drawn wagons, often called "sandwich wagons." These mobile eateries originated on the East

Coast where, by the late 1800s, hundreds of converted wagons were peddling inexpensive meals to pedestrians and workers. Most important, food wagons gained a following by staying open late at night, after restaurants had closed. Chicago had many wagons, described by a newspaper in 1894 as institutional as baked potato or fried fish stands in England. Chicago wagons had cooking gear on board and served foods through a service window on one side of the vehicle. Foods were those that could be eaten out of hand, especially fried egg or ham sandwiches, "hamburger steaks," cheese sandwiches, and lots of fried chicken.

The business could be lucrative. George Corey, whose lunch car stood at the 39th Street elevated station, made more money than most downtown restaurants during the Columbian Exposition in 1893. Others were similarly successful, one hauling in $55 (5- to 6-weeks' wages for wagon operators) on the night of the "Gentleman Jim" Corbett and John L. Sullivan boxing match in 1892. All was to change, because wagons and pushcarts competed with established restaurants and were said to clog the already crowded streets. Chicago, along with other cities, passed ordinances restricting the horse-drawn vehicles because they were claimed to be unsanitary. By 1902, the numbers of vendors and wagons were greatly diminished in the downtown area. However, as manufacturing moved further west and south of the city, food wagons followed. By the 1920s, many were motorized. After the 1950s, they came to be called food trucks, and pejoratively, "roach coaches." But they now had refrigeration and heating devices to help serve lunch to working people in factories, warehouses, and other venues.

Other lunch wagons became permanent. Attempting to circumvent the city ordinances, many lunch wagon entrepreneurs began to place their wagons in semipermanent locations. By the 1920s, the popular style of Chicago's Pullman Palace Car Company's railroad dining car was being emulated in the manufacture of permanent eateries across the country. This experience led to the creation of the term "diner." Diners typically were set up with service counters and stools in front of them. The desire to capture more customers in this era led to cleaner, more attractive interiors, table seating, restrooms, longer lunch counters, and courteous service. A latter-day (1993) classic dining car at 501 S. Wells St. serves as home to the Tutto Italiano restaurant. The Silver Palm on N. Milwaukee Ave. is an actual railway dining car.

Although Chicago never had the classic diners of the East Coast, today it has many diner-style eateries, with menus like the lunch wagons of old: soups and numerous griddled dishes such as eggs, ham, cheese sandwiches, and steaks. Notables include Lou Mitchell's, located at 565 W. Jackson St. at the beginning of Old Route 66, and in its eighty-sixth year of service; The Chicago Diner on N. Halsted St.; and The White Palace Grill at S. Canal St. and Roosevelt Road.

Contributors: Philip Wojciak and Bruce Kraig
See also: Fast Food/Quick Service; Lou Mitchell's Restaurant

BIBLIOGRAPHY
Gutman, Richard J. S. *American Diner, Then and Now*. Baltimore: The Johns Hopkins University Press, 1993.
"History and Culture of The American Diner." American Diner Museum. http://www.americandinermuseum.org/site/history.php.
"Viands at the Curb: Hungry People Fed by the Nocturnal Sandwich Wagon." *Chicago Daily Tribune*, April 15, 1894.

Lutz's Café and Bakery

Opened in 1948 by Swiss-born Fred Lutz and his wife Mariele, Lutz's, at 2458 Montrose Ave., is one of Chicago's iconic bakeries. After the Lutzs' retirement, their children ran the store until 2002, when it was bought by current owners John Tzortzis and Howard Gould. They continue making the bakery's traditional European-style pastries, cookies, and cakes, such as sacher, marzipan, and other tortes; stollen; strudel; *kolachky*; and a signature strawberry whipped-cream cake. Customers can enjoy a light lunch of soup, sandwiches, or quiche in the bakery's Old World café or its outside patio, followed by Viennese-style coffee service with a silver pot of coffee and a dish of whipped cream.

Lutz is probably best known for its *baumkuchen* ("tree cake" in German) that, in July 2010, was featured on Food Network's *Kid in a Candy Store*. This three-foot-tall confection is made by dipping a spit into a sponge cake batter of almond paste, marzipan, and rum, roasting it for 90 seconds, then dipping it again, and repeating the process 22 times until it resembles a big log. Once a Christmas delicacy, the cake now is sold year-round and includes a chocolate-covered version. The unique rotisserie, one of three in the country, was manufactured in Berlin in 1945.

Contributor: Colleen Sen
See also: Baking and Bakeries; Germans

BIBLIOGRAPHY
Carlozo, Lou. "Chicago's Lutz Bakery Takes the Cake after Food Network Episode." *Daily Finance*, July 13, 2010.
Zell, Fran. "Pastries Sing Viennese Tune." *Chicago Tribune*, May 15, 1975.

Magazines (See: Media, Print)

Malted Milk Shake

In 1873, London-born brothers William and James Horlick settled in Racine, Wisconsin, and then in Chicago, where they founded J & W Horlick's Food Company. They set out to create a dried whey and malt powder that would not ferment and could be used as a nutritional supplement. In 1875, they got a patent for Horlick's Infant and Invalid Food that could be mixed with fresh milk. But since fresh milk was not a reliable commodity at the time, William Horlick developed powdered milk. Powdered milk combined with malt powder could be prepared with water. Horlick's Malted Milk gained favor with explorers because it was lightweight and nonperishable; it traveled to both poles with Admiral Richard E. Byrd.

In 1922, Ivar "Pop" Coulson was working at the soda counter in a Chicago Walgreens Drug Store when he combined malted milk powder with the store's own brand of vanilla ice cream. His recipe called for 1–1/2 ounces chocolate syrup, 3 scoops of vanilla ice cream, 5–1/2 ounces cold milk, and 1 heaping tablespoonful of malt powder, all blended and served in a 10-ounce glass with a generous mound of whipped cream. The drink, known as a malted milk shake, malt shake, malted, or simply a malt, became widely popular at U.S. soda fountains and remains a popular ice-cream treat.

Contributor: Deborah Pankey

See also: Walgreen, Myrtle and Charles

BIBLIOGRAPHY

Giles, Diane. "Malted Milk Traces History to Racine's Horlick Brothers." *Kenosha News*, December 31, 2012.

"The Milkshake That Shook Up America." Walgreens. http://www.walgreens.com/topic/history/hist4.jsp.

Mandel, Abby

Her mission could be found in "The Weekend Cook," the column Mandel launched on September 14, 1986, in the *Chicago Tribune*, writing: "I'll help you cook and entertain with style, but never anxiety."

It was pure Abby Mandel, embracing that mission in the vast number of cooking classes she taught and the cookbooks she wrote. And it was apparent to readers of

OLD-FASHIONED CHOCOLATE MALTED MILK SHAKES

Here is the Walgreens version:

"In a frosty malt can, combine 1 1/2 ounces chocolate syrup, 3 #16 dips of vanilla ice cream and 5 1/2 ounces cold milk. Add one heaping tablespoonful of malt powder. Place can on mixer only until mixed. Do not over mix. Pour into a 10-ounce glass, about 2/3 full. Top with a generous portion of whipped topping. Serve remainder of malted in a shaker along with the glass to the guest with straws and a package of fountain treat cookies."

—DEBORAH PANKEY

her columns in the *Tribune, Chicago Sun-Times* ("Turned On Kitchen"), and *Bon Appetit*, which introduced cooks to a then-new kitchen gizmo, the food processor.

Perhaps her most important legacy is the Green City Market, which she founded in 1998 to connect consumers and restaurateurs to local farmers and producers, and to support local sustainable agriculture. There were nine farmers at that first market on the passageway along the South Side of the iconic Chicago Theatre. These days, dozens of farmers and producers are on hand for the market's summer homes at the southern end of Lincoln Park and at Green City Market, in the West Loop, or at its winter quarters in the Peggy Notebaert Nature Museum.

Born Abby Evarts in Holyoke, Massachusetts, she cooked as a youngster, but went on to earn degrees in sociology (Smith College) and social work (Wayne State University). It was at a Smith College benefit she organized that she met Julia Child, was introduced to a food processor, and found her culinary calling. She trained at restaurants in France, Switzerland, and Belgium.

She founded the Best of the Midwest Market in 1989; it ran for 11 years under the auspices of The American Institute of Wine & Food. She won a prestigious James Beard Foundation Award for her 1989 book, *More Taste than Time*. And she was involved in culinary organizations including The American Institute of Wine & Food (national board member, Chicago chapter board member) and Les Dames d'Escoffier (Chicago chapter president, and president of Les Dames d'Escoffier International, 1999–2001).

In her final *Tribune* column, October 16, 2005, she wrote: "There's a special camaraderie that can only come from people who love talking together about cooking and good food." Abby Mandel Meyer brought those people together. She died in 2008 at 75.

Contributor: Judy Hevrdejs

See also: Farmers Markets; Green City Market

BIBLIOGRAPHY

Guy, Sandra. "Abby Mandel Meyer: Chef, Food Columnist Started Lincoln Park Organic Market." *Chicago Sun-Times*, August 14, 2008.

Will, Joanne. "A New Book from the Dear Abby of the Food Processor Crowd." *Chicago Tribune*, April 2, 1981.

Manny's Coffee Shop & Deli

Located on Chicago's Near West Side, the family-owned Manny's is considered the biggest, best known, and oldest deli in the city, popular among regular folk and politicians, including President Barack Obama.

The restaurant's roots can be traced back to 1942, when Russian-born brothers Jack and Charlie Raskin opened a deli, called The Purity, at Van Buren and Halsted Streets. The siblings specialized in Jewish American steam-table cuisine (but not kosher) served up fast and in big portions: behemoth corned beef sandwiches, smoked whitefish, blintzes, kishke, and knishes.

Manny's came into existence shortly after World War II, when the Raskin brothers split up so that Jack could open his own restaurant on Roosevelt Road near the bustling Maxwell Street Market. Jack named the eatery after his teenage son, Emanuel (Manny, to family and friends). The address changed several times, and then in 1965, Manny's landed at its present site, 1141 S. Jefferson St. (Manny's opened a second location in 2002 at Midway Airport.)

Today, Ken Raskin, proprietor and son of the late Manny, can be seen working the rooms, greeting customers who have known him since he was a little boy. Ken's wife, Patti, and son, Danny (fourth generation), have joined full-time. Manny's is among the last of that unique style of urban eatery, the home-style, family-run cafeteria attracting patrons from all walks of life. In June 2016, Manny's opened a full-fledged deli selling traditional Jewish foods for takeout, including Manny's own brand of corned beef and pastrami, bagels, prepared foods, and cookies.

Contributor: Scott Warner

See also: Delicatessens; Jewish

Manny's Coffee Shop and Deli is Chicago's most famous deli. Courtesy of Manny's Coffee Shop and Deli.

BIBLIOGRAPHY

Eng, Monica. "At Manny's Deli in Chicago, President-elect Barack Obama Is Served Corned Beef with a Side of Applause." *Chicago Tribune*, November 22, 2008.

Mantuano, Tony

Since the opening of the 4-star Spiaggia restaurant in 1984 by Levy Restaurants, Chef Mantuano has been in the forefront of Chicago's fine-dining explosion. With a background in food—his family owned an Italian grocery store in Kenosha, Wisconsin—Mantuano, not surprisingly, ended up being a chef, even though he studied music at the University of Wisconsin-Milwaukee. Earning top reviews from area newspapers and multiple awards, including Best Chef Midwest from the James Beard Foundation in 2005 and a Michelin star, Mantuano is known for raising the level of Italian dining with Spiaggia. His simple but sophisticated dishes use prime, often imported, Italian ingredients. And, as one reporter noted, not a meatball in sight.

In 1991, he left Spiaggia to open Tuttaposto on Franklin Street, a more casual Mediterranean restaurant. But after five years, he closed the place and soon returned to Spiaggia as chef/partner. Mantuano also runs Cafe Spiaggia, a casual sister to the larger restaurant next door (980 N. Michigan Ave.) More recently, he opened Bar Toma on Pearson Street, Piano Terzo in the Art Institute of Chicago's new Modern Wing, and River Roast overlooking the Chicago River. He also owns Mangia Trattoria in Kenosha with family members. With his wife, Cathy, he has written two cookbooks, *The Spiaggia Cookbook: Eleganza Italiana in Cucina* and *Wine Bar Food: Mediterranean Flavors to Crave with Wines to Match*. He has appeared in numerous television shows, including Bravo's *Top Chef Masters*.

Contributor: Carol Mighton Haddix

See also: Restaurants and Fine Dining

BIBLIOGRAPHY

Schnitzler, Nicole. "Chicago Chef Tony Mantuano Will Never Forget His Grandmother's Homemade Fusilli." *Food Republic*, March 10, 2015. http://www.foodrepublic.com/2015/03/10/chicago-chef-tony-mantuano-will-never-forget-his-g.

Margie's Candies

Peter George Poulos, a Greek immigrant, opened the Security Sweet Shop, at 1960 N. Western Ave. in 1921, selling candy and ice cream. His son George practically grew up in the shop and, in 1933, after George's marriage, the shop was renamed Margie's in honor of his new bride, Margie Michaels. After George's death in 1954, Margie took control of the company while still working 15 hours a day in the shop. After Margie's death in 1995, her son Peter took over and, following the same successful formula of the Western Avenue store, opened a second Margie's at 1813 W. Montrose Ave. Both stores are in operation today. The stores feature marble soda fountain counters and Tiffany lamps with photographs and newspaper clippings covering the walls. Stuffed animals are all around.

Margie's serves homemade, hand-dipped candies and ice cream made from family recipes and is known for both the quality of the products and the décor. Margie's has more than 50 varieties of sundaes on the menu using fresh and natural ingredients and imported fresh nuts and fruits. The Atomic Buster, a jumbo sundae made with hot fudge and fruit, is a Margie's original. The waffle cones are made in-house. A "Before Dessert" section of the menu includes hot and cold sandwiches and salads.

During each decade of Margie's existence, a variety of celebrities visited. Roy Rogers, Kim Novak, Jim Belushi, the Beatles, and the Rolling Stones, among a host of others. Margie's has appeared on television from time to time including a WTTW's *Check, Please!* episode in 2001.

Contributor: Geraldine Rounds

See also: Candy; Greeks

BIBLIOGRAPHY

Hoekstra, Dave. "60 Years of Sweet Dreams at Margie's." *Chicago Sun Times*, February. 12, 1993. www.margiesfinecandies.com.

Markets (See: Supermarkets and Grocers; Wholesale Markets)

Mars, Incorporated

The story of Mars begins in Minnesota with a little boy afflicted by polio, who learned how to hand-dip chocolates from the mother who was also teaching him his ABCs. Born in 1882, Frank C. Mars had graduated to selling candy by the age of 19. A year later, he was doing well enough to get married, and, in 1904, he and his wife had a son named Forrest Edward Mars.

Frank's focus changed from selling to making butter cream candies while living in Tacoma, Washington. After returning to Minneapolis, he built a successful chocolate and nougat business. Always researching new ideas, Frank hoped to connect with the era's malted milk craze. With the help of his son, Forrest, he succeeded, and in 1923, he introduced the Milky Way, advertised as "a double malted milk in a candy bar." It was an immediate hit.

Success demanded greater manufacturing capacity. So in 1929, Frank Mars moved Mars, Inc., to 2019 N. Oak

Park Ave. in Chicago, bringing along 200 of his workers. Son Forrest, now 25, came along and worked for his dad for the first of the Chicago years. In 1930, the company introduced Snickers, named for Frank's favorite horse. In 1932, 3 Musketeers was introduced, originally three separate pieces in chocolate, strawberry, and vanilla. During World War II, strawberry and vanilla were hard to come by, so Mars switched to all chocolate but retained the name.

Frank and Forrest did not agree on how to run the business, so in 1932, Forrest was given seed money for his own company. He moved to the United Kingdom and created Mars Limited, with a candy bar similar to the Milky Way called the Mars Bar (deep-fried Mars Bars becoming a Scottish and later worldwide phenomenon). Forrest then developed candy-coated bits of chocolate that he called M&Ms. When Frank died in 1934, he excluded his son Forrest and left the company to his second wife, Ethel (now the name of Mars's upscale chocolate division), and their daughter Patricia. After some years, Forrest returned to the company as chairman of Mars, Inc., and merged the company with his company, Food Manufacturers, Inc., in 1964.

Forrest Mars bought Uncle Ben's Rice in 1942 and other food-related businesses, including pet food. All were combined with Mars, Inc., in 1964, but chocolate remained the cornerstone. New brands were steadily added or acquired, and the company expanded beyond the U.K. and U.S. markets. The trend has continued under the Mars family direction. In 1986, Mars acquired Chicago's Dove Candies and, in 1990, introduced Dove Chocolates. In 2008, Mars acquired the William Wrigley Jr. Company.

The company's commitment to its "Five Principles"—quality, responsibility, mutuality, efficiency, and freedom—has been reflected in everything from purchasing Seeds of Change and launching the Rainforest Alliance to refusing to advertise snacks to children under 12.

Today, Mars, Incorporated, is one of the world's leading food companies, but it remains best known for its confectionary division, Mars Chocolate. Though the main office of Mars Chocolate is in New Jersey, the Chicago factory is still in operation in its original Spanish-style buildings. The 29 brands of candy now produced by Mars are among the best known in the world.

....

Contributor: Cynthia Clampitt

See also: Candy; Dove Bar; William Wrigley Jr. Company

BIBLIOGRAPHY

Brenner, Joël Glenn. *The Emperors of Chocolate: Inside the Secret World of Hershey and Mars*. New York: Random House, 1998.

Goddard, Leslie. *Chicago's Sweet Candy History*. Mount Pleasant, S.C.: Arcadia Publishing, 2012.

Marshall Field's

On April 15, 1890, Marshall Field's became the world's first department store with an on-premise restaurant. The South Tearoom on the third floor was an instant hit, and within a year, the restaurant was serving 1,500 guests a

---

MRS. HERING'S CHICKEN POT PIE
....

Prep: 20 minutes
Cook: 25 minutes
Makes: 4 servings

These individual pot pies are perfect for a luncheon. If you like, add a pinch of dried tarragon to the sauce ingredients. Adapted from the *Marshall Field's Cookbook*.

   1 sheet frozen puff pastry dough or pie dough, thawed
   3 tablespoons butter
   1/4 cup flour
   2 cups chicken broth
   Kosher salt, to taste
   Freshly ground black pepper, to taste
   12 ounces cooked chicken breast, cut into strips
   1/4 cup tiny frozen peas, thawed

   1/4 cup diced cooked carrot

1. Heat oven to 450 degrees. Place four individual casseroles with 1 1/2- to 2-cups capacity on a baking sheet. Cut circles from the pastry to fit the tops of the casseroles. Make two 1-inch slashes in the center of each pastry circle. Set aside.

2. Melt butter in a medium pan; stir in flour. Cook, stirring, 1 minute. Add broth, whisking until smooth. Heat to a boil; cook until thickened, 1 to 2 minutes. Season with salt and pepper. Add chicken, peas, and carrots; heat until hot.

3. Divide the mixture among the casseroles. Top with a pastry round, tucking the edges in. Place the baking sheet with casseroles in the oven. Bake until puffy and golden, 20 to 25 minutes. Serve hot.

The cover of Marshall Field's childrens' menu. Photograph by Colleen Taylor Sen.

day. When the restaurant moved to a 17,000-square-foot space on the seventh floor, the name was changed to the Walnut Room, a nod to the imported walnut paneling on the walls.

Signature dishes such as chicken salad and chicken pot pie were on the menu from the beginning. A traditional afternoon tea, complete with sandwiches and sweets, was a popular twentieth-century addition. But of all the edibles associated with Marshall Field's, none is more important than Frango mints. Field's was also a must stop for packaged gourmet foods and wines. Today it (now Macy's) offers many dining options in the basement and the seventh-floor food court with spots for such celebrity chefs as Rick Bayless and Marcus Samuelsson.

Contributor: Barbara Revsine

See also: Cooking Classes; Department Store Dining; Frango; Moody, Harriet Brainard; The Walnut Room

BIBLIOGRAPHY

Greene, Joan. *Marshall Field's Food and Fashion*. Portland: Pomegranate Books, 2005.

Siegelman, Steve. *The Marshall Field's Cookbook*. San Francisco: Book Kitchen, 2006.

Maxim's de Paris

Maxim's was one of Chicago's first nationally recognized fine-dining restaurants. It was located in the basement of the Astor Tower building, 24 E. Goethe St. Maxim's was conceived by Nancy Goldberg, wife of leading Chicago architect Bertrand Goldberg, and she operated it from 1963 until she sold the business in 1982.

Maxim's was an homage to the original Paris restaurant on Rue Royale. The Chicago place brought classical French cuisine to the city. Set on creating the same Parisian menu and Belle Époque interior, Nancy Goldberg (née Florsheim) imported chefs and staff from France to serve a celebrity and socialite clientele such dishes as *daube de boeuf Provençal*, sole Albert, smoked eel with horseradish, and *coquilles Saint-Jacques*. The extensive wine list, uncommon in Chicago at the time, contained such bottlings as Château la Tour Blanche 1957, Château Angelus 1959, and Château Haut-Brion 1926.

Maxim's was awarded 5 Mobil stars during its heyday. It housed Chicago's first disco, with a record collection handpicked by Régine, the reigning queen of Paris nightlife. And it helped launch the Chicago restaurant careers of Georges (Kiki) Cuisance, Bernard Cretier, and Jean Joho. Maxim's success mirrored significant trends in the 1960s: the growing popularity of French cuisine, fueled in part by Julia Child's 1963 television cooking program; and more widely traveled consumers and favorable exchange rates.

After several changes of ownership, Maxim's reverted back to Goldberg in the late 1980s; she then ran it as a special events venue until her death in 1996. It was donated by Goldberg's children to the City of Chicago in 2000 and named the Nancy Goldberg International Center. Maxim's then was acquired for $1.37 million in 2013 by restaurant owner Brendan Sodikoff (Au Cheval, Green Street Smoked Meats, Gilt Bar) and other investors, who planned a restoration and reopening.

Contributors: Mary La Plante and John Carruthers

See also: French; Restaurants and Fine Dining

BIBLIOGRAPHY

Rose, Don. "Some Like It Haute: Maxim's de Paris When It Was Hot and When It Was Not." Chicago: Chicago Department of Cultural Affairs, Maxim's and the Nancy Goldberg International Center report, 2001.

Will, Joanne. "Unmistakably Maxim's." *Chicago Tribune*, June 20, 1976, Section 9.

Maxwell Street Market

The area around Maxwell Street on Chicago's Near West Side has been a "gateway" community since the

View of Maxwell and Halsted Streets, the heart of the old Jewish community, 1950s. Courtesy of Lake County (Ill.) Discovery Museum, Curt Teich Postcard Archives.

mid–nineteenth century, changing in character with every wave of newcomers that washed through. Nearby, Jane Addams founded her Hull House to help Irish, German, and other immigrant groups acclimate to the urban environment.

Spared the flames of the Great Fire of 1871, Maxwell Street started to reflect the demographics of increasing numbers of Eastern European Jews who were starting to live in the area. Pushcarts began to line the neighborhood around Maxwell and Halsted. This was the beginning of Maxwell Street Market.

With the Great Migration of the 1920s, the community became home to a growing African American population. The market became central to the development of electrified Chicago Blues, and vendors continued to sell a variety of diverse merchandise and food.

Food offerings varied, based on which immigrant group predominated in the local population at the time. The most well-known and enduring of all foods served at the market is undoubtedly the Maxwell Street Polish, a bright red sausage, griddled with onions, served on a bun with mustard and, sometimes, pickles and sport peppers. The sausage, a combination of beef and pork, is a spicier version of the traditional Polish kielbasa. Jimmy Stefanovic owned a stand at the corner of Maxwell and Halsted in the late 1930s, and he's credited with the introduction of the Maxwell Street Polish. Now called Jim's Original, this

stand moved to nearby Union Street when the original market area was razed and renovated to become University Village. Its cousin with an identical menu, the Express Grill, is just a half-block south on the same street. Owing to the University of Illinois expansion, the market was moved to Canal Street and then to Des Plaines Avenue, between Roosevelt and Harrison.

Reflecting Chicago's changing immigrant populations, Maxwell Street Market is now largely Mexican, offering some of the finest regional Mexican street food vendors in the United States. Notable offerings included tamales Oaxaquenas (large squares of dense corn masa filled with shreds of chicken and topped with crema and salsa); mole rojo, plump chunks of pork in a deep and delicious red mole sauce, served at Rubi's and Manolos; handmade tortillas; churros (long pastry tubes filled with chocolate, vanilla, or strawberry and deep fried); *birria* (goat meat slow-cooked in a stew); and *horchata* (a cold beverage of rice, or sometimes other grain, almonds and sugar). One of the best things about the market is that it's always changing. In a few years hence, what is now a wonderful source for Mexican foods may be an equally wonderful source of Middle Eastern or Chinese cuisine.

Contributor: David Hammond

See also: African Americans; Jews; Mexicans; Sausages

BIBLIOGRAPHY

Berkow, Ira. *Maxwell Street: Survival in a Bazaar*. Garden City, N.Y.: Doubleday, 1977.

Grove, Lori, and Laura Kamedulski. *Chicago's Maxwell Street*. Chicago: Arcadia, 2002.

McCormick, Cyrus Hall

Cyrus Hall McCormick (1809–84) was the inventor of a mechanical small-grain harvester and other machinery that revolutionized American agriculture. Born and raised in Virginia where he and his father invented an efficient horse-drawn grain reaper, McCormick moved to Chicago in 1847. He realized that the rapidly expanding agricultural production of the Midwest, with its wide open prairies, was made for his machines. In 1847, McCormick partnered with the Gray and Warner foundry to build a factory on the north bank of the Chicago River. Production took off, and the plant employed 300 people. The Great Fire of 1871 destroyed the factory, but McCormick, working closely with his wife, Nancy ("Nettie") Fowler McCormick, rebuilt an even bigger factory on the Southwest Side. Here, production of all the machines' parts was centralized rather than licensed out to subcontractors as other manufacturers did. The new factory eventually employed 7,000 workers and was Chicago's largest.

The McCormick Company expanded in three ways. One was to buy up smaller companies that had new and better farming technologies. The second was the McCormick's research, leading to its own new machines. For instance, harvesters and side-cutting mowers with a single operator sitting at the back of the horse team, and a cutting-and-rake device that left bundles of stalks on the ground. Combines that reaped, bundled, and tied grain and grasses for fodder followed to further revolutionize grain production. Third, Cyrus McCormick was a brilliant marketer who knew the value of advertising. After his machine won an award at London's 1851 Crystal Palace Exhibition, he widely advertised his triumphs in colorful pamphlets, handbills, and posters. Many others followed.

After the founder's death, the company had many ups and downs. Though employees were paid relatively high wages for the time, labor unrest during an economic depression led to a strike in 1886. It was brutally put down by police, which led to a protest rally on May 4, an event that would be known ever after in labor history as the Haymarket Riot (and later judicial murder). In 1902, McCormick joined with the Deering and Plano companies to form International Harvester, now called Navistar. It soon became the largest manufacturer of agricultural machinery in the world, supplying 80 percent of the American market by 1929. Since then, all the Chicago plants closed and the city is no longer the world's harvester capital.

....

Contributor: Bruce Kraig

See also: Labor and Unions

BIBLIOGRAPHY

Hutchinson, William T. *Cyrus Hall McCormick: Seedtime, 1809–1856.* New York: Century, 1930.

McDonald's Corporation

In 1945, brothers Richard and Maurice McDonald opened a barbecue restaurant with a large menu in San Bernardino, California. In 1948, however, the brothers temporarily closed shop to reorganize their operation; when they reopened, they had a smaller menu and a 15-cent hamburger. The focused menu and high-value hamburger caught the eye of Oak Parker Ray Kroc, a Multimixer salesman. The brothers were clients of Kroc's, who soon learned that they were looking for a nationwide franchising agent. In 1955, Kroc opened his first McDonald's in Des Plaines, Illinois (400 N. Lee).

After about one year in operation, Kroc hired Fred Turner to work the counter. Turner was responsible for streamlining and refining the McDonald's Speedee Service System, an assembly-line production process that enabled each location to turn out hamburgers and other menu items quickly, efficiently, and consistently.

McDonald's has long been favored by people who appreciate that hamburgers and fries taste exactly the same wherever you are in the world. Turner began a tradition of exacting standards and quality control, explicitly clarifying the characteristics of McDonald's items. Though Kroc must be recognized as the man behind this tremendously successful corporation, it is fair to say that Turner provided the nuts-and-bolts implementation of Kroc's vision that made his dream a reality.

In 1958, McDonald's had sold 100 million hamburgers; in 1959, the company opened its 100th restaurant in Fond du Lac, Wisconsin.

In 1961, Kroc bought out the McDonald's brothers' interest in the company as well as their name, which Kroc believed was critical to his company's continued success. Also in that year, Hamburger University (HU) was opened, making McDonald's the first restaurant company to maintain a global training center. HU was founded by Turner on the principles of Quality, Service, Cleanliness, and Value (QSC&V). Originally located in the basement of a McDonald's restaurant in Elk Grove, Illinois, HU has since graduated over 80,000 students with degrees in Hamburgerology. Turner remained with the company throughout his life, later becoming chairman and chief executive officer; he died in 2013.

McDonald's entered international markets in 1967 with restaurants in Puerto Rico and Canada. Today, McDonald's operates in 119 foreign markets.

Jim Delligatti, a franchisee in Pittsburgh, introduced the iconic Big Mac in 1968, saying he needed a sandwich that would appeal to the hearty appetites of his working-class clientele. The Big Mac was the first in a series of menu innovations that continue to this day. In 1973, the Quarter Pounder and Quarter Pounder with Cheese were introduced, with the Egg McMuffin following in 1975. The Happy Meal was first served in 1979, and it represents the company's focus on children.

During the early '60s, entertainer Willard Scott appeared in several television spots as "Ronald McDonald, the Hamburger-Happy Clown." Ronald McDonald became the McDonald's "mascot" and later the figurehead for one of the most extensive corporate giving campaigns in American corporate history. The first Ronald McDonald House opened in Philadelphia in 1974 to serve the needs of children and their families. Today, Ronald McDonald

House Charities provides young people with housing and medical attention. If families are unable to pay for services, fees are waived.

Ray Kroc died in 1984. In 1985, McDonald's became one of the 30 companies comprising the Dow Jones Industrial Average.

Though originally located in Chicago's Loop, McDonald's Corporation moved in 1971 to what came to be called McDonald's Plaza in Oak Brook, Illinois. Later, the firm grew beyond this space and established an expansive campus in a wooded area of Oak Brook, featuring a hotel, training center, and additional corporate offices; 35,000 McDonald's outlets now operate worldwide. In June 2016, McDonald's announced it would move its headquarters from Oak Brook to 1045 W. Randolph St. in Chicago's West Town neighborhood, close to restaurants and bars that would attract millennials as employees. The move is expected to be completed by spring 2018.

Contributor: David Hammond

See also: Fast Food/Quick Service; Kroc, Ray

BIBLIOGRAPHY

Kroc, Ray, and Robert Anderson. *Grinding It Out: The Making of McDonald's.* Chicago: H. Regnery, 1977.

Love, James. *McDonald's: Behind the Arches.* New York: Bantam. 1995.

Meade, Mary

In the 1930s, the *Chicago Daily Tribune* began using this pen name for its food writers and cooking editors. Many newspapers and food companies used aliases for women writers or spokeswomen (i.e., Betty Crocker), perhaps because management thought they would not work long and leave to marry and raise families; but the familiar byline would go on. One of the first writers to use the name Mary Meade was Virginia Rich, who wrote a column briefly for the *Tribune* after college graduation. She left to get married and later wrote culinary mystery books. Ruth Ellen Church was the longest tenured food editor writing under the Meade byline, from 1936 to 1974. When Church retired, the Meade byline also was retired. The name appeared on a series of cookbooks and pamphlets published by the newspaper during those years.

Contributor: Carol Mighton Haddix

See also: Church, Ruth Ellen

BIBLIOGRAPHY

"Ruth Ellen Church, 81, Food Critic and Author." *New York Times,* August 23, 1991.

Bornhofen's butcher shop on the Far North Side opened around 1912. Courtesy of the Rogers Park / West Ridge Historical Society.

Meat and Poultry

When they arrived in the middle of the 1800s from Ireland, Germany, Scandinavia, and other places to settle in this new city called Chicago, immigrants brought with them whatever they could carry. What they couldn't carry, they built: houses, churches, shops, and institutions from the old country. They also brought skills and the need to make a living. One skill that provided well: butchering.

Buying a chicken from a farmer for 10 cents, plucking its feathers, discarding its head (feet and innards optional), and perhaps sectioning the bird into parts and selling them to villagers could net the butcher a 20-cent profit, with fat left over for rendering. Similar profits were found for other birds—and, except for the feathers, for domestic mammals. Butchers prospered. The system worked. In a few places it worked better and, for a century, nowhere on a grander scale than it did in Chicago.

The city's first meat market was built in 1829 by Archibald Clybourn on the North Branch of the Chicago River near what is now Wolf Point. An early customer was Fort Dearborn, and, by 1836, the profits enabled him to build a brick 20-room mansion within sniffing range of what would be Chicago's first stockyard.

The growing city soon became a transportation hub (the lake, rivers, canals, stagecoaches, and, beginning in 1848, railroads). Livestock, corn, and other feed were shipped in; some of the feed went into incoming cattle and hogs, which stayed a while before being slaughtered, packaged, and shipped, mostly east.

The opening of the Union Stock Yards in 1865, and the great packing houses that followed, concentrated much of the industry to the neighborhood southwest of the city's

THE PERILS OF MEAT SHOPPING

Madam Grandin visits Chicago for the World's Fair and goes shopping in 1893:

"Markets in Chicago are unlike those in France in that you can purchase everything under one roof.

Across from Mrs. A.'s house there was a grocery store that was rather pompously named 'Empire Grocery.' Fruit, vegetables, bread, fish, meat and other staples were sold there, with each product displayed in a separate area. The entire market was very clean and the meat counter was kept dark in order to keep flies away.

In another butcher shop, the same precautions were not taken. I requested a quarter of beef and the butcher took it out of an enormous meat locker.

Upon arriving home, I unwrapped the meat from the package and found that my steak was literally covered on all sides with crushed flies. In the short amount of time that it took for the butcher to cut, weigh, and prepare the meat, the flies had stuck to it!"

—MADAM LÉON GRANDIN, *A PARISIENNE IN CHICAGO, IMPRESSIONS OF THE WORLD'S COLUMBIAN EXPOSITION*, 52.

—BRUCE KRAIG

downtown. At its peak, 45,000 men and women worked in the slaughterhouses, packers, and related industries . . . then went home to their houses and tenements in the Back of the Yards, Bridgeport, and Brighton Park and did what folks eventually in all city neighborhoods did: They went to the local butcher for a chicken or a pork roast or sausages like the ones from the Old Country.

Not so much today, thanks to the supermarket. Gepperth's Meat Market opened on Halsted Street in the city's Lincoln Park neighborhood in 1906 where it remains to this day. There were other stand-alone butcher shops in the neighborhood at the time.

In 1910, the Shaevitz brothers opened three kosher meat markets on the city's predominantly Jewish West Side. By the 1930s, according to the Shaevitz website, "there were hundreds of kosher markets" in the city. The family's remaining market moved north to Devon Avenue in the West Rogers Park neighborhood in the 1950s; the Shaevitzes opened a branch in north suburban Highland Park in 1983—and six years later closed the Devon store.

On Clark Street near Touhy Avenue in Rogers Park, in a neighborhood where "there was literally a kosher butcher shop on every block or every other block," according to Romanian Kosher Sausage Company manager Mark Shainwald, there was now one, the city's last: Romanian Kosher Sausage Company. But not the last *butcher*. When Shaevitz left Devon Avenue, Zabiha Meat Market moved in to serve the street's predominantly Indian and Pakistani customers.

Ray Lekan, whose father, Sigmund, opened Paulina Meat Market on the North Side in 1949, remembers there being more than 25 butcher shops in the predominantly German neighborhood at the time. When Sigmund Lekan died in 2008, there was one: Paulina Meat Market.

In a dynamic city, demographics change. So, too, have buyer habits, as shoppers gravitate to supermarkets and, more recently, mega-retailers for their meat products. Specialty and ethnic markets hang on. Paulina Meat Market, which stocks just about everything meaty and can procure and prepare more to order, is one of them. Gene's Sausage Shop and Deli, with two Chicago locations, both north, specializes in European cuts and sausages. Polish is the first language in Kurowski's Sausage Shop, on Milwaukee Avenue in the Avondale neighborhood on the North Side, a shop that isn't just sausages—and if you don't find it there, there's Endy's Deli, just up the street.

One of the few live poultry stores in Chicago, ca. 1970. Courtesy of the Chicago History Museum, ICHi-85011; M.J. Schmidt.

CRAFT OF CHARCUTERIE MAKES A COMEBACK

Who knows why exactly, but the art of making meat products has returned. A backlash to commercially made sausages, pâtés, terrines (Spam, anyone)? Perhaps. Part of the locally sourced food movement? Yes. Whatever the reason, Chicagoans are happy to sample the new versions of such Old-World foods. Butchers and chefs across the city are curing, smoking, and aging their own versions of what once were ethnic meat stalwarts.

Restaurants serve appetizer boards of rustic pork pâté and tender head cheese. West Loop Salumi, 111 W. Randolph St., is a production firm with a retail counter that supplies area restaurants with its house-made products. Owner Greg Laketek makes several types of sausages, from Italian finocchiona to Spanish chorizo, dry curing them for up to 18 months. Such operations, and the many others embracing the art, seem appropriate in a town that once was stockyard central.

CAROL MIGHTON HADDIX

Holzkopf's Meat Market, on Broadway in Edgewater, is a modern throwback to Lakeview's departed German shops. Joseph's Finest Meats, on far-west Addison Street in the Dunning neighborhood, isn't all-Italian, but its sausage tells a different story.

Chicago hasn't entirely abandoned its hog-butcher heritage. Peoria Packing House, founded in 1990 as a distribution operation on Lake Street near the city's traditional Fulton and Randolph Street Markets, began slaughtering, butchering, and packaging hogs there in 1993. Almost around the corner, goats and lambs transition from life to edibility at the Halsted Packing House. Meanwhile, the fourth generation of the Kurzawski family still makes Leon's Sausages and owns Slotkowski sausages and the upscale Amylu chicken sausages in its ATK Foods plant on West Lake Street. The Chiappetti family began offering fresh-slaughtered lamb and veal on Halsted Street north of the stockyards in 1943; the yards left, but not the Chiappettis, now in their third generation as meatpackers.

Steady demand for live poultry continues, some of that demand cultural and some culinary. John's Live Poultry, on the city's Northwest Side, has been providing killed-to-order chickens, plus turkeys, geese, ducks, and rabbits, for half a century. Alliance Poultry Farms, in East Ukrainian Village, opened before World War II as a kosher market and now follows Islamic traditions (similar to kosher) in its slaughter ritual, as does Aden Live Poultry, in Albany Park. Brighton Park on the Southwest Side, a neighborhood once home to many who worked in the old Stock Yards, today is home to Windy City Poultry. There are others.

The glory days of Swift and Armour and Sandburg may be past, but this city is still in the butcher business, ever since Archibald Clybourn sliced and chopped his way to profits and into Chicago history.

Contributor: Alan Solomon

See also: Meat and Poultry; Union Stock Yards

BIBLIOGRAPHY

Mayer, Harold M., and Richard C. Wade. *Chicago: Growth of a Metropolis*. Chicago: University of Chicago Press, 1969.

Saiyed, Gulnaz. "Fresh for the Fearless: Live Poultry in Chicago." http://www.stevedolinsky.com, January 27, 2012.

Vonnegut, Sarah. "Chicago's Last Kosher Butcher." *The Red Line Project*, March 7, 2011.

Meatpacking (See: Food Reform Legislation, Meat and Poultry, Union Stock Yards)

Media

The proposition that Americans' demonstrable taste for fast food on the one hand and obsession with celebrity chefs on the other was caused by the media is certainly a debatable hypothesis. There is no doubt, however, that print and electronic mass communication has brought broad knowledge of consumable options to the American public. Interest in culinary trends and everyday cooking tips began with newspaper stories and recipe columns as early as the 1870s. Celebrity cooks such as Juliette Corson were widely followed from the later decades of the nineteenth century onward.

The popularization and development of the radio in the 1920s and of television in the 1950s did more to create a common culinary knowledge that bridged historic gaps of ethnicity, geography, and even religion. Chicago manufacturers, merchants, and food processors were uniquely positioned in the Midwest to team with cooks, promoters, and entertainers to take early advantage of the dramatically expanded audiences provided by the new technologies.

From earnest newspaper home economists in the 1940s to today's combatants in Kitchen Stadium, those with stories to teach and tell about what and how we eat have found welcoming platforms.

Contributor: Elizabeth D. Richter

NEW

In 1997, Jim Leff and Bob Okumura founded Chowhound. com in New York City, an online national food discussion board that supported continuous conversations among food enthusiasts across the country. The board was divided into larger regions and cities, and anyone could participate in the discussions because Chowhound required no registration. As time went on, a group of regular posters on the Chicago board of Chowhound started their own listserv for backchannel discussions and posts that might be considered inappropriate for Chowhound (for instance, Chowhound was not a good venue for talking about food or cocktail recipes, and the management did not approve of planning social events that took focus away from the Chowhound board).

From this listserve, LTHForum.com was launched in 2004. The name "LTH" stands for "Little Three Happiness" because on Cermak in Chicago's Chinatown there were two restaurants directly across the street from one another, both named Three Happiness. The larger restaurant was a multistory tourist stop that served decent-enough food; the smaller (or "little" Three Happiness: LTH) served grittier Cantonese chow from a mom 'n' pop storefront. LTH was dedicated to all those little places that deserved attention but received almost none. LTHForum.com continues to grow and had more than 18,000 registered members in 2015.

Former Chowhound participant Steve Plotnicki started Opinionated About, a food discussion site that covers restaurants across the country; other former Chowhounds went on to found egullet.com. Other website discussion boards and blogs that focused on Chicago have been active in Chicago over the past decade, including Eater, Menupages, Serious Eats, Tasting Table, and Grub Street. However, many of those sites—including Tasting Table and Grub Street—have basically pulled out of Chicago to refocus their coverage on the New York dining scene. Only Eater continues to deliver anything like comprehensive coverage of Chicago.

Multiple blogs were spawned by former Chowhounds, including Mike Gebert's fooditor.com and skyfullofbacon. com, sites focusing primarily on food in the Chicago area, and thelocalbeet.com, edited and published by Robert Gardner. There are, however, hundreds of Chicago-based blogs, and many are conveniently collected, listed alphabetically and by category, on Chicagofoodbloggers.com and on the Gaper Block food section gapersblock.com/drivethru/, the latter not current past 2016.

Yelp provides what Chowhound used to offer: local crowd-sourced reviews and discussions of restaurants, though perhaps with less objectivity. Bleader, the food blog of the *Chicago Reader*, continues to be active.

Contributor: David Hammond

BIBLIOGRAPHY

Gebert, Mike. "Farewell, Serious Eats Chicago, " *Chicago Reader*, August 8, 2013.
Kass, John, "These Restaurants Get It Right." *Chicago Tribune*, April 10, 2011.

PRINT

If a good newspaper is a nation talking to itself, as playwright Arthur Miller noted in 1961, then a good newspaper's food pages carry on an engaging conversation with readers about what they are eating and cooking, how they are cooking, and who is doing the cooking. And in Chicago, the city of big shoulders and bigger appetites, it has been a lively conversation that has been going on for 100-plus years.

More than a collection of recipes, the food pages and food sections found in Chicago's print media—newspapers, magazines, community periodicals—reflect changes in the city, culture, science, and the world, echoing the tenor of the day from world wars to the Depression, from the growth of supermarkets to technological advances that made in-home refrigerators and freezers readily available, on to the microwave ovens and food processors indispensable to many a cook today.

The first food stories that appeared in print were a mix of recipes developed by newspaper staffs, usually a mix of home economists and journalists. They still are. In 1849, a one-paragraph recipe for baked ham appeared in the *Chicago Daily Tribune*. By 1910, the *Tribune*'s pages featured more recipes, household hints, and excerpts from cookbooks pulled together by Caroline S. Maddocks (aka Jane Eddington), including one in 1918 titled: "Food Facts and Hints for the Patriotic Housewife."

Often recipes arrived from readers via contests that newspapers conducted over the years. At the *Chicago Daily News*, the *Daily News Cook Book* was published in 1896 and offered "Seasonable, Inexpensive Bills of Fare for Every Day in the Year," with "1000 prize menus with recipes . . . contributed by the women of America. By its use families of moderate means can get out of the ruts that lead to dyspepsia through the dead level of monotony," the preface promised.

In 1930, the *Chicago Daily Tribune* regularly ran a variety of cooking-related contests, including "Untangle This Food Mixture! Win a Prize," courtesy of Miss Meta Given, the *Tribune*'s cooking editor who had scrambled ingredients for three recipes. A year later, an advertisement in the paper announced: "Don't Miss Tomorrow's Tribune Food Section," promising articles by culinary editor, Mary Meade, and Everett Swingle, who had been checking fruit and vegetable prices at the market, plus a piece by Betty Browning on "lake fishermen who toil in the shadows of the skyscrapers."

"Mary Meade," the pseudonym for several different food writers and editors appeared in print until 1974. "When Mary came on the scene, we had six full-time employees who answered letters and telephones from readers," food editor Ruth Ellen Church told a reporter in 1988. "Mary got all sorts of fan mail. Quite a girl." Church, in addition to writing as Meade for many years, wrote nine cookbooks under her own name, hundreds of cooking articles, and America's first newspaper wine column. The *Chicago Tribune* has had an on-site test kitchen for more than 75 years; it is one of the few newspaper test kitchens in the country. Recipes were tested, usually by home economists, and photographed for publication. The kitchen has enjoyed its share of facelifts in the 1940s, 1970s, and 1990s.

In the early 1940s, food stories kept readers up to date on food rationing, while helping them cope with the challenges of sugar and meat shortages. By the late 1940s, Morrison Wood was writing a cooking column dubbed "For Men Only," often reflecting dishes popular in restaurants of the day. One such recipe? Flaming sweet potatoes. "Carry into the dining room while flaming," Wood wrote. "The sight will cause oh's and ah's from the guests, and the taste, gulps of pleasure."

By the 1950s, food editors were focusing not just on recipes but on consumer and nutrition issues as well, with articles such as one in March 1955, "The Egg and You: How Poultry Farms Serve Your Table," by *Chicago Daily News* food editor Isabel DuBois, who explained how eggs are graded and their nutritional value.

Stand-alone food sections arrived in Chicago in February 1957 when the *Chicago Tribune* announced in an advertisement: "Weekly Food Section Will Begin Friday. Tribune to Give Tips on Recipes and Shopping." It was believed that "This Weekly Illustrated Food Guide" was "the first time that such a section devoted exclusively to food has been published weekly by any metropolitan daily newspaper." There would be a large photograph on the cover and "the Inquiring Camera Girl" would visit food stores asking shoppers their opinions on food. A 22-page food section appeared and the excitement continued the next week, with the *Tribune*'s Miss Food Guide showing up at supermarkets around town.

In 1957, two retired advertising executives launched *Bon Appetit* magazine in Chicago. It was sold in 1975 to Knapp Communications in Los Angeles.

With the 1960s, an array of prepared foods, the expanded frozen food sections of supermarkets, and more women heading to the workplace shifted the focus of some food sections. As Ruth Ellen Church wrote in *Mary Meade's Modern Homemaker Cookbook*, a volume that used bottled, canned, and frozen foods with abandon: "Our modern homemaker has ninety-six more 'things to

do' than her Mom had. Even if she does not go to work every day, she is family shopper, launderer, errand runner, housekeeper and chauffeur. She needs all the meal-getting help available. . . . Today's family doesn't always have its meals around the dining table," Church wrote, blaming too many meetings, too much tempting television, and too much getting home late. "In the pace of today's living," she pointed out, "we must all be careful that mealtime doesn't degenerate into something resembling a stop at a filling station to gas up the car."

Yet family cooking was only one aspect of newspaper food sections. By the 1970s, there were four newspapers in Chicago and as many distinct food sections. They celebrated the city's vibrant ethnic communities with guides to groceries in those neighborhoods as well as the vast array of restaurants. Sections embraced new cooking appliances, sometimes testing them, and always guided cooks through the basics of the microwave oven and food processor. And they tracked food prices and planned menus for readers.

By the end of the decade, our appetite for flavors beyond the Midwest region was so strong that the number of cooking schools available in the Chicago area expanded. Newspaper food sections became coaches for those trying their hand at preparing unfamiliar recipes. Home entertaining figured prominently as well, with party planning tips, recipes for groups, cocktail and wine suggestions, and more filling the pages. Home cooks were routinely saluted. Consider the headline on a February 1985 story by the *Chicago Sun-Times*' Bev Bennett: "Cheesecake Whiz Shares Secrets of Her Success: Mother of Nine Has Collection of More than 200 Recipes for the Rich Dessert."

By the 1990s, fitness and nutrition became more important and continued to be so into 2000 and beyond. Fad diets were scrutinized. Food lifestyles—vegetarian, vegan, raw—became part of the conversation. So did the role food and meals play in our culture and in our family.

While some print food coverage has moved to digital, there are some things that haven't changed. Think those early recipe contests in the 1930s were a fluke? Think again. The *Chicago Tribune*'s holiday cookie contest has been popular for 30 years.

Contributor: Judy Hevrdejs

BIBLIOGRAPHY

Church, Ruth Ellen. *Mary Meade's Modern Homemaker Cookbook.* Chicago: Rand McNally and Co., 1966.

Eddy, Kristin. "Serving Food News for 150 Years." *Chicago Tribune,* July 16, 1997.

Sheridan, Margaret. "Whatever Happened to . . . Flashes in the Pan: Once Rebuffed in the Name of Progress Some Are Making a Comeback." *Chicago Tribune,* July 21, 1988.

RADIO

During the 1920s and 1930s, both battery-run and house-current–operated radios rapidly became fixtures in American homes. They were purchased in stores or by mail-order to the degree that, by 1930, nearly one-half of U.S. homes owned a radio. In addition, that same year, Chicago's pioneering Galvin Manufacturing Corporation (Motorola) began producing automobile radios so motorists could listen to their favorite programs.

The proliferation of radios fueled consumer demand for on-air programs, some geared for the homemaker, such as Aunt Sammy's *Housekeeper's Chat*, brainchild of the USDA Bureau of Home Economics. Some radio culinary shows were sponsored by companies involved in the food or food-related industries, such as General Mills's *Betty Crocker Cooking School of the Air*, and General Foods' daily show with Frances Lee Barton. In addition to touting specific products, these cooking programs dispensed nutrition information, recipes, menu plans, advice on meal preparation, and food presentation techniques. As stations increased their broadcasting strength, they also afforded homemakers across the nation opportunities for recipe exchanges. Sometimes individual programs' recipes were compiled and then made available to listeners helping to bring about effective homogenization and standardization of American cuisine.

On April 12, 1924, WLS radio, a Sears, Roebuck and Company enterprise, went live from its studio in Chicago's downtown Sherman Hotel (the transmitter was in Crete, Illinois). The call letters were an acronym for "World's Largest Store." Its target audience lived throughout the Corn Belt. Early content included programs of high interest to farmers, as well as a cooking show ostensibly broadcast from the "Sears Bungalow Studio."

In 1927, WLS became the Chicago outlet for the National Broadcast Company's Blue Network. One year later, station ownership passed to Burridge D. Butler's *Prairie Farmer* magazine, becoming known as the WLS–Prairie Farmer station. Broadcasts from its Chicago studio included Helen Joyce and June Merrill's *Homemaker's Hour*; Mrs. Julian Heath's *Cooking Talk*, Ann N. Goudiss's *Forecast School of Cookery*, with Anne Williams and Sue Roberts in *Tower Topics Time*. By 1932, WLS radio's "cooking family" included Leone Heuer, a Sears Roebuck and Company representative who talked about good things to eat; Martha Logan, nutrition expert for Swift & Company; and homemaker, Martha Crane, whose recipes were aired on *Homemaker's Time*.

WLS also broadcast music productions, sometimes sponsored by food-related companies such as market leader Northwestern Yeast Company of Chicago. Between 1929 and 1930, the *Yeast Foamers Show* featuring the Yeast Foamer singers and orchestra, reached the American public from NBC's Chicago facility on Washington Boulevard. The show went off the air following J. P. Morgan's merger of the Northwestern and Fleischmann's Yeast companies with the Royal Baking Powder Company, Widlar Food Products, and Chase and Sanborn Coffee into Standard Brands.

Radio cooking shows diminished in number as television gained in popularity. By the latter 1950s, they had almost disappeared. Coverage of food events, trends, general interest stories, and restaurant reviews are found on many Chicago radio stations such as WBEZ's *Chewing the Fat* podcasts.

Contributors: Ellen F. Steinberg and Jack H. Prost

BIBLIOGRAPHY

Dunning, John. *On the Air: The Encyclopedia of Old-Time Radio.* New York: Oxford University Press, 1998, 51.

Evans, James F. *Prairie Farmer and WLS: The Burridge D. Butler Years.* Urbana: University of Illinois Press, 1969.

WLS. http://www.wlshistory.com/.

TELEVISION

From the earliest days of television, cooking shows have been produced in Chicago. Though not the national center of cooking show production, Chicago programs have contributed significantly to the evolution of the genre.

Chicago may have produced the nation's very first broadcast cooking segments on the pioneering experimental station W9XBK, reaching just a few hundred sets in the early 1940s. In 1944, the station (now commercially licensed WBKB) produced *Cooking by the Dial*, featuring Commonwealth Edison's Kay Newman as chef. The station (becoming WLS-TV, better known as ABC-7) set the educational yet commercial tone for cooking shows to come. Commonwealth Edison sponsored the show to promote its "all electric kitchen appliances," establishing a much copied and profitable sponsorship model.

Local stations across the country quickly mounted the inexpensive, easy-to-produce format of a female host instructing her primarily female viewers on creating popular recipes. WGN-TV boasted one of the earliest, *Chicago Cooks with Barbara Barkley*, which debuted on its first day of live broadcasting in April 1948. Sponsored by Kelvinator appliances and S.O.S. cleaning pads, the program seamlessly integrated the message. A *Chicago Tribune* critic noted that Barkley "folds them [commercials] in as smoothly as an egg white." Like her counterparts around the country, Barkley was a home economist; she had previously worked for Sears and the Milk Foundation. Kay Middleton, a Canadian food writer and editor, replaced her in 1951.

WGN-TV also attracted female viewers to its *Women's Magazine of the Air*, launched in 1949, which included cooking demonstrations from Flower Vocational High School. Radio-based personality Helen Joyce made her name as cohost of *Feature Foods* on WLS and then moved to WGN-TV to host *The Femme Show*, covering a wide variety of topics for women, from 1935 to 1952.

While the predominant cooking show experts were women, Chicago's first network cooking show, *Creative Cookery*, had a male host, François Pope, assisted by his two sons. The program aired on WBKB Channel 4 (later on WNBQ Channel 5, today's WMAQ-TV, aka NBC-5) from 1951 through 1963. Born in France, he was married to Antoinette Pope, founder of the famed Antoinette Pope School of Fancy Cookery. Despite her success, he maintained that the finest cooks were men.

Overlapping *Creative Cookery* by a year, Boston-based Julia Child, though not a chef herself, challenged that claim on public television's *The French Chef* and raised public television's profile as a cooking-show powerhouse. The public television platform later provided Chicago its next male cooking star.

Jeff Smith, a Methodist minister and host of a low-budget local cooking show in Tacoma, Washington, inspired Chicago's public station WTTW with his engaging on-air personality. The station upgraded the production values and produced the show for PBS in 1983. Broadcast nationally for more than a decade, *The Frugal Gourmet* became PBS's most popular culinary show, laying the groundwork for the personality-driven, cable-based Food Network. Smith left WTTW for San Francisco in 1992 at the peak of his popularity. The show continued for another five years.

WTTW continued to explore other television cooking series and produced NPR host Verta Mae Grosvenor's *America's Family Kitchen* for PBS for two seasons in 1996 and 1998. Today, the station coproduces the restaurant review show *Check, Please!*, which is now in local production around the country. The station also produces local documentaries on Chicago food specialties.

As a distributor in the 1990s, WTTW provided PBS with a series of documentary specials on international culinary traditions in China, Korea, India, and Mexico, produced by Food for Thought (Chicago) Productions. It now distributes *Mexico: One Plate at a Time*, with award-winning chef Rick Bayless, to PBS affiliates. Bayless and other chefs often appear in cooking demonstrations on WTTW's *Chicago Tonight*. One of Chicago's premier chefs, Charlie Trotter, produced four seasons of the series *The Kitchen Sessions* for PBS distribution before his untimely death in 2013.

Chicago's local commercial stations regularly cover culinary topics in local newscasts. James Beard Award winner Steve Dolinsky produced and reported *Good Eating* on cable channel CLTV for eight years and now produces the *Hungry Hound* reports three times a week for ABC-7 as well as a podcast in collaboration with chef Rick Bayless. Vince Gerasole of CBS-2 also has won James Beard Foundation awards for his reporting on culinary topics. Wayne Johnson contributes culinary hints on *Wayne's Weekend* segments for NBC-5.

....

Contributor: Elizabeth D. Richter

BIBLIOGRAPHY

Collins, Cathleen. *Watching What We Eat: The Evolution of Television Cooking Shows.* New York: The Continuum International Publishing Group Inc., 2009, 35.

Kaufman, William I. *Cooking with the Experts.* New York: Random House, 1955.

Wolters, Larry. "Cookery Show Is Appetizing Television Fare." *Chicago Tribune*, May 23, 1950.

Melman, Richard

As founder and chairman of Lettuce Entertain You Enterprises (LEYE), Rich Melman (born 1942) oversees an organization that changed forever the way Chicago dines. He is also regarded as one of the nation's most innovative restaurant creators. His eclectic organization now owns, licenses, or manages more than 100 locations, most in Chicago and several in six other states. The restaurants range from fast food (M Burger) to 4-star dining (Everest), and include Asian, Italian, American, French, and other concepts as well.

Melman grew up in Chicago's Logan Square neighborhood. As a teenager he worked at his father's delis on the North Side. Together with Jerry Orzoff, a Chicago real estate agent, Melman formed Lettuce Entertain You Enterprises, and opened R. J. Grunts, in 1971, an informal eatery in Lincoln Park that brought wit and novelty to dining. Grunts offered macrobiotic food along with burgers, ribs, and shakes. Grunts also featured an expansive salad bar, the first in Chicago. The restaurant proved highly profitable and helped pave the way for dining out as entertainment, a trend that swept this country in the early 1970s.

Melman and Orzoff opened more restaurants with whimsical and appetizing names such as Lawrence of Oregano and Jonathan Livingston Seafood. In 1976, the partners took on fine dining when they bought the legendary Pump Room on Chicago's Gold Coast. Orzoff died in 1981.

In 1986, Melman opened Café Ba-Ba-Reeba! and introduced Chicago to Spanish tapas; he popularized risotto in Chicago with the opening of Scoozi in River North and launched the city's first restaurant frequent-dining club. His fine-dining restaurants include Everest, the former Ambria, and L20 (now called Intro).

Melman often visits his restaurants, where he can be seen, dressed in blue jeans and sneakers, seating customers and helping busboys clean tables. He was awarded the James Beard Foundation's Lifetime Achievement Award in 2015.

Melman and his wife Martha have three children—Jerrod, Molly, and R. J.—who are all successful restaurateurs with LEYE.

....

Contributor: Scott Warner

See also: Lettuce Entertain You Restaurants; Restaurateurs and Restaurant Groups

BIBLIOGRAPHY

Mautner, Julie. "Grilled for a Minute: Rich Melman." *Food Arts*, August 29, 2012.

Rice, William. "Let Them Entertain You." *Chicago Tribune*, September 1, 1991.

Mexicans

All histories of Mexicans in Chicago start with official immigration records from 1916–19. Economic and political upheavals in Mexico, as well as severe labor shortages in the United States, led to the conscription of a large number of single men to work in steel mills, railways, or the meatpacking industries. Women did housework or cooked at boarding houses and company messes.

By the 1920s, three principal Mexican concentrations were well-established: around the Hull House settlement on Halsted, near meatpacking and rail companies of Back of the Yards, and around South Chicago's steel mills. Butchers and groceries such as El Gardenia (1120 S. Peoria St., opened in 1921) and La Tienda Colorada (4530 S. Ashland Ave., with stores in four neighborhoods by 1929) offered increasingly larger selections from the Mexican pantry. They sold earthenware cazuelas as well as the metate, the traditional mortar to grind lime-cooked corn (nixtamal masa) for tortillas. But convenience products such as Tamalina (a dehydrated corn flour product) and canned goods also were available. Tortillerías as a specialized business were a recent development in the United States, as in Mexico, and were established in Chicago from the late 1920s. El Azteca in South Chicago advertised its services as a mill for fresh masa ("molino para nixtamal") in an advertisement from 1928. Bakeries such as El Chico at Clark and Oak offered bolillos (rolls), pan dulce (pastries), and hot chocolate. Home-based artisans produced mole pastes, chorizo (pork sausages) or chicharrón (fried cracklings).

Boarding houses or home kitchens catered to single men by serving humble everyday meals and packing workday lunches. A university survey in 1928 counted 14 storefront eateries near Hull House. Popular restaurants included La Ideal and El Rancho Grande in South Chicago, which served as many as 50 regular diners daily. Antojitos Mexicanos on W. Taylor St. listed pozole (a stew of hominy and pork), or sopes (griddled cake of corn masa, served open-faced with toppings). Longer menus offered

MEXICAN STREET FOOD

Mexican street food has become a part of the fabric of Chicago food culture. By the 1920s, Mexicans were frequenting the open-air Maxwell Street Market and soon carved out a dominant presence. Stalls offering Aguascalientes-style *barbacoa* (steam-roasted lamb) or Guanajuato's *empanada de sesos* (brain, inside a round of *masa*, folded, pleated closed, and fried crisp) continue this market's long-storied tradition of immigrant foods, many of which have become Chicago icons.

In the neighborhoods, street stalls, located at specific corners and on specific days and times, offer Morelia-style *gaspacho* (jicama, mango, pineapple, or other fruits finely diced and mixed with citrus juice and other condiments as a kind of fruit soup) or *tacos de cabeza al vapor* with the rich variety of different parts (beef cheek, sweetbread, eyeball) of steamed whole cow's head to please the connoisseur. Increasingly elaborate and baroque setups may include griddles, vats of oil for frying, or gas-powered spits on sidewalks.

One family, famous on the West Side for decades at successive sites, serves dozens of rare specialties of Guerrero, including *tamales nejos* (in Chicago, often seen as flat disks or triangles wrapped in banana leaf) and *atole de ciruela* (gruel of *masa de nixtamal*, flavored with hogplums), generating long lines expanding by word of mouth. Tented shelters and milk crates as impromptu seats push the limits of local zoning. Pushcart vendors selling *elotes* (corn-on-the-cob with a variety of dressings) or *paletas* (ice pop) in flavors of fruits such as *mamey* or *nanche* are a common sight, asserting a vibrant urban presence during a period when street peddling has been marginalized to invisibility in the larger culture.

—RICHARD S. TAN

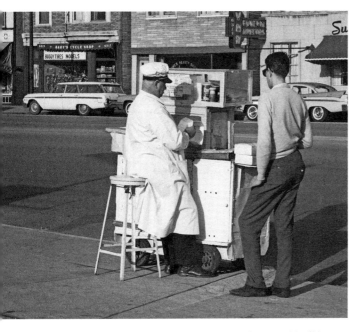

Hot Tamale vendor, 6300 North Clark St., ca. 1960. Courtesy of the Chicago History Museum, ICHi-85008; Norman A. Tegtmeyer.

higado de res (beef liver), torta de sesos (brain fritters in a light tomato-chile sauce), albondigas (meatballs), and other mestizo classics from the central plateau states that were the source of the largest number of immigrants.

Promoted for decades by the Mexican elite as a symbol of national and culinary identity, mole poblano (customarily served with chicken in Chicago) might be highlighted as a weekend special. Although the turn-of-the-century craze for Texan chili had subsided by the 1920s, many "chili parlors" such as Mexican Joe's were in business and were ridiculed in a Mexican community newspaper. "Hot tamales" could now be found in the phone book, listed under "h." Being the closest to downtown, the vibrant and colorful slums around Hull House were a convenient destination for non-Mexicans seeking adventure and exotic immigrant food. The blocks near the corner of Polk and Halsted were referred to as "tamaletown," considered a slur and denounced in an editorial in *México*, a local newspaper, in 1930. Labor shortages during World War II and immigration reforms in 1965 allowed many Mexicans legal entry, although large numbers of undocumented workers also arrived. By the 1980s, Chicago's Mexican population was, along with Los Angeles and Houston, the largest of any metropolis in the United States. Each new generation of immigrants strengthened and renewed connections to traditional and regional cuisines.

The razing of the Hull House district in the 1960s displaced established businesses. Though Mexicans were in Pilsen in the 1920s, they now moved there in large numbers, replacing the Eastern European communities that dominated the area. Many food businesses that opened during this period are still identified with Pilsen today: Casa del Pueblo Supermarket (1960), Restaurante Nuevo Leon (1962), and several specialists of carnitas in the style of Uruapan (pork, often whole hog, slow-cooked in its own fat) from the 1970s. Pilsen became the banner Mexican neighborhood and a center for Latino activism. By the late 1970s, adjacent neighborhoods, anchored by streets like Cermak and 26th, also became predominantly Mexican. In the neighborhood now called La Villita, 26th St. became the second most important commercial street (in gross sales) in Chicago after the Magnificent Mile.

Food wholesalers, consolidators, importers, and multimillion-dollar food processing businesses established in the postwar period included Azteca Foods (1962, refrigerated tortilla business) and V & V Supremo (1964, packaged cheeses in traditional styles). As tastes changed, traditional Mexican produce such as cactus paddles, fresh tamarind pods, and calabacitas (a variety of summer squash) became standard items in many Chicago grocery chains. Large Mexican supermercados (such as Carnicería Guanajuato or El Guero) opened in immigrant-dense neighborhoods and offered increasingly specialized items, including culinary herbs such as *verdolaga (purslane), huauhzontle (chenopodium or goosefoot), and papaloquelite (skunk weed)*. In-house butchers sold specific Mexican cuts, regional blood sausages, and housemade goat barbacoa (a popular kitchen version of traditional pit-roasted meat).

The repertoire of Mexican dishes popular at midcentury including carne a la tampiqueña (grilled steak with roasted peppers) and milanesa de res (thin breaded steaks), which were offered by rival restaurants to attract both Mexican and Anglo customers. The Pepe's franchise (founded in 1962) offered crossover favorites like enchiladas and chicken flautas. Tacos de carne asada, rarely seen in Mexico except in northern states, cemented its supremacy as the most popular item in taquerías. Starting in the late 1970s, the overstuffed burritos popular in California became a favorite food among college students in gentrifying Lincoln Park.

In addition to Pilsen and La Villita, at least two dozen commercial strips of Mexican businesses have transformed the streetscape in neighborhoods such as Albany Park, Humboldt Park, Logan Square, Back of the Yards, Rogers Park, and on Commercial Avenue in South Chicago. Starting in the 1950s, immigrants from Santiago Papasquiaro in Durango arrived in larger numbers, settling in pockets of the South Side and also in Avondale and Belmont-Cragin. Groceries in these areas offer the *chuales* (kernels of parched corn) and *carne seca* (dried salted beef) of their cuisine. Eateries serve their delicate traditional burritos,

Mexican street food stand in the Maxwell Street Market. Photograph by Bruce Kraig.

made with freshly griddled wheat tortillas and stuffed with *chile pasado* (a stew of the regional sun-dried chile) or homemade cheeses like cuajada and requesón.

From the late 1970s, immigrants from Ciudad Hidalgo in Michoacan settled in many different areas as well but would become most visible along Clark Street in Rogers Park where signs on windows entice passersby with offers of *corundas con puerco en salsa verde* (flat or triangular tamales wrapped in banana leaf, served with pork stew). Business names such as Carnicería La Mixteca Poblana or Restaurante Oaxaca flaunt regions of origin, but also suggest the local dishes available. Immigrants from the area around Teloloapan and Iguala in Guerrero state arrived preponderantly after 1994. A customary artisanality marks their foodways, and their dynamism and business acumen are expressed in the more than 100 food businesses they have opened throughout the city, ranging from street food carts to the highest level of fine-dining restaurants. The endless stream of new arrivals strengthens the connection with home villages and ensures a supply of provisions from the regional larder. This strong sense of home identity ensures the preservation of distinct regional culinary practices. Because of this, representation of Mexico's culinary diversity is arguably greater in Chicago than anywhere else in the United States.

Mexicans living in Chicago have been employed in hotels in the Loop and in the catering and service industries from the 1920s. Mexicans contributed to Chicago's rise as a great restaurant city in the 1980s. Carlos Nieto started as a busboy and became owner of the much-awarded 4-star Carlos'. Guillermo Tellez became chef de cuisine at Charlie Trotter's. Spiaggia, the 4-star Italian restaurant, was almost completely staffed for over two decades with Mexicans from a single village. Mexicans today also staff the humblest

mom-and-pop ethnic food businesses, preparing kimchi or making Vietnamese *banh mi.*

A series of restaurants emerged from the mid-1980s ambitious to elevate Mexican cuisine to fine dining. Restaurants such as Las Cazuelas, Rick Bayless's Frontera Grill and Topolobampo, Priscilla Satkoff's Salpicon, Geno Bahena's restaurants, and Clementina Flores at Sol de Mexico moved away from the clichés and canons of Mexican food. Bayless's successful operations in particular would serve as much-admired, much-copied templates in coming decades for "high-end Mexican" throughout the world. Mobility and exchange between "high" and "low," the strength and diversity of traditional cuisines, and the immigrants' dynamism—all these contribute to the vibrancy of Mexican Chicago at the beginning of the twenty-first century.

Contributor: Richard S. Tan

BIBLIOGRAPHY

Arredondo, Gabriela. *Mexican Chicago: Race, Identity and Nation, 1916–39.* Urbana: University of Illinois Press, 2008.

Innis-Jiménez, Michael. *Steel Barrio: The Great Mexican Migration to South Chicago, 1915–1940.* New York: New York University Press, 2013.

Jirasek, Rita Arias, and Carlos Tortolero. *Mexican Chicago.* Charleston, S.C.: Arcadia Publishing Co., 2001.

Middle Easterners

The 1893 World's Columbian Exhibition brought the first major wave of Middle Easterners to Chicago. In the century since, immigrants from the Middle East have made their way to Chicago at various intervals from Palestine, Jordan, historic Assyria, Iraq, Syria, Lebanon, Egypt, Yemen, and Turkey. They have come seeking prosperity, to connect with predecessor family and friends, and to escape turmoil in their home countries.

THE MEANING OF HALAL

The Arabic word *halal* means permissible or lawful, and in Islamic law it means foods that Muslims are allowed to eat, as opposed to foods that are *haram* or forbidden. The latter category includes pork and alcohol. To make other kinds of meat halal, the animal or bird must be slaughtered in a ritual way known as *zabiha.* In Chicago, restaurants, butcher shops, and grocery stores that serve a Muslim clientele advertise that their food is both halal and zabiha.

—COLLEEN SEN

An influx of Christian and Muslim Palestinians arrived from the West Bank in the late 1960s, tripling the size of the Arab community in Chicago. Middle Eastern Muslims have tended to flock to the Southwest Side and Christians to the Northwest Side of the city. An estimated 220,000 people of Middle Eastern descent, both Christian and Muslim, live in the six-county Chicago area. While Lebanese Americans are the largest group nationally, Palestinians are the largest group in Chicago. More Palestinians live in Chicagoland than anywhere in the United States.

Most Iranians in Chicago are Persian-speaking Muslims who arrived in the wake of the 1979 Islamic Revolution in Iran. Assyrians are Aramaic-speaking Christians from historic Assyria, currently part of northern Iraq, southeastern Turkey, and northwestern Iran, and their Chicago community is the largest in the United States.

The earliest Syrian community in Chicago, consisting mainly of Melkites (Greek Catholics), was founded in 1894. Lebanese Americans, initially Eastern-Rite Maronite Catholics, followed in the 1900s; a later wave in the 1970s was of various religious backgrounds, including Muslim, settling throughout the city. Egyptians are scattered, but Coptic Christians congregate in Burr Ridge, while Muslims congregate in Northbrook. Turks, non-Arabic, form a small segment of the Middle Eastern population in Chicago and are scattered throughout the northwest suburbs.

Most of the immigrants brought their food preferences with them. For the most part, they eat Mediterranean-style foods. Healthful offerings of fresh fruits, vegetables, legumes, grains, and lean meats—with an emphasis on seasonality and a deep tradition of preserving—are the hallmarks of this ancient cuisine. Some commonly used ingredients include olives and olive oil, pita bread, bulgur, sesame seeds and tahini, dates, sumac, chickpeas, lamb, pine nuts, flower waters, and mint. *Za'atar*, a blend of wild thyme, sumac, and sesame seeds is a characteristic spice, typically topping flatbreads. Most meals are accompanied by piquant, pink, pickled turnips.

A *maza*, or a spread of numerous small plates, is a great way to taste a variety of dishes at one time. *Maza* typically includes hummus, *labneh* (thickened yogurt), *tabbouleh*, *kibbeh*, and stuffed grape leaves, among many others. Traditional main courses include grilled kebabs of lamb or chicken with rice, *kofta* (grilled spiced ground lamb), falafel, and many flavorful preparations of chickpeas, lentils, and fava beans. Breads play a starring role in a Middle Eastern meal, from puffy pita to chewy flatbreads and stuffed savory pies. Dessert typically includes fresh fruit, and on special occasions, pastry such as baklava and cookies flavored with flower waters. *Arak*, anise liqueur, is enjoyed with *kibbeh nayeh*, a mix of ground lamb or

beef, spices (each region has its own spice blends), and bulgur wheat, often eaten raw.

Arab employment and ownership in trading and shopkeeping, a niche that was established more than 100 years ago by Lebanese and Palestinian immigrants, remains strong in Chicago today. Restaurants and food stores selling Middle Eastern products can be found on the major Arab and Assyrian commercial district running on Kedzie Street, from Montrose to north of Lawrence Avenue. The entrepreneurial Lebanese Ziyad family expanded out of the community, beginning with an imported food store on the South Side in 1966. Ziyad Brothers imports a line of Lebanese specialty ingredients, which are sold nationally from its large warehouse operation in Cicero.

Middle Eastern food in Chicago has become ever more popular because of its flavors and perception as a healthful cuisine. These tastes are catered to by numerous well-priced, casual restaurants including Grape Vine, a small Palestinian storefront restaurant, grocery, and bakery on John Humphrey Drive; Persian restaurants Noon Al-Kabab on Kedzie, Pars Cove, Reza's, Doostan, and Masouleh; and Lebanese restaurants such as Maza on North Ashland, Taste of Lebanon on West Foster, Semiramis on North Kedzie, and Kan Zaman on North Wells. There are numerous butcher shops, many Halal, on North Kedzie, along with Lebanese-owned Al Khayam bakery, grocery, and restaurant—a major source for ingredients, tools, and baked goods. The Lebanese Middle East Bakery and Grocery on West Foster also offers ingredients, pita bread, and other traditional baked goods. A good way to sample Chicago's Turkish fare is the annual Turkish fest held every August at Daley Plaza.

Other popular spots for Middle Eastern cuisine in Chicago are Shawarma Gardens on Division, Old Jerusalem on North Wells, Olive Mountain Restaurant in Evanston, Al Bawadi Grill in Bridgeview, and fast-food lunch options at Mezza Grill locations throughout the Loop. The Oasis Café in the Jeweler's mall on North Wabash is another Middle Eastern favorite of the lunchtime crowd.

Church festivals are a source of authentic Middle Eastern cuisine in Chicago, such as the enormous annual festival of Our Lady of Lebanon Maronite Catholic Church in Lombard every September.

....

Contributor: Maureen Abood

See also: Specialty Stores

BIBLIOGRAPHY

Arab American Institute. http://www.aaiusa.org/pages/demographics/.

Cankar, Louise. "Immigrants from the Arab World." *The New Chicago: A Social and Cultural Analysis*. Philadelphia: Temple University Press, 2006.

Hanania, Ray. *Arabs of Chicagoland*. Mt. Pleasant, N.C.: Arcadia Publishing, 2005.

Middleby-Marshall Company

The Middleby Oven Company began in 1888 as a manufacturer of portable commercial ovens. The growth of large-scale bakeries in urban locations created a wealth of opportunities for Middleby in the late nineteenth century. It produced ovens that could be quickly assembled on site rather than custom built—an innovative concept for the time.

Middleby became the largest manufacturer of commercial bake ovens in the United States by the turn of the twentieth century. Joseph Middleby and John Marshall set up one of their first locations on W. Van Buren St. in Chicago in the 1890s. They moved their main operation to W. Adams St. by the 1920s. In the 1930s, Middleby introduced one of the earliest rotary pan ovens in the country—a system that brought food through different temperature zones in the oven using a system akin to a Ferris Wheel. These ovens ensured an even cooking process through the use of natural convection.

Middleby-Marshall continues to produce more pizza ovens than any other manufacturer in the world at their Elgin plant at 1400 Toastmaster Drive. They can count more than 180,000 pizza ovens in operation at locations ranging from Papa John's to Pizza Hut. Middleby-Marshall also pioneered the use of touch-screen controls in commercial cooking equipment.

Middleby-Marshall now owns 40 firms involved in equipment manufacture and food packaging systems. Some of its brands include Blodgett Ovens, the largest maker of commercial convection ovens in the world; Viking Range, the first company to offer professional grade ranges for the home; Turbo Chef, one of the first companies to offer speed ovens that combine convection cooking with microwave technology and conduction; Nieco, makers of automated broilers for businesses such as Dairy Queen; Toastmaster, the earliest originator of the pop-up toaster in 1923; and South Bend Range, the third largest commercial range maker in North America after Garland and Vulcan-Hart.

....

Contributor: Stefan Osdene

See also: Equipment, Commercial

BIBLIOGRAPHY

http://www.fundinguniverse.com/company-histories/the-middleby -corporation-history/.

https://middlebycooking.wordpress.com/.

Milling

The rivers and lakes in the Chicago region were natural locations to place water mills and windmills in order to grind locally produced grains such as wheat, corn, and oats. The earliest milling method used stone wheels for grinding. By 1800, the first nonnative settler in the region, Jean Baptiste Point DuSable, had a bakehouse with millstones located just north of the Chicago River.

Steam-powered flour mills began to take over in Chicago during the 1830s, and milling became one of Chicago's most important food businesses. Illinois was a top producer of both whole and milled corn and wheat. The mid-1800s saw shipments move from the "breadbasket' Midwest by way of the Great Lakes to the East. After the Civil War, growing railroad networks quickly carried the grains to eastern millers. Large grain silos rose along the Chicago River and, later, the Calumet River, to hold wheat, corn, barley, and other grains before they were shipped by rail or barge around the country. (Only two grain facilities—the Archer Daniels Midland Plant and the Illinois International Port Grain Elevators at the Port of Chicago—remain in operation within the city limits.)

Eventually, most grains were not milled locally; rather they were moved east to Buffalo and New York and, later, west to the Mississippi River with firms such as the Minneapolis Milling Company, which later became General Mills. Large wheat flour mills, with prices that undercut local mills, slowly began to drive small mills out of business.

But the Imperial Milling Company, begun in 1879 at 16th Street and Dearborn Avenue to process oats, became part of a cereal processing powerhouse, after merging with many area mills. It was called the American Cereal Company and then the Quaker Oats Company in 1901. Quaker grew through the 1900s and produced ready-to-eat cereals, pasta, dog foods, and, later, Gatorade. In

Middleby-Marshall oven in a bakery in West Virginia. Courtesy of Stefan Osdene.

THE HISTORIC GRAUE MILL

Frederick Graue, born in Germany, arrived in the United States, settling in what was Fullersburg, Illinois., now Oak Brook, in the 1840s. He purchased a burned-down lumber mill, and, brick by brick, built a mill with clay taken from his nearby farm. He imported buhr stones from France, and in 1852, the waterwheel mill began grinding wheat, corn, and other grains produced by local farmers. Salt Water Creek provided the power for the mill for three generations of the Graue family. The mill was valued by the local community not only for grinding grains but also for making syrup during the Civil War and apple cider at the turn of the century. Although never formally recorded, oral histories reveal stories that Graue allowed his mill to be a safe place for runaway slaves on the Underground Railroad as they journeyed to a free Canada.

Technology changes made the mill obsolete and eventually the building was abandoned. The DuPage County Forest Preserve District restored it in the 1940s. In 1950, the district leased the property to the DuPage Graue Mill Corporation, an organization formed by local residents, who opened a museum. The mill was listed in the National Register of Historic Places in May, 1975, and in 1981 was named an Illinois Historic Mechanical Engineering Landmark, the only grist mill so named in the United States.

—JENNY LEWIS

2001, it was purchased by PepsiCo Inc. of New York, but headquarters remain in Chicago.

Other millers in the region included the Argo Corn Products Company in Argo (now Summit), Illinois. Begun in 1910, it processed corn into corn starch and, by 1930, had became the largest corn refinery in the world.

The artisan bread movement in Chicago has led to a resurgence in small milling operations in bakeries and restaurants. Chefs and bakers are using flours made from ancient grains; heirloom, organic, sustainably grown grains; and gluten-free ingredients. One example is Nellcote restaurant chef Jared Van Camp, who grinds flour in-house. And the owners of Baker Miller Bakery and Millhouse, Megan and David Miller, are trying to resurrect one of Chicago's earliest businesses, but on a small scale, with their new Baker Miller Flour Company.

Contributor: Jenny Lewis
See also: Baking and Bakeries; The Quaker Oats Company

BIBLIOGRAPHY

Lewis, Jenny. *Midwest Sweet Baking History: Delectable Classics around Lake Michigan*. Charleston, S.C.: History, 2011.

Witter, David. "Grain of Truth: Taking Stock of the Relics of Chicago's Era as the World's Stacker of Wheat." New City. January 2, 2015. http://newcity.com/2010/06/02/grain-of-truth-taking-stock-of-the-relics-of-chicagos-era-as-the-worlds-stacker-of-wheat/#sthash.l72df9se.dpuf.

Molecular Gastronomy

The term *molecular gastronomy* was coined in 1988 by physicist Nicholas Kurti, but the father is considered to be Adrian Feria, chef at El Bulli restaurant in Spain (although he prefers to call his cuisine *deconstructivist*). In the late 1990s and early 2000s, chefs adopted advanced technologies and products in order to change the textures of ingredients and present familiar flavors in unfamiliar presentations. Chicago has embraced molecular gastronomy perhaps more than any other North American city; the main proponents have been Grant Achatz of Alinea and the late Homaro Cantu of Moto and Ing.

Molecular gastronomy (sometimes called *modernism*) can include the use of foams, made in an immersion blender or with the use of a surfactant such as lecithin; flash freezing and shattering ingredients with liquid nitrogen; *sous vide* (low temperature) cooking using a thermal immersion circulator; spherification (shaping liquids into spheres); the emulsification of ingredients with lecithin; the injection of unusual fillings with a syringe; menus on edible paper made from soybeans and potato starch; and unusual combinations of flavors such as sweet and savory. The presentation style often is whimsical and may feature accompanying a dish with aromas or serving food on unusual serving pieces, such as metallic skewers or steel-string swings.

For example, in Chicago, Cantu used a powerful laser to cook the interior of fish while leaving the outside raw, and to create "inside out bread" with a doughy exterior and crusty interior. One of Achatz's signature presentations is a pillow filled with the fragrance of Earl Gray tea placed under a diner's plate that, when punctured with a needle, releases a floral aroma.

The influence of molecular gastronomy has spread. Other Chicago chefs, including Graham Elliot, Iliana Regan, and Curtis Duffy, have adopted some of these practices. Foams have become ubiquitous. Sous-vide cookers and immersion blenders now are manufactured for home cooking. Also for home cooks, Chicago's Spice House sells small amounts of lecithin, xanathan gum, and other ingredients needed to make foams, gels, and spheres.

Contributor: Colleen Sen
See also: Achatz, Grant; Alinea; Cantu, Homaro; Restaurants and Fine Dining

BIBLIOGRAPHY

Stein, Joel. "The Miracle Worker: Chicago Chef Grant Achatz." *Time*, December 20, 2010.

This, Hervé. *Molecular Gastronomy: Exploring the Science of Flavor*. New York: Columbia University Press, 2005.

Vettel, Phil. "How Cantu Changed Chicago's Culinary Scene." *Chicago Tribune*, April 15, 2015.

Montgomery Ward

Aaron Montgomery Ward started his business in Chicago in 1872, 14 years prior to the formation of Sears and Roebuck, and it would become the nation's first major retailer to sell merchandise via mail-order catalog.

Ward concentrated on a rural consumer basis in the early years. He offered a wider array of products than consumers could find in general mercantile stores. He also offered prices cheaper than other retailers and relied heavily on volume sales rather than high profit margins. Ward's first group of customers consisted of Grange members who formed cooperative purchasing groups to save money on dry goods.

Sears and Montgomery Ward vied for the position of the nation's leading mail-order retail outlet in the twentieth century, with Sears in the lead after 1900. Montgomery Ward's consumer durables included everything from china to linens to kitchen appliances. The firm contracted out the manufacture of kitchen equipment to various companies in Chicago, such as A. F. Dormeyer. Montgomery Ward lacked the extensive range of sub-branding that Sears pioneered with brands such as Kenmore appliances and Craftsmen tools. Beginning in 1926, Montgomery Ward capitalized on its brand-name recognition by opening a number of retail outlets throughout the country.

Montgomery Ward purchased most of its products in bulk quantities at wholesale prices from manufacturers rather than specifically designing a given product line and having it made to their specifications. Permissive return policies and flexible modes of payment contributed to the company's success. From 1908 to 1974, Montgomery Ward occupied a large complex known informally as the Catalog House at 618 W. Chicago Ave. Following bankruptcy in 2001, Montgomery Ward ceased to be a brick-and-mortar operation. It has continued to operate as an online-only retailer since 2004.

Contributor: Stefan Osdene

See also: Equipment, Home

BIBLIOGRAPHY

Cherry, Robin. *Catalog: The Illustrated History of Mail Order Shopping*. New York: Princeton Architectural Press, 2008, 18–19.

Ferguson, Rebecca N. *The Handy History Answer Book*. Canton, Mich.: Visible Ink Press, 2006, 343–44.

Moo & Oink

A small, locally owned chain of meat and grocery stores, Moo & Oink primarily caters to the African American market. It started in the 1930s as a wholesaler called Calumet Meat near the Union Stock Yards. It was founded by the Lezak and Levy families who had been in the meat business for 150 years, working as kosher meat sellers and schochets (ritual slaughterers) in Europe. Calumet used the slogan "Home of Moo & Oink." They later created cartoon cow and pig mascots, before finally adopting Moo & Oink as a business name in the 1970s.

The chain once consisted of four stores, on the South and West Sides and in a south suburb. Beginning in the 1980s, Moo & Oink became known to a wider cross section of Chicago through a series of memorable late-night television commercials. The unconventional ads featured dancers wearing cow and pig costumes and hoofing it to a catchy jingle composed by Richard Pegue, a radio host on WVON and WGCI. Fresh meats comprised much of their business, but they also were known for prepared products such as buckets of handwashed chitterlings ("Cleanest little chitlin in America. So clean they cook in half the time"), and hot links, as well as other sausages like Moooo Doggy all-beef franks. The company suffered severe financial problems in its final years and closed its stores in 2011, though some products bearing the Moo & Oink brand continue to be sold by Best Chicago Meat Company.

Contributor: Peter Engler

See also: African Americans; Supermarkets and Grocery Stores

BIBLIOGRAPHY

Balu, Rekha. "Have a Cow, Man! Or Chicken or Pig." *Crain's Chicago Business*, November 30, 1996.

Lynch, LaRisa. "Moo and Oink Scrambling to Find Buyer." *Austin Weekly News*, August 10, 2011.

Moody, Harriet Brainard

When she was 11 years old, Harriet Converse Tilden (1857–1932) moved to Chicago from Ohio with her family. After school at Cornell University, a marriage to, and then divorce from, Edwin Brainard, she taught English literature at the West Division and Hyde Park high schools and served as a Fellow at the University of Chicago. Her home in North Kenwood became a literary salon where intellectuals and artists gathered, among them poet and playwright, William Vaughn Moody, whom she married in 1909, one year before his death.

In 1890, finding a teacher's income insufficient to support herself and her widowed mother, Harriet Moody founded a gourmet food service and catering company, the Home Delicacies Association. Quickly, the Association began catering meals and providing baked goods for Pullman diners, transatlantic steamship lines, Marshall Field & Company, and Selfridge's in London. Her dishes included chicken and lobster salads, creamed chicken, calves brains, bouillon, 11 kinds of bread, and numerous desserts that included Nesselrode pudding, cream puffs, eclairs, and ice creams. In addition, Moody established the Field Museum cafeteria, operated the Near North Side White Elephant Shop tearoom in conjunction with a Chicago charity, and supplied foodstuffs to the Northwestern University Settlement's short-lived Coffee House and Bakery. By 1896, the Association was also training housemaids and operating a cooking school. At this point, the company had become so successful it purchased the 300-year-old recipe for Napoleon's favorite rum cake for $35,000.

In 1921, the Association opened Le Petit Gourmet restaurant in basement quarters at 619 N. Michigan Ave., serving meals and poetry. Association plans for 1927 included opening another restaurant, Au Grand Gourmet, at E. Delaware Place. However, the company, no longer under Moody's direction, collapsed during the Great Depression. The location was later the first version of the celebrated Chez Paul, which opened at the end of World War II.

In 1930, Harriet Moody wrote 16 food-related articles for the *New York Herald Tribune*. Then, in 1931, she published *Mrs. William Vaughn Moody's Cookbook*, a compilation of her best recipes. Prior to her death in 1932, she organized cooking classes for the deaf under the auspices of the Illinois Department of Vocational Education.

Contributors: Ellen F. Steinberg and Jack H. Prost

See also: Catering; Marshall Field's

BIBLIOGRAPHY

Hard, Anne. "Poetry and Pies." *New York Herald Tribune*, June 22, 1930.

Harriet Brainard Moody Papers (1899–1932). Special Collections Research Center, University of Chicago Library.

Moody, Harriet Converse. "The Million Dollar Cook Book." *New York Herald Tribune*, June 29, 1930.

Morton, Arnie

The son of a restaurateur and the father of several more (Peter, Amy, Michael, and David), Arnold "Arnie" Morton (1922–2005) was, for decades, a driving force in Chicago's restaurant scene. Morton often described himself as a "saloon keeper," a descriptive that reflected his humility but was at odds with his accomplishments, since the "saloons," in this case, were trend-setting restaurants catering to an A-list clientele.

Morton created the Playboy Clubs in partnership with Hugh Hefner and Victor Lownes, brought chef Jean Banchet to the Midwest to head up the kitchen at the Playboy Club in Lake Geneva, launched the Morton's of Chicago Steakhouse chain in 1978, and persuaded both mayor Jane Byrne and the local restaurant community to support the initial Taste of Chicago on July 4, 1980.

At Morton's Steakhouse, he pioneered the "large steak/giant potato" format that became an industry standard. And for years, the Chicago edition of the "Ladies Who Lunch" lunched at Arnie's, where the ambiance was as sophisticated as their attire, and owner Arnie Morton was typically on hand to make sure they received the anticipated level of service and cuisine. Ever the gracious host, he made everyone feel like an honored guest.

Contributor: Barbara Revsine

See also: Playboy Club; Restaurants and Fine Dining; Restaurateurs and Restaurant Groups; Steak and Chop Houses

BIBLIOGRAPHY

Gibbard, M. Daniel. "Arnold 'Arnie' Morton: Chicago Feasted on His Dreams." *Chicago Tribune*, May 29, 2005.

Oliver, Myran. "'Arnie' Morton, 83; He Worked the Room at His 'Steakhouses for the Rich.'" *Los Angeles Times*, May 31, 2005.

Morton Salt, Inc.

A major producer of salt, headquartered at 123 N. Wacker Dr., Chicago, Morton employs nearly 2,700 people. According to its website, Morton produces salt "for culinary, water softening, household and road de-icing, food processing, chemical, pharmaceutical, and numerous industrial uses."

Thanks to an advertising campaign launched in 1914, starring the umbrella-toting Morton Salt girl and the slogan, "When It Rains It Pours," Morton has long been one of the more recognizable brand names in the United States. The company dates back to 1848 and the arrival in Chicago of Alonzo Richmond, who opened Richmond & Company, a sales agent for Onondaga Salt. In 1889, Joy Morton purchased a major share of the venture, renaming it Joy Morton & Company. His company was renamed Morton Salt Co. in 1910.

An anticaking agent was added to the salt in 1911, sparking that famous ad campaign of 1914. In 1924, Morton introduced iodized salt to help prevent goiters. Joy Morton was the son of J. Sterling Morton, the originator of

Arbor Day, and Joy established, in 1922, the Morton Arboretum in Lisle. His son, Sterling Morton, put up money in 1961 to build the Morton Wing of the Art Institute of Chicago.

Morton merged with Norton Pharmaceutical in 1969, becoming Morton-Norton Products and then merged in 1982 with Thiokol Corp. to become Morton Thiokol, Inc., only to reemerge in a 1989 spin-off as Morton International Inc. The company sold itself to Rohm & Haas Co. in 1999. Dow Chemical later bought up Rohm & Haas, but sold Morton to Germany's K+S Group, the world's leading producer of salt, for $1.67 billion in 2009.

Contributor: Bill Daley

BIBLIOGRAPHY

Heise, Kenan. "Daniel Peterkin Jr., 82, Turned Salt Firm into Industry Giant." *Chicago Tribune*, May 11, 1988.

Hughless, Mike, "$1.7 Billion for Morton: German Salt Firm Hopes Deal Will Expand Its Reach." *Chicago Tribune*, April 3, 2009.

Mother-In-Law

This uniquely Chicago sandwich is a tamale covered with chili, usually served in a hot dog bun. The same term can refer to a chili tamale in a cup and occasionally to a tamale in a bun without chili (sometimes the canonical Chicago hot dog toppings are used). The tamales are almost invariably commercial extruded products, not traditional Mexican ones, often from Tom Tom Tamale (in business since 1937) or Supreme Tamale (since 1950). Although chili-covered tamales are found throughout the Chicago area and beyond, the peculiar name is associated with the South Side. According to the owner of Tom Tom, the term goes back at least to the 1950s (in the Back of the Yards neighborhood) but is likely older. As the story goes, it got its name because the snack, like the relative, is well known for causing indigestion.

Contributor: Peter Engler

BIBLIOGRAPHY

Engler, Peter (under pseudonym of Rene G). "Mother in Law = Tamale with Chili." LTH Forum.com. May 31, 2005. http://www.lthforum.com/bb/viewtopic.php?p=33703#p33703.

Nahabedian, Carrie

One of Chicago's top female chefs, Nahabedian is co-owner of NAHA restaurant, 500 N. Clark St., and Brindille, 534 N. Clark St. In 2000 at NAHA, she created an elegant American restaurant with a menu that also gave a nod to her Armenian background. Brindille, opened in 2013, is her smaller, more upscale French-influenced restaurant. Both are run in partnership with her cousin, Michael Nahabedian.

Beginning in high school, Nahabedian interned at the Ritz-Carlton Chicago and went on to work at well-known places such as Le Français, Le Perroquet, and La Tour, and as executive chef at The Four Seasons Biltmore in Beverly Hills. She won a Best Chef: Great Lakes award from The James Beard Foundation in 2008 and multiple Michelin stars. She is a board member of Green City Market and a member of Les Dames d'Escoffier.

Contributor: Carol Mighton Haddix

See also: Restaurants and Fine Dining

BIBLIOGRAPHY

"The Big Heat: Chicago's Food and Drink Fifty 2015." *New City Resto*, April 16, 2015. http://resto.newcity.com/2015/04/16/the-big-heat-chicagos-food-and-drink-fifty-2015/4/.

National Live Stock and Meat Board

Chicago's central location in the country and its access to waterways and rail transit made it an ideal location for livestock sales, processing, and shipment. In 1865, Chicago established its first stockyards—a key industry in this burgeoning industrial city that would remain a strong presence well into the mid–twentieth century. The National Live Stock and Meat Board began in Chicago in 1922 as a cooperative group made up of many of the key players in meat production and marketing: slaughterhouses, canners, meatpackers, farmers, butchers, wholesalers, and retailers. This organization initially sought to counteract claims that meat caused gout and rheumatism.

This coalition of organizations and individuals—including the National Swine Growers' Association and the United Master Butchers of America—lobbied for greater meat consumption in America. Their first advertising agenda emphasized what they described in 1922 as a "Farm to Table" campaign. It touted the nutritional and taste benefits of meat. This group supported scientific research into the health benefits of meat, funding academic research on the topic.

The board also published cookbooks and informational manuals on meat, including *Tempting Meat Recipes* (1934), *Cashing in on Pork: A Modern Merchandising Manual*, (1937), and *Home Freezer: Freezer Guide* (1980). Their 1940 movie short *Meat and Romance* helped to promote their agenda in movie theaters throughout the nation. This organization continued to promote meat well into the 1990s, launching the now famous "Beef: It's What's for Dinner" campaign with actor Robert Mitchum in 1992. The organization merged with the National Cattlemen's Beef Association in 1996 and ceased to operate as a separate enterprise.

Contributor: Stefan Osdene

See also: Meat and Poultry; Union Stock Yards

BIBLIOGRAPHY

Bray, Robert W. *History of Meat Science*. http://www.meatscience.org/about-amsa/history-mission/history-of-meat-science (originally published in 1997 for the 50th Anniversary History of the Reciprocal Meat Conference).

"Farm to Table" Meat Campaign, Interests from Producer to Retailer Get Together. *The National Provisioner*, Vol. 66, No. 11, 1922. Chicago: National Provisioner, 1–3.

National Restaurant Association

The National Restaurant Association (NRA) is the largest food-service trade association in the world, representing nearly 500,000 restaurant businesses. Based in downtown Chicago from 1919–2012 and now headquartered in Washington, D.C., this national organization supports entrepreneurship and pro-restaurant regulations (such as lobbying against raises in the minimum wage) at the local, state, and national level. The National Restaurant Association Show remains an annual event in Chicago, drawing more than 40,000 food-service professionals from around the world. In 1987, the NRA Educational Foundation was formed as a philanthropic subsidiary that offers professional development and certification programs for culinary arts, restaurant management, food safety, and employability skills.

Contributor: Tia M. Rains

BIBLIOGRAPHY

http://www.restaurant.org/Home.

Native Americans

Chicago was named for a food. The Miami and Illinois nations, who lived in the Chicago area at the time of the first European contact, called the Des Plaines River *šikaakwa siipiiwi* "Ramp River" for the abundance of *allium tricoccum* found along its banks. The French explorer La Salle recorded an approximation of the river name as *Checagou;* the designation was later transferred to the Chicago River and then extended to the settlement founded at the river's mouth.

The traditional foods of the Miami, Illinois, and other local nations (Potawatomi, Ojibwa, Meskwaki, Sauk, Kickapoo, Mascouten) included not only ramps but also venison, rabbit, buffalo, raccoon, squirrel, turkey, duck, goose, fresh water fish and eels, turtles, corn and hominy, beans, squash, goosefoot, purslane, milkweed, Jerusalem artichokes, prairie turnips, sunflower seeds, black walnuts, pawpaws, persimmons, prickly pear cactus, and many sorts of berries. Maple syrup was harvested as a sweetener; medicinal teas were made from cedar, sage, and other plants. This diet changed greatly with European settlement of the Midwest. An emblematic Native American dish of the postcontact era is frybread, made from a simple dough of flour, salt, baking powder, and water or milk; some cooks add a bit of sugar as well. The dough is formed into flat disks 4 inches or more in diameter, often with a small hole in the center, and fried in oil, shortening, or lard. Frybread may be eaten plain or topped with powdered sugar or honey, or with savory toppings.

In the 2010 census, approximately 27,000 Chicagoans reported full or partial Native American ethnicity, about 1 percent of the city's population. A significant part of Chicago's Native American population arrived in the city during the 1950s, when Chicago was one of the original four destination cities designated by the federal relocation program, intended to remove Native Americans from reservations. Members of more than 50 tribes moved to Chicago, especially from the Algonquian and Siouan groups of the upper Midwest. The American Indian Center of Chicago was established in Uptown in 1953 by newly arrived Native Americans and has played a crucial role in establishing a pan-Indian identity among Chicago Native Americans.

Powwows sponsored by the American Indian Center or other organizations are the most accessible occasions for outsiders to sample Native American dishes. Frybread and Indian tacos (ground beef, shredded cheese, lettuce, tomato, and salsa on frybread) are always offered by vendors; buffalo burgers, corn soup, or wild rice soup may be available as well. The St. Kateri Center, a Catholic ministry in North Center named for the first Native American saint, hosts an Indian taco sale a few times during the year. Though elsewhere in North America it is possible to find high-end Native American restaurants, such as chef Nephi Craig's Summit in Sunrise Park, Arizona, no comparable establishment currently exists in Chicago.

The American Indian Center and other midwestern native groups have been active in the food sovereignty movement: planting communal gardens, teaching young people about traditional foodways, and reviving heirloom varieties of produce. Beyond the Native American community, an increased interest in local products has resulted in greater availability of indigenous foods such as ramps, black walnuts, native persimmons, and pawpaws at Chicago's farmers markets.

Contributor: Amy Dahlstrom
See also: Wild Onion

BIBLIOGRAPHY

Lagrand, James B. *Indian Metropolis: Native Americans in Chicago, 1945–1975*. Urbana: University of Illinois Press, 2005.

McCafferty, Michael. "A Fresh Look at the Place Name Chicago." *Journal of the Illinois State Historical Society* 96.2 (Summer, 2003): 116–29.

Tanner, Helen Hornbeck. *Atlas of Great Lakes Indian History*. Norman: University of Oklahoma Press, 1987.

Newspapers (See Media, Print)

Nielsen-Massey Vanillas, Inc.

The family-owned Nielsen-Massey Vanillas, Inc., one of the world's premier vanilla manufacturers, has a long history in the flavors business, much of it in Chicago. The company was founded in 1907 by Richard Massey in Sterling, Illinois. The business, then called Massey's, sold vanilla to firms to help cover the noxious fumes of cleaning products. In 1917, Chatfield Nielsen Sr. joined the operation and the company's focus changed to offering vanillas and flavors to food manufacturers. Shortly thereafter, the operation moved to Webster Street on Chicago's North Side to be near the city's transportation hub. Richard Massey died in 1954, and Nielsen Sr. bought the company from Massey's heirs.

Chatfield Nielsen Jr. (Chat) joined his father's business in 1958. In 1963, the company name changed to Nielsen-Massey Vanillas, Inc. In the 1970s, Chat succeeded his father. The company got a major boost in 1982 when Chuck Williams, founder of the Williams-Sonoma chain, visited Chicago and sampled Nielsen-Massey Vanilla at a Chicago baking school. Williams offered to sell the product to the public through his stores, and Nielsen-Massey Vanillas began reaching consumers on a national scale. The company moved from Chicago to a bigger facility in Lake Forest in 1984 and expanded further when it moved to Waukegan in 1992, the same year that Chat died. Chat's wife, Camilla, who had joined the business in 1979, took over management, and oversaw the building of the company's European facility in 1993 in Leeuwarden, Netherlands, to better serve European customers.

Today, the company sells nearly 80 products, including vanilla beans, powders, pastes, and extracts from Madagascar, Tahiti, and Mexico. Nielsen-Massey celebrated its 100th anniversary in 2007 by publishing *A Century of Flavor*, a vanilla-inspired cookbook featuring sweet and savory recipes, such as crab cakes with vanilla remoulade. Camilla retired in 2005. The company is now run by her three children, Craig, Matt, and Beth, the third generation of Nielsens to steward the company.

Contributor: Scott Warner
See also: Flavorings

BIBLIOGRAPHY

A Century of Flavors. Waukegan, Ill.: Nielsen Massey Vanillas, Inc., 2007.

Organizations, Other Culinary Groups

The Culinary Historians of Chicago (CHC) was founded in 1993 by Bruce Kraig, professor of history at Roosevelt University; culinary historian Gloria Billick; *Chicago Tribune* food editor Carol Mighton Haddix; and Linda Calafiore, founder of the Cooking and Hospitality Institute of Chicago (later Cordon Bleu). The organization was incorporated as a not-for-profit educational organization "committed to the study of the history of food and drink in human cultures." The first meeting, held at Roosevelt University, featured an illustrated talk by Chef Louis Szathmary on the history of Chicago restaurants. The following year, the organization held its first large conference on the foods of the Columbian Exposition. Subsequent meetings were held at the Chicago History Museum and later Kendall College.

The Chicago Foodways Roundtable was started in 2005 as an offshoot of CHC for programs that CHC could not schedule or accommodate. Speakers have included leading chefs, cookbook authors, and academic scholars.

ChicaGourmets! is a dining club started in 1997 by Don Newcomb, a retired professor of horticulture. The group holds some 30 events a year at local restaurants, ranging from small ethnic restaurants to top fine-dining establishments. In 2015, it celebrated its 1,000th program with a meal at Tallgrass in Lockport, Illinois.

The American Institute of Wine and Food (AWF) was founded in 1981 by Julia Child, Robert Mondavi, Richard Graff, and others as a national nonprofit educational organization devoted to improving the appreciation, understanding, and accessibility of food and drink. The Chicago chapter was one of 27 chapters nationwide. Events included dinners, lectures, neighborhood tours, and programs devoted to special topics, such as risotto and bread. For several years, starting in 1988, the AIWF Chicago chapter sponsored the Best of the Midwest Market, which was one of the predecessors of the Green City Market.

Slow Food Chicago was informally launched in 1998 and formally founded in 2001 as a chapter of Slow Food USA, the national representative of Slow Food International based in Italy. The purpose of the organization is "to link the pleasures of the table with a commitment to protect the community, culture, knowledge and environment that make this pleasure possible." The Chicago chapter hosts dozens of events and initiatives every year, including workshops, book discussions, tastings, and farm-to-table dinners, and is one of the sponsors of the preSERVE garden in North Lawndale.

....

Contributor: Colleen Sen

See also: Community Gardens

BIBLIOGRAPHY

Gerst, Virginia. "For the Foodie Who Has Most Everything." *Chicago Tribune*, December 17, 2003.

Organizations, Professional

The city of Chicago has a long history in the ingredient and food processing industries, and many professional food organizations were founded within the city's limits. One of the first was the National Confectioners Association, which was formed in 1884 by 69 representatives of confectionary manufacturing firms as a trade association to support the needs of candy manufacturers. Now located in Washington, D.C., the association calls itself one of the oldest and largest trade associations in the country. It sponsors an exposition of candies and other snack foods annually at McCormick Place in Chicago.

In 1945, the Future Homemakers of America was founded in Chicago with the intent of unifying home economics clubs in high schools in the United States. Now

called the Family, Career and Community Leaders of America (FCCLA) and based in Reston, Virginia, it is the only nonprofit, in-school student organization for junior high and high school students in family and consumer science education.

The Institute of Food Technology (IFT) was formed in 1939 to promote communication among food science and technology professionals. It is now the largest professional organization for food science and technology in the world and hosts an annual meeting and food expo that attracts more than 20,000 people from around the world. Headquarters remain in Chicago at 525 W. Van Buren St.

The American Dietetic Association was formed in 1917 at a meeting in Cleveland, Ohio, and ultimately landed in Chicago. Originally created to help maximize food resources and improve health and nutrition during World War I, the association has evolved over the years to an organization of dietetic professionals. In 2012, the organization officially changed its name to the Academy of Nutrition and Dietetics and maintains Chicago offices at 120 South Riverside Plaza, as well as an office in Washington, D.C.

Several other food organizations were conceived in Chicago, including Les Dames d'Escoffier Chicago (1982), National House Furnishing Manufacturers Association (1928), National Restaurant Association (1919), and the Chicago Food and Nutrition Network (1942). All maintain presences in Chicago.

....

Contributor: Tia M. Rains

BIBLIOGRAPHY

http://www.eatright.org/.
http://www.fccla.com/.
https://www.ift.org/.

Ovaltine

A brand of milk flavoring made with barley malt and egg started in Switzerland as Ovomaltine. In 1865, Swiss doctor Georg Wander discovered the nutritional benefits of malt extract, but it didn't taste good. In 1904, his son Albert, a pharmacist, added whey and beet extract to make a more palatable product. During World War I, it was used in Allied hospitals in Europe to meet soldiers' nutritional needs. Once cocoa was added, it appealed to mothers whose kids didn't like plain milk. Enjoyed cold or hot, an 8-ounce serving provides a healthy dose of vitamins A, C, D, B1, B6, and niacin and phosphorus.

In 1917, the Wander Firm opened a plant in west suburban Villa Park, a town chosen for its good water, access to farm product, and transportation routes. According to local lore, the company provided Ovaltine and milk to employees and those in need during the Great Depression. In the late 1930s, Ovaltine sponsored radio shows, *Little Orphan Annie* and *Captain Midnight,* and its popularity soared. The suburban plant closed in 1986 when domestic manufacturing moved to Minneapolis. In 2001, the factory was turned into apartments and the 217-foot smokestack, a village landmark, was imploded.

Contributor: Deborah Pankey

BIBLIOGRAPHY

Grondin, Kathryn. "Ovaltine Smokestack Becomes Dust in Villa Park." *Daily Herald*, October 30, 2008.

History of Beverage. April 8, 2010. www.beveragehistory.com/2010/04/history-of-ovaltine.html.

Oyster Bars

With an amazingly long history that dates back further than the fourth century BC, oysters [*Ostrea edulis*] were savored by, among others, the Vikings, Greeks, and Romans, as well as Medieval and Renaissance kings and queens. To no one's surprise, in the nineteenth century enjoyment of these highly prized bivalves became the fashionable savories of the bourgeoisie. Oyster saloons and bars, usually tucked away below street level and identified by only a flying white flag, were ubiquitous in London and other major European cities. The New World echoed the clamor, and native oysters [*Crasostrea virginica*] were consumed with relish on both the Atlantic and Pacific coasts.

That the oyster found a congenial home in Chicago, in the "heartland" of the United States, is a bit more surprising. But in 1852, with the railroad's conquest of the land between the two coasts, oysters packed in sawdust-filled barrels could be ordered by Abraham Lincoln for his political gatherings in southern Illinois and could also be purchased, shucked, and preserved in sealed cans. Chicago's Brunswick restaurant listed raw "Oysters half shell" in 1867. Later, ice-carrying "refrigerated" train cars made oysters even more abundant in the nation's interior.

The famous restaurateur and author George Rector published an account of the arrival by train of the first Long Island oysters in *The Girl From Rector's.* By 1888, basement saloons, like the one at Wabash and 22nd Street, were known to serve oysters as late as 2 a.m., to the satisfaction of proprietor George H. Smith and documented by the *Tribune* (December 4, 1888).

No doubt Rector's Cafe Marine at the World's Columbian Exposition in 1893 reaffirmed his historical role in popularizing oyster consumption in Chicago, but other city establishments such as the Boston Oyster House,

Booth Fisheries was a major fish and oyster packer begun in 1850; it was bought by Sara Lee in 1985. Courtesy of the Chicago History Museum, ICHi-85010.

Race Brothers New England Oyster House, and Burke's European Hotel had already satisfied the appetites of local oyster aficionados. At 25 cents a dozen for raw oysters and 60 to 75 cents for broiled and sauced oysters, the oyster craze flourished among urban dwellers. While elegant and discriminating hostesses, like Mrs. Potter Palmer, served bluepoints on the half shell, arranged on specially designed oyster plates, the man on the street could savor oysters cheaply in saloons and taverns until World War I suddenly interrupted access to many coastal oyster beds here and abroad.

Fortunately, the postwar era ushered in renewed appreciation of oysters and a proliferation of oyster bars. Prohibition, however, and its attendant anti-saloon leagues made the case for poor oyster sales in speakeasies and "mob" establishments. Further complicating the enjoyment of oysters in Chicago's leading seafood houses, such as Gus Mann's Ranibo [*sic*] Sea Food Grotto at 117 S. Dearborn St., were the Depression years and the popularity of venues like New Orleans that popularized the appeal of raw oysters and the development of oyster recipes from Antoine's Rockefellers to the quintessential French Quarter "po boys."

By the mid–twentieth century, shrimp had become the shellfish of choice, due in large measure to the publicized pollution of coastal oyster beds and the subsequent health concerns about contaminated oysters. But the scare diminished, and the presence of many varieties of oysters on today's local menus, such as at the Cape Cod Room in the Drake Hotel and well-known oyster bars, such as Shaw's Crab House on Hubbard Street (which holds an annual Oyster Fest), the Kinzie Tavern, and G. T. Fish and Oyster on Wells Street, shows that oysters continue to please Chicagoans, whether served on the half shell or in trendy dishes such as the Pearl Tavern's "Rockefella," which features baked oysters hidden under a herbed *paté a choux*, topped with cheese and dried prosciutto chips. As for the future, oysters will continue to captivate both Chicago connoisseurs and residents who savor the "taste of the whole ocean" with each oyster consumed.

Contributor: Joan Reardon
See also: Restaurants and Fine Dining; Seafood Restaurants

BIBLIOGRAPHY

Meyer, Arthur L., and Jon M. Vann. *The Appetizer Atlas: A World of Small Bites*. Hoboken, N.J.: John Wiley and Sons, 2003.

Reardon, Joan. *Oysters: A Culinary Celebration*. New York: The Lyons Press, 2000.

Willard, Pat. *America Eats! On the Road with the WPA*. New York: Bloomsbury, 2008.

Palmer, Bertha Honore

Bertha Honore (1849–1918) was born in Louisville, Kentucky. A nineteenth-century Chicago society leader, she was best known during her lifetime for her role as president of the Board of Lady Managers of the 1893 World's Columbian Exposition; her work on behalf of women's rights and other causes; her social triumphs, especially hobnobbing with European royalty; and her museum-quality collection of French Impressionist paintings, many of which are now at the Art Institute of Chicago.

Today, Mrs. Palmer also is remembered for her dinner parties—she was fond of chafing-dish creations—and for a new version of the brownie. Desiring a portable and tasty chocolate dessert fairgoers could enjoy with their box lunches, she asked for something special from the chefs at the Palmer House, the grand hotel built by her husband, Potter, at 17 E. Monroe St. in Chicago's Loop. The result: a walnut chocolate brownie brushed with apricot glaze.

Contributor: Bill Daley
See also: Columbian Exposition

BIBLIOGRAPHY

Erens, Patricia Fae. "When Potter Was King and Bertha Was Queen." *Chicago Tribune*, November 30, 1969.

MRS. POTTER'S ROMAINE PUNCH

This recipe for a frozen punch seems to be the only recipe ever attributed to Bertha Palmer. It is from Carrie Shuman's book *Favorite Recipes*, gathered for the 1893 Columbian Exposition.

—BRUCE KRAIG

From Mrs. Potter Palmer, of Chicago, president, Board of Lady Managers:

"Boil together one quart of water and one pint of sugar for about half an hour; add the juice of six good sized lemons and one orange; strain and set away to cool. Then prepare the following: Boil together one gill of sugar and one gill of water for eighteen minutes. While the syrup is cooking, beat the whites of four eggs very stiff, and into these pour the hot syrup very slowly—beating all the time, and continue to beat a few minutes after it is all in. Set this away to cool. Place the first mixture in the freezer and freeze by turning it all the time for twenty minutes. Then take off the cover, remove the beater and add one gill of sherry, two tablespoonfuls Jamaica rum and the meringue, mixing this well with a spoon into the frozen preparation. Cover again and set away until time to serve. Serve in punch glasses, as a course between entrees and roast."

Palmer House

The nation's oldest continuously operating hotel, the Palmer House opened in 1871 and burned days later in the Great Fire; it was rebuilt in 1875. Although not provable and unlikely, it is said the brownie was invented there when Bertha Palmer requested dessert for ladies attending Chicago's 1893 Columbian Exposition. In 1925, the third Palmer House was built, and it became known for extravagant dining in its Empire Room, which purportedly offered alcohol even during Prohibition. After Prohibition was repealed, the Empire Room became a supper club, hosting presidents and kings. Today, the Palmer House's fine-dining restaurant is Lockwood, winner of a 2014 OpenTable Diner's Choice award.

Contributor: David Hammond

BIBLIOGRAPHY

Hall, Susan Bard. "For Nearly 125 Years, The Palmer House Has Built Its Own Empire." *Chicago Tribune*, September 19, 1995.

Pancake Houses

There is no shortage of pancake houses in Chicago and surrounding areas, but probably the most revered in the area is Walker Bros. The Original Pancake House. Its first location was on Green Bay Road in Wilmette, opened in 1960. Serving legendary dishes such as the caramelized apple Pancake or Dutch Baby pancake, the restaurant also is unique due to its ornate woodwork and stained-glass windows, giving it a comfortable and inviting feel. Often credited as the first of the Original Pancake Houses in the United States, it is actually a franchise that was started in Portland, Oregon, in 1953 by Lester and Doris Highet.

The Walker brothers, Victor and Everett, who owned four snack shops in Evanston, were inspired by the pancake business and negotiated with the Highets to use the Walker Bros. name for their first franchise in Illinois. Since opening, the restaurant has had several famous celebrity guests, including Robert Redford, Bill Murray (who grew up only a few blocks away), and Phil Donahue. The Oscar-winning movie *Ordinary People* included scenes at the restaurant. In 2014, the Wilmette location remains the most lucrative of the six area Walker Bros. pancake houses and the highest grossing of the entire Original Pancake House franchise. The award-winning chain remains consistently ranked as one of the best pancake houses in the Chicago area.

Other pancake houses popped up in the Chicago area about the same time as the first Walker Bros. location. International House of Pancakes (IHOP), founded by Al and Jerry Lapin, franchised their Los Angeles–based restaurant concept in the early 1960s. The Golden Nugget Pancake House, originally launched in Florida by Howard N. Quam, opened in 1966, at 2971 N Lincoln Ave. A Chicago native and once a blackjack dealer at the Golden Nugget Casino in Las Vegas, Quam decided to focus on accessibility; The Golden Nugget is known for being open 24 hours a day. There are now seven Golden Nuggets, all located in the Chicago area.

Contributor: Tia M. Rains

BIBLIOGRAPHY

Borrelli, Christopher. "A Holy House of Pancakes." *Chicago Tribune*, November 18, 2010.

The Parthenon (See: Greeks; Saganaki)

Patel Brothers

The largest U.S. Indian grocery chain with 51 stores, including three in the Chicago area, Patel Brothers started in a small storefront at 2043 West Devon in

---

DUTCH BABY, A POPULAR VERSION OF PANCAKE

A Dutch baby pancake, also known as a German pancake, is a revered menu item at local pancake houses. Resembling more of a popover than a traditional pancake, the Dutch baby is made with a slightly different combination of eggs, flour, milk, and sugar, and then baked, often in a cast iron skillet or cake pan. The light and fluffy treat typically is served with fresh squeezed lemon, butter, and confectioners' sugar, but other toppings work well, too, such as raspberry syrup, maple syrup, and fresh berries.

TIA M. RAINS

German pancakes

Prep: 10 minutes
Cook: 30 minutes
Makes: Two 9-inch pancakes
Adapted from a recipe from an old blender cookbook.

4 eggs
1 tablespoon sugar
1/2 teaspoon salt
2/3 cup flour, sifted
2/3 cup milk
2 tablespoons soft butter

1. Heat oven to 400 degrees. Butter two 9-inch cake pans well. Put eggs in a food processor or blender container; cover and process until light yellow in color. Remove cover and add remaining ingredients; process until smooth, about 10 seconds.

2. Pour into prepared pans; bake 20 minutes. Reduce heat to 350 degrees; bake until puffed and golden, 8–10 minutes. Slide onto hot plates. Sprinkle with fresh lemon juice and confectioners' sugar.

The flagship store of Patel Brothers, a South Asian grocery store. Photograph by Ashish Sen.

September 1974. The founders were brothers Tulsi and Mafat Patel, immigrants from a village in Gujarat. In 1986, they opened a much larger flagship store at 2610 Devon. Products include fresh and frozen fruit and vegetables, many not found in standard grocery stores, canned and fresh pickles, spices, dairy products, oils, lentils, rice, flours, fresh and frozen breads, ready-to-eat packaged foods, and, since 1989, frozen goods. A typical Patel Brothers store today has nearly 60 freezers of frozen products from all over India. The stores do not sell fresh meat or fish, although a few of the frozen products may contain fish or seafood.

The brothers are also part owners of Raja Food, which repackages food and sells it to other companies, and Swad Food, which distributes over 200 items imported from India, Britain, Australia, and other countries. Today, a second generation is involved in the company's operations.

Contributor: Colleen Sen

See also: South Asians

BIBLIOGRAPHY

Cross, Robert. "A World of Flavors: The Complex Mixture of Chicago's Nationalities Means Global Shopping for All." *Chicago Tribune*, June 27, 1991.

Peapod

Home delivery of groceries has been part of Chicago's shopping landscape at least since the mid–nineteenth century. But brothers Andrew and Thomas Parkinson nudged the grocery store onto home computers—and eventually mobile devices—when they cofounded the online grocery delivery business called Peapod in Evanston in 1989.

A consumer too busy to roll a shopping cart down grocery store aisles could order groceries via a home or work computer with help from a modem. At a prescheduled time, a pea-green truck (often driven by the brothers or family members) would arrive at the front door with the grocery order. By 1996, the brothers moved the e-commerce site onto the Internet, launching www.peapod.com. In 2010, they released apps designed for mobile devices so shoppers could order from a smartphone or tablet. In 2014, they set up a digital innovation center, the Peapod Propulsion Labs, in Chicago.

In the 25 years since its birth, Peapod's green trucks remain. But the company has expanded into 24 markets. Headquartered in Skokie, it is working on several fronts: delivering to businesses, offering pickup sites for those who cannot be tied down to a 2-hour delivery time frame, and partnering with local artisans and small-batch vendors. It also has teamed with Seattle startup Gatheredtable.com, which creates menus geared to family size and needs, with items on the grocery list delivered to the homes via Peapod.

Peapod is a wholly owned subsidiary of Royal Ahold. The Netherlands-based food retailing giant was the majority stockholder when it bought the remaining Peapod shares in 2001. The founding brothers are at the helm: Andrew (president and general manager) and Thomas (senior vice president and chief technology officer Systems Development/Management).

Contributor: Judy Hevrdejs

See also: Delivery Services

BIBLIOGRAPHY

Cook, John. "Howard Schultz-backed Gatheredtables Launches Meal Planning Service, Partners with Peapod." *Geekwire.com*, October 16, 2014.

Sweeney, Brigid. "How Peapod Plans to Beat Amazon and Walmart." *Crain's Chicago Business*, January 20, 2014.

Weary from shopping and a day's work, women sit in a National Tea Company store in the late 1930s. Courtesy of the Chicago History Museum, ICHi-50900; Elisabeth Felsenthal Kornblith.

Pepper and Egg Sandwich

The "pepper 'n' egg" is a meatless sandwich found at Italian beef stands and other sandwich shops. Like the "Catholic dog"—a hot dog bun with the usual Chicago condiments but no sausage—it is allowed to those observing days of abstinence during Lent or on Fridays (especially in the days before Vatican II). Many traditional eateries offer it only at those times, but others serve it daily. It consists of scrambled eggs cooked with large chunks or strips of sautéed or roasted green bell pepper—the same sweet peppers used on an Italian beef—served in a length of Italian bread or a crusty long roll. Ideally, the eggs are cooked to order, either in a small omelet pan or on a flattop griddle, though some high-volume businesses are known to make batches in advance. Seasonings are often little more than salt, black pepper, and a bit of dried oregano. Hot or mild giardiniera may be added (or even cheese or other ingredients), either during cooking or as a garnish, but the sandwich is intended to be somewhat austere. Places known for their sandwiches are Pompeii and Bacchanalia in Little Italy, Ferros and Geos' Cafe in Bridgeport, Buono Beef (various locations), and Johnnie's Beef in Elmwood Park.

Contributor: Peter Engler

See also: Italians

BIBLIOGRAPHY

Kass, John. "Time for Peppernegg Lovers to Vote for Favorite Sanguich." *Chicago Tribune*, February 27, 2014.

Samors, Neal, and Eric Bronsky. *Chicago's Classic Restaurants*. Chicago: Chicago's Books Press, 2011.

Pfeiffer, Jacquy

An internationally acclaimed French pastry chef, award-winning cookbook author, and documentary subject, Chef Jacquy Pfeiffer is cofounder of The French Pastry School in Chicago. The school is considered to be one of the world's premier pastry-chef training facilities. Pfeiffer, along with Chef Sébastien Canonne, founded the school in 1995 and became part of Kennedy-King College, part of the City Colleges of Chicago, in 1999. Earlier, Pfeiffer had gained renown for his pastry work. Born in Alsace in 1961, Pfeiffer apprenticed at leading pâtisseries in Strasbourg and Alsace. He achieved international experience by working for the royal family in Saudi Arabia and later for the Sultan of Brunei and the Hyatt Regency Hong Kong.

Pfeiffer came to Chicago in 1991 to work for the Fairmont hotels and later the Sheraton hotels. Among his achievements are being named one of the Top Ten Pastry Chefs in America by both *Chocolatier* and *Pastry Art & Design* magazines (1997); winning the silver medal with the U.S. Team at the Coupe du Monde de la Pâtisserie in Lyon, France 1997); having the featured role in the *Kings of Pastry* documentary in 2009; and winning awards in 2014 for his book, *The Art of French Pastry*, from the International Association of Culinary Professionals, the James Beard Foundation, and the Gourmand Best in World Cookbook Award.

Contributor: Scott Warner

See also: Baking and Bakeries; Cooking Classes; Restaurant Awards and Honors

BIBLIOGRAPHY

Pfeiffer, Jacquy, and Martha Rose Shulman. *The Art of French Pastry*. New York, N.Y.: Alfred A. Knopf, 2013.

Phil Smidt's

For nearly 100 years, Phil Smidt's restaurant in Hammond, Indiana, just across the Illinois border, was where Chicagoans went to celebrate special occasions and to enjoy the restaurant's famous dishes, served family style: cornmeal-battered fried perch or frog legs, accompanied by parsley tartar sauce. Meals opened with a "5-star" tray of side dishes—pickled beets, cottage cheese, cole slaw, potato salad, and kidney beans. The signature dessert was gooseberry pie. Although perch and frogs legs accounted for three-fourths of the meals, the menu also featured fried chicken, walleye pike, snow crab, and steaks.

The restaurant was opened in 1910 by German-born Smidt when he began frying his customers' catch of Lake Michigan perch in a clapboard building with three tables. In the 1940s, the restaurant moved to a sprawling building at 1205 North Calumet Ave. Its seven dining rooms, painted pink and black, could accommodate 450 customers. After Smidt died, his son Pete ran the restaurant for a while, but then donated it to Calumet Community College. After 1980, it was sold and reopened several times, but competition from a nearby casino diverted customers and it closed for good in 2007.

Contributor: Colleen Sen

See also: Fish and Seafood

BIBLIOGRAPHY

David, Marjorie, "Phil Smidt's Means Frog Legs—and a Whole Lot More." *Chicago Tribune*, November 15, 1996.

Knoblauch, Mark. "Perch, Frog Legs Still Worth the Trip to Phil Smidt's." *Chicago Tribune*, May 23, 1983.

Picnics and Parks

Picnics evolved from the traditional lavish outdoor meals enjoyed by the wealthy, including medieval hunting feasts and Victorian garden parties. Picnics as Americans know them today date to the middle of the nineteenth century.

Family eating in a picnic grove, late nineteenth century. Courtesy of the Rogers Park / West Ridge Historical Society.

Their popularity comes from enjoying the outdoors, especially following a long Chicago winter. There was also the pleasure of dining al fresco, often while sitting on blankets spread out on the grass or at picnic tables.

In the second half of the nineteenth century, Chicago had several picnic groves located along rivers and streams on the North and Northwest Sides of Chicago. Ogden's Grove, Wright's Grove, Brand's Park, Hoffman Park, and Schuetzen Park were popular summer destinations for immigrant groups, labor organizations, benevolent societies, even anarchists. They especially were popular with Germans. In 1869, for example, those from the Swabian region of Germany organized the Cannstatt Festival in Ogden's Grove. It featured parades, floats with historical characters, pillars made from produce, music, dancing, beer and wine bars, and traditional dishes, such as sauerkraut, dumplings, potato salad, sausages, buttered almond cake, and *stippels*, sweet bread similar to coffee cake. Everyone brought food to share. The Irish, Poles, Italians, Lithuanians, Russians, and others held their own picnics.

As these groups became assimilated in the early twentieth century, picnic foods became more standardized and Americanized. The emphasis was on "finger food" and "fun food" that required a minimum of utensils and could be prepared in advance or purchased from nearby stores. A 1909 picnic-basket menu in the *Chicago Tribune* featured pressed chicken, saratoga (potato) chips, bread, sardine and lettuce sandwiches, stuffed olives, cheese, and devil's food cake.

Today the most common picnic foods are hot dogs and hamburgers, a variety of sandwiches, roast chicken, potato chips, potato salad, pasta salads, cole slaw, relishes, pickles, and cookies, brownies, or fruit, especially watermelon. And ethnic groups still celebrate their holidays with their own foods. For example, every summer Russian-speaking Chicago-area residents meet in Harms Wood in Skokie to enjoy piroshki and borsch.

Today, 40 picnic groves in Chicago parks offer picnic table seating. Although the parks do not provide barbecue grills, almost all of them allow people to bring their own. The Chicago Park District requires parties of more than 50 to have a permit to reserve their space. People line up on New Year's Day to make sure they obtain a permit for a summer date. Popular venues are Grant Park, Lincoln Park, and Millennium Park. Picnickers bring food from home or buy it in nearby stores that serve deli sandwiches and salads or take out more exotic fare, such as Middle Eastern hummus and *falafel* or Indian tandoori chicken. Many companies provide readymade picnic boxes. Recent developments include the purchase of food from food trucks offering prepared foods of many types, and the practice of "tailgating," in which food is served from the back of an SUV or pickup truck at a sporting event.

At the other end of the scale is Ravinia Park in Highland Park, where elaborate and elegant meals have become part of the tradition. Many concertgoers enjoy gourmet dishes served on china, with linen napkins, silverware, and flower centerpieces. Dishes may include caviar, paté de foie gras, poached salmon, or beef tenderloin. Over time, a competitive spirit developed as picnickers strive to outdo each other in the lavishness and elegance of their meals. One couple, for example, tried to replicate a dinner given by the Shah of Iran. In 2014, Ravinia partnered with Terlato Wines to sponsor the DIY Ultimate Picnic Contest where contestants could show their creative talents via tableware, imaginative displays, flower arrangements, and food. The winner received a season pass to Ravinia.

Contributors: Arlene Swartzman and Colleen Sen

See also: Germans; Tailgating

BIBLIOGRAPHY

Hooker, Lisa. "Packing a Symphony of Exotic Tastes for Once-a-Year Feast at Ravinia." *Chicago Tribune*, June 30, 1985.

Maes, Nancy. "Fine Picnics Never Go out of Style." *Chicago Tribune*, May 22, 1986.

Newberry Library. "The Cannstatt Festival: Immense Crowd at Ogden's Grove." *Chicago Foreign Language Press Survey*. http://flps.newberry.org/article/5418474_9_0067.

Pizza

By the middle of the eighteenth century, chewy thin-crusted pizza was a well-established street food in Naples. A wave of Italian immigrants brought the beloved concoction to American shores in the late nineteenth century, where it took hold in New York City. In Chicago, the first pizzeria was Granato's (later called Pizzeria Napolitana) at 907 West Taylor Street, opened by the Neapolitan Granato family in the early 1930s. It survived until 1961 when the building was razed for the construction of the University of Illinois Circle Campus. But it wasn't until American soldiers returned from World War II that pizza made serious footprints from coast to coast. And nowhere was it bigger than in Chicago, where deep-dish, the ultimate Chicago-style pizza, was born.

Although there are several stories about the origins of deep-dish pizza, the most accepted version is that Ric Riccardo Sr. (born Richard Novaretti in Italy), who owned a very popular Northern Italian restaurant and bar on Rush Street, partnered with Ike Sewell, the executive of a distillery company, to open a pizzeria. Sewell was all in, but he wanted big, brawny, knife-and-fork food. And after repeated trials, they came up with deep-dish pizza: a one-inch-thick crust, a thick covering of mozzarella, a take-no-prisoners layer of sausage, an abundance of chunky plum tomatoes, and a final sprinkle of cheese. One theory holds that the deep-dish pizza was inspired by the thick, tomato-sauced pizza breads made in local Italian bakeries. There is some question about whether Riccardo and Sewell, who were not cooks and knew nothing much about pizza, actually created it themselves. One plausible candidate was Adolpho "Rudy" Malnati, the restaurant's bartender. Whoever the actual cooks were, Riccardo and Sewell directed the creation and branded and marketed it.

CHICAGO-STYLE DEEP-DISH SAUSAGE PIZZA

Prep: 45 minutes
Rise: 1 hour, 40 minutes
Cook: 30 minutes
Makes: One 14-inch pizza, about 6 servings

Feel free to use pepperoni or sweet Italian sausage, or both, in this recipe, adapted from *The Great Chicago-Style Pizza Cookbook*, by Pasquale Bruno Jr. (McGraw Hill, 1983).

Dough:
1 1/2 packages active dry yeast
1 1/2 cups warm water (105 to 115 degrees)
1 tablespoon sugar
3 1/2 cups unbleached all-purpose flour
1 teaspoon salt
1/4 cup corn or olive oil, plus more for brushing, drizzling
1/2 cup warm water

Topping:
1 can (28 ounces) crushed tomatoes, drained
1 teaspoon each: dried basil, dried oregano
1/2 teaspoon salt or to taste
10 ounces mozzarella cheese, thinly sliced
1/4 cup freshly grated Parmesan cheese
1/2 pound Italian sausage, casing removed, crumbled

1. For dough, dissolve yeast in 1 cup of the warm water. Stir in sugar; set aside. Combine flour and salt in a large bowl. Make a well in the center. Stir in the yeast mixture, the oil, and remaining 1/2 cup warm water until dough forms a rough ball and cleans the sides of the bowl.

2. Turn dough out onto a floured surface. Knead dough, dusting with flour if too sticky, until smooth and soft, 5 to 6 minutes. Dust dough and a large, clean bowl with flour. Put dough in bowl; cover with plastic wrap and towel. Let rise in warm place until doubled, about 1 1/2 hours.

3. Meanwhile, for topping, combine tomatoes, basil, oregano and salt. Set aside. Heat oven to 475 degrees. Turn dough out of bowl; knead about 2 minutes. Let dough stand, covered, about 10 minutes. Oil bottom and sides of a 14-inch round, 2-inch deep pizza pan. Spread dough in pan until it covers the bottom. Press edges of dough up sides to form a lip around the pan edge. Pierce dough bottom with a fork at 1/2-inch intervals. Bake exactly 4 minutes; remove from oven. Brush crust lightly with olive oil.

4. Lay slices of mozzarella evenly over crust. Spoon tomatoes over cheese. Sprinkle Parmesan over tomatoes. Distribute pepperoni or flattened sausage pieces evenly over filling, Drizzle 1 tablespoon olive oil over top. Bake on bottom oven rack 5 minutes. Move pizza to upper third of oven. Bake until crust is lightly browned and sausage is cooked through, 15 to 20 minutes. Let cool slightly before slicing.

Their Pizzeria Riccardo opened in 1943 in the basement of an old mansion at 29 E. Ohio St.

But Chicagoans were having none of a pizza that took 30 to 45 minutes to cook. Sewell took to giving free samples on the sidewalk to lure customers in. Just when it looked like the business would fold, according to one story, a reporter who happened to be a World War II veteran discovered the place—and wrote about it. Actually, Riccardo's was one of the main hangouts for the city's newspaper reporters and workers, and Riccardo and Sewell persuaded them to write about the new pizza joint. That's when deep-dish Chicago-style pizza turned the corner. The first restaurant became so popular that Sewell opened Pizzeria Due in 1955 in another Victorian mansion just a block away from the original (619 N. Wabash St.) and Riccardo's was renamed Pizzeria Uno.

Many Uno and Due alumni started their own pizza parlors. Alice Rae Redmond, the original pizza chef, teamed up with two cab drivers and a Sicilian butcher who owned a building on nearby Superior Street. They launched Gino's East in 1966. At Gino's, the crust was equally thick but more of a polenta-based beast than Uno's or Due's. New locations were added and today there are 11 locations of the Gino's chain in the Chicago area, Wisconsin, and Texas.

In 1970, bartender Malnati, who ran the day-to-day operations with his son Lou, asked Sewell if Lou could secure his future by buying in. Sewell said no, and that was the end of their friendship. Lou Malnati's soon opened in Lincolnwood, a north suburb of Chicago. Malnati had vine-ripened plum tomatoes canned exclusively for his store; the buttery-crusted pies were slightly thinner than their progenitors', but they still stood tall at two inches. Lou Malnati died in 1978, and his sons Marc and Ric took over the business. Malnati's has grown to 14 dine-in and 25 carryout operations and ships frozen pizza nationwide.

A Malnati offshoot is Pizano's, which sprung up in Chicago in 1991, owned by Rudy Malnati Jr., a half- brother of Lou Malnati. Pizano's crust has a more pastrylike texture than its relatives' crusts, but it, too, has legitimate ties to the original deep-dish recipe developed for Pizzeria Uno.

Double-crusted pizzas, called stuffed pizzas, were developed by the Giordano's and Nancy's chains in the mid-1970s, and made the dish even deeper. Edwardo's came along in 1978 and pioneered offbeat toppings such as pineapple and spinach.

Neapolitan pizza and wood-oven–fired cracker-thin pizza recently have appeared in Chicago. Among newer and often upscale places are Spacca Napoli on W. Sunnyside; Nonnina on N. Clark St.; Coda di Volpe on N. Southport St.; Eataly, the Italian food market; Rosangela's Pizzeria (famous for its cracker crust) in Evergreen Park; Acanto in the Loop; Forno Rosso on N. Harlem (Neapolitan-style soft crust); Antica Pizzeria on N. Clark; Coalfire in West Town and Lake View (coal-fired ovens); Macello (Pugliese-style) on Lake Street; and Santullo's Eatery (New York style) on W. North Avenue.

In 1979, Ike Sewell sold his deep-dish company to Aaron Spencer, who moved the headquarters to Boston. Spencer's iteration is called Uno Chicago Grills, and there are now hundreds around the country, but few Chicagoans accept them as the real deal. Despite the recent inroads by Neapolitan pizza and wood-oven–fired pizza in town, deep-dish pizza is Chicago's own, and it's here to stay.

Contributors: Penny Pollack and Bruce Kraig

BIBLIOGRAPHY

Mariani, John. *The Dictionary of Italian Food and Drink*. New York: Bantam Doubleday Bell Publishing Group, 1998.

Pollack, Penny, and Jeff Ruby. *Everybody Loves Pizza*. Cincinnati: Emmis Books, 2005.

"Who Invented Deep Dish? Search to Find the Creator of City's Trademark Pie Yields Dueling Claims." *Chicago Tribune*, February 18, 2009.

Playboy Club

The members-only Playboy Club opened on February 29, 1960, at 116 E. Walton St., bringing to real life Hugh Hefner's pinup magazine. Waitresses wore the required "Bunny" uniform: revealing corset, bunny ears, and tail. Excellent liquor, filet mignon, and live jazz were on the menu. The subject of a now-famous 1963 *Show* magazine article by feminist Gloria Steinem, the club was later replicated in 25 states and abroad. The Chicago location, which moved to N. Michigan Ave. and then to N. Lincoln Park West, closed on June 30, 1986. Playboy Enterprises, Inc., planned to resurrect the club on the Near North Side after 2013 but financial difficulties made that a distant prospect.

Contributor: Janet Fuller

See also: Private Clubs and Restaurants

BIBLIOGRAPHY

Slania, John T. "The Real Playboy Club: Former Bunnies, Performers and Hugh Hefner Remember the Chicago Hangout." *Timeout Chicago*, September 7, 2011.

Polish

The first Polish settlers arrived in Chicago in the 1850s after the early Germans and Irish. Three more waves of immigrants came, fleeing political and religious persecution and a lack of work. They quickly found jobs in the steel mills and stockyards and built modest homes to form some of the first ethnic neighborhoods.

The largest wave came between the end of the Civil War and the late 1920s and was called *za chlebem*, the bread immigration. The immigrants left Poland when there was not enough to eat. Most were from the Polish Highlands area outside of Warsaw. In addition to industrial labor jobs, these immigrants often became involved in politics and insurance businesses. After World War II, another wave arrived, made up of middle-class people with a higher level of education and able to speak English, and they quickly assimilated. A final wave in the 1980s brought educated and upwardly mobile immigrants.

Most were Roman Catholic and immediately formed their own Polish churches, many of which survive today. These parishes were located near places of employment and formed pockets on the South, Southeast, and Northwest Sides, especially along the "Polish Highway" of Milwaukee Avenue, stretching from downtown to the city limits. About 1 million Poles now live in the Chicago metropolitan area; however, many Polish families have left the city proper and live in nearby suburban areas, such as Oak Park, Morton Grove, and Park Ridge.

Retail establishments opened near the churches to serve the Polish-speaking population. The area near Division, Ashland, and Milwaukee was once referred to as Polish Downtown. Further north, near the intersection of Milwaukee and Belmont lies Avondale, known as *Polska Asada* (Polish Village), which continues to operate as a true village with many residents and businesses intact.

In addition to church-based organizations, fraternal organizations offered services such as employment assistance and banking, and a welcome gathering place; Polish Roman Catholic Union of America (PRCUA), Polish National Alliance (PNA), and Polish Women's Alliance (PWA) are all active today. Most of these organizations sponsor festivals, such as Taste of Polonia around Labor Day. In early May, a citywide parade celebrates Polish Constitution Day. October is designated Polish Heritage Month in Chicago, highlighting food, the arts, and contributions of the Poles to the fabric of the city. The festivals, open to the public, offer a way to taste traditional and authentic foods made by home cooks and restaurants.

Shopping is an old-country experience in these neighborhoods. Bobak's, located near the old stockyards for more than 50 years, offers catering, a restaurant, and deli and grocery items alongside dozens of types of cured meats. Kasia's Deli on Chicago Avenue features her signature pierogi as well as other deli items. Endy's Deli in

POLISH EASTER MEALS (*ŚWIĘCONKA*)

Perhaps no holiday in the Polish calendar includes more pageantry than Easter. The entire day is spent together as a family, and newer immigrants have always been invited to share the meal with those more established. Preparations begin far ahead of time and focus on the presentation of an elaborately decorated basket containing eggs, bread, butter (in the shape of a Pascal lamb), and other ingredients. The baskets are taken to the church on Holy Saturday for a blessing by the priest. These ingredients later are used to make Easter breakfast or dinner.

The base for a *biały barszcz* (white borscht), served at breakfast or to begin the dinner, starts with rye bread moistened and set to ferment for hours, lending a distinctive sour flavor to the buttermilk and dill soup. Easter dinner features Polish-style ham, sausages, boiled potatoes with dill, hard-cooked eggs, beet salad, and rye bread, along with any number of other side dishes. A *baranek* (Pascal Lamb) cake ends the meal along with traditional pastries, such as *kolaczki*, *babka*, and *chrusciki*.

—JUDITH DUNBAR HINES

Avondale is small but complete. And Oak Mill Bakery, on North Avenue and at six other locations, and the newer Delightful Pastries, with three Chicago locations, fulfill the desire for traditional Polish pastries of every kind.

Restaurants located near workplaces sprang up to feed hungry laborers with inexpensive meals of soup, sausage, and bread. Many still exist. Some feature a wide selection of choose-it-yourself dishes for a set price; this "Polish all-you-can-eat buffet" concept originated in Chicago. One more recent example is Sawa's Old Warsaw Restaurant in Broadview, opened in 1973.

Whether at home or in a restaurant, traditional Polish food was based on inexpensive and homegrown ingredients such as cabbage, dairy, and fruits. No true Polish dinner would be complete without *kapusta* (cabbage as sauerkraut or rolled to enclose meat and rice) and a variety of hearty breads, usually rye. Meats are smoked, roasted, or boiled pork, beef, and poultry. Game, such as goose or rabbit, often appeared on menus; men of the Old Country were active hunters. Foraged mushrooms find their way into sauces and soups, pierogi, and other entrees.

Soups are important in lunches or as a separate course of a larger meal. There are many variations of borscht, including some that begin with a sour, fermented rye base, *kvass*, and may be made with buttermilk. Dill is a common herb used in sauces, potatoes, and meats, as is caraway.

In Polish homes, holiday meals are still extensive and labor intensive. A traditional Christmas Eve dinner, or *Wigilia*, offers up to 11 courses (always an uneven number) of nonmeat dishes. Easter preparations begin a few days early with the assembly of a basket of items to be taken to the church on Easter Saturday to be blessed by the priest. Holiday meals and everyday get-togethers end with pastries like *kolaczki* or poppy seed *babka*, but today hosts are more likely to buy them from a bakery than make them at home.

Paczkis, doughnuts stuffed with cream or jelly, are examples of a traditional food that has moved far beyond the ethnic neighborhoods. Originally, they were a pre–Ash Wednesday treat, designed to use up sweet and rich ingredients not allowed in the home during Lent. Today, a Polish bakery can make and sell as many as 15,000 on the day before Ash Wednesday, declared Paczki Day throughout Chicago.

Contributor: Judith Dunbar Hines

See also: Baking and Bakeries; Festivals; Sausages

BIBLIOGRAPHY

Granacki, Victoria, and The Polish Museum of America. *Chicago's Polish Downtown*. Mt. Pleasant, S.C.: Arcadia Publishing, 2004.

Holli, Melvin, and Peter D'A. Jones. *Ethnic Chicago*. Grand Rapids: William B. Erdmans Publishing Co., 1995.

Kaplan, Jacob, Daniel Pogorzelski, Rob Reid, Elisa Addlesperger, and Dominic Pacyga. *Avondale and Chicago's Polish Village*. Mt. Pleasant, S.C.: Arcadia Publishing, 2014.

THE "CHICAGO MIX" CONTROVERSY

Surprisingly, "Chicago Mix" did not originate in the Windy City. Candyland, Inc., in St. Paul, Minnesota, created the popular blend of flavored popcorns in 1988—and trademarked the name. Candyland owner Brenda Lamb, who created the combination, said she picked the name "Chicago Mix," because she felt it would have wider appeal than "St. Paul Mix." Unlike most Chicago purveyors who mix caramel and cheese-laced popcorn, Candyland's version includes their seasoned popcorn, not just cheese corn and caramel corn. Candyland's desire to protect their trademark led to some legal wrangling. Now, if you visit a Garrett's shop for this treat, you'll find them selling it as "Garrett Mix."

—CYNTHIA CLAMPITT

Popcorn

Popcorn entered the United States through New England's seaports in the early 1800s, most likely picked up in South America by whalers and traders. However, the modern popcorn industry didn't begin until 1893, when Charles "C." Cretors introduced the first popcorn machine—and the first hot-buttered popcorn—at the Columbian Exposition in Chicago. The machine made popping corn easy, adding butter made it a joy, and popcorn began to transition from homegrown novelty to booming business.

As the passion for popcorn spread, Chicago-based C. Cretors & Company sold its popcorn machines. Housed in handsome carts or wagons, the machines offered a great opportunity to people who wanted to start their own businesses. Carts could be maneuvered by individuals, or large wagons were drawn by horses. After 1909, they were fitted with automobile engines. Thousands of men and women got their start selling popcorn from Cretors's wagons.

Patent protection ran out on Cretors's invention in 1909, and others began to copy the popper. Competition bred invention, and popcorn machines soon appeared in shops and movie theaters. The poppers made numerous popcorn-related businesses possible, such as Cracker Jack, which got its start in Chicago.

One shop that began selling popcorn in 1921 has become a Chicagoland icon. The Little Popcorn Shop in Wheaton was once an alley that E. Claire Brown thought was the perfect location for selling popcorn and candy. The alley, which was only 49 inches wide, was roofed over and named the In-Between Shop. The shop changed hands, as well as its name, when Brown died, but the Little Popcorn Shop still focuses on buttered popcorn and penny candy—and is still only 49 inches wide.

In 1949, what would become one of Chicago's best-known popcorn shops was opened at 10 West Madison Street. Garrett Popcorn Shops created their caramel, cheese, and buttered popcorns based on family recipes. Since 1949, Garrett's has seen a lot of growth, as well as growing competition from other popcorn shops, such as Nuts on Clark and Mother Butter's.

With the development of large, industrial poppers, Chicago-area companies began packaging popcorn. Mellos Snacks, a family-owned wholesaler that offers gift tins and private label packages of all the classics (butter, cheese, caramel) started in 1946 and is still located in downtown Chicago. Numerous other Chicago-area companies followed suit, including The Popcorn Factory and Gary Poppins.

The family that started it all is still producing popcorn poppers, with the great-grandson of C. C. Cretors now running the operation. Even when it outgrew a downtown space, the company stayed close, moving in 2014 to the Chicago suburb of Wood Dale.

Early motorized popcorn wagon after Cretors design, ca. 1910. Courtesy of the Chicago History Museum, ICHi-85007; Robert E. Moulton.

The popcorn industry is firmly anchored in the Midwest and its cornfields, and especially in the Chicagoland area. The Popcorn Board, a nonprofit organization that works to raise public awareness of the joys of popcorn, and The Popcorn Institute, a trade association of U.S. popcorn processors, are in Chicago. A web search of "popcorn shops, Chicago" turns up hundreds of locations.

Given popcorn's history and continued popularity, it is not surprising that, in 2003, the Illinois General Assembly established popcorn as the official snack food of Illinois.

Contributor: Cynthia Clampitt

See also: Cracker Jack; Equipment, Commercial

BIBLIOGRAPHY

Clampitt, Cynthia. *Midwest Maize: How Corn Shaped the U.S. Heartland*. Urbana: University of Illinois Press, 2015.

Smith, Andrew F. *Popped Culture: A Social History of Popcorn in America*. Washington, D.C.: Smithsonian, 2001.

Pope, Antoinette and François

By the time François Pope walked in front of the TV cameras in 1951 to launch the *Creative Cookery* show with sons Frank and Robert, the Antoinette Pope School of Fancy Cookery had already been teaching Chicagoans how to cook for decades. In 1930, Antoinette Pope began holding cooking classes for friends in the family's home and cofounded the school with her husband François. Eight years later, a *Chicago Daily Tribune* advertisement for Antoinette Pope's Schools of Fancy Cookery (there were two locations then) announced afternoon and evening classes were available, with lessons costing $1 each. Among the topics: cake decorating, vegetable carving, and candy making.

When class sizes outgrew the teaching areas within the Popes' home, they moved the school to a 3,000-square-foot space at 316 N. Michigan Ave. in 1942. Outfitted with kitchens, laboratories, an auditorium for 150 students, and reception rooms, the school remained at that site almost 30 years.

The Popes produced several cookbooks, including *Choice Recipes for the Discriminating Hostess* (1936) and *Antoinette Pope School Candy Book* (1949). But it was *The Antoinette Pope School Cookbook*, published in 1948, that proved a bestseller. A Marshall Field & Company newspaper ad announced an autograph session with the Popes at the retailer's State Street store, noting the new book featured "Specialty dishes and other recipes that contribute to the success of the hostess . . . including French, Italian, Cantonese and Scandinavian dishes." With more than 40 years of experience "creating new recipes and improvising on old," the aim of the Popes' cookbooks was to give students a knowledge of the fundamentals of cooking and the keys to fancy cookery.

If the couple proved a culinary force in Chicago with their school and cookbooks (as well as a variety of prepared foods they sold, from frozen pizzas to fruitcakes), their fame spread nationwide with their TV show that ran for 12 years on local and network stations. In a television era dominated by cooking shows starring home economists, François, wearing a suit (he reportedly felt it was more "dignified"), would whip up a complete meal in 60 minutes. "The most remarkable cooking program in the history of radio and television," trumpeted a full-page ad in the Hollywood trade paper *Variety*.

Antoinette (born in Seneca, Italy) married François (born in Valentigney, France) in Chicago in the early 1920s. François' father was a chef, his mother loved to cook, and they had a cafe in Paris. So young François was scrambling eggs at the age of six. It was François' parents who taught Antoinette to cook. François died in July, 1971, at the age of 75. Antoinette died at 97 in 1993.

Contributor: Judy Hevrdejs

See also: Books and Publishers; Cooking Classes; Media, Television

BIBLIOGRAPHY

Brownson, JeanMarie. "Chicago's Chef: Antoinette Pope's Schools and Books Led Generations of Men and Women into the Regimen of the Kitchen. *Chicago Tribune*, May 27, 1993.

Collins, Kathleen. *Watching What We Eat: The Evolution of Television Cooking Shows.* New York: The Continuum International Publishing Group Inc., 2009.

Popeil Brothers

The Popeil (pronounced *poh-PEEL*) family crossed over into mainstream America with Dan Aykroyd's *Saturday Night Live* lampoon of the Popeils with fictional products such as the "Bass-O-Matic." But the Chicago-based family did create the Veg-O-Matic, Whip-O-Matic, and Kitchen Magician that were popularized in 1970s fast-talking television ads.

The Popeils learned their shtick on Maxwell Street in Chicago. Founder Samuel "S. J." Popeil (1915–84) was born in New York City to Polish-Jewish immigrants. Between 1942 and 1945, S. J. and his brother, Raymond, moved to Chicago and sold gadgets on Maxwell Street.

In 1945, they established the Popeil Brothers manufacturing firm and built a factory on State and Lake Streets. S. J. was a classic tinkerer, a gourmet Rube Goldberg. He improvised on products he already saw. The detailed, sleek construction of Popeil products such as the Inside-the-Eggshell Egg Scrambler has attracted modern-day fans of midcentury design.

His son Ronald also learned to hustle as a 16-year-old on Maxwell Street. In the mid-1950s, the Popeils took their act to the F. W. Woolworth Co. store at State and Washington, then the largest grossing Woolworth's in America. Ron would set up a demonstration table near the entrance of the store and put kitchen gadgets near the cosmetic department to attract women. Ron often recruited his older brother, Jerry, to work the other end of the department store. Ron earned $1,000 a week when the average monthly salary in his field was $500.

With the popularity of television, Ron Popeil (born 1935) became the face of the company. In 1964, he founded his own Ronco Teleproducts, headquartered in Chicago's Playboy Towers. Most of the Ronco products, such as the smokeless ashtray, were battery-operated, but batteries were a bad sales pitch. Ron Popeil told viewers his merchandise was "cordless electric."

The Popeil name resurfaced in another light in 1974, when S. J.'s wife, Eloise Little Popeil, was convicted of plotting to have two hit men murder S. J. in their 10-room Drake Towers apartment on Chicago's Gold Coast. S. J.'s estimated worth then was between $10 million and $150 million, according to published reports. The Popeils were divorced, and she served a 19-month prison sentence. But wait . . . there's more! They remarried after her release from prison.

The Popeil Brothers company was sold in 1979 to Milwaukee businessman Saul Padek, who liquidated it.

Ronco Teleproducts was forced into bankruptcy in 1984, although Ron was able to repurchase the colorful inventory. Although he does not own Ronco, Ron Popeil still invents and pitches cooking products. His 5 in 1 Cooking System, a unique food fryer, can be seen on many of America's infomercial television venues.

Contributor: Dave Hoekstra

BIBLIOGRAPHY

Ron Popeil. *The Salesman of the Century.* New York: Delacorte Press, 1995.

Potbelly Sandwich Works

A sandwich chain based in Chicago, Potbelly boasts warm sandwiches, a neighborhood feel, and service within eight minutes. It began in 1977, when Peter Hastings started serving sandwiches in his North Lincoln Avenue antiques store (complete with an old potbelly stove) in the hopes of boosting business. Lines of customers soon formed. Hastings began toasting his sub sandwiches and then adding soups and desserts. He also brought in local musicians to play at the lunch hour. In 1996, Bryant Kiel bought the shop and began an expansion of the concept that today includes more than 300 Potbellys worldwide.

Each restaurant offers a limited menu of the freshly made, toasted sandwiches, soups, salads, and hand-dipped ice cream. After becoming one of the fastest-growing firms in Chicago, it went public in 2013. Revenue rose to nearly $86 million by early 2015. The firm is still growing and expects to open at least 48 new stores in 2015. Each will have its own potbelly stove in the center of things.

Contributor: Carol Mighton Haddix
See also: Fast Food/Quick Service

BIBLIOGRAPHY

Zillman, Claire. "Quiznos and Potbelly: A Tale of Two Sandwich Chains." *Fortune.* http://fortune.com/2014/03/18/quiznos-and-potbelly-a-tale-of-two-sandwich-chains/.

Printer's Row Restaurant

Michael Foley opened Printer's Row, at 555 S. Dearborn St., in 1981, taking a gamble in the South Loop neighborhood of the same name, where few ventured at the time. Once home to many publishing and printing firms in the late 1800s, the area of old warehouses was just beginning to attract loft developers. Printer's Row restaurant helped revitalize it, with a clublike decor, fine service, and an intriguing menu of midwestern ingredients prepared with Chef Foley's flair for combining flavors.

Few chefs at the time sourced ingredients from local farms and producers, but Foley searched out the best vegetables, game, fish, and cheeses from Midwest suppliers, creating a unique network. The restaurant became a leader in what the national press called a "new American cuisine" in the 1980s and earned a 3-star review from the *Chicago Tribune.*

The menu often mixed flavors from other regions and countries, with ingredients such as bok choy, Tex-Mex spices, or Thai curry pastes. Game played a large role, such as a roasted venison chop topped with a sun-dried cherry and rosemary marmalade or a duckling served with corn crepes. Wild mushrooms were sautéed with pine needles, and grilled salmon was paired with pink peppercorn sauce. After 23 years of operation, the restaurant closed in 2004.

Contributor: Carol Mighton Haddix

See also: Foley, Michael; Restaurants and Fine Dining

BIBLIOGRAPHY

Fonda, Daren. "Printer's Row, Chicago, Ill." *Cigar Aficionado,* November-December 1998.

Mandel, Abby. "Michael Foley's Midwest Quest." *Midwestern Table.* November-December 1996.

Private Clubs and Restaurants

Chicago is home to many private clubs and restaurants. The Standard Club is the oldest in the city, having been founded in 1869 as a business club. Following were The Union League Club, The Metropolitan Club, The University Club, and several business clubs, all located in the Loop. They attract members from the Board of Trade, area law firms, and others from the business community. The Cliff Dwellers, The Arts Club of Chicago, and Soho House attract members from the arts community. Dining at many of the clubs offers fine wines, classic prime steaks and seafood, and formal decor and service. Some clubs, struggling with decreasing membership in recent years and competition from local restaurants, have revamped menus and rules to attract younger members.

Prospective members for all clubs must be put up for membership by two existing members, and members pay an initiation fee plus monthly fees for access to the dining room, meeting rooms, and special events such as the annual Boxing Night at The Standard Club and the homecoming gala at The Union League Club. Soho House is the newest private club, opening in 2014 in the West Loop. It is a hotel and club chain, with casual restaurants available to the public as well as members. The Chicago location of Soho House is the largest; other locations can be found in London, New York, and Los Angeles.

Les Nomades is a fine-dining French restaurant in Streeterville that used to be a private dining club. It was opened in 1978 by legendary Chicago restaurateur Jovan Trboyevic. The current owner, Mary Beth Liccioni, bought the restaurant in 1993 with her then-husband, acclaimed chef Roland Liccioni, and they opened it to the public.

Contributor: Chandra Ram

See also: Playboy Club; Restaurants and Fine Dining

BIBLIOGRAPHY

Putnam, Seth. "Examining Chicago's Top 5 Private Clubs." *Michigan Avenue Magazine.* http://michiganavemag.com/living/articles/chicago-top-private-high-society-clubs.

Werner, Laurie. "Chicago's Soho House Opens and It's Not Just Members Only." *Forbes.* http://www.forbes.com/sites/lauriewerner/2014/08/19/chicagos-soho-house-opens-and-its-not-just-members-only/.

Prohibition

In 1918, Congress passed the 18th Amendment to the Constitution, making the transportation, manufacture, and sale of most kinds of "intoxicating liquor" illegal in the United States. The amendment was enforced by the Volstead Act passed in October 1919, which went into effect on January 17, 1920. Some alcoholic beverages were legal under specific circumstances, such as "near beer" and sacramental wine and alcohol for medicinal purposes. It was also perfectly legal to store and drink alcohol in one's own home, which is what many people

Authorities disposing of illegal beer. Wikimedia Commons.

did. This legislation remained in place until 1933, when the law was repealed

Americans loved their drink. Even in the colonial era, drinking was more than a way to socialize. It was built into the workday. Drinking in excess became the problematic norm that some increasingly argued was in direct conflict with religious ideals. By the 1830s, with the rise of the American Temperance Society and its offshoots, organized calls not just for temperance but outright Prohibition began, resulting in a wave of legislation in some states (most later repealed) that restricted or banned the sale of alcohol.

Women picked up the fight in the 1870s. The Women's Christian Temperance Union pursued prohibition while advocating for and establishing antialcohol educational and social service initiatives. The Anti-Saloon League, formed in the late 1890s, laid significant groundwork for national prohibition by working to elect dry candidates. Further efforts led to the passage of local option bills, which dried up counties or portions of some cities, including in Chicago, and eventually extended to a number of states.

Proponents argued that Prohibition would reduce crime, corruption, poverty, and other societal problems associated with alcohol and limit the influence of the burgeoning immigrant populations in cities across America. It hardly worked out that way. In Chicago, the law ushered in one of the most colorful eras in the city's history, one where politicians and policeman were in cahoots with mobsters who controlled the flow of bootlegged liquor, and Mayor William "Big Bill" Thompson, who served two terms during Prohibition, looked the other way.

Drinking became de rigueur in many levels of society. Hip flasks were popular. Regular folks, if they weren't making their own hooch at home, frequented speakeasies, the illegal barrooms that proliferated across the city. Women bellied up to the bar alongside men without worrying that their behavior would be frowned upon as it was before. All were welcome, male and female, rich and poor.

After Prohibition went into effect, thousands of doctors and pharmacists in Chicago applied for licenses to sell "medicinal" liquor. By the mid-1920s, the city had some 20,000 speakeasies and 15 breweries.

Chicago's gangs had been in business before Prohibition, but if there was a golden era for them, this was it. When Prohibition began, James "Big Jim" Colosimo, an Italian immigrant and restaurateur, controlled the city's gambling and prostitution rackets. He was gunned down at his restaurant, the victim of a hit many believed was ordered by his business partner and nephew Johnny Torrio, who wanted in on this huge new opportunity—alcohol. Torrio and other gang leaders quickly and effectively built up their bootlegging operations, staking claims over sections of the city. There were at least a dozen gangs by the mid-1920s, distinguished by ethnicity. Irishman Dion O'Banion headed the North Side Gang. In Little Italy, the Genna brothers made their name in industrial alcohol.

The gangs regularly paid off policemen, politicians, and judges. Chicago's own police chief estimated that 60 percent of his force was on the take from bootleggers. Territorial disputes among the gangs inevitably led to violence, and lots of it. In the first four years of Prohibition, there were an estimated 200 gang killings; by Prohibition's end, Chicago counted 800 deaths linked to the so-called Beer Wars. Mayor William Dever, who served from 1924 to 1927 in between Thompson's terms, worked to enforce Prohibition by closing speakeasies, but this did little to curb the gang violence and regular citizens' thirst for booze and general disregard of the law.

And Torrio's syndicate was about to get bigger. He had hired a bold, young bodyguard from New York, Al Capone, and moved operations to the suburb of Cicero. After Torrio survived a shooting and spent nine months in jail, he retired to Italy and left Capone in charge. Capone went on a tear, moving in on rival gangs, arranging assassinations, and spreading his influence to speakeasies, brothels, racing tracks, distilleries, and breweries in the city and suburbs. With control of the liquor supply line from Canada and elsewhere firmly in hand, Capone built his empire into a $70-million-a-year operation.

He was comfortable in the public eye and presented himself as a family man who lived on South Prairie Avenue. He bought and distributed clothing and food for the needy and opened soup kitchens during the Great Depression. Though he spared no rivals, it was said that he sometimes paid the hospital bills of his injured enemies. The tipping point came with the notorious St. Valentine's Day Massacre of 1929 in which Capone's men, dressed as policemen, staged a raid on a building at 2122 N. Clark St. that was a transfer point for beer and shot to death seven men. The incident put Chicago under a microscope and raised calls for an end to the violence.

In 1931, Capone was convicted of federal tax evasion. He served more than six years in prison and moved to Florida upon release, where he kept a vacation home. He suffered from dementia, a complication from syphilis, and died in 1947.

Bootlegging continued until Prohibition was repealed on December 5, 1933, with the ratification of the 21st Amendment. A good number of Chicagoans gathered at bars and large downtown hotels to toast the occasion. But Prohibition's effect would linger, with organized crime's influence in Chicago now solidified and the Depression still weighing heavily on people's moods and wallets.

....

Contributor: Janet Fuller

See also: Bars, Taverns, Saloons, and Pubs; Beer, Breweries, and Brewpub; Gangsters; Speakeasies; Spirits and Distilleries, Supper Clubs and Roadhouses

BIBLIOGRAPHY

Aylesworth, Thomas G., and Virginia L. *Chicago: The Glamour Years (1919–1941)*. New York: Gallery Books, 1986.

Behr, Edward. *Prohibition: Thirteen Years That Changed America*. New York: Arcade Publishing, 1996.

Hill, Jeff. *Prohibition: Defining Moments*. Detroit: Omnigraphics, 2004.

Spinney, Robert G. *City of Big Shoulders: A History of Chicago*. DeKalb, Ill.: Northern Illinois University Press, 2000.

Pullman Porters

Industrialist George Pullman founded the Pullman Palace Car Company in Chicago in 1867 to manufacture elegant sleeping and dining cars. He also provided luxury services to middle- and upper-class passengers traveling by rail. Pullman hired porters to provide the best services possible. He sought out former slaves and the descendants of slaves to fill the positions for what was becoming a hugely profitable company.

By 1925, the Pullman Co. was the second largest employer of blacks in the country, employing more than 12,000. Many of the black workers were college-educated employees who could not find jobs in a segregated workforce; others were attracted by the steady work and the large tips that supplemented a very meager salary.

In August of 1925, black workers organized The Brotherhood of Sleeping Car Porters (BSCP) with A. Philip Randolph and Milton Webster as leaders. Though demands for better working conditions and wages continued to be generally ignored in society at large, the BSCP was effective in gaining better pay and safer working conditions for its members.

Positive experiences for these workers included meeting people from all walks of life, traveling with family members who took advantage of railroad discounts, and sampling regional delicacies while touring the United States. Traveling to New Orleans while working on the Illinois Central introduced workers to gumbo. A trip between Detroit and Miami offered some workers a tropical vacation and a chance to return home with fresh oranges. A Pullman commissary car attached to the B & O Capital Limited tempted workers with fresh seafood from the Chesapeake Bay.

Dining was an important part of railway travel, and African American chefs and waitstaff were critical to the experience. Railroad companies set up rigorous training programs for cooks and service personnel. Some were run by distinguished chefs and caterers such as George Rector and Chicago's C. H. Shirecliffe. A strict hierarchy

Late-nineteenth-century flyer advertising food service on Pullman Palace cars. Library of Congress.

ran from chef to second cooks, pantrymen, and several orders of waiters.

African American personnel became adept in the hospitality industry, and many later served in major hotel kitchens or became entrepreneurs, opening their own restaurants. One chef, who worked for the private Pullman cars from 1883 to 1907, wrote and published a cookbook, considered one of the first by an African American. Rufus Estes documented his career and an era with almost 600 recipes in *Good Things to Eat as Suggested by Rufus: A Collection of Practical Recipes for Preparing Meats, Game, Fowl, Fish, Puddings, Pastries, Etc*. Estes later went on to become chef to tycoon John "Bet-a-Million" Gates and the U.S. Steel Co.

Contributor: Donna Pierce

See also: African Americans; Transportation

BIBLIOGRAPHY

Estes, Rufus. *Good Things to Eat as Suggested by Rufus: A Collection of Practical Recipes for Preparing Meats, Game, Fowl, Fish, Puddings, Pastries, Etc.* Chicago: Published by the Author, 1911.

Tye, Larry. *Rising from the Rails.* New York: Henry Holt and Co., 2004.

Pump Room

The Pump Room served as a magnet for a galaxy of Hollywood stars for nearly 40 years. Opened by Chicago hotelman Ernie Byfield on October 1, 1938, the Pump Room was the centerpiece of Byfield's elegant Ambassador East Hotel built in 1926 at State Parkway and Goethe Street on the city's Gold Coast. Byfield, a born showman, staged the Pump Room with crystal chandeliers, sprawling white leather booths, costumed waitstaff, and dramatically presented food.

Byfield counted among his regulars Humphrey Bogart and Lauren Bacall, who had their wedding breakfast in the Pump Room, Elizabeth Taylor, Judy Garland, Bette Davis, Frank Sinatra, and many others. Crowds came to dine near the stars, who were seated in Booth One right off the entrance. The food and service were the strong supporting cast. Byfield dressed his waiters in red swallow-tailed coats and garbed the coffee boy in emerald cloth and a white satin turban plumed with ostrich feathers. They showcased imaginative fare such as chicken Portolla, curried in a coconut shell; steak Diane, made at tableside; crabmeat à la Byfield; roast pheasant, clad in its original plumage; and the showstopper, a flaming sword dish—Shashlik Caucasian—"performed" by a half-dozen waiters, each armed with rapiers covered with flaming chunks of lamb, weaving their way through the tables.

Diners often capped their meals by dancing to the music of David LeWinter's band in the '40s and to Stanley Paul's in the '60s. But over time, the hotel's luster

Waiter and doorman at the Pump Room. Courtesy of the Chicago History Museum, HB-07185; Photograph by Hedrich-Blessing.

faded, along with that of the Pump Room. In 1976, Lettuce Entertain You founder Rich Melman acquired the Pump Room as his first fine-dining restaurant, only to sell it in the mid-1980s. The restaurant and the hotel went through several more incarnations until New York–based hotelier Ian Schrager bought the Ambassador East in 2010, completely remodeled it, and reopened it in 2011 with a new identity as the Public Chicago Hotel. He kept the Pump Room's name after holding a public vote of Chicagoans, who overwhelmingly chose to keep it. Today, the Pump Room sports a modern chic look with dark-stained oak floors and Italian resin orbs, and a farm-to-table menu created by New York award-winning chef Jean Georges Vongerichten. A wall of photos showing long-gone celebrities now welcomes diners at the new street-level entrance, reminding all those who enter that this was once the Camelot of all Chicago eateries.

Contributor: Scott Warner

See also: Lettuce Entertain You Restaurants; Restaurants and Fine Dining

BIBLIOGRAPHY

Kogan, Rick. *Sabers & Suites The Story of Chicago's Ambassador East.* Chicago: Rick Kogan Publisher, 1983.

FROM BATH TO CHICAGO

Chicago hotelman Ernie Byfield named his legendary eatery after the Pump Room in Bath, England, an eighteenth-century British gambling and watering place. It was Bath's focal point, the first fashionable spot where the aristocracy and actors socialized together. Nearly 200 years later, Chicago's Pump Room also filled that bill, as the city's society members went social climbing after the actors.

—SCOTT WARNER

Q

The Quaker Oats Company

Officially formed in 1901, Quaker Oats has roots in several Midwest cities, including Chicago. The name originally was held by The Quaker Mill Company of Ravenna, Ohio, which had the first U.S.-registered trademark for a breakfast cereal in 1877. In 1881, Henry Parsons Crowell (1855–1944) purchased Quaker Mill, and in 1885, partnered with two of his competitors, Robert Stuart and Ferdinand Schumacher, to form the Consolidated Oatmeal Company. The image of a full-figure and severe-faced man dressed in "Quaker garb" appeared on the company's packages. The Imperial Mill, built in 1879 at 16th and Dearborn Streets in Chicago, was in part owned by Stuart and became part of the partnership. However, other competitors worked strategically to undermine the efforts of Consolidated, which eventually collapsed in 1888. Shortly thereafter, seven of the nation's largest mill owners came together to form the American Cereal Company, controlling most of the country's oats market, with Schumacher in the role of president and Crowell as vice president. In 1899, Schumacher lost control of the company to Crowell and Stuart, who diversified their portfolio into other cereal grains.

In 1901, American Cereal became known as The Quaker Oats Company, headquartered in Chicago, with annual sales of $16 million. Crowell, known as "the cereal tycoon," held several managerial positions in the company from 1888 until 1943. In 1922, Robert Stuart's oldest son, John, became president, a post he held for 34 years, growing the business substantially through foreign operations, new brands, and acquisitions. In 1921, a chemical division was formed to harness the solvent properties of oat husks. By the early 1900s, Quaker Oats became the largest cereal manufacturer in the world. Over time, Quaker Oats diversified their portfolio, acquiring both food and other consumer product businesses, such as Aunt Jemima Mills (1925–present), Fisher-Price toys (1969–91), Jos. A. Banks Clothiers, Brookstone mail-order company Eyelab (1981–86); Stokely-Van Camp, makers of Gatorade and Van Camp pork and beans (1983); and Snapple (1994–97). Gatorade became the company's best seller by 1987.

Quaker became the first food company to successfully petition the U.S. Food and Drug Association for a food-specific health claim after investing millions of dollars into research on the health benefits of oats. In 1997, oatmeal packages could bear the claim: "Soluble fiber from oatmeal as part of a low saturated fat, low cholesterol diet, may reduce the risk of heart disease." A commitment to research was also evident in the formation of the Gatorade Sports Science Institute (GSSI) established in 1985 at the Quaker Oats Research & Development facility in Barrington, Illinois. GSSI partnered with top universities across the country studying the effects of nutrition on athletic performance and hydration.

In 2001, PepsiCo, based in Purchase, New York, acquired The Quaker Oats Company for $14 billion, purportedly for the Gatorade business, creating the fourth largest consumer goods company in the world. Other major brands now include a number of ready-to-eat cereals (e.g., Cap'n Crunch, Life); Quaker rice cakes and granola bars; Rice-A-Roni; and Near East rice and pasta side dishes. Chicago remains the headquarters for Quaker Oats, located at 555 W. Monroe St.

The iconic Quaker Man, originally selected to identify the brand with integrity, honesty, and purity, continues to grace the cylindrical oats packages. Known as Larry, the symbol has changed slightly over the past 100 years, most recently in 2012 by "trimming his famous coif and revealing more radiant skin from daily oatmeal masks."

Contributor: Tia M. Rains

See also: Organizations, Professional

BIBLIOGRAPHY

"Quaker Oats Co." *Encyclopedia of Chicago*. www.encyclopedia
.chicagohistory.org/pages/2821.html.

Smith, Andrew F. *Eating History: Thirty Turning Points in the Making of American Cuisine*. New York: Columbia University Press, 2009

(R)

Radio (See: Media, Radio; Media, Television)

Rector, Charles E

Born in Lewiston, N.Y., to a family of hoteliers, Rector (1844–1914) was one of Chicago's and the nation's leading restaurateurs in the late nineteenth and early twentieth centuries. He enlisted in the Union army and fought in some of the bloodiest battles of the Civil War. Saving his money from working as a civil servant in Washington, D.C., and a streetcar motorman in New York City, he decided to seek his fortune in Chicago in the late 1860s. After working in the famous Boston Oyster House beginning in 1873 and as assistant superintendent of dining for the Pennsylvania Railroad, he opened his own restaurant in a basement at the corner of Clark and Monroe streets, just a block away from the Boston Oyster House. The venture was financed by Chicago's leading liquor dealer, Chapin and Gore (who also financed Kinsley's).

The restaurant became one of the premier dining places in the country, serving fresh oysters brought in from the East Coast and seafood such as Lobster Newburg, a dish made with cream, egg yolks, and cayenne pepper sauce that was said (erroneously) to have been created by the restaurant. So beloved was the fare that Rector was given the sole restaurant concession on the 1893 World's Columbian Exposition fairgrounds. Rector accumulated millions of dollars, putting them into a new building and

Founded in 1873, the Boston Oyster House was one of Chicago's premier restaurants. Courtesy of the Chicago History Museum.

restaurant on the original site. It was a great success. He sold out in 1911 and moved all his operations to a grand restaurant he had built in New York in 1899. The New York restaurant was even more famous than the Chicago business. As in Chicago, Rector then decided to build a grand hotel and restaurant at 44th Street and Broadway. Opened in 1910, it was a bust and within a year Rector was bankrupt. He died in 1914, but the restaurant lived on until 1929 in the hands of his son, George, a famous cookbook author and raconteur.

Contributor: Bruce Kraig

See also: Oyster Bars

BIBLIOGRAPHY

Rector, George. *The Girl from Rector's.* New York: Doubleday, Page and Co., 1927.

"Rectors New York." *The Washington Herald*, February 23, 1911.

RECTOR, DIAMOND JIM BRADY, AND LILLIAN RUSSELL

The Columbian Exposition made Charles Rector nationally famous. He was granted the restaurant concession at the Café de la Marine (Marine Café) within the fairgrounds, where he served "all animals from Water." It was a huge success, especially when his friends Diamond Jim Brady and Lillian Russell came for lunch and ate so much fresh corn that the cobs were said to have been mounded up around them. Fairgoers regarded this modern corn pyramid as one of the fair's top spectacles.

—BRUCE KRAIG

Refrigeration

Chicago, dependent upon the production of perishable foods such as pork and beef, became a center of innovation for the early mechanical refrigeration industry. The first such machines, developed during the 1870s but not perfected until the 1890s, weighed tons but could produce tons of ice per day or prevent whole warehouses full of animal carcasses from decaying too quickly. Previous to these machines, packers used ice for refrigeration. That simple technology was dirty (because the ice was often dirty), inefficient, and took up lots of space.

Breweries installed Chicago's first refrigerating machines during the 1870s because reliable cold allowed them to make lager beer in large quantities during summer for the first time. The Chicago packers introduced mechanical refrigeration into their warehouses during the 1880s as experiments. But meatpackers did not turn to refrigerating machines until the 1890s, when the technology became more reliable. These machines allowed packers to chill meat much faster than they could when using only ice, thereby improving the slaughterhouses.

Fred W. Wolf of Chicago became a mechanical refrigeration pioneer when he obtained American rights for a successful German patent in 1881. At first, he imported German machines for brewers in Chicago and Milwaukee but, in 1887, he founded the Fred W. Wolf Company, which built these German-style machines in the United States for the first time. His son, Fred W. Wolf Jr., would go on to work on an early prototype of the electric household refrigerator during the 1910s.

The Hercules Iron Works of Chicago was a Wolf competitor; it won the contract for the ice rink and cold storage facility at the Columbian Exposition. Unfortunately, that facility exploded shortly before the fair officially began, killing 17 people, including 9 firemen who came to fight it. The cause of that blaze was an explosion of gas from leaking ammonia pipes, a common hazard of refrigerating machines from that era. Within a few years, the Hercules Iron Works went out of business, even as the refrigeration equipment industry grew rapidly.

Chicago also was the site of another refrigeration-related tragedy in 1929. A string of deaths occurred in apartment buildings across the city when refrigerators leaked methyl chloride, an odorless, poisonous gas used as a refrigerant in some early models. Because methyl chloride poisoning makes people feel abnormally warm, the victims' bodies were found mostly undressed. This problem led directly to the development of Freon, an effective artificial refrigerant with no side-effects, other than destroying the Earth's ozone layer (but scientists did not discover that problem until many decades later).

....

Contributor: Jonathan Rees

See also: Beer, Breweries, and Brewpubs; Ice Houses

BIBLIOGRAPHY

Anderson Jr., Oscar Edward. *Refrigeration in America: A History of a New Technology and Its Impact*. Princeton: Princeton University Press, 1953.

Rees, Jonathan. *Refrigeration Nation: A History of Ice, Appliances and Enterprise in America*. Baltimore: The Johns Hopkins University Press, 2013.

Regulations

Chicago's transformation from a small village of hundreds in the 1830s to more than 100,000 by the 1850s kept food suppliers busy. Chicago, like many urban centers in the early years of their development, was growing so fast there were few systems of food distribution or food safety. Public officials were called upon to organize specific market locations for citizens to access food. In 1837, a public health department was formed that began inspecting the markets.

But as farming was pushed outward from the city and the family cow for milk became obsolete, Chicagoans had to rely on a fragile food support system. Shoppers themselves had to check the quality and safety of foods. Some cookbooks had directions on how to find an "acceptable or unadulterated product." Supplies of milk were so scarce and contaminated, many residents gave their children beer, or later, canned milk (sweet and evaporated), as these were hermetically sealed. The infant death rate due to contaminated milk pushed Chicago to create the first dairy inspections in the country in 1867. In 1909, Chicago became the first to mandate compulsory milk pasteurization, but this proved difficult to enforce because of conflicting laws between the city and the state. The city had passed stricter regulations than the state, and although Chicago had a larger inspecting staff, it could not command uniform standards from the 12,000-some dairies in the region that supplied milk.

Food production in Chicago became big business, especially with the creation of the Union Stock Yards. Railroads gave Chicago a great advantage in importing food and competing with other cities' meat butchering. But the growth of the stockyards meant more dumping of carcasses and animal by-products into the river.

Before the Pure Food and Drug Act of 1906 was implemented into national law, state law mandated most food laws. Originally, the Pure Foods Movement was grassroots, looking to eliminate unsanitary slaughterhouse conditions. Chicago-area women's groups brought local attention to Upton Sinclair's 1906 novel, *The Jungle*. The book exposed the Chicago meatpacking and slaughterhouse conditions to the world, and prompted President Theodore Roosevelt to send officials to Chicago to investigate, and to state, "its publication would be well-nigh ruinous to our export trade in meat." A drawn-out legislative battle ultimately resulted in rules on accurate product labeling, outlawing misbranded or adulterated foods, and listing specific ingredients of food products.

On the same day in 1906, the Meat Inspection Act also was enacted. At first it asked for voluntary inspections of livestock. The Oscar Mayer Company was one of the first Chicago companies to comply. Later, inspection of livestock before and after slaughter became mandatory. Sanitary standards were established. The U.S. Department of Agriculture hired more than 1,300 inspectors nationwide at 163 establishments, including those in Chicago. Poultry was added in 1957, under the Poultry Products Inspection Act. The law expanded further in 1967 with the Wholesome Meat Act and Wholesome Poultry Act, which set a minimum of sanitation standards for state inspections of meat and poultry plants. The Federal Food, Drug, and Cosmetic Act of 1938 replaced the Pure Food and Drug Act and demanded more specific standards for foods.

Food laws have been in place in the city of Chicago for some time. Chicago-area food handlers and supervisors are mandated by their local jurisdictions to follow these laws. Food sanitation licenses are required for nonprofit and for-profit establishments. Under the Department of Public Health, education, training, and exams are given for Chicago's food licenses. Occasionally, food abuse and/or food errors in preparation or handling are addressed through lawsuits. Food trends, such as the arrival of ethnic food carts, modern food trucks, and the debate over serving foie gras in restaurants also have pushed the city council to establish specific rules for food-related issues.

Contributor: Jenny Lewis

See also: Dairy Industry; Food Reform Legislation; Food Safety; Food Trucks and Carts; Meat and Poultry; Sanitation

BIBLIOGRAPHY

Duis, Perry R. *Challenging Chicago: Coping with Everyday Life, 1837–1920*. Urbana: University of Illinois Press, 1998.

Wade, Louise Carroll. *Chicago's Pride: The Stockyards, Packingtown, and Environs in the Nineteenth Century*. Urbana: University of Illinois, 1987.

Reis, Leslee

Until her untimely death at age 47 in March, 1990, Reis played an important role in the city's rapidly expanding culinary scene. She opened her flagship restaurant, Café Provençale, in Evanston in 1977. Her subsequent restaurants, all in Evanston, included Leslee's and Bodega Bay, both of which closed in 1988.

Reis's culinary career began when she volunteered to do dishes for Julia Child, who was about to make her television debut. Then a doctoral candidate in biochemistry at Harvard University, Reis eventually studied cooking at the Cordon Bleu in Paris. Not long after, she and her husband Andrew moved to Evanston in 1966, where she

opened a catering business, followed by Café Provençal 11 years later.

While it is hard to know whether Reis actually "invented" the wine dinner, there's no debating her role in making it popular. Her creativity, like her intelligence, was immediately apparent. She completed her doctoral studies when she was 23. She was a founding board member of the Chicago chapters of both Les Dames d'Escoffier Chicago and the American Institute of Wine and Food.

Contributor: Barbara Revsine

See also: Restaurants and Fine Dining; Restaurateurs and Restaurant Groups

BIBLIOGRAPHY

O'Neill, Molly. "Leslee Reis, 47, Dies; Illinois Restaurateur Won Many Awards," *New York Times*, March 28, 1990.

Restaurants and Fine Dining

Chicago has had many forms of dining establishments since its early years, though dining out has changed significantly. Area restaurants have fed Chicagoans well, from the first early 1800s taverns on the Chicago River to the later fancy Loop hotels and steak, chop, and oyster houses. From its steak-and-potatoes beginnings, the city soon expanded its menu with fancy French food, regional American food, fusion food, farm-to-table food, and molecular gastronomy.

By the mid-1800s, office workers packed the downtown Chicago Loop, and lunchtime dining systems sprang up. Service had to be quick because lunch hours typically

Chicago was full of German-style restaurants well into the twentieth century; chop suey was also a major trend in Chicago dining at the turn of the century. Courtesy of the Chicago History Museum, ICHi-85015.

lasted only 30 minutes. A hierarchy of dining establishments sprang from these lunchrooms: Five-and-dime stores and drugstore lunch counters, diners, smorgasbords, and cafeterias. These restaurants fostered a revolution in public dining, with traits that remain today at such places as Oak Brook–based McDonald's: They were fast and cheap.

Fast-food chains eventually replaced the old cafeterias and lunchrooms. But small, local chains also flourished. Portillo's, begun by Dick Portillo in 1963 as The Dog House in Villa Park, expanded through the years to include 38 locations. Other quick-service local firms include Pot Belly's, Pockets, and Al's Beef (home of the famous Italian beef sandwich). Ethnic influences helped change the restaurant scene in the late 1800s and into the 1900s. As immigrants arrived, many opened restaurants featuring their native country's fare. And some of them and their descendants helped create Chicago's iconic foods, including Jewish all-beef hot dogs, Italian beef sandwiches, and deep-dish pizza.

But more dramatic changes came to Chicago dining beginning in the last three decades of the twentieth century. The many Continental and French menus in town began to give way to new American fare. Some of the classic old-time dining rooms closed: The Bakery, the College Inn, Fritzel's, Jacques, Red Star Inn, and Don Roth's Blackhawk Inn downtown, home of the "spinning salad bowl." By the early 2000s, Chicagoans' growing sophistication about food and a crop of new, young chefs created one of the fine-dining capitals of the world.

A list of the most influential fine-dining restaurants from the last few decades must begin with Le Perroquet (1973–91). One of Chicago's most well-known, but controversial, restaurateurs, Jovan Trboyevic designed it for formality: menus written in French only, traditional service, and classic and nouvelle French dishes such as duck Perroquet and signature soufflés. Trbojevic later opened Les Nomades (1978–present) as a private dining club with a formal French menu. Mary Beth and Roland Liccioni bought the restaurant in 1993 and opened the restaurant to the public, continuing the well-regarded French menu.

In the same year that Le Perroquet opened, French chef Jean Banchet created Le Français (1973–2007) in Wheeling and then rebuilt it as a French country restaurant after a fire in 1975. By 1980, *Bon Appetit* declared it the best restaurant in America and a destination for fine French country cuisine. Banchet is credited with putting Chicago on the map for food lovers. In succeeding years, other French dining places thrived, including Carlos', L'Auberge, La Cheminee, L'Escargot, La Fontaine, Le Bordeaux, and Le Titi de Paris. Ambria (1980–2007), located in the Belden-Stratford Hotel

Gordon Sinclair of Gordon's Restaurant. Photograph by Cheri Eisenberg.

in Lincoln Park, was known for a luxurious French dining experience under chef Gabino Sotelino and Rich Melman of Lettuce Entertain You Enterprises. Carlos and Debbie Nieto were well-known restaurateurs in Highland Park because of their elegant French Restaurant, Carlos', which they ran for 30 years (1981–2011). They regularly were rated number one for food by *Zagat*, and their award-winning wine program attracted many wine lovers and purveyors.

New American cuisine gained importance around the nation in the '70s and '80s, including Chicago. The dapper Gordon Sinclair was the impresario of new American dining with his restaurant, Gordon (1976–99), which featured rich velvet curtains and his signature fried artichokes.

This was the training ground for many star chefs, including Charlie Trotter, Carrie Nahabedian, Norman Van Aken, and Don Yamaguchi. When Michael Foley and his father opened their restaurant, Printer's Row (1981–2004), in the neighborhood of the same name, they regularly slept in the restaurant to ward off burglars in what was a dicey area. Foley's modern American cooking quickly attracted more

THE RESTAURANT SCENE IN THE LOOP, 1879–87

In his book on Chicago history, written for the 1933–34 World's Fair, Henry Justin Smith waxed nostalgic about the Loop dining scene:

"To decent but convivial places, like Billy Boyle's chophouse, Rector's (with its goldfish aquarium as an ornament), Burcky and Milan's, the Boston Oyster House (lobster a specialty) flocked people to eat and stare. They might expect to see, though more likely at Chapin and Gore's, such a sport patron as Malachi Hogan, such a nighthawk as 'Billy' Pinkerton (son of the great Allan), such a theater man as Will J. Davis; and possibly—just passing through—such an international hero as the prize-fighter, John L. Sullivan. On Dearborn Street there was a saloon, kept at first by Joseph Mackin, then by a man whose wit flowed over and later filled a book. This saloonkeeper's real name was James McGarry; the book was 'Mr. Dooley.'"

BRUCE KRAIG

supportive fans, and the restaurant became the place young cooks went to learn from Foley's innovative cooking style.

Chicago is full of Italian restaurants, but Spiaggia (1984–present) is undisputedly the most upscale. Paul Bartolotta was the opening chef, earning 4 stars and a James Beard award for his Northern Italian cooking. Tony Mantuano took over when Bartolotta left, adding innovations such as a cheese cave, and continuing to receive accolades and even visits from President Obama. Accolades also came to Arun's Thai Restaurant (1985–present), located on Chicago's Northwest Side and operated by chef/owner Arun Sampanthavivat. It has been called the best Thai restaurant in the country by *Zagat* and the *Wall Street Journal* and is known for the artful food presentations, serene atmosphere, and elegant collection of Thai artifacts. Everest (1986–present) appeared the following year, but in a most unusual location: on the top floor of the Chicago Stock Exchange. Chef/owner Jean Joho opened Everest in partnership with Lettuce Entertain You Enterprises. The restaurant boasts Joho's French/Alsatian cooking, one of the strongest Alsatian wine programs in the country, tuxedoed servers, and dramatic skyline views.

Charlie Trotter, an icon in Chicago dining, created one of the first all-degustation menus at his eponymous restaurant (1987–2012), which received the highest accolades. He furthered Chicago's reputation as a culinary destination, helping train a generation of influential chefs in his notoriously tough kitchen.

Topolobampo (1989–present) is one of the few Mexican fine-dining restaurants in the United States, furthering chef/owner Rick Bayless's mission to teach diners that Mexican food is more artful than tortilla chips and burritos. The menus feature food inspired by historic periods in Mexico's history, and the restaurant boasts an award-winning wine and tequila list to complement the cuisine.

Evanston's Trio restaurant (1993–2006) was the launching pad to fame for every chef who led its kitchen. Owner

ON THE DINING MAP?

A curious recurring theme in articles about Chicago restaurants is the number of successive restaurants that are said to have "put Chicago on the dining map." The cycle repeats itself every decade or so. In the 1980s, Mimi Sheraton wrote in the *New York Times* and *Bon Appetit* magazine that Jean Banchet's Le Français was the best restaurant in the United States, while James Villas writing in *Esquire* called Jovan Trboyevic (at Le Perroquet and Les Nomades) "Absolutely, Positively The Finest Restaurateur in America." Somehow, though, the oft-repeated honor was bestowed upon Charlie Trotter. The *New York Times* called him "the chef who put Chicago on the fine-dining map," and one of his own websites modestly said he "helped put Chicago's dining scene on the epicurean map."

Louis Szathmary's The Bakery attracted national attention before Banchet and Trboyevic, and an earlier restaurant, Imperial House, at 50 E. Walton St., put Chicago on the dining map in the 1950s. Sometimes the map is drawn in retrospect. Fifty years after Maxim's opened in 1963, Andrew Gill on WBEZ radio called it "the restaurant that put Chicago on the haute cuisine map."

And over the last decade, it probably is impossible to count how many times Alinea has put Chicago "on the fine-dining map."

Exactly who keeps this mythical dining map is a bit of a mystery, along with the question of why, once put on the map, Chicago apparently keeps needing to be put back on, but the comment recurs from Chicago-based writers, as well as from afar.

—RICHARD WARREN SHEPRO

Henry Adaniya opened the restaurant with chefs Rick Tramonto and Gale Gand and then promoted Shawn McClain to chef when they left. After McClain left to open Spring, Adaniya hired a young Grant Achatz, launching the career of one of the most influential chefs in the world. Fine dining in Chicago was a formal affair until Paul Kahan opened Blackbird (1997–present), where he and his partners merged ingredient-driven, high-end food with a sleek, stylish atmosphere that was anything but stuffy. Kahan trained his cooks to maximize flavors from a few ingredients in order to better show them off and helped popularize the farm-to-table ethos that drives restaurants today.

What Charlie Trotter started, Grant Achatz took to the next level at Alinea (2005–present), which has been named the best restaurant in the United States and one of the top 10 restaurants in the world. Achatz changed the nature of fine dining with his experimental cuisine, inspiring a generation of cooks to play with texture and temperature as they transform ingredients into entirely new products.

Accolades also followed the opening of the Randolph Restaurant Row spot Grace (2012–present) for Curtis Duffy's elegant, artistic tasting menus and stylish interior design. The *Michelin Guide* awarded it 3 stars for its intricate cuisine using unusual, seasonal ingredients. Duffy's journey to open the restaurant was documented in the film "For Grace." Most recently, two newcomers in Fulton Market grabbed Michelin stars in 2016: Smyth, from chef/owners John and Karen Shields, with 1 star, and Oriole, from chef/owner Noah Sandoval, with 2 stars.

Contributors: Chandra Ram and Carol Mighton Haddix

See also: Restaurant Awards and Honors; Specific restaurant names and types of restaurants—Dairy Restaurants; Delicatessens; Department Store Dining; Fast Food/Quick Service; Lunch Counters; Pancake Houses; Seafood Restaurants; Smorgasbords; Steak and Chop Houses; Supper Clubs and Roadhouses; Tapas and Small Plates

BIBLIOGRAPHY

McKeever, Amy. "Chefs Weigh In on the Influence and Importance of Awards." *Chicago Eater*, May 14, 2014. http://www.eater.com/2014/5/14/6225357/chefs-weigh- in-on-the-influence-importance -of-awards.

Pollack, Penny. "Best Chicago Restaurants Ever." *Chicago Magazine*, April 15, 2010. http://www.chicagomag.com/Chicago-Magazine/May- 2010/40-Best- Chicago-Restaurants- Ever/.

Restaurant Awards and Honors

Chicago regularly attracts attention for several restaurant and chef honors, most notably the James Beard Awards, The World's 50 Best Restaurants list, *Food & Wine* magazine's Best New Chef honors, and the *Michelin Guide*. The James Beard Awards are considered by many to be the most prestigious honors in the restaurant world. They are presented each May by the James Beard Foundation at

its annual gala, which took place in New York City from its inception in 1990 until 2014. It moved to Chicago in 2015 and 2016 after extensive lobbying and financial support from the Illinois Restaurant Association and City of Chicago tourism department.

Chicago is well represented in the Beard nominations each year, usually with three or four finalists in the "Chef: Great Lakes" regional category, as well as finalists in the journalism and cookbook categories and the national chef awards, which have been won by Chicago chefs, including Grant Achatz (Alinea), Rick Bayless (Frontera Grill), Mindy Segal (HotChocolate), Jimmy Bannos Jr. (The Purple Pig), and Paul Kahan (Blackbird). Chicago chef Art Smith (Table 52) was given the Humanitarian of the Year award in 2007 for his work with the charity he founded, Common Threads. James Beard Awards also are given for Outstanding Restaurateur, which Donnie Madia (One Off Hospitality) won in 2015. Chicago restaurateur Rich Melman (Lettuce Entertain You Enterprises) won the Outstanding Restaurateur award in 2011 and the Lifetime Achievement award in 2015. Achatz, Kahan, and Jean Joho (Everest) have been inducted into the James Beard Foundation's Who's Who of Food and Beverage in America.

Several Chicago chefs have been named to *Food & Wine* magazine's Best New Chef honors, including Achatz, Kahan, Stephanie Izard (Girl & the Goat), Dave Beran (Next), and Jason Vincent (formerly of Nightwood). Achatz also is a regular honoree for Alinea on the "World's 50 Best Restaurants" list compiled by *Restaurants* magazine each year. The *Michelin Guide* launched its first Chicago edition in 2010 and has given updates to the guide every few years since. Alinea and Chef Curtis Duffy's Grace are the two Chicago restaurants awarded 3 stars, the highest honor.

Aside from national and international honors, local awards are given to chefs and others in the restaurant industry by the Cystic Fibrosis Foundation at its annual Grand Chefs Gala. The awards are named for Jean Banchet, the late former chef/owner of Le Français, and voted on by local chefs. As well, several Chicago publications present their own annual chef and restaurant awards, including the *Chicago Tribune*'s Dining Award, *Chicago Reader*'s Best of Chicago, *Chicago Magazine*'s Best Restaurant, *Time Out Chicago*'s Food & Drink Award, and *NewCity*'s Best of Chicago.

Contributor: Chandra Ram

BIBLIOGRAPHY

McKeever, Amy. "Chefs Weigh In on the Influence and Importance of Awards." *Chicago Eater*. May 14, 2014. http://www.eater.com/2014/5/14/6225357/chefs-weigh-in-on-the-influence-importance -of-awards.

Restaurant Critics

It could be argued that restaurant criticism, as a profession, began to coalesce in the last three or four decades of the twentieth century. That this coincided with an increasing American hunger for dining out—especially at whatever joint was the priciest, most exclusive, most authentic, or even cheapest—is no accident. People wanted help on where to go and what to order and, perhaps most crucially, what to expect.

So it was in Chicago, as elsewhere, and also as elsewhere, restaurant criticism historically was "often little more than advertising," according to the *Chicago Reader*. John Drury, a *Chicago Daily News* reporter, wrote a popular "intimate guide" to Chicago's restaurants in his 1931 book, *Dining in Chicago*. Carl Sandburg wrote the foreword to the book.

When restaurant columnist James Ward started at the *Chicago Sun-Times* in the mid-1970s, he was appalled at local criticism. It needed a sense of fun, he said, and it "simply was not critical."

Enter *Chicago Magazine*'s Allen Kelson and his wife, Carla. The Kelsons famously personified the new anonymous and more rigorous attitude toward reviewing, even going so far as to stash a microphone under Allen's tie so they could take notes while dining. They became the most visible and important critics in town, so visible that a column from the famed Mike Royko mocked some of their criticisms. Restaurants reviewed by the Kelsons were rated on a scale of 1 to 10, and whether the restaurant advertised or not made no difference in whether it was included in the magazine's dining list. Other media outlets today have standards nearly paralleling those of *Chicago Magazine*, with critics visiting restaurants anonymously and paying for all meals.

At the *Chicago Tribune*, longtime staffer Kay Loring transitioned from the "Front Views and Profiles" column to restaurant reviewing, which she continued doing as a freelancer after retiring in 1971. Johnrae Earl became the Tribune's dining critic in 1974. He also was a food columnist and senior copy editor at the newspaper. After his death in 1978, food writer Fran Zell served as the *Tribune*'s chief restaurant reviewer into the early 1980s, followed by Paul A. Camp, and the current, longtime critic, Phil Vettel. Vettel's reviews run in the newspaper and online and are augmented by regular restaurant segments on WGN-TV, in which his face is never shown. Other *Tribune* staffers have performed as ancillary critics over the years. "Cheap Eats," for example, was a beat tackled by a rotating cast of *Tribune* food writers before morphing into "The Cheap Eater" in 2009 with Kevin Pang. William Rice was a *Chicago Tribune* food and wine writer, not a reviewer. But his coverage of Chicago chefs and restaurants, beginning in the mid-1980s, had extra influence because of his national reputation built as food editor of the *Washington Post* and editor of *Food & Wine* magazine.

After the *Chicago Sun-Times*, Ward moved to WLS-Ch. 7 news, where he did televised reviews for 20 years. The late Pat Bruno became the *Sun-Times* reviewer in 1984, a post he held until he left in 2011. He often focused on Italian restaurants, which was his heritage. Vettel, his competitor for years, said Bruno's reviews were "very linear" and he "loved his puns and his wordplay." Bruno, who died in 2012, was succeeded by Michael Nagrant, who left the paper in May 2013 and is now a freelance restaurant critic for the *Tribune*'s *RedEye* newspaper.

Social media applications have made everyone a critic—just look at the success of Yelp! and its user reviewers; photo-sharing sites like Instagram, loaded with dining shots; and, to some extent, *Check, Please!*, the public television series in which ordinary people get to be the reviewers.

Still, a number of influential voices rise above the din, offering insight and opinions in print, online, broadcasting, or a mixture of those, people such as writers Michael Gebert, Mike Sula, and Julia Thiel at the *Chicago Reader*; food journalist David Hammond; and WLS-Ch. 7's Steve Dolinsky, whose *Hungry Hound* segments have long served to introduce Chicago-area restaurants of all stripes to a large audience.

More voices and more outlets for expression also have changed the rules of reviewing. Anonymity is less regarded as essential. With a push to be first fueled by an unceasing 24/7 news cycle, more and more reviews are being written earlier and earlier after a restaurant opens—putting additional pressure on establishments to be on top of their game from the moment they open the doors. Printed columns are augmented with photo galleries, podcasts, and video clips.

The nature of the job produces some squabbling among critics. Jeff Ruby, now *Chicago Magazine*'s chief dining critic, compared the climate in Chicago to that in New York. In Chicago, critics have the same petty grudges, "but like good Midwesterners, we do our backbiting in private." Too many critics are focused on doing their jobs right to worry about or focus on the competition, Ruby theorized.

Contributor: Bill Daley

BIBLIOGRAPHY

Jensen, Trevor. "James Ward 1932–2009: Restaurant Critic on Channel 7, Author and Magazine Editor." *Chicago Tribune*, February 29, 2009.

Ruby, Jeff. "Chicago Restaurant Critics Talk Food Fights." *Chicago Magazine*, July 2012.

Schlesinger, Toni. "Dining for Dollars." *Chicago Reader*, February 1, 1980.

Vettel, Phil. "Pat Bruno, Longtime *Sun-Times* Restaurant Critic, Dies." *Chicago Tribune*, October 31, 2012.

Restaurateurs and Restaurant Groups

Successful restaurateurs have created and re-created Chicago's restaurant scene over the years as the city's tastes have evolved. In the 1860s, John Wright's restaurant at Crosby's Opera House was a magnet for the city's elites. The same decade saw Phillip Henrici open his Viennese Cafe and H. M. Kinsley begin his first venture in the city. Kinsley's restaurant became known as the equal of Delmonico's in New York.

In the late 1800s, John Z. Vogelsang's namesake German place and Charles Rector's Oyster House were among the nation's finest. Henrici had opened multiple restaurants, but in the 1950s, Henrici's was bought out by the Chicago cafeteria chain, Thompson's. Founded by John R. Thompson in 1892, the chain grew to 49 units in Chicago and 109 nationally at the time of Thompson's death in 1927. Later successful restaurateurs included Dario Toffenetti, who started his business in 1914 and, by the 1960s, had a half-dozen restaurants in the city and another on New York's Times Square.

Today, the most influential restaurateur in Chicago is Rich Melman, who founded Lettuce Entertain You Enterprises (LEYE) with his business partner, the late Jerry Orzoff, when they opened R. J. Grunt's in Chicago's Lincoln Park neighborhood in 1971. They were successful from the start and opened four more restaurants within five years. Orzoff died in 1981, and Melman continued to open more restaurants; by the mid-1990s, LEYE became known for its consumer-friendly, midrange concepts including Café Ba-Ba-Reeba, serving Spanish tapas; Shaw's Crab House, featuring a variety of seafood; Scoozi, with an Italian menu and wood-fired pizza oven; and Papagus, featuring Greek food. The company was also successful with counter-service–casual concepts such as Corner Bakery, Wow Bao, and Big Bowl.

Melman also partnered with chefs for fine-dining restaurants such as Everest and Brasserie Jo with Jean Joho, Ambria and Mon Ami Gabi with Gabriel Soletino, Tru with Gale Gand and Rick Tramonto, and L2O with Laurent Gras. He brought on his sons, R. J. and Jerrod Melman, as partners in the company, and they added to the LEYE name with restaurants like HUB 51, designed for a younger demographic. In 2015, Melman reopened the shuttered L2O as Intro, a restaurant with a new chef and menu every three months, designed to train aspiring chef/restaurateurs in the company's highly regarded management system. LEYE now owns or operates more than 100 restaurants in Illinois, California, Arizona, Maryland, Virginia, Minnesota, and Nevada.

Larry Levy of Levy restaurants was once considered the primary competition to LEYE, with restaurants including Bistro 110, Spiaggia, Café Spiaggia, and Jake Melnick's, but the company moved most of its attention to its national on-premise sports and entertainment division.

KDK Restaurants was at the center of the creation of Chicago's Randolph Market district as a hub for edgy fine dining in the 1990s. Former partners Jerry Kleiner, Howard Davis, and Dan Krasny launched their company in 1990, and thrived with popular concepts including Red Light, Vivo, and Marché on Randolph Street, and Opera and Gioco in the city's South Loop neighborhood. Krasny left the partnership in 1999 after a three-year court battle, taking ownership in Vivo with him. After its restaurants began to falter and were cited for failing to pay taxes, KDK dissolved in 2011. Former KDK chef Michael Kornick created his own company, DMK Restaurants, in partnership with David Morton, son of Arnie Morton of the Morton's Steakhouse chain. Their restaurants include DMK Burger Bar, Fish Bar, Ada Street, and County Barbecue.

One Off Hospitality, founded in 1996, is considered one of the most successful chef-driven restaurant groups in the country. Partners Donnie Madia, Paul Kahan, Eduard Seitan, and Rick Diarmit began the company with their critically acclaimed Blackbird restaurant and expanded it with more restaurants and bars, including Avec, Nico Osteria, The Publican, Publican Quality Meats, Big Star, Dove's Luncheonette, and Violet Hour.

The Boka Restaurant Group is another chef-driven restaurant group, founded in 2005 by Rob Katz and Kevin Boehm and their chef/partners including Stephanie Izard, Giuseppe Tentori, and Lee Wolen. The group's restaurants include some of the city's most popular, such as Girl & the Goat, Boka, G. T. Fish & Oyster, Momotaro, and Swift and Sons steakhouse. They partnered with B. Hospitality Co's John Ross, Chris Pandel, and Phillip Walters to open Balena. B. Hospitality Co. operates Bristol and Formento's as well.

Brendan Sodikoff has emerged as another successful concept-driven restaurateur. He cooked with chefs including Thomas Keller and Alain Ducasse before meeting Melman and joining LEYE as a test-kitchen chef. He left LEYE in 2010 to open his first restaurant, Gilt Bar, which was an immediate success. He quickly opened more restaurants under the Hogsalt Hospitality name, and his often-packed restaurants, including Maude's Liquor Bar, High Five Ramen, Doughnut Vault, Au Cheval, and Bavette's, are not considered chef-driven, but they are much in tune with the food zeitgeist.

Nick Kokonas and Grant Achatz have been leaders in the fine-dining realm since partnering to open Alinea, one of the most highly regarded fine-dining restaurants in the world, in 2005. Kokonas had been a regular guest at Evanston's Trio when Achatz was the chef there and offered to help him open his own place when the time came. After the success of Alinea, they partnered to open Next, a restaurant that changes its menu three times a year, in 2011. They followed that with The Aviary, a cocktail lounge; the Office, a private bar within The Aviary; and a more casual restaurant, Roister. Kokonas developed a ticket sales system to sell dining reservations much like concerts and sporting events sell event tickets. The ticketing system, called Tock, is being used by other restaurants around the country.

Contributor: Chandra Ram

See also: Restaurants and Fine Dining; Specific restaurant and restaurateur names

BIBLIOGRAPHY

"Restaurant Partnership KDK Falters as Last Venues Are Shuttered." *Crain's Chicago Business.* http://www.chicagobusiness.com/article/20110402/ISSUE01/304029961/restaurant-partnership-kdk-falters-as-last-venues-are-shuttered.

Wells, Pete. "Grant Achatz to Open a Restaurant and a Bar." *New York Times.* May 3, 2010. http://dinersjournal.blogs.nytimes.com/2010/05/03/grant-achatz-to-open-a-restaurant-and-a-bar/.

Ricketts Cafeteria

Nothing fancy, just hearty American cooking—that was the hallmark of the Ricketts family's restaurants, popular with diners over four generations. In 1898, Mary Ricketts, a widow, opened the first one, a four-table spot with a countertop, at Clark Street and Chicago Avenue. Her sons, John, Ernest and Ash, went on to open cafeterias at 1004 N. Clark St. and 2727 N. Clark St. and a more upscale spot at 103 E. Chicago Ave. Customers counted on the broad menus of homemade fare, the friendly and fast service, and affordable prices. Later generations of Ricketts also ran restaurants in Maywood, Wheeling, and Glenview until the 1980s.

Contributor: Janet Fuller

See also: Cafeterias and Lunchrooms

BIBLIOGRAPHY

Samors, Neal, and Eric Bronsky, with Bob Dauber. *Chicago's Classic Restaurants: Past, Present & Future.* Chicago: Chicago's Books Press, 2011.

Hevrdejs, Judy. "A 3d Generation Ricketts Reminisces about Tastes." *Chicago Tribune,* October 5, 1978.

R. J. Grunts (See: Lettuce Entertain You; Melman, Richard)

Rosen, Sam and Fred

Sam's Wines was a nationally known store in the Lincoln Park neighborhood of Chicago. Famous for its vast selection of wines, both familiar and lesser-known, Sam's business started out at the turn of the twentieth century.

Sam Rosen immigrated to Chicago from Russia and began by working in retail stores until, in 1942, he opened his first bar. His son, Fred, took over the business in 1956. Wedged between Cabrini Green Housing projects and the Gold Coast, Sam's catered to both audiences, with high-end wines and lower-end spirits in the same store.

Fred's sons, Brian and Darryl, worked in the store for most of their lives. They bought the business from Fred in 2003, but he continued to have an office and manage the business.

The family feud between the Rosen brothers became the talk of the business community, and in 2007, the store was sold to Arbor Investments, a private-equity firm. In 2009, Sam's was bought by longtime rival Binny's Beverage Depot. In 2011, the Rosen brothers opened Evolution Wine and Spirits in the Bucktown neighborhood, the third location for this Illinois chain.

Contributor: Clara Orban

See also: Wine Distribution and Sales

BIBLIOGRAPHY

Fields-White, Monée. "Sam's Wines Succumbs to Rival Binny's." *Crain's Chicago Business,* October 9, 2009. http://www.chicagobusiness.com/article/20091009/NEWS07/200035757/sams-wines-succumbs-to-rival-binnys.

Jones, Sandra. "Sam's Wines Wraps Up Equity-Firm Deal." *Chicago Tribune,* May 12, 2007, http://articles.chicagotribune.com/2007-05-12/business/0705111796_1_rosen-family-fred-rosen-sam-rosen.

Roth, Don

Don Roth (1913–2003) was a leading Chicago restaurateur with his Blackhawk Restaurant on Wabash Avenue in the Loop. Founded by his father Otto in 1920, it became a cultural hot spot under Don's direction. Using his experience as a theatrical booking agent, he enhanced the restaurant's reputation as a venue for live music. When he dropped the live music format in 1952, Roth turned the spotlight on the Blackhawk's food. Two items, the prime rib carved tableside and the "Spinning Salad Bowl," prepared tableside, got the most publicity. A bottled version of the salad dressing is still available.

Changes in demographics eventually prompted a move to River North and the opening of a second Blackhawk restaurant in suburban Wheeling. The downtown restaurant closed in 1984, the suburban venue in 2009.

Roth was one of the creators of Taste of Chicago. He also wrote dozens of stories for the *Chicago Tribune*'s travel section in the 1950s and '60s, reporting on the cuisine of such places as London. He was president of the Chicago and Illinois Restaurant Association and served on the boards of many local and national cultural and professional institutions.

Contributor: Barbara Revsine
See also: Blackhawk Restaurant; Restaurateurs and Restaurant Groups

BIBLIOGRAPHY
Kogan, Rick, "Don Roth, 1913–2002: Restaurant Ace Changed the Way Chicago Dined." *Chicago Tribune*, November 23, 2003.

Russians

Russian immigrants can be divided into two distinct groups: ethnic Russians and Russian Jews, though U.S. immigration authorities historically used the designation to describe Belarusian, Ukrainian, Polish, non-Russian Jews, and Germans. As a result, it is hard to identify the number of Russian immigrants who settled in Chicago. While most of the ethnic Russian and Russian Jewish immigrants settled on the East Coast, Chicago had the Midwest's largest influx of ethnic and Jewish Russians.

Russian Jews made their way to Chicago's South Side between 1861 and 1880, arriving in larger numbers to escape persecution in the 1880s. Between 1881 and 1920, they arrived in greater numbers, initially residing around Maxwell Street, where they created a bustling outdoor market. By 1930, Russian Jews comprised 80 percent of the Jewish population in Chicago. They began moving further away from the city center into the West Rogers Park and Albany Park neighborhoods, along Division Street and into suburban Mount Prospect, Glenview, and Northbrook.

During the twentieth century, ethnic Russians had claimed, as their own, "Little Russia" in the West Town neighborhood, an area bordering West Division, Wood, and Leavitt Streets. In the 1970s and 1980s, Devon Avenue on Chicago's North Side was home to several Russian restaurants and delis, but most have moved to Skokie. Typical Russian dishes served in those restaurants and in homes include *shashlyk* (meat kebabs), *pirozhki* (meat- or vegetable-filled dumplings), *kotlety* (ground meat cutlets), vegetables such as cabbage and beets, caviar, and fish (salted, pickled or smoked and often part of a *zakuski* (hors d'oeuvres) table. Vodka is the drink of choice.

Restaurants serving Russian cuisine include old-school Russian Tea Time, a Loop stalwart for beef stroganoff and vodka flights; scarlet-hued Versailles in Buffalo Grove for borscht and chicken Kiev; Rolling Meadows's club-meets-banquet-hall La Mirage; buffet-style Old Lviv Restaurant, 2228 W. Chicago Ave.; and Zhivago, a Skokie eatery known for its live music and duck with cherry sauce. A recent addition, Deka Restaurant, 401 E. Dundee Rd., Wheeling, combines Russian and French cuisines, including dishes such as caviar and veal-stuffed dumplings.

Contributor: Jennifer Olvera
See also: Jews

BIBLIOGRAPHY
"Chicago Restaurant History." LTHForum. Katarzyna Zechenter. "Russians." *Encyclopedia of Chicago*. http://www.encyclopedia.chicagohistory.org/pages/1104.html.
http://www.lthforum.com/bb/viewtopic.php?p=349450.

Saganaki

In Greece, it's a popular appetizer of sliced and fried kasseri cheese. In Chicago, it's all that, but add a little brandy, a lit match, and a few shouts of "Opa!" Dibs for the flaming version of this dish goes to The Parthenon restaurant, 314 S. Halsted St., in the city's Greektown neighborhood. Chris Liakouras, cofounder of the restaurant with his brother, Bill, is credited with creating this dramatic presentation shortly after the restaurant opened in 1968. Parthenon closed in 2016.

Contributor: Bill Daley
See also: Greeks

BIBLIOGRAPHY
Johnson, Charles J. "Parthenon Blazes a Trail: Greektown Pillar Was Cutting Edge When It Opened." *Chicago Tribune*, March 13, 2014.

SAGANAKI

Prep: 5 minutes
Chill: 1 hour
Cook: 5 minutes
Makes: 1 serving

A single appetizer serving, in the style of the Parthenon restaurant, Chicago.

    1 egg, beaten
    2 tablespoons milk
    1 piece Kasseri cheese or other firm Greek cheese, cut
        in a triangle
    1/4 cup flour
    1 tablespoon butter or vegetable oil
    1 shot glass Metaxa or Ouzo, warmed
    1/2 lemon

1. Beat egg in shallow bowl; beat in milk. Dip cheese into egg mixture. Place flour on a plate; dip cheese into flour to coat both sides; shake off excess flour. Place on a plate. Refrigerate at least 1 hour.

2. Heat butter in heavy skillet until foamy. Add cheese; fry until lightly browned, about 2 minutes. Turn; fry other side until browned.

3. Turn off heat; remove skillet to a sturdy rack or board. Pour metaxa over cheese; carefully light the metaxa with a long, lit wooden match. Let metaxa flame briefly. Sprinkle flames with a squeeze of lemon juice to douse. Serve hot with Greek sesame bread.

Sage, Gene

Gene Sage (1926–99) was instrumental in the creation of Chicago's contemporary food scene. His first spot, Sage's One North, was a restaurant and singles bar located in the heart of the city's financial district. A success virtually from the get-go, the restaurant offered a mix of good food and good service with an ambiance to match. It was a format that would serve Sage well throughout his career, as appropriate for a business lunch as it was for a romantic evening on the town.

Gene Sage graduated from UCLA in 1949 with a master's degree in political science. His father had just opened a restaurant in downtown Chicago, and the newly minted college graduate decided to spend a few days helping him out. A "few days" turned into a lifetime.

Sage eventually opened nine Chicago-area restaurants, including Eugene's and Mon Petit on North State Street, Sage's East in the Lake Shore Drive Hotel, Sage's West in Downers Grove, and Sage's Sages in Arlington Heights. He retired after closing Sage's Sages on New Year's Eve, 1997.

Contributor: Barbara Revsine
See also: Restaurateurs and Restaurant Groups

BIBLIOGRAPHY

Breslin, Meg McSherry. "Restaurateur Gene Sage, 73. Wizard at Promoting Business." *Chicago Tribune*, January 27, 1999

Sam's Wine and Spirits

This nationally famous Chicago establishment got its start in 1943 when Sam Rosen, an immigrant from Russia who had worked in bars and taverns, opened a liquor store at Chicago and Ashland. The business had two other locations before moving into an old saloon at North and Halsted in the mid-1950s; its 118-foot bar was the longest in the United States. One of Rosen's staff, a wine lover, started stocking fine wines. Eventually, the store, renamed Sam's Wine and Spirits, became a wine store that happened to sell liquor. It was famous for its cramped, rather disorganized premises and knowledgeable staff.

By 2001, Sam's was the largest-grossing liquor store in the United States. It had become Chicagoans' go-to place for wine and a tourist destination, featured on the cover of *Time* magazine. In 2005, it received *Wine Enthusiast*'s Retailer of the Year Award. Following Sam's death, the store was operated by his son Fred and later by his grandchildren Brian and Darryl. In 1986, Sam's moved to 1000 W. North Ave. and, subsequently, into a larger store at 1720 N. Marcey St. that also featured a gourmet market and cigars. In 2007, the store was sold to Arbor Investments, a private equity firm. Sam's opened outlets in Downer's Grove, the South Loop, and Highland Park, but the last two were closed in 2009. Later that year, the company was sold to Binny's Beverage Depot.

Contributor: Colleen Sen
See also: Wine Distribution and Sales

BIBLIOGRAPHY

Fields-White, Monée. "Sam's Wines Succumbs to Rival Binny's." *Crain's Chicago Business*, October 9, 2009. http://www.chicago business.com/article/20091009/NEWS07/200035757/sams-wines -succumbs-to-rival-binnys.

Guy, Sandra. "Sam's Has Had Many Locations, Lots of Media Moments." *Chicago Sun Times*, August 16, 2004.

Sandwiches

Chicago has a long and rich history of sandwich innovation and appreciation that continues to this day. Hot dogs are probably Chicago's best-known sandwich and rank among the city's most famous foods. Vienna Beef brand frankfurters dressed with the canonical seven toppings are most familiar, but there's much more to the story. Italian beef sandwiches, filled with thinly sliced roast beef dripping with spicy natural jus and mounded with hot giardiniera, are one of the glories of Chicago street food and widely available throughout the region. Pepper and egg, a rare meatless Chicago sandwich, is a Lenten replacement for Italian beef. Chicago can take credit (or blame) for commercializing the gyros sandwich, another ubiquitous staple of the area's fast-food scene.

Other sandwiches have much more restricted distributions. Chicago isn't often thought of as a burger town—"cheezborgers" from Billy Goat Tavern aside—but the Big Baby cheeseburger has had a steady following among the blue-collar citizens of the Southwest Side for almost half a century. The mother-in-law, a hot dog bun stuffed with a commercial tamale covered with chili, has a long history on the South Side but is virtually unknown elsewhere, by that name at least. A specialty of African American neighborhoods on the South and West Sides, the Jim Shoe is a submarine sandwich overflowing with corned beef, roast beef, and gyros. The jibarito (hee-bah-REE-toe), a sandwich that uses fried plantains instead of bread, is still found mostly in Puerto Rican neighborhoods.

Contributor: Peter Engler

See also: Gyros; Hot Dogs; Italian Beef; Jibarito; Jim Shoe; Mother-In-Law; Pepper and Egg Sandwich; Potbelly Sandwiches

BIBLIOGRAPHY

Bruno, Pat. *Chicago's Food Favorites: A Guide to Over 450 Favorite Eating Spots*. Chicago: Contemporary Books Inc., 1986.

Sanitation

In its first century, Chicago grew incredibly fast. In a quickly growing city built largely in a swamp, public health and sanitation were a great challenge and often a central concern of the city government. In 1836, just three years after Chicago was incorporated as a town, the Chicago Hydraulic Company was given permission to pipe water from Lake Michigan and run mains through the streets The river (not the lakefront) is also the city's harbor and was originally its sewer as well. Because the land was so flat with a thick layer of clay, waste had nowhere to drain. In 1855, the city hired a Boston engineer to design a system of sewers. They flowed into the Chicago River, bringing about cleaner streets but greatly dirtying the river and the lake and fouling the city's drinking water. Successive unsuccessful attempts were made to reverse the Chicago River in order to move Chicago's waste toward the Mississippi River system rather than toward Lake Michigan, using an existing canal. In 1900, the Chicago Sanitary and Ship Canal opened, along with a series of locks at the mouth of the river, reversing the flow of the main and south branches and providing a long-term improvement in Chicago's water supply.

While providing sanitary water was the city's earliest public health concern, protecting its food supply was close behind. In the mid–nineteenth century, before germ theory was widely known, most Chicago food regulations focused on adulteration and freshness. In 1857, a fish inspector was funded to certify barrels of fish shipped to the city. Inspections of other food shipped in barrels, such as flour and meat, followed, focusing mainly on the food's weight and conditions. In 1867, the Chicago Board of Health was organized. It placed sanitary inspectors throughout the city who looked at meat shipped to Chicago and at meatpacking plants.

In the late nineteenth century, city inspectors paid increasing attention to the milk supply. What was known as "the milk problem" was considered a natural outcome of urbanization. As cities grew, less space was available for livestock. At the same time, milk was increasingly considered an essential food, particularly for children. The early laws focused on adulteration of milk by skimming and adding chalk or other materials to whiten it, or worse, adding formaldehyde to delay souring. With the discovery of the germ theory of disease, milk was often blamed for disease outbreaks, including a 1907 outbreak of scarlet fever. This led to regulations for keeping milk clean and separating it from possible infection by humans or cows. In 1908, Chicago became the first city in the world to mandate that all milk, except milk from tuberculin-tested cattle, be pasteurized. While this mandate was fought by the state legislature, Chicago city workers approved all farms that sold fluid milk into the city into the 1970s.

In the twentieth century sanitation legislation increasingly followed federal guidelines. This began with the formation of the predecessor of the Food and Drug Administration in 1906, which took over much of the regulation of meatpackers. In general, the sanitation tasks of the Department of Public Health mainly focus on the inspection of restaurants and groceries.

Contributor: Daniel Block

See also: Dairy Industry; Food Safety

BIBLIOGRAPHY

Block, Daniel R. "Public Health, Cooperatives, Local Regulation, and the Development of Modern Milk Policy: The Chicago Milkshed, 1900–1940." *Journal of Historical Geography* 35 (2009): 128–53.

Duis, Perry R. *Challenging Chicago: Coping with Everyday Life, 1837–1920.* Urbana: University of Illinois Press, 1998.

Pierce, Bessie L. *A History of Chicago, Vol. 1: The Beginnings of a City 1673–1848.* Chicago: University of Chicago Press, 2007 [1937].

Sara Lee Corporation

From its beginnings as a bakery, Sara Lee has grown into a corporation that markets food products (frozen and fresh baked goods, coffee, fresh and processed meats) as well as personal and household products. Its North American headquarters is in downtown Chicago. The North American research and development center is in Downers Grove, under the name *The Kitchens of Sara Lee.*

The roots of Sara Lee started in 1935 with Charles Lubin (1904–88). A native Chicagoan, Lubin began in the baking business at the age of 14 as an apprentice to a baker in Decatur, Illinois. Together with his brother-in-law, he bought the three existing Community Bake Shop stores for $1,500. They expanded to seven stores by 1949. In that year, Lubin created a rich cheesecake that was twice the price of any others in his market. He defended the product, saying: "Our goal was to make a product so delicious you couldn't resist it. There is no substitute for plenty of butter, eggs and milk in the recipe." He was vindicated by success, as his company made more than $20 million per year by the mid-1950s.

He named his first cheesecake after his 8-year-old daughter, Sara Lee, and renamed the company The Kitchens of Sara Lee. New products and innovations were added over the years including the All Butter Pound Cake in 1951; a pioneering process for freezing baked goods that preserved quality; and a foil pan in which to bake, freeze, and distribute baked goods. The company franchised routes within a 300-mile radius of Chicago in 1954 and expanded delivery to 48 states the next year.

Sara Lee was acquired by Consolidated Foods Corporation in 1956 and was headed by Lubin as CEO until 1965. In 1964, the company opened a production plant in Deerfield, Illinois. The facility included R&D labs, test kitchen, machine shop, and an in-home preparation test kitchen. A year later it was named one of the top ten new manufacturing plants by *Factory Magazine*. TV ads added to the popularity of the brand, and the now-iconic jingle "Nobody doesn't like Sara Lee" first appeared in 1968. Consolidated Foods acquired Chef Pierre, Inc., pie makers (1978) and later merged their

"fruit based technology" with Sara Lee (1988). In 1985, Consolidated Foods was renamed Sara Lee Corporation, and the name Kitchens of Sara Lee became Sara Lee Bakery. Fresh-delivered products (meaning direct delivery from plant to point of sales) were added to its line and California markets received the first fresh delivery when it was initiated in 1993. A 120,000-square-foot campus, The Kitchens of Sara Lee, named in honor of the company founded by Charles Lubin, was opened in 2009 in Downers Grove. This was the first time the company had all its food and beverage R&D under one roof, but it was not to last. Sara Lee decided to sell its bakery division in 2010 to the Mexican food giant, *Grupo Bimbo*. In 2012, the remaining part of the company split again into two entities: Hillshire Brands (meats) and D. E Master Blenders 1753 (coffees). Hillshire then merged with Arkansas-based Tyson Foods in 2014. Hillshire relocated its headquarters to a newly rehabbed building at 400 S. Jefferson St. in 2016.

Contributor: Geraldine Rounds

See also: Consolidated Foods Corporation

BIBLIOGRAPHY

Kendall, Peter. "Charles W. Lubin, Sara Lee Founder." *Chicago Tribune,* July 17, 1988. http://articles.chicagotribune.com/1988–07–17/news/8801150451_1_sara-lee-corp-charles-w-lubin-frozen.

"Sara Lee Fresh Bakery—The Story of Sara Lee." www.saraleebread.com/story-of-sara-lee.

Sausages

Even on a culinary skyline that includes Italian beef, gyros, and deep-dish pizza, sausage reigns supreme in Chicago. The city's time as the center of the country's meatpacking industry is responsible for the establishment of a continuing national production industry, as well as an extensively documented love of encased meats among local eaters.

Local sausage production began with German butchers in the 1850s. Oscar F. Mayer and his brother Gottfried came from Germany to open his butcher shop on Sedgewick Avenue in 1883. They were one of many German sausage makers who have long since departed Chicago. Among the remaining companies is the redoubtable Paulina Meat Market founded by Sigmund Lekan in 1949. Paulina makes a huge variety of German and other sausages ranging from andouille to debreziner, Nuremberger bratwurst, rinderwurst, Swiss and German thuringers, and weisswurst. Gepperth's, founded in 1906, also makes classic German sausages including knackwurst, bockwurst, bratwurst, and perhaps the only South African *boerewors brats* in the city. Since 1960, the Bavarian Stiglmeier

Sausage Co. in Wheeling has made German-style products, especially Bavarian weisswurst and brats.

Jewish immigrants took up the sausage business beginning in 1860 when David Berg established his butcher shop on Wells Street. He sold kosher beef franks to local baseball fans as early as 1901. The Vienna Sausage Company was started by brothers Samuel Ladany and Emil Reichl in 1894, after they had moved to the city from Budapest the year before. The company moved into a larger facility on Halsted Street in 1920 and moved again to a facility at the intersection of Damen, Elston, and Fullerton Avenues in 1972 when the neighborhood was gutted to make way for UIC facilities. They stayed at that facility until an overhaul of that infamous intersection forced them to find new facilities in Bridgeport. Other Jewish companies, such as Best Kosher and Sinai 48 and Wilno, were sold to larger companies and no longer exist.

The Slotkowski Sausage Company, founded in 1918 by Joseph Slotkowski, proved instrumental as producers of the city's Polish sausages—similar to a hot dog, but with larger-diameter hog casings and more aggressive spicing. Slotkowski had brought his son Leonard into the business by the time the company opened a factory on West 18th Street. Following the elder Slotkowski's death in 1956, the company expanded production to more than 100 products as the popularity of the company's sausages boomed with the city's Polish population. The company fought declining margins until Slotkowski sold it to Joseph Halper in 1986. It was acquired at bankruptcy auction by ATK Foods in 1992, which still produces andouille, garlic sausage, kielbasa, and kiszka under the Slotkowski name.

ATK Foods began as Leon's Sausage company in 1924. Leon Kurzawski came from Austria where he learned the art of sausage making. Located at 1143 West Lake St., the company grew especially well under the leadership of Leon's granddaughter, Amylu Kurzawski. Sausages by Amylu, an all-natural chicken sausage line, became so popular that the company expanded into gourmet sausage products that are sold in big box stores and groceries across the country.

Crawford Sausage Company at 2310 S. Pulaski Ave. was founded in 1925 by a group of Czech sausage makers. Originally serving the West Side Bohemian community, the company markets its Daisy Brand in markets across the Chicago region. They still make Czech specialties such as *debreziner* (called Debs), *prasky*, *jaternice*, and *jelita*.

Another immigrant contributor to the sausage culture of Chicago was Macedonian-born Jimmy Stefanovic, who moved to the city in 1939 and took over his uncle's hot dog stand at the corner of Maxwell and Halsted streets. Rechristening it as Jim's Original, Stefanovic focused on

selling Polish sausages (made to order by Slotkowski) with sweet grilled onions and mustard. A shot of the stand is featured in the 1980 film *The Blues Brothers*. Jim's Original relocated twice—first in 2001, then in 2005 to a location on Union Avenue where it still stands.

Bobak Sausage Company has produced sausages in the city since 1967, starting in the Back of the Yards neighborhood, moving to a facility in Archer Heights in 1989, and relocating again to West Garfield Park in 2015. The company opened a handful of Polish supermarkets in the city and nearby suburbs in the late 1990s before a bitter and public family feud between brothers Stanley, John, and Joseph Bobak proved a drag on the business. The flagship store at 5275 Archer Ave. closed in March 2015. Bobak is one of the remaining Polish sausage makers that once dotted the city's North and South Sides. Among the best known remaining in the early twenty-first century are Gene's Sausage Shop and Delicatessen, Harczak's Polish Deli, Kurowski's Sausage Shop, Andy's Deli, and Wally's Market.

Contributor: John Carruthers

See also: Germans; Hot Dogs; Jews; Meatpacking; Polish

BIBLIOGRAPHY

ATK Foods. "Our Brands." http://www.atkfoods.com/our-brands/slotkowski.

Bowen, Dana. "City of Pork." *Saveur*, October 2007. http://bobak.com/press/.

Isackson, Noah. "Leonard Slotkowski, Chief of Sausage Firm." *Chicago Tribune*, January 2000. http://articles.chicagotribune.com/2000–01–16/news/0001160243_1_polish-sausage-meats-hot-dogs.

Scala Packing (See: Italian Beef)

Scandinavians

The five Nordic countries—Norway, Sweden, Denmark, Finland, and Iceland—have close historical and cultural ties, including foods. Climate, lifestyle, and isolation have shaped Scandinavian food. Lengthy, dark, and cold winters have always been a basic fact of life. Surviving depends on food stored during the short growing season, hence preserved food is abundant; the best known are the preserved fish dishes lutefisk and gravlax. The short growing season is why traditional Scandinavian cuisine includes only small amounts of green vegetables. Seafood, wild game, lamb, cheese, cabbage, apples, onions, berries, and nuts are historic staples of the Scandinavian diet.

Other food preferences that Scandinavian immigrants brought to America were fish, pork, and poultry, as well as beets, potatoes, cucumbers, horseradish, and broiled, baked, and smoked apples. Dairy was always in season: cheeses, yogurt and whipped cream. Spices and herbs included chives, thyme, cardamom, juniper berries, parsley, and fennel. Dill, the "garlic of the North," was added to everything from pickled fish to crisps. Much of the cookery was plain, simple farm fare, hearty whole-grain breads, and rich seafood stews—food meant to sustain during the winter.

Chicago's exposure to Scandinavian cuisine started with Swedish, Danish, and Norwegian immigration beginning in the 1840s. At the turn of the twentieth century, Chicago had the second largest Swedish and the third largest Norwegian population of any city in the world. By 1930, more than 65,000 Swedes, 55,948 Norwegians, and some 18,000 Danes lived in the city and its near suburbs (Finns were never a large population). Populations moved over time so that the Norwegian-Danish Northwest Side became largely Polish in the twentieth century. The North Side was heavily Swedish, but today Swedish food, drink, and history remain alive mostly in the Andersonville neighborhood and the area around North Park University on the North Side. Merchants and locals turn out for the traditional Midsummer, Saint Lucia, and Christmas celebrations. Christmas is celebrated at restaurants with dishes such as lutefisk, meatballs, and ham, preferably arranged on a buffet-style smorgasbord table, surrounded by baked goods and perhaps accompanied by *brännvin* (distilled spirits). The Norwegian Lutheran Memorial Church in Logan Square, the only remaining Norwegian-language church in the city, holds similar celebrations with similar foods. Tre Kronor restaurant on Foster is famous for its Julbord, a Christmas buffet featuring eight varieties of smoked herring, reindeer meat, lutefisk, and other delicacies.

The smorgasbord is Sweden's main contribution to Chicago's restaurant history. During the late nineteenth and early twentieth centuries, a number of smorgasbord restaurants catered to lunch crowds in and around the Loop. One of them was turned into a "Cafeteria," and before long, many cafeterias were serving American dishes to the same clientele.

The Swedish Bakery on North Clark Street, opened in the late 1920s by a family named Johnson, is famous for Swedish coffee cakes, cookies, sweet rolls, toast, petit fours, and marzipan cakes. Suddenly closing in early 2017, the bakery did traditional baking, using ingredients such as cardamom, saffron, anise, fennel, orange peel, and almond paste. Wikstrom's Specialty Foods, a Scandinavian shop, was open for 47 years in Andersonville, but now they only sell online. They are famous for glogg, Swedish meatballs, limpa bread, cardamom coffee cake, sausages, ring bologna, *sju sorter kakor*, Swedish herring, lingonberries, *julekaka*, and Swedish coffee. No specifically Norwegian bakeries

or food stores exist in Chicago, though Kirsten's Danish Bakery in suburban Burr Ridge makes Danish pastries and specializes in the iconic kringle.

Of many Scandinavian restaurants that once served Chicago, such as the Kungsholm Restaurant and Puppet Theater at 100 E. Ontario St. (the present Lawry's Steakhouse) and Nielsen's Danish restaurant in Elmwood Park, only one or two survive. Ann Sather launched her first Chicago restaurant on Belmont Avenue in 1945, featuring pancakes and her famous cinnamon rolls. Today, Tom Tunney continues Ann Sather's Swedish American traditions at five locations around the city. The Swedish furniture chain IKEA, which has branches in suburban Schaumburg and Bolingbrook, is known for its Swedish food products, including meatballs, salmon, herring, and condiments.

Contributor: Margaret Laport

See also: Ann Sather Restaurants; Cafeterias and Lunchrooms; Smorgasbords

BIBLIOGRAPHY

Anderson, Philip J., and Dag Blanck. *Swedish-American Life in Chicago: Cultural and Urban Aspects of an Immigrant People, 1850–1930*. Urbana: University of Illinois Press, 1992.

Lovoll, Odd S. *A Century of Urban Life: The Norwegians in Chicago before 1930*. Northfield, Minn.: Norwegian American Historical Society, 1988.

Schaefer's Wine, Food, & Spirits

One of the Chicago area's oldest and most highly rated wine stores, Schaefer's origins go back to January 1, 1936, when George J. Schaefer Sr. opened a tavern at what is now 9965 Gross Point Rd. in Skokie. It originally was called The Boundary because it bordered the dry communities of Evanston and Wilmette. In the mid-1940s, he turned it into a package liquor store and renamed it Schaefer's. A wine room opened in 1959. Following Schaefer's death the same year, the store was managed by his wife Eileen and later by his children, George Jr. and Gene Schaefer Flynn. In the 1960s, the store began selling cheese, olive oil, and other gourmet food items. George Jr. died in October 2009; in February 2009, Schaefer's was bought by Bill Graham, a longtime customer, who expanded the selling floor and added a new event and tasting space. George's granddaughter Anja carries on the family tradition as Schaefer's executive vice president,

Contributor: Colleen Sen

See also: Wine Distribution and Sales

BIBLIOGRAPHY

Megan, Graydon. "George J. Schaefer: 1944–2008." *Chicago Tribune*, October 21, 2008.

Schlogl's

A German American fixture, Schlogl's was known as much for its clientele as its food. The restaurant was founded by Joseph Schlogl in 1879 at 37 N. Wells St. and was decorated in an old-world Germanic style with large, heavy wooden tables and chairs and a lack of natural light countered by cut-glass chandeliers. Given its proximity to the headquarters of the *Chicago Daily News*, Schlogl's was a legendary gathering place for Chicago's newspapermen and literary elite, including Carl Sandburg, Theodore Dreiser, and Ben Hecht. In the 1920s, some critics dubbed it "Chicago's Algonquin Club." Regulars were drawn, in part, by a promise of free meals on Fridays if their bylines appeared in print that day.

Menu items included the "Stewed Chicken a la Schlogl," the apple pancake, and hamburger steak fried in butter, in addition to a roster of typical German American fare such as spaetzle and hasenpfeffer. The menu featured the phrase "Owls to order," a running joke inserted by ownership as a comment upon the adventurousness of its menu.

Longtime *Chicago Tribune* political correspondent Arthur Sears Henning (of "Dewey Defeats Truman!" fame) described Schlogl's in his 1954 memoirs for the paper as one of two Chicago restaurants that remained unchanged over a half-century. Author Harry Hansen likewise sketched a picture of the famous literary hotspot as "unchanged since the day it reared upon smoldering embers and charred walls." By the early 1950s, Schlogl's was no longer a literary salon. It was shut down in 1959 when its liquor license was suspended because a bartender shot a customer, and it finally closed in 1961.

Contributor: John Carruthers
See also: Germans

BIBLIOGRAPHY
Smith, Alison J. *Chicago's Left Bank*, Chicago: Henry Regnery, 1953.

Schnering, Otto

Nicknamed the "U.S. Candy Bar King," Schnering (1891–1953) was born in Chicago, the son of an affluent German-born businessman. He graduated from the University of Chicago and, in 1916, founded the Curtiss Candy Co. in the back of a hardware store, making candy in a five-gallon kettle using his own recipes. He developed several new products, including the Polar Bar, Jolly Jacks, and Kandy Kane. Kandy Kane's success enabled him to build a factory in Streeterville, and by 1928 Curtiss Candy was producing 1 billion candy bars a year with 3,500 employees in three Chicago factories.

Manufacturing efficiencies and the bulk purchase of ingredients made it possible to produce a 5-cent candy bar at a time when other bars cost 10 cents. His greatest success was the Baby Ruth. In the 1940s, Schnering began buying farmlands in McHenry County, initially as a source of milk and butter for his candy business, but eventually he became a full-time farmer who raised animals on his 10,000-acre farm, the largest in Illinois. This led to the founding of Curtiss Breeding Services, the first large artificial insemination cattle-breeding company in the United States.

Contributor: Colleen Sen
See also: Candy

BIBLIOGRAPHY
Chmelik, Samantha. "Otto Y. Schnering." In *Immigrant Entrepreneurship: German-American Business Biographies, 1720 to the Present*, Vol. 4, edited by Jeffrey Fear. German Historical Institute. http://www.immigrantentrepreneurship.org/entry.php?rec=111.

School Lunches

In 1910, the Chicago Board of Education authorized the expenditure of $1,200 to begin an experimental program of serving hot lunches to children in six elementary schools. The number of participating schools grew rapidly and, by 1921, Chicago had the most intensive school lunch program in America, which included feeding 31,000 elementary school students and most high school students. Community groups such as Hull House and other settlement houses, including the Back of the Yards council, also ran lunch programs. The Back of the Yards neighborhood was one of the first to get federal surplus foods during the late 1930s and early 1940s. Parent groups or PTAs ran some of the programs, and home economics teachers ran others, often as training for female students.

In 1946, President Truman signed the National School Lunch Act into law. Until then, Congress had made year-to-year appropriations and school boards were reluctant to rely on them. Federal programs came to represent an uneasy pact between farm state politicians who wanted to find an outlet for agricultural products and politicians from urban districts who wanted to feed hungry students. For most of the program's existence, the U.S. government has reimbursed districts for meals served, depending on the economic status of the recipient—some qualifying for free lunch and others qualifying for reduced or full-priced meals. In 2015, the federal reimbursement rate for a lunch served to a child who qualified for free lunch was $2.98. Many believe that this equation of reimbursements based on "participation" led many schools to serve meals that would get the most participants, rather than offer the most nutrition.

For much of the twentieth century, high schools served lunches cooked by "lunch ladies" in often large, well-equipped kitchens. Most students also had the freedom to buy food off-campus, and all could bring lunch from home. But by the late 1980s, school administrators realized they could reduce labor, make more money, and increase participation (and thus federal reimbursements) by offering prepackaged, heat-and-serve entrees. Soda machines and extensive a la carte canteens also grew during these years.

The "lunch ladies" were replaced by low-wage workers whose main job was to open packages and warm food. By the late 1990s, Chicago Public High School students could eat a pile of nachos or a pizza slice, fries, and chocolate milk for lunch every single day of their high school career without variation. This combination was the most popular choice through 2010, when school food reformers complained about the lack of healthful meals. Nationally, childhood obesity rates had tripled since the 1980s. Chicago's obesity rates were higher than the national average—an average of 20 percent of the city's children were obese in 2010–11.

Chicago Public Schools eventually cut their nacho service down to two days a week. The 2010 Healthy Hungry-Free Kids Act (which went into effect in 2013) moved schools from nutrient-based menus (with nutrient targets) to food-based menus, requiring more whole grains; dark, green, leafy, and orange vegetables; and reduced reliance on fruit juice for fruit servings. CPS complied with these rules, even before the 2013 deadline, but many of the vegetables ended up in the garbage. Students complained that the limp, overcooked veggies lacked flavor and salt. In 2013, a new director and former Aramark executive took over. Aramark snagged the nation's largest school food contract—a new consolidated CPS contract—that same year. Although the company promised to save the district money and provide better food, by 2014, the top entrees at CPS were still highly processed fare, including chicken nuggets, chicken patties, hamburgers, and nachos.

Contributor: Monica Eng

BIBLIOGRAPHY

Levine, Susan. *School Lunch Politics: The Surprising History of America's Favorite Welfare Program*. Princeton: Princeton University Press, 2010.

Poppendieck, Janet. *Free for All: Fixing School Food in America*. Berkeley: University of California Press, 2011.

Schulman, Eli M.

Born in Chicago in 1910, Schulman's entry into the restaurant business was almost an accident. In 1940, Schulman, who had worked in retail and in politics, saw a foreclosure notice on the door of his favorite neighborhood restaurant at Ogden and Kedzie. He bought the building and named the restaurant Eli's Ogden Huddle. That started an almost 50-year career in the restaurant business that took him to Chicago's North Side at Argyle and Sheridan Road in the 1950s, to the Rush Street area in 1962 with the opening of Eli's Stage Delicatessen, and then, in 1966, to Streeterville with the opening of Eli's the Place for Steak.

Eli's the Place for Steak was known not only for great steaks, but also for shrimp à la Marc (named after his son) and liver Eli. Regular customers included the who's who of Chicago and beyond, such as politicians Mayor Richard J. Daley and Jesse White, sports figures Mike Ditka and George Halas, celebrities Frank Sinatra and Liza Minnelli, and journalists Irv Kupcinet and Rick Kogan. But perhaps today, Schulman is best known for the dessert he created for his restaurant: Eli's Chicago's Famous Cheesecake.

Contributor: Scott Warner

See also: Eli's Cheesecake

BIBLIOGRAPHY

Kogan, Rick, "Eli Schulman, 78, Chicago Restaurateur." *Chicago Tribune*, May 8, 1988.

Seafood Restaurants

When New Englanders settled in Chicago in 1831, they brought with them a passion for East Coast oysters, which then became a staple in Chicago after the first rail shipments from the east. In 1842, the first lobster shipments arrived in Chicago. Residents began eating crustaceans at home and, later, at newfangled "lobster palaces." By 1857, Chicago also was home to seven "oyster depots" and four "oyster saloons."

In 1883, Rector's Oyster House, opened by Charles E. Rector at Clark and Monroe Streets, was the first to serve oysters on the half shell. His son, George, who took over the popular restaurant, later told the story in his book, *The Girl From Rector's*. Before long, oyster houses were serving other fresh seafood and freshwater fish as they became readily available.

But it wasn't until 1923 that the first themed seafood restaurant was born. Gus Mann opened a Chicago seafood eatery, Rainbo Sea Food Grotto, at 117 S. Dearborn St., that was adorned with maritime trappings, such as fishnets and portholes, with waitresses wearing sailor uniforms. The concept was wildly popular, and other seafood-themed restaurants began opening nationally.

In the 1920s, Ireland's Oyster House opened on LaSalle Street, selling fresh-daily oysters and planked Lake Superior whitefish. The popular restaurant had an almost 60-year run until it closed in the 1980s. The popular Cape Cod Room opened in 1933 in the Drake Hotel, attracting visiting celebrities as well as locals. It closed in 2016 after its 83-year run.

Also in the 1920s, quintessential South Side "shrimp shacks" appeared, including Troha's at 4151 W. 26th St. The storied Calumet Fisheries, 3150 W. 95th St. at the 95th Street "Blues Brothers" Bridge, opened in 1948. Calumet received a James Beard Foundation Award as an America's Classic icon in 2010. Commonplace on shrimp shack menus were fried, smoked, and fresh seafood. Calumet smokes fish on site over wood fires.

Ben's Shrimp House on North Avenue found itself at the center of a controversy when it came under fire from Jay McMullen, husband of then-mayor Jane Byrne. His son attempted to write a check to pay for his meal at Ben's, and employees refused to accept it. Not long after, Ben received anonymous threats that his business would close, coupled with a surprise visit from the health department. Today, a handful of shrimp shacks remain, including Calumet, Troha's, and Lawrence's Fisheries on S. Canal St.

Chicago now receives its seafood, much of it soon after it is caught, through O'Hare International Airport, from all U.S. coasts and around the world.

Modern-day restaurants, such as Shaw's Crab House and Bob Chinn's Crab House in Wheeling, keep the spirit of those early oyster houses alive, featuring fresh-shucked oysters, pricey seafood towers, and fresh-plucked fish.

Other newer spots bring creativity to the genre: G. T. Fish & Oyster, 531 N. Wells St. with a small-plate format; an expense-account must, Joe's Seafood Prime Steak and Stone Crab, 60 E. Grand Ave.; and Hugo's Frog Bar and Fish House in Chicago, Naperville, and Des Plaines. Two other suburban spots are Tin Fish, in Tinley Park, and Oceanique in Evanston. Finally, newcomers include mfk, 432 W. Diversey Pkwy, with Spanish-influenced seafood; and Sink/Swim, 3213 W. Armitage Ave.

....

Contributor: Jennifer Olvera

See also: Fish and Seafood

BIBLIOGRAPHY

Nagrant, Michael. "A Fish Story: Chicago's Seafood History Lives on through Its Shrimp Houses." *New City*. http://resto.newcity.com/2010/07/06/a-fish-story-chicagos-seafood-history-lives-on-in-its-shrimp-houses/.

Calumet Fisheries are the best known of Chicago's numerous fish shacks. Courtesy of Meathead, AmazingRibs.com.

Sears, Roebuck and Company

Richard Sears and Alvah Roebuck founded Sears and Roebuck in 1886. They moved their operations from Wisconsin to Chicago in 1887 and offered their first retail catalog in 1893. Sears revolutionized retail sales by reaching a broader and more dispersed audience than any previous American merchandiser—though rivaled by the earlier Chicago company, Montgomery Ward.

Their mail-order catalog business catered to consumers in every corner of the country. The growth of railways and mail services such as the parcel post enabled Sears to supplant the function of dry goods and general merchandise stores in rural areas. Sears' strategic location in the middle of the country allowed the company to supply consumers in western markets with merchandise that had previously been difficult to find. From the late nineteenth century through the early twentieth century, Sears catalogs offered virtually anything and everything for the American household, including an array of kitchen products: stoves, cookware, eating utensils, apple peelers, and Hoosier storage cabinets.

Clothing manufacturer Julius Rosenwald joined Sears in 1895 and remained at the helm of its leadership until his death in 1932. He turned Sears into a publicly traded company in 1905. He also oversaw the creation of brick-and-mortar Sears stores in the 1920s that reached a broader demographic than rural consumers.

The expansion of Sears's retail network during the 1920s provided a boon for the company's appliance business. It began private-label kitchen products under its own brand names, such as Energex, Kenmore, and Coldspot, shortly before the Great Depression. Sears worked with Chicago manufacturers, such as Russell Electric and Chicago Electric, to produce these products. By the 1930s, Sears had a full line of appliances made specifically to its own design parameters. Famed designer Raymond Loewy redesigned Sears's Coldspot refrigerator in 1934, giving Sears a reputation for creating cost-effective, attractive, and modern appliances. The Kenmore name supplanted Coldspot as Sears's largest appliance brand in the postwar era. Kenmore continues to be the number one brand in terms of major appliance market share as of 2014.

Sears ran its operations from a 41.6-acre complex for almost seventy years at a location bounded by Kedzie Avenue, Harvard Street, Central Park Avenue, and the Chicago Terminal Transfer Railroad. From 1973 to 1994, Sears corporate headquarters occupied the Sears Tower at 233 South Wacker Drive (now the Willis Tower)—the world's tallest building at the time.

....

Contributor: Stefan Osdene

See also: Equipment, Home; Montgomery Ward

BIBLIOGRAPHY

Cherry, Robin. *Catalog: The Illustrated History of Mail Order Shopping*. New York: Princeton Architectural Press, 2008, 20–23.

Emmet, Boris, and John E. Jeuck. *Catalogues and Counters: A History of Sears, Roebuck, and Company*. Chicago: University of Chicago Press, 1974.

Settlement Houses

The idea behind this concept was that civic-minded citizens, clergy, students, and, in general, people of privilege actually settle in poor neighborhoods. Through their example and good works, they would introduce moral strength, a semblance of education and hope for a better future into the uncertainty of late-nineteenth-century urban existence.

The model was in London's East End slum: Toynbee Hall, which opened in 1884. Two years later, America's first settlement, the Neighborhood Guild, came to New York's Lower East Side. In 1889, Jane Addams and school friend Ellen Gates Starr visited Toynbee, returned to Illinois, and applied their own vision—"an experimental effort"—to Hull House, Chicago's first Settlement House, on the city's Near West Side. Among many other social efforts, the two founders opened a dining hall next to Hull House and created a public dispensary providing food for the sick and a daycare center. Starr taught cooking lessons for the mostly Italian neighbors, emphasizing nutrition and accessible foods. "It is part of the new philanthropy to recognize that the social question is largely a question of the stomach," said Addams. Today, settlement houses

serve as food pantries and offer nutritional information, cooking classes, and prepared meals.

By 1900, there would be 19 settlement houses in the city, and more to come. First to follow Hull House was the Northwestern University Settlement House (1891) on Chicago Avenue. Maxwell Street Settlement House, a few blocks south of Hull House, opened in 1893 to help its largely Jewish district. Mary McDowell left Hull House to open The University of Chicago Settlement (1894) near the Union Stock Yards and its predominantly Bohemian, Polish, and Slavic worker-families. Churches were a major force: Most Christian denominations, along with Jewish agencies, opened or helped support the early settlements.

The welcomes weren't universal. "Strangers of a different part of town and another nationality have no business to come into the neighborhood and start something the people had not asked for," said one man in a Bohemian neighborhood. But come they did, and some carried their work into the twenty-first century. By 1922, the Chicago Federation of Settlements and Neighborhood Centers had grown to a 36-member organization.

Hull House is no more, but Chicago Commons, with roots to 1894, continues at 10 sites in four neighborhoods. Northwestern, at 1400 W. Augusta Blvd. since 1901, is still doing its good deeds. Erie House, the earliest of them, founded in 1870, also continues its work, now among a Hispanic population.

What they all originally shared was a commitment to help a population that flooded into Chicago from Europe, Mexico, and rural America in search of jobs and a new life—and found challenges ranging from language to crime to simply locating a place to bathe. Exacerbating all that were labor clashes, slumlords, and politicians eager to exploit.

"There are the evils of sweatshops and crowded factories to guard against, prostitution to cope with, the fascinating saloon to outwit," wrote Josephine Raymond in an 1897 study of the city's settlement neighborhoods. "All sides of life must be responded to." The responders were the settlement houses, with their kitchens and kindergartens, cooking classes and kindnesses, providing safe havens—and transition.

....

Contributor: Alan Solomon

See also: Addams, Jane; Hull House

BIBLIOGRAPHY

Addams, Jane. *Twenty Years at Hull-House*. New York: Signet Classics, 1961.

"Changing Neighborhoods: Photographs of Social Reform from 7 Chicago Settlement Houses." Richard J. Daley Library of the University of Illinois at Chicago. www.uic.edu/depts/lib/specialcoll/exhibits/7settlements/main.htm.

Philpott, Thomas Lee. *The Slum and the Ghetto: Immigrants, Blacks and Reformers in Chicago, 1880–1930*. Belmont, Calif.: Wadsworth Publishing Company, 1991.

ICONIC CHICAGO SHRIMP DISH

Although the original recipe is lost to time, this is an approximation of the De Jonghe Restaurant's famous shrimp dish, adapted from a recipe that appeared in the *Chicago Tribune* in 1985.

Shrimp de Jonghe

Prep: 30 minutes
Cook: 15 minutes
Makes: 4 servings

   1 stick (1/2 cup) unsalted butter, melted
   1 1/2 cups fine, fresh breadcrumbs
   2 cloves garlic, minced
   2 tablespoons minced parsley
   1 tablespoon minced shallot
   1/2 teaspoon paprika
   1/8 teaspoon ground red pepper
   1 bay leaf

1 1/2 pounds large raw shrimp, peeled, deveined
2 tablespoons dry sherry or white wine
1/4 teaspoon salt

1. Heat oven to 400 degrees. Mix half of the melted butter and breadcrumbs in small bowl. Stir in garlic, parsley, shallot, paprika, and red pepper. Set aside.

2. Add remaining butter and bay leaf to a large skillet; heat over medium high heat until frothy. Add shrimp; cook, turning shrimp once, until pink, about 3 minutes. Place shrimp in a large bowl; discard bay leaf. Add remaining half of the melted butter, sherry, and salt. Toss to mix.

3. Spoon half of the shrimp mixture into a buttered 1 1/2-quart baking dish. Top with half of the breadcrumbs. Top with remaining shrimp mixture. Top with remaining breadcrumbs. Bake until crumbs are lightly browned, about 10–15 minutes.

Shrimp de Jonghe

Although no one knows exactly when this dish was invented, it has been called one of Chicago's oldest iconic dishes, and one of the tastiest. It teams lightly cooked shrimp with garlic, butter, a touch of sherry, and breadcrumbs, all baked in the oven until crispy and hot. Italian trattorias, steakhouses, and other restaurants throughout Chicago and suburbs serve shrimp de Jonghe as an appetizer or entree.

The name hails from the de Jonghe brothers, who immigrated from Belgium in 1893 to create a restaurant for the 1893 Columbian Exhibition. After its success, Henri, Pierre, and Charles moved their restaurant to the Loop and, in 1899, opened De Jonghe Hotel and Restaurant at 12 E. Monroe St. Their gourmet food—perhaps including shrimp de Jonghe by that time and prepared by their chef Emil Zehr—drew the city's elite for the next two decades. But in 1923, the brothers ran up against the dry liquor laws of the day, and the hotel was closed down by the feds, never to reopen.

Contributor: Carol Mighton Haddix
See also: Restaurants and Fine Dining

BIBLIOGRAPHY

Camp, Paul A., and JeanMarie Brownson. "The Heavenly Recipe That Helped Make Henri De Jonghe Immortal." *Chicago Tribune*, January 27, 1985.

Siebel, John Ewald

Born in Hofcamp, Düsseldorf, Germany, John Ewald Siebel (1845–1919) moved to Chicago in 1866, with his PhD in physics and chemistry. He became chief chemist at Belcher's Sugar Refining Company. After that business failed, he worked, circa 1868, for the Chicago Municipal Building Commission while operating the John E. Siebel Chemical Laboratory. In 1873, he was hired as gas inspector for the City of Chicago's Gas Committee. Simultaneously, he worked as an analytic chemist for Cook County, holding both those positions for seven years.

Partnering with Chicago brewer, Michael Brand, Siebel founded the Midwest's first scientific school for brewers in 1882. However, this enterprise was not successful. In 1890, Siebel opened the Zymotechnic Institute, whose name changed in 1910 to The Siebel Institute of Technology.

The initial focus of the institute was technical. Courses taught in both German and English were offered on raw materials, brewing, malting, fermentation, engineering, refrigeration, and bottling. Brewers could expect to spend six months at the Institute before graduating, while engineers studied for three months. In addition, shorter courses of two months each were offered for malting, bottling, and postgraduate work.

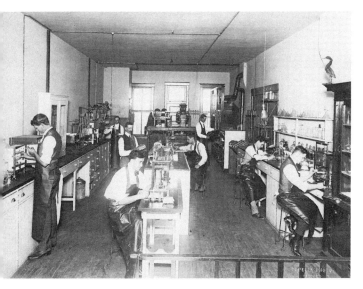

Siebel Brewing Academy students at work in the laboratory, 1910. Courtesy of the Chicago History Museum, ICHi-85012.

Because of Prohibition, the school's focus shifted to educating bakers and millers, and the curriculum included all aspects of baking, refrigeration, engineering, milling, nonalcoholic carbonated beverages, and related topics. The Institute also offered "The Home Study Course in Scientific Baking."

With the repeal of Prohibition in 1933, the Institute returned to its original concentration: educating students of malt beverages in the theory and practice of brewing and providing associated laboratory services. By this time, Dr. Siebel's five sons were involved in the business, working to expand its scope and keep abreast of the progress in the brewing industry.

The Institute, with involvement of the fourth generation of the Siebel family, continues to promote the brewing industry through instruction, research, and analysis. Recent additions to the curriculum include courses on beer styles, home brewing, and craft distillation. The Siebel Institute of Technology and World Brewing Academy currently operates out of facilities at Kendall College, 900 N. Branch St.

Contributors: Ellen F. Steinberg and Jack H. Prost
See also: Beer, Breweries, and Brewpubs; Germans

BIBLIOGRAPHY

Arnold, John Paul, and Frank Penman. *History of the Brewing Industry and Brewing Science in America*. Chicago: U.S. Brewers Association, 1933, 15–21.

http://www.breweryhistory.com/journal/archive/121/bh-121-081.htm.

Sinclair, Gordon

Gordon Sinclair was working in public relations when a psychic predicted he would become a famous restaurateur. After working part-time as a maître d' to see whether he liked it, he opened his flagship restaurant Gordon in 1976. While Sinclair's forte was the front of the house, he was a keen judge of culinary talent. Every chef who ever worked for him, beginning with Norman Van Aken and including Michael Kornick, Michael Foley, Carrie Nahabedian, and Charlie Trotter, turned in a bravura performance. His restaurant raised the standard for Chicago dining and became a showcase of contemporary American cuisine.

Sinclair also was an urban pioneer. Choosing to open his first restaurant on the 500 block of North Clark Street when the area was littered with derelicts and seedy bars helped to jump-start the trend-setting neighborhood's gentrification.

Gordon's clientele was as worldly as they were food-savvy. They smiled at the salacious artwork in the restrooms, appreciated the avant-garde option of ordering half-portions of select dishes, cheered the groundbreaking ban on cellphones, and displayed an endless appetite for the restaurant's flourless chocolate cake and artichoke fritters. He closed the restaurant and retired in 1993. The space is now home to Carrie Nahabedian's Naha.

Contributor: Barbara Revsine
See also: Chefs; Restaurants and Fine Dining; Restaurateurs and Restaurant Groups

BIBLIOGRAPHY

Dailey, Pat. "Agricultured." *Chicago Tribune*, September 30, 1990.

"Gordon Sinclair." *Food Arts*, October 1996.

http://articles.chicagotribune.com/1990-09-30/news/9003220062 _1_michigan-rural-community-gordon-restaurant.

Sinclair, Upton

Few writers have had a more significant impact on Chicago and the nation than Upton Sinclair (1878–1968). Born in Baltimore and raised in New York City, Sinclair was brilliant and full of writing energy. He entered college at age 13, paying his way by publishing magazine stories and writing pulp fiction adventure novels. His 90 novels plus plays and articles amount to some 8 million words.

Well versed in telling a good story and with an encyclopedic grasp of details, Sinclair turned to his true passion: social justice. At the turn of the century, so-called (by President Theodore Roosevelt) "muckrakers"—investigative journalists who wrote about the corruption of

Gilded Age capitalism—reached wide audiences and drove reforms. Sinclair had become a Socialist in 1902 and was sent by the Socialist weekly *Appeal to Reason* to Chicago to investigate the meat-processing industry in 1904. The author spent seven months undercover writing a series of stories, novelistic in style, called *The Jungle*. Sinclair's purpose was to show the appalling conditions to which workers were subjected. Published by Doubleday, Page & Company in 1906 (after the firm was sure that it could withstand lawsuits from Armour & Company), the novel became a sensation. The unspeakable filth and working conditions in the Union Stock Yards shocked the nation, and calls for reform were immediate.

But calls for reform in the meatpacking industry were not new. Chicago newspapers had published articles on unsanitary conditions in the meat industry since the 1850s. Harvey Washington Wiley, the chief chemist in the U.S. Department of Agriculture had been pushing for government actions since his appointment in 1882. It took a sensational novel to bring real action. President Theodore Roosevelt invited Sinclair to the White House and appointed a commission to look into the author's allegations. They were found to be true, and Congress passed both the Meat Act and the Pure Food and Drug Acts in 1906. The laws called for Federal inspection of meats, other foods, and drugs under the Food and Drug Administration.

The Jungle has never been out of print or lost its power to jolt the reader. The reforms had lasting impact on the nation's food supply systems, though Sinclair thought that they were too weak and only benefited big business. Besides, the book's purpose was to help the working men and women of America. Sinclair's most famous comment was: "I aimed at the public's heart, and by accident I hit it in the stomach."

Contributor: Bruce Kraig

See also: Armour & Company; Swift & Company; Union Stock Yards

BIBLIOGRAPHY

Arthur, Anthony. *Radical Innocent: Upton Sinclair*. New York: Random House, 2007.

Sinclair, Upton. *The Jungle*. New York: Doubleday, Page and Company, 1906 (and many subsequent editions).

Singh, Alpana

Although not a Chicago native, Alpana Singh has made her mark on the Windy City. Singh moved from California to Chicago in 2000 to take the sommelier position at Jean Joho's Everest Restaurant. In 2003, she became the youngest woman to pass the final level of the Master Sommelier exam. She later became Director of Wine and Spirits with Lettuce Entertain You.

From 2003 to 2013, Singh hosted the Emmy Award–winning show *Check, Please!* on Chicago's PBS station, WTTW Channel 11. She also appeared in an ongoing wine and spirits Q&A segment on WTTW's *Chicago Tonight*. In 2014, she appeared as a judge on the Food Network's *Food Truck Face Off*.

Singh added "restaurateur" to her already impressive resumé with the December 2012 opening of The Boarding House in River North, which made *Chicago Magazine*'s 2013 Best New Restaurants list. Singh herself was awarded the *Wine Enthusiast* 2013 Sommelier of the Year Wine Star Award and named one of *Food & Wine*'s Sommeliers of the Year 2013. Seven Lions, Singh's second restaurant, opened on Michigan Avenue in early 2015. In 2016, she opened Terra & Vine in Evanston.

Singh is the author of *Alpana Pours: About Being a Woman, Loving Wine, and Having Great Relationships*. She is a member of the Board of Directors of Choose Chicago and helped bring the Beard Awards to Chicago in May of 2015.

Contributor: Julie Chernoff

See also: Media, Television

BIBLIOGRAPHY

Alpana Singh. http://www.alpanasingh.com.

Boarding House. http://boardinghousechicago.com.

Smelt

Smelt are seven- to nine-inch-long freshwater fish from the *osmeridae* family, found in the Great Lakes. They spawn on the shoreline of Lake Michigan, and their season runs from around mid-March to mid- or late April. Netting smelts is a traditional April 1 pastime for Chicagoans prepared to brave the chilly early spring weather, using nets and buckets to collect the fish while tailgating on the shore. It is tradition to bite the heads off the first smelt caught each season. The smelt population has significantly diminished in the last several years, due to environmental issues and low water levels. The mild-flavored fish most often are served in local restaurants or at home lightly battered with flour or crushed crackers, panfried, and eaten whole. Tartar sauce is a common side.

Contributor: Chandra Ram

See also: Alliance for the Great Lakes

SMELT

Battered, fried smelt with lemon-garlic mayo dip:
Prep: 10 minutes
Chill: 30 minutes
Cook: 4 minutes
Makes: 4 appetizer servings

Use a Chicago craft beer for this batter, if you like. This batter also can be used on other small fish fillets, such as perch.

2 cups flour
1 1/2 teaspoons salt
1 teaspoon Old Bay seasoning
1/4 teaspoon freshly ground black pepper
1 bottle (12 ounces) beer
1 pound smelt, cleaned
1/4 cup canola oil

Lemon wedges
Garlic mayo, see recipe

1. Mix 1 1/2 cups of the flour, salt, Old Bay, and pepper in a bowl. Whisk in the beer slowly to avoid lumps. Refrigerate until cold, about 30 minutes.

2. Dust smelt with the remaining 1/2 cup flour. Shake off any excess. Heat a large, cast-iron skillet. Add oil to skillet; heat to 350 degrees. Dip smelt into batter; place in hot oil in small batches. Cook 2 minutes; turn. Cook until golden brown, about 2 to 3 minutes. Drain on paper towels. Season with salt. Serve with lemon wedges and garlic mayo for dipping.

Garlic mayo: Crush 2 cloves of garlic into a small bowl. Sprinkle with 1/4 teaspoon salt and zest of 1 lemon. Stir in 1/2 cup mayonnaise. Chill to meld flavors, about 30 minutes.

BIBLIOGRAPHY

http://gentlejanuaries.wordpress.com/2009/05/19/the-fish-the-myth-the-legend-smelt—fishing-and-tradition-in-chicago%E2%80%99s-lake-michigan/.

Sticha, Sarah. "The Fish, the Myth, the Legend: Smelt Fishing and Tradition in Chicago's Lake Michigan." Thesis, University of Chicago, 2009.

Smorgasbords

Swedish smorgasbords were one of the most popular dining experiences in Chicago from the 1920s through the 1950s. Economic and industrial problems in Sweden led to mass exodus to other countries between 1840 and 1930, and Chicago became home to many of the thousands of Swedes immigrating to the United States. By 1910, one-fifth of the people born in Sweden lived in the United States, and Chicago had the second-largest Swedish population in the world, second only to Stockholm. Many of them opened smorgasbords in the Loop and neighborhoods. Sweden House on East Ohio Street was one of the city's best-known smorgasbords.

The McCormick mansion on East Ontario Street, now the site of Lawry's The Prime Rib, was purchased in 1937 by Fredrik Chramer, a Danish restaurateur. He renovated the building in Swedish Modern style and opened Kungsholm, one of the city's most iconic smorgasbords with a puppet theater. It closed after his death in 1960.

At a smorgasbord, for a set price, a diner could sample any number of dishes from a buffet, such as bread, butter, cheese, herring, meatballs and headcheese. The food was typically offered in three courses, starting with bread and cold meats and cheeses, followed by chilled seafood, and then warm dishes such as fried sausages, potato casseroles, and meatballs. Later, Polish restaurateurs copied the popular concept with their own smorgasbords of Polish dishes.

Contributor: Chandra Ram

BIBLIOGRAPHY

Gustafson, Anita Olson. "Swedes." *The Encyclopedia of Chicago History*. Chicago History Museum, 2005. http://www.encyclopedia.chicagohistory.org/pages/1222.html.

Snowden, John

At Dumas Pere l'École de la Cuisine Française, founded by John Snowden (1914–80), the focus was classic French cooking, the schedule was rigorous, and the owner/instructor was both skilled and demanding. Although designed primarily for dedicated amateurs, Dumas Pere was the training ground for many top-tier chefs, including John Terczak, Sarah Stegner, George Bombaris, and John Hogan.

Not much is known about Snowden's early life, but as an African American interested in French cooking in the mid–twentieth century, his opportunities were limited. He wound up working on cruise ships, in a hotel in Switzerland, and at various restaurants worldwide. By the time he took a job at a French restaurant in Chicago's racially diverse

Interior of the Triangle Soda Fountain, ca. 1920s. Courtesy of the Chicago History Museum, ICHi-85002; Walter A. McDougall.

Hyde Park neighborhood, he was a skilled chef, conversant with every aspect of French cooking. He opened his own French restaurant, Le Provençal, in Hyde Park in 1951.

Snowden opened the original Dumas Pere in Chicago's gentrifying Old Town neighborhood in the late 1950s. A move to north suburban Glenview came next, where he ran the successful cooking school with an on-site restaurant open to the general public. After Snowden's death in 1980, his sons Juan and Manuel kept the school open for a brief time.

Contributor: Barbara Revsine
See also: Cooking Classes

BIBLIOGRAPHY

Levin, Cheryl. "In Memory of John Snowden." *Chicago Tribune*, December 29, 1980.
Simms, T. Prescott, "John Snowden: Prince of the Palate." *Chicago Tribune*, April 24, 1974.

Soda Fountains

Soda fountains emerged in drugstores in the early nineteenth century, when soda water was considered to be a health aid and potential cure for illnesses like colic and dyspepsia. Carbonated waters were prized for their abilities to soothe stomachs, but gaining access to naturally carbonated mineral water from volcanic springs was difficult and expensive. Pharmacies stocked mineral water and, soon, the machines necessary to carbonate regular water. The fountain attendants who operated the machines became known as "soda jerks," because of the jerking action they made when pulling the soda draft arm.

Soon, druggists were adding flavored syrups to the carbonated water and then to ice cream. The soda fountain went from having medicinal purposes to becoming an important source of revenue for drugstore owners, and a family-friendly social hub for customers. The equipment soon went from utilitarian to decorative, and the water was charged and dispensed in onyx or marble boxes with Victorian and Art Deco designs, sometimes with Tiffany lighting or Favril glasswork above.

Once drugstore owners saw the potential for a steady stream of customers and more revenue, sandwiches and dishes like hot dogs, griddled sandwiches, and root beer floats became part of the menu, and an all-American social and dining tradition, perfect for a country embracing isolationism, was born.

Chicago was home to the soda fountain industry, with leaders such as Sam Schy, who started his business in 1919 after he won the Chicago distributorship for Liquid Carbonic. He renamed the business American Soda Fountain, which is still operating, and sold and repaired fountain equipment all over the country. Fizzy chocolate soda is thought to have been created by a Chicagoan, Frederick Sanders Schmidt, who lost his soda fountain after the Chicago Fire in 1871 and moved to Detroit.

Charles Walgreen helped soda fountains thrive when he decided to add food to his soda fountain menus around 1910. His wife, Myrtle, prepared sandwiches with egg salad and beef tongue, soups, and cakes and pies for his Chicago drugstores.

Soda fountains thrived until the early 1970s, when Americans fled cities to settle in the suburbs, and city centers lost their appeal. Vending machines offering sodas almost anywhere trumped charm with convenience, and drugstores and pharmacies began to phase out their soda fountains. Walgreens closed the soda fountains in its stores in the 1980s.

Homer's in Wilmette, Illinois, was founded before World War II and continues to operate, with a mail-order business as well as the traditional soda fountain. Today, newer businesses such as Bobtail Ice Cream, with five locations in the Chicago area, hope to capitalize on the nostalgia of soda fountains.

Contributor: Chandra Ram

See also: Malted Milk Shake; Soft Drinks; Walgreen, Myrtle and Charles

BIBLIOGRAPHY

Funderburg, Anne Cooper. "Sundae Best: A History of Soda Fountains." Madison: The University of Wisconsin Popular Press, 2002.

Kass, John, "Chocolate Soda's Origins Are Open to Sweet Debate." *Chicago Tribune*, August 23, 2014. http://www.chicagotribune.com/news/columnists/ct-kass-met-0824–20140823-column.html.

Sodikoff, Brendan

One of the most enterprising restaurateurs of the last few years, Sodikoff has opened a succession of popular restaurants, beginning in the River North neighborhood in 2010. His Hogsalt Hospitality group has opened 10 establishments and counting, beginning with Gilt Bar, nestled on Kinzie Street behind the Merchandise Mart, and moving on to Bavette's Bar and Beef a few doors down, Maude's Liquor Bar on Randolph, Au Cheval diner on Randolph at Halsted Street, Roxie's by the Slice on Milwaukee Avenue, and Green Street Smoked Meats (and High Five Ramen in the basement) near Randolph. He also opened The California Clipper in a former speakeasy and The Doughnut Vault, a tiny take-out bakery behind Gilt Bar.

After high school in Southern California, Sodikoff took off for Paris and cooking school at the École Ritz Escoffier, then trained with chefs Alain Ducasse and Thomas Keller, and then worked as test kitchen chef for Lettuce Entertain You. By then, Sodikoff was ready to start his own restaurant empire. He has made a success of finding old buildings and transforming them into unique, fun destinations where customers often wait hours to get in the doors for stellar food and drinks. One website magazine wondered if Chicagoans might tire of "Sodikoff-saturation."

Contributor: Carol Mighton Haddix

See also: Restaurants and Fine Dining; Restaurateurs and Restaurant Groups

BIBLIOGRAPHY

Viera, Lauren. "Brendan Sodikoff: 40 under 40, Class of 2014." *Crain's Chicago Business.* http://www.chicagobusiness.com/section/40-under-40–2014?recipient=Sodikoff.

Soft Drinks

Chicago has a reputation as a hard-drinking town, but it has a few notable soft drinks. One of the largest brands of bottled water started here, as well as some unique contributions to soda pop (which Chicagoans, in common with much of the Midwest, call "pop").

In the nineteenth century, most Chicagoans drank untreated water from Lake Michigan. Before the reversal of the Chicago River in 1900, raw sewage flowed into the lake and the water was frequently contaminated with the effluvia of slaughterhouses and factories. Waterborne diseases, such as typhoid, cholera, and dysentery, were common. People bought bottled spring water instead, as George J. Schmitt noted as he worked as an assistant at the Gale and Block Drug Store in the Palmer House hotel. So, in 1888, he partnered with Otis Hinckley to start a home-delivery service for bottled water.

Hinckley & Schmitt Bottled Water Co. bought water from White Rock Spring in Waukesha, Wisconsin, and delivered it directly to Chicago customers. The partners

A BASEMENT CREATION: DAD'S ROOT BEER

Dad's was developed in the 1930s by partners Barney Berns and Ely Klapman in the basement of Chapman's Chicago-area home. Making root beer at home was a popular pastime in the early twentieth century. The first trademark for Dad's Root Beer Co. was granted in 1939. The soft drink soon earned a following in the Midwest and, by the 1940s, became popular throughout the United States.

The firm's plant was located in Avondale, compete with a large sign on the roof that claimed "Dad's tastes like Root Beer should." Dad's was the first product to use the six-pack carrier invented by the Atlanta Paper Company in the 1940s. Dad's also introduced the half-gallon bottle and marketed the line as a family, advertising bottle sizes as "Junior" (7, 10, or 12 ounces), "Mama" (16 ounces), and "Papa" (32 ounces). The image of the young boy featured on the "Junior" size bottle is Barney Berns's son, Gene Berns.

Ely's son, Jules Klapman, took over and expanded the brand internationally. But the Klapman and Berns families sold rights to IC Industries in the 1970s. Then, the Monarch Beverage Company of Atlanta acquired Dad's in 1986. At that time, Dad's sold 12 million cases annually and held the second largest share of the root beer category behind A & W. In 2007, Dad's Root Beer was purchased by Hedinger Brands, LLC and licensed to The Dad's Root Beer Company, LLC. The company headquarters now is in Jasper, Indiana. Dad's Root Beer still is sold in stores almost 80 years after its basement creation.

JUDITH DUNBAR HINES

also pioneered watercooler service for offices. As business increased, they began using railroad tank cars to bring the water to Chicago, bottling it at first on Franklin Street, and then at 420 W. Ontario St., a large plant they built in 1911. This remained corporate headquarters until 1968. As time went on, they added additional spring waters and beverages to their line, including the speakeasy favorite White Rock brand water in its famed brown bottle with a label picturing the nymph Psyche on the rock.

The Hinckley and Schmitt families remained involved with the company until the mid-1990s. In 1981, the firm was sold to Anjou International Co., a French firm, but CEO George J. Schmitt, the founder's grandson, continued to helm Anjou's Chicago-based Hinckley & Schmitt Bottled Water Group until 1996, by which time it was the third-largest bottled-water company in the United States, boasting annual sales of more than $175 million. After sales and mergers, in 2005 the firm wound up owned by Kelso & Co., an investment fund based in Atlanta. However, the brand, now called Hinckley Springs, still bottles at 6055 S. Harlem Ave. in the Clearing neighborhood, one of 25 plants across the country.

Schoenhofen Edelweiss Brewing Co. at 18th Street and Canalport Avenue in Pilsen, introduced Green River soda in 1919, and turned full-time pop bottler after the Volstead Act went into effect on January 16, 1920, pouring its bright green lime drink into old beer bottles. The drink was such a hit that Eddie Cantor sang about it in that year's Ziegfeld Follies: "For a drink that's fine without a kick, Oh, Green River / It's the only drink that does the trick, just Green River." By Prohibition's end in 1933, only Coca-Coca exceeded Green River's Midwest fountain sales. Upon returning to beer brewing, though, Schoenhofen made Green River a second priority. Sales dropped, and the brewery closed in 1950. Green River, however, kept going with a variety of owners and sometimes spotty distribution. In 2011, the brand was acquired by California-based Wit Beverage Co., which also makes Goose Island soda pop.

Arthur Canfield began producing soda pop in a plant at 67th Street and South Chicago Avenue in 1924, but the A. J. Canfield Co. remained a little-known local producer until 1984, when it reformulated a flavor first produced in 1972 to use aspartame as a sweetener. After dieting Chicago columnist Bob Greene raved about Canfield's Diet Chocolate Fudge soda, claiming "a sip of the stuff is like biting into a hot fudge sundae," the pop company went from regional to national success. Greene's column sparked such a fudge frenzy that there were shortages of the flavor and the company sold 2 million cans of it in 1985. E. J. "Manny" Wesber, chief chemist and vice president of research and development at A. J. Canfield Co., created Diet Chocolate Fudge. Canfield's current flavors also include Diet Chocolate Cherry, Diet Swiss Creme, 50/50 (grapefruit/lime), ginger ale, tonic water, and regular and flavored seltzers. A. J. Canfield remained family-owned until 1994. Today, Canfield's is a regional brand licensed by the Dr. Pepper Snapple Group, bottled in Northlake and sold primarily in the Chicago area, where it enjoys a passionate following.

Another firm, Filbert's Old Time Draft Root Beer, began in 1926 when George Filbert moved from his milk, coal, and ice delivery service to making root beer and delivering it in barrels to restaurants. Business expanded during Prohibition. Using the same family recipe and batch-brewed process, Charlie's grandson Ron Filbert still makes Filbert's at 3430 S. Ashland Ave. in Bridgeport, along with 25 other pop flavors. The soft drinks are sold in glass bottles at the plant. Root beer is still available in quarter- and half-barrels.

Coca-Cola was invented by pharmacist John Pemberton in Georgia in 1886, but if it were not for a Chicago invention, Coke might never have achieved its phenomenal success. Until 1933, ordering a Coke meant that a soda jerk pumped some syrup into a glass and topped it off with cold seltzer. The process tended to make the drink vary widely. At the Century of Progress Exposition, the Chicago World's Fair that year, Coca-Cola introduced the first automatic fountain dispenser, which created a well-blended Coke with the pull of a handle. What's more, the dispenser could be packed with ice, making the perfect "ice-cold Coca-Cola." The Coke machine, aka the Dole Master Dispenser, was the product of the Dole Valve Co., 1923–1933 Carroll Ave. in Chicago. The innovation was a huge hit—helped along, no doubt, by the millions of free drinks Coca-Cola dispensed to fairgoers.

A number of smaller bottlers existed in Chicago over the course of its history, including some newer "upscale" ones. Lasser's began bottling in 1879 in the De Paul area. Its root beer was especially prized because the company aged its own roots in barrels. Squeezed out of the market by large brands, it went out of business in 1985, its factory turned into lofts. O-So Grape began in 1946 and bought Dr. Swett's Root Beer in 1949. One of the oldest root beer brands, Dr. Swett's had been bottling root beer in Boston and New York since the 1880s. O-So Grape went out of business after lawsuits by major bottlers in the late 1950s and is today owned by the Homer Soda Company of Homer, Illinois. Recently, artisanal soft drinks have appeared. In 2009, pastry chef Gale Gand created Gale's Root Beer. Flavored with cinnamon, ginger, and vanilla, it is bottled in and distributed from Chicago. Consultant and author Bruce Cost, well-known for expertise in Chinese ingredients, bottles his Bruce Cost Ginger Ales using fresh ginger. And as in days past when beer companies made root beer, WBC Goose Island Root Beer is made locally and sold nationally.

Contributor: Leah A. Zeldes
See also: Beer, Breweries, and Brewpubs; Prohibition

BIBLIOGRAPHY
Filbert's. "The History of Filbert's Root Beer." filbertsrootbeer.com/History.htm.
Wit Beverage Co. "Green River Finds New Home at WIT Beverage Company," July 28, 2011. www.greenriversoda.com.
Zeldes, Leah. "Chicago Put the Pop in Pop." *Intercity Intelligencer*, June 4, 2013.

Sotelino, Gabino

Together with Richard Melman and Lettuce Entertain You Restaurants (LEYE), chef Gabino Sotelino helped create some of Chicago's best restaurants: Ambria (1980), Café Ba-Ba-Reeba! (1985), Mon Ami Gabi (1998), and its predecessor Un Grand Café (1981). Ambria anchored the city's fine-dining scene throughout its tenure, while Ba-Ba-Reeba! has the distinction of being the area's first tapas bar. And when the partners swapped out Un Grand Café for the more casual Mon Ami Gabi, they created an enduring appetite for the deceptively simple cooking of Parisian bistros. A Las Vegas edition of the restaurant opened in the Paris Hotel in 1999.

Sotelino was born in the Basque region of Spain. He began working at the Ritz Hotel in Madrid when he was 13, and by the age of 20 had become an apprentice chef at the posh Plaza Athénée in Paris. Stints with various hotel groups throughout the world came next, followed by an opportunity to head up the kitchen at Le Perroquet (1974), one of Chicago's best restaurants. He left in 1977 to become executive chef of the world-famous Pump Room, then part of LEYE, before moving on to Ambria. It was the beginning of a beautiful partnership.

Contributor: Barbara Revsine
See also: Chefs; Lettuce Entertain You Restaurants; Pump Room; Restaurants and Fine Dining

BIBLIOGRAPHY
Vettel, Phil. "Excellent, Nouvelle-Tinged Dishes Earn 4 Stars for Sotelino's Ambria." *Chicago Tribune*, July 26, 1991.

Soul food

The term *soul* has been used as a signifier of African American culture since the nineteenth century. Soul food is recognized as an amalgam of dishes found in black (and white) communities across the American South. The usual elements of soul food include fried chicken, catfish, chitterlings/"chitlins" (pork intestines), pig feet, hot links, black-eyed peas, macaroni and cheese, greens, okra, candied yams, cornbread, wheat flour biscuits, banana pudding, peach cobblers, and crisps, among others. Some dishes are spicy, as in Louisiana Creole, or in cooked mustard greens with pot liquor; others are blander.

An early use of the term *soul food* to describe specific dishes enjoyed by African Americans can be traced back to pioneering black journalists such as Gertrude Gipson.

In her *Los Angeles Sentinel* column in 1960, she described a popular Los Angeles bartender's refusal to eat anything but cottage cheese: He "claims he can't eat the 'soul food' like Ham and Grits." A year after Gipson's first mention of soul food in a newspaper, Chicago native Masco Young advised *Philadelphia Tribune* readers to consider themselves square if they had not heard about soul food.

In Chicago, the *Chicago Defender*'s first soul food reference came in a 1966 column by Joseph "Ziggy" Johnson, in which the dancer and writer, a Chicago native, recommended an eating establishment with the description that "Mom's kitchen has 'soul' food.'" The first *Chicago Tribune* soul food mention came in a 1967 story headlined: "Dee Jay Jones Cooks Up Soul Food." Two recipes, soul chili spaghetti and peppered Swiss steak, were used to illustrate soul food, following the story about the legendary WVON disc jockey who would go on to become the station's program director.

The earliest restaurants in the largely black community on the South Side featured the kinds of dishes found in regional southern restaurants. Fresh fish, shrimp, crabs, barbecued chicken, and biscuits, as one might find in Louisiana and the coastal Carolinas were commonly advertised by restaurants such as the Dixie Fish and the Georgia Food and Fish Hut. Other restaurants made specialties: Hanson's Chitterling Shack and Arletta's Creole Food were among many. Sunday dinners and after-church brunches were commonly advertised as southern home-style cooking.

African American immigration to Chicago increased dramatically during and after World War II, many of the newcomers coming from rural Mississippi and Arkansas. They brought their own styles of barbecue, hot links, biscuits, and fried chicken, and those dishes merged with the established cuisine to become "soul food." Robinson's Ribs in Oak Park is an example of the Western Mississippi style of barbecue. Chicken and fish shacks appeared everywhere in the black communities of the South and West Sides to serve the enlarged communities with "home cooking" that was recognizably their own.

Army & Lou's, 422 E. 75th St. was the city's premiere soul food destination. It opened in 1945 as one of the first African American–owned restaurants in the Midwest and closed in 2011. The restaurant was named after original owners Armstrong and Louise. Regular guests included Muhammad Ali, Dr. Martin Luther King, and Smokey Robinson, and their photos appeared on a "Wall of Fame." Army & Lou's was known for its smothered fried chicken and a sharp macaroni and cheese with ground pepper. The macaroni and cheese recipe is now used at Baker's Keyboard Lounge in Detroit.

Strong women who lived in the neighborhood were the faces of these restaurants.

WHAT SEPARATES SOUTHERN FOOD AND SOUL FOOD?

The question was posed to Edna Stewart, the late, longtime owner of the iconic restaurant, Edna's, on Chicago's West Side.

"The soul food version of the same dish has more flavor," she said. "It tastes better because of the ingredient called soul."

—DONNA PIERCE

Gladys' Luncheonette opened at 4527 S. Indiana in 1946, owned by Gladys Holcomb. Her biscuits and black-eyed peas became a go-to item for artists like Redd Foxx, Jackie Wilson, and Sam & Dave, who were appearing at the nearby Regal Theater. During the 1940s and 1950s, word about Gladys's ample servings of pork chops and spaghetti got out to teams traveling the Negro Baseball League circuit. A portrait of former Chicago Mayor Harold Washington adorned the restaurant wall more than a dozen years after his death.

Edna Stewart opened her first soul food restaurant, Edna's, with her father Samuel Mitchell, Sr. in 1966 in the Far West Side Austin neighborhood before moving to Kedzie and Madison. The restaurant's specialties included fried catfish and chicken, short ribs, Arkansas-style biscuits, okra, and collard greens. Edna's was a meeting place for Dr. King and a young Rev. Jesse Jackson as they mapped out strategies to combat housing discrimination. Edna insisted that they eat for free. Edna's benevolence included her hiring of convicted felons to work in the kitchen.

Helen Maybell Anglin, who died in 2009 at the age of 80, was owner-entrepreneur of the Soul Queen Restaurant, 9031 S. Stoney Island. The effervescent Anglin had her waitresses wear gold paper crowns and made sure she wrote all her recipes down by hand. Anglin also ran a Soul Queen at Cermak Road and South Michigan Avenue, which closed in the mid-1980s. The Stoney Island Soul Queen closed in early 2009. The Soul Queen was known for its candied yams, liver and gravy with fresh onion, and panfried catfish with cornmeal breading.

Chicago's West Side neighborhood evaporated even faster than South Side neighborhoods, due in part to the West Side riots following the April 1968 assassination of Dr. King. And people continue to pack up and go. Eating habits and urban neighborhoods changed dramatically in the 1990s and early 2000s, resulting in the closure of all the legacy soul food restaurants in Chicago. Queen of the Sea on Blue Island Avenue (originally H&H Diner), Izola's on east 79th Avenue, Gladys' Luncheonette, and Army and Lou's on east 75th street are among the casualties. Following Edna Stewart's death, Edna's closed in August 2011, but in December it was reopened as Ruby's around the corner at 3175 West Madison by Henry and Gloria Henderson and some former employees.

Demographics changed. According to the 2010 U.S. Census, there were 181,000 fewer African Americans in the city in 2010 than in 2000—a 17 percent decline—and inroads by corporate restaurants are the main cause of the apparent decline in soul food restaurants. Fortunately, southern-style restaurants and many chicken shacks remain as reminders of a unique Chicago cuisine.

The Chicago soul food restaurants of today have veered from many of the rich offerings such as chitlins and ham hocks from midcentury glory days. The eclectic Soul Vegetarian East, aka "Soul Veg," opened in 1982 at 203 E. 75th St. as one of America's first vegan soul food restaurants and has since influenced other vegan soul food establishments in the Midwest. Soul Veg pioneered the use of kale, and their tasty "jerk chicken" is made with tofu. Pearl's Place, 3901 S. Michigan Ave., offers "down home southern cooking" in a modern supper club style and offerings like lemon chicken rice soup, fried green tomatoes, and roast turkey, an increasingly popular item in soul food restaurants.

An even greater departure is the popularity of fine southern-style cooking restaurants in trendy North Side neighborhoods at places like Big Jones (Andersonville) and Feed (Humboldt Park.) that many critics and customers label as soul food. Soul food will continue to evolve, but its core sense of community and spirituality should never be forgotten.

Contributors: Dave Hoekstra and Donna Pierce

See also: African Americans

BIBLIOGRAPHY

Hoekstra, Dave. *The People's Place: Soul Food Restaurants and Reminiscences from the Civil Rights Era to Today*. Chicago: Chicago Review Press, 2015.

Miller, Adrian. *Soul Food: The Surprising Story of an American Cuisine One Plate at a Time*. Chapel Hill: University of North Carolina Press, 2013.

Poe, Tracy N. "The Origins of Soul Food in Black Urban Identity: Chicago, 1915–1947." *American Studies International. February 1999*, Vol. XXXVII, No. 1, 4–33.

Soup Kitchens

A soup kitchen is a place where food, usually soup and bread, is served for free to the needful public. Soup kitchens began in the United States in the 1870s in poor communities, but they became widespread nationally in 1929, shortly after the crash of the stock market on October 29 and the onset of the Great Depression. American citizens from all walks of life lost their invested savings and livelihoods. The economic policies and relief efforts instituted by President Herbert Hoover were inadequate to stem the disastrous effects of the severe economic downturn. By 1932, 12 million Americans, approximately 25 percent of the work force, found themselves unemployed with no financial reserves.

The first soup kitchens were funded and operated by religious organizations and private charities. These relief centers served mostly bread and soup, which could be thinned as needed by adding water. The Capuchin Services Center in Detroit opened on November 2, 1929, and began serving between 1,500–3,000 people every day. The Volunteers of America ran soup kitchens in every large city in America.

One of the first and most thriving soup kitchens in 1930 was located in Chicago and was funded and operated by the notorious Chicago crime figure Al Capone, who acquired a financial fortune from his activities as a Chicago bootlegger during the American government's Prohibition experiment (1920–33). By 1930, Al Capone was nearing federal indictment on tax evasion charges and needed some good publicity. The early years of the depression provided an opportunity. Capone made personal visits to his new charitable enterprise located at 935 S. State St., shaking hands and providing encouragement to the poor and needy. The kitchen served three meals each day, often feeding over 1,000 people. On Thanksgiving Day in 1930, Capone's soup kitchen fed an estimated 5,000 indigent citizens of Chicago. One year later, after his conviction of federal tax evasion, Capone was occupying a prison cell at Cook County Jail. The building was demolished 25 years later and is now a parking lot.

Soup kitchens remain as an integral part of the charitable and volunteer efforts for the care of the homeless and needy families in Chicago. The Greater Chicago Food Depository is among the largest and operates in several locations across the city. A Just Harvest at 7649 N. Paulina St. serves some 55,000 meals a year. A number of community religious and secular organizations run soup kitchens, such as A Just Harvest and Franciscan Outreach. The most famous is the Salvation Army, three of which operate in the downtown Chicago area.

Contributor: Philip V. Wojciak

See also: Depression Food; Food Pantries

BIBLIOGRAPHY

The Chicago Crime Scenes Project (December 2008) "Capone's Soup Kitchen." http://www.Chicagocrimescenes.blogspot.com/2008/12/capone.html.

United States History. "Depression-era Soup Kitchens." http://www.u-s-history.com/pages/h1660.html.

South Americans

Almost 38,000 Chicago Hispanics identified themselves as being of South American origin, according to the 2011–13 American Community Survey. The majority (just more than 20,000) came from Ecuador. This group has more than doubled in size since the 2000 census population count. Colombians remain the second largest group, with approximately 8,500 Chicagoans identifying themselves as being of Colombian origin, followed by Peruvians at approximately 3,700. Chicago's South American community also includes a diverse mix of immigrants and descendants from Argentina, Brazil, Venezuela, Chile, and Bolivia, and some arrivals from Uruguay and Paraguay.

Roughly 60 percent of Chicago's South American immigrants are foreign-born, and of those just more than 40 percent arrived in Chicago since 2000. South American arrivals, unlike Mexicans, Puerto Ricans, and some Caribbean populations, have settled across Chicago's North Side, rather than congregating in specific neighborhoods.

Argentinian and Brazilians have become increasingly well known in Chicago for their steak culture. A string of Brazilian steakhouse chains have capitalized on the *churrascaria* and *gaucho* culture of the southern and central areas of South America. These smorgasbords of meat parade cuts of beef, lamb, pork, and chicken on spits before seated customers, re-creating the environment of the gauchos from the pampas, cowboys of the South American plains that extend from Patagonia to Southern Brazil.

In addition to large downtown Brazilian steakhouses, several neighborhood Argentinian restaurants, such as Tango Sur in Lakeview and its sister outpost Folklore in West Town, specialize in meat with less show. The national accompaniment for steak, however, is *chimichurri*. This green sauce—a mix of parsley, garlic, and olive oil that occasionally verges on paste—is at the heart of Argentinian meals. Accompaniments tend toward potatoes: mashed, roasted, and, sometimes, fried, revealing strong continental influences and midwestern acculturation.

Substitute *gauchos* with *llaneros*, and *pampas* with *llanos*, the plains across southern Colombia and Venezuela, and similarities across South America reveal themselves. Colombian restaurants, such as Pueblito Viejo in Lincoln Square, La Brasa Roja in Albany Park, Las Tablas in Lakeview and Irving Park, and Sabor a Café in West Rogers Park, celebrate this culture, referencing the llanero cowboys and their grassland lifestyles in their décor. Heaping servings of beef, pork, blood sausage, roasted chicken, and often rabbit, at times served as one platter with a boiled potato and

arepa (and even a fried egg), offer the Colombian equivalent of a lumberjack lunch. The *arepa*, a grilled cornmeal patty, generally served plain, can also be fried, stuffed with meat and egg, sweetened, or baked with cheese.

Colombian Bakery Mekato's, next door to Pueblito Viejo in Lincoln Square, offers a full display of the snack-sized savory and sweet specialties of Colombia, like *arepas*, including a range of guava pastries, *carimañolas* (meat filled yucca-dough fritters), and *empanadas*. *Empanadas* are a pan–South American treat, varying in preparation according to national customs. Colombians traditionally fry and use corn meal dough, while Argentinians and Chileans bake with flour dough. Fillings range but often include chicken, ground or shredded beef, or, especially in the south of the continent, ham and cheese, or spinach.

Meanwhile, indigenous influences on South American cuisine are highly visible in the prominence of legumes and potatoes: as the black bean is a mainstay of Cuban food, and the pinto bean of Mexican food, so is the *cargamanto* (*borlotti*) bean to Colombians. As the cradle of domestication some 6,000 years ago in the Andes, Peruvian cuisine features the potato prominently, perhaps unsurprisingly, given the ancient Andean predilection for the tuber. Potatoes might stand alone as in *papas a la huancaina*, a dish of boiled potatoes covered in a cheese and olive sauce; or *papas rellenas*, potatoes stuffed with meat; or the potato might just serve to thicken Peruvian secos or stews. Ingredients for many of these and other South American dishes can be found in markets such as La Unica on West Devon Avenue, El Condor on North Milwaukee Avenue, or El Mercado Meat Market on North Southport Avenue.

Finally, the integration of Caribbean seafood into the South American diet also acknowledges the diaspora of flavors. Peruvian cuisine also is a blend of sea and land, but in this case it is fostered by Peru's prime location near a Pacific upwelling that brings cold, nutrient-rich waters up from the deep to the ocean's surface to support a rich fish population. Peruvian restaurants in Chicago, such as Machu Picchu in Lakeview, Tanta in River North, and Ay Ay Picante in Albany Park, mirror this fusion, offering fried fishes, shellfish, and ceviche, marinated raw seafood, alongside hearty chicken and beef specialties, such as *anticuchos*, skewered meat, most popularly of beef heart, and warming stews.

Contributor: Andres Torres

BIBLIOGRAPHY

Fabricant, Florence. "For Chileans, Passion Translates to Empanadas." *New York Times*, April 14, 2009.

http://earthobservatory.nasa.gov/Features/ElNino/elnino2.php.

Senyel, Kelly. "Brazil: Ready for Its Culinary Close-Up." *Gourmet Live*, September 19, 2012.

South Asians

People of South Asian origin—a census category that includes Indians, Pakistanis, Bangladeshis, Sri Lankans, Bhutanese, and Nepalese—are one of the fastest growing Asian American ethnic groups in the Chicago area. About 171,000 South Asians live in the suburban six-county area, including 43,475 in the city of Chicago. In Chicago, more than three-quarters of South Asians are of Indian descent, 18 percent are Pakistanis, 1.5 percent Bangladeshi, and 1.5 percent Nepali, with smaller communities of Sri Lankans and Bhutanese. In recent years, many South Asians have moved to the northwest and western suburbs, especially Des Plaines, Mount Prospect, Schaumburg, and Naperville.

A few South Asians came to Chicago as students and businessmen in the first decades of the twentieth century, but a 1924 federal law banned immigration from South Asia. The majority arrived after the immigration reforms of 1965, which removed geographical restrictions and encouraged the immigration of professionals and family members.

The first Indian grocery store was opened by Sarjit Singh Sikand in 1967 at 2911 N. Broadway. Until then the only source of South Asian spices and other ingredients was Conte di Savoia on Roosevelt Road. Sikand at first sold imported items to Conte's owner. When business far exceeded his expectations, Sikand opened Indian Gifts and Food at Belmont and Sheffield. In 1973, he opened a restaurant at the same location, which initially served kabobs and other tandoori items and later some South Indian dishes. The majority of his customers were Americans, many of whom were tasting Indian food for the first time.

Other early restaurants included House of India (1963), originally on North Lincoln and later at 1746 N. Wells St.; Brothers, a modest storefront on Belmont Avenue (late 1960s); Bengal Lancers, a fine-dining restaurant on North Clark Street (1970); and Gaylords at 678 N. Clark (1972), the first North American branch of an Indian chain. All are closed, except Gaylords, which is now on East Walton Street and no longer associated with the chain. The first Indian restaurant on Devon Avenue, which became the region's main South Asian shopping district, was Standard India restaurant. Opened by the Kamboj family in 1983, it later moved to Belmont Avenue, but closed in 2014 following the death of the owner.

Today, Indian restaurants in the Chicago area range from small holes-in-the-wall to fine-dining establishments. Buffets are common, especially at lunch. The most popular dishes include *samosas* (small filled pastries), *tandoori* chicken, butter chicken (roasted chicken in a gravy), *saag panir* (farmer's cheese cooked with spinach), *biryani* (rice

A DEVON AVENUE CLASSIC

This rich, spicy dish is a favorite of Chicago's South Asian Muslims and is available on many restaurants on Devon Avenue and elsewhere.

Nihari (Beef stew with ginger)

Prep: 30 minutes
Cook: 2 hours, 15 minutes
Makes: 4 servings

  2 large onions, sliced
  1 tablespoon vegetable oil
  1 pound boneless beef chuck, cut into 1 1/2-inch cubes
  1 piece (1-inch) fresh gingerroot
  3 cloves garlic
  1 teaspoon each: chili powder, salt
  2 teaspoons flour
  Garam masala (spice mixture):
  8 black cardamom seeds, removed from pods
  8 black peppercorns

6 cloves
1 piece (2 inches long) cinnamon stick
1 teaspoon cumin seeds
Sliced ginger, sliced green chilies, chopped cilantro, optional

1. Heat the oil in a Dutch oven over medium heat; add onions. Cook until golden, about 5 minutes. Add the beef; cook 30 minutes, stirring often. Meanwhile, process ginger and garlic in a food processor or blender with a little water until smooth. Add to the meat; cook 10 minutes. Add the chili powder and salt; cook 30 minutes.

2. For the garam masala, place spices in a heavy skillet over medium heat. Heat, stirring often, until fragrant; let cool. Grind the spices in a spice or coffee grinder to make a fine powder. Place in small bowl; mix in flour and a little water. Stir into the beef mixture; add 4 cups of water. Mix well; cook, tightly covered, over very low heat until the meat is tender, about 1 hour. Transfer to serving dish; top with sliced ginger, chilies and cilantro. Serve with Indian bread.

Sukhadia Sweets on Devon Avenue serves traditional Indian sweets and snacks. Photograph by Ashish Sen.

and meat), and such wonderful Indian breads as *naan*, *parathas*, and *puri*. Some restaurants, especially South Indian ones, serve only vegetarian dishes, but most also offer dishes of chicken and mutton (a term that can mean lamb or goat). Beef and pork are excluded for religious reasons. A growing number of restaurants in the Chicago area serve regional food, including Gujarati (Annapurna), Hyderabad (Hyderabad House), and the Chettinad community (Karaikudi). Indian sweet and snack shops include Sukhadia's and Tahoora on Devon Avenue. Chinese-Indian restaurants, such as Umania Chinese on Devon, serve spicy-hot Indian-Chinese food. Modern takes on Indian street food dishes can be found at Hakka Bakka on Fullerton and Bombay Wraps, with stores on East Ohio and North Wells

In 1974, Mafat and Tulsi Patel opened their first store at 2034 W. Devon Ave., followed by a larger flagship store at 2610 Devon Ave. Today, it is the largest Indian grocery chain in the United States. Other stores followed, including Kamdar Plaza, butcher shops serving halal meat for Muslims, Bangladeshi fish markets, and grocery stores serving a multiethnic clientele. In recent years, business has dropped off somewhat on Devon as more South Asians move to the suburbs and stores follow.

Chicago is home to around 8,000 Pakistanis (with more than 18,000 living in Cook County) and while Indian and Pakistani cuisines share much in common—some restaurants bill themselves as "Indo-Pak restaurants"—there are some differences. Generally, Pakistani cuisine is more meat-heavy and somewhat greasier than Indian

dishes (except for kabobs). Pork and alcohol are forbidden, and most restaurants offer halal/zabiha meat that is slaughtered according to Islamic law. Restaurants owned by Indian Muslims have a similar fare. Typical dishes include *nihari* (a rich spicy meat stew traditionally eaten for breakfast), *chapli kebab* (spicy beef patty), *haleem* (cooked rice and grains that is a favorite during the fasting month Ramadan), *biryani*, many varieties of kabob, and *naan*, *parathas*, and other breads.

The earliest Pakistani restaurants were Tasty Eats on Montrose Avenue and Bundoo Khan on Devon Avenue, which opened in the mid-1980s, both now closed. The late 1970s and early 1980s saw a large influx of Pakistani immigrants who settled on the North Side. Restaurants serving Pakistani/Indian Muslim food on Devon Avenue include Sabri Nihari (winner of a Michelin Bib award in 2015 and 2016), Usmania, Lahore Food & Grill, Khan BBQ, Bismillah, and Ghareeb Newaz (which now has a branch near the UIC campus). Dhabas—small establishments offering a limited menu whose main clients are taxi drivers—include Sheesh Mahal on Maplewood and Tabaq on Clybourn. Like the restaurants, grocery stores also advertise themselves as Indian and Pakistani. Awami Bazaar and Mehrab are two well-known grocery stores on Devon Avenue. Both are also butchers and purveyors of halal/zabiha meat.

Chicago's Bangladeshi community is small—around 4,000 in the Greater Chicago area. In the past ten years, two restaurants opened—Sonargaon on Devon Avenue and Radhuni on Clark Street—but eventually closed.

However, in 2015, Mithai Restoran (now called Haandi) opened on Devon, serving typical Bangladeshi dishes such as rezala and hilsa fish and a selection of the famous Bengali sweets. Several Bangladeshi grocery stores (Fish Corner, Devon Fish House, and Shahjalal Grocery) on Devon Avenue sell imported fish beloved of Bengalis.

Nepalis have opened several restaurants in Chicago and suburbs serving both Indian and Nepali dishes, which tend to be milder than Indian dishes. Distinctive Nepali dishes are *kwati* (a stew made from nine beans), *alu tama bodi* (a stew of beans, potatoes, and sour bamboo shoots), and chicken *chowela* (pieces of boneless chicken marinated in herbs and spices). Cumin on Milwaukee has won a Michelin Bib award.

Contributors: Sharif Islam and Colleen Taylor Sen

See also: Patel Brothers

BIBLIOGRAPHY

Lautman, Victoria. "A Guide to Devon Avenue." *Chicago Magazine*, January 5, 2011.

Sen, Colleen. "Incense and Spice: Traveling to That Exotic Crossroads called Devon Avenue." *Chicago Tribune*, September 9, 1993.

South Water Market (See: Wholesale Markets)

Southeast Asians

While the history of most Southeast Asian immigrants in Chicago is relatively short compared to European immigrants, their culinary mark can be seen around the city with scores of Thai restaurants, an increasing number of Vietnamese restaurants and sandwich shops, and Southeast Asian touches and influences in restaurants at many different dining levels.

The vast geographical area of Southeast Asia is made up of the countries of Burma, Indonesia, Laos, Malaysia, Thailand, Vietnam, Philippines, and more. While some immigrant groups started coming to Chicago in the late 1800s and early 1900s, by far the vast majority came after the historically significant Immigration and Nationality Act of 1965 was passed by Congress during the Johnson Administration. It allowed, for the first time, larger numbers of immigrants from Asia. Malaysians, for example, have been immigrating to Chicago since the 1970s, largely for jobs and to secure educations.

This was coupled with an influx of refugees from the Vietnam War (including Laotians and Cambodians) and the bloody rule of the Khmer Rouge and contributed to a wave of Southeast Asian immigrants to Chicago from the late 1960s through the 1990s. Many Vietnamese, Cambodians, and Laotians settled in Uptown, creating an ethnically distinctive neighborhood referred to as Argyle Street or New Chinatown. While the area has ties to Chicago's Chinatown on the South Side of the city, and has a few Chinese businesses, it is predominantly Southeast Asian. Concentrated around a few blocks are Vietnamese noodle shops and restaurants, bakeries, Chinese BBQ and Southeast Asian markets, and a large beautiful mural depicting and celebrating 100 years of immigrant history in this part of Uptown. Markets include the large and well-stocked Vietnamese market Tai Nam. For more than 30 years, Thai Grocery was a staple market in the Argyle area and was one of the first Southeast Asian–owned businesses in the area. Thailand Food Corp. is a source for many Thai ingredients, wholesale and retail. A variety of small Southeast Asian markets can be found around the city as well.

The Malaysian Americans are comprised of people from a variety of ethnic origins, including Malay, Malaysian-Chinese, and Malaysian-Indian. The cuisine primarily blends the fare of three cultures: Malay, Chinese, and Indian. Malaysia's signature dish is *laksa*, a curry-based noodle dish, for which there are regional variations throughout the country. The Chicago area is home to a small handful of restaurants representing Malaysian cuisine, including Penang Malaysian Cuisine in Arlington Heights and Asian Noodle House in Hoffman Estates.

In the case of Indonesian cuisine, rice is a focus; pork appears rarely because many Indonesians are Muslim. Indonesian dishes often begin with a coconut milk and oil base and may be wrapped in banana or coconut leaves. Indonesian dishes can be found at Rickshaw Republic in Lincoln Park. Laotian food, with its similarities to Thai and Vietnamese food, is even rarer in the area, found in only one restaurant, Spicy Thai Lao in Burbank.

With the ubiquity of Thai restaurants (and their often repetitive menus), eager foodies latched onto an exciting subset of dishes that came to be known through sometimes secret (and now not so secret) Thai language menus. A handful or more restaurants around the city, including Spoon Thai on Western Avenue and TAC Quick Thai on Sheridan Road, are known for having "Thai language menus" that feature especially authentic or hard-to-find Thai dishes. Thai food is regional, and recently Isan dishes from north Thailand, such as distinctive sausages, have become popular. Chicago also is home to Arun's, a fine-dining staple in the local restaurant scene since 1985, and one of the first restaurants to elevate Thai cuisine in the country.

Vietnamese restaurants have gained in popularity in Chicago for the past decade; sandwiches, such as the *banh mi* baguette, have become popular for their exciting blend of flavors and textures, and noodle soups, such as *phô*, became increasingly known and loved. Le Colonial downtown and Pasteur in Uptown were on the early side of a trend toward capitalizing on colonial nostalgia and creating a more upscale dining experience. Now Southeast Asian flavors can be seen on restaurant menus at all levels of dining, from humble storefronts and food trucks selling street food to Michelin 3-star gems.

While the concept of "fusion" food may have run its course in the American restaurant scene, the cuisines of Southeast Asia lend themselves to the sometimes subtle, sometimes assertive blending and borrowing of flavors from various parts of the world. Malaysian food, for example, wouldn't be what it is without the tantalizing combination of Indian, Chinese, and Malay flavors. With the exception of Thailand, all the cuisines of Southeast Asia have been heavily influenced by colonization. A surge in popularity and excitement around restaurants such as Fat Rice in Logan Square (with Macau's mix of Southeast Asian, Chinese, Indian, and Portuguese) reflect that Chicagoans are eager to embrace the mash-up of colonial and traditional Southeast Asian flavors.

Contributors: Jennifer Olvera and Rebecca Wheeler

See also: Arun's; Filipinos

BIBLIOGRAPHY

Education Malaysia Chicago. http://www.emchicago.org/web/.

"Indonesian-American." Every Culture. http://www.everyculture.com/multi/Ha-La/Indonesian-Americans.html#ixzz3PqWzD9U7.

Khim, Borita. "Cambodians." *The Ethnic Handbook: A Guide to the Cultures and Traditions of Chicago's Diverse Communities*. Cynthia Linton, ed. Chicago: Chicago Area Ethnic Resources, 1996.

Spanish

Few Spaniards settled in Chicago through most of the nineteenth to the mid–twentieth centuries, but after changes in immigration laws in 1965 a few thousand settled in the city and suburbs. Some were skilled workers, others academics and business people, and most notably some were restaurateurs. In their Iberian Peninsula homeland, seafood, lamb, excellent breads, olive oil, and wine are all staples. These were brought to Chicago both by immigrants and by Americans' discovery of olive oils and well-priced wines, especially in the 1970s and '80s. No doubt American tourism to Spain led to the development of interest in Spanish food.

Because Spanish restaurant cuisine shares features with Italian and French food, ingredients and techniques were familiar to Chicago diners. While Spanish regional cuisine is varied, a few dishes have become iconic here: *tortilla Española* (an omeletlike cake of eggs, potatoes, and onions); gazpacho (cold tomato soup), *paella de Marisco* (seafood and rice); *jamon Serrano* (cured ham); and chorizo (pork sausage). Olive oils, alioli, *sofritos*, and rice dishes have been on fine-dining menus since the 1920s.

In the early 1930s Chicago, there were Spanish restaurants such as Casa De Alex, 58 E. Delaware Place, but they made no major impact. It wasn't until the 1980s that Spanish cuisine reentered the dining scene. Gabino Sotelino, in partnership with Rich Melman of Lettuce Entertain You restaurants, decided to open an authentic Spanish restaurant, Café Ba-Ba-Reeba!, in 1985. He brought in Chef Emilio Gervilla. Born in Granada, Spain, Gervilla was the first chef to bring tapas and Andalusian cuisine to Chicago. The Café's success inspired Gervilla to open his own tapas place in Hillside, Emilio's Tapas, followed not long after by two more locations, on Ohio Street and on Clark Street. In 1992, another popular tapas restaurant, Café Iberico, opened on LaSalle Street.

By 2016, about a dozen tapas bars were found in Chicago, including Black Bull in Wicker Park, Café Marbella in Jefferson Park, Tapas Valencia in the South Loop, Bulerias Tapas Bar in Lakeview, La Taberna Tapas on Halsted Street, Vera on the Near West Side, Mercat a la Planxa on Michigan Avenue, and Paola's Vinum on Jefferson Street. Solera on West Randolph marries a wine bar concept with an updated Spanish menu of small and large plates. The popularity of small plates in many of Chicago's restaurants today is a result of the tapas phenomenon and, thus, Spanish cuisine.

Contributor: Margaret Laport

See also: Lettuce Entertain You Restaurants; Restaurants and Fine Dining

BIBLIOGRAPHY

Emilio's Tapas. http://www.emiliostapas.com.

"Lettuce Tell You Our History." Lettuce Entertain You. http://www.leye.com.

Speakeasies

By some estimates, speakeasies numbered at least 10,000 and flourished in Chicago during Prohibition. To gain entry to these illegal drinking spots, one had to discreetly say a password or phrase through a peephole in the door. Like snowflakes, no two were exactly alike, except that in every one, alcohol flowed freely.

Speakeasies lurked in the back rooms and basements of legitimate businesses across Chicago. They had hidden doors or soundproof walls and were located down unassuming alleys or in backyards, allowing them to slip under the radar, though police often took bribes in exchange for looking the other way. At big speakeasies downtown, patrons dressed up. The small, neighborhood ones served the crudest booze. Some innocently labeled themselves "soft drink parlors."

The city's underground network of freight and service tunnels facilitated the delivery of alcohol to speakeasies. Despite their illicit nature and association with gangs that supplied the booze, speakeasies were mostly decent places that welcomed women and men, a change from the pre-Prohibition all-male tradition. Belligerent behavior was not tolerated. The more exclusive ones offered music or other live entertainment and, sometimes, good food.

This was the era of the cocktail—bootlegged liquor on its own tasted pretty awful. Gin drinks were popular, thanks to the generous supply of "bathtub gin." Cocktails born from behind the speakeasy bar include the French 75, made with gin, lemon juice, simple syrup, and Champagne; the Mary Pickford, named after the silent movie star, and starring rum, pineapple juice, and grenadine; the Bacardi Cocktail, with white Bacardi rum, lime juice, and grenadine, and the Sidecar, with Cognac, Cointreau, and lemon juice. Other cocktails poured before Prohibition but popularized in the 1920s (and enjoying a comeback in recent years) included the Old-Fashioned and the Tom Collins.

When Prohibition repeal came on December 5, 1933, people packed the bars to celebrate, though it was by most accounts a more subdued occasion than the evening

before Prohibition took effect 13 years earlier, when drinking was a race against the clock. Speakeasies that had not already gone out of business did not last much longer in the Depression, but others survived and got their liquor licenses.

Some of the city's most storied speakeasies exist today as bars and restaurants. These include the Green Mill Cocktail Lounge, 4802 N. Broadway; Green Door Tavern, 678 N. Orleans; The Hideout, 1354 W. Wabansia; Schaller's Pump, 3714 S. Halsted, and Twin Anchors, 1655 N. Sedgwick.

Contributor: Janet Fuller

See also: Private Clubs and Restaurants; Prohibition

BIBLIOGRAPHY

Bentley, Chris. "A Shot of History: Ingredients of the Chicago Speakeasy." WBEZ.org, August 7, 2014. http://www.wbez.org/series/curious-city/shot-history-ingredients-chicago-speakeasy-110616.

Coughlin, Francis. "Speakeasy and Carry a Big Character Reference." *Chicago Tribune*, December 4, 1966.

Sawyers, June Skinner. *Chicago Sketches: Urban Tales, Stories and Legends from Chicago History*. Chicago: Wild Onion Books, 1995.

Specialty Stores

During the early 1800s, Chicagoans had to visit multiple food stores on a daily basis to feed their families. In the absence of refrigeration, perishables were purchased practically daily from independent retailers across the city. In 1839, the city's first public market was constructed by Joseph Blanchard on State Street between Lake and Randolph. Retailers of meat, produce, and other grocery items rented out stalls to sell directly to the public in a centralized location. This concept received a warm reception from Chicagoans, and two additional markets were built in the 1840s: one on Market Street and the other on State Street, in what eventually became known as the Market Building. They were not to last, as the wholesale food markets shifted to Water St. (now Wacker Drive) and, in the 1920s, the South Water St. area and a smaller one on Randolph St.

One of the most prominent specialty stores at the turn of the century was Stop & Shop, originally founded in 1872 as Tebbetts and Garland and located on 18th and Wabash.

Around 1916, it was purchased by an Iowan furniture store owner, Aaron Younker, who changed the name to Stop & Shop. It changed hands again in 1925, landing at its ultimate location at 16 W. Washington. Stop & Shop was a unique store at the time, catering to Chicago's upper

Exterior of a Stop & Shop grocery store, ca. 1960. Courtesy of the Chicago History Museum, ICHi-69984; Glenn E. Dahlby.

class by selling difficult to obtain specialty items that could not be found elsewhere. Hillman's, owned by the same people, was more of a conventional operation and was located in the basement of the same building. Both closed in the 1970s, much to the disappointment of many Chicagoans who favored this local treasure.

Over the 1900s, the number of independent food stores declined rapidly. By 1987, there were only 3,638 retailers within the city versus 17,000 in 1933. Large superstores, with footprints up to 100,000 square feet, resulted in lower costs that were passed on to shoppers. Smaller retailers could no longer compete, ending in consolidation and bankruptcy for many.

However, some smaller, more specialty-type markets were established in the Chicago area in the mid-1900s and continue to operate in and around the city. For example, Treasure Island, opened by Christ Kamberos and his brother Frank in 1963, was modeled after the European shopping experience. It was deemed by the famous chef Julia Child as "the most European supermarket in America." Originally located at 3460 N. Broadway, the chain has grown to seven stores across Chicagoland offering upscale cheeses, meats, produce, and grocery staples from domestic and European manufacturers.

Foodstuffs is another specialty market with a European feel, selling fine chocolates, breads and pastries, and unique culinary ingredients, in addition to a large and diverse array of prepared foods. The store originated in Glencoe, a northern suburb of Chicago, in 1979 by Carole Segal, cofounder of Crate and Barrel (with her husband, Gordon Segal). In 2014, Foodstuffs had a total of four independent gourmet stores in the suburbs.

After decades of consolidation and centralization in the grocery business, there has been a recent resurgence in specialty retail markets that focus on high-end, ready-to-eat, or locally produced goods. In fact, specialty food stores have been one of the fastest growing industries across the United States, and the only grocery sector showing significant growth in the Chicago market in recent years. Such stores appeal to people who value quality, freshness, and a more intimate shopping experience.

Fox & Obel, one of the first of its kind in the high-end, gourmet food markets, opened its doors in the River East area of Chicago in 2001, the creation of Ari Fox, Ken Obel, and Gary and Meme Hopmayer. Fox & Obel featured locally grown organic produce, fresh seafood, artisan breads and pastries, fine cheeses, and regionally famous food-to-go, plus an attached café that was *Zagat*-rated. The prices matched the upscale feel of the products and modern interior. However, this did not deter a very loyal customer base who would visit the store regularly.

Unfortunately, the store filed for bankruptcy and closed its doors in 2013 amid controversy related to the private equity investors who were involved with the business.

Since Fox & Obel, a bevy of other high-end food stores have quickly infiltrated the well-off neighborhoods of Chicago. In 2004, Debbie Sharpe opened the Goddess and Grocer on Damen Avenue in Wicker Park. Sharpe, a former caterer to rock and royalty, like Madonna and The Rolling Stones, has grown the business into four locations featuring a deli and a selection of upscale grocery items, including cookies, desserts, pastas, sauces, dressings, and wine and beer.

Plum Market opened in 2013 in Old Town, featuring locally made products, as well as an array of natural, organic, and specialty products. Started by Matthew and Marc Jonna in Michigan, the store aims to provide customers with a unique shopping experience. Similarly, Mrs. Green's Natural Market opened in Lincoln Park in the fall of 2013. Mrs. Green's appealed to shoppers who value sustainable and environmentally friendly foods, but business was slow and it closed in 2016. Olivia's Market on Wabansia in Bucktown (opened in 2004) is a small neighborhood store that specializes in local fresh produce, fancy charcuterie and cheese, and flowers.

Other retail stores specializing in a limited number of offerings have seen mixed success. For example, Pastoral Artisan Cheese is a European-inspired specialty store stocking high-quality domestic and international cheeses, freshly baked breads, and small production wines and handcrafted beers. Since the first store opened in the East Lakeview neighborhood in 2004, two other locations have opened in other parts of the city, as well as a bistro attached to their flagship Lakeview store. Argo Tea, founded in the Lincoln Park area, is another success story, expanding to over 25 locations across the U.S.

Contributor: Tia M. Rains

See also: Supermarkets and Grocery Stores

BIBLIOGRAPHY

Gilmore, Paul. Grocery Stores and Supermarkets. http://www.encyclopedia.chicagohistory.org/pages/554.html.

http://www.goddessandgrocer.com/our_story.php.

Telfer, Tori. "Inside Chicago's Speciality Store Boom." http://chicago.racked.com/archives/2014/01/29/contributor-tori-telfer-xx-2013.php.

The Spice House

The Spice House is a specialty spice shop with five locations: two in Milwaukee, Wisconsin, and three in Illinois: Chicago, at 1512 North Wells (opened 2000), Evanston,

The Spice House sells single spices and over 300 blends. Courtesy of The Spice House.

and Geneva. The business was started by Bill and Ruth Penzey in Milwaukee in 1957. In 1991, they sold it to their daughter and son-in-law Patty and Tom Erd. Penzey's Spices, owned by Patty Erd's brother, is a national retailer of spices with a store in the Chicago suburb of Naperville.

The Spice House sells single spices and over 300 blends, including a series based on Chicago's ethnic neighborhoods, featuring Back of the Yards garlic pepper (their best-selling blend), Argyle Street Asian Blend, Chicago Deep Dish Pizza Pizzazz, Greektown "Billy Goat" Seasoning, and Pullman Pork Chop Seasoning.

Tools of their trade include large stainless steel scoops, mixing bowls, sifting screens with different mesh sizes, some old-style stone and shearing mills, and most important, their human senses. They grind and mix what they anticipate selling every week, so that the products are very fresh. For example, to make curry powder, each store grinds its own ingredient separately and then they mix them all in a large stainless steel bowl. They sift the blend three times and hand-mix it 1,500 times to ensure full flavor development. Spice House also has a national catalogue and an online business. Customers include home cooks and the city's leading chefs.

Contributor: Colleen Sen

See also: Flavorings

BIBLIOGRAPHY

Dedmun, Amy Dewall. "Curry Comes in Many Flavors." *Journal Sentinel*, March 17, 2015.

Yates, Victoria. "History Adds Spice to Life at the Spice House." *Medill Reports Chicago*, March 14, 2012.

Spirits and Distilleries

Long before Prohibition began in 1920, Illinois was a hotbed of distillery activity—not surprising, given its close proximity to midwestern grain fields barley, rye, and corn—and waterways. Early Chicago was a whiskey town as befitted some of its Scotch-Irish settlers and the 1840 Irish immigrants. Kentucky was close enough to supply bourbon. Samuel Miller and Archibald Clybourne established the Miller House in 1831, a store that also was one of the city's three earliest taverns. By 1860, there were eight distilleries in Chicago, but the city was soon overtaken by whiskey-dense Peoria (which had 73 distilleries pre-Prohibition). Still, Chicago paid the second-highest U.S. whiskey tax in the country.

The city continued to see an explosion of businesses selling alcoholic beverages until Prohibition pushed the trade underground. Political fortunes were made and broken by Prohibition. In the late 1870s, Mayor Joseph Medill dealt with the powerful German saloon keepers, who favored only candidates supporting their livelihoods. In the first decade of the twentieth century, Mayor Edward F. Dunne had to contend with the strong Sunday Closing League, intent on closing bars and taverns one day a week to foster temperance. During Prohibition, Mayor Big Bill Thompson beat his opponent the reform Mayor William Dever in 1927 because of his opposition to the 18th Amendment. In truth, Prohibition was scorned and evaded in Chicago.

After Prohibition began, all the distilleries were shut down. When it was ended in 1933, Chicago's distilleries did not spring back into action. In fact, some of Chicago's neighborhoods and many of the neighboring towns—including Wilmette, Oak Park, and Evanston, the latter once home to Frances E. Willard and the Women's Christian Temperance Union—remained dry until the 1970s.

In the early part of the twenty-first century, the craft cocktail movement took off, and with it, the demand for locally crafted spirits. In 2004, husband and wife team Sonja and Derek Kassebaum opened North Shore Distillery, Chicagoland's first post-Prohibition craft distillery in suburban Lake Bluff. They now produce vodka, gin, aquavit, and absinthe, all extracted from midwestern grains.

When Koval Distillery opened its doors in 2008, it was the first distillery started within the Chicago city limits since the mid-1800s. Robert and Sonat Birnecker distill their whiskeys, gin, vodka, and brandies solely from organic grains; all are made on site in their custom-built 5,000-liter copper still made by German still-maker Kothe.

Next came the DiPrizio family's Chicago Distilling Co. on Milwaukee Avenue (2010), followed by Paul Hletko's

FEW Spirits in Evanston (2011), named in honor—or perhaps gentle mockery—of Frances E. Willard herself.

Letherbee Distillers was launched in 2012 by bartender Brenton Engel, who favored an artisan distillery dedicated to craft botanical spirits such as gin, fernet, absinthe, and the wormwood-based Bësk.

The latest additions to Chicago's burgeoning craft distillery movement are CH Distillery, founded by Termain Atkinson and Mark Lucas, and Rhine Hall, a handcrafted brandy distillery fueled by the obsession of father-daughter team Charlie and Jenny Solberg, who use locally sourced produce to create their old-country–style fruit brandies. More are sure to follow.

Contributor: Julie Chernoff

See also: Bars, Taverns, Saloons, Pubs; Prohibition

BIBLIOGRAPHY

Bohlmann, Rachel E. "Prohibition and Temperance." *Encyclopedia of Chicago.* http://www.encyclopedia.chicagohistory.org/pages/1238.html.

Thiel, Julia. "Distilleries Are on the Rise in Chicago, but Will the City Soon Reach Its Saturation Point?" *Chicago Reader.* http://www.chicagoreader.com/chicago/distilleries-new-koval-letherbee-malort-ch-quincy-street/Content?oid=12786430.

Steak and Chop Houses

Chicago's storied steakhouses are a testament to its past dominance in the cattle shipping and meat processing industries, which lasted from the Civil War to the 1920s.

Although Chicago stood as the headquarters of the meatpacking industry at that time, the chophouse and steakhouse concepts predate the Union Stock Yards, which opened in 1865. They can be traced back to London in the 1690s, when restaurants first served portioned meat called "chops." Steakhouses—which served "beefsteak" in dining hall-like settings—made their way to the United States, specifically New York, during the second half of the nineteenth century.

By the time Carl Sandburg dubbed Chicago the "hog butcher for the world," the Union Stock Yards were already in full swing. Meatpacking plants were slaughtering pigs and cows for human consumption at a frenzied pace, and major companies—including Nelson Morris, Armour, and Swift—opened plants in Chicago.

Naturally, some of that meat made its way into Chicago restaurants, such as the iconic, erstwhile Stock Yard Inn, a Tudor-style hotel built in 1912 at Halsted and 42nd Streets. It featured several restaurants, including the Sirloin Room, where diners could select their own steaks. The meat was then branded with a hot iron. Choosing your own steak tableside remains a tradition that lives on

today at Gibson's Steakhouse on Rush Street, the Morton's chain, and others.

The city's oldest surviving steakhouse, Gene & Georgetti's, located on Franklin Street in River North and with a branch in Rosemont, is a family-run business that opened in 1941. Owner Tony Durpetti married into the family, and today he continues to uphold the tradition, serving steak from its original supplier and hand-cutting meat on site, all in a building that dates back to 1872. The meat is not seasoned, it is simply seared in a very hot gas oven. While diners wait to indulge, they do so amid a pictorial history of Chicago via the muraled wall that adorns the main dining room.

Barney's Market Club on West Randolph, which was opened in 1919 by Barney Kessel and closed in 1991, was known as a politician's hangout, where staffers responded to everyone, "Yes Sir, Senator!" Later came stalwarts such as That Steak Joynt, Chicago Chop House, Lawry's The Prime Rib, and Morton's The Steakhouse. Now a chain of 70-some restaurants, Morton's was founded by Arnie Morton and Klaus Fritsch, who met while working at the Playboy Club. The original, grotto-like location still stands at 1050 N. State St., at the corner of Rush Street.

In the twenty-first century, steakhouses abound, from the humble (think old-timer Golden Steer in Forest Park) to glossy and glam Chicago establishments, such as Primehouse, RPM Steak, Mastro's, Swift & Sons, GT Prime, and the celebrity-frequented Chicago Cut, with its on-site aging room, reinterpreted steakhouse menu, and accoutrements that range from foie gras to truffle salt and blue cheese fondue. As is the case with most steakhouses in Chicago and beyond, carved prime rib is a prominent feature.

Contributor: Jennifer Olvera

See also: Meat and Poultry; The Stockyard Inn; Union Stockyards

BIBLIOGRAPHY

"The Birth of the Chicago Union Stock Yards." Chicago Historical Society. http://www.chicagohs.org/history/stock.html.

Reichl, Ruth. "For Red Meat and a Sense of History." *New York Times,* January 21, 1994.

Stegner, Sarah

One of the city's top chefs and a two-time James Beard Award winner (Rising Star of the Year in 2004, Best Midwest Chef in 1998), Sarah Stegner's cooking combines French sophistication and technique with fresh Midwest products. Born in Evanston in 1974, she studied at the Dumas Pere Cooking school in Glencoe. In 1984, she was hired as an intern in the Ritz-Carlton Hotel Chicago, where she worked under executive chefs Fernand Gutierrez and George Bumbaris. In 1990, she became the chef of the hotel's Dining Room restaurant, which won many awards, including Second Best Hotel Dining Room in the World by *Conde Nast Traveler* and 4-star ratings by the *Chicago Tribune* and *Chicago Magazine*.

Stegner's love of local ingredients led her to become a founder and board member of Chicago's Green City Market in 1999. In 2004, she and Bumbaris opened Prairie Grass Café in Northbrook. Stegner described their goal: "to bring the culinary technique that we mastered in the world of fine dining to the more accessible level of casual dining." A signature winter dish is shepherd's pie made with grass-fed beef and Swiss chard and topped with Yukon Gold potatoes, butternut squash, and parsnip puree. In 2009, Stegner and Bumbaris opened a second restaurant, Prairie Fire, in Chicago; it closed in 2011.

Contributor: Colleen Sen

See also: Chefs; Restaurants and Fine Dining

BIBLIOGRAPHY

Jarvi, Jake and Eliza, "SR Dinner Date: Prairie Grass Café," *Sheridan Road*, Vol. 6, Issue 8.

"Sarah Stegner," www.prairiegrasscafe.com/sarah-stegner.

The Stock Yard Inn

The massive Union Stock Yards on Chicago's Southwest Side closed in 1971, but Chicago's reputation as a "meat and potatoes" town lingers on. In its heyday, the stockyards processed more than 80 percent of the nation's meat, fueling the development of the "steakhouse" as a popular restaurant format. There were a lot of good steakhouses, but none captured the meat culture better than the restaurants in the Stock Yard Inn.

Located at 42nd and Halsted, the large Tudor-style hotel opened in 1912. At its busiest, the hotel was home to a trio of restaurants, all offering meat-centered menus. Diners in the Sirloin Room were able to pick their own steaks, branding them with their initials to eliminate mix-ups once they were cooked. The decor in the Matador Room focused on bullfighting, while the Saddle and Sirloin Club showcased agricultural icons. The meat was prime, the servings substantial. Options ran the gamut from a half-pound burger with grilled onions and Cheddar fries ($20) to Chateaubriand for two ($90).

With the closing of the Union Stock Yards, the inn's customer base dwindled. Dinner was served for the last time on November 15, 1976, and the building was demolished the following January.

Contributor: Barbara Revsine

See also: Restaurants and Fine Dining, Steak and Chop Houses; Union Stock Yards

BIBLIOGRAPHY

Vettel, Phil. "That Steak Mystique." *Chicago Tribune*, October 6, 1991.

Sunbeam Corporation

One of the most recognizable household brands in the nation began in 1897 with the founding of the Stewart-Warner Corporation in Chicago by John K. Stewart and Thomas Jefferson Clark. They incorporated as Chicago Flexible Shaft Company, making commercial animal clippers and shearing equipment. As a sideline, in 1910 they introduced the first electric iron, named Sunbeam in a customer contest.

The name became popular after the firm introduced the Mixmaster electric mixer in 1931 under the Sunbeam brand. More than 60,000 units were sold that first year; by 1936, more than a dozen attachments had been added and production was up to 300,000 units annually. A freestanding electric juicer was introduced in 1932, and a seven-cup electric coffee maker came out two years later.

The company incorporated as Sunbeam Corporation in 1946 and continued to thrive and introduce new inventions for the home, including the first pop-up toaster and electric fry pan.

In 1980, the Oster Company was acquired by Sunbeam, and Sunbeam-Oster Company Inc. was formed, combining Sunbeam's products with the famous Osterizer blender, vaporizers, and hair dryers.

Sunbeam had sales of more than one billion dollars and was the best-known brand of small electrical appliances in the country when they were bought by Allegheny International, Inc., in 1981. A series of mergers, buyouts, and moves followed, and most of the Chicago-area factories were closed and the headquarters moved out of the area.

Contributor: Judith Dunbar Hines

See also: Equipment, Home

BIBLIOGRAPHY

Achilles, Rolf. *Made in Illinois: A Story of Illinois Manufacturing.* Oak Brook: Illinois Manufacturers' Association, 1993.

"History of Sunbeam-Oster Co. Inc." Funding Universe. http://www.fundinguniverse.com/company-histories/sunbeam-oster-co-inc-history/.

Supermarkets and Grocery Stores

Early Chicago groceries were available only through general stores, where shoppers could find imported coffee,

Before self-service supermarkets, each grocery item was taken from a shelf and handed to customers. Courtesy of the Rogers Park / West Ridge Historical Society.

tea, sugar, dried fruit, and spices next to the tools and fabrics. The Miller House was an early dry goods store that also was the city's first tavern, located at Wolf Point. Fresh ingredients came from what Chicagoans could grow themselves or purchase from the few public markets that, starting in 1839, sold produce, dairy foods, meat, and poultry. But as the city boundaries stretched further from the town center and the public markets, small retail markets sprang up in the neighborhoods.

By the late 1800s, the city's food retailing landscape was peppered with corner grocery stores, often run by families and often reflecting the needs of their neighborhoods, from the foods they offered to the services they provided and the gathering places they nurtured. Many were opened by immigrants and catered to their immigrant customers. Shop assistants collected products for customers, and many stores offered home delivery via bicycle. Adding to the mix were specialty stores, such as butchers and bakers. As the street railways reached the suburbs, independent groceries sprang up there.

A growing number of chain stores began appearing in the early 1900s, from Chicago-based National Tea Co., Jewel Tea Co., and Dominick's to retailers from other states, including A&P and Piggly Wiggly, which introduced the self-service concept.

Supermarkets firmly planted themselves in Chicago in the 1940s. By the 1950s and 1960s, they blossomed into supersized stores worthy of their name, each with its own personality. Much more than self-service operations, supermarkets offered shoppers a vast array of foods, plus in-house butchers and bakers and fresh produce, as well as extended hours, all under one roof. Dawson's Trading Post, a behemoth created by a New Jersey retailer at 8200 S. Chicago Ave., touted (though shouted is more appropriate, judging by superlatives and exclamation points) in a 1934 *Chicago Daily Tribune* advertisement: "Open Every Night Until 9 p.m."

Several factors fed into the rapid growth of supermarkets in the 1950s and 1960s in Chicago and its suburbs: advances in home refrigeration and freezing (daily shopping was no longer a necessity), a proliferation of automobiles (large parking lots were a draw for customers), shopping carts, branded products, and the city's location at the center of the nation's railroads.

The supermarket became an icon of American life after World War II. As the number of supermarkets grew, so did the variety. There were stores with local roots, family-owned operations, and co-ops. Groups such as Chicago-based Independent Grocers Alliance (IGA) (1926) and Joliet-based Centrella Grocers (1917) helped improve the buying power of smaller independent grocers as more and more supermarkets based beyond the Chicago area entered the market.

Dozens of today's supermarkets began as family-run operations. Prisco's Family Market (1927) in Aurora is a part of the community's history. It created a cookbook with full vintage photos, *Prisco's Family & Friends' Cookbook*. Sunset Foods (est. 1937) was opened in Highland Park by John J. Cortesi and his uncle, Adeodata Fontana. By 1954, a second store opened on Green Bay Road. The Sunset staff would take care of the checkout and deliver items to the shopper's car. Sunset now has supermarkets in Northbrook, Lake Forest, Libertyville, and Long Grove.

Exterior of a modern Jewel Foods supermarket. Photograph by Colleen Sen.

Brothers Herb, Dave, and Mel Potash as well as their father, Max, and their sister, Marian, first opened Pleezing Foods at Clark and Schiller Streets on the city's North Side (1950). Then came a second store, Potash (1525 N. Clark St.) and, in 1962, Potash Bros. Food and Liquor (875 N. State St.). Treasure Island Foods chain (est. 1963), now with seven stores, was started by the Kamberos family as a European-style supermarket. County Fair Foods (1964) was opened by Bill and Joan Baffes and is now headed by their son, Tom, in the Beverly/Morgan Park neighborhood at 10800 S. Western Ave. Butera Market (1968) was a family-owned business with 11 supermarkets and originally known as Butera Finer Foods, now headquartered in Elgin. Pete's Fresh Market (1970) began as a produce stand on Chicago's South Side and has grown into a full-service, family-owned group of 12 supermarkets, with more in the works. Catering to the large Hispanic population is Carnicerias Jimenez (1975) with 8 locations in Chicago and 2 in the suburbs. And there's Tony's Finer Foods (1979), which opened with one store on Fullerton Avenue and now has 13 supermarkets in the family-owned business.

While many supermarkets have served the Chicago area for decades, evolution continues to change the food retailing landscape. Sometimes supermarkets leave and don't return. National Tea closed in 1997. A&P is gone. And longtime city favorites, Stop & Shop and Hillman's, grocers established in 1925 and 1927, respectively, no longer exist. Kroger's has come and gone. Sometimes chains leave and their abandoned stores are taken over by regional firms, as in the case of Piggly Wiggly and Eagle Foods.

Other food retailers have grown or moved into the market, especially since the demise of Dominick's in 2013: Whole Foods (1993), Meijer (2011), Woodman's (2010), Heinen's (2012), Plum Market (2013), Trader Joe's (2000), Aldi (1979), and Mariano's (2011).

In recent years, hypermarkets selling groceries also have arrived, such as Walmart and Target, as well as membership clubs Costco and Sam's Club. According to the industry's Food Marketing Institute, in 2013, the median supermarket size was 46,500 square feet and the average number of items carried was 43,844. That is a far cry from a typical Chicago corner store in the 1920s.

....

Contributor: Judy Hevrdejs

See also: Dominick's Finer Foods; Jewel-Osco; Mexicans; Specialty Stores; Treasure Island Foods

BIBLIOGRAPHY

Deutsch, Tracey. *Building a Housewife's Paradise: Gender, Politics, and American Grocery Stores in the 20th Century.* Chapel Hill: University of North Carolina Press, 2012.

Heller, Laura. "Supermarket Spring Has Finally Come to Chicago." *Forbes*, May 1, 2014.

Millman, Nancy, Phuong Le. "No Upsets by Upstarts in Supermarket Wars." *Chicago Tribune*, April 9, 1998.

Supper Clubs and Roadhouses

The supper club most often is associated with Wisconsin and Minnesota, but from the 1930s through the 1970s, the supper club scene in Chicago included destinations such as Chez Paree, 610 N. Fairbanks; Club DeLisa, 5521 S. State St.; and Bisaetti's, 1625 W. Irving Park. Hugh Hefner also used elements of a supper club to create his Playboy Clubs.

The supper club is a place of escape. Standard characteristics include a relish tray, linen napkins, a Friday night fish-fry, and prime rib on Saturday. Live entertainment was a key component of the midcentury supper club, which accounted for its presence in Chicago. People made a commitment to spend several hours at a supper club. This contributed to its "clubby" atmosphere: arrive around 4 p.m. for a couple of cocktails, adjourn to "supper" (a rural term), then return to a lounge or separate entertainment area for more drinks and live music. Tougher DUI laws and higher costs for live entertainment doomed many supper clubs.

The South Side of Chicago would never be confused with the north woods, but Club DeLisa (1937–58) had all the trappings of a supper club, inviting people to dine and dance, gamble in the basement, and get their photos taken by roving photographers. The dimly lit, surreptitious atmosphere was popular with the African American gay community. Sonny Blount (who later became legendary jazz bandleader Sun Ra) was in the house band during the mid-1940s (and liked to eat purple food because he believed it made people healthier).

Keyboardist Lonnie Simmons held court for many years at Biasetti's (1942–2005). Although it was called a steakhouse, it was actually a supper club with its dark-at-any-time-of-the-day lighting and football helmets hanging above the bar. Simmons was featured in *Jet* magazine turning out the lights on the last night of the Club DeLisa.

The Chez Paree was a big deal, with a bar called "The Tropical Circle" and a separate entertainment room that featured headliners such as Sammy Davis Jr. and Louis Prima. The Chez Paree debuted in 1932 on the Near North Side of Chicago and shut down in 1960. In keeping with the clandestine and dark trappings of a supper club, Chez Paree was popular with Chicago mobsters.

Mobsters also preferred roadhouses in secluded areas away from the city. Roadhouses are like supper clubs with less food and more "action" and alcohol.

FitzGerald's is one of the best known music clubs in America, but the building goes back to the early 1900s. It was a roadhouse on West Roosevelt Road in Berwyn, which lined up against the border of Al Capone's

Cicero. The wood frame building—which looks just like a house—became The Hunt Club and in the 1960s was known as the Deer Lodge. It promoted "Air Conditioning" and "Dancing Nightly," while business cards promised it was a destination "Where a Doe Can Make a Buck."

Capone's Hideaway was a roadhouse restaurant nestled along the Fox River outside of west suburban St. Charles. It closed in 2012 after a 38-year run. It was born in the 1920s as Reitmayer's Resort, a getaway summer destination for Capone and his posse. The joint offered homebrewed beer laced with bathtub gin. Because it served alcohol during Prohibition, it was not a roadhouse or a supper club—it was a speakeasy.

An Illinois footnote to the midcentury roadhouse and supper club scene includes the dozens of "lake clubs" popular around Lake Springfield in central Illinois. The most popular spot was simply called the "Lake Club," which opened around 1940 and ran until 1968. Entertainers such as Cab Calloway, Bob Hope, and Chico Marx headlined the club because it was a stopping point between appearances in St. Louis and Chicago. The club had a dining room, a dance floor, a back room with craps and slots and a cop working the front door. The Lake Club was co-owned by a former prize fighter nicknamed "Rocky," who helped create the big, proprietary personality often associated with supper clubs.

Contributor: Dave Hoekstra
See also: Gangsters; Playboy Club

Workers dressing beef at the Swift plant, 1890s. Library of Congress.

A MODEL OF MODERNISM

Gustavus Swift established separate plants for each element of the company, from lard and oleomargarine manufacture to marketing. Each division reported to a central office whose watchword was "efficiency." Swift's organization was the model of the modern factory system, something Henry Ford observed when visiting Chicago's meat plants. Ford took the idea of moving belts and specialized disassembly stations and then applied it to his new automobile assembly line in Michigan.

—BRUCE KRAIG

BIBLIOGRAPHY

Hoekstra, Dave. *The Supper Club Book: A Celebration of a Midwest Tradition*. Chicago: Chicago Review Press, 2013.

Swift & Company

Gustavus Franklin Swift (1839–1903) founded one of America's largest and best-known meat and general food processing companies. Swift perfected refrigerated food transportation, but his greatest importance was in his organizational concepts and methods: Swift was a father of America's modern food processing and distribution systems.

Swift was born and reared in Cape Cod, Massachusetts, and, with little schooling or opportunities available, he went to work as a butcher's apprentice at age 14. Dogged in everything, he built a successful wholesale business with James A. Hathaway. Always frugal, he learned how to manage resources, thus preparing himself for his role as America's "dressed beef king."

Seeking business opportunities, Swift moved to Buffalo and finally to Chicago in 1875 because the city had become the meat-processing center of the nation. Americans wanted fresh meat, and Swift gave it to them at reasonable costs. Since only 60 percent of a slaughtered animal would become food, why not process meat in Chicago and ship only the high-profit carcasses? The remaining animal parts could be made into products to be sold by his company. His famous phrase was "now we used all of the hog except his grunt."

To use his facilities efficiently, meat shipped in warm seasons required stable temperatures. Refrigeration systems had been introduced to market facilities and unsuccessfully tried on railcars by Chicago packer G. H. Hammond in 1874. Swift asked his engineer friend,

Andrew J. Chase, to build a refrigerated system using ice blocks set on top of the car. It was a success: Swift & Company undersold everyone, made huge profits, and became the country's leading meat producer in the 1880s.

Swift's innovations were part of new methods of mass production that established modern American food systems. Swift developed an efficient multidecked disassembly line at his Chicago plant for food animals. Carcasses were attached to overhead traveling belts to individual stations, each station doing one task alone. At the end of the line, carcasses were loaded into the waiting boxcars for transportation. The company was adept at creating new markets outside of Chicago for new cuts of meat ready for shipping in refrigerated cars.

Like the friendly Chicago rival Armour & Company, Swift produced branded meats—Swift Premium—chickens, eggs, butter, shortening, margarine, various soaps, shoe polish, and violin strings among others. Its Silver Leaf lard was the leading national brand before lard fell out of culinary fashion in the 1970s. Long a major advertiser in print media, Swift & Company was a pioneer in television advertising, sponsoring the *Swift Show* in 1948. Swift ended Chicago production in the mid-1950s. The company was sold to Con Agra in 1987 and headquarters moved to Greeley, Colorado. Today, Swift is a wholly owned subsidiary of a Brazilian food company, JBS S.A.

Contributor: Bruce Kraig

See also: Armour & Company; Union Stock Yards

BIBLIOGRAPHY

Swift, Louis F., in collaboration with Arthur Van Vlissingen Jr. *The Yankee of the Yards, the Biography of Gustavus Franklin Swift.* Chicago: A. W. Shaw and Co., 1927.

Wade, Louise Carroll. *Chicago's Pride. The Stockyards, Town and Environs in the Nineteenth Century.* Urbana: University of Illinois Press, 1987.

Szathmary, Louis

As chef/owner of one of Chicago's most acclaimed restaurants, The Bakery, Louis Szathmary (1919–96) helped shine the nation's culinary spotlight on Chicago. Szathmary influenced American fine-dining standards, became one of the first U.S. "celebrity chefs," established one of the premier culinary archives in the United States, and was a pioneer in frozen food technology.

Born in Hungary, Szathmary earned a master's degree in journalism and a doctorate in psychology from the University of Budapest and then was drafted into the Hungarian Army during World War II. Szathmary immigrated to

Louis Szathmary was the chef/owner of one of Chicago's most celebrated restaurants, The Bakery. Photograph by Skrebneski.

the United States in 1951 and took a job as a short-order cook, but was soon catering to the rich and famous on the East Coast. In 1959, Szathmary moved to Chicago to work for Armour & Company, where he developed a number of frozen food lines.

Szathmary began to see his real niche as a restaurateur. In 1963, with his wife and partner, Sadako Tanino, Szathmary opened The Bakery Restaurant in an aging building on the Near North Side of Chicago. The food was Continental; a signature dish was beef Wellington with Cumberland sauce.

Szathmary wrote seven cookbooks and kept 31 apartment rooms upstairs from the Bakery filled with his historical and eclectic collection of food books. When he retired in 1989, Szathmary donated 30,000 of the books and materials to establish the Culinary Archives and Museum at Johnson and Wales University in Providence, Rhode Island. The museum is referred to as the "Smithsonian" of food archives.

Contributor: Scott Warner

See also: The Bakery Restaurant; Chefs; Restaurants and Fine Dining

BIBLIOGRAPHY

Rice, William. "Louis Szathmary, Noted Chef, Ex-restaurant Owner." *Chicago Tribune*, October 05, 1996.

Warner, Scott. "Remembering Chef Louis." *Chicago Sun-Times*, October 11, 1997.

Tailgating

Tailgating involves setting up a picnic on a car's tailgate (especially a station wagon) and traditionally occurs before a sporting event to fuel the participants before, and sometimes after, the game. It usually takes place in a parking lot adjacent to the game location.

If one defines tailgating more generally as eating before/while watching a contest, some trace the practice back to Manassas, Virginia, to the Battle of Bull Run in 1861, the first major battle of the Civil War. Supporters of the Union army headed to the front in carriages filled only with picnic baskets to watch what was expected to be a rapid defeat of the Confederates. As the battle turned into a bloody southern victory, horrified spectators fled back to Washington, D.C. Other tailgating roots include the inaugural intercollegiate football game between Princeton and Rutgers in 1869, thought to be the first evidence of fans wearing team colors, in this case red scarves converted to turbans—a custom seen today in the plethora of team paraphernalia. But it was in the 1960s that tailgating as we know it, according to some experts, was invented by fans from Georgia heading to games at Florida State University in Tallahassee, which was located near no bars. BYO was necessary.

Tailgating at a local high school or university sporting event is usually fairly straightforward; one just needs to bring food to designated parking lots in time for a favorable location. The Chicago Fire soccer games provide popular tailgating opportunities with just a few rules and reminders. It takes more than 400 words, however, to list the rules for tailgating at Soldier Field for a Chicago Bears football game. These rules include which parking lots are open and when (tailgating is not allowed during the game itself), the need to buy both game tickets and parking lot tickets, size of space allowed, rules on alcoholic beverages (just in the parking lot), the ban on open fires and deep fryers, and so forth. Of course, one has to buy a game ticket and a parking space. Tickets can range from $100 to $500 or more, plus $18 and up for parking.

Even the simplest tailgate party takes planning. Weather and food require gear. From umbrellas and blankets to the simplest small disposable pop-up grill or a massive party-friendly grill on a trailer hitch, everything must be brought to the location. Typical foods are meats such as hamburgers, hot dogs, bratwurst, and steaks accompanied by roasted corn, potato salad, chips, and, if tailgaters nod toward health, green salads.

For the truly adventurous, such delights as Krispy Kreme donuts thrown on the grill, football-shaped meatloaf, stadium-shaped cakes, and Bloody Marys garnished with whole cheeseburgers have been reported. Trucks tricked out with complete bars and hearses retrofitted for Bears fans enliven the rows of SUVs.

Tailgating etiquette is important. One must be prepared to share food, not only with a neighboring party, but most importantly, with security guards and police. Cooperation is the word of the afternoon.

The family picnic on the tailgate of the station wagon in the definition above has largely given way to SUVs and trucks with ample room for elaborate buffets. Tailgating at Chicago professional sporting events now reaches new levels with organizations such as Corporate Tailgate. Luxury buses bring guests to the game, equipped with televisions, couches, and everything needed for a VIP experience. Needless to say, no host or guest sweats over the grill, whether hot dogs or filet mignon is ordered. A photographer can even be added to memorialize the day.

Tailgating also offers attractive sponsorship activities. Miller Lite, the *Chicago Tribune*, and WBBM Newsradio 780 AM produce "The Ultimate Tailgate" experience for Bears fans. Included in the free admission to the area are Bears alumni appearances and autographing sessions, free giveaways, and, of course, food and drink—for purchase.

Contributor: Elizabeth D. Richter

See also: Picnics and Parks

BIBLIOGRAPHY

"10 Commandments of Chicago Bears Tailgating." AXS. http://www.axs.com/the-10-commandments-of-chicago-bears-tailgating-16345.

Chicago Bears. http://www.chicagobears.com/events/ultimate-tailgate.html.

Takeout

Modern American takeout is credited to a convergence of sociology and packaging. *Takeout* means dishes prepared in a restaurant and packed for customers to eat in their own homes, offices, cars, and other off-premises locations. It can also mean drinks as accompaniment to food or on their own.

From their earliest days until Prohibition, Chicago's taverns and bars sold beer for people who brought pails specifically to be filled. Novelist James T. Farrell, writing about Irish families in Washington Park in the first third of the twentieth century, mentions "buckets of suds" as an ordinary thing. Sometimes the bars threw in some prepared food. Workers on their way to industrial jobs often stopped in at sandwich joints to have food put into their lunch buckets.

So popular was takeout that a packaging revolution changed the ways that foods could be transported from restaurants, especially Chinese places. The iconic, small, waxy paper carton for Chinese takeout (and modified for pizza in the 1950s) was invented on November 13, 1894, in Chicago. The inventor, Frederick Weeks Wilcox, patented a "paper pail," a single piece of paper, origami folded into segments, nearly leakproof and with a dainty wire handle on top. The intent was to replace the wooden pails that held shucked oysters. This new paper carton was an inexpensive and sanitary way to transport them. Chinese chop suey places adapted these early in the twentieth century and have used them ever since.

The 1950s saw a boom in takeout dining. Returning WWII GIs settled their families in the suburbs where they had many distractions: televisions, yard work, and things to do . . . other than cook. Takeout was popular alongside cake mixes, TV dinners, and convenience foods. Today, takeout has become an important part of the Chicago dining scene, helped by the advent of easy, online ordering.

Contributor: Margaret Laport

BIBLIOGRAPHY

Greenbaum, Hilary, and Dana Rubinstein. "The Chinese-Takeout Container Is Uniquely American." *New York Times*, January 13, 2012.

Lee, Jennifer. *The Fortune Cookie Chronicles*. New York: Twelve Books, 2008.

Tapas and Small Plates

Spanish lore credits the origin of tapas—*el tapeo*—with humble beginnings in Seville and, ironically, with empty plates. Bartenders would cover (*tapar*) drinks with a small plate to protect them from flies. Then, they began placing a simple slice of ham on the plate, which delighted bar patrons. Seeing the possibility of more patrons, bar-owners started serving different *tapas*, hence starting the national phenomenon of Spain.

Tapas in Spain are generally served at the bar, and are typically a grazing exercise. They mix hot and cold, and often the items contain one or two bites of fish, cheese, pork, or vegetables. Some common tapas that are also served in Chicago include:

- *Calamares*: fried squid rings
- *Patatas bravas*: fried potato wedges served with a spicy alioli sauce

- *Ensaladilla*: potato salad with mayonnaise and either tuna or prawns
- *Tortilla*: potato omelet
- *Jamón Iberico*: thinly sliced salt-cured ham
- *Albóndigas*: meatballs—most often pork, but also beef or seafood

Most notable are three restaurants that started the tapas trend in Chicago including Café Ba-Ba-Reeba! (1985), Emilio's Tapas (1988), and Café Iberico (1992). Tapas establishments can be credited with giving rise to other small-plate restaurants in the early 2000s, including those offering other cuisines such as Italian and new American.

Contributor: Margaret Laport
See also: Chefs; Restaurateurs and Restaurant Groups; Specific Restaurant Names

Taste of Chicago

For a sample of everything from barbecued turkey legs to Cajun alligator and Oreo cookie cheesecake, with a yoga tent to work off the calories, Taste of Chicago is the well-established summer destination. From a one-day Fourth of July event on North Michigan Avenue in 1980 to today's multiday food fest attracting over a million hungry participants to Grant Park, Taste (its abbreviated nickname) has been called "the world's largest food festival."

Originally conceived by restaurateur Arnie Morton, the food festival was initially a sidebar to the much larger ChicagoFest, which had been established by Mayor Michael Bilandic in 1977. ChicagoFest is no more, but Taste has survived and grown, with bumps along the way, under the administrations of four mayors. It was clear after year one, in which some 250,000 attendees swelled the crowd beyond the expected 100,000 and grossed $300,000, that North Michigan Avenue was too small. In 1981, Taste moved to Grant Park, where it has been ever since.

Despite its initial popularity, Taste was put on hold in 1983 while Mayor Harold Washington's administration sought corporate sponsors. A new and enlarged Taste reappeared in 1984 with the disappearance of Chicago-Fest. Music, however, did not vanish and, in 1985, live music expanded and over the years such stars as Carlos Santana, Stevie Wonder, Wayne Newton, and Wilco would appear. By 1988, Taste had grown to 10 days.

By 1991, the restaurant community was enthused about the opportunity to reach new customers. Over 300 restaurants competed for 77 slots. The popularity of Taste continued to expand. By 1997, a record crowd of 3.46

million customers parted with $12 million, enjoying everything from pizza to lobster. Two years later, attendance reached 3.68 million.

New challenges appeared in 2004 and 2005 with shootings in and near the park. Food poisoning affected over 300 in 2007, and the 2008 shooting of five people near the site raised safety issues. In 2009, in the shadow of an economic downturn, the city cut vendor slots from 74 to 56 and sought healthier food options and smaller portions. With the cancelation of the traditional July 3rd fireworks in 2010, attendance continued to dwindle and, by 2011, just 2.35 million marked the lowest attendance in 25 years.

Lower attendance also impacted the bottom line, already reflecting a deficit for the previous five years. In 2012, just 36 restaurants participated. The next year, however, marked a financial turnaround with a profit of $272,000, attributed to great weather, the appearance of food trucks for the first time, and participation by such celebrity chefs as Graham Elliot and Stephanie Izard.

The 2014 Taste featured 64 restaurants, including pop-up restaurants and 16 food trucks. Eli's Cheesecake, the only original vendor still participating, celebrated its 34th year at Taste with a giant 1,000-pound cheesecake. Seeking to control costs, Mayor Rahm Emanuel cut Taste from 10 days to 5 and moved it away from the July 4th weekend. The weather did not cooperate, and heavy rains canceled the Taste on the key Saturday, resulting once again in a losing year, with a deficit of $169,404 and just 1.1 million attendees.

Opinions vary as much as the culinary offerings:

"Highly overrated, highly overpriced, heavily crowded and very annoying. Best way to describe this phony festival that is a tourist trap and a lure for bored suburbanites."

"Great for tourists who have never experienced such a large outdoor food festival or even Chicagoans who just have yet to try it out."

The Taste model has inspired many other cities to establish their own food festivals. From Toronto to Denver to Cincinnati, food lovers can find similar events around the country and Canada.

Contributor: Elizabeth D. Richer
See also: Festivals

BIBLIOGRAPHY

History of Taste, back to 1980, "How Taste of Chicago Ballooned, then Shrank." *Chicago Tribune*, July 16, 2011.

Yue, Lorene. "Taste of Chicago Favorites to Cost More." *Crain's Chicago Business*, June 16, 2009.

Tea (See: Coffee and Tea)

Television (See: Media, Television)

Terlato, Anthony J.

The chairman of the Terlato Wine Group—the parent company of several businesses "specializing in the marketing and production of exceptional wines"—has been instrumental in creating an American market for fine wines, both foreign and domestic. It is an accomplishment that would have been hard to predict when Terlato started working at Leading Liquor Marts, his father's store on Chicago's North Side. His first coup came when a New York–based importer agreed to work with him if he took 600 cases of a Portuguese rosé called Lancers. He sold every bottle, and doors started to open.

Terlato was working at Pacific Wine Company, his father-in-law's wine bottling firm, when he and Robert Mondavi became friends. In 1967, Mondavi's Fume Blanc became the first California wine in Pacific's portfolio. As the domestic business grew, Terlato began eyeing the imports. He revamped Paterno Imports, a family business focused on olive oil and, in 1979, signed on the makers of Santa Margherita Pinot Grigio, the first of many luxury brands acquired.

At the urging of his sons, Bill and John, both active in the family business, Terlato bought the Rutherford Hill winery in 1996. This was followed by the acquisition of Chimney Rock Winery and Terlato Vineyards, partial ownership of wineries in France and Australia, and other companies. Like the other branches of the company, the list of vineyards owned in full—or in part—by the Terlato family is a work in progress.

In 1995, the company purchased Tangley Oaks in Lake Bluff, an estate that includes a 26,000-square-foot house built by Philip D Armour III in 1916 and 61/2 acres. It was named to the National Register of Historic Places in 1996.

Contributor: Barbara Revsine
See also: Wine Distribution and Sales

BIBLIOGRAPHY

Terlato, Anthony. *Taste: A Life in Wine*. Evanston: Agate, 2008.

Toffenetti, Dario

One of Chicago's most successful restaurateurs and remarkable characters of the twentieth century, Italian-born Dario Toffenetti (1889–1962) immigrated to Chicago in 1910. Along the way, he worked selling cooked potatoes in Wisconsin mining camps, and that dish became a staple of his later restaurants. Young Dario's first Chicago job was as a busboy at the famed Sherman House restaurant where he learned the value of service. With $3,500 saved up, he opened a small restaurant in 1914 on Clark Street near Randolph Street called The Triangle. His specialty was "ham and sweets" and to promote the fare he stood in the restaurant's window publicly carving large hams. Large plate-glass windows were features of his restaurants, and he pioneered the open kitchen concept. He also learned a good deal about marketing from the night school courses in business that he took at Northwestern University.

Toffenetti's restaurants were moderately priced and served middle-class patrons and families. These were not quick-service cafeterias or fancy restaurants but, with inexpensive breakfasts priced at 25 cents in the 1930s and dinners such as hot roast ham with sweet potatoes at 75 cents, his clientele were assured of decent meals that they could afford. He is reported to have said in his Italian accent: "And the customers say to me, 'Dario, you serve too much food. I can't eat it all.'"

Toffenetti was also a master of marketing language. His menu items were described in florid terms, saying that only a poet laureate could describe the glories of each dish. Among his signature dishes was strawberry shortcake described as "tempting red translucent berries have arrived this morning to be made for you in the most magnificent of all desserts." Another signature dish was spaghetti served in a meat sauce, the recipe having been found "in the archives among the ruins of the ancient castle of the count of Bonpensler in Bologna." The spaghetti was also described as "one hundred yards of happiness." As for potatoes, he sold so many baked potatoes that the Idaho potato growers gave him a special achievement award.

Invited to the New York World's Fair, his restaurant was such a hit that he opened a large place on Times Square in 1940. The menu was the same as in his eight Chicago locations and one in St. Petersburg, Florida. Toffenetti died of a sudden heart attack in 1962 (ironically in front of the Sherman House Hotel). Run by his brothers and nephews, the restaurant chain continued on, but by the late 1960s it was fading. The New York location was sold to Nathan's Famous in 1968, and the Chicago units were closed in the early 1980s.

Contributor: Bruce Kraig

See also: Restaurants and Fine Dining; Restaurateurs and Restaurant Groups

BIBLIOGRAPHY

Morabito, Greg. "A Trip to Toffenetti, Times Square's 1000 Seat Restaurant." *New York Eater*, Aug 28, 2012. http://ny.eater.com/2012/8/28/6558333/a-trip-to-toffenetti-times-squares-1000-seat-restaurant#4251212.

"Toffenetti, Chain's Owner Is Dead." *Chicago Tribune*, January 17, 1962.

Tootsie Roll

This candy is a chewy chocolate-tasting confection that does not melt during transportation. This single product formed the foundation of the Chicago-based Tootsie Roll industries, one of the largest candy companies in the world. After decades of growth with its core confection plus Tootsie Roll Pops, the company bought up such well-known products as Dots Gum Drops, Charleston Chews, Sugar Daddies, Junior Mints, Andes, and Double Bubble.

The first penny candy to be individually wrapped, Tootsie Roll was developed as an alternative to chocolate in 1896 New York City by an Austrian immigrant, Leo Hirshfield. He named the candy after his daughter, Carla, whose nickname was Tootsie. The company itself was called The Sweets Company of America. In 1935, when Sweets Company was in trouble, Bernard Rubin acquired it and moved the factory to Hoboken, N.J. Rubin remained the president until his death in 1948, after increasing the sales volume twelvefold. Since 1962, the Gordon family has been in control. In 1966, the company opened a large factory in Chicago, centralized operations, and renamed the company Tootsie Roll Industries, Inc. At its helm for 50 years was Chairman Melvin Gordon and his wife, Ellen; Chairman Gordon died in 2015 at age 95 and was the oldest CEO listed on NYSE or the Nasdaq. Because the Gordons keep a tight rein on the company, little about the company's business and operations has been made public. Tootsie Roll Industries remains a more than century-old success, with more than 64 million Tootsie Rolls produced daily at its Chicago plant.

Contributor: Geraldine Rounds

See also: Candy

BIBLIOGRAPHY

Abad-Santos, Alexander. "The Sweet Secret Life of Tootsie Rolls." *Wire*. http://www.thewire.com/business.

TOOTSIE ROLLS IN WARTIME

Penny Tootsie Rolls were popular with migrants during the Dust Bowl 1930s because they were so cheap. Since World War I, they have been put in soldiers' field rations because they did not melt. Korean War GIs nicknamed tootsie rolls "mortar shells," a cause for confusion. Once, when they requested more mortar shells in preparation for battle, they received the candy instead of real ammunition.

—GERALDINE ROUNDS

Kesling, Ben. "Tootsie's Secret Empire." *Wall Street Journal*. http://www.online.wsj.com/news/articles.

Tortillas and Tortillerias

Today Chicago is hailed nationally as a major center for artisanal tortillas, but the industry started from slender roots. From 1910 through the 1960s, Mexican laborers were brought to Chicago under contract to work for railroads, steelyards, local factories, and food processors. As Mexicans immigrated to the city in the 1960s, tortillerias began opening on the South Side of Chicago, using age-old techniques and modern machinery.

Corn tortillas are made from soaking dried corn in lime and water, the process known as *nixtamalization*. The process breaks down the corn, making it easier to grind into masa dough. The masa is flattened and cooked on a griddle to become a tortilla. The first corn tortillas date back about 12,000 years. Flour tortillas began when the Spaniards arrived in Mexico in 1519, bringing with them wheat and lard.

Corn tortillas in their simplest forms are made of masa and little else and can be identified in the grocery store in their paper wrappers. Corn tortillas containing preservatives to extend their shelf life are wrapped in plastic.

Some of the first tortillerias in Chicago included Del Rey, El Milagro, El Popocateptl, and Sabinas. El Milagro was established in 1950 by Raul Lopez, a day laborer on the railroads. El Popocateptl was founded in 1954 by Antonio and Ernesto Avina. Nuevo Leon was established in 1975 by Oscar and Maria Martinez. Tortilleria Atotonilco was established in 1984 by Oscar Munoz and produced tortillas from their own corn. All four still operated in 2016. The largest area's tortilla maker is Azteca Foods, founded by Art Velasquez and partners in 1969. In 1984, the company, then called Azteca Corn products, was sold to Pillsbury, which spread products across the nation and abroad. In 1989, the Valasquez family bought the company back, renaming it Azteca Foods.

By 1979, Tortilleria Del Rey was the largest tortilla factory in Chicago, with more than 110 workers. Labor organizer Rudy Lozano fought for worker rights in the factory when he found poor working conditions. Unfortunately, to stop workers from organizing, Del Rey invited the federal Immigration and Naturalization Service to raid the facility. Lozano continued fighting for worker rights and was organizing a consumer boycott in 1983 of the Del Rey tortillas, when he was killed outside his home. Del Rey ultimately was shut down in 2009 by the federal Food and Drug Administration due to violations.

By 2005, tortilla shipments in the United States reached $1.91 billion and the Chicago tortillerias continued to grow. In 2014, there were seven large tortillerias in the Chicago area, including La Banderita in Bedford Park, Los Comanches in Cicero, and Masa Uno (owned by the Del Rey family) in Berwyn. Most make various masa products and flour tortillas.

Contributor: Kelsey Coday

See also: Azteca Foods Inc.; Mexicans

BIBLIOGRAPHY

"Berwyn's First Tortilla Bakery." *Chicago Tribune*, July 30, 2014.

Fernandez, Lilia. *Brown in the Windy City*. Chicago: University of Chicago Press, 2012.

"Stack 'em Up." *Chicago Tribune*, February 27, 2002.

Tours and Tourism

Visitor interest in the city's edibles, on the hoof or in the pot, is not a new concept for Chicago. Even before the 1893 World's Columbian Exposition attracted tourists to Chicago, guests—some of them famous—insisted not only on viewing the acres of livestock pens at the Union Stock Yards but also on seeing what went on in the slaughterhouses. Actress Sarah Bernhardt's enthusiastic, if theatrical, description of the hog butchering, for example? "A horrible and magnificent spectacle."

The Yards are gone (closed in 1971) and so are most of the meatpackers and many of the manufacturers—but not the fascination with Chicago food. Industrial tours include peeks at the source of a couple of the city's iconic brands: Vienna Beef, home of the city's classic hot dogs and other sausages, at its North Side plant; and Eli's Cheesecake, at its bakery on the Northwest Side. Less venerable but nonetheless worth the time (and the nominal fee): Intelligentsia

CHICAGO FOODSEUM

Although Chicago is one of the world's great food cities, there has never been a physical museum dedicated to the city's food history. In 2014, a young Internet entrepreneur, Kyle Joseph, and his partner, Suzie Fasulo, decided to do something about it. Putting together a largely volunteer team of experts in food history, museum design, marketing, business entrepreneurship, publicity, and Internet savvy, Joseph led the incorporation of the Chicago Foodseum as a nonprofit entity in 2015. The first version of the museum was a four-month-long pop-up in Block 37 at Daley Plaza dedicated to "Hot Dog and Encased Meats of the World." The museum has a sophisticated website filled with information from food history to videos about cookery, restaurants, and much more. See http://www.foodseum.org/.

—BRUCE KRAIG

Coffee's roasting operation on the Near West Side; and Half Acre Beer Company, North Side brewer of lagers, ales, and other adult beverages, both of which welcome the curious and thirsty.

The most compelling factor that sets Chicago apart from most other American cities is its cultural diversity, which begets culinary variety at all price levels. An ever-growing selection of food tours—a chance to sample goodies grouped by neighborhood, ethnicity or a particular food—has provided accessibility (and a shortcut) to much of what the city has to serve.

Among the offerings (all subject to change): pizza tours, hot dog tours, cupcake tours, "Chicago favorites" tours, and chocolate-lovers tours. There are Chinatown tours, Old Town tours, Gold Coast tours, Bucktown & Wicker Park tours, Argyle Street (pan-Asian) tours, Devon Avenue (Indian and Pakistani) tours. Tours by bus, bike, Segway, and foot. A few names of tour firms, out of many, include Chicago Food Planet, Tastebud Food Tours, Chicago Pizza Tours, and Spice of Life Tours.

One pizza tour samples only deep-dish pies—the style that (right or wrong) has come to represent "Chicago pizza." Another features a variety of styles, from thin to deep-dish to stuffed. Another adds beer and wine. Another takes you into the kitchens.

There are Progressive Dining tours (starter at one restaurant, entrée at the next, dessert at the next). At least one outfit will guide four diners (minimum) into the kitchens to meet chefs who will present their Michelin-star–level samples—for a Michelin-star–level price. What would Sarah Bernhardt do? Something horribly magnificent.

Contributor: Alan Solomon

BIBLIOGRAPHY

Miller, Donald L. *City of the Century: The Epic of Chicago and the Making of America*. New York: Simon and Schuster, 1997.
Tour. www.choosechicago.com.
www.chicagotours.us.
www.chicagofoodplanet.com.
www.rebeccawheeler.com.
www.chicagopizzatours.com.
www.conciergepreferred.com.
www.zerve.com/d/chicago.

Trade Shows

Chicago's central location within the American Midwest made it an ideal location for trade shows that showcased food products and food-related equipment. The agricultural bounty of this region and its emphasis on food processing, transportation, and manufacturing fostered an environment conducive to the marketing of food and its associated wares. Chicago represented one of the largest consumer markets in the country after 1900 and possessed a large array of nationally syndicated publications, advertisers, and media outlets that impacted the practices of consumers throughout the country. Formal trade fairs such as the International Home and Housewares Show as well as events like the Columbian Exposition of 1893 and the 1933–34 Century of Progress provided venues for the display of the most cutting-edge products and practices in American Foodways.

The 1893 Columbian Exposition in Jackson Park contained a number of exhibitions, such as an all-electric kitchen that served as thinly veiled displays for manufacturers wishing to present their newest technologies/products. Like a conventional trade show, manufacturers purchased spaces where they created displays designed to appeal to domestic consumers and potential distributors of their goods. The American Electrical Heating Corporation of Boston—one of the pioneering makers of electrical heating appliances—outfitted the all-electric kitchen with everything from chafing dishes and frying pans to electric range-tops and water heaters. This display represented one of the earliest if not the first examples of electrical cooking in the United States, well before most consumers had access to even the most basic electrical power networks.

This exposition also helped to popularize such food products as Cream of Wheat, Shredded Wheat, Quaker Oats, Hershey Chocolates, Cracker Jack, and Aunt Jemima pancake mix. Nancy Green—a former slave—appeared in character as Aunt Jemima at this event for the first time. She cooked pancakes for a wide audience of hungry consumers, helping to cement this iconic brand figure into the American consumer imagination, generating a lucrative stream of income for the R. T. Davis Milling Company. The national publicity generated by this exposition helped exhibitors reach a consumer audience that stretched from coast to coast. Geographically based exhibits also presented an array of foreign foods at the Exposition, perhaps broadening the palates of fairgoers to a more diverse range of global cuisines.

Like the Columbian Exposition, the 1933–34 Century of Progress World's Fair in Chicago also served as a trade venue for manufacturers seeking to present their newest products. Companies such as General Electric displayed their most modern kitchen technologies, including their iconic monitor-top refrigerator, the first mass-produced refrigerator with a sealed compressor and easily transportable body. Other major makers of household appliances such as Westinghouse displayed their newest products, many of which emphasized a streamlined or art deco appearance that characterized Depression-era design. These virtual showrooms of housewares served as an important marketing guise for the nation's largest manufacturers.

Since 1927, Chicago has served as the location of the International Home and Housewares Show—the largest display of domestic appliances and kitchenware in the country. Although the origins of this show may be traced back to the Home Furnishing Goods Exhibition of 1906 held in New York City, this show grew significantly in scale after relocating to the Windy City. Chicago provided a more centralized location for many of the manufacturers displaying their wares because the Midwest comprised the nation's largest manufacturing base prior to and after the Second World War. The International Housewares Association (IHA) has been the officially sanctioned organizer of this show since 1938. Iconic products such as the Waring blender, aluminum bakeware, Fiestaware, the microwave oven, the crockpot, and the George Forman grill first entered the marketplace through this venue. The IHA show continues to be one of the most important venues for the introduction of new food-related products and technologies. It has been held at McCormick Place since 1961.

Contributor: Stefan Osdene

See also: African Americans; Equipment

BIBLIOGRAPHY

Bathelt, Harald, Francesca Golfetto, and Diego Rinallo. *Trade Shows in the Globalizing Knowledge Economy*. Oxford: Oxford University Press, 2014.

Matranga, Victoria K., James Beck, and Karen Kohn. *America at Home: A Celebration of Twentieth-Century Housewares*. Rosemont, Ill.: National Housewares Manufacturing Association, 1996.

Tramonto, Rick

One of the partners behind the popular Tru restaurant just off the Magnificent Mile, chef Tramonto opened the restaurant in 2000 with his then-wife and pastry chef Gale Gand and with Rich Melman of Lettuce Entertain You. The restaurant was an immediate success, serving Tramonto's modern American dishes in a elegant, art-filled dining room. His caviar "staircase" presentation particularly impressed the critics. The restaurant earned a 4-star review from the *Chicago Tribune* and *Chicago Sun-Times*. Tramonto won the Best Chef Midwest award from the James Beard Foundation in 2002.

Tramonto learned classic cooking from many well-known chefs. After dropping out of high school in Rochester, New York, and working at Wendy's, he eventually moved to New York City, where he worked at Tavern of the Green, Gotham Bar & Grill, and then Charlie Trotter's in Chicago. He and Gand worked at Stapleford Park Hotel in England, then at Evanston's Trio restaurant, earning

4 stars, before opening Tru. Tramonto and Gand also opened Brasserie T in Northfield. Then, in 2005, Tramonto opened Osteria di Tramonto, Tramonto's Steak & Seafood, and RT Sushi Bar & Lounge in Wheeling, Illinois, in the Westin Hotel, all now closed. After leaving Tru, he partnered with chef John Folse to open Restaurant R'evolution in New Orleans, in 2012 and a second location in Ridgeland, Mississippi, in 2014. He has appeared on many television shows and is the author of seven cookbooks and a memoir, *Scars of a Chef.*

Contributor: Carol Mighton Haddix

See also: Restaurants and Fine Dining; Restaurateurs and Restaurant Groups

BIBLIOGRAPHY

"Rick Tramonto of Tru-Biography." Starchefs. http://www.starchefs.com/cook/chefs/bio/rick-tramonto.

Transportation

Chicago has been mid-America's dominant hub for the transportation of agricultural products and many other foods since the late nineteenth century. Even in its earliest days, the city showed considerable promise as a budding center for the trading of consumable goods. After it was incorporated as a city in 1837, a buoyant market emerged for grain, livestock, produce, and other feed sales along the southern bank of the Chicago River, near present-day East Wacker Drive. Vessels carrying foods began regularly arriving from large cities of the Eastern Seaboard via the Erie Canal and over the Great Lakes. Food shipments from the region's interior grew sharply after the Illinois & Michigan (I&M) Canal opened in 1848. The I&M spurred the expansion of farming through much of Illinois by creating a continuous water route between the Great Lakes and the Mississippi River basin.

Chicago's first railroad, the Galena & Chicago Union railroad, began operating in 1848, which set off a frenzy of track laying that pushed its transportation role to enormous heights. As the cost of shipping plummeted, the grain trade surged. By 1880, the city had tracks radiating from it in nearly every direction.

For the next half-century, railroads remained the dominant force in the transportation of food. The Illinois Central Railroad and Wabash Railways reached deep into the highly productive farmland in the central part of the state, while westward-focused lines, such as Chicago, Burlington & Quincy Railroad and Chicago & North Western Railway (C&NW) became veritable lifelines to rural areas of the Upper Midwest and Great Plains. Routes from the East converged with those oriented toward the west on the city's Near South and Near West sides, creating a

Chicago Transit Company flyer, 1920s to '30s. Archive.org.

transportation-laden area that gradually became one of the country's foremost hubs for food-related shipping and production. The Union Stock Yards, at Exchange and Halsted Streets, grew to enormous proportions and even had its own "L" route, the now-abandoned Stock Yards Branch. The city's Meatpacking District, home to such giants as Armour & Co., Swift & Co., Wilson Packing Company, and others sprouted up in this part of the city. Annually, they generated thousands of carloads of packed beef, pork, and other products, with much of it shipped in refrigerated cars beginning in the 1880s.

Chicago also gained distinction as the "Candy Capital" on account of its abundant transportation links that supplied flour, sugar, and other basic ingredients to candy makers producing such familiar consumables as Mars and Snickers bars, Cracker Jack, Curtiss, Wrigley's gum, Tootsie Rolls, and Frango Mints. Dairy products and fresh produce, meanwhile, were shipped from outlying areas for packaging and sale in the city, often on "milk run" trains or electric interurban railways.

Gradually, the growing size and reliability of trucks made over-the-road shipping an attractive alternative to rail and maritime services. Trucks had the ability to speed up the delivery of foods that could spoil or had limited shelf lives, as well as reach small businesses not served by rail. Many candy producers, for example, switched to trucks to bring their sweet delicacies to market while still using trains to bring in sugar and other basic ingredients. The need to create greater order in the city's fruit and vegetable markets, meanwhile, culminated in the 1925 opening of the massive South Water Street Market, on the Near Southwest Side.

As highways improved and the shift to truck transportation kicked into high gear after World War II, dramatic changes in retail distribution occurred. One of the country's first supermarkets, located in an auto-oriented shopping mall, was built in Park Forest, a south suburb incorporated in 1949. The first McDonald's restaurant opened in suburban Des Plaines in 1955. By the early 1960s, trucks operating from massive distribution centers along a newly opened express system shouldered almost the entire burden of keeping fruit stands, restaurants, and supermarkets stocked. The massive Chicago International Produce Market, another Southwest Side facility, opened in 1971, and had much more spacious loading docks for trucks than the more tightly configured South Water Market it replaced.

Large corporations relying on both trucks and trains modernized some of the region's largest food-production

Santa Fe Railroad grain elevator on the Atchison, Topeka & Santa Fe Railroad slip on the south side of the Sanitary and Ship Canal, Chicago, Cook County, Ill., 1968. Library of Congress.

facilities, with a particularly large number in corn processing. Ingredion Corporation, a major supplier of corn syrup, operates a massive corn-refining plant in suburban Bedford Park. El Milagro, Inc., a producer of tortillas, tostadas, chips, and taco shells, has modern facilities in Pilsen and Little Village. ACH Food Company facility in suburban Summit processes Argo brand cornstarch and corn oil.

Today, much grain is shipped on river barges and on deep draft vessels moving on the Great Lakes. Although the massive elevator at the International Port District on Lake Calumet is now idle, a 14-silo elevator along the Little Calumet River in Burns Harbor, Indiana, remains heavily used. An increasing amount of grain also moves in containers by rail to coastal ports, where the containers are stacked onto enormous oceangoing vessels.

Only a few perishable items generally arrive in Chicago by airplane, due to the comparatively high costs of air cargo. Significant quantities of fresh fish, including live lobsters, wild salmon, and fresh tilapia, are shipped to O'Hare International Airport, much of it as "belly cargo" on passenger airplanes. Upon arrival, the fish is trucked to nearby distributors to be cleaned or filleted, packaged, and delivered to high-end restaurants, often in a span of only a few hours. (Fresh fish shipped on ice generally must be cooked within 48–72 hours.) Frozen fish, less susceptible to spoilage, generally can be shipped by boat, train, or truck.

Shifting customer tastes have altered the way food has been transported and sold. Portions of the former C&NW terminal were repurposed as the Chicago French Market, known for its upscale and organic food, in 2009. The municipal government began issuing permits, with restrictions, in 2012 to food-truck operators who requested the ability to sell freshly prepared food on city streets. Restaurants now often use bicycles to speed up delivery of takeout orders in the congested Greater Loop area. And a comprehensive delivery system also emerged to bring organic foods, often purchased over the Internet, directly to the customer's door.

Contributor: Joseph Schwieterman

See also: Candy; Union Stock Yards; Wholesale and Distribution

BIBLIOGRAPHY

Mayer, Harold, and Richard Wade. *Chicago: Growth of a Metropolis.* Chicago: University of Chicago Press, 1969.

Solzman, David M. *The Chicago River: An Illustrated History and Guide to the River and Its Waterways.* Chicago: University of Chicago Press, 2006.

Young, David M. *The Iron Horse and the Windy City: How Railroads Shaped Chicago.* DeKalb: Northern Illinois University Press, 2005.

Trbojevic, Jovan

One of Chicago's great restaurateurs, Jovan Trbojevic (1921–2010) fled his native Yugoslavia during World War II. His facility with languages and cooking skills got him jobs at different hotels and restaurants around the world, including Jacques in Chicago and Sardi's in New York. In 1967, he found backers for his first restaurant in Chicago, Jovan, on Huron Street. It was, one of the first restaurants to feature a fixed-price dinner, a lot of vegetables, and what may have been the city's first espresso machine.

A visit to Europe led to an interest in nouvelle cuisine and, in 1972, he opened Le Perroquet, a fine-dining restaurant on Walton Street. In 1978, he opened Les Nomades as a private dining club. (Membership was only $1, but was by invitation only.) He sold Le Perroquet in 1984 and Les Nomades in 1993. Many leading chefs honed their skills in his kitchens, including Gabino Sotelino, Michael Foley, Mary Sue Milliken, and Susan Feniger. The name has been revived for the restaurant in the Washburn Culinary Institute at the South Shore Country Club.

Contributor: Colleen Sen

See also: Chefs; Private Clubs and Restaurants; Restaurants and Fine Dining; Restaurateurs and Restaurant Groups

BIBLIOGRAPHY

"Jovan Trboyevic." *Food Arts*, June 1996.

Vettel, Phil. "Chicago Fine Dining Pioneer Jovan Trboyevic Dead at 89." *Chicago Tribune*, January 13, 2010.

Treasure Island Foods

Chicago's patchwork of ethnic neighborhoods—Italian, Greek, Chinese, Mexican, and more—always boasted grocery stores stocked with foods reflecting their communities. Then along came the brothers Kamberos, Christ and Frank, plus partners William Allen and William Benjamin. They gathered some of those foods—the grape leaves, the rice vinegars, and mustards of many colors—and lined them up on shelves not far from the Tide detergent and Cheez Whiz and then seasoned it all with ambience in their first store, Treasure Island Foods, which opened in 1963 at 3460 North Broadway in Chicago.

It was a hit. The brothers were, wrote a *Chicago Tribune* columnist a few months after the opening, "the talk of the supermarket trade, coast-to-coast. Their new north-side Treasure Island, with fantastic innovations, is such an overnight smash, two national mags are readying pieces."

Produce was always important in the store's mix. "We try to carry everything that grows, whether we can sell it or not," Christ Kamberos told one reporter. When they opened the North Wells Street store, the team emphasized imported foods (think caviar and paté), as well as an extensive selection of wine, beers, and liquors. They added more stores and in-store cooking classes. Today, Treasure Island Foods has six stores in Chicago plus one in Wilmette. The company is now run by Maria Kamberos, wife of the late Christ Kamberos, who died October 27, 2009.

....

Contributor: Judy Hevrdejs

See also: Specialty Stores; Supermarkets and Grocery Stores

BIBLIOGRAPHY

Lyon, Herb. "Tower Ticker." *Chicago Tribune*, April 11, 1963.
Rasmussen, Carol. "Treasure Island: Chicago's Treasure Trove of Exotica." *Chicago Tribune*, March 10, 1983.

THE TROTTER PROJECT

After the death of well-known chef Charlie Trotter in 2013, members of his family, friends, and a group of alumni of his restaurant joined together to form The Trotter Project. It aims to continue Trotter's practice of mentoring youth interested in the culinary arts with internships and other programs. The project undertook a three-year capital campaign to fund its programs. It is based in Charlie Trotter's old restaurant and office space on Armitage Avenue in Lincoln Park. In 2015, United Airlines joined the project as a corporate sponsor; chef members of the project will work with United to create new menus for the airline.

—CAROL MIGHTON HADDIX

Trotter, Charlie

The chef and restaurateur Charlie Trotter (1959–2013) was quoted as saying, "If it isn't broken, then break it." Trotter made his reputation on a cuisine in which, according to Molly O'Neill (*New York Times*), "the complexity of his recipes pushes the outer limits of culinary sanity." The cuisine, however, won Trotter international acclaim and almost every major culinary award for his namesake restaurant, his books, and his television series.

Trotter was reared in the northern Chicago suburb of Wilmette. On his prom night in 1976, while dining at The Bakery restaurant in Chicago, Trotter had an epiphany. Seeing the dramatic persona of the impeccably toqued chef Louis Szathmary, Trotter declared that one day he, too, would be a chef.

At the University of Wisconsin, Madison, where he majored in political science, Trotter began cooking for friends. After graduation, he pursued a culinary career full time. With no formal experience, Trotter was given his first break at Sinclair's, in Lake Forest, training under the chef Norman Van Aken. Trotter then began a self-styled apprenticeship, working in restaurants in Florida and San Francisco. Trotter moved to France and ate out frequently at Michelin-rated 3-star restaurants.

In 1987 with his father's financial backing, Trotter purchased a 1908 Victorian house in Chicago's Lincoln Park neighborhood. Trotter remodeled the building into the elegant, wood-paneled fine-dining establishment that bore his name. Likening his food to improvisational jazz, Trotter changed menus daily and never repeated a dish. The cuisine was based on classical French techniques, but Trotter freely used Asian and other international influences in his tasting menus. His cuisine relied on natural vegetable juices and stocks, purees, and infused oils instead of cream and butter sauces, which Trotter said neutralized flavors. Trotter emphasized freshness, using organically grown grains and vegetables, meats from free-range animals, and line-caught fish.

Trotter published more than 15 books and taught cooking on his award-winning PBS TV show. He regularly invited inner-city schoolchildren to experience fine dining at his restaurant and awarded culinary scholarships through his philanthropic foundation. He won numerous awards, among them the James Beard Foundation's Outstanding Chef in the United States (1999). *Wine Spectator* magazine cited Charlie Trotter's as the best restaurant in the world for wine and food.

Trotter closed the restaurant on its 25th anniversary in 2012. He said he wanted to travel and to pursue a graduate degree in philosophy. But Trotter suffered from high blood pressure and struggled with depression. He died on November 5, 2013, after suffering a stroke at his home.

Contributor: Scott Warner

See also: Chefs; Restaurants and Fine Dining; Restaurateurs and Restaurant Groups

BIBLIOGRAPHY

Brown, Rochelle. *The Chef, the Story, and the Dish*. New York: Stewart, Tabori, and Chang, 2002.

Warner, Scott. *Trotter, Charlie. The Oxford Encyclopedia of Food and Drink in America*. Oxford: Oxford University Press, 2004.

Turano Baking Company

In 1962, three brothers, Mario, Carmen, and Eugenio Turano merged their two Chicago bakeries: Campagna and Turano became one bakery/production facility in Berwyn. The name was eventually changed to Turano Baking. Italian old-world breads, plus French and Vienna breads, pizza, and Kaiser rolls, gave them a strong presence in the Chicago market. By 1967, their Mama Susi pizzas and fresh and frozen breads were sold throughout the Midwest. The Turano family expanded into Georgia and Florida in 2009. The unique partnership in Florida was the first of its kind: Turano produced the buns for McDonald's, but when the buns reached the freezer, they became the property of the bread distributor, Martin-Brower. Turano's large Berwyn facility still produces classical Italian and American pastries and cookies, as well as 2 million pounds of bread a week. Its retail outlet is open 24 hours, seven days a week.

Contributor: Jenny Lewis

See also: Italians

BIBLIOGRAPHY

Gorton, Laurie. "Turano Baking: . . . And Now: Soft Buns." *Baking Business.com*, March 1, 2011. http://www.bakingbusiness.com/Features/Company%20Profiles/Turano%20Baking%20plant.aspx?cck=1.

Twinkies

The "cream"-filled golden sponge cake was introduced in 1930 by Continental Baking Company. Originally sold plain to be made into strawberry shortcakes, the baking molds lay disused when the berries were out of season. The complex process of injecting whipped sweet banana cream into the cake was devised by bakery manager, Jimmy Dewar. Legend has it, he gave them the name "Twinkies" after he saw a billboard for Twinkle Toe Shoes. During World War II when bananas were rationed, the company switched to its now-familiar vanilla-flavored cream filling. Since the filling is not made with dairy products, Twinkies' shelf life was about 26 days (currently 45 days), not the 70 years or so as is rumored in urban myths.

In 2012, Hostess filed for Chapter 11 bankruptcy protection, and production ceased. The company was sold to investors, and after a little more than a year, Twinkies were back on the shelves and selling at the rate of half a billion a year. Originally made in the suburb of Schiller Park, they are no longer baked in the Chicagoland area. The company also makes popular baked snacks Ding Dongs and Ho Hos.

Contributor: Craig Goldwyn

See also: Baking and Bakeries

BIBLIOGRAPHY

Jorgensen, Janice, ed. *Encyclopedia of Consumer Brands, Volume 1: Consumable Products*. Detroit: St. James Press, 1994.

Ukrainians

The initial wave of Ukrainian immigration occurred from the 1880s through World War I and included peasants from eastern Galicia and Subcarpathia in the Austro-Hungarian Empire. The next waves followed the collapse of the Austrian empire after World War I. In the late 1980s, more immigrants arrived from the Soviet Republic of Ukraine.

By 2000, the census identified 45,036 residents of the Chicago area as having Ukrainian ancestry. Although they were concentrated in the West Town neighborhood called Ukrainian Village, many later settled throughout Lake, DuPage, and Cook counties. To this day, however, the Ukrainian Village neighborhood remains an epicenter for Ukrainian culture, housing churches, stores, schools, and associations, as well as the Ukrainian Institute of Modern Art and the Ukrainian National Museum.

The Ukrainian Village Fest, complete with traditional foods and a beer garden serving Ukrainian beer, is held in September on Superior Street and Oakley Boulevard.

Some of those traditional foods include dishes such as *varenyky* (meat-, vegetable-, or fruit-filled dumplings), *kotlety* (minced meat cutlets), stuffed or pickled cabbage and sauerkraut, borshch (beet soup), and *paska* (Easter bread). Such traditional foods can be found at Chicago eateries such as Old Lviv Restaurant, Shokolad Pastry & Cafe on W. Chicago Ave., and Magic Jug on W. Irving Park Rd.

Ann's Bakery and Deli on Chicago Avenue is a go-to place for house-made breads and pastries. Rich's Deli, on N. Western Ave., and Ukraina Deli, on W. Chicago Ave., offer hot and cold prepared foods, sausages, and cheese. Also, Eastern European delis throughout Chicago often will carry Ukrainian sausages and other foods.

Contributor: Jennifer Olvera

BIBLIOGRAPHY

Zechenter, Katarzyna. "Ukrainians." *Encyclopedia of Chicago*. http://www.encyclopedia.chicagohistory.org/pages/1279.html.

Underground Dinner Clubs

Sometimes called pop-up restaurants, underground dinner clubs in Chicago became popular in 2005, as the public's interest in chefs and restaurants encouraged experimentation in dining. At the same time, a weak economy and real estate market made it more difficult for young cooks to open their own restaurants. They began to host dinners in their homes and invite guests to pay for a one-night-only dining experience. The dinners hold appeal for people looking to discover the next great rising chef talent, and to try an intimate "speakeasy" dining experience.

The restaurants are promoted online and via membership-only email lists. They often feel like dinner parties, with participants bringing their own wine, beer, or cocktails and sitting at communal tables. The underground nature of the clubs comes from the fact that they are not cleared by the health department and take place in private homes or other spaces not zoned for food service. Dinner locations are often not revealed until the day of the event.

Some of the most popular and successful underground dinner clubs in Chicago have included X-Marx, Sunday Dinner Club, Sobremesa, and El Ideas. The club scene has yielded several of the city's most in-demand restaurants. Abraham Conlon and Adrienne Lo of X-Marx opened Fat Rice in Chicago's Logan Square neighborhood; the restaurant was named one of *Bon Appetit*'s ten best new restaurants in the country in 2013. Christine Cikowski and Joshua Kulp launched Sunday Dinner Club in 2005 and then quit their restaurant cooking jobs to take their supper club "above board" and move it out of Cikowski's living room

and into an official dedicated space. Likewise, Jake Bickelhaupt and Alexa Welsh of Sous Rising opened 42 Grams to great acclaim. Iliana Regan of One Sister, Inc., opened Elizabeth in the Lincoln Square neighborhood after success cooking 12-course meals in her apartment, and she has developed a national reputation for her skills in foraging mushrooms and esoteric ingredients such as cattails and yarrow and serving them in an experimental fine-dining atmosphere.

Established chefs also host underground dinners; Stephanie Izard hosted a series of "Wandering Goat" dinners before opening her restaurant, Girl & the Goat.

Contributor: Chandra Ram

BIBLIOGRAPHY

Borelli, Christopher. "Underground Dining in Chicago Not So Underground Anymore." *Chicago Tribune*, May 20, 2010.

Union Stock Yards

By 1848, this still-new place called Chicago—population 20,000—was already known as a hog butcher, with its rail sidings and holding pens. But railroads were moving the nation west; livestock producers, with farms and ranches where the spaces were wide and open and cheap, were shipping their animals east to the population centers. And opportunity called from all directions.

Massachusetts native Benjamin P. Hutchinson arrived in Chicago in 1858 to begin a meatpacking and grain-shipping company in Bridgeport. The wheat business always interested him, because wheat was the seed of life, he said, but the meat business led to his contribution to Chicago's economic history (he later went bankrupt, but not before cornering the wheat market in 1888). In the early 1860s, Hutchinson made a great deal of money packing meat for the Union Army during the Civil War. So did his competitor, Nelson Morris, a German of Jewish heritage who began in meatpacking in 1854 and then founded his own company in 1859. He became one of the founders of the Union Stock Yards. By 1859, Chicago had gone from shipping 683,600 pounds of pork the decade before to 2.7 million pounds.

In 1864, with the Civil War grinding to an end, nine railroad companies combined to pay owner and ex-mayor John "Long John" Wentworth $100,000 for an unattractive 320 acres south and west of the Chicago city limits. The patch was bounded by what would become Pershing Road (then 39th Street) 47th Street, Racine Avenue, and Halsted Street; more parcels would be added. The stockyards were a major part of a revolution in American food production. From a business perspective, centralized processing was an economy of scale producing cheaper meat, while the network of rail systems to and from the city gave access to national markets. Packers such as Gustavus Swift and Philip Armour created factories where animals were slaughtered, disassembled, and packed, every part of them used. Henry Ford, seeing this, devised his assembly-line production methods. New machines made the operations possible, from animal hoists to moving overhead lines, refrigeration, chopping and grinding machines, huge boiling vats, and more. The places were hell-like, but efficient for their time.

The Union Stock Yards opened on Christmas Day, 1865. They closed officially on July 31, 1971. In between, fortunes were made and lost; slaughterhouses, packers, and tanneries would provide jobs first for Irish and Germans, and then for Poles, Lithuanians, Slovaks, and all who could stand the blood, gore, and stench; rivers and streams were fouled beyond imagination; strikes were won and broken; and Chicago's livestock industry was celebrated in poetry by Carl Sandburg and reviled in muckraking by Upton Sinclair, with his stories of furtively canned horsemeat, tubercular cattle, and crippled workers.

Fires were frequent. One, in 1910, killed 21 firemen and three civilians. There was Bubbly Creek: An essentially currentless arm of the South Branch of the Chicago River at the Yards' border, it would become a notorious repository for wastes whose slow decay generated major bubbles. The creek never froze, but sometimes it would burn. On warm summer nights, breezes from the southwest would carry the unmistakable aroma of the

stockyards to Comiskey Park, home since 1910 of the Chicago White Sox, two miles away. But actual cowboys worked the pens, and there were all those live animals—so naturally, the Yards became a tourist attraction.

The business of the Union Stock Yards was the business of processing animals into food and by-products. Phillip Armour built a plant there in 1867. Eight years later, Gustavus Swift set up shop, and Nelson Morris and G. H. Hammond would follow. By 1900, the industry employed 25,000 workers and produced more than 80 percent of the country's meat. By 1919, the number of workers had swelled to more than 45,000.

Sandburg declared the city "Hog Butcher for the World" in 1914. Five years later, in 1919, plants in Chicago butchered 7.9 million hogs—and more than 2 million cattle. Through 1933, from 13 million to 18 million head of livestock arrived annually, to be herded, slaughtered, processed, and distributed.

The 9,000-seat International Amphitheater, built on the grounds in 1934, hosted five national political conventions, an annual livestock show and rodeo, pro basketball, auto shows, boat shows, Elvis Presley, and the Beatles. The Sirloin Room of the Stock Yard Inn would provide elegant reinforcement of Chicago's reputation as a great steak town.

And then the world changed. More efficient plants were built closer to the breeders. Wilson & Company closed its Chicago operations in 1955. Swift and Armour followed. By 1971, the cattle market had closed—but more

View of the entrance to the Union Stock Yards, ca. 1890. Courtesy of Lake County (Ill.) Discovery Museum, Curt Teich Postcard Archives.

symbolically, in 1970, the last hog was butchered. The pens are gone. So are the Amphitheater and the Stock Yard Inn. It took a few years, but eventually the smell was gone, too. The last true remnant: The limestone Union Stock Yard gate (1875).

Contributor: Alan Solomon

See also: Lithuanians; Meat and Poultry; Sanitation; Sinclair, Upton

BIBLIOGRAPHY

Hogan, John F., and Alex A. Burkholder. *Fire Strikes the Chicago Stock Yards: A History of Fame and Folly in the Jungle*. Charleston: The History Press, 2013.

Slayton, Robert A. *Back of the Yards: The Making of a Local Democracy*. Chicago: University of Chicago Press, 1986.

University of Illinois Extension

Formerly called The Cooperative Extension Service, the organization has been channeling information from the University of Illinois, Urbana-Champaign, to the farms, homes, and gardens of Illinois, including the Chicago area, for 100 years. It has delivered on its mission through pamphlets and the Internet, through work with established and newly minted farmers, rural and urban 4-H programs, and community-based classes in cooking, gardening, farming, nutrition, and more.

That mission, set out in the Smith-Lever Act of 1914, established the Service as a way to disseminate research, knowledge, and resources beyond the campuses of the nation's land-grant universities and colleges. Today, University of Illinois Extension (its name changed in the 1990s) is part of the nationwide Cooperative Extension System of the National Institute of Food and Agriculture at the U.S. Department of Agriculture. There are 12 Extension offices located in the Chicago area counties of Cook, Lake, McHenry, DuPage, Will, and Kane.

Its vast reach wasn't always so. In 1927, for example, Extension staff teamed with the railroads to offer the "Cow, Sow, and Hen Special." Railcars outfitted with exhibits of animals and equipment traveled the state so Extension staff could offer classes and demonstrations. By the 1930s, telephone and radio helped county Extension agents deliver information. In 1961, Extension was offering a new "dial-a-number telephone encyclopedia of homeowners' hints" to Chicago and Cook county residents, with daily messages providing homemaking hints, gardening tips, and weekend bargain food buys. The first Illinois Extension website was launched in 1996. Today, Extension even has a YouTube presence.

Extension information available today has kept pace with people's changing needs and problems. While farming and homemaking skills dominated at the Extension's birth, today those programs are joined by more popular programs on the environment, nutrition, cooking, home management, master naturalist, and master gardener. The first master gardener program began in Will County in 1975. In 2010, Extension reorganized its agricultural educators to focus on small farms and local food systems, a reflection of the increase in farmers markets.

Another part of the service, 4-H, had been geared toward young people in rural areas. In 1956, it began a move into Chicago, announcing plans to bring the 4-H "learning by doing" philosophy to urban areas, offering projects such as vegetable gardening, entomology, cooking, sewing, and floriculture. Today, 4-H has added expanded science, technology, and engineering projects. In 1964, Extension made new efforts to bring "to Chicago residents programs in home economics and family living." In 2012, the service celebrated its 150th year.

Contributor: Judy Hevrdejs

See also: Agriculture, Urban; Chicago High School for Agricultural Sciences

BIBLIOGRAPHY

Rasmussen, W. D. *Taking the University to the People: Seventy-five Years of Cooperative Extension*. Ames: Iowa State University Press, 1989.

Vegetarianism

Groups of religious-based vegetarians began immigrating from England to the United States in the late 1700s. In the mid-1800s, The Seventh-Day Adventist church had its beginnings in New England. One of its members, John Harvey Kellogg, took charge of the Battle Creek Sanatorium in Michigan in 1876 and turned it into the most popular vegetarian spa in the world. Kellogg was one of the many speakers at the Columbian Exposition, held in Chicago in 1893. As part of the exposition, about 200 vegetarian delegates met for the first World Vegetarian Congress.

The Chicago Vegetarian Society (CVS) also participated at the exposition. Founded in 1890, it was the first group in Chicago to promote meatless eating. In a letter to *The

Vegetarian Messenger (Manchester, England), a member wrote, "The Chicago Vegetarian Society was founded with 5 members, and according to a newspaper, they now claim 100,000 persons in Chicago alone who are vegetarians as the result of the Society's working." At the turn of the century, the city was recognized as the center of the vegetarian movement in the United States.

At some point, CVS went defunct but reemerged in 1943, stating its purpose was to spread vegetarianism throughout Chicago, "across the country, around the world and through the universe." But the cause didn't keep the group active for long; it disbanded and then regrouped only briefly in 1980.

In 1895, a second vegetarian organization appeared in Chicago, the Vegetarian Eating Club. Its yearly celebration at the University of Chicago became one of the country's first turkey-free Thanksgiving banquets. Although it is not known how long the eating club was in existence, its tradition of a turkey-free holiday continues in various groups around the country to this day.

In 1906, Upton Sinclair published *The Jungle*, exposing the deplorable conditions of the animals at the Chicago Union Stock Yards. The popularity of the book was one spark leading to the passage of the Pure Food Act and the Meat Inspection Act, and it also pushed many Americans toward a vegetarian diet. In 1902, per capita meat consumption in the United States was 225 pounds. By 1921, it had fallen to 170 pounds, a 24 percent decline. It was after World War I that the movement slowed down in Chicago and around the country. And then the Great Depression marked the end of "the golden era of vegetarianism." It would not revive until the 1960s.

Chicago's first modern-day vegetarian business opened in 1971, the very year the Union Stock Yards closed. The Bread Shop, in East Lakeview, began as a whole-grain bakery, with an adjacent bulk food store. There was no division of labor at the Bread Shop. All workers waited on customers, lifted 50-pound sacks of flour, kneaded the bread dough totally by hand, and had an equal say in all business decisions. They were each paid $7 a day—and a free loaf of bread. A vegetarian restaurant, the Bread Shop Kitchen, later opened across the street. A meal there cost $1.50.

The Bread Shop closed after 25 years, but former employees moved on to run some of today's vegetarian-focused businesses: two Chicago General Nutrition Centers, Evanston's Blind Faith Café, and The Chicago Diner. In 1975, another shop opened, Rainbow Grocery at 946 W. Wellington St., which carried bulk foods such as nuts, grains, and flours, as well as a selection of vegetables.

Vegetarian Times, based in Oak Park, printed its first edition—a four-page handout—in 1974 and went on to become a national glossy magazine filled with

CHICAGO EDUCATIONAL VEGETARIAN GROUPS HAVE GROWN FROM ONLY ONE IN 1970 TO THE FOLLOWING TODAY

Chicago Raw Food Community: Educational events, RawLucks, Festivals, Retreats. http://www.meetup.com/rawchicago community.

Chicago Veg: Chicago's largest educational group, a 501 C 3 recognized nonprofit. http://www.meetup.com/chicagoveg.

Chicago Vegan: Laid-back group that explores and learns the vegan lifestyle. http://www.meetup.com/Chi-Vegan-Meetup.

Chicago VeganMania: A yearly, full-day celebration of vegan culture and food, including speakers and food demos. http://www.chicagoveganmania.com.

Healthy Dining Chicago: A community education and outreach effort offering meat-free cooking classes and a dining guide. http://www.healthydining.org.

LGBTQ Vegan Dining: Dining group for LGBTQ community. http://www.meetup.com/lgbt-vegan-dining.

Meat Free Mondays: Meets monthly for a meat-free meal or potluck. http://www.meetup.com/meatfreemondays.

No Oil Vegan Support Group: Meetings for education, social support, and recipe sharing. http://www.meetup.com/no-oil -vegan.

Vegan Chicago: Meetings, dine-outs, book club, family activities. http://www.meetup.com/vegan-chicago.

—KAY STEPKIN

photography and helpful articles on cooking vegetarian. In 2013, it celebrated its 400th issue.

Original Soul Vegetarian restaurant, 203 E. 75th St., opened in the Chatham neighborhood in 1981. Although it is run by a community of Black Hebrews, who take their diet from Genesis in the Old Testament, it is not a religious community. According to owner Arel Israel, "our mission is to improve the health of all humanity. This is Illinois' first vegan restaurant."

Victory's Banner was open in Evanston from 1981–86, and reopened in 1999 in Roscoe Village at 2100 W. Roscoe St. Owner Pradhan Balter, a follower of Indian meditation master Sri Chinmoy, considers the restaurant "a manifestation of my spiritual beliefs." Several Indian restaurants on Devon Avenue and the suburbs serve vegetarian fare.

In 1985, Karyn Calabrese opened Karyn's Raw, the city's first raw food restaurant, at 1901 N. Halsted St. It is now the longest-standing raw food restaurant in the country. She currently has three vegan restaurants, including Karyn's Cooked, in Chicago.

Since the 1970s, vegetarian restaurants have not only grown in Chicago, but grown upscale, from brown rice and veggies to Chef Charlie Trotter's groundbreaking 1988 vegetable tasting menu (and his later cookbooks, *Charlie Trotter's Vegetables* and *Raw*) and on to modern spots such as Shawn McClain's upscale Green Zebra, on W. Chicago Ave. The fast-food chain Native Foods opened its first spot in 2011 and now has six locations in Chicago. Urban Vegan is a Thai restaurant that opened its first location, on W. Montrose Ave. in 2011, and its second, location, on W. Fullerton Ave., in 2013.

Today vegetarianism is so mainstream that Mana Food Bar, 1742 W. Division St., in Wicker Park does not even use the V-word in its advertising, preferring the word "meatless."

Contributor: Kay Stepkin

BIBLIOGRAPHY

Iacobbo, Karen, and Michael Iacobbo. "*Vegetarian America: A History.*" Westport, Conn.: Praeger Publishers, 2004.

Terkel, Studs. "The Age of Charlie Blossom." *Working: People Talk about What They Do All Day and How They Feel about What They Do.* New York: Pantheon Books, 1972.

Victory Gardens (See: Agriculture, Urban; Wartime)

Vienna Beef

A multimillion-dollar worldwide business, Vienna Beef began with two Jewish immigrant sausage makers from Hungary peddling their family recipe at the 1893 World's Columbian Exposition in Jackson Park.

The efforts of Samuel Ladany and Emil Reichl at the fair were so successful that they decided to establish their business in Chicago. They originally called their enterprise the Vienna Sausage Manufacturing Co., choosing the name "Vienna" because that city had a reputation for fine sausage makers.

The partners' first location was a small, three-story building on Halsted Street in the Maxwell Street Market area. They expanded the business into a block-long facility where they stayed until 1972 when they built their plant at 2501 N. Damen Ave. In 2015–16, the company built a new plant and factory store in a redesigned former Sara Lee hot dog factory at 1000 W. Pershing Rd.

Vienna's early success may have been due to using only beef and more flavorful spicing in their sausages. In its early period, Vienna began selling to other retailers and stand operators. Henry Davis (né Davidovich), a longtime VP of sales, sparked business by advising stand owners, loaning them money, and helping them with construction and signage. The vendors reciprocated by agreeing to sell only Vienna products. Because of Davis's techniques, Vienna dominated the market, supplying stand owners with the "Vienna Beef Hot Dog" logo.

The Depression likely had a positive effect on the hot dog market; hot dogs could be bought for as little as a penny apiece. The hot dog surge continued through WWII, when meat rationing increased demand for foods like hot dogs.

In 1950, Vienna began selling its products nationwide. The demand was so great that the company opened distribution facilities in eight other American cities and production facilities on the West Coast. Vienna further expanded by supplying chain stores and supermarkets. Thanks to advances in refrigeration, meats could now be stored longer and be sold in smaller, self-serve packages.

Both Jules Ladany and his brother, William, succeeded their father Samuel in running the company. Jules Ladany died in 1979 and was succeeded by his son-in-law, Jim Eisenberg. Eisenberg and Jim Bodman, who had joined Vienna in 1964, bought the company from the Ladany family and continue to run it to this day. Scott Ladany is now a vice-president.

Over the years, the company expanded its line of products to Polish sausage, Italian beef, and corned beef. In addition, the company makes nonmeat products (pickles, soups, chili, and condiments). It also now markets products internationally. Today, practically every Chicago neighborhood has at least one Vienna hot dog stand, and if you enter sports stadiums in Chicago and others around the country, there's a good chance you'll see Vienna hot dogs for sale.

Contributor: Scott Warner

See also: Hot Dogs

BIBLIOGRAPHY

Eisenman, Herbert, and Jerold Levin. "Hot Dog! Jewish Participation in Chicago's Meat Industry." *Chicago Jewish History*, Summer 2012.

Walgreen, Myrtle and Charles

Charles R. Walgreen fought in the Spanish American War, but returned to Chicago in 1898, after contracting yellow fever. Once recuperated, he took a job as a pharmacist on Cottage Grove Boulevard near Bowen Avenue in the same neighborhood where Myrtle Norton was living. Born in 1870 in Carbondale and growing up on a farm, Myrtle learned the homemaking arts. She moved to Chicago in 1896. The couple met at a pharmacists' outing. About the same time, Charles used his military pension, plus a loan from his father, to purchase the drugstore where he worked in 1901 for $6,000. He called it Walgreens. The couple soon became engaged and married on August 18, 1902.

After a brief move to the West Coast, the newlyweds returned to Chicago, where Myrtle took pride in her cooking abilities. For their fifth anniversary, Myrtle chose a set of aluminum cooking pots. When she extolled their value, Charles bought a salesman's overstock of 300 pans and Walgreens began selling small aluminum pans for 15 cents each.

At home, Charles often discussed his ideas for expansion and new products with his wife. When the opportunity presented itself, he proposed a partnership in the first store with a former employee, enabling Walgreen to purchase a second store in 1909, this one for $15,000. When the store next door became available, Charles also bought it, cut through the wall, and built an ice-cream fountain, making the ice cream in the basement. Chocolate sodas and banana splits (for 20 cents) were popular, but when an employee added two scoops of the homemade ice cream to the chocolate soda, he invented the chocolate malted milkshake. Customers surrounded the counter three-deep to enjoy them.

When demand for the ice-cream treats declined one winter, Myrtle suggested her husband might expand the offerings by selling soup, sandwiches, cakes, and pies. For five years, she rose early every morning to shop, cook, and make fresh sandwiches and pots of soup, which she delivered to the store. As this idea became popular, Charles added a lunch counter in every store, built a commissary, and hired cooks. But Myrtle still went to the store to taste the offerings and make improvement suggestions. Myrtle once said, "[C]ooking is a deep satisfaction. . . . A lot of happiness was stirred, beaten and rolled into that food."

These business innovations have been preserved in an exhibit in the Museum of Science and Industry, installed in 1986 to celebrate Walgreens's 85th anniversary. In 1984, Walgreens opened its 1,000th store; today, there are stores around the world, but the soda fountains were discontinued in the 1980s. The Walgreens moved to the North Shore, raised two children, and built a country estate in Dixon, Illinois. Charles died in December 1939. Myrtle became a pilot, photographer, philanthropist, and master gardener before her death in August, 1971.

Contributor: Judith Dunbar Hines

See also: Lunch Counters; Malted Milk Shake; Restaurants and Fine Dining; Soda Fountains

BIBLIOGRAPHY

Hogan, Terry. "Charles R. Walgreen, One of Galesburg's Own." *The Zephyr*. http://www.thezephyr.com/backtrack/cwalgreen.htm.

http://www.thezephyr.com/backtrack/cwalgreen.htm.

Walgreen, Myrtle, and Margueritte Harmon Bro. *Never a Dull Day*. Washington, D.C.: Henry Regnery Company, 1963.

The Walnut Room

The first reputed restaurant in a department store opened in 1907 in Marshall Field's flagship store at 111 N. State St. It is now known as Macy's State Street. A soaring 45-foot decorated and lit "Great Tree" has made The Walnut Room a must-do stop over the holidays for generations of Chicagoans. The restaurant was born out of a chicken pot pie shared by a store clerk, Mrs. Hering, with two hungry customers with no place to eat. Word spread and Hering was soon selling her pot pies at the millinery department counter.

A store manager named Harry Selfridge—these were the days before he found mercantile fame and fortune in London—saw the possibilities in offering food in-house and urged Marshall Field to open a small third-floor tea room on April 15, 1890. Fifteen tables were set up, and 56 women came for a lunch; options included corned beef hash, chicken salad, and chicken pot pies. After the operation was relocated to a larger 17,000-square-foot dining room on the seventh floor, the room known as the South Tea Room quickly began to be called "The Walnut Room" for its Circassian walnut paneling. The name became official by 1937. Chicken pot pie is on the menu still.

Contributor: Bill Daley

See also: Department Store Dining; Moody, Harriet Brainard

BIBLIOGRAPHY

Siegelman, Steve, *The Marshall Field's Cookbook*. San Francisco: Book Kitchen, 2006.

Armour's Veribest Package Foods

The convenience of ready-cooked foods to be served cold, or with a few minutes heating, is appreciated by all housekeepers. Veribest Package Foods are prepared by expert Armour chefs in Armour's sanitary kitchens and include many delicacies difficult and expensive to prepare in the home. They are not only time-savers, but add variety to the menu. The housewife with a shelf of Armour's Veribest Foods is protected against any emergency. The Veribest Foods sold under the Oval Label include so wide a choice that almost the entire menu, day after day, can be satisfactorily arranged from them.

The uniform high standard of all these products, whether vegetable, fruit, meat, or fish, begins in the initial step of their preparation,—that is, in the selection. In the meat products, only choice portions of the highest grade meats are chosen. Fresh meat shrinks some fifty per cent in cooking. Armour's Veribest Meats are therefore *all* food, without waste, and the Armour methods of preparing and canning preserve all the original juices and fine flavor.

On pages 56–57 of this book will be found a complete list of Veribest Package Foods and on the following pages are many appetizing and novel methods of serving these.

Veribest products from "The Business of Being a Housewife." https://archive.org/details/businessofbeingh00male.

Wartime

During the Civil War (1861–65), food shortages were commonplace, north and south, though it was thought that civilians and soldiers from the north ate better than those from the south. Most soldiers lived on a limited diet of a baked flour and water blend called hard bread, plus beef, navy beans, and coffee. Civilians in Chicago and other large cities made do with what they could buy in poorly stocked markets or could grow in small plots in their yards. People learned to live without common ingredients or got creative about substitutes. But the rapid industrialization of food production as a result of war efforts made it possible to preserve foods and distribute them, via railroads, to consumers throughout the country.

Although food rationing did not exist on the home front during World War I, there were campaigns encouraging residents to limit food consumption, an approach that effectively reduced national consumption by 15 percent. The government and food companies published recipe booklets with simpler versions of classic recipes, often using less expensive food substitutes. "Meatless Tuesdays" and "Wheatless Wednesdays" saw recipes using corn flour, buckwheat, potato flour, and oatmeal, while main dishes included rice, spaghetti, beans, and soybeans. Chicago's Armour & Co. published recipes for meat and vegetables using their bargain canned products such as a luncheon beef stew made from sliced onions, potatoes, and cans of Veribest Tomato Soup, luncheon meat, peas, and seasoning sauce. Restaurant menus became notably smaller and with simpler preparations such as plain broiled steaks with baked potatoes and a vegetable or salad.

Three types of rations were used by American forces during World War I, starting with the "ironration" in 1907. It consisted of three 3-ounce cakes made from beef bouillon powder and parched, cooked wheat, three 1-ounce bars of sweetened chocolate, and packets of salt and pepper. Because food for soldiers in the trenches was often ruined by gas attacks, a trench ration featuring canned meats was introduced. That gave way to the "reserve ration," which initially consisted of 12 ounces of bacon or a pound of canned meat, two 8-ounce cans of hard bread or hardtack biscuits, ground coffee, sugar, salt and pepper, and cigarettes with rolling papers.

During World War II, domestic consumption was strategically limited to allow governments to equally distribute resources to many people. In 1942, President Franklin Delano Roosevelt encouraged Americans to grow fruits and vegetables to supplement the food supply during wartime. Nationwide, citizens rose to the occasion, planting victory gardens and crops to help prevent a food shortage. At the peak of the movement, more than 20 million plots existed nationwide.

Chicago played a key role in the government's wartime campaign to replenish scarce produce, sparking at-home growing and food preservation, both from bounty grown on school grounds and in community plots. It is estimated that more than 250,000 people began gardening at home, and 90 percent of those gardeners had never gardened before.

The Chicago Horticultural Society, in partnership with the Chicago Park District, supported the creation of 15,000 victory gardens on vacant sites within the city. In 1943, Chicago produced 55,000 pounds of food from these gardens. Excess food grown in home and public gardens was canned and used to supplement available food once the winter months arrived. By 1944, victory gardens produced 40 percent of vegetables grown in the United States. Even citizens without yards were planting in window boxes. Planting victory gardens also helped ensure there was enough food for American soldiers fighting throughout the world. It helped Chicagoans stretch their ration coupons because store-bought, canned vegetables—and store-bought items in general—were subject to rationing. Because trains and trucks were being used to transport soldiers, weapons, and vehicles, Chicagoans made a concerted effort to eat locally grown produce, and schools planted gardens on their grounds and incorporated grown-on-site produce into school lunches.

Today, Peterson Garden Project keeps the spirit alive. Inspired by Chicago's victory gardens of World War II, this twenty-first-century initiative takes cues from the city's past. There are about 650 community garden plots, with 2,400 participants, scattered throughout the Chicago area.

Contributor: Jennifer Olvera

See also: Agriculture, Urban

BIBLIOGRAPHY

"Victory Gardens at a Glance." National World War II Museum. http://www.nationalww2museum.org/learn/education/for-students/ww2-history/at-a-glance/victory-gardens.html.

Wolford, Ron. "Tending 'Defiant Gardens' During Wartime." University of Illinois Extension, September 2, 2007. http://web.extension.illinois.edu/cook/eb21/entry_1336/.

Water

Since Chicago's early days as a trading post through to its transition as a major hub in the global twenty-first-century service economy, water has played a critical role in the city as a drinking source, transportation medium, commercial asset, and recreational and industrial tool. Prior to the development of a national rail network, the Chicago River and Lake Michigan connected the city to the outside world and propelled the region to global status.

Until the mid–nineteenth century, the Chicago River flowed into Lake Michigan, but the construction of the Illinois & Michigan (I & M) Canal was the first step in reversing this flow, which was ultimately achieved with the completion of the Chicago Sanitary & Ship Canal in 1900. This engineering marvel effectively separated Chicago's drinking system (Lake Michigan) from its drainage system (the Chicago River). The I&M Canal also linked the U.S. interior by water from the Gulf of Mexico, up the Mississippi River, through the Great Lakes system, and finally to the Atlantic Ocean.

Though the Chicago area had been a minor trading post and portage site for centuries, Chicago's rise as a modern metropolis can be directly tied to the first plans for a canal in the early nineteenth century. Speculation not only drove up land values and attracted settlers and investors, including Chicago's first mayor, William Butler Ogden, but also provided the impetus for one of the first orthogonal plans of the city.

Securing fresh drinking water was complicated by Chicago's rapid growth and heavy industrialization. Industry

at the time clustered along the river and canal, freely discharging waste into the waterways, which was seeping into Lake Michigan and contaminating the region's drinking water. The food industry, namely the meatpackers, were a highly visible offender from their outpost in today's Bridgeport and Back of the Yards neighborhood, where they so heavily polluted a fork of the Chicago's River's South Branch that the section became popularly known as Bubbly Creek for the gases that would bubble to the surface as a result of the massive decomposition of meatpacking by-products.

To compensate for rising pollution, Chicago began to build intake cribs farther out in Lake Michigan. Whereas water collection used to take place close to the lake's edge, intake cribs were built two miles out into the lake, where they continue to collect water today. Additionally, in the early twentieth century, the city began to invest in sophisticated wastewater treatment and water purification plants to continue to secure the quality of drinking water. Today, the James W. Jardine Water Purification Plant just north of Navy Pier is the world's largest water treatment plant.

In addition to the extraordinary feats of reversing the river's flow, tunneling under the lake about two miles out to build intake cribs and building some of the world's most sophisticated treatment facilities, Chicago even went to the extraordinary length of raising its streets 50 feet in the nineteenth century in order to build sewers that would successfully drain across the city's flat plains.

Protecting a critical source of drinking water and improving conservation and treatment efforts also have helped preserve Lake Michigan as a destination for recreational fishing. After decades of strong growth, though, fishing deteriorated as a commercial pursuit in the mid–twentieth century.

Prior to the coordinated regional efforts, fish in local waterways were at risk not just from pollution but also from overfishing and invasive species. Aquatic hitchhikers have been a downside of Chicago's booming international maritime commerce since the late nineteenth century. Several nonnative species have been introduced to the Great Lakes system via ballast tanks in cargo ships. Today, they present one of the preeminent threats to regional biodiversity, especially as the threat of overfishing has largely been controlled.

One species that fell prey to the triple threat of pollution, overfishing, and invasive species (in this case the sea lamprey) was the lake trout, which was extirpated from Lake Michigan in the 1950s. Historically a popular food fish, the lake trout has been unable to reestablish a self-sustaining population, and the State of Illinois has been stocking the lake with lake trout since 1965. The state also stocks Lake Michigan with hundreds of thousands of other top predator fish, including Chinook salmon, coho salmon, rainbow trout, and brown trout.

Foreign species, such as the zebra mussel, quagga mussel, sea lamprey, round goby, and ruffe pose a threat to the aqua system's native species, such as the yellow perch. But some, such as pacific salmon, were introduced purposefully to provide recreational fishing opportunities and also to control the population of smaller fish that traditionally served as a food source for Lake Michigan's top predator species. Other popular species fished off the shores of Chicago include smelt, perch, and several varieties of bass.

Until the 1920s, Chicago's vast maritime trade clogged the central branch of the Chicago River as schooners, and then steamers, introduced Chicago to an array of international foods, products, and people. In 1921, work began on a new port for the city, 20 miles south of downtown, where modern freighters now dock, bringing more than 18 million tons in trade each year, mostly of raw materials such as steel and stone. Chicago is one of the busiest inland ports in the world. Additionally, the Port of Chicago harbors some of Illinois' largest grain storage facilities, with a capacity of about 14 million bushels. However, finished products and perishables such as food now tend to move by air, or overland by truck or train. With its major transportation hubs (O'Hare Airport, key national railroad interchanges, and strong interstate highway connections), Chicago remains a relevant and key port.

Contributor: Andres Torres

See also: Transportation; Zebra Mussels

BIBLIOGRAPHY

Chicago Maritime Museum. http://www.chicagomaritimemuseum.org/.

Egan, Dan. "Commercial Fishing, Once a Great Lakes Way of Life, Slips Away." *Los Angeles Times*, August 30, 2011.

Hudson, John. *Chicago: A Geography of the City and Its Region*. Santa Fe, N.M.: The Center for American Places, 2006.

Weber-Stephen Products Co.

Best known for its iconic kettle grill, the Palatine, Illinois–based company manufactures a variety of grills and grilling accessories sold worldwide. The Weber grill story began in 1952, when George Stephen Sr. began selling "George's Barbecue Kettle," which he had first fashioned out of a metal buoy. Stephen worked for Weber Brothers Metal Works in Chicago and earned enough money from grill sales to buy the company, creating Weber-Stephen Products Co. in 1959. The company remained family-owned until December 2010, when it was announced that BDT Capital Partners LLC had acquired a majority share of the company. The chain of Weber Grill restaurants, however, remains owned by the Stephen family. (Locations include 539 N. State St. in Chicago, and in Lombard, Schaumburg, and Indianapolis, Indiana.)

Just like the little black dress, Weber's black kettle charcoal grill is an eternal classic—and comes in various sizes. But over the years the company has added color and gussied up the grill by mounting it into, among other things, a faux wishing well, wrought-iron patio furniture, or even a wooden cart. It introduced gas and electric grills (in 1971 and 1973, respectively).

The company's first cookbook was 1999's *Art of the Grill*. Weber has issued 11 cookbooks in the United States as of 2014, most of which were written by Jamie Purviance, a California-based grilling expert. According to Weber, the best-selling book, with more than 1 million copies sold, is 2005's *Weber's Real Grilling*.

Weber has focused considerable effort on customer support. About a half-million calls annually come into its customer-care center in Schaumburg. It also developed a social media presence, notably with its "Weber Nation" blog.

Contributor: Bill Daley

See also: Equipment, Home

BIBLIOGRAPHY

Daley, Bill. "Weber World! Once Humble Grill Becomes a Cultural Icon in Back Yards around the Globe." *Chicago Tribune*, May 26, 2004.

Lashinsky, Adam, "Byron Trott: The Billionaires' Banker." *Fortune Magazine*. http://fortune.com December 29, 2014.

Wholesale and Distribution

From almost the beginning, Chicago has been a center for wholesaling and distribution of foods. At first, this was because of its location at the border of America's frontier. Raw materials, including grains, dairy, and meats, flowed in from across the West, were processed in the city, and then were shipped to the East Coast and beyond. As William Cronon states: "Whether breaking up shipments from the East or assembling bulk shipments from the West, (Chicago) served as the entrepôt—the place in between—connecting eastern markets with vast western resource regions." While its situation on the frontier may have sparked Chicago's massive mid–nineteenth century growth, it was its role as America's central city that allowed this growth to continue through the early twentieth century, building the city as a national and global economic power.

South Water Market, Fulton Street Market (the nearby market for meats), and Randolph Street Haymarket (where hay and local produce were sold) were the hubs of the wholesale food trade in late nineteenth and early twentieth-century Chicago.

South Water Market stretched along the south bank of the main branch of the Chicago River. There, large "commission houses," which earned money by contracting with farmers and manufacturers to resell goods on commission, backed up against the river. Foodstuffs came via the river or by wagons on South Water Street that arrived from the rail lines. This traffic, combined with the normal central city bustle, made congestion a constant issue.

The Burnham Plan of 1909 recommended that South Water Market be removed and replaced by a double-decker boulevard, and that produce sales be moved to a municipally owned wholesale market away from the city's core. While most of the Burnham Plan never came to fruition, in 1925, a new South Water Market, with good access to both rail lines and the street, was built between Racine and Morgan and 14th and 16th Streets. The next year, Wacker Drive opened on the site of the original South Water Market. By 1949, South Water was the second largest wholesale produce market in the country, supplying the metropolitan area and acting as a repackaging and shipping point for shipments to the east and south. Competing sites soon developed, including the Chicago Produce Terminal, a train yard where incoming produce was sorted, located about two miles southwest of the market.

By 1950, issues with the second South Water Market were becoming apparent. The southeastern United States was growing as an area for produce production. More importantly, with the growth in the use of refrigerated trucks for long-distance hauling, shipments to secondary markets did not have to go through a central market like Chicago but could be delivered directly to warehouses and distribution centers in smaller cities. In addition, large supermarket chains increasingly had their own distribution systems and did not rely on central "terminal" markets like South Water. Chicago's own Jewel Tea, for instance, had a large warehouse on South Ashland next to the Chicago Union Stock Yards, serving both its national grocery delivery business and its growing group of supermarkets.

The Fulton and Randolph markets located mostly west of North Halsted Street, were once host to wholesale vendors who sold fruits, vegetables, meat, fish, dairy products, eggs, and other food products to neighborhood markets and downtown hotels and restaurants. As early as 1857, the street was designed wider than usual to accommodate an open-air wholesale farmers market. In the 1920s,

business expanded after the moving of the downtown Water Street Market and the further widening of Randolph all the way to Ogden Avenue. Products sold over the decades included giant wheels of Wisconsin cheese, crates of Michigan plums, and barrels of pickles. Later, wholesale produce vendors occupied storefronts along Randolph Street. The last one closed in 2013. However, the retail butcher shop, Olympia Meats, founded in the 1960s, is still open.

Two blocks to the north, Fulton Market specialized in animal products. In the 1870s, wholesale items included butter, eggs, fish, meat, and poultry. Meatpackers of the Union Stock Yards had branch operations here in order to be closer to downtown and the North Side. With the rise in freight truck transportation, meatpacking operations expanded in the 1950s because of the market's proximity to the highway. Small- to midsize companies sold dressed meat or made specialty meat products, such as corned beef, variety meats, and beef jerky. As of August 2015, several historic businesses still resided there, including Variety Meats, Peer Foods (formerly Buehler Foods), and Isaacson and Stein, the last remaining fish market.

In 2001, the state-of-the-art Chicago International Produce Market was built, located along the Chicago Ship and Sanitary canal, the Stevenson Expressway (I-55), and train lines. It is the largest in the Midwest and much more efficient than the previous market, being designed for today's larger trucks. However, the new market has a lesser aim than the original or second South Water Markets. While some of the tenants of the new market have an international reach, Chicago, in general, does not strive to be the central produce wholesale market of the United States but instead focuses primarily on serving the Chicago area and the Midwest.

....

Contributors: Daniel Block and Amanda Scotese

See also: Transportation

BIBLIOGRAPHY

Butterworth, James D. *A Study of the Changes in the Volume of Fresh Fruits and Vegetables Handled by Middlemen Operating in the Chicago South Water Market, 1939–1949*, PhD Dissertation, Northwestern University, 1950.

Cronon, William. *Nature's Metropolis: Chicago and the Great West.* New York: W. W. Norton and Company, 1991.

Duis, Perry R. *Challenging Chicago: Coping with Everyday Life, 1837–1920*. Urbana: University of Illinois Press, 1998.

Wild Onion

If Chicago had been named by botanists, it would be called *Allium tricoccum*. Also known as the ramp, wild leek, wild garlic, and *ail des bois*, this onion relative grew thickly in the area that was to become Chicago when the first

Europeans visited. *Chicago* is a corruption of a French misspelling of the word for this plant in the language of the Miami and Illinois native tribes. First recorded by seventeenth-century explorer Robert Cavelier, sieur de La Salle, the name was explained by his comrade, naturalist-diarist Henri Joutel in his 1687 account of their last expedition:

"We arrived at a place which is named Chicagou, which, according to what we learned, has taken its name from the quantity of garlic which grows in this district, in the woods . . . a species of garlic in quantity which is not entirely like that of France, having its leaf broader and shorter, and is also not so strong, though its taste closely approaches it but is not like the little onions or the onion of France."

Early historians thought that the *chicagou* plant—*ail sauvage*, in French—was *Allium cernuum*, the nodding wild onion, but research by John F. Swenson in the 1990s showed the correct plant was the ramp.

Contributor: Leah A. Zeldes

See also: Native Americans

BIBLIOGRAPHY

Joutel, Henri. *Journal, 1684–1688*. Dolph Briscoe Center for American History, University of Texas at Austin.

Swenson, John F. "Chicagoua/Chicago: The Origin, Meaning, and Etymology of a Place Name," *Illinois Historical Journal* 84 (Winter 1991): 235–48.

William Wrigley Jr. Company

The Chicago-based firm created in 1891 by William Wrigley Jr. sells more than Juicy Fruit gum today. In the United States, in addition to the familiar chewing gum titles, its brands include Life Savers, Skittles, Starburst, and Altoids. Internationally, locals can buy Wrigley's Rondo in Kazakhstan, Boomer (a bubblegum) in Cambodia, Airwaves (a "vapor release" gum) in Switzerland, Pim Pom (a lollypop) in Bhutan, Kenman in Australia, Big G in Botswana, Squeeze Pops in Guam, Cool Air in Mauritius, Big Boy in Fiji, and others.

Yet when Wrigley arrived in Chicago at 29 with a wife, daughter, $32 in his pocket, and a rich father back in Philadelphia, his intention was to sell not gum, but soap and baking powder, produced by his dad's company. As an incentive to customers, he threw in a little gum as a bonus— "Everybody likes something extra, for nothing"—then discovered they liked the gum more than the soap or powder.

So in 1892, with a little help from a moneyed uncle, he went into the gum business. Early brands were Sweet Sixteen Orange and Lotta Gum. A year later, he had Juicy Fruit (introduced at Chicago's World's Columbian Exposition) and Spearmint under the Wrigley brand, and he prospered.

Built in 1911, Wrigley's 175,000-square-foot factory operated until 2006. The Central Manufacturing District: Chicago Junction Railway Service: A Book of Descriptive Text, Photographs & Testimonial Letters about Chicago Junction Railway Service and the Central Manufacturing District—the center of Chicago, "The Great Central Market," 1915. https://archive.org/details/centralmanufactu00cent.

By 1916, he owned a piece of the Chicago Cubs, and three years later he controlled it all—including the ballpark that would eventually carry his name.

Wrigley invested early in advertising ("Tell 'em quick and tell 'em often."), built the Wrigley Building (1921), put workers on a five-day week in 1924—a revolutionary concept—and died in 1932 at 70. "He was proud of Chicago—proud of being in business in Chicago," friend and rental car-taxi baron John Hertz said upon the man's death. "He once told me he would not take the throne of England if it meant he had to leave Chicago."

Son Philip K. took over. Among the developments under his watch: the Doublemint Twins (1939); the All-American Girls Professional Baseball League (1943–44); and, in 1944, pulling Spearmint, Juicy Fruit, and Doublemint off the open market (because of wartime scarcity of ingredients), and distributing what *could* be produced free to service members. Full production resumed after the war.

Under Philip's successor, William Wrigley, production and distribution went international. In 2007, the company's sales exceeded $5 billion for the first time, and in 2008, under chairman Bill Wrigley Jr., the company became a subsidiary of candy giant Mars, Incorporated. The Wrigley family sold the Cubs to Tribune Co. in June 1981. Company headquarters is still in Chicago but no longer in the Wrigley Building. And no member of the family has been offered the throne of England.

Contributor: Alan Solomon

See also: Candy

BIBLIOGRAPHY

Boyle, Robert. "A Shy Man at a Picnic." *Sports Illustrated*, April 14, 1958.

Solomon, Alan. *A Century of Wrigley Field: The Official History of the Friendly Confines.* New York: Major League Baseball, 2013.

Wilson & Company

One of the largest meatpackers in the United States from 1917 to the 1950s, Wilson & Company was named for its founder, Thomas E. Wilson (1868–1958). A Canadian farm boy, Wilson immigrated to Chicago where he was employed by Nelson Morris & Company, one of the Union Stock Yards' original meatpackers. He worked his way up the corporate ladder, eventually becoming company president. Offered the presidency of a failing national company, Sulzberger and Son, in 1916, he took the position and renamed the company Wilson & Company. Within a year, the company rebounded to become the equal of Armour and Swift in production. By the 1930s, Wilson employed 5,000 people and was one of the top 50 American companies. Wilson was famous for its Wilson's Certified Hams and Corn King bacon, hot dogs, and other deli meats.

As a sideline, Wilson purchased the Ashland Manufacturing Company, a maker of sporting goods. Because Wilson had hides and pigskins, a firm making baseball gloves, shoes, basketballs, and footballs was a natural fit. The business took off, changed its name to Wilson Sporting Goods Company in the 1930s, and became America's leading sporting goods manufacturer. Wilson stopped its Chicago slaughtering operations in the late 1950s but remained a major national meat company through the 1960s. It was sold to a conglomerate in 1967, and its headquarters were moved to Dallas, Texas. The company was sold piecemeal over the next 20 years with only Corn King hams, a Tyson Foods subsidiary, remaining as a food brand name. Wilson Sporting Goods remains a vibrant Chicago business.

Contributor: Bruce Kraig

See also: Union Stock Yards

BIBLIOGRAPHY

Fowler, Bertram. *Men, Meat, and Miracles.* New York: Julian Messner, 1952.

Wilson, Warren J. *Tied to the Great Packing Machine: The Midwest and Meatpacking.* Iowa City: University of Iowa Press, 2007.

Wilton Enterprises

This Woodridge, Illinois, company has grown into an international corporation and the largest cake-decorating education company in the United States. Since 2007, the company has been owned by one of the nation's largest private equity firms, Tower-Brook Capital, and generally

Decorating class at Wilton School of Cake Decorating and Confectionary Art, 1947. Courtesy of Wilton Industries.

is considered the largest and most diversified company in the craft industry.

Wilton was started in 1929 by candy maker, Dewey McKinley Wilton, who made pulled-sugar confections. Wilton developed the Wilton Method of cake decorating and offered its first course in his family's dining room. Following its success, he moved operations to Lodge Hall, 59th and Halsted Sts., Chicago, and in 1946, opened a school in Woodridge.

Today, the school educates 1,400 students a year from 88 countries and all 50 states. Its educational marketing arm hires almost 4,000 teachers for its stores across the United States. As of 2008, 262,000 people were instructed in the art of cake decorating. In 2012, Wilton created 2,500 cake idea projects annually. The company also sells baking supply products such as pans and decorating equipment to accompany its classes.

Wilton's offices were moved in 1964 to West 115th Street, Chicago, and then again in early 1980s to Woodridge. Candy making classes were added, and the company name changed to Wilton School of Cake Decorating and Confectionary Art.

Wilton publishes an annual Cake Decorating yearbook and holds a yearly tent sale (1985 to present). In 1993, the company built a new facility in Darien, Illinois, with an adjacent retail store. The new century saw Wilton expand to the web with a video show called, *Bake, Decorate, Celebrate*, and online classes. Wilton merged with many firms, making supplies for scrapbooking, paper-based craft, tag books, scrapbooks, paint-by-numbers, beading, rubber stamping, and needlecraft. Licensing agreements include Disney, Marvel, Nickelodeon, Sesame Street, Warner Brothers, American Girls Crafts, and Martha Stewart Crafts. Further expansion, in 2013, included the Simplicity Creative Group.

Contributor: Geraldine Rounds

See also: Cooking Classes

BIBLIOGRAPHY

"Wilton Expands Crafting Reach with Simplicity Deal." *Chicago Tribune*, January 2, 2013.

Wilton Home. "A History of Wilton." http://www.wilton.com/about/history.cfm.

Wine and Wineries

Chicago has always been an important brewer for the nation, but not a winemaker. Wine grapes were not as easy to grow as grain and hops in the northern Midwest climate. Although wine has been made in Illinois since the 1850s, mostly downstate, serious winemaking did not kick off near Chicago until the 1990s. By then, winemakers had learned how to grow mostly hybrid grape varieties hardy enough to withstand the cruel winters of northern Illinois.

Until the second half of the twentieth century, wine primarily was consumed in private homes or during ethnic festivals and holidays. Many immigrants brought home winemaking traditions to Chicago, especially the Italians. The Germans and others from Central Europe frequented *weinstuben* (wine taverns) that served on-tap imported German wines or wine made by midwestern German farmers. Imported wine was expensive and available only to the affluent in restaurants such as Kinsley's and at Chicago's best hotels. The first California wines appeared in Chicago in the 1870s.

Under Prohibition, which began in 1919, boxes of compacted grapes from California, Michigan, and elsewhere were sold in Chicago as "wine bricks" for use in home winemaking, which was exempt from the ban on alcohol production. In 1923, it was estimated Chicagoans produced about 12,500,000 gallons of homemade wine, equivalent to about 4–1/2 gallons per person.

Another loophole was for religious rituals, which led to an increased demand for exemptions to Prohibition based on religious affiliation. This led some wags to comment that the city had become a haven for the religiously devout. The *Chicago Tribune* reported in 1923 that over 1 million gallons of still and sparkling wines "were purchased in this city by persons who technically were forced to claim they needed the stuff in their drive to keep Satan behind them."

Although Illinois had been the fourth largest producer of wine in the country, with the end of Prohibition,

WINE DINNERS, A TREND NO MORE

Wine is more the focus than the food (although pairing them well is a goal) in these dinners. Once a popular marketing tool for restaurants and a cause for a festive night out for customers, they have peaked in popularity (the economic crisis of the mid-2000s did them in). When the winemaker is present, they're often called a "winemaker dinner," but these, too, have become less well considered by the winemakers themselves who are commonly requested to donate the wines being served. An Internet site, Local Wine Events, lists many dinners available in Chicago and across the nation: http://www.localwineevents.com.

—BILL ST. JOHN

wine production was slow to return. It would take many decades before commercial wineries would return to Illinois, much less Chicago. Recently, however, wineries have been springing up in many new locations. Both the greater Chicago metropolitan area and the city of Chicago itself are now home to wineries, and in some cases, vineyards.

Within the city limits, City Winery opened in Chicago after a successful beginning in New York. Located on Randolph Street, City Winery hosts concerts, has an extensive restaurant, and offers patrons the chance to make their own wine. Another winery in the city's Beverly neighborhood on the Far South Side, Wild Blossom Meadery is most famous for its mead, an ancient drink made from fermented honey.

Outside the city limits, several wineries and vineyards call the Chicago area home: Fox Valley Winery, Valentino Vineyards, The Village Vintner Winery and Brewery, Cooper's Hawk, Glunz Winery, and Lynfred Winery. Several of these grow grapes, make wine on the premises, serve food, and host events and entertainment. Many other wineries are further from the city. Illinois' wine industry is growing as more people recognize the increasing quality of its wines.

Contributor: Clara Orban

BIBLIOGRAPHY

Burns, Edward. "Wine Bootleggers: Millions in Graft but Game Has Died." *Chicago Tribune*, March 27, 1927.

Orban, Clara. *Illinois Wines and Wineries: The Essential Guide*. Carbondale: Southern Illinois University Press, 2014.

Wine Bars

Deciding what is a "wine bar" in Chicago goes a way toward explaining the term, and both its history and role. No establishment ever has succeeded at offering for sale merely a select and long list of interesting wines by the glass without also offering at least some food. But many a restaurant, obviously more focused on food, has developed that long list of interesting wines by the glass and has also come to be called a "wine bar."

For instance, the first of the genre, Geja's Café (est. 1965), is commonly called "Chicago's first wine bar" and still fancies itself thus, but nonetheless advertises itself and is thought of by the majority of its patrons as a fondue restaurant. Thomas Bentley in 1980 opened Bentley's Wine Bar/Café on the corner of Willow and Halsted in Lincoln Park. It became the center of wine interest in Chicago in its day; it served wine only, no liquor. Bentley's closed in 1985.

Other wine bars followed in the wake of Bentley's, but also were short-lived, including Johanna's at 10 E.

GROWING GRAPES IN THE FOX VALLEY

Dick Faltz, owner of the Oswego, Illinois, Fox Valley Winery, is one of the most prominent winemakers in Illinois today. Faltz and his family planted vines on their farm in the Fox River Valley in 2000. In 2003, they opened a tasting room, after the formerly "dry" township was rezoned to allow wine sales for the first time since the 1930s. They grow several varieties of hybrid grapes, such as Frontenac, St. Pepin, and Traminette, and they also are experimenting with *vitis vinifera* grapes, such as chardonnay and pinot noir. Falz specializes in small-lot, single-vineyard wines that showcase the terroir of Illinois. Some wines also are made from grapes brought in from Michigan or farther afield. A winner of numerous awards, the winery hosts many classes and events throughout the year.

—CLARA ORBAN

Delaware, well-liked for its annual Champagne tasting, wide range of wines, and light snacks; and Rudi's Wine Bar near Ashland and Fullerton, with its French Quarter atmosphere.

In 1994, husband and wife Tom MacDonald and Jana Asfour opened Chicago's most ambitious wine bar, Webster's Wine Bar in Lincoln Park. It recently moved to new quarters in Logan Square, taking the place of yet another wine bar that had previously occupied the space, Telegraph.

For more than 30 years, Pop's for Champagne has operated a wine bar devoted to sparkling wines, first near DePaul University, now on State and Ohio. It sports more than 250 sparkling wines on its list. Other contemporary openings for wine bars include Ampersand Wine Bar on North Damen Ave., Eno in the Intercontinental Hotel, Bin 36 on Jefferson Street, Quartino on State Street, and Vera on Lake St.

Contributor: Bill St. John

BIBLIOGRAPHY

Geja's Cafe. https://www.gejascafe.com/.

Pops for Champagne. http://popsforchampagne.com/.

Webster Wine Bar. http://websterwinebar.com/.

Wine Classes

Wine education opportunities abound throughout the Chicago region. For example, many restaurants or retail establishments hold ad hoc wine education pop-ups, perhaps led by a traveling winery representative essentially touting product, but nonetheless passing on wine knowledge. Most any Saturday morning at many area wine shops, a passerby can pick up a wine information tidbit along with a sample of wine.

Chicago's longest-serving wine education professional was Patrick Fegan, who established The Chicago Wine School in 1984, although he had been teaching about wine in taverns and restaurants since 1974. His school enjoyed permanent residence on South Halsted Street from 2001–7, but later operated in places as varied as restaurant private dining rooms, business boardrooms, and private living rooms. Fegan estimated that he taught more than 25,000 students in the Chicago area since he began lecturing in the '70s. He died in 2016.

The American Wine School, affiliated with the London-based Wine & Spirits Education Trust (WSET), offers regular sessions for beginners as well as the more knowledgeable in several area locations, including Binny's Beverage Depot in Lincoln Park.

Mark Gruber has long taught wine appreciation classes through Northwestern University's Norris Center. Many wine shops also offer classes, such as Diana Hamann's The Wine Goddess shop in Evanston, Lush Wine & Spirits in three locations, Binny's Wine Depot locations, and many others. Kristin Savino's Vino di Savino offers wine education classes around Chicago and Northwest Indiana. Since 2003, Bill St John has taught classes at his Lincoln Park wine school, St. John on Wine.

For professionals, many local culinary schools offer classes about wine, beer, and spirits, such as in Kendall College's Beverage Management program. And for those interested in making wine, Bev-Art Brewer and Winemaker Supply in the Beverly neighborhood offers the how-to's as well as equipment.

Contributor: Bill St. John

BIBLIOGRAPHY

American Wine School. http://americanwineschool.com/
wset-classes/chicago/.

The Chopping Block. http://www.thechoppingblock.net/wineShop/
wineshop.htm.

Wine Distribution and Sales

The greatest irony of the 21st Amendment (1933) to the Constitution of the United States, commonly called "Repeal," is that it made getting a post-Prohibition drink more difficult to obtain than during those glory days of the Grand Experiment itself. In 1933, Repeal devolved to the individual States of the Union the power over distribution and sales of beverage alcohol (wine included, of course) that had once been the purview of the federal government.

After Repeal, Illinois and many other states adopted what came to be called a "three-tier" system to regulate and tax the distribution of beverage alcohol. The three-tier system keeps producers, wholesalers, and retailers independent of each other; producers sell to licensed wholesalers, who in turn sell to licensed retailers, who in turn sell to consumers (at liquor stores, for example, or wine shops, restaurants, or taverns). Alcohol sales may neither skip a tier nor proceed in an opposite direction.

In the 1930s and after Repeal, several wholesale liquor, beer, and wine distributors that had existed as such before passage of the National Prohibition Act were granted licenses to reoperate under the new three-tier system. One exists to this day, under the same name since it was established in 1888, Louis Glunz Wines.

Early wine distribution in Chicago from the period after Prohibition until the 1960s, when Chicago did become both a national and international wine market, was of wine that had been produced in states such as California or New York and then shipped in bulk to Chicago and bottled there by distributors such as Romano Bros. Beverage Co. and A. Fantozzi & Sons Wine Importers.

The 1960s (into the 1970s and 1980s) ushered in a new world of wine distribution for Chicago. Anthony Terlato, first at his in-laws' Pacific Wine Company and Paterno Imports, and then at his own Terlato Wines, sought out and brought to Chicago high-end, already-bottled wines from Europe and California. Similarly, Gerald Hirsch at Wines Unlimited, a branch of the liquor distributor Federated Distributors (and later at Heritage Wines, which he founded in 1981), brought to Chicago many of the finer wines of Europe and the West Coast.

But from 1980 until the early 2000s, like an enormous bellows breathing in` to consolidate or out to diversify, wine distribution in Chicago fell to a few very large companies (such as Wirtz Beverage that in 1999 employed 1,500 people) or broke out into dozens of smaller firms that represented only a few wine labels. Consolidation leads to splintering off, more often than not, because wineries dislike the liquor-dominated mentality of large distributors. Later, smaller companies, struggling in a fractured marketplace, get gobbled up in a new wave of consolidation.

The largest sweep occurred in 2002 when Southern Wine & Spirits, the nation's largest wine and liquor distributor (35 markets; 14,500 employees) entered the Illinois market by taking up Chicago's Romano Brothers Beverage Co., then the 12th largest wine and liquor distributor in the United States.

The history of wine retail in Chicago mirrors these same waves, except in one important way: more and more outlets are available for wine sales with the building of new grocery and convenience stores. After 2014, when the Illinois legislature moved the allowed hours for the sale of alcohol on Sunday from 11 a.m. to 8 a.m., and allowed issuance of a "late hour" licensee to sell alcohol until 5 a.m. on a Sunday, it is technically illegal to purchase wine in the city of Chicago for a mere three hours each week—from 5 to 8 a.m. Sunday mornings.

Consolidation also is commonplace in wine retail sales. Gone are legendary names in wine retail such as Armanetti's (some remain as franchises), Gold Standard, Chalet, Zimmerman's, and Sam's Wines & Spirits; many have been absorbed by Binny's Beverage Depot and its 31 locations, most in the Chicago area.

....

Contributor: Bill St. John

BIBLIOGRAPHY

Wine and Spirits Distributors of Illinois. http://www.wineandspirtis.com.

Wine Service

At the 1893 World's Columbian Exposition, Spain proudly showcased the aggressive growth of its wine industry over the previous decade by sending a large display to the fair. The German Empire also sent a comprehensive selection from every wine region. Several German winemakers brought libraries of old wines stretching back to legendary 1763 and 1811 vintages. But there were also wines from far-flung or emerging regions such as New South Wales or even Peru. The Ottoman Empire sent 22 exhibitors, including two wineries from the Bekaa Valley (now Lebanon). Chilean wines were highly praised by judges. Japan made an impression with 47 examples of rice brews (sake, mirin).

As wine stewards and other service workers at restaurants and large hotels emerged as a class, and became professionalized, this expanded geography of wine of the 1890s would be systematized and diffused as applied knowledge in industry journals, such as in the wine steward's manual written by John Tellman serialized in the Chicago-published *Hotel Monthly* from 1898. Other articles from this journal or from *Chicago Hotel Reporter* discussed inventory systems or fine points of blending, bottling, and other cellar work, which were key everyday tasks for wine stewards in the nineteenth century. John Goins, an African American headwaiter with over two decades of experience in Chicago-area hotels and restaurants wrote an invaluable guide for waiters, including detailed instructions on the correct sequence of wine service and the proper temperature for serving Sauternes or Burgundy.

Of course, not all those exhibited wines would find a way into the American market. A global recession of wine prices, which had been presaged by shortages due to grapevine diseases and labor unrest during the 1890s, would end up stretching half a century into the postwar period. The collapse of the wine market in Europe because of the two World Wars, and in the United States because of Prohibition followed by the Great Depression, made impossible the intensive investment necessary for the production of quality wines anywhere in the world. It would not be until the 1960s that non-European wines would slowly make their way into restaurant wine lists, with California leading the charge.

Wine stewarding from the 1970s now required not just a mastery of classic wine regions but also a grasp of the so-called "New World wines" and an understanding of Asian, Latin, California, and other cuisines, emerging into the forefront. Even wine lists at very traditional French restaurants, such as Bob Bansberg's when he was sommelier at Ambria (1980–2007), now included sections of Australian wines, Oregon Pinot Noirs, or Lebanon's Chateau Musar. Sommelier Henry Bishop curated the progressive Italian wine list at Spiaggia (1984–2006) but also crafted the early wine lists tailored to match the Mexican cuisine at Frontera Grill. He was also a pioneering champion of wines from lesser-known winemaking states such as Arizona or Michigan. Charlie Trotter opened his restaurant in 1988, and his pioneering of the long-form tasting menu was nationally influential. But so was his pioneering of the matched suite of wines that drew from a now seemingly infinite universe of global wines to pair with the lavish series of courses featuring unrepeatable combinations of ingredients drawn from throughout the world. From the 2000s, sake became a regular pairing option at top Chicago restaurants, such as in Joe Catterson's wine program at Alinea (2004–15).

....

Contributor: Richard S. Tan

BIBLIOGRAPHY

Goins, John. "The American Colored Waiter." *Hotel Monthly*, Chicago, March 1901 and April 1901.

Sturm, A. "Sammelausstellung des deutschen Weinbaues" in *Amtlicher Bericht über die Weltausstellung in Chicago 1893*, Vol. 1. Berlin: Reichsdruckerei, 1894.

Tellman, John. "The Practical Hotel Steward." Series. *Hotel Monthly*, Chicago, June 1898–December 1899.

World's Columbian Exposition, Chicago, Illinois. 1893: Report of the Committee on Awards of the World's Columbian Commission. Washington D.C.: U.S. Government Printing Office, 1901.

Zebra Mussels

The zebra mussel, so-called because of the stripes on its shell, is one of the more pernicious invasive creatures in the Great Lakes. Native to Russia and Ukraine, it and its relative, the quagga mussel, arrived in ballast tanks of freight ships in the 1980s. These are efficient filter feeders and because they reproduce prolifically—in 2014, there were an estimated 950 trillion quaggas on Great Lakes bottoms—they have cleared large areas of lake waters. Clearer waters allow sunlight to penetrate deeper into lakes, promoting the growth of algae and microorganisms. Some of these organisms are poisonous to other species, including fish and humans. Native fish and shellfish stocks have plummeted, and numerous bird deaths have been linked to this pollution. Because of special tentaclelike organs, zebra mussels can cling to almost anything. They have clogged Chicago's water intake pipes and, by clamping on clam's shells, have killed large numbers of them. Zebra and quagga mussels have few predators, though yellow perch have a taste for them. They are edible, but because they contain so many pollutants, health authorities discourage people from dining on them. In 2014, a common soil bacteria was found to be a zebra and quagga killer, but only limited trials have been done so far to test its effectiveness.

Contributor: Bruce Kraig

See also: Alliance for the Great Lakes

BIBLIOGRAPHY

Alexander, Jeff. "Zebra Mussels Are Transforming the Great Lakes and Fueling Rampant Algae Growth." *Bridge Magazine*, August 12, 2012. http://www.mlive.com/environment/index.ssf/2012/08/zebra_mussels_are_transforming.html#comments.

Appendix A

PERIOD KITCHEN, DINING ROOM, PANTRY, AND RECIPES RESOURCES

Chicago is replete with historic homes that are open to the public. Each of these homes had a kitchen and a dining area; many of them still do. These rooms and their furnishings offer a glimpse into the culinary lives of Chicagoans past. Some of the current institutions also contain libraries and archives with collections of cookbooks and recipe manuscripts. Several of them offer tours or special programs with costumed interpreters. The following symbols are used for the list of these homes and what one can find in them today.

Symbols Key:

🍴 Kitchen

🍽 Dining Room

🥘 Butler's Pantry or Work Room

📖 Cookbook Library

📑 Manuscript and Recipe Archives

🧍 Costumed Interpreters and Programs

🔑 Available for Rentals

🎞 Available for Film and Photography with Arrangement

🎁 Giftshop

Historic Farms

GARFIELD FARM, 1841. Garfield Rd., LaFox, IL 60147. 630.584.8485. Open Wed and Sun 8-4 Jun–Sept and other times by appointment. garfieldfarm.org.

KLINE CREEK FARM, 1890-1900. 1N600 County Farm Rd., West Chicago, IL 60185. 630.876.5902. Open Thurs–Mon 9-5 and by appointment. Some pieces in the collection date as recently as the 1920s. There are two kitchens; one is a reproduction summer kitchen. dupageforest.com.

PRIMROSE FARM, 1930S. 5N726 Crane Rd., St. Charles, IL 60175. 630.513.4370. Open Mon–Sat 8-3. Open dawn to dusk; staffed Mon–Sat 8-3. Drop-in tours and programs Wed and Sat. primrosefarmpark.com.

VOLKENING HERITAGE FARM, 1880S. 201 S. Plum Grove Rd., Schaumburg, IL 60194. 847.985.2102. This is a living, working farm interpreting German heritage in the Midwest. It has extensive food history and foodways programs. Parkfun.com.

WAGNER FARM, 1920. 1510 Wagner Rd., Glenview, IL 60025. 847.657.1506. Open Mon–Sat 9-5, Sun 9-3. wagnerfarm.org.

Historic Houses and Historical Societies

AURORA HISTORICAL SOCIETY, WILLIAM TANNER HOUSE, 1857. 317 Cedar, Aurora, IL 60506. 630.897.9029. Open Wed and Sun Apr–Sept and by appointment. aurorahistory.net.

BRADLEY HOUSE KANKAKEE, FRANK LLOYD WRIGHT'S FIRST PRAIRIE-STYLE HOUSE, 1900. 701 South Harrison Ave., Kankakee, IL 60901. 815.936.9630. Open Fri–Sun for tours at noon, 1:00, 2:00, 3:00, and by appointment, closed Jan–Feb. This site was the Yesteryear restaurant, 1953–83. The current collection includes historic menus and other memorabilia. wrightinkankakee.org.

CHARLES GATES DAWES HOUSE, 1920S. 225 Greenwood St., Evanston, IL 60201. 847.475.3410. Open for tours Thurs–Sun 1-4. Research room Tues–Thurs and Sat 1-4 and by appointment. evanstonhistorycenter.org.

CHARNLEY-PERSKY HOUSE MUSEUM, LATE NINETEENTH CENTURY. 1365 North Astor St., Chicago, IL 60610. 312.573.1365. Open for tours Wed and Sat noon–1:30 Apr–Oct and by appointment. charnley-perskyhouse.org.

CLARKE HOUSE, CHICAGO'S OLDEST HOUSE, CA. 1836. 1827 S. Indiana, Chicago, IL 60616. 312.326.1480. Open Wed–Sun 9-5, tours at noon and 2:00. The collection also contains excellent examples of settlement-era crockery and utensils. clarkehousemuseum.org.

FRANCES WILLARD HOUSE, 1865. 1730 Chicago Ave., Evanston, IL 60201. 312.994.4000. Open for tours 1st and 3rd Sun 1-4 or by appointment. 847.328.7500. franceswillardhouse.org.

FRANK LLOYD WRIGHT HOME, 1889, AND STUDIO, 1898. 951 Chicago Ave., Oak Park, IL 60302. 312.994.4000. Open for Tours Daily 10-4, Gift Shop 9-5. flwright.org.

GLESSNER HOUSE, 1893. 1800 S. Prairie Ave., Chicago, IL 60616. 312.326.1480. Open for tours Wed–Sun 1:00 and 3:00. The Glessners also collected menus and these are a rich resource for researchers visiting the Glessner House. glessnerhouse.org.

HEMINGWAY BIRTHPLACE, 1890S. 339 North Oak Park Ave., Oak Park, IL 60302. 708.524.5383. Open Sun–Fri 1-5, Sat 10-5. ehfop.org.

JANE ADDAMS HULL HOUSE, 1889. 800 S. Halsted, Chicago, IL 60607. 312.413.5353. Open daily 8:30-3. hull-housemuseum.org.

KEITH HOUSE, CA. 1870. 1900 S. Prairie Ave., Chicago, IL 60616. 312.907.7909. This is a historic event venue, hours by reservation or event. keithhousechicago.com.

KINDER HOUSE, DES PLAINES HISTORICAL SOCIETY, 1907. 789 Pearson, Des Plaines, IL 60016. 847.391.5399. Open Tues–Fri 10-5 and Sun 1-4. 847.391.5399. desplaineshistory.org.

THE LAURENT HOUSE, 1952. 4646 Springbrook Rd., Rockford, IL 61114. 815-877-2952. Open for tours 1st and 3rd weekend of the month, hourly 11-3. This is Frank Lloyd Wright's only home designed for a person with a disability. This home is fully furnished with all original Wright-designed furniture and textiles. laurenthouse.com.

MADLENER HOUSE, CA. 1901. 4 W. Burton Place, Chicago, IL 60610. Open Wed–Sat 11-6. 312.787.4071. This historic house at one time had kitchen, dining room, and butler's pantry, although they are no longer interpreted as such. The site does have historic images that depict the original uses. grahamfoundation.org/madlener_house.

MAYSLAKE PEABODY, CA. 1921. 1717 W 31st St., Oak Brook, IL 60523. 630.850.2363. Open Mon–Fri 8-4 and Sat 9-1, Closed Sun. This is a historic event venue. mayslakepeabody.com.

MCCORMICK MANSION, FIRST BUILT 1896, RENOVATED 1936. 1S151 Winfield Rd., Wheaton, IL 60189. 630.668.5161. Open Tues–Fri 10-4 (Oct–Apr), 10-5 (May–Sept) Sat noon–4 (Feb–Apr), 11-5 (May–Oct), 11-4 (Nov–Dec) Closed all of Jan. Cantigny.org/museums/Robert-r-mccormick-museum.

MT. PROSPECT MUSEUM, DIETRICH FRIEDRICHS HOUSE, 1906. 101 S. Maple St., Mt. Prospect, IL 60056. 847.392.9006. Open Tues–Thurs 10-3:30. Closed weekends except for special events. mtphist.org.

NAPER SETTLEMENT, 1831. 523 South Webster St., Naperville, IL 60540. Open Apr–Oct Tues–Sat 10-4, Sun 1-4, Nov–Mar Tues–Fri 10-4. 630.420.6770. This site consists of multiple buildings, three of them have period room setting kitchens: Mitchell Mansion, 1890s; Halfway House, ca. 1900; and the Log House, 1830s. The permanent collection houses the extensive Cookbook and Manuscript Archives. napersettlement.org.

NATIONAL PUBLIC HOUSING MUSEUM, 1950S. 1322 West Taylor West, Chicago, IL 60607. 773.245.1621. Site officially opens in 2017, please phone or see website for details. nphm.org.

PARK FOREST HISTORICAL SOCIETY CO-OP, 1950S. 227 Monee Rd., Park Forest, IL 60466. 708.481.4252. Open Wed and Sat 10:30-3:30 and by appointment. parkforesthistory.org.

PLEASANT HOME, 1897. 217 Home Ave., Oak Park, IL 60302. 708.383.2654. Open for free viewing Wed. 10-12; for tours Thurs–Sun at 12:30, 1:30, and 2:30; last tour not available Dec–Feb. pleasanthome.org.

PULLMAN HOUSE PROJECT, CA. 1880. 11141 S. Cottage Grove Ave., Chicago, IL 60628. 773.660.2341. Active renovation and interpretations of various sites within this historic district are ongoing. Please contact for current information. pullman-museum.org.

RICHARD H. DRIEHAUS MUSEUM, CA. 1880. 40 East Erie St., Chicago, IL 60611. 312.482.8933. Open Tues–Sun 10-5. driehausmuseum.org.

RIVER GROVE HISTORICAL HOUSE, 1874–1924. 8455 W. Grand Ave., River Grove, IL 60171. 708.453.8000. Hours by appointment. The house was added to over time and is interpreted as such. The dining room is interpreted as 1900 and the kitchen, pantry, and mud room as 1924. rivergrovehistory.org.

ROBIE HOUSE, CA. 1910. 5757 S. Woodlawn Ave., Chicago, IL 60637. 312.994.4000. Open for tours Thurs–Mon 10:30-4, Gift Shop Thurs–Mon 9:30-5:30. flwright.org.

ROLLING MEADOWS 1950S HOUSE, CA. 1952. 3100 Central Rd., Rolling Meadows, IL 60008. 847.577.7086. Open Winter Wed 10-2, Sun 1-4. ci.rolling-meadows.il.us.

SCHMIDT-BURNHAM LOG HOUSE, CA. 1830, INTERPRETED AS 1853. Crow Island Woods, Willow Rd., Winnetka, IL 60093. 847.446.0001. By appt and special days. Winnetkahistory.org.

SCHWEIKHER-LANGSDORF HOME AND STUDIO, BUILT 1938, FURNISHED 1940–70S. 645 S. Meacham Rd., Schaumburg, IL 60193. 847.923.3866. Hours by appointment only and for special tours and events by arrangement. This site has outdoor natural areas including five acres of prairie meadow and garden space with fruit trees, iris, and peonies. schweikherhouse.org.

Libraries and Special Collections for Cookbook and Cooking Manuscripts

Most historical societies and museums have small collections of cookbooks, manuscript cookbooks, and recipe archives. Consult your local institution for specific inquiries. Local libraries may also contain unexpected resources. It is best to inquire in the specific community where research is focused. The following are general sources for these materials within the Chicago area.

THE HAROLD WASHINGTON LIBRARY, 400 S. State St., Chicago, IL 60605. 312.747.4300. Mon–Thurs 9-9, Fri and Sat 9-5, Sun 1-5. Special Collections Mon and Tues 12-6, Fri and Sat 12-4. chipublib.org. Circulated Materials from any library in the CPL system may be ordered online and checked out at any library. Special Collections, noncirculating, and rare-books materials may be viewed only at the Harold Washington Library Branch.

THE NEWBERRY LIBRARY. 60 West Walton St., Chicago, IL 60610. 312.943.9090. Research hours Tues–Sat 9-5. Researchers must obtain a Reader's Card. newberry.org.

THE RYERSON AND BURNHAM LIBRARIES, ART INSTI-TUTE OF CHICAGO. 111 South Michigan Ave., Chicago, IL 60503. 312.443.7279. Public Research Hours Mon–Wed 1-5pm, Thurs 10:30-8pm, Fri 1-5pm, Closed Sat and Sun. artic.edu.

THE UNIVERSITY OF CHICAGO JOHN CRERER LIBRARY, 5730 S. Ellis, Chicago, IL 60637. 773.703.8701 (general information) On-campus access only to members of the public with a legitimate research need to consult the collections. Members of the public must establish their research need with the library in order to be granted access. lib.uchicago.edu.

Appendix B

U.S. PRICES AND SALARIES, 1890–2015

	AVERAGE ANNUAL SALARY ALL WORKERS, $	BUTTER ($/LB)	EGGS ($/DOZEN)	ROUND STEAK ($/LB)
1890	445 (11,421)	0.26 (6.67)	0.21 (5.39)	0.12 (3.08)
1900	438 (11960)	0.26 (7.10)	0.21 (5.73)	0.14 (3.82)
1910	574 (14,166)	0.39 (8.63)	0.34 (8.39)	17.4 (4.20)
1920	1407 (16,752)	0.70 (8.33)	0.68 (8.51)	0.40 (5.01)
1930	1388 (19,792)	0.46 (6.56)	0.52 (7.41)	0.43 (5.91)
1940	1315 (22,216)	0.42 (9.10)	0.45 (7.60)	0.36 (6.08)
1950	3180 (31,871)	0.74 (7.42)	0.67 (6.71)	0.94 (9.42)
1960	4816 (38,745)	0.74 (5.95)	0.65 (5.23)	1.05 (8.45)
1970	6670 (41,851)	0.77 (4.83)	0.67 (4.20)	1.30 (8.16)
1984	15,751 (45,579)	1.99 (5.75)	0.91 (2.65)	2.86 (6.55)
1990	23,602 (44,270)	2.10 (3.94)	0.99 (1.86)	3.41 (6.40)
2000	42,148 (58,286)	2.80 (3.94)	0.96 (1.35)	3.50 (4.42)
2010	51,144 (55,852.73)	3.42 (3.75)	1.66 (1.82)	4.41 (4.83)

Source: U.S. Bureau of the Census, Historical Statistics of the United States, Colonial Times to 1970, Bicentennial Edition, Part 2, Bureau of Labor Statistics, 2011; 2015.

1984 data. http://www.foxbusiness.com/features/2011/05/05/10-everyday-grocery-items.html.

This table shows how food prices have declined in real terms over the past 130 years. While prices of basic foodstuffs such as butter, eggs, and round steak were low in current terms, they represented a significant outlay for average workers. In 1901, food averaged around 40 percent of a consumer's income. However, this percentage declined steadily to around 34 percent by the 1930s. Prices of butter and eggs declined during the depression, but meat remained expensive. Today Americans spend about 13 percent of their household income on food because food prices have declined and household incomes have risen. Prices in parentheses are 2016 dollars.

Some Chicago Menu Prices (comparable 2016 prices in parentheses)

1893:

A dozen raw oysters at the Boston Oyster House at the corner of Clark and Madison cost 25 cents ($6.41) with the price doubling if they were fried and increasing to 77 cents ($19.76) if broiled with mushrooms. The most expensive item on Rector Oyster House's menu was sirloin steak for two, $1.75 ($44.92).

1939:

Dinner at Walgreens, consisting of soup or cocktail; roast loin of pork, chopped chicken with noodles, or grilled tenderloin: veggies; potatoes; salad; dessert; and coffee, cost just 50 cents ($8.45).

A special supper featured "chop suey chinese style" with French fried noodles, desserts, and rolls for 35 cents ($5.91).

Sandwiches ranged from 15 cents ($2.53) for cheese, ham, liver sausage, or PBJ to 25 cents ($4.22) for a three-decker chicken salad.

1950:

A sandwich at Woolworth's lunch counter ranged from 30 cents ($2.96) for ham, egg, or American cheese to 66 cents ($6.60) for a three-decker chicken salad sandwich.

A regular banana split cost 25 cents ($2.50), but a super jumbo version with 3 scoops of ice cream and crushed fruits would set you back 39 cents ($3.90).

1959:

Typical German entrees at Red Star Inn (pot roast, schnitzel, Koenigsberger Klops) ranged from $2.25 to $3.50 ($18–$28). The most expensive item was filet mignon at $4.95 ($40.51).

1960:

Fritzel's offered a businessman's special lunch (chicken chop suey, banana cream tart, and stewed fruit compote) for $1.50 ($12.27), perhaps accompanied by a daiquiri at 80 cents $6.55) or a glass of imported champagne for $1.50 ($12.27).

EARLY 1970S:

You could enjoy a bowl of Maxim's famous billibi soup for just $1.50 ($7.50). The most expensive items on the menu (written entirely in French) were timbale de langouste Newburg or homard Cardinale for $8.50 ($42.50).

2016:

At French bistros such as Kiki's and Bistronomic, for example, soups and appetizers ranged from $7.75–$12, while entrees such as steak au poivre ranged from $28–$34. The famed Cape Cod Room charged $12 for red snapper soup and $64 for Dover sole, prepared tableside, with Drake meuniere sauce.

At the lower end of the dining scale, Chicago hot dogs that were 25–50 cents at ballparks in the 1970s were now $5.75 at Wrigley Field and a bargain $4.00 at the White Sox ballpark.

Selected Bibliography

The literature on Chicago history is voluminous, and that dealing with all aspects of food not far behind. This bibliography lists a number of books used by the editors and authors of Food City's entries, but it is not exhaustive. Some are not specifically Chicago-related but have information that relates to the city's food story. Rather, we present the list for further reading and encourage anyone doing research in Chicago's food history to use these books as starting points.

General Histories

Andreas, Alfred Theodore. *History of Chicago*, Volume I. Chicago: A. T. Andreas, 1884.

———. *History of Chicago*, Volume II. Chicago: A. T. Andreas Company, Publishers, 1885.

———. *History of Chicago*, Volume III. Chicago: A. T. Andreas Company, Publishers, 1886.

Block, Daniel R., and Rosing Howard. *Chicago A Food Biography.* Lanham, Md.: Rowman, Littlefield, 2015.

Bundy, Beverly. *The Century in Food: America's Fads and Favorites.* Portland, Ore.: Collectors Press, 2002.

City of Chicago, Department of Development and Planning. *The People of Chicago: Who We Are and Who We Have Been.* Chicago, 1976.

Cronon, William. *Nature's Metropolis: Chicago and the Great West.* New York: W. W. Norton and Company, 1991.

Cutler, Irving. *Chicago, Metropolis of the Mid-Continent*, 4th Edition. Carbondale: Southern Illinois University Press, 2006.

Danckers, Ulrich, Jane Meredith, John F. Swenson, and Helen Hornbeck Tanner. *A Compendium of the Early History of Chicago: To the Year 1835 When the Indians Left.* River Forest, Ill.: Early Chicago, Inc., 2000.

Duis, Perry. *Challenging Chicago: Coping with Everyday Life, 1837–1920.* Urbana: University of Illinois Press, 1998.

Grossman, James, Ann Durkin Keating, and Janice L. Reiff, eds. *The Encyclopedia of Chicago.* Chicago: University of Chicago Press, 2004 (online edition: http://www.encyclopedia.chicagohistory.org).

Hudson, John C. *Chicago: A Geography of the City and Its Region.* Santa Fe, N.M.: Center for American Places; Chicago: University of Chicago Press, 2006.

Hurlbut, Henry H. *Chicago Antiquities: Comprising; Original Items and Relations, Letters, Extracts, and Notes Pertaining to Early Chicago; Embellished with Views, Portraits. Autographs, etc.* Chicago: Henry H. Hurlbut, 1881.

Mayer, Harold, and Richard Wade. *Chicago: Growth of a Metropolis.* Chicago: University of Chicago Press, 1969.

Miller, Donald L. *City of the Century: The Epic of Chicago and the Making of America.* New York: Simon and Schuster, 1996.

Pacyga, Dominic A. *Chicago: A Biography.* Chicago: University of Chicago Press, 2009.

Parton, James. *Triumphs of Enterprise, Ingenuity, and Public Spirit.* Hartford, Conn.: A. S. Hale and Co., 1871.

Pierce, Bessie Louise. *History of Chicago*, Vol. I–III. Chicago: University of Chicago Press, [1937, 1940, 1957] 2007.

Pierce, Bessie Louise, and Joe Lester Norris. *As Others See Chicago; Impressions of Visitors, 1673–1933.* Chicago: University of Chicago Press, 1933.

Quaife, Milo Milton, *Chicago and the Old Northwest, 1673–1835: A Study of the Evolution of the Northwestern Frontier, Together with a History of Fort Dearborn.* Chicago: University of Chicago Press, 1913.

Smith, Henry Justin . *Chicago's Great Century 1833–1933.* Chicago: Published for A Century of Progress by Consolidated Publishers, Inc., 1933.

Trager, James. *The Food Chronology.* New York: Owl Books, 1997.

Dining and Drinking

Bronte, Patricia. *Vittles and Vice.* Chicago: Henry Regnery Co., 1952.

Dedmon, Emmett. *Fabulous Chicago.* New York: Atheneum, 1983.

Drury, John. *Dining in Chicago.* New York: John Day Company, 1931.

———. *Where Chicago Eats.* New York: Rand McNally and Co., 1953.

Duis, Perry. *The Saloon: Public Drinking in Chicago and Boston, 1880–1920.* Urbana: University of Illinois Press, 1983.

Kraig, Bruce, and Patty Carroll. *Man Bites Dog: Hot Dog Culture in America.* Lanham, Md.: Taylor Trade Publishing, 2014 [2012].

Lait, Jack, and Lee Mortimer. *Chicago Confidential.* New York: Crown Publishers, 1950.

Skilnik, Bob. *The History of Beer and Brewing in Chicago, 1833–1978.* West Conshohocken, Pa: Infinity Publishing, 2002.

Ethnic Chicago

Cruz, Wilfredo. *City of Dreams: Latino Immigration to Chicago.* Lanham, Md.: University Press of America, 2007.

Cutler, Irving. *The Jews of Chicago: From Shtetl to Suburb.* Urbana: University of Illinois Press, 1996.

Danahey, Mike, and Allison Hantschel. *Chicago's Historic Irish Pubs.* Charleston, S.C.: Arcadia Publishing, 2011.

Fernandez, Lilia. *Brown in the Windy City.* Chicago: University of Chicago Press, 2012.

Gabaccia, Donna R. *We Are What We Eat: Ethnic Food and the Making of Americans.* Cambridge: Harvard University Press, 1998.

Ganakos, Alexa, and Katherine Bish. *Greektown Chicago: Its History, Its Recipes.* St. Louis, Mo.: G. Bradley Publishing, 2005.

Granacki, Victoria, and the Polish Museum of America. *Chicago's Polish Downtown.* Mt. Pleasant, S.C.: Arcadia Publishing, 2004.

Grossman, James R. *Land of Hope: Chicago, Black Southerners, and the Great Migration.* Chicago: University of Chicago Press, 1989.

Holli, Melvin G., and Peter d'Alroy Jones, eds. *Ethnic Chicago: A Multicultural Portrait.* Grand Rapids, Mich.: W. B. Eerdmans Publishing Company, 1994.

Philpott, Thomas Lee. *The Slum and the Ghetto: Immigrants, Blacks and Reformers in Chicago, 1880–1930.* Belmont, Calif.: Wadsworth Publishing Company, 1991.

Reed, Christopher Robert. *Black Chicago's First Century.* Columbia: University of Missouri Press, 2005.

Steinberg, Ellen, and Jack Prost. *From the Jewish Heartland: Two Centuries of Midwest Foodways.* Urbana: University of Illinois Press, 2011.

Memoirs

Bowen, Louise de Koven. *Growing Up with a City.* Introduction by Maureen A. Flanagan. Urbana: University of Illinois Press, 2002.

Cleaver, Charles. *In Reminiscences of Chicago during the Forties and Fifties.* Edited by Mabel McIlvaine, William Bross, Charles Cleaver, Alfred Theodore Andreas, and Joseph Jefferson. Chicago: R. R. Donnelley and Sons Company, 1913.

King, Caroline B. *Victorian Cakes, A Reminiscence with Recipes.* Introduction by Jill Gardner. Berkeley, Calif.: Harris Publishing Company, 1984 [1941].

Kinzie, Mrs. John H. *Wau-bun, the Early Day in the Northwest.* New York: Derby and Jackson, 1856.

Steinberg, Ellen F. S., and Eleanor H. Hanson. *Learning to Cook in 1898: A Chicago Culinary Memoir.* Detroit: Wayne State University Press, 2007.

Recipes and Home Cooking

Gray, Grace Viall, *A Century of Progress in Cooking.* Chicago: Gray Institute of Home Economics, 1934.

Haddix, Carol Mighton. *Chicago Cooks: 25 Years of Food History with Menus, Recipes, and Tips from Les Dames d'Escoffier Chicago.* Evanston, Ill.: Surrey Books, 2007.

Lovegren, Sylvia. *Fashionable Food: Seven Decades of Food Fads.* Chicago: University of Chicago Press, 2005.

Shapiro, Laura. *Something from the Oven: Inventing Dinner in 1950s America.* New York: Viking, 2014.

World's Fairs

Ganz, Cheryl R. *The 1933 Chicago World's Fair: A Century of Progress.* Urbana: University of Illinois Press, 2008.

Gustaitis, Joseph A. *Chicago's Greatest Year, 1893: The White City and the Birth of a Modern Metropolis.* Carbondale: Southern Illinois University Press, 2013.

Lewis, Arnold. *An Early Encounter with Tomorrow: Europeans, Chicago's Loop, and the World's Columbian Exposition.* Urbana: University of Illinois Press, 1997.

Special Topics

Goddard, Leslie. *Chicago's Sweet Candy History.* Mount Pleasant, S.C.: Arcadia Publishing, 2012.

Pocius, Marilyn, *A Cook's Guide to Chicago.* Chicago: Lake Claremont Press, 2002.

Smith, Andrew F. *Popped Culture: A Social History of Popcorn in America.* Columbia: University of South Carolina Press, 1999.

Wade, Louise C. *Chicago's Pride: The Stockyards, Packingtown, and Environs in the Nineteenth Century.* Urbana, Ill.: University of Illinois Press, 1987.

Contributors

Editors

CAROL MIGHTON HADDIX was food editor of the *Chicago Tribune* from 1980 to 2011. Under her direction, the Good Eating section won yearly best-section awards and nominations from the Association of Food Journalists. Haddix is a founding member of Les Dames d'Escoffier Chicago, a professional food society. She is a member of the Culinary Historians of Chicago and the James Beard Foundation, where she was a member and former chairman of the Beard Book Awards committee. She has edited many Tribune cookbooks, including *Good Eating's Best of the Best: Great Recipes of the Past Decade from the Chicago Tribune Test Kitchen*, *Chicago Tribune Good Eating Cookbook*, and *Ethnic Chicago Cookbook*. She wrote the introduction for and edited *Chicago Cooks: 25 Years of Food History with Menus, Recipes, and Tips from Les Dames d'Escoffier*. Prior to joining the *Tribune*, Haddix worked for the *Detroit Free Press*. She holds a bachelor's degree in home economics and communication arts from Michigan State University.

BRUCE KRAIG is professor emeritus in history at Roosevelt University in Chicago, where he taught a wide variety of courses in history, anthropology, and popular culture. He also taught culinary subjects at the culinary school of Kendall College, Chicago. Kraig has appeared widely in the electronic media as writer and on-camera host and narrator for a multiaward-winning PBS series on food and culture around the world. Publications range from books and articles in academic journals on European and world prehistory through American history. He has written hundreds of articles on food in newspapers and journals. His books about cookery and culinary history include the following: as author, *Mexican-American Plain Cooking*, *The Cuisines of Hidden Mexico*, *Hot Dog: A Global History*, *Man Bites Dog: Hot Dog Culture in America* (with Patty Carroll); as editor, *Cooking Plain: Illinois Style* (2012); and as coeditor, *Street Food around the World: An Encyclopedia of Food and Culture* (with Colleen Sen) (2013) and *A Rich and Fertile Land: America's Food* (2017). He is the editor of the "Heartland Foodways" book series for the University of Illinois Press. He has lectured at the Pillsbury Bake-Off, Smithsonian Institutions' Museums on Main Street projects, the Australian Symposium on Gastronomy, and has spoken before the Library of Congress on food history and, one of his favorite topics, baseball history.

COLLEEN TAYLOR SEN is a food and travel journalist and food historian specializing in Asia and the Indian Subcontinent Her articles have appeared in the *Chicago Tribune*, *Travel and Leisure*, *Food Arts*, *Chicago Sun Times*, and many other publications. She is the author of six books, including *Food Culture in India*, *Curry: A Global History*, *Turmeric: The Wonder Spice*, *A Guide to Indian Restaurant Menus*, *Street Food around the World: An Encyclopedia of Food and Culture (*with Bruce Kraig), and, most recently, *Feasts and Fasts: A History of Food in India*. Colleen Sen has a BA and MA from the University of Toronto and a PhD from Columbia University, all in Slavic Languages and Literatures. She has been decorated by the French government with the Ordre des Palmes Académiques.

Contributors

MAUREEN ABOOD is author of *Rose Water & Orange Blossoms: Fresh and Classic Recipes from My Lebanese Kitchen* (Running Press 2015), and her award-winning blog by the same name at maureenabood.com, where she also offers a full line of Lebanese ingredients.

ANN KATHLEEN BARNDS is an artist, gardener, former community organizer, and urban planner with many years of experience working (and eating) in neighborhoods across Chicago.

DANIEL BLOCK is a professor of geography at Chicago State University and the coauthor of *Chicago: A Food Biography*.

ANTHONY F. BUCCINI is an historical linguist and food historian with many academic publications in the two disciplines; he has taught in the fields of general linguistics and Germanic, Romance, and Celtic philology at the University of Chicago and was awarded the Sophie Coe Prize in Food History in 2005.

ELLIE CARLSON is a museum curator and historical performer who caters in costume. She researches, collects, practices, and produces historic recipes with period-appropriate ingredients and tools. Her website is elliepresents.com where her cookbooks and other materials are available.

JOHN CARRUTHERS has written about food and grilling for *Serious Eats*, *Newcity*, and two cookbooks from Running Press. He runs Chicago-based grilling club ManBQue, occasionally caters, and is two-time hot dog cookoff champion of Chicago, and thus the world.

JULIE CHERNOFF is an editor and food writer and has worked for chefs Wolfgang Puck and Rick Bayless; she is past president of the Chicago Chapter of Les Dames d'Escoffier.

CYNTHIA CLAMPITT is a writer, speaker, and food historian for a wide range of media and is the author of *Midwest Maize: How Corn Shaped the U.S. Heartland*.

J. PETER CLARK, PhD, had a distinguished career developing new technologies in the private sector and writing and lecturing on food-processing matters with a focus on advancing processing technologies to mitigate food insecurity.

KELSEY CODAY, a recipe and product developer for Chef Rick Bayless, has cooked in sweet and savory kitchens throughout Chicago and written about food, science, and policy.

AMY DAHLSTROM is a linguist at the University of Chicago who has published extensively on Algonquian cultures and languages, languages spoken or formerly spoken over much of the Northeast and Midwest including the Chicago area. In the field of food history, she is the author of the Swedish entry in *Ethnic American Food Today: A Cultural Encyclopedia*.

BILL DALEY is a food and feature writer for the *Chicago Tribune*.

JIM DEWAN is an instructor at Kendall College Culinary School, a columnist for the *Chicago Tribune*, and author of *Prep School: How To Improve Your Kitchen Skills and Cooking Techniques*.

ROBERT DIRKS is emeritus professor of anthropology at Illinois State University. His recent book, *Food in the Gilded Age: What Ordinary Americans Ate*, concerns the late-nineteenth-century eating habits of communities in various parts of the United States, including Chicago.

CHARLA DRAPER is a former food editor for *Ebony* and *Southern Living* magazines; she has contributed to *Cooking Light* and *Cooking Pleasures* magazines. She has appeared on the *Today Show* and *WLS-TV*. Draper's blog is ChowChow&Soul.com.

MEGAN E. EDWARDS is an archaeologist and student of the historical anthropology of food. She is currently wrapping up a PhD in anthropology at the University of Chicago, where she is working on early modern developments in Irish whiskey.

MONICA ENG, who reports on food, health, and ethnic culture in Chicago for *WBEZ* Chicago Public Radio, previously covered these topics at the *Chicago Tribune* and the *Chicago Sun Times*.

PETER ENGLER has worked at the University of Chicago for 20 years doing research in genetics, and he spends his spare time exploring Chicago, focusing on the South Side's food and history.

JOSHUA EVANS is pursuing an MA in history at Roosevelt University. His graduate thesis focuses on Chicago's Uptown neighborhood.

JANET RAUSA FULLER writes about food and cooking for *Epicurious* and *DNAinfo* Chicago and was for many years the food editor of the *Chicago Sun-Times*.

ROBERT GARDNER is a cofounder of the Chicago-based food site, LTHForum.com, and publishes a website based on spreading his passion for local food, thelocalbeet.com.

MICHAEL GEBERT, after a long career as a copywriter, is a freelance video producer for the *Chicago Reader*, award-winning food writer, and blogger for *Grub Street*, *Sky Full of Bacon*, and other online and print publications.

ERIK S. GELLMAN is associate professor of history and associate director of the St. Clair Drake Center for African and African American Studies at Roosevelt University in Chicago and is working on a collaborative food and labor history project about the organizing campaigns of the union UCAPAWA/FTA in the 1930s and 1940s.

CRAIG "MEATHEAD" GOLDWYN is a writer, barbecue and wine judge, and owner/operator of a barbecue and grilling website, AmazingRibs.com.

REBECCA S. GRAFF, assistant professor of anthropology at Lake Forest College, is a historical archaeologist with research interests in late-nineteenth- and early-twentieth-century Chicago, including archaeological work on the 1893 World's Columbian Exposition and the Louis Sullivan and Frank Lloyd Wright–designed Charnley-Persky House.

RITA GUTEKANST and Marguerite Lytle are founders of Limelight Catering, offering innovative cuisine with local and sustainable practices for Chicago social occasions.

DAVID HAMMOND is dining and drinking editor for *Newcity/Chicago*; a regular contributor of food-related articles for the *Chicago Tribune*, *Chicago Sun-Times, Wednesday Journal,* and *Rivet Radio*; and a founding member and lead moderator of LTHForum.com.

ELEANOR HANSON was cofounder of FoodWatch Trend Tracking and Consumer Insights and a director of the Kraft Foods Consumer Kitchens.

JUDY HEVRDEJS is a food and features writer at the *Chicago Tribune*.

JUDITH DUNBAR HINES is a food consultant and former Director of Culinary Arts, City of Chicago Department of Cultural Affairs.

DAVE HOEKSTRA is a Chicago author/producer, a radio host on WGN-radio, and a former columnist/critic at the *Chicago Sun Times*.

MARY LA PLANTE is a writer and award-winning documentary film producer whose global nonprofit media relations and advocacy work has taken her to four continents, producing stories on fair-trade chocolate and coffee, clean water, education, and humanitarian relief.

MARGARET LAPORT, a Chicago native and the marketing director for Gourmet Garden Herbs and Spices, previously led branding and research programs for several fresh fruit and vegetable brands including Dulcinea Farms.

ROBERT LAUNAY is professor of anthropology at Northwestern University, the author of two books on Muslim minorities in West Africa, and is studying French foodways in the Midwest.

JENNIFER LEWIS, CCE, CHE, is a culinary and hospitality instructor at Washburne Culinary Institute, Chicago, and researches culinary history and leads candy tours. She is the author of *Midwest Sweet Baking History: Delectible Classics around Lake Michigan*.

GEORGE MACHT, retired professor/coordinator of the Hospitality Administration Program at College of DuPage; tour director of Culinary Adventure and Discovery, escorting groups to many of the most interesting food and culturally enriching destinations around the globe.

JANINE MACLACHLAN is author of *Farmers' Markets of the Heartland* from University of Illinois Press. Her writing and recipes have appeared in *Relish, Cooking Light, Country Living*, and 14 Tribune Company publications.

SARAH MUIRHEAD is a journalist covering food, farming, and agribusiness for Penton Agriculture's weekly publication, *Feedstuffs*.

JOSH NOEL is a travel and beer writer for the *Chicago Tribune*.

JENNIFER OLVERA is a food and travel writer, columnist, and author of *Food Lovers' Guide to Chicago*.

CLARA ORBAN, professor of French and Italian at DePaul University, has published widely on Italian and French literature and culture, has written a novel, and published two books on wine, including *Illinois Wines and Wineries: The Essential Guide* (2014).

STEFAN OSDENE earned his doctorate in art history at UW-Madison in 2014 and is a historian of material culture based in Madison, Wisconsin.

SARAHLYNN PABLO cofounded and writes for *Filipino Kitchen*, a multimedia blog and pop-up dinner series focusing on Filipino food and culture.

DEBORAH PANKEY is the former food editor at the Arlington Heights *Daily Herald*.

DONNA BATTLE PIERCE, a 2015 recipient of a Harvard Nieman Foundation Visiting Fellowship, was an assistant food editor and test kitchen director for the *Chicago Tribune*. Her syndicated column "Black America Cooks" appears in the *Chicago Defender* and other African American publications.

PENNY POLLACK is dining editor for *Chicago* magazine (1994–present) and coauthor of *Everybody Loves Pizza*.

JACK H. PROST, a native Chicagoan with an interest in local ethnic dining, is professor of anthropology, University of Illinois at Chicago, and has published articles and books on biological anthropology, culinary history, and midwest Jewish foodways.

TIA RAINS, PhD, is a nutrition scientist with over 15 years of experience in the food and beverage industry. She has authored over 50 scientific articles and book chapters on food and nutrition-related topics.

CHANDRA RAM is the editor of *Plate* magazine, a member of Les Dames d'Escoffier, and recipient of the McAllister Editorial Fellowship.

JOAN REARDON, PhD, is a culinary historian and award-winning author of cookbooks and culinary biographies on M. F. K. Fisher, Julia Child, and Alice Waters.

JONATHAN REES is professor of history at Colorado State University–Pueblo. He is the author of *Refrigeration Nation: A History of Ice, Appliances and Enterprise in America*.

BARBARA REVSINE has written for *Food Arts*, the *New York Times*, *Wine Spectator*, *Travel & Leisure*, and most Chicago-based print publications. She writes the blog, Pantry-to-Plate, covering every aspect of the food scene.

ELIZABETH D. RICHTER is coeditor of *The Green City Market Cookbook* and president of The Richter Group, a

strategic communications consulting firm that helps clients tell their stories through compelling messaging, effective branding, and targeted delivery.

MIKE ROSSMEIER is a commercial banker and has been involved in the financing of companies in the food industry, including food production, manufacturing, distribution, and retailing, and also the manufacturing of food-processing equipment.

GERALDINE ROUNDS is an educator, culinary historian, and consultant, formerly with Naperville School District 203, and adjunct professor at Benedictine University. She has 20 years of experience teaching food courses and has written numerous food-related curricula and television programs.

JOSEPH SCHWIETERMAN is a professor in the School for Public Service, Department of Public Policy, and Sustainable Urban Development program at DePaul University. He is an expert in the fields of public policy, transportation, and urban planning and is the author of numerous books and peer-reviewed articles on the development of cities and transportation.

AMANDA SCOTESE's passion for Chicago architecture, history, and culture inspired her to create Chicago Detours, a tour company that explores stories and places that even locals don't know.

RICHARD SHEPRO, lecturer at the University of Chicago, has also taught at Harvard University; his articles have been published in the *Proceedings of Oxford Symposium on Food and Cookery*, *Food & Wine*, and numerous other publications.

ALAN SOLOMON is a freelance writer and the author of *A Century of Wrigley Field: The Official History of the Friendly Confines*. He was a reporter and editor at four newspapers, including the *Chicago Tribune*, and winner of more than 60 writing awards, including a James Beard Foundation Award for food writing.

ELLEN F. STEINBERG, PhD (University of Illinois-Chicago), a native Chicagoan finds everything related to the city worth investigating. Between "eating locally" and gardening, she writes articles and books based on her anthropological and culinary historical research.

KAY STEPKIN founded The Bread Shop, Chicago's first modern-day vegetarian business, and was the host of the "Go Veggie! with Kay" TV cooking series and the Veggie

Cook columnist for the *Chicago Tribune*. She is the president of the nonprofit organization Go Veggie!.

MICHAEL STERN (with **JANE STERN**) is the distinguished author of well-known books on food, such as *Roadfood: The Lexicon of Real American Food*, and runs Roadfood.com.

BILL ST. JOHN has written and taught about wine for more than 40 years.

MIKE SULA, winner of the James Beard Foundation's MFK Fisher Distinguished Writing Award, is a food writer for the *Chicago Reader*.

ARLENE SWARTZMAN, PhD, is an educator and writer specializing in business and professional communication who has written on urban parks, community-based health, domestic violence, and community policing.

RICHARD S. TAN is a sommelier and currently is working on a book on early colonial Mexican cuisine.

ANDRES TORRES is an urban policy and communications consultant and a former director of community outreach, Chicago Office of Tourism and Culture.

MARY VALENTIN is an artist, culinarian, food stylist, and lifelong Chicagoan. She has been an adjunct instructor at Kendall College and is currently the chair of the Food Photographers and Stylists section of the IACP. Mary teaches and lectures around the world on food in art, food styling, and food photography.

LAUREN VIERA contributes stories on travel and leisure for the *Chicago Tribune*, *Condé Nast Traveler*, *T Magazine*, and others. She is currently working on her first book, which documents the twenty-first-century cocktail craze.

KIMBERLY VOSS is associate professor at the University of Central Florida and a researcher of food journalism history.

SCOTT J. WARNER, a freelance food writer, is president of the Culinary Historians of Chicago and is a member of the International Association of Culinary Professionals.

REBECCA WHEELER teaches ethnic cooking classes for home cooks, leads food tours in Chicago's diverse neighborhoods, and runs rebeccawheeler.com.

PHILIP WOJCIAK is a Chicago South Side native, vice president sales executive with 35 years of experience in the national print industry, and a recent graduate of Roosevelt University with an MA in History.

LEAH A. ZELDES has been covering the Chicago food scene for over 25 years, first as the longtime food editor for Lerner Newspapers and more recently as a freelancer for the *Chicago Sun-Times*, the *Daily Herald*, *Red Eye*, and a wide variety of other local, regional, and national media.

Index

HEARTLAND FOODWAYS

The University of Illinois Press
is a founding member of the
Association of American University Presses.

_____

Text designed by Jennifer S. Holzner
Composed in ITC Garamond Book 9/11.5
with Trade Gothic and Univers display
by Lisa Connery
at the University of Illinois Press
Cover designed by Jennifer S. Holzner
Cover illustration: © iStock.com / kai813,
alblec, Margolana
Manufactured by Sheridan Books, Inc.

University of Illinois Press
1325 South Oak Street
Champaign, IL 61820-6903
www.press.uillinois.edu